The
United States
Congress

The
United States
Congress

E. Scott Adler
UNIVERSITY OF COLORADO–BOULDER

Jeffery A. Jenkins
UNIVERSITY OF SOUTHERN CALIFORNIA

Charles R. Shipan
UNIVERSITY OF MICHIGAN

 W. W. NORTON & COMPANY
NEW YORK · LONDON

W. W. Norton & Company has been independent since its founding in 1923, when William Warder Norton and Mary D. Herter Norton first published lectures delivered at the People's Institute, the adult education division of New York City's Cooper Union. The firm soon expanded its program beyond the Institute, publishing books by celebrated academics from America and abroad. By midcentury, the two major pillars of Norton's publishing program—trade books and college texts—were firmly established. In the 1950s, the Norton family transferred control of the company to its employees, and today—with a staff of four hundred and a comparable number of trade, college, and professional titles published each year—W. W. Norton & Company stands as the largest and oldest publishing house owned wholly by its employees.

Editor: Peter Lesser
Project Editor: Linda Feldman
Assistant Editor: Anna Olcott
Managing Editor, College: Marian Johnson
Managing Editor, College Digital Media: Kim Yi
Production Manager, College: Sean Mintus
Media Editor: Spencer Richardson-Jones
Media Editorial Assistant: Michael Jaoui
Marketing Manager, Political Science: Erin Brown
Design Director: Rubina Yeh
Designer: Juan Paolo Francisco
Photo Editor: Ted Szczepanski
Director of College Permissions: Megan Schindel
Permissions Assistant: Patricia Wong
Composition: Westchester Publishing Services
Manufacturing: Sterling Pierce

Permission to use copyrighted material is included on page C-1.

Library of Congress Cataloging-in-Publication Data

Names: Adler, E. Scott, author. | Jenkins, Jeffery A., author. | Shipan, Charles R., 1961- author.
Title: The United States Congress / E. Scott Adler, Jeffery Jenkins, Charles Shipan.
Description: First edition. | New York : W. W. Norton & Company, [2019] | Includes
    bibliographical references and index.
Identifiers: LCCN 2018049362 | ISBN 9780393680195 (pbk.)
Subjects: LCSH: United States. Congress. | United States—Politics and government.
Classification: LCC JK1021 .A46 2019 | DDC 328.73—dc23 LC record available at
    https://lccn.loc.gov/2018049362

W. W. Norton & Company, Inc., 500 Fifth Avenue, New York, NY 10110-0017
wwnorton.com
W. W. Norton & Company Ltd., Castle House, 15 Carlisle Street, London W1D 3BS

1 2 3 4 5 6 7 8 9 0

For our families:
Pam, Anna, and Rose
Lisa
Kathy, Jeff, and Becca

We thank them for their support, love, and encouragement, and for reminding us that as important and interesting as Congress is, there are other things that are far more important and interesting.

Brief Contents

Contents

3 Representation

4 Elections

5 Committees

6 Parties

7 Policy Making

8 The Legislative Effectiveness of Congress and Its Members

9 Congress and the President

10   Congress and the Bureaucracy

11   Congress and the Courts

12 Interest Groups

About the Authors

E. SCOTT ADLER is Professor of Political Science at the University of Colorado, Boulder. His current research uses theoretical models of legislative organization to examine congressional agenda setting and committee power. He is the author of *Why Congressional Reforms Fail: Reelection and the House Committee System* (University of Chicago Press, 2002), which was awarded the Alan Rosenthal Prize from the Legislative Studies Section of the American Political Science Association, and *Congress and the Politics of Problem* Solving (Cambridge University Press, 2012, co-authored with John Wilkerson). He is also co-editor of *The Macropolitics of Congress* (Princeton University Press, 2006). He has published articles in the *American Journal of Political Science*, *Legislative Studies Quarterly*, and *Urban Affairs Review*. Adler is co-PI of the Congressional Bills Project, which has compiled and coded data on all bills introduced in Congress since World War II. From 2006 to 2007, Adler was a Visiting Professor at the Center for the Study of American Politics and Department of Political Science, Yale University. He received a BA from the University of Michigan in 1988 and a Ph.D. from Columbia University in 1996.

JEFFERY A. JENKINS is Provost Professor of Public Policy, Political Science, and Law, Judith & John Bedrosian Chair of Governance and the Public Enterprise, Director of the Bedrosian Center, and Director of the Political Institutions and Political Economy (PIPE) Collaborative at the University of Southern California. He previously held tenure-stream positions at the University of Virginia, Northwestern University, and Michigan State University. His research interests include American political institutions and development (with a special emphasis on Congress and political parties), lawmaking, separation of powers, and political economy. Much of his work takes a positive political theory (or rational choice) approach and examines how political actors pursue their interests while being constrained by formal and informal institutional arrangements. His current work involves papers on the ideological content of federal lawmaking in the postwar era, and book projects on how civil rights policy has been dealt with in Congress over time and how the Republican Party evolved in the South after the Civil War. Jenkins holds a PhD in political science from the University of Illinois at Urbana-Champaign and an MS in mathematical methods for the social sciences from Northwestern University. He has been a postdoctoral fellow at Princeton University and Michigan State University. He currently serves as the Editor-in-Chief of *The Journal of Politics*.

CHARLES R. SHIPAN is the J. Ira and Nicki Harris Professor of Social Sciences and Professor of Political Science in the College of Literature, Science, and the Arts, with a courtesy appointment at the Ford School at the University of Michigan. Prior to joining the faculty at Michigan, Shipan served on the faculty at the University of Iowa, and he has also held positions as a research fellow at the Brookings Institution, as a visiting research fellow at Trinity College in Dublin, and as a visiting fellow at the U.S. Studies Centre at the University of Sydney. He is the author of *Designing Judicial Review*, co-author of *Deliberate Discretion?*, and has written numerous articles and book chapters on political institutions and public policy. He is currently engaged in a comparative study of antismoking laws in the United States and Switzerland and an examination of the effects of bipartisanship on public policy. Shipan received a BA in chemistry from Carleton College and an MA and PhD in political science from Stanford University.

Preface

Congress is *always* in the news. Not a day goes by without the House, the Senate, or individual members of Congress, doing something—taking action (or not), making statements, holding hearings—that attracts the attention of both traditional and social media. The focus of this attention might be the attempt (and failure) to address thorny issues related to immigration. It might be about changing tax or health policy. Or perhaps it might be reactions to the latest tweets from President Trump on issues like tariffs, Russian interference in the 2016 election, or the latest appointments to the federal courts. For close observers of politics, there is never a dull moment on Capitol Hill.

The three of us would characterize ourselves as close observers of politics. But although we avidly consume the latest news and social media reports about Congress, we do so from a particular perspective. Yes, we read newspapers and online magazines, listen to podcasts, and follow politicians and journalists on Twitter—but our focus goes well beyond these activities. We have also devoted our careers to conducting and publishing research about this central institution of American government. It is the combination of these two perspectives— observing what is happening in Congress, while also engaging in and producing new analyses of Congress—that led us to realize that the time is ripe for a fresh look at the "first branch" of American national government. Why does Congress so often fail to pass new policies? Why does it sometimes succeed? Why are there endless internal squabbles and machinations between Democrats and Republicans on Capitol Hill? How should we understand the role of parties and congressional committees? Why does Congress sometimes seek to rein in the other branches, but at other times defer to them? What role do elections and interest groups have on the internal operations and output of Congress?

These are questions that we regularly think about, ones that we have studied in our own research. But more than that, they are also the sorts of questions that we regularly get from students. We constantly touch on these issues when we teach our own courses. Yet existing books on Congress do not consistently approach these questions in a way that we and our students are looking for. It is this gap that led us to write this book.

To be able to answer these important questions, as well as countless others, requires a comprehensive understanding of how Congress works. Some of this understanding can come from knowing the basic functions and institutions of Congress—how members get elected, what parties and committees do, what tools exist for dealing with the other branches, and so on. In this book, we provide this essential information, the nuts and bolts about how the institution works, which serves as a good start for understanding Congress. But it's only a start. We also want students to be critical thinkers, to be able to analytically assess, understand, and evaluate Congress (and politics more generally) for a lifetime.

In our view, for students to acquire this analytical ability they need to gain an appreciation of the rich and exciting research on Congress. This body of research goes well beyond studies that we have conducted ourselves and includes work done by an exceptionally talented and diverse group of scholars. It is this broad set of exciting studies that we engage with, explain in an accessible way, and sometimes critique, throughout this book. Our goal is to use and communicate this research to address a deceptively simple overarching question: How do we know what we know about Congress? That is, while we want to convey facts about Congress, we also want to disseminate to a broad audience the arguments, theories, and evidence that congressional scholars regularly produce. In doing so, we talk about Congress not just in descriptive terms, but in the analytical way that political scientists do.

Of course, the accumulated research on Congress is vast, at times unwieldy, and sometimes internally inconsistent. Thus, to effectively communicate this material, we emphasize three main themes that provide a fundamental underpinning for an evaluation of any particular aspect of Congress: *governing*, *representation*, and *separation of powers*. We save detailed discussions of these themes for the substantive chapters of this book, but here it's worth setting out a brief description of what we mean by each theme.

- *Governing*: Citizens see Congress as the nation's primary institution for democracy and governing. The Framers also saw it that way, which is why the Constitution identifies Congress as the first branch of government. Much of the recent hand-wringing regarding gridlock and lack of legislative productivity is predicated on the notion that the House and Senate should be more effective in their governing responsibilities. Governing is, in large part, lawmaking, but also includes bureaucratic oversight, influencing public opinion, and establishing policy priorities as an agenda for the nation. Governing in Congress requires collective decision making and a certain level of cooperation. Throughout this book, we examine the aspects of congressional organization, bicameral structure, and the electoral system that both help and hinder collective choice.

- *Representation*: Governing is predicated on the notion of representation, which is the fundamental link between lawmakers and their constituents. But representation is not merely a bilateral relationship between voters and their member of Congress. There are many constituencies that lawmakers must respond to—stakeholders within their districts or states, such as businesses and organized groups; ideological and policy-interested groups outside their districts or states; potential reelection supporters; party leaders; the president; and more. For members of Congress, having to satisfy multiple constituencies often makes collective action and collective choice a challenge. Put simply, representation and governing can sometimes be at odds.

- *Separation of powers*: Although Congress is the first branch of the federal government, it is not the only branch. Lawmakers on Capitol Hill must negotiate the broader institutional labyrinth created by the Framers—including the president, the bureaucracy, and the courts, and their shifting powers over time. How do shifts in these relationships alter the strategies of individual lawmakers and the collective activities of the legislative body? Governing further entails interaction outside these branches. Most notably, bureaucrats and interest groups have multiple venues for access to the governing process, which can add to the difficulty of passing laws and influencing policy.

These three themes, which appear in nearly every chapter in this book, help both to organize our approach to any particular topic and to provide continuity across topics.

Again, in exploring these themes and in covering the topics found in each chapter, we go well beyond description and examples—although we freely acknowledge their importance—and present an explicitly *political science* view of Congress, one that involves asking questions, developing theories, creating arguments, collecting data, and assessing evidence. Too often, there is a gulf between how Congress is taught, or presented, in textbooks, and how political scientists analyze it. We aim to bridge this gulf. We do this in part by including, in each chapter, a section called **How We Study**, which delves deeply into a specific course of study and explains how it has added to our knowledge of Congress.

But more generally, this approach of focusing on, and introducing students to, political science underpins every page of this text.

Our unique approach allows us to provide students with the current state of knowledge on standard topics, such as congressional elections or the relationship between Congress and interest groups. But it also allows us to delve more deeply into topics that scholars have devoted increased attention to in recent years, such as legislative effectiveness, policy making, and the relationship between Congress and government agencies. In addition, we stress that in order to understand the House and Senate now, we have to understand how they operated in the past. We do this in part through a chapter that focuses on congressional development. But we also include in each chapter a specific section called **Then and Now**, which takes a key aspect of that chapter—for example, how the filibuster has been used in the Senate—and examines how that congressional activity, process, or structure has changed over time.

In all of this, we strive for balance. In part, this means that we balance description and examples with analysis and presentations of research. It also means that we balance a focus on the current Congress with a focus on the past, and that we balance discussions of our three themes. But it also means that we strive for balance in our overall assessment of Congress. Finding aspects of Congress to criticize is not difficult—and we don't shy away from such criticisms. At the same time, there are things the institution does well, and we note these too. Furthermore, sometimes when Congress is criticized along one of the dimensions that we explore—say, governing—it is because that aspect of its job has come into conflict with another, like representation. This is not to excuse failures; rather, it is to indicate, and to appreciate, why they might occur.

Ultimately, we hope this book will pique the interest of students to further pursue questions regarding Congress, representation, or even governing in general. Perhaps even better, it could serve as a useful resource for the next generation of scholars, practitioners, and voters. We know that many factors affect whether students become interested in politics. Sometimes that interest eventually translates into going to graduate school and making the study of politics a vocation or pursuing a career in the world of politics or policy making, or simply being a politically informed citizen. We believe our book—which combines facts and social science—will serve as a good introduction to both the world of congressional politics and the important insights gained from the academic study of Congress.

At this point, one task remains for us in this preface—acknowledging the enormous and invaluable help we received during the writing of this book. In part, this book is the product of the many conversations and interactions the three of us have had over the years. But more than that, it is a product of the more general scholarly conversation that we have been fortunate to be part of over the years—a conversation that has taken place with the generous community of scholars who study Congress. This conversation has occurred at conferences, at research presentations, through journals and reading each other's papers, via email and social media, and—most recently, and most directly, for this book—through the exceptionally insightful set of reviews that an outstanding set of scholars provided on each chapter in this book. These reviews improved the manuscript in countless ways—correcting errors, providing new insights, alerting us to studies we had neglected or hadn't known about, suggesting different emphases, and often filling holes we didn't even know existed. In many ways all the scholars (and students) who contributed to this endeavor can lay some claim to this sizable collective effort and achievement. For these and other contributions, we are extremely grateful and offer our thanks to the following reviewers:

David Bateman, Cornell University
Jim Battista, SUNY Buffalo
William Bianco, Indiana University
Sarah Binder, George Washington University
Bethany Blackstone, University of North Texas
Barry Burden, University of Wisconsin–Madison
David Canon, University of Wisconsin–Madison
Jamie L. Carson, University of Georgia
Jason Casellas, University of Houston
Jennifer Hayes Clark, University of Houston
Meredith Conroy, California State University, San Bernardino
Michael Crespin, University of Oklahoma
James M. Curry, University of Utah
Charles J. Finocchiaro, University of Oklahoma
Jeremy Gelman, University of Nevada, Reno
Matthew Green, Catholic University of America
Jeff Grynaviski, Wayne State
Peter Hanson, Grinnell College
Laurel Harbridge-Yong, Northwestern University
Thomas Hayes, University of Connecticut
Rebekah Herrick, Oklahoma State University
Gary E. Hollibaugh, Jr., University of Notre Dame
Kristin Kanthak, University of Pittsburgh
Stephanie Dean Kerce, Emory University
Aaron S. King, University of North Carolina at Wilmington
Gregory Koger, University of Miami
John Lapinski, University of Pennsylvania
Tim LaPira, James Madison University

Jennifer Lawless, American University

Jeffrey Lazarus, Georgia State University

Jason MacDonald, West Virginia University

Bryan Marshall, Miami University

Robert McGrath, George Mason University

Natasha Altema McNeely, University of Texas, Rio Grande Valley

Scott Meinke, Bucknell University

Kenneth W. Moffett, Southern Illinois University Edwardsville

Nathan Monroe, University of California, Merced

Timothy Nokken, Texas Tech University

Ian Ostrander, Michigan State University

Jeffrey Peake, Clemson University

Brittany N. Perry, Texas A&M University

Eleanor Powell, University of Wisconsin–Madison

Molly Reynolds, The Brookings Institution

Josh Ryan, Utah State University

Emily Schilling, University of Tennessee, Knoxville

Scot Schraufnagel, Northern Illinois University

Joel Sievert, Texas Tech University

Gisela Sin, University of Illinois, Urbana-Champaign

Peverill Squire, University of Missouri

Andrew J. Taylor, North Carolina State

Gregory Wawro, Columbia University

Alan Wiseman, Vanderbilt University

Jennifer Victor, George Mason University

Jose D. Villalobos, University of Texas at El Paso

In addition to these reviewers, we are also deeply appreciative to the following scholars, who provided a helpful mixture of suggestions, insights, and data: Michael Berry, Jamie Carson, Sara Hagedorn, Peter Hanson, Jennifer Lawless, Josh Kennedy, Barbara Koremenos, Jason MacDonald, Rob McGrath, Nolan McCarty, Anthony Madonna, Scott Meinke, Ian Ostrander, Dan Ponder, Andy Rudalevige, Josh Ryan, Judy Schneider, and Sean Theriault. And we are particularly grateful for the useful feedback we received on early drafts of chapters from students in the following classes on Congress: Scott Minkoff's class at SUNY New Paltz, Adam Cayton's class at the University of West Florida, and Tim Nokken's class at Texas Tech University.

We benefited from outstanding research assistance and feedback from a number of students, including Adam Cayton, Jared Cory, Ryan Dawkins, Stefani Langehennig, Ben Lempert, Sinead Redmond, Rebecca Shipan, and James

Strickland. We also thank the Hoover Institution, which provided several weeks over the years for collaborative work on Stanford University's beautiful campus.

Finally, we have been fortunate to work with an incredible team at Norton, starting with Peter Lesser, whom we thank for his excellent insights, positive attitude, general encouragement, and—not least—his amazing patience (accompanied, when necessary, by subtle—or not-so-subtle—nudges). The book is also much better due to the careful and cheerful editorial efforts of Anna Olcott and Samantha Held. Our project editor Linda Feldman went above and beyond to ensure the high quality of the book, and production manager Sean Mintus kept us on schedule. We thank media editor Spencer Richardson-Jones, associate media editor Michael Jaoui, and media editorial assistant Tricia Vuong for coordinating the media components.

E. Scott Adler
Jeffery A. Jenkins
Charles R. Shipan

The
United States
Congress

1

Representation and Governing in a Separated System

If we were to choose a single act by Congress to define contemporary politics and policy making on Capitol Hill, it would be the Patient Protection and Affordable Care Act (ACA). The ACA, or "Obamacare," was the signature legislative achievement of the Barack Obama presidency and quickly became the most heated political issue of our generation. In its original form, the ACA mandated health insurance for all Americans, expanded eligibility for Medicaid, and made significant reforms to the system of health delivery and insurance. Enacted in 2010, the ACA epitomized how the contemporary Congress works. It has also been a primary battleground between the executive and legislative branches, and a leading topic of debate during every election since its passage. Since 2010, Republicans in Congress have made repealing or dismantling Obamacare their political mission.

Following the 2008 election, debate began over how a large Democratic majority in both the House and the Senate, along with a new Democratic president, would revamp the U.S. health care system. Congress had not enacted such a sweeping change to health care policy since the adoption of Medicaid and Medicare in the mid-1960s. In the first two years of Bill Clinton's presidency

Congressional Democrats faced fierce opposition from Republicans, members of their own party, and the American public during the passage of the Affordable Care Act. Since it was enacted, the Affordable Care Act has remained a contentious issue for politicians and voters.

(1993–94), an effort to reform health care failed, in part because it was perceived as being directed from the White House rather than from Congress. President Obama, aware of the prior failures and having just been elected president after serving in the Senate, left the details of policy making to his former colleagues on Capitol Hill.

Over the coming year, health care reform dominated news in Washington and beyond. Through the summer of 2009, Democratic leaders in Congress struggled to placate their members, whose reform priorities varied considerably. They also sought to gain the support of at least some Republicans to claim the bill had bipartisanship backing. While an effort at bipartisanship quickly faded in the House, Senate Democratic leaders continued negotiating with moderate Republicans through the early fall of 2009.

Lawmakers approached the congressional recess in August without a clear plan. And in the absence of specific bill language, speculation and rumors about the content of the law began to spread. When meeting with constituents during the recess, Democratic members quickly discovered that many of them were opposed to, and often angry about, the potential changes the law might make to the existing health care system. Many Democrats were thus left in an uncomfortable position, forced to choose between support for the party's long-standing goal of expanding access to health care and constituent sentiment to resist change.

Nonetheless, Democratic leaders in Congress, with public backing from President Obama, continued to seek support for the bill. In the House, Democratic leaders struggled to gain the necessary votes to pass their version of the bill, with heated debate centering on abortion coverage and the inclusion of a public (government-based) health insurance option. As the House vote neared, a vigorous attempt to secure a majority ensued. The White House exerted pressure on representatives, and House Democratic leaders made implicit threats to prevent the measure from failing. Ultimately, enough Democrats held together to pass the measure by a slim margin: 220–215. Those Democrats who voted against the bill were mostly from the more conservative "Blue Dog" coalition or represented districts that Republican presidential candidate John McCain (R-AZ) had won in the prior year's election.

In the Senate, the path to success was just as difficult. Democrats had a 60-vote majority and thus could defeat a Republican filibuster, but they needed to keep every single member on board. Ultimately, Senate Democratic leaders had to drop provisions that had wide party appeal—such as the public health insurance option—because one or two Democratic members would not support them. In late December 2009, after a marathon month of lawmaking, the Senate adopted its version of health care reform without any support from Republican senators.

Soon after New Year's Day, Democratic leaders began meeting with White House officials and President Obama to resolve differences between the House and Senate versions of the bill. In the midst of the intense negotiations, proponents were dealt a potentially fatal blow. On January 19, 2010, Scott Brown, a Republican, won the special election to fill Democrat Ted Kennedy's Senate seat in Massachusetts following Kennedy's death. As a result, Republicans now had enough votes in the Senate to employ a filibuster and kill the legislation. The Democrats were left with only one option: negotiating compromises that would be adopted in the House and then attaching these changes to what is known as a *budget reconciliation measure.* This option would allow the bill to be adopted in the Senate with a simple majority and thus avoid the possibility of a filibuster. While some considered this procedure to be extraordinary, Congress had used reconciliation numerous times in the recent past to enact major laws that might have otherwise been killed by a Senate filibuster. Examples included the continuation of health insurance for employees after they leave their jobs (Consolidated Omnibus Budget Reconciliation Act, or COBRA) in 1985, the Children's Health Insurance Program in 1997, and three tax cuts during the George W. Bush administration (2001, 2003, and 2006).[1]

It took several more weeks of painstaking negotiations, but in the end, House Democrats passed the Senate version of the bill and the reconciliation act on March 21. President Obama signed the law on March 23. Two days later the Senate held up its end of the deal and on March 25 it passed the reconciliation, which Obama signed five days later.

Usually, passage of legislation in both chambers and a signature by the president would be the end of the political story. But the ACA hardly qualifies as usual. Republicans successfully mobilized opposition to the legislation through the first year of the Obama presidency, and they kept the pressure on the Democrats throughout the congressional term. The ACA became the primary focus of the 2010 midterm elections,[2] and the Republicans capitalized on this opposition, picking up 6 seats in the Senate and a staggering 63 seats in the House. This "shellacking," as President Obama referred to the election results, gave the Republicans majority control of the House and thus ended the Democrats' unified control of government.[3]

Since 2010, Republican opponents of the ACA have kept up the pressure. In the House, Republicans have held nearly 70 votes to repeal the legislation. Provisions of the ACA have been the subject of three different Supreme Court decisions (which mostly, although not entirely, upheld the language of the statute).

Following the 2016 election, Republicans took control of the presidency and both chambers of Congress. During the first year of President Donald Trump's administration, one of the party's primary goals was to "repeal and replace" Obamacare. An intense effort by House and Senate Republican leaders in the spring and summer of 2017 to scuttle the ACA ultimately failed. In the end, Republican leadership in the Senate was unable to craft a bill that appealed to enough of its members to secure a repeal. However, as part of the massive tax reform law passed in 2017, Republican leaders were able to repeal one of the ACA's key provisions: a mandate that individuals must have health insurance or pay a penalty. Many predicted this change would destabilize the market for affordable health insurance and lead to more people being uninsured. Time will tell whether this prediction was accurate.

As the events surrounding the ACA make clear, the work of Congress can be extraordinarily complicated. Sometimes, it is a wonder that legislation passes at all. Lawmakers are expected to represent their districts, states, and other interests while overseeing the operations of a massive and sprawling federal government. Congress must do all of this while navigating a set of shared powers with the other federal branches of government, most notably the president and executive branch agencies. And when crafting laws, members of Congress also must consider the possibility, or even the likelihood, of future judicial action to assess the constitutionality of legislation. In this context, it is not hard to see the difficulties that members of Congress face in performing their duties on Capitol Hill and at home with constituents.

At the same time, Congress is an extraordinarily powerful lawmaking body. Unlike most governing systems around the world, not only does the United States separate legislative and executive authority but it also grants exceptional privileges and autonomy to its lawmaking body to influence the issue agenda and to control the direction and shape of policy changes. While members of Congress face a difficult set of duties and expectations, they do so within the world's most powerful legislative body.

This book's goal is to foster an appreciation and understanding of how Congress works—and when it seemingly does not—and why any of that matters. This is no simple task given the complicated array of rules and laws that govern congressional procedure and the many responsibilities of our lawmakers in Washington.

This chapter highlights what we believe should be the key features of an in-depth analysis of the U.S. Congress. We start by defining the core democratic principles that define Congress: representation, separation of powers, and governing. We also make the case that knowing the historical context and using the best available information and most advanced analytical techniques to assess the quality of Congress's performance are critical to a proper understanding of this complex and fascinating lawmaking body.

CONGRESS AT THE CORE OF DEMOCRATIC PRINCIPLES: REPRESENTATION, SEPARATION OF POWERS, AND GOVERNING

The primary imperative of Congress—the goal that it must achieve collectively as an institution, as well as the objective of individual lawmakers—is *representing* various constituents within a complicated web of *separated institutional powers* to *govern* the nation. This is the goal the Founding Fathers sought to achieve after their rebellion against the tyranny of the British Empire. They soon discovered that designing such a system would be complicated, controversial, and fraught with a seemingly endless array of pitfalls. Understanding representation, separation of powers, and governing is central to understanding Congress today as well as in the past.

Representation

There is no principle more central to our democracy than *representation*, which is the link between citizens (constituents) and the political agents (lawmakers) they select to act on their behalf. Representation is critical in any consideration of

U.S. politics, and it can take different forms. When thinking about how law-makers translate what their constituents want into policy actions, we might perceive a representation spectrum. On one end, lawmakers follow their con-stituents' preferences, faithfully doing what their constituents would want them to do. When lawmakers behave in this way, we say that they act as *delegates*. At the other end of the representation spectrum, lawmakers pursue their con-stituents' interests but not necessarily their will. In some cases, constituents' preferences are not fully formed or even discernible. Thus lawmakers must rely on their own judgment and make independent decisions. When lawmakers behave in this way, we say that they act as *trustees*.[4]

If representation is the link between constituents and lawmakers, what con-stitutes a constituent? Each member of Congress is elected from a specific geo-graphic unit: a state or district. We consider the citizens of those units to be the geographic constituency that members of Congress represent. Yet there are other constituencies to keep in mind. Sometimes, members of Congress focus on particular subgroups within their larger geographic constituency. They might also respond to groups of individuals with shared interests—perhaps racial or religious groups—who may not necessarily reside in their districts or states. And they might sometimes represent the interests of the nation as a whole.

In fact, there was considerable debate during the construction of the Constitu-tion about the nature of congressional representation. It was perhaps *the* central question the Framers of the Constitution considered during the Philadelphia Con-vention (see Chapter 2). *The Federalist Papers*, a collection of 85 essays written by Alexander Hamilton, James Madison, and John Jay between 1787 and 1788, reveal the logic of the Constitution's proponents.[5] These essays were developed to per-suade the states to support the ratification of the Constitution. In *Federalist 10*, Madison makes the case for a large and diverse republic that sends a sizable set of delegates to Congress to speak for them. He contends that a representative democracy, as opposed to lawmaking through direct democracy, is a necessity in a republic with varied and often narrow interests because representatives chosen by the people are likely to be "more consonant of the public good." Within the republic they were creating, Madison writes, Congress was intended "to refine and enlarge the public views, by passing them through the medium of a chosen body of citizens, whose wisdom may best discern the true interest of their country, and whose patriotism and love of justice will be least likely to sacrifice it to temporary or partial considerations."[6] In other words, the interests and voice of the people need to be filtered and clarified through elected representatives.

Throughout U.S. history, debates about representation emerge again and again. In this book, we investigate the question of representation from many angles. For example, what mechanisms enable us to translate constituency opinion or inter-ests into actions by those who do the governing or lawmaking? In our democracy, elections are the principle way of controlling public officials.[7] But do elections work as intended? That is, do elections—and the threat of being voted out of office—lead members of Congress to better represent their constituents? How has voting changed for legislators? For example, what were the causes and consequences of the Seventeenth Amendment, which instituted the popular election of senators? What are the challenges and triumphs of representing the interests of those who have sometimes been shut out of our political system—people of color, women, and others?

Separation of Powers

Another principle of U.S. democracy embodied in Congress is the idea that government authority and oversight are distributed among a set of governing institutions. The consent of the governed motivated the Framers to craft sufficient representation of varied interests. But perhaps equally important were the Framers' fears about the power of an unchecked central authority. After all, they were breaking away from a British monarchy they believed to be tyrannical. These fears motivated the Framers to focus on separating powers rather than concentrating them in a single body. As Madison declared in *Federalist* 51, "The accumulation of all powers, legislative, executive and judicia[l] in the same hands, whether of one, a few, or many, and whether hereditary, self–appointed, or elective, may justly be pronounced the very definition of tyranny."[8]

Not surprisingly, the Framers steadfastly incorporated this *separation of powers*, along with its associated system of *checks and balances*, into the Constitution. As the Framers saw it, institutions should have the ability to counteract one another, thereby preventing any one branch of government from becoming too powerful and eventually subsuming the others. Madison writes, "The great security against a gradual concentration of the several powers in the same [branch], consists in giving to those who administer each [branch], the necessary constitutional means, and personal motives, to resist encroachments of the others. . . . Ambition must be made to counteract ambition. The interest of the man must be connected with the constitutional rights of the place."[9]

In this book, we explore Congress's place at the center of a government where powers are not only divided but also interconnected and dependent on one another. The authority to make law is a responsibility shared between Congress and the president, often with validation or input by the courts. Congress and the president also share a responsibility for ensuring the day-to-day operations of a vast government bureaucracy. The two branches often exercise their powers of governance in union, but sometimes, as we explore in Chapter 9, conflicts emerge.

Another great innovation of the U.S. Constitution was to embed fundamentally different perspectives and motivations within the design of the branches of

Congress is empowered by the Constitution to create laws that respond to constituents' policy goals of the time. When suffragists fought for the right to vote in the early 1900s, they lobbied Congress to advocate for their enfranchisement.

government. Each branch's authority is derived and constituted in a completely different way, with each relying on a different constituency. Members of Congress are beholden primarily to their geographic constituency; the president usually sees the entire nation as his or her constituency; federal judges, given that they are not elected, are not directly beholden to any constituency (although they do depend on Congress and the president for their budgets, structure, and enforcement of decisions). Different powers and motivations help each branch maintain distance from, and influence over, other branches.

Governing

Congress's governing ability most clearly locates it at the center of U.S. democracy. Does Congress keep the federal apparatus funded, does it renew and update existing laws and agencies, does it pave new directions for government so that federal policy can adapt to changes in the world and society's evolving needs? Or is Congress hamstrung, limping from crisis to crisis, barely able to keep the lights on or federal departments and programs from shutting down every year or two?

The Framers at the Philadelphia Convention focused much more on Congress than on the executive and judicial branches because they intended to make Congress the lynchpin of a new governing structure. As such, the section of the Constitution that enumerates the structure and powers of Congress (Article I) is the first, and by far the longest, portion of the Constitution. Among the extensive powers and authority expressly granted to Congress in the Constitution are the responsibility for taxing and spending, borrowing money and taking on government debt, regulating interstate and foreign commerce, constructing a federal court system, declaring war and supporting a standing military, impeaching and trying presidents, overriding presidential vetoes on legislation, confirming high-level executive branch and judicial appointments, and ratifying treaties with other nations.

However, it is the Constitution's "necessary and proper" clause (sometimes called the "elastic" clause) that gives Congress its preeminent governing authority:

> *To make all Laws which shall be necessary and proper for carrying into Execution the foregoing Powers, and all other Powers vested by this Constitution in the Government of the United States, or in any Department or Officer thereof.*

Congress's exercise of this power over more than two centuries has led to its dominance in the federal policy–making process.

Interestingly, it is often in Congress's governing responsibilities where its representation imperative collides with the separated powers of the branches. Congress struggles to govern at times because its members must also be responsive to district constituents, while the president, with a diverse electorate and a national mandate, is in a better position to define and carry out a policy agenda.

CONGRESS AND AMERICAN POLITICS THROUGHOUT HISTORY

Over time, Congress has played a leading role in most major changes in federal policy. In addition, the centuries-long debate over the influence of the various branches of government has almost always revolved around Congress's role vis-à-vis other governmental actors. Throughout this book, we discuss the history of Congress and its implications for our analysis and understanding of Congress today.

When we look at congressional history, some key ideas emerge. First, a central goal of the American Revolution was the creation of a democratic system with a representative legislature at its core. Decades of rule by the British Crown and a lack of citizen participation in colonial governing led to a groundswell for revolution in the early 1770s. Although the First Continental Congress was composed of an unelected set of intellectual and business elites, state conventions eventually selected delegates to represent the colonies. It took time and a faltering economy for the post–Revolutionary War Continental Congress (which was based only on state-level representation) to be replaced by today's Congress (which is based on both state-level and population-based representation). Throughout this book, we explain the logic and implications of Congress's organization and representational structure, which has existed now for over 225 years.

Second, Congress has been the principal actor in policy making since the Founding of the United States. Consider, for example, the primary issue of debate during the nation's first century: slavery. Slavery was an all-consuming and divisive issue at the Founding. In many ways, the structure of Congress specified in the Constitution—a bicameral legislature with different forms of representation (states versus congressional districts) for the House and Senate—can be attributed to disagreements among the states on the matter of slavery. And only a few years after ratification of the Constitution, Congress acted to foster and perpetuate slavery. It did so by first reinforcing the slave clause of the Constitution with the Fugitive Slave Act of 1793—guaranteeing the return of a fugitive slave to her owner—which it revised and strengthened in 1850. And as the country expanded west, Congress extended the reach of slavery via the Missouri Compromise (1820), the Compromise of 1850, and the Kansas–Nebraska Act (1854), which provided for the admission of new slave states into the Union. After the Civil War broke out, Congress's role changed dramatically. First, Congress ended slavery via legislation that would become the Thirteenth Amendment (1865). Then, following the war, Congress worked to build a post-slavery society, first by granting explicit legal rights to freed slaves in the Civil Rights Act of 1866 (enacted over President Andrew Johnson's veto). Later that year, Congress passed legislation that would become the Fourteenth Amendment (ratified in 1868), providing citizenship and equal protection to all citizens. And through the Reconstruction Acts (1867 and 1868), Congress defined the terms by which southern states would be admitted back into the Union—including the requirement that they ratify the Fourteenth Amendment and adopt new state constitutions granting voting rights to black men.

We also see Congress at the center of many other federal policy decisions over the course of the nation's history. The monumental expansion of federal authority in managing the economy and assisting in the lives of struggling Americans as a response to the Great Depression of the 1930s, for example, was in many respects driven by lawmakers on Capitol Hill.[10] And Congress has been at the core of landmark changes to our electoral system through the expansion of constitutional voting rights[11] and improved ballot access,[12] regulation of election administration,[13] and restrictions on candidate and party campaigns.[14] Stated simply, if something important is happening in U.S. political life, Congress is often deeply involved.

Third, the historic evolution of American democratic principles is inextricably linked to congressional continuity and change. For example, the relative power between Congress and the president/executive branch has shifted back and forth over time. In the nineteenth century, for example, strong-willed presidents such as Andrew Jackson and Abraham Lincoln often battled Congress on a range of matters. In the early twentieth century, the presidency became a more powerful institution, as Theodore Roosevelt and Woodrow Wilson often asserted executive influence against a skeptical Congress on various domestic and international issues. And while the influence of the presidency continued to expand throughout the twentieth century, especially under Franklin D. Roosevelt and Lyndon B. Johnson, Congress was present to offer resistance and sometimes rein in that expansion by imposing permanent restrictions on what many viewed as unconstitutional abuses of presidential power in the 1960s and 1970s.[15]

THIS IS NOT YOUR GRANDPARENTS' CONGRESS

The primary focus of this book is how Congress works today. The insights we provide in these pages move beyond the conventional wisdom and idealized depictions of the "textbook Congress" that appear in typical civics books, popular culture, or the Schoolhouse Rock cartoon "I'm Just a Bill." The Congress of today is notably different than the Congress of a generation or two ago.

Take, for example, the separation of powers between Congress and the executive branch. Over time, Congress has relinquished influence to the president. Some of this has occurred via conscious delegation on Congress's part—as the nation's political economy has expanded greatly over the centuries, Congress has needed to offload some governing authority to the executive branch. But some political observers contend that Congress's recent inability to achieve some of its most basic duties—enacting budgets, reauthorizing expiring federal programs and agencies, and ensuring that the Treasury may continue to borrow money to keep the government solvent—is another reason power has shifted away from Congress and toward the president. For example, the President's Office of Management and Budget and even federal departments themselves (such as the Department of Agriculture and the State Department) have had the ability to set the spending agenda, often with minimal input from congressional leaders and committees. Moreover, dysfunction on Capitol Hill has resulted in accelerated congressional staff turnover and decreased institutional memory on how

The government shutdown in January 2018 exemplified the dysfunction of the contemporary Congress. Deep partisanship led to the inability of the U.S. Senate to reach an agreement on the budget, resulting in a government shutdown. President Trump and the Republicans blamed Democrats for the shutdown, and Democrats like Senate Majority Leader Chuck Schumer (D-NY) blamed Trump and the Republicans.

programs are reauthorized. This situation provides the White House with the upper hand in policy negotiations and the execution of the budgetary process. Taking stock of the balance of power and the causes of congressional dysfunction will be a topic to which we return throughout this book.

At the same time, the story of the contemporary Congress is the story of extraordinary partisanship. Throughout congressional history, parties have been central players in establishing our core democratic principles. In terms of representation, parties provide a way for voters to understand where politicians stand on particular issues, focus candidates' efforts during elections, and support politicians' campaigns. In a separation-of-powers system, parties often coordinate shared goals across government branches and act as a mechanism for negotiating and bargaining. With respect to governing, parties define agendas, organize the process of lawmaking on Capitol Hill, and assemble the majorities necessary for congressional action.

Yet parties' roles in Congress have evolved in recent years in ways that have fundamentally redefined lawmaking and lawmakers. Both in Congress and in public, parties are now more polarized than at any other point in the modern era.

Partisanship has become more "tribal" in recent years as support for partisan teams has often outweighed commitments to values and ideology. For example, when Congress enacted the sweeping overhaul of tax policy at the end of 2017, the measure was passed without a single Democratic lawmaker in either chamber supporting it.[16] In contrast, the last major tax reform, which took place during the Reagan presidency in 1986, was the result of bipartisan negotiations and passed with the support of Republican and Democrat majorities. Similarly, voters are reluctant to stray from their partisan camps. For example, in the 2017 special election Senate race in Alabama, Republican voters were faced with the choice of voting for party candidate Roy Moore, who had been accused of sexual assault and misconduct, or voting for his Democratic challenger Doug Jones and losing the seat to the Democrats. Ninety-one percent of Republicans ended up voting for Moore.[17] (He still lost.)

In recent years, defections from the partisan agenda in Congress have been uncommon. When they do occur, they are rarely motivated by shared goals across the partisan aisle or even within a single party. For instance, at the end of 2015, John Boehner stepped down from his position as Speaker of the House after repeated battles with hard-line Republican conservatives who were unhappy with his use of bipartisan votes to keep federal programs funded and the government from shutting down.

Lawmakers have viewed parties differently throughout our history, but the current place of parties in representation and governing is unique. Throughout this book, we explore how parties influence or change the way that voters, lawmakers, and Congress as a whole operate.

HOW DO WE KNOW WHAT WE KNOW ABOUT CONGRESS?

Congress has long been a center of attention in political science research. As the academic discipline of political science emerged in the late nineteenth and early twentieth centuries, it focused on Congress—the primary governing and representative institution in the United States and widely considered the most powerful legislature in the world. To appreciate the insights that generations of congressional scholars have produced, and to think critically about those insights, it is important to know how scholars approach their work. Rather than taking the knowledge generated by congressional scholars as a matter of fact, we believe it is important to examine how these experts come to know what they know.

Among the earliest works was research conducted by Woodrow Wilson. Before becoming president of the United States (or even president of Princeton

University), Wilson gained his insights on the American political landscape by writing a PhD dissertation on the importance of Congress in a separation-of-powers system and the need to reconsider its institutional advantages. That study, titled *Congressional Government* (published in 1885),[18] remains one of the most widely cited books on Congress today.

As the social sciences began to embrace the availability of data, the earliest applications of statistical techniques to the study of politics were quantitative analyses of congressional roll call votes.[19] One particularly influential study, conducted by sociologist Stuart Rice in 1924, created a widely used measure of *voting bloc unity* (that is, which members tend to vote with whom in Congress) that contemporary scholars continue to use in a wide variety of legislative studies.[20] In the 1950s, as the field of political science expanded, studies of public opinion and voting behavior became the fastest-growing areas of political science research. Also in the 1950s, the seminal American National Election Study—still the leading survey of political opinion today—began gathering a wealth of data from presidential and congressional races. Beginning in the early 1960s, scholars interested in understanding representation matched data on voters' opinions with policy activities, specifically congressional roll call votes.[21] Around the same time, scholars began studying the attitudes of members of Congress on the functioning of the institution and potential reforms in Congress itself.[22] The field of public opinion research today is massive, and understanding how opinions translate into action is now ubiquitous in nearly every aspect of modern society, from commerce to politics.

In the 1950s and 1960s, scholars interested in studying the factors influencing election outcomes gravitated to congressional races because they offered an enormous number of cases (435 House races and 33 or more Senate races every two-year election cycle) to test the effects of constituency conditions, lawmaker behavior, and incumbency.[23] This work resulted in massive data collection at the congressional district level over numerous decades and across a wide variety of conditions. A parallel line of research that began about the same time focuses on the role that parties play in organizing lawmakers and directing the work of Congress.[24]

The mid–twentieth century also saw the creation of game theory, which explores the incentives of, and strategic interactions between, individuals. Not surprisingly, Congress was fertile ground for its development. In the mid-1950s, scholars seeking insights into the notion of power—a critical concept in the study of politics—based their conclusions on the process of voting in the U.S. Senate.[25] Eventually, as students of Congress grew increasingly interested in the importance of "institutions"—or how rules, structures, and processes affect political outcomes—they began to apply game theory and other related theories like spatial voting theory, which holds that members of Congress can be arrayed ideologically on a line from left to right, to examine the committee system and the role that parties play in legislative politics.[26]

To test these theoretical concepts, researchers needed to estimate lawmakers' ideological positions. Congress was an ideal venue because of the availability of thousands of roll call votes. The "revealed" preferences of every member could be derived from how they voted, which meant that researchers could situate each lawmaker's ideology relative to every other lawmaker's.[27] The techniques developed for estimating ideology in Congress eventually extended to other political venues where voting occurs, such as the courts, state legislatures, and foreign lawmaking assemblies.[28]

Not all research advances have taken place in the realm of statistical studies of large congressional data sets. In the 1950s and 1960s, political science began introducing sociological and anthropological techniques, and broadening its methodology to examine politics through the use of in-depth case studies and participant observation. Congress was one of the many venues used for this kind of qualitative research. In the mid-1950s the American Political Science

In groundbreaking work beginning in the 1960s, political scientist Richard Fenno (left) followec lawmakers in and out of Washington to study how they interact with, and represent, constituents. Here, Fenno is pictured with Representative Barber Conable (R-NY).

Association (APSA) began placing scholars, called congressional fellows, in the offices of members of Congress to work as regular staff. Researchers were thus able to observe lawmakers in their "natural habitat," which led to the collection of novel data and the creation of hundreds of unique studies from an insider's perspective.[29] An extraordinary amount of the research cited in this book was produced by scholars who early in their careers served as congressional fellows.[30] Perhaps the most gifted observer of the behavior of members of Congress, Richard Fenno followed lawmakers around their districts and constructed what is still considered the most important study of representative interactions with constituents.[31]

Not long after the development of the congressional fellowship, APSA sponsored the Study of Congress Project, which resulted in a large series of detailed case studies illuminating aspects of congressional organization and operations, ranging from party leadership to the culture of specific House and Senate committees.[32] Many of the scholars who had spent so much time doing close-up observation on "the Hill" became key players in the congressional reform movements of the 1970s and 1990s.[33]

In recent years, new avenues of research have been made possible through emerging data and information now available on the Internet. The increased accessibility of data has raised prospects of answering long-standing questions in new ways and addressing questions never before considered. Detailed content coding of roll call votes has allowed us to investigate how much congressional behavior is truly ideological and how much is simply parties staking out positions on policies and organizing their members as "teams."[34] Innovations in computational social science and text analysis have led to path-breaking studies of lawmaker press releases that reveal differing styles of representation.[35] Scholars have used the plethora of data about lawmaker behavior, such as cosponsorship of bills or membership on internal policy caucuses, to examine the networks of members of Congress and how they influence the laws that are made.[36] Similarly, by combining advanced statistical techniques with extensive data on contributions to congressional campaigns, scholars have mapped the ideological positions of incumbents and challengers for congressional seats.[37] And researchers have also begun to draw on the mass of information available through new online activities. For example, we see that members of Congress reinforce polarizing viewpoints by sharing ideologically divisive news on their social media feeds.[38]

POLITICAL NOISE, POLITICAL SCIENCE, AND THE SCIENTIFIC PROCESS

Each year, dozens of books by political journalists and historians recount the travails of lawmaking on Capitol Hill. Add to these books the nightly reflections (and shouting matches) about politics and policy on cable news and you have a media landscape filled with opinion, prediction, and partisan rancor. What is usually missing are the analyses and insights about politics gleaned from sustained social scientific inquiry. Knowing how the political scientists cited in this book do their work can help us better understand their findings and cut through the exaggerated political noise in the United States today.[39]

The scholars cited in this book start with critical questions: Do party structures influence lawmakers' actions, or is their behavior the result of shared ideologies? Are committees still meaningful in the legislative process? Is Congress productive? Why don't we see more women and people of color in Congress? How influential is the public in shaping congressional behavior? How influential are interest groups, political parties, and presidents? They then pose hypotheses to guide their research. With hypotheses in hand, the scholars then consider the best ways to measure causes and effects.

The process of testing these hypotheses can take years and involve extensive data collection and sophisticated analysis. And while there is often debate about the best ways of conducting a study—as is the case in any scientific endeavor—the insights are often unique and can be meaningful for understanding how Congress works. We build on these scholarly works to explain the activities on Capitol Hill and beyond.

THE PLAN OF THIS BOOK

What should you expect from this book? First and foremost, each chapter centers on what we believe to be the most important topics in studying Congress: how members of Congress run their campaigns and get elected, what committees do, the nature of the interactions between the president and Congress, interest groups' ability to influence the lawmaking process, and whether individual lawmakers and Congress as a whole are effective. In each chapter, three overarching themes guide our exploration of Congress.

First, the core democratic principles of *representation, separation of powers, and governing* serve as each chapter's point of departure. These principles are the backbone of American democracy. When Congress does not meet its responsibilities with regard to these core democratic principles, there is cause for concern.

Each chapter in this text is therefore structured around explaining an aspect of one or more of these principles. For example, when we study parties in Congress, we describe how parties facilitate the representation process, how parties can help (or hinder) cooperation and oversight between the branches of government, and how parties articulate a governing agenda for lawmakers and the public. When we study congressional committees, we explore the degree to which these panels of policy specialists are at the center of congressional oversight of executive branch agencies and responsible for the formulation of laws. As you read, the core principles of representation, separation of powers, and governing will help you organize and make connections between key concepts.

There is one caveat each chapter does not necessarily focus on all of the core principles in the same depth. For example, when we study the interactions between Congress and the president, we are by definition focusing on separation of powers and governing. Although representation plays a part in the priorities and actions of lawmakers and the president, it takes a back seat to the other two democratic principles.

Second, throughout this book, we place today's Congress, which is seemingly so different from the "textbook" legislature, in its historical context. Accordingly, in each chapter, we offer a section titled "Then and Now." These sections explore how Congress has changed over the course of years, decades, or even centuries. Sometimes, these changes have occurred quickly. Sometimes, they are slow-moving transformations that are perceptible only with many years of hindsight. Our goal in underscoring the evolution of Congress over time is to understand why Congress has changed and what that means for Congress today and in the future.

Third, to be fully conversant in the actions and accomplishments of the contemporary Congress, it is not enough to merely know the facts about the institution. It is also important to understand how political scientists know what they know. Each chapter thus includes a "How We Study Congress" section that delves into a specific question relevant to the subject of that chapter, how social scientists approach that question, and the resources and tools they use to search for answers. We hope these sections will help you develop a deep understanding of cutting-edge research and the newest and most important findings by congressional scholars.

Let's begin.

2

The Historical Development of Congress

Observers of contemporary American politics, both experts and amateurs alike, agree that Congress is significantly polarized by party. Democrats and Republicans in Congress rarely see eye to eye on important policy matters and regularly disagree about the right direction for the country. Partisanship has also affected how Congress relates to the other two branches of the federal system. How seriously to investigate executive decisions often comes down to whether the president and Congress share the same party affiliation. For example, a Republican House spent four years investigating whether Democratic president Barack Obama's State Department, led by Hillary Clinton, was responsible for security lapses surrounding the terrorist attack on the U.S. Consulate in Benghazi, Libya, in 2012. Yet the Republican House and Senate in 2017 was slow to investigate charges of Russian tampering in the 2016 U.S. presidential election and that country's ties to Republican president Donald Trump and members of his administration. Moreover, filling vacancies on the Supreme Court has emerged as one of the most partisan issues of the twenty-first century. For instance, in 2016, the Republican Senate refused to consider Obama's choice of Merrick

SOUTHERN CHIVALRY — ARGUMENT VERSUS CLUB'S.

Partisan politics in Congress is not unique to the modern era. Several years before the start of the Civil War, animosity between the parties turned violent when proslavery Democrat Preston Brooks (SC) attacked antislavery Republican Charles Sumner (MA) on the floor of the Senate.

Garland to replace deceased (Republican appointee) Antonin Scalia. The following year, however, the Republican Senate seated Trump's nominee, Neil Gorsuch, and changed the Senate rules prohibiting a filibuster on Supreme Court nominees to do so.

While these events underscore how Congress today is deeply and, perhaps, hopelessly divided by party, it would be wrong to characterize contemporary American politics as unique. American politics at other points in history has been similarly polarized, and Congress has seen its share of heated (and sometimes overheated) partisanship. Prior to the Civil War, it was not uncommon for members of Congress, deeply divided over slavery, to carry pistols into the chamber in anticipation of personal challenges. And in 1857, those differences erupted in actual violence when Democratic representative Preston Brooks (SC) beat Republican senator Charles Sumner (MA) nearly to death on the Senate floor over a speech that Sumner made sharply criticizing slaveholders, including Brooks's cousin Democratic senator Andrew Butler (SC). These divisions became insurmountable three years later. After Republican Abraham Lincoln was elected president, Democrats from the Deep South resigned from Congress after their states—which were unwilling to be governed by an antislavery president—seceded from the United States.

In addition, changing chamber rules to achieve partisan ends has been a standard strategy of party leaders in Congress across time. Toward the end of the nineteenth century, for example, Speaker of the House Thomas Reed (R-ME) believed "the best system is to have one party govern and the other party watch," and he used strong-arm tactics to ensure that his Republican majority would be able to get their way. Reed reinterpreted House rules to limit the procedural rights that the Democratic minority possessed, after which the Republicans steamrolled them on a number of policy issues. The Democrats cried foul over Reed's tactics but could do nothing about it. And when the Democrats regained the majority, they adopted the same strategy that Reed had used.

To understand contemporary politics in Congress thus requires us to understand the past. This is true for two reasons. First, it is common for commentators to believe that what happens in Congress today is unprecedented. Sometimes it may be. But often it is not, as the aforementioned examples suggest. To properly evaluate the distinctiveness of contemporary congressional action and behavior requires a long view and a detailed understanding of congressional history. Second, the contemporary Congress and how it relates in the constitutional order to the executive (president and bureaucracy) and the judiciary (the Supreme Court and lower federal courts) has changed over time. While Congress was designed to be the nation's leading institution, and operated as such for much of our history, its relative position has declined in recent years as the executive and judiciary have grown in prominence and power. That shift has occurred gradually and requires a historical understanding to identify key points and causes. The contemporary Congress also reflects changes in the social and political fabric of the United States—changes that affect whom members represent and how they are elected. Studying the contemporary Congress without a solid understanding of how the institution has developed over time—both internally and externally within a changing nation and a federal system of shared powers—runs the risk of misinterpreting contemporary actions and events by failing to contextualize them properly.

This chapter is divided into four sections. The first section provides a short summary of Congress's constitutional foundations, with the next three sections covering three distinct eras in American congressional history. The three eras document how Congress's governing and representational roles in the constitutional order have changed over time. The Framers of the Constitution created a separated system of federal power, but clearly envisioned Congress playing the leading role in that system. For the first era of American congressional history, until the start of the Civil War, Congress indeed was the dominant institutional actor. That began to change in the second era, which extended through the first three decades of the twentieth century, as presidents began to assert their influence. In the current era, which begins with the New Deal, the executive and judiciary have continued to grow in power to the point that Congress—especially a polarized Congress that struggles to act—is often rivaled in important matters of governance.

CONSTITUTIONAL FOUNDATIONS

From the first moments the colonists rebelled against Great Britain's monarchy, the essential question at the heart of the insurrection was how to place a representative body of lawmakers at the center of governing. Chafing at the imposition of excessive taxes imposed by King George III in the 1760s and 1770s, colonists gathered in Philadelphia in the fall of 1774 to discuss and coordinate their resistance to rule by the British Crown. The primary point of contention was that governing had been done by decree of a foreign monarchy without any direct representation of the people being governed.

In what became known as the First Continental Congress, each colony sent a group of unelected representatives composed of intellectual and business elites to Philadelphia to lay out a plan for boycotting British products and resisting the king's decrees. These plans also set in motion the creation of what would develop into statewide conventions acting in place of the colonial assemblies that the British had disbanded. Eventually, those conventions selected delegates to the Second Continental Congress, also in Philadelphia, in the spring of 1775. That legislative body now had a full-on insurrection to manage, requiring the creation of more formal governing bodies in the colonies, the construction of a coordinated military, and the raising of funds to finance the war effort.

The members of the Second Congress would sign the Declaration of Independence in 1776 and, more important from a governing perspective, draft the Articles of Confederation. In stark contrast to the governing authority that existed in most other places in the Western world, the Articles sanctioned a legislative body composed of representatives of the various states assembled into a confederation. Starting with its ratification by all the states in 1781, the Congress created under the Articles was the sole instrument of a national government. However, while the colonists had emerged victorious in the Revolutionary War, the new confederation government faced a massive public debt, a struggling economy, and widespread discontent with its performance. The congressional institutions under the Articles proved to be too weak to allow for effective governing: all important decisions required supermajorities, laws passed by Congress were not binding on the states, and limited rules of procedure meant that legislating was nearly impossible.[1]

Consequently, 55 delegates from the 13 states met again in Philadelphia in 1787 to consider an initial revision of the Articles.[2] While the delegates had no mandate to redraft the governing document for the new nation, after much deliberation, this is exactly what they decided to do. Organizing themselves into a Constitutional Convention, the delegates all agreed that the national government needed to be strengthened and that Congress needed stronger internal institutions. But there were disagreements between delegates from large (more populous) and small (less populous) states about how representation in the new national legislature would be designed. While the large states wanted representation to be based exclusively on population, and the small states desired equal representation for each state, a compromise was ultimately reached whereby they would split the difference: Congress would be bicameral, with representation in the lower chamber (the House of Representatives) based on population and in the upper chamber (the Senate) based on equality. Members of the House would be elected directly by the people, while members of the Senate would be chosen by state legislatures.

In drafting what would become the U.S. Constitution, the delegates—often called the Framers—established a federal system in which the national government would be supreme over state governments. And while they saw the need for both a national executive and a national judiciary, the Framers also clearly established the national legislature as the most important institution within the new federal system. That said, to protect against the possibility of majority tyranny, institutional powers were separated and checks and balances among the three branches were created. The Congress was the chief lawmaker, and a set of powers—to lay and collect taxes, to borrow and coin money, and to regulate commerce—was specifically enumerated (Article I, Section 8). The president was given the power to veto acts of Congress (Article I, Section 7), which Congress could override by a two-thirds vote in each chamber. The president and Senate would share authority on treaty making, ambassador appointments, cabinet-level executive appointments, and judicial appointments (Article II, Section 2). The courts, by comparison, were woefully underdeveloped: only a Supreme Court was specified (Article III, Section 1), and no power of "judicial review"—the ability to declare a law unconstitutional—was created. Only later, in the *Marbury v. Madison* case in 1803, did Chief Justice John Marshall "discover" judicial review.

Thus within this new constitutional order, the Framers clearly considered Congress to be supreme. The president was a significantly weaker number two: a factor, but not a direct precipitator of policy. The Supreme Court was a distant third. This then was the constellation of forces when the First Federal Congress assembled in the spring of 1789.

THE ANTEBELLUM ERA (1789–1861)

The years from the constitutional founding through the Civil War mark the first period of U.S. congressional history. Congress, at this time, was the preeminent power in the federal government. The nation's political-economic growth and development during these decades was accomplished largely, but not exclusively, by congressional statute. Congress as an institution changed considerably during this time from a body that was built on norms and temporary structures to one that was guided by rules and where permanent structures conducted business.[3]

Political parties in Congress also emerged during this time, created by ambitious politicians to help expedite governing. And three different party systems spanned the era. Partisans in Congress would routinely battle over the federal government's role in the economy, with Federalists, and later Whigs, advocating for a more activist federal government to help develop the nation and Jeffersonian Republicans supporting a weaker federal government that would leave more decision-making power to the states. In time, an issue that both parties sought to keep off the legislative agenda—slavery—emerged to threaten the continued existence of the new nation. Congressional deals postponed the inevitable for several decades, but eventually slavery tore the nation apart.

The Early Years

On March 4, 1789, the First Federal Congress convened. Over the next four decades, Congress would develop in ways that would create the foundation for the institution we see today. In its earliest years, Congress was not overly complex. The number of representatives and senators was relatively small, decisions were deliberative, and political parties were nonexistent. The House was considered the unruly body, while the Senate was viewed as the more high-minded and dispassionate body.

Very quickly, however, congressional leaders realized that discussing and debating each bill or issue as a body (or a "committee of the whole") was extremely time consuming. Thus leaders in both the House and Senate quickly moved to create committees to handle legislative business. For much of the Congress's first 30 years, "select" committees dominated. These committees were temporary, often created to perform a single task, such as drafting a piece of legislation, and expired at the end of a Congress's two-year cycle. By the mid-1810s, the use of "standing" committees grew, both in the House (where the change was more gradual) and the Senate (where the change was more rapid). Standing committees were permanent bodies existing beyond the bounds of a given Congress; their permanent nature would allow them to serve as repositories of information and expertise, both of which congressional leaders learned were important for policy making. By the late 1820s, standing committees dominated both chambers.

Parties in Congress also emerged quickly. In the First Congress, legislative activities were organized around leading figures in the new nation: Alexander Hamilton, Thomas Jefferson, and James Madison. Despite possessing a majority in Congress, Hamilton's proponents, who sought a strong national government, often found themselves stymied on the floor by Jefferson and Madison's supporters, who preferred stronger states' rights. The core problem was that Hamilton's followers struggled to stick together on key votes, while Jefferson and Madison's followers were able to raise issues strategically to split the Hamiltonian coalition apart.

As a result, Hamilton and his lieutenants began to develop the institutional machinery that would constitute the nation's first political parties: informal whip systems to share information, informal caucuses to communicate the importance of remaining unified on major issues, and informal floor leader positions to align member behavior during congressional proceedings and votes. Stated differently, a bond of partisanship was created, whereby members were educated on how they would be better off in the long run if they coordinated their actions and voted together. Soon thereafter, Hamilton's proponents began winning consistently on key policy votes and thereby became a formidable legislative coalition. Jefferson and Madison's forces responded to the Hamiltonians' newfound governing success by adopting the same institutional techniques.[4]

By the mid-1790s, an institutional party system was in full swing as parties became the means by which Congress governed. Hamilton's proponents began calling themselves Federalists, while Jefferson and Madison's followers referred to themselves as Jeffersonian Republicans. The two parties reflected different groups in society and thus had different visions for the nation's future. The Federalists, based in the Northeast, were more elite focused and represented business, financial, and commercial interests, while the Jeffersonian Republicans, based in the South, were the party of the common people and represented agrarian and worker interests. This period in which Federalists and Jeffersonian Republicans vied for political control would be known as the First Party System. For the first decade of the new nation, the Federalists were the majority party in Congress. With Thomas Jefferson's election as president in 1800, the Jeffersonians took control of Congress, and the Federalists were relegated to a permanent minority.

This era also saw the emergence of the first strong Speaker of the House of Representatives, Henry Clay of Kentucky. Clay was one of a group of young members from the South and West known as the "War Hawks," who pressured President James Madison to enter into war with the British (in what became known as the War of 1812). Over time, Clay saw the speakership as a means of achieving power in the federal system and as a stepping-stone to higher positions, such as the presidency. Before Clay, Speakers were more reticent about using the authority of the office in a strict partisan or individualistic way and often demurred to the wishes of strong presidents (such as Thomas Jefferson) on matters of policy. Clay made the speakership a partisan office and showcased—through the creation of new standing committees, the granting of new rights to committees, and the strategic allocation of committee assignments—how it could be an independent position of power. For example, Clay created a new set of "oversight" committees to monitor expenditures in the executive Departments of State, Treasury, and War, thus enhancing the position of Congress (especially the House) in the constitutional order.[5]

The Second Party System and Slavery

From the 1830s through the mid-1850s, a new party system operated in Congress and in the nation: the Second Party System, in which Whigs faced off against Democrats on the national stage. The Whigs replaced the Federalists and were similar philosophically. They were the big-government party of the time and sought to use the power of the federal government in an activist way. To help develop the nation's economy, they proposed protecting the country's infant industries through a high tariff, linking population centers and markets through the federal funding of internal improvements (such as national roads and canals), and providing financial stability for the nation through the creation of a national bank and banking system. The Democrats, as the descendants of the Jeffersonians, were the small-government party. They preferred lower tariffs to help expedite trade and the sale of agricultural products overseas, internal improvements to be the exclusive jurisdiction of the states, and banking to be decentralized and thus locally controlled. The Democrats were led by President Andrew Jackson (TN) and his successor, Martin Van Buren (NY), while the Whigs were led by (now Senator) Henry Clay, former president and now House member John Quincy Adams (MA), and Senator Daniel Webster (MA).

Unlike during the First Party System, when the Federalists and Jeffersonians were largely institutional parties (or "parties in Congress"), both the Democrats and Whigs were mass parties, with extensive connections throughout the nation's states and localities. Suffrage rights were broadened considerably in the early nineteenth century, and wealth and property restrictions were largely done away with, making participatory democracy considerably less elite. Finally, the Democrats and Whigs were both interregional parties, with wings in both the North (the free states) and the South (the slave states).

To maintain interregional harmony, leaders in both parties sought to focus political conflict on issues that divided them from each other—tariff rates, internal improvements, banking—rather than on issues that divided along regional lines. However, a regional issue—slavery—was always bubbling under the surface and threatening to tear both parties apart. The slavery issue during the Second Party System was governed initially by a law enacted toward the end of the First Party System. The Missouri Compromise (1820) admitted Missouri into the Union as a slave state, admitted Maine into the Union as a free state, and established Missouri's southern border as the dividing line for slavery rights (prohibited above this line, allowed below) in the remainder of the Western territory acquired via the Louisiana Purchase (1803). The Missouri Compromise, and subsequent statehood decisions, established a rough system of parity in free versus slave states, which provided the southern (slave) states with an implicit policy veto in the Senate over bills that might restrict slavery in the future.

By the late 1830s, the slavery issue reared up again. Antislavery activists in the North began sending petitions to Congress for the elimination of slavery. Southern lawmakers sought to prevent these petitions from being read by forcing Congress to adopt a "gag rule." And while southerners were successful initially, northern members eventually chafed at their constituents being silenced and chose to repeal the gag rule.[6] This case highlighted the growing tension between governance (both parties agreeing to keep slavery off the agenda to maintain interregional harmony) and representation (individual members of Congress seeking to satisfy the wishes of their constituents, even on divisive issues) in the young nation.

By the early 1840s, the tenuous basis of the Missouri Compromise was eroding, and southerners looked further west for more land to populate and extend slavery.[7] Led by Democratic president James Polk, the Democratic majority in Congress—over the objections of the Whigs—sought to annex the Independent Republic of Texas, which Mexico still considered part of its nation. As a result, Mexico and the United States went to war. And after several years of hostilities, the United States extracted by treaty huge tracts of Mexican land in the West (California and the territory that would become New Mexico, Arizona, Utah, Nevada, and parts of other states). Eventually, Congress adopted a series of laws to decide the slavery status of these newly acquired Western territories. Known together as the Compromise of 1850, these laws established the right of "popular sovereignty," allowing the people of the territories to decide for themselves whether slavery would be allowed or prohibited.

The Compromise of 1850 would put significant pressure on the interregional dynamics of the two parties. Slavery had become a lightning rod issue in mass politics, and pro- and antislavery forces fought to extend or abolish slavery in the West. Members of Congress were often torn between following their parties—and establishing a coherent governing strategy—and representing the wishes of their constituents back home. Slavery inserted a regional wedge between the parties, and most members eventually voted with their region (free or slave) rather than with their party. Democratic leaders were able to convince enough northern Democrats to support the Compromise of 1850 to get the deal done. These northern Democrats were known as "dough faces," or "northern men with southern principles." On the Whig side of the aisle, the compromise votes revealed fatal fissures in the party, exposing the tenuous nature of the inter-regional coalition.

Four years later, proslavery forces continued their search for new land. This time, congressional Democrats sought to undo the basis of the Missouri Compromise by making the free territory within the remaining Louisiana Purchase land open to slavery via popular sovereignty. Once again, Democratic leaders coerced a small majority of northern Democrats in the House to support the deal (known as the Kansas-Nebraska Act), while the Whigs were split perfectly by region (northerners against, southerners for). While the Democrats would be hurt (in the North) by their continued support of slavery extension, the Whigs would not survive at all. Slavery extension had exposed the Whigs as too fractured to be a viable governing coalition. As a result, the Whigs' national organization collapsed, and northern and southern party members sought new partisan homes.

The Rise of the Republicans and the Third-Party System

As the Whig Party collapsed, a new major party emerged to take its place. The growth of antislavery popular politics in the North, helped along by the Democrats' continued push to extend slavery, eventually led members of various antislavery minor parties and groups (such as the Liberty Party, the Free Soil Party, and the Northern Whigs) to combine their efforts under one banner.[8] This new party—the Republican Party—was a wholly northern party, organized explicitly around antislavery principles.[9] The Republicans achieved their first major victory in the House speakership election of 1855–56, when antislavery candidate Nathaniel Banks of Massachusetts was elected after 2 months and 133 ballots. Over the next few years, the Republicans' popularity grew in the North as the proslavery Democratic Party weakened. The *Dred Scott* decision in 1857, proffered by a proslavery Supreme Court, helped Republican Party growth by establishing (in an extreme and subsequently criticized decision) that slavery was a fundamental (constitutional) right that Congress could not legislate. The following year, the Democrats suffered their first slavery-extension defeat, when attempts to convert the Kansas Territory into a proslavery state failed in both a House vote and a popular referendum. Finally, in 1860, Republican Abraham Lincoln of Illinois was elected to the presidency.

Lincoln's election was too much for the proslavery forces, and 11 southern states seceded from the Union and formed their own government: the Confederate States of America.[10] Yet Lincoln and the Republicans tried to reunify the country before it was too late. In early 1861, both the House and Senate, now controlled by the Republicans, passed (by the necessary two-thirds vote required to change the Constitution) legislation for a proposed Thirteenth Amendment that would have preserved slavery rights for all time in states where it already existed. Lincoln supported this proposed amendment after he ascended to the presidency later that year.[11] The amendment was never ratified, however, and the southern states were determined to strike out on their own.[12] President Lincoln was equally determined to keep the Union together. As a result, the American Civil War began.

THE CIVIL WAR THROUGH THE EARLY 1930s

The years spanning 1861 (the beginning of the Civil War) and 1932 (the election of President Franklin Delano Roosevelt) represent the middle period of congressional history. During this time, great changes occurred throughout the country. Coming out of a bloody Civil War, the United States needed to rebuild, and a period of Reconstruction ensued. New citizenship and voting rights were granted to the former slaves, and the southern states, which had seceded, were formally brought back into the Union. At the same time, the nation was industrializing at a rapid pace, which created a host of new political and economic issues involving the regulation of business and the rights and obligations of citizens in the new, modern economy. By the early years of the twentieth century, the United States was well on its way to being a world power, and governmental infrastructure began expanding to meet those needs. At the heart of all these changes was Congress.

The Civil War

During the Civil War, Congress often found itself in an unusual position, playing second fiddle to the president in matters of governance. As discussed earlier, despite a constitutional role that was clearly subservient to Congress, the president had occasionally played a meaningful role in national policy making. Sometimes, this had occurred via direct presidential action, as when Thomas Jefferson purchased the Louisiana Territory from France in 1803. But often, this had occurred because of congressional deference to the occupant of the White House (as during the Jefferson, Jackson, and Polk presidencies). But once the southern states had seceded and war was declared to keep the Union together, the president—Abraham Lincoln—as commander in chief took center stage. At the same time, Congress, led by Republican majorities in both chambers, was determined to remain relevant.[13]

Much of Lincoln's authority stemmed from pressing political realities. Because the Civil War began when Congress was not in session, Lincoln was forced to step in and make a series of important policy decisions by executive decree. For example, after the Confederate capture of Fort Sumter (off the coast of Charleston, South Carolina) in April 1861, Lincoln was quick to mobilize for the impending war, immediately calling up 75,000 volunteers to quell the rebellion and declaring martial law (by suspending the writ of habeas corpus) between Washington, D.C., and Philadelphia. Recognizing the need for legislative validation, Lincoln called Congress into an emergency session in early July 1861, wherein lawmakers informally ratified his executive actions in the context of war powers that were necessary to preserve the Union. Congress then produced a revenue act to finance the war effort and a conscription act—the first draft in American history—to build an army.

Thus early in the war, the president was the guiding force in national policy making, with Congress seemingly forced into a secondary role. Yet Republican majorities in the House and Senate were not content with playing second fiddle. For example, they sought to oversee President Lincoln's handling of the war effort through the creation of the Joint Committee on the Conduct of the War. Made up of strongly antislavery Republicans (who became known as "Radicals") from both chambers of Congress, the Joint Committee investigated all aspects of major Civil War battles and frequently pursued aggressive second-guessing of military strategy. Moreover, the Joint Committee was often successful in replacing key generals with individuals more in line with their own political preferences. This repeatedly led to disasters on the battlefield.[14]

Amid the war, congressional Republicans also continued to pursue their prime policy goal: the elimination of slavery. In the first year of the war, the Republican-led Congress set the course for abolition by passing two confiscation laws (freeing slaves in the context of Confederate "property" seizure) and a compensated emancipation law specific to the District of Columbia. These congressional enactments helped establish abolition as the ultimate goal of the Union war effort and set the groundwork for Lincoln's Emancipation Proclamation (issued in September 1862 to take effect on January 1, 1863), which freed all slaves in territory still under rebellion. Congress then moved to abolish slavery entirely via legislation that would become the Thirteenth Amendment, which was passed and ratified in 1865.

Reconstruction and Its Aftermath

In time, thanks largely to a significant manpower advantage, the Union would emerge victorious in the Civil War. As a result, national political leaders turned their attention to the next major challenge: North-South reconciliation. As noted, thanks to war demands and commander-in-chief responsibilities, the presidency had risen in the nation's constitutional order. Whether such an activist presidency would carry over into peacetime was the question. The early postwar years would provide the answer, as the president and Congress clashed over how the conquered Confederate South should be "reconstructed" and reintegrated into the Federal Union. In the end, Congress established complete control over Reconstruction policy, reversing early presidential efforts and overcoming subsequent presidential opposition and vetoes. This early postwar period was Congress's high-water mark in terms of authority in the nineteenth-century constitutional order and returned the presidency to the relatively weak position of the prewar era (where it would remain until the early twentieth century).

Shortly before the war ended, John Wilkes Booth, a Confederate sympathizer, assassinated Lincoln. Vice President Andrew Johnson, a former "War Democrat" from Tennessee, ascended to the presidency. Johnson's plan for reuniting North and South was amicable (and likely would have mirrored Lincoln's plan): if the states that had seceded were prepared to pledge their allegiance to the United States and recognize the legality of the Thirteenth Amendment, he was prepared to welcome them back. Radical Republicans in Congress had a much different idea, seeking instead a fundamental rebuilding of southern society that would be both liberating (elevating former black slaves to political equality with whites) and punitive (preventing former white leaders from regaining power). To organize and direct their efforts in this regard, the Radicals created the Joint Committee on Reconstruction, a 15-member select committee.

Johnson and Congress locked horns over these different visions. Thanks to Johnson's inept leadership and reports that former Confederates were attempting to create institutions ("Black Codes") that would economically subjugate the former slaves, the Radical Republicans emerged victorious. Enjoying supermajorities in both chambers of Congress following the elections of 1866, the Republicans passed legislation that would become the Fourteenth Amendment (guaranteeing federal citizenship to former slaves along with due process and equal protection under the law) and the Fifteenth Amendment (disallowing race, color, or previous condition of servitude as criteria for restricting voting rights). And in four Reconstruction Acts, they carved up the South into military zones and established martial law in order to compel southern whites to accept black citizenship and voting rights. Moreover, the Radicals directed the military to be proactive in registering African Americans to vote and in doing so helped create a viable southern wing of the Republican Party.

In establishing a Radical Reconstruction, the Republican-led Congress steamrolled Johnson. For example, all four of the Reconstruction Acts were adopted over a Johnson veto. And the readmittance of several southern states, reconstructed per the Radicals' wishes, was also accomplished by overriding Johnson. In all, Johnson issued 21 regular vetoes during his presidency, and Congress overrode 15 of them. Eventually, the Radicals grew tired of Johnson's intransigence and in early 1868 sought to impeach him.[15] In the end, they fell one vote short of the two-thirds vote necessary for conviction in the Senate, and Johnson survived.[16] But he was rendered relatively ineffective for the remainder of his term, and the presidency itself was minimized in the larger constitutional order.

Thanks to enfranchisement and aggressive registration efforts, African Americans in the South quickly remade the region. The "freedmen" voted in large numbers and helped establish strong Republican governments throughout the former Confederate states. While many of these southern Republican politicians were white, African Americans were also elected to a substantial number of offices. Between 1870 and 1876, 632 African Americans served in southern state legislatures, 14 in the U.S. House, and 2 in the U.S. Senate.[17] Thus African American suffrage also led to significant descriptive representation—with the election of politicians who "looked like them," and could relate to and understand the experience of African Americans in a deeper way.

Radical Reconstruction would not last, however. Southern whites and the Democratic Party worked hard to challenge the new Republican governments, and violence and intimidation were used to dampen African American voting power. Congress actively investigated such illegal activities, delegating power to the president to protect African Americans and preserve the sanctity of the voting process. While these efforts produced some success, there were many countervailing pressures at work. White southerners continued to press for white supremacy, and northern support for Reconstruction ebbed amid an economic depression that began in 1874. As white voters in the North tired of the near-daily newspaper "drama" of Reconstruction, Democrats began winning elections and taking back state governments in the South. By 1877, the transition was complete: in exchange for the Democrats conceding to the disputed presidential election of 1876 being decided in favor of Republican Rutherford Hayes, the Republicans, by then nicknamed the "Grand Old Party" (GOP), ended the stationing of the army at southern polling places. Shortly thereafter, Democrats took over the last three Republican-controlled state governments in the South.[18]

While Reconstruction ended officially in 1877, African American rights did not disappear overnight. Although white southerners continued to use violence and intimidation to suppress African American voting, there were still some Republican electoral successes in portions of North Carolina, Tennessee, and Virginia. Indeed, from 1877 to 1900, five additional African Americans from the South were elected to the U.S. House. That said, white southern Democrats were ever watchful for a GOP resurgence. So when Republicans in the 51st Congress (1889–91) were nearly successful in passing a new Federal Election Law to enforce African American voting rights in the South, the Democrats moved away from ad hoc strategies of violence and intimidation and toward legal remedies. Starting in 1890 in Mississippi, statutory and constitutional changes at the state level were made to disenfranchise African Americans. These changes, which included poll taxes, literacy tests, and residency requirements, became known as Jim Crow laws, and by 1908, all states in the South had adopted some form of them.[19] They did not discriminate explicitly by race—and thus sidestepped the provisions of the Fifteenth Amendment—but were extremely effective at eliminating African American participation in the South and by extension Republican representation in Congress.[20]

In the end, Jim Crow laws eliminated voting rights for African Americans in the South for generations, and the region became a one-party Democratic state for the first half of the twentieth century.[21] As African American voters in the South were disenfranchised, African American members of Congress also disappeared. Republican George H. White (NC), who left the House in 1901, would be the last African American member of Congress from the South to serve during this era. An African American would not represent a southern state in Congress again until 1973, when Democrats Barbara Jordan (TX) and Andrew Young (GA) were seated in the House.

The Gilded Age and Progressive Era

The half-century spanning 1870 to 1920 combined multiple traditions in American society. As noted earlier, this period included the end of Reconstruction and the period of white "redemption" in the South. But in other parts of the country, different trends were under way. One such trend was an upsurge in industrialization and national economic development. As the nation expanded economically, large gaps between rich and poor emerged. This period of significant income inequality has been referred to as the Gilded Age. A second trend was, in many ways, a response to the first. The economic expansion and development during the Gilded Age concentrated wealth in the hands of a few and bred rampant political and economic corruption. As a result, reformers emerged and sought social, economic, and political change in the country. This period of changing societal priorities and democratizing political processes has been referred to as the Progressive Era.

With the Civil War over and the institutions of Reconstruction in place, the Republicans in Congress turned their attention to national economic policy. Republicans, like the Whigs before them, believed the federal government should promote economic development. Thus federal spending on national infrastructure—railroads, canals, and rivers and harbors—grew considerably in the 1870s and 1880s. While new federal spending expanded, interest-group lobbying also grew as businesses sought out politicians in Washington to "grease the wheels" for their favored projects.[22] This lobbying bred corruption, both in President Ulysses S. Grant's administration and in Congress.[23]

The federal government's expansion in the national political economy, along with the subsequent rise in interest-group activity (and opportunities for corruption), also had an effect on congressional career patterns. As government power and influence began to shift from the states to the federal government, politicians began to adjust their aspirations accordingly. Prior to the Civil War, ambitious politicians normally sought a career in the party rather than in Congress. Consequently, political careers often had a leapfrog quality to them as politicians moved back and forth between local, state, and federal elective (and appointed) positions. As federal policy making grew and Congress's role in major economic decisions expanded, ambitious politicians began to view Congress as a final destination or a place to build a lengthy career. By the end of the nineteenth century, a "congressional career" had become the norm for most members of Congress.[24]

Along with the rise of careerism were other changes to the electoral environment that provided members of Congress with more direct control over their political lives. For example, in the 1880s, state-sponsored ballots began to replace party ballots. During the party-ballot era, the two parties created and distributed ballots, which gave them considerable control over the electoral process. Such ballots were often color coded and listed only the given party's candidates for each office, which both limited voters' choices and revealed their party preferences to all who might be watching (and thus created incentives for vote buying and intimidation). The state-sponsored (or "Australian") ballot introduced secrecy into the process and gave electoral authority to the state governments.[25] Voters were now provided with "official" ballots that listed multiple party candidates for each office, and they could split their tickets (select different party candidates for various offices) if they so desired—all without anyone being able to observe their voting choices.

The emergence of the Australian ballot firmed up the electoral connection by creating a direct link between House members and their constituents. Voters could now reward or punish individual representatives for their behavior in office. In the party-ballot days, by contrast, voters were largely restricted to casting votes for an entire party ticket. Thus House members now had an increased incentive to be responsive to their constituents' preferences and to seek out institutions that would signal their efforts and achievements. As a result, congressional seniority on standing committees increased substantially around the turn of the twentieth century, as committees were seen as a vehicle by which members could build policy expertise and claim credit for policy achievements.[26]

Whereas the Australian ballot affected elections, an additional reform took hold in the first two decades of the twentieth century that affected nominations: party primaries began to replace party nominating conventions. Primaries allowed citizens to determine directly who would represent the party for elective offices, such as the House of Representatives. This move to direct representation *within* the party had two main effects: (1) it reduced the power of party leaders to screen candidates and influence the substantive direction of the party, and (2) it helped reduce intraparty conflict, as factional groups were more likely to accept democratic decisions by the people rather than nondemocratic decisions by a select group of party actors.[27]

At the same time, the internal party organizations in the House and Senate were solidifying in a conservative direction. In the 1870s and 1880s, collective decision making in Congress was often hampered by the minority party, as their procedural rights were plentiful and strong. The minority took advantage of this, especially in the House, to hinder the majority party's pursuit of its agenda and to extract considerable policy concessions along the way. The period of strong minority party power ended in 1890 with the House speakership of Thomas Reed (R-ME). Reed reinterpreted the House rules to limit the power of the minority. The Republicans then adopted a series of changes to the House rules—over the strenuous objections of the Democrats—that codified and enhanced Reed's rulings. These "Reed Rules" allowed the majority party to govern effectively, shunting the minority aside and establishing a two-decade period of strong party government in the House.[28] In the Senate, a Reed-style revolution did not occur, as a single leader did not emerge to promote efficient governing. Instead, a four-person Republican team—known as the "Senate Four"—was created to mimic the leadership developments in the House.[29]

The strong party rule by Republicans in Congress between 1890 and 1910 was directed toward promoting conservative interests (such as those of eastern bankers and financial elites), and thus was increasingly challenged by Republicans with more progressive leanings, both in Congress and by Republican president Theodore Roosevelt.[30] After being stymied for years under Speaker Joe Cannon (IL), who followed Reed in governing the House with an iron fist, the progressive Republicans in the House joined with Democrats to strip Cannon of most of his power—such as the ability to make committee assignments—and shift authority in the chamber away from the majority party leadership and toward the standing committees.[31] This shift would typify politics for most of the remaining twentieth century, as *committee government* characterized how power was structured in the House. And seniority was the new way of attaining chairs and achieving influence within the committee system.[32]

The revolt against Cannon ushered in a decade of significant progressive change, some internal to Congress and some resulting from Congress's actions. A split in the Republican Party between President William Howard Taft's conservative faction and ex-president Theodore Roosevelt's progressive faction led to progressive Democrat Woodrow Wilson's election to the presidency in 1912. The factionalism within the GOP also carried over into Congress, as narrow Democratic majorities in both chambers rode in on Wilson's coattails. This unified Democratic government lasted six years and was the by-product of Republican divisions. As a result, Democrats in Congress looked to Wilson to create a broad agenda that would allow them to survive and thrive, if and when the GOP mended its intraparty fences.

Wilson took on a "prime minister" role during this time, meeting regularly with House and Senate party leaders, and directing their policy efforts. As a result, the Democrats tried to create a "binding party caucus" on some policy issues during the Wilson years, wherein Democratic lawmakers were formally expected (or bound) to support the party's decisions on the floor.[33] This brief period represents the closest thing to a system of "parliamentary government" in American history. And while this experiment did not work as intended and was abandoned quickly (with the Democrats' loss of unified government following the 1918 midterms), the Democrat-led Congress was successful at adopting a series of progressive reforms during the Wilson years, including the creation of a new federal banking system, new antitrust legislation, and the first child labor laws.[34] Moreover, the role as national policy leader that Wilson adopted would become (after a brief retrenchment in the 1920s) the standard for presidents thereafter and help define the modern political era.

In the Progressive Era, Congress also addressed major governing and representational issues through enactments that would become constitutional amendments. The Sixteenth Amendment provided for a federal income tax, which gave the federal government a new revenue stream and (over the next two decades) helped eliminate a prime source of intra- and cross-chamber governing difficulties in Congress: the regular revision of the protective tariff. The Seventeenth Amendment democratized the Senate by replacing indirect elections (and thereby eliminating the state legislatures' role) with direct elections. Like House members, senators would now be chosen directly by the citizenry, and senators would consequently behave more in keeping with a constituency-based electoral connection.[35] The Nineteenth Amendment provided voting rights for women, thereby doubling the number of voters in federal elections. While more than three-quarters of the states had provided women with some degree of voting rights by then, often these were limited to local or school elections. Jeannette Rankin (R-MT) was the first woman to be elected to Congress—as a member of the House—in 1916. Rankin was instrumental in leading the House debate on legislation that would prohibit the states and the federal government from denying the right to vote to citizens on account of sex, which would become the basis of the Nineteenth Amendment.

Conservative Revival

By the start of the 1920s, the progressive movement had lost steam. Theodore Roosevelt had died, and the conservative and progressive wings of the Republican Party had begun to cooperate again. As a result, the Republicans were able to dominate elections, and they enjoyed unified control of government for the entire decade. Moreover, the conservative wing of the party called the shots, buoyed by the economic boom that was felt in all sectors of the economy.

The last vestiges of progressivism in the Republican Party were effectively eliminated during this time. A number of midwestern Republicans fought against the conservative party leadership in the House, opposing the speakership election of Republican William Gillette (MA) in 1923 and backing Progressive Robert La Follette's (WI) presidential campaign instead of GOP nominee Calvin Coolidge in 1924. The conservative leaders in the Republican Party quickly asserted their authority, however, and punished the Progressive defectors accordingly. Speaker Nicholas Longworth—Gillette's successor—stripped them of their committee seniority and banished them from the party conference until they pledged their loyalty.[36] These sanctions eventually brought the Republican progressives in the House in line, while Republican progressives in the Senate held out a while longer.[37] The Republican Party would thenceforth be a conservative governing authority. Progressivism, which had existed in both parties since the nineteenth century and counted Theodore Roosevelt as an important leader, would only exist in a meaningful way in the Democratic Party going forward.

Two statutory changes also occurred during the 1920s that affected Congress's governing and representational roles. First, in 1921, Congress passed the Budget and Accounting Act, which required the president to submit an annual budget for the entire federal government to Congress. The act also created the Bureau of the Budget, which later became the Office of Management and Budget, to help the president assemble budgetary requests from agencies and consolidate and organize those requests. The 1921 act is generally viewed as the starting point for the "institutional presidency" (or the modern presidency), which possesses independent sources of expertise and information (staff) and is linked to other facets of the federal government. While individual presidents, such as Theodore Roosevelt and Woodrow Wilson, had exerted influence in the early twentieth century, the 1921 act started a trend toward empowering the *office of the presidency* with substantial capacity and authority, which increasingly made it a governing rival to Congress. Second, in 1929, a new Apportionment Act was passed, which capped the size of the House of Representatives at 435 members. Prior to that, the size of the House had increased in a near-continuous fashion after every decennial census, to the point that the chamber's ability to govern effectively was threatened. House size, with one exception, has been permanently capped at 435 ever since.[38] With continued growth in the U.S. population, this "435 cap" has meant that House members represent larger and larger constituencies over time.

While economic prosperity defined the "Roaring Twenties," a cataclysmic conclusion was waiting at the end of the decade. In October of 1929, a stock market panic and crash—driven by excess stock speculation, lax banking and financial regulation, risky corporate mergers, and plummeting consumer confidence—led to a growing series of personal and corporate bankruptcies and bank failures. The economy sank into a full-scale depression, with double-digit unemployment, housing foreclosures, and additional business collapses. The Herbert Hoover administration and the Republican Congress were slow to respond, and the depression deepened. Eventually, the Republicans lost the House in 1930, and the Democrats, behind the presidential candidacy of Franklin Delano Roosevelt (FDR), swept the 1932 elections and gained unified control of the federal government. Indeed, the Democrats would have sizeable majorities in both the House and Senate—and two years later, supermajorities. FDR and the Democrat-led Congress would have a profound effect on American society, and their "New Deal for the American People" would usher in a new era in American national governance.

THEN AND NOW
LAME-DUCK SESSIONS OF CONGRESS

The timing of congressional sessions—when members of Congress come together to meet and legislate—has influenced the nature of both representation and governance. Here we document the rise and fall of the regularly occurring *lame-duck session of Congress* (because of the adoption of the Twentieth Amendment in 1933) and the rise of a new ad hoc lame-duck session that has been a staple of modern congressional politics for the past 25 years.[39]

The lame-duck session of Congress traces its origins back to the nation's constitutional founding. Article I, Section 4, stipulated that Congress would assemble at least once per year, with the first Monday in December established as the date of convening. This led to the adoption of a two-session format, with a first ("long") session extending from December through late spring/early summer and a second ("short") session extending from December through noon on March 4, the official end date of the given Congress.[40]

The December convening decision resulted in an odd institutional arrangement, as the short session of a given Congress met *after* many states held their elections to the *next* Congress. This was especially true after the passage of the Apportionment Act of 1872, which stipulated that all federal elections be held on the *same* day, the first Tuesday after the first Monday in November. As a result, the short session was composed of three different member types: those who had won reelection, those who had lost their reelection or higher-office bids, and those who had decided to retire. The short session thus became known as the *lame-duck session*, because it was populated in part by members who would be exiting the chamber in a few months. These exiting members (or lame ducks) were no longer formally tied to their constituents, but they still enjoyed all the privileges of reelected members, such as the ability to cast roll call votes, thus creating a clear agency problem in representation.

The number of lame ducks in short sessions was often considerable. For example, in the period between 1877 and 1933 (representing the post-Reconstruction/pre–New Deal era), lame ducks constituted around 30 percent of the House on average. In some Congresses, lame ducks represented a *majority* of the chamber. Given the size of this group and the aforementioned agency problem, lame-duck sessions were often unpredictable affairs, frequently characterized by spotty attendance (because of the absence of lame ducks) and procedural delaying tactics used to string business along until the Congress's expiration. A more serious concern was fraud, as lame ducks were sometimes charged with selling their votes, most notably to the president in exchange for executive appointments.

Such vote-buying allegations, which threatened good governance and grew significantly during the Gilded Age, eventually led to efforts to reconfigure the congressional calendar. In the late 1880s, proposals were offered to seat members far earlier in the calendar year—January rather than December—which would eliminate the underlying agency problem, but they went nowhere. Such reform efforts continued into the 1890s, but the status quo always prevailed. Most members could not be persuaded that the current institutional design was working poorly. And despite the best efforts of the progressive press, arguments for a constitutional amendment to abolish lame-duck sessions did not resonate with the citizenry.

Reform efforts returned in force in the second decade of the twentieth century. Filibusters ended all four lame-duck sessions during President Wilson's administration, raising the hackles of the progressive press as well as many politicians. In 1922, the issue came to a head with the passage of a ship subsidy bill, a controversial piece of legislation supported by President Warren G. Harding and passed with votes from a considerable number of Republican lame ducks—votes that Harding was accused of buying with promises of executive appointments.[41] Angered by these accusations and the politics of the shipping bill more generally, Senator George W. Norris (R-NE), a strong proponent of reform, introduced a resolution to move the starting date of Congress forward—harkening back to the proposals decades earlier—and eliminate the lame-duck session. Thanks to growing public support, Norris pushed his resolution through the Senate, but he was blocked by the conservative Republican leadership in the House. This pattern continued for the next four Congresses. Finally, in 1932, Norris succeeded. On his sixth attempt, his resolution was passed in both the Senate and the (now Democrat-controlled) House. And within a year, the Twentieth Amendment was ratified by three-quarters of the states and officially took effect in 1933.

The Twentieth Amendment significantly reconfigured the congressional calendar.[42] The opening of Congress was moved to early January, and the lame-duck (short) session was eliminated and replaced by a second long session that also convened in January. The consequence was the firming up of the representative-constituency relationship—the timing of sessions was altered so that elections to the next Congress would normally take place during the adjournment *between Congresses*, instead of during the adjournment *between sessions of a given Congress*, as Figure 2.1 shows. Thus electoral accountability was strengthened, with *all* members of Congress in office only for periods that occurred between elections. Agency problems (threats of vote buying, low attendance, and the like) were thereby reduced, increasing the likelihood of good governance.

While the Twentieth Amendment eliminated the regularly occurring lame-duck session, a different kind of lame-duck session was still possible. That is, the Twentieth Amendment did not preclude Congress from reconvening in the time between the November elections and the seating of new members the following January. While a given Congress was now made up of two long sessions, a variety of factors could force lawmakers to extend that second session into the November–January time gap that was intended (by proponents of the Twentieth Amendment) to serve as an inter-Congress adjournment. And this new form of lame-duck session—an added postelection portion of the second session—has in fact occurred on 21 occasions between 1935 and 2016.

Post–Twentieth Amendment (or "contemporary") lame-duck sessions were convened sporadically during much of the twentieth century. In the 29 Congresses

FIGURE 2.1 Sequence of Congressional Sessions and Elections, Pre- and Post– Twentieth Amendment

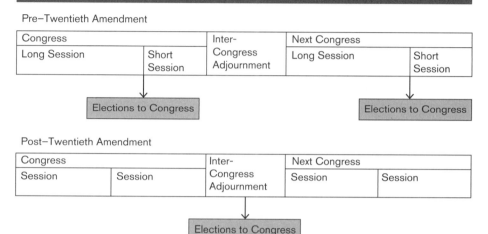

between the 74th (1935–36) and 102nd (1991–92), only 10 included a lame-duck session. This uneven pattern has changed in recent years, however, as a more regularized postelection, lame-duck session has emerged. In the last 13 Congresses—the 103rd (1993–94) through the 115th (2017–19)—12 have included a lame-duck session. More specifically, each of the last 11 Congresses has included a lame-duck session. A postelection, lame-duck session has thus become institutionalized.

Lawmakers have convened contemporary lame-duck sessions for a variety of reasons. Three of the first four lame-duck sessions following the Twentieth Amendment met for reasons related to World War II. Others have been ad hoc to deal with specific issues that have arisen, such as censure of Senator Joseph McCarthy (R-WI) in the 83rd Congress (1953–55), passage of a new General Agreement on Tariffs and Trade treaty in the 103rd Congress (1993–95), and impeachment proceedings against President Bill Clinton in the 105th Congress (1997–99). Still others have been convened to complete important business that was cut short by external events, such as dealing with President Nixon's domestic agenda in the 91st Congress (1969–71), which was stalled by the Vietnam War, and completing a number of important domestic and international policies in the 93rd Congress (1973–75), which were delayed by the Watergate scandal.

Increasingly, however, party leaders have viewed contemporary lame-duck sessions as a means to provide political cover for fellow partisans. Leaders will delay consideration of some issues (and, more important, votes on those issues) until after the November elections so that their members will not have to take unpopular positions before voters go to the polls. The primary "problem" issue that leaders push into lame-duck sessions has involved spending-related legislation, specifically appropriations bills. Other "difficult" issues have included a gasoline tax (which provoked a lame-duck session filibuster), a congressional pay raise, immigration reform, and bankruptcy reform. In recent years, Congress has also used the lame-duck session to create a Department of Homeland Security (107th Congress, 2001–03) and complete an auto bailout of General Motors and Chrysler (110th Congress, 2007–09).

As contemporary lame-duck sessions have become regular events over the past two decades, it is important to remember the reasons for the passage of the Twentieth Amendment: Senator Norris made a strong case that the agency problem in lame-duck sessions could (and did) lead to representational breakdowns and the passage of policy outcomes that were contrary to the wishes of the people. More generally, Norris and his reform colleagues believed that the very existence of a lame-duck system, with a set of representatives no longer electorally tied to their constituents and thus possessing a different incentive structure, was a recipe for governing disaster, whether or not fraudulent behavior was obvious always and everywhere.

Norris's concerns are seemingly valid again today. Decisions about the continued use of lame-duck sessions should be informed ones, weighing the benefits of a given Congress meeting in the period between the November elections and the January convening of a new Congress against the costs of policy making when an agency problem in representation is present. As a result, a systematic understanding of the representational elements and policy consequences of contemporary lame-duck sessions should be important goals not only for scholars of Congress but also for the general citizenry.

Critical Thinking

1. Why might we be less concerned about agency problems in lame-duck sessions today relative to the pre–Twentieth Amendment era?
2. If we were searching for evidence that agency problems are affecting lame ducks in the modern Congress, where would we look? What data might we collect, and how would we analyze it to determine if problems exist?
3. Why might we think that party leaders in the nineteenth century—either congressional leaders or presidents—might have more influence on the behavior of lame ducks than party leaders do today?

THE NEW DEAL THROUGH THE PRESENT

The years spanning 1933 (the beginning of the New Deal era) through the present represent the third period of congressional history. During this time, the nation—and the federal government's role in it—changed profoundly. The New Deal established a welfare state in the United States as a way to relieve Americans' suffering during the worst economic depression in the country's history. The Second World War in the 1940s and a Cold War in the decades after threatened American security. The Democrats were almost exclusively the majority party in Congress through the 1970s, but the liberal policy momentum of the New Deal era was stymied by occasional Republican presidents (Eisenhower and Nixon) and more seriously by a "conservative coalition" of southern Democrats and Republicans. Despite this, a variety of liberal policy achievements (together referred to as the "Great Society") were produced in the 1960s, notably in the area of civil rights. Democratic dominance of national politics ended with Republican Ronald Reagan's presidential election in 1980, and since 1994, the Republicans have usually been the majority party in Congress. While this has meant more conservative policy generally, liberal achievements have still occurred, such as the Affordable Care Act during the first Congress of Barack Obama's presidency.

Congress has been a major force in contemporary policy achievements, but the constitutional order has shifted in the current (third) period of congressional history. The executive branch has grown in size and power since FDR's presidency, with the federal bureaucracy playing a greater role in policy decisions and implementation. In addition, an activist Supreme Court emerged in the 1950s and 1960s to lead the way in ushering in new social change. The Court's liberal tendencies shifted in a more conservative direction in the ensuing decades, but the Court's willingness to be at the forefront of policy change remained. In recent decades, Congress has become more divided by party and more polarized ideologically, which has hampered its ability to perform its traditional governing responsibilities. This has incentivized the executive and judiciary to step in and exert more governing authority.

The New Deal

Upon ascending to the presidency, Roosevelt wasted little time in responding to the many problems that the nation faced: 25 percent unemployment (more than 12 million people out of work), a 50 percent drop in farm prices, and state banking near collapse. Over his first 100 days in office, during an emergency session, FDR worked with the Democrat-controlled 73rd Congress (1933–35) to produce a number of landmark laws that he promised would represent a

"New Deal for the American People." This 100-day burst represented a new era in activist federal government, as laws were adopted to, among other things, stabilize the banking system, alleviate low farm prices, provide relief to needy families, and offer jobs to unemployed men in conservation-related projects. By the end of FDR's first two years in office, Congress had passed additional legislation to prop up the home mortgage industry, regulate the securities industry, and provide easier farm credit. The work of the 73rd Congress is often referred to as the First New Deal.

The following Congress, the 74th (1935–37), was more ambitious and more liberal in its scope. Its policies came to be known as the Second New Deal. Whereas the First New Deal sought to manage the underlying emergencies of the depression head on, the Second New Deal had the broader goal of creating significant social change in society. FDR believed the depression was caused, in part, by an underlying system of inequality, and he pushed Congress for legislation that would better level the playing field. Congress responded with (1) the Social Security Act, which provided a system of old-age and survivors' pensions and unemployment compensation; (2) the National Labor Relations Act, which guaranteed organized labor's right to bargain collectively; and (3) the Revenue Act, which increased surtax, estate, and progressive tax rates on high-earning Americans. The 75th Congress (1937–39) continued with legislation in this same vein, passing the Federal Food, Drug, and Cosmetic Act, which required accurate labeling of ingredients and proof in advertising in the areas of food, drugs, and cosmetics, and the Federal Fair Labor Standards Act, which provided a federal minimum wage and maximum workday and prohibited child labor.

The 75th Congress also saw conflict between the branches of government, as FDR grew frustrated with a Supreme Court that declared portions of his New Deal agenda unconstitutional. FDR proposed gaining the power to "pack" the Court with as many as six new Supreme Court justices. This caused a split in Congress, with southern Democrats and Republicans opposing the move. FDR responded by lobbying the country (via radio-based "fireside chats") in an attempt to move public opinion toward his position. Ultimately, Congress refused to produce the legislation necessary to increase the size of the Supreme Court, but the justices—perhaps concerned that their power would be diminished if they didn't support the president more consistently—became more accepting of various New Deal programs. While this achieved Roosevelt's initial goal of protecting and furthering the New Deal agenda, the Court-packing overreach helped create a "conservative coalition" in Congress composed of southern Democrats and Republicans that would prevent further liberal moves on domestic policy, especially those in the area of labor policy. The conservative coalition would be an impediment to liberal policy initiatives in Congress for the next several decades, as the seniority system in Congress often provided

THE GALLOPING SNAIL

As this cartoon depicts, the Great Depression inspired President Roosevelt to push the often slow-moving Congress to enact sweeping domestic policy legislation. This era saw a dramatic increase in the power of the executive branch at the expense of Congress.

southern Democrats with powerful committee chairs, which they used to block legislation that might liberalize civil rights policy.

Then, in the following Congress, the 76th (1939–41), a new law—the Administrative Reorganization Act—would create a significant change in the nation's constitutional order. In adopting the act, which FDR strongly supported, Congress provided the president with the ability to hire additional senior staff and reorganize the executive branch (including federal agencies and the federal bureaucracy) for efficiency reasons. FDR used this authority to create the Executive Office of the Presidency, which included a variety of important support staff (initially the White House Office and the Bureau of the Budget) that expanded greatly over time. Overall, the Administrative Reorganization Act—building on the earlier Budget and Accounting Act—helped expand the institutional presidency and formed the basis of an increasingly powerful, better staffed, and efficient executive branch that could compete with, and often rival, Congress in national policy-making authority.

World War II and Its Aftermath

In early December 1941, the United States entered World War II. Over the next several years, Congress passed a number of laws to support the war effort.[43] Among them were the First and Second War Powers Acts, adopted shortly after the nation's entry into the war, which provided the president with additional power to organize the executive branch so that he could effectively manage his commander-in-chief duties.

By the end of the war, the presidency had become a powerful force in domestic and international politics. Once peace was at hand, Congress quickly sought to rein in the executive branch and reorganize and strengthen its own institutions. In the 79th Congress (1945–47), the Democratic majority enacted the Administrative Procedure Act, which created and codified standards for executive agency behaviors and operations, and provided for judicial review of agency decisions. They also passed the Legislative Reorganization Act of 1946, which streamlined the committee systems in the House and Senate, and strengthened professional staff and information services.

The following Congress, the 80th (1947–49), was the first GOP-controlled Congress since the late 1920s. The Republicans, with the help of southern Democrats, sought to continue reining in the executive branch. They also sought to undo some aspects of the New Deal. The Twenty-Second Amendment limited to two the number of times an individual can be elected president, thereby preventing another FDR from emerging (he was elected four times). The Presidential Succession Act established the Speaker of the House and the president pro tempore of the Senate as the next two individuals in line for the presidency after the vice president. Finally, the Taft-Hartley Act weakened the national position of organized labor by allowing states to pass right-to-work laws and prohibiting unions from contributing to political campaigns.

Civil Rights and the Great Society

The 1950s were mostly a period of divided government. Compared to the New Deal era, domestic legislative achievements were modest. The Federal-Aid Highway Act of 1956, which helped construct the modern interstate system, was the most lasting and important enactment. But change was coming on another policy front. In 1954, the Supreme Court ruled in *Brown v. Board of Education of Topeka* that public school facilities separated by race were inherently unequal and thus unconstitutional (overturning an 1896 ruling by the Court in *Plessy v. Ferguson*). This was a major victory for the African American civil rights movement, and it paved the way toward eliminating Jim Crow–based segregation in the South. It also put pressure on Congress to produce new civil rights legislation. In 1957, Republicans, seeing potential electoral gains among black voters in the North, joined with northern Democrats to push through a new Civil Rights Act, the first of its kind since 1875. While it was mostly symbolic—a new Commission on Civil Rights was created, a Civil Rights Division was placed in the Justice Department, and the attorney general was given injunction power in the face of state-level, voting-rights abuses—the new act set the stage for further, and more substantive, action.

The 1960s saw a new liberal moment in American society. All branches of government—the presidency, led by John F. Kennedy and Lyndon B. Johnson (LBJ); the Supreme Court under Chief Justice Earl Warren; and Congress—would work independently and together to craft liberal policy. In Congress, where the size of the liberal wing of the Democratic Party grew substantially after the 1958 midterm elections, the chief battleground was civil rights. In 1960, Congress adopted a new Civil Rights Act that slightly strengthened the voting-rights provisions in the 1957 act. The Kennedy administration and liberal Democratic leaders in Congress then began work on creating a more substantive set of civil rights policies. The first success was the Twenty-Fourth Amendment (passed in 1962, ratified in 1964), which eliminated the poll tax, a chief means of disenfranchisement in southern elections. Kennedy's assassination in 1963 left LBJ to continue to press for civil rights. Backed by large numbers of northern Democrats and assisted by a substantial group of Republicans, he threw his full weight behind the next set of congressional achievements: (1) the Civil Rights Act of 1964, which outlawed discrimination based on race, color, religion, sex, or national origins and prohibited unequal application of voter registration requirements, and (2) the Voting Rights Act of 1965, which eliminated any further deterrents to voting, including literacy tests and voter qualifications.[44] Southern Democrats fought these legislative initiatives aggressively, but they no longer possessed the numbers or institutional power to prevent change from occurring. Three years later, in 1968, Congress passed a final

In the 1960s, Democratic leaders in Congress collaborated on a number of significant civil rights reforms with Presidents Kennedy and Johnson. Johnson signed the Civil Rights Act of 1964 surrounded by the bill's congressional sponsors and civil rights leaders, including Martin Luther King Jr.

Civil Rights Act that eliminated discrimination in the sale, rental, or financing of housing.

The push for civil rights was only one element in LBJ's policy agenda.[45] After his election in 1964, with large Democratic majorities in both the House and Senate, he sought new social welfare policies that would augment, and perhaps rival, the New Deal programs. LBJ's policy agenda, called the Great Society, focused on alleviating poverty. The 89th Congress (1965–67) responded to the president's agenda by passing a number of landmark laws, including (1) the establishment of Medicare (health coverage for the elderly) and Medicaid (health coverage for the needy and disabled), (2) the Elementary and Secondary Education Act and the Higher Education Act to help students from needy families get better public education all the way through college, and (3) the Child Nutrition Act, which provided breakfast to children in poor areas.

Despite controlling the presidency and large majorities in Congress, however, the Democrats never quite achieved all that they might have. The liberal moment eventually passed. The escalating costs of the military conflict in Vietnam, which LBJ actively supported, led Congress to rein in domestic spending, and the racial discord caused by urban riots throughout the North soured the public on further Great Society initiatives.

Watergate and Congressional Reassertion

Republican Richard Nixon was elected president in 1968, and divided government would characterize the first half of the 1970s. The Democrats held majorities in both chambers of Congress for the entire decade, giving them more than a quarter century of continuous control. Initially, Nixon and the Democratic Congress worked together on several policy areas, including the environment, transportation, and nuclear arms limitation.[46] Voting rights were also extended via the Twenty-Sixth Amendment, which lowered the voting age in all federal, state, and local elections to 18 years old.

During his second term, Nixon was involved in a scandal dubbed "Watergate" after a break-in (and subsequent cover-up) at the Democratic National Committee headquarters in the Watergate Hotel in Washington, D.C. The president and many of his White House associates were implicated in the conspiracy, and Nixon was eventually forced to resign. He was replaced by Vice President Gerald Ford. In response to the scandal, the 93rd Congress (1973–75) took steps to reassert authority vis-à-vis the executive branch, through (1) the War Powers Resolution, which required the president to consult with Congress before committing troops in a military action (adopted over Nixon's veto); (2) the Budget and Impoundment Control Act, which created budget committees in both chambers to analyze the president's budget, established a Congressional Budget Office to help compile budgetary information, and prevented the president from indefinitely rejecting congressionally approved spending; and (3) an expansion of the Freedom of Information Act, which increased transparency in federal agencies and provided deadlines for them to meet public information requests (adopted over President Ford's veto).

As Congress responded to presidential scandal, the other branch of the federal government—the Supreme Court—continued to assert itself. Following the *Brown v. Board of Education* decision in 1954, the Court issued a series of decisions in the 1960s expanding civil liberties and civil rights.[47] And in 1973, the Court in *Roe v. Wade* moved into social policy by striking down state laws that criminalized or restricted access to abortion, declaring that a right to privacy existed in the Constitution (via the due process clause of the Fourteenth Amendment). Through this decision, the Court signaled that they were willing to "legislate" on important policy topics.

Amid this turmoil in the constitutional order, Congress continued to reorganize itself. A New Legislative Reorganization Act in the 1970s made all roll call votes public, reduced the power of committee chairs, enhanced information technology, increased congressional staff, and expanded the Congressional Research Service. Internal reforms also occurred within the Democratic Party Caucus in the early 1970s as liberal members worked to expand their authority by weakening the seniority system (as the automatic method for achieving committee chairs) and decentralizing committee power while expanding the authority of subcommittees.

The demographic makeup of Congress also began to change during this time. As the social dynamics in American society started to shift in the 1960s, and women and minorities began to challenge preexisting power structures that were dominated by white men, the composition of Congress was ultimately affected. During the 1970s, the number of women and African Americans elected to the House grew. Congress was still an overwhelmingly white, male institution, but the change was significant, and since then a gradual but consistent increase has occurred in the number of female, African American, Latino, and Asian American representatives.

The last portion of the 1970s witnessed unified Democratic government, as former Georgia governor Jimmy Carter was elected president. Carter had a stormy relationship with his fellow Democrats in Congress—often relying instead on his own circle for advice and counsel—but several important laws were nonetheless passed during these years. For example, Congress created a Department of Energy, began the deregulation of the airline industry, expanded environmental protections, and prevented the spread of nuclear weapons.

The Reagan Revolution

After Carter, Republicans won the next three presidential elections (1980, 1984, and 1988), with former California governor Ronald Reagan leading a Republican resurgence. Reagan's landslide victories in 1980 and 1984 also produced a Republican Senate—which stayed in GOP hands for six years—breaking the pattern of more than a generation of Democratic rule. The House remained Democratic, however, and divided government characterized the entirety of Reagan's presidency, along with the four years under his successor, George H. W. Bush. President Reagan worked with the Democrats in the House to, among other things, increase defense spending and reform the personal and corporate tax system.[48]

The 1980s also marked the beginning of the partisan polarization in Congress that we still observe (and that continues to grow) today. Over the decade, the two parties became more internally homogenous and more polarized from each other, as the full effects of the Voting Rights Act, along with Reagan's election, would push conservative southerners into the Republican Party and make southern Democrats in Congress—now composed mostly of moderate whites and liberal African Americans—look more like northern Democrats. Liberal Republicans in the North also largely disappeared during this time. In effect, thanks to the help of some external events, the two parties were better able to sort themselves ideologically. Since the late 1950s, the Democrats in Congress were mostly a liberal party, and the Republicans were mostly a conservative party, but each had members that ran the full ideological gamut. During the Reagan era, the Democrats became a strongly liberal party and the Republicans a strongly conservative party, and this ideological separation has only increased since then. And with this increasing homogeneity of preferences, party members, especially in the House, became more willing to delegate power to their leaders to structure the legislative agenda to pursue shared policy goals, which had the effect of reinforcing the underlying ideological homogeneity.[49]

In addition, the GOP's takeover of the Senate led Democrats to organize and coordinate their messaging activities, as they worked to better frame for the public the differences between the two parties. And in the House, younger Republicans, tired of being the "permanent minority party" in the institution, clashed with more-senior Republicans over strategy, with the younger members seeking a more confrontational approach. Eventually, the younger members would win out, electing Newt Gingrich, a well-known partisan instigator, as Republican minority whip in 1989. And the House GOP's confrontational approach would be mimicked by Republicans in the Senate. Back in the minority after the 1986 elections, the Senate Republicans increasingly pursued a strategy of obstruction in which they were more willing to use the filibuster to slow down or stymie Democratic measures.[50] These activities in both chambers epitomized the growing polarization that was occurring in Congress.

Bill Clinton and the Contract with America

The early 1990s saw the United States enter a military conflict in the Middle East. Responding to Iraq invading the nation of Kuwait, President George H. W. Bush sought Congress's approval in removing Iraqi forces. Congress passed the Persian Gulf Resolution, providing the president with said authority, along with appropriations to fund Operation Desert Shield and Operation Desert Storm, covering the costs of the war. The 102nd Congress (1991–93) also passed a new Intelligence Authorization Act, which required that the president report all covert activities to Congress. This was, in part, a response to the Iran-Contra scandal that dogged the Reagan administration in its final years, when arms were covertly and illegally sold to Iran and the proceeds diverted to the Contra rebels in El Salvador.

While Bush's popularity was very high after the Persian Gulf War, it eroded quickly because of an economic recession at home. As a result, former Arkansas governor Bill Clinton defeated Bush in the 1992 presidential election, and Clinton enjoyed unified Democratic control of government during his first two years in office. While the 103rd Congress (1993–95) did not produce the comprehensive national health care law that Clinton sought, it did respond with major legislation that reduced the budget deficit, established background checks on handgun purchases, initiated a "don't ask, don't tell" policy regarding homosexuality in the U.S. military, and provided significant funds to states to fight crime.[51]

Despite these considerable Democratic policy achievements, the Republicans enjoyed great success in the 1994 midterm elections—so much so that they won majority control of both the House and Senate for the first time since the early 1950s. The Republicans claimed their electoral success was due to the Contract with America, a set of proposed conservative policy reforms the GOP introduced during the congressional campaign that they promised to enact should they become the majority party.[52] Led by new Speaker of the House Newt Gingrich, the Republicans set out to put various Contract elements into effect. Some were successful, such as the Congressional Accountability Act, which required that all federal laws apply equally to Congress (that is, no special status for members of Congress), and the Line-Item Veto Act, which provided the president (until it was struck down by the Supreme Court) with the power to eliminate particular provisions of spending bills. Other Contract priorities were not successful, however, such as imposing term limits on members of Congress. The Republicans also made a number of internal changes to Congress, reducing the number of committees, eliminating some committee staff, and imposing term limits on committee chairs. These internal changes had the effect of reducing committee (and subcommittee) power and concentrating more authority in the hands of party leaders.

From a policy perspective, the Republican Congress often had an adversarial relationship with President Clinton. Yet congressional Republicans and Clinton managed to work together to produce some truly important legislation during the last six years of Clinton's presidency. This included the Personal Responsibility and Work Opportunity Reconciliation Act of 1996, which was a major reform to the federal welfare system; the Balanced Budget Act of 1997, which created entitlement-program savings and reduced the federal deficit; and the State Children's Health Insurance Program, which provided matching funds to states

The Republicans swept the House and Senate in 1994 on the political strength of their "Contract with America," a proposed conservative policy agenda spearheaded by Speaker of the House Newt Gingrich. Future Speaker of the House John Boehner stands just to Gingrich's right.

for health coverage of low-income children. But Congress and the president also clashed repeatedly. For example, disputes over spending in the 1996 federal budget negotiation led to two government shutdowns (in mid-November 1995 and late December 1995). Public opinion polls suggested that Americans largely blamed congressional Republicans for these shutdowns.[53]

Conflict between congressional Republicans and President Clinton reached a fever pitch in Clinton's second term in office. As relations between Republicans and Democrats in Congress became increasingly strained, with filibustering in the Senate continuing to rise, information emerged about an extramarital affair between Clinton and Monica Lewinsky, a White House intern. Republicans sought to impeach Clinton on the basis of perjury (stemming from his testimony about the affair) and obstruction of justice. The House succeeded in impeaching him on the two counts, but the Senate failed to muster the required two-thirds vote to convict.[54] Clinton thus remained in office. The GOP had overreached, and House Republicans were increasingly fed up with Speaker Gingrich's leadership. Amid rumors of a potential ouster, Gingrich stepped down from the speakership, in part because of the GOP's loss of five House seats in the 1998 midterms—after internal polls suggested they would gain more than 20 seats.

Deeply Divided in the Twenty-First Century

The presidential election of 2000 was the closest in American history, a virtual tie between Texas Governor George W. Bush and Vice President Al Gore. The outcome came down to a handful of votes in Florida and the manner in which those votes—amid a recount—would be tallied. Eventually, the Supreme Court stopped the recount and decided the election for Bush on a 5–4 vote.[55] President Bush enjoyed unified Republican government during much of his first six years in office.[56] The biggest challenge that Bush and the GOP-led Congress faced was the September 11, 2001, terrorist attacks that destroyed the World Trade Center, damaged the Pentagon, and left thousands of Americans dead. Very quickly, Osama Bin Laden and al Qaeda were implicated, and Congress authorized the use of force against them and those who provided them with aid (the Taliban in Afghanistan). A year later, as part of the Global War on Terror, Congress authorized the president to take military action against Iraq to remove Iraqi president Saddam Hussein and eliminate the country's nuclear capability.[57] The Global War on Terror effort also helped produce important legislation at home. Congress passed the USA PATRIOT Act, which provided U.S. law enforcement and intelligence agencies with more power and discretion to prevent incidents of domestic terrorism (at the cost of individual civil liberties). It also passed the Homeland Security Act, which created a new cabinet-level department and transferred major portions of 22 existing agencies to it to prevent domestic terrorist attacks.

Bush's domestic agenda was affected by the Global War on Terror, but he and the Republican-led Congress still managed to pass a number of major initiatives. For example, a considerable personal tax cut was adopted before September 11.[58] Shortly thereafter, Congress passed a major education bill, the No Child Left Behind Act, which established standards for states in reading and math for students in grades 3 through 8. It also passed a campaign reform bill, the Bipartisan Campaign Reform Act, which limited the amount of money that corporations, unions, and individuals could contribute to political parties. Later in Bush's first term, Congress adopted legislation that placed limitations on abortion rights and added a voluntary prescription drug benefit for Medicare beneficiaries.[59]

The Democrats retook the House and Senate in 2006, and the Senate Republicans in the 110th Congress (2007–08) responded by more than doubling the number of filibusters from the previous Congress—an all-time high (by a considerable amount) at that time.[60] The Democrats then swept the Republicans out of government in 2008 behind the presidential candidacy of Democratic senator Barack Obama (IL). Initially the Democrats held a major advantage in the 111th Congress (2009–10), as they controlled 60 seats in the Senate (before

Senator Ted Kennedy's death) and thus could prevent any GOP filibusters. Their signature achievement during this time was the Patient Protection and Affordable Care Act (or "Obamacare"), the comprehensive federal health insurance law that we discussed in Chapter 1.[61] Other major legislative achievements included the American Recovery and Reinvestment Act, an economic stimulus bill to combat the effects of the Great Recession; the Dodd-Frank Wall Street Reform and Consumer Protection Act, which established a process of identifying and reducing the risks of financial institution failure; and the Don't Ask, Don't Tell Repeal Act, which eliminated the Defense Department's policy on homosexuality.[62]

The Republicans won back the House in 2010, and the last six years of Obama's presidency were characterized by divided government and high levels of partisan polarization. Governing was more difficult, as the GOP was determined to limit Obama and the Democrats' legislative achievements. In this way, the congressional Republicans during the Obama years were different from the congressional Republicans during the Clinton years. While Gingrich and the Republicans clashed with Clinton on numerous occasions, they were also willing to make deals with him when it was in their interest to do so. The post-2008 Republicans had no interest in working with Obama and actively sought to prevent his reelection.[63]

Once in office, the House Republicans sought deficit reduction, especially the younger Tea Party–affiliated members who were elected on an anti-government agenda, and the two parties worked on a "grand bargain" to reduce spending and produce more than $3 trillion in deficit reduction. A Budget Reform Act was signed, but implementation of the necessary reductions in government spending and/or tax increases was put off until the last minute and threatened to take the federal government over the "fiscal cliff," risking governmental default. As a result, Congress passed a stopgap measure, permanently extended the Bush-era tax cuts, and modestly raised taxes on the wealthy. Around the same time, the Supreme Court in *Citizens United v. FEC* (2010) overturned key provisions of the Bipartisan Campaign Reform Act of 2002—specifically, those that prohibited corporations and unions from funding "electioneering communications" (broadcast ads that mention a candidate in any context) within 30 days before a primary or 60 days before a general election. While some believe the Court decision was a victory for free expression (by equating political speech with First Amendment rights), one consequence was that election spending by corporations was no longer limited, increasing political tensions in what was already a highly polarized environment.

The remainder of the Obama presidency saw additional conflict. After Obama's reelection in 2012, the Senate Republicans in the 113th Congress (2013–15) tripled the number of filibusters from the preceding Congress—nearly doubling

Although the first two years of President Trump's administration have had the support of unified government and Republican leadership in both the House and Senate, the president has faced dissent from a largely unified Democratic Party, led by House Minority Leader Nancy Pelosi (above) and others.

the previous all-time high.[64] In October 2013, the government shut down for more than two weeks, again over appropriations and spending levels. Constant GOP filibustering of Obama's executive branch nominees led Democratic Majority Leader Harry Reid (NV) to invoke the "nuclear option" and eliminate filibuster rights on all appointments below the level of Supreme Court nominees. House Republicans, in an attempt to curry favor with their constituents back home, staged dozens of fruitless roll call votes to repeal Obamacare. And in perhaps the most blatant application of partisanship yet, after the Republicans took back the Senate in 2016, they refused to consider Obama's nominee for the Supreme Court—Merrick Garland—after the death of Justice Antonin Scalia. Such a refusal was unprecedented in president-Senate relations on Supreme Court nominations.

In 2016, Donald Trump was elected president, and the Republicans maintained majority control of both the House and Senate. Through the first year of the Trump administration, the Republicans tried to undo the signature achievement of the Obama administration—the Affordable Care Act. While the Republicans in the House managed to successfully pass a bill that would have repealed and replaced Obamacare, the Republicans in the Senate came up just short.[65] Nonetheless, the Republicans produced some successes. The Republican

Senate confirmed a slate of Trump's conservative cabinet-level appointments, over the near-unanimous objections of Democrats. (Thanks to the Democrats' "going nuclear" in 2013, they could not block any of these nominees.) Majority Leader Mitch McConnell (KY) later invoked the nuclear option on Supreme Court nominations in order to sidestep a Democratic filibuster and confirm Neil Gorsuch, a Trump nominee. And, finally, the Republicans passed a major tax reform bill, reducing tax rates for both businesses and individuals. In addition, the bill included a provision repealing the individual mandate—a crucial component of the Affordable Care Act.[66] Thus while the Republicans were unable to roll back Obamacare directly, they may have found a way to kill it indirectly.[67] As of this writing, the fate of the Affordable Care Act remains to be seen.

HOW WE STUDY
IDEOLOGY IN CONGRESS

To study Congress at different points in time and across time, political scientists have sought ways to understand the basis of representatives' and senators' decision making. One way is to argue that legislators have preferences on policy and, more generally, preferences *across* policy areas—which we call *ideologies*. We typically think of ideology in terms of left-right positions on a line. A representative with a liberal ideology would be on the left; a representative with a conservative ideology would be on the right. A liberal ideology would be consistent with positions such as being pro-choice on abortion and supportive of more-restrictive gun laws. A conservative ideology would be consistent with the opposite positions: being pro-life on abortion and opposed to restrictions on gun ownership.

Figure 2.2 illustrates how we might think of these concepts. Here we consider ideological positions on a line, where the underlying issue is gun control. The leftmost (or liberal) point is consistent with the position of no access: no one is allowed to have a gun. The rightmost (or conservative) point is consistent with the position of no restrictions: anyone who wants a gun can have one with no governmental interference. The median position is the middle (or center) of the space and is the midpoint of these two extreme positions. On most policy issues in the United States, people—and parties—typically have left-of-center or right-of-center positions. But rarely does anyone hold the most extreme positions. For example, on the question of guns, most people believe some restrictions are necessary, but they disagree as to whether there should be more restrictions (the left-of-center position) or fewer restrictions (the right-of-center position). In this

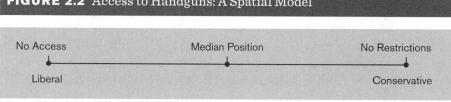

FIGURE 2.2 Access to Handguns: A Spatial Model

book, we refer to such preference and policy comparisons along a line as *spatial models*.

To study ideology in a systematic way requires some way of measuring it. Legislators could be asked questions, perhaps in a survey, to get a sense of their preferences on a range of issues. But that method creates measurement difficulties. First, legislators may answer questions strategically (or not at all), based on how they think the survey analysts (or their constituents) believe they should respond. For example, on sensitive topics such as race or gender, legislators might yield to *social desirability* concerns and provide more liberal answers than they would otherwise give. Second, survey-based ideology measures are limited temporally and can only be used to study the contemporary Congress. If we wanted to compare legislators' ideologies in foregone eras to those today, survey-based measures would not be helpful.

An alternate way to measure legislators' ideologies is to use roll call voting data. That is, we can track how legislators vote in Congress and use their votes to draw conclusions about their ideologies. Roll calls on the floor of Congress are public—they can be observed by constituents, interest groups, and the media—and often have direct policy consequences. As such, a vote is a clear signal about how a legislator views an issue. Individual roll call votes have been a staple of legislative proceedings going back to the First Congress in the late eighteenth century, making them extremely useful for constructing an across-time measure of ideology.

The simplest measure of ideology that can be created from roll call votes is a basic rating that shows, for some number of votes, how often a legislator voted with the liberal or conservative position. For example, assume that we are analyzing how legislators voted on 10 roll call votes, and we establish whether the "yea" or "nay" position on each corresponds to the liberal position. We would then calculate how many times, over these 10 votes, each legislator voted for the liberal position. If a legislator voted for the liberal position on 7 of the 10 votes, then he would receive a rating of 70. By contrast, if a legislator voted for the liberal position on only 2 of the 10 votes, then she would receive a rating of 20.

The range of ideological positions would span from 0 to 100, with 0 being a perfect conservative ideology and 100 being a perfect liberal ideology.

Interest groups often create ratings (or "scores") based on a set of carefully chosen roll calls, as a way to assess how members of Congress vote on issues that they care about. Examples of interest groups that produce regular legislative ratings include the Americans for Democratic Action (ADA), the American Conservative Union (ACU), the League of Conservation Voters, the National Taxpayers Union, and the AFL-CIO's Committee on Public Education. Interest-group scores, then, correspond to how often members of Congress supported positions in line with that group's stated preferences on specific issues.

ADA and ACU scores, which are based on a range of roll call–based issues, are often used as measures of basic left-right (liberal-conservative) ideology. They have been important in a number of political science studies across time. But these scores, and really any interest-group scores, introduce the problem of *artificial extremism*. That is, interest-group scores, by their nature, are based on roll call votes that are selected because they draw stark differences between liberal and conservative positions. Stated differently, the vote positions themselves—the "yea" and "nay" positions—represent ideologically distinct alternatives, often very liberal and very conservative positions. This type of roll call selection is useful for identifying those legislators who are truly liberal or conservative. But moderate legislators are not given moderate policy positions to vote for; instead, they must vote for the liberal or conservative positions. This setup tends to make moderates appear to be more extreme—either more liberal or more conservative—than they really are.[68]

Scholars have responded to artificial extremism concerns by searching for other roll call–based ways of measuring legislator preferences. A solution has been to use ideology measures derived from procedures that use all (or nearly all) roll call votes in a given Congress, not just a handful of votes that are intended to create stark liberal-conservative differences. A large sample of roll call votes allows a variety of policy positions to be presented to members of Congress, including moderate positions. Stated differently, incorporating many different types of roll calls allows legislators to be differentiated in a more fine-grained way. These approaches can identify conservatives and liberals, but they can also identify true moderates, right-leaning and left-leaning moderates, and so on. In other words, a true—or truer—distribution of ideological types can be identified, instead of just two groups (one conservative and one liberal).

The "gold standard" for broad roll call–based ideology measures is NOMINATE scores, created by political scientists Keith Poole and Howard Rosenthal. NOMINATE scores, which range from −1 (most liberal) to +1 (most conservative), are based on a statistical technique from psychology and incorporate all nonunanimous roll call votes in a given Congress. The statistical technique is more complicated than a simple rating, but the output is similar in that legislators who vote more alike are placed nearer to one another on the left-right scale.

Figures 2.3 and 2.4 illustrate two phenomena: (1) the artificial extremism concerns with interest-group scores and (2) how NOMINATE scores can differentiate members more precisely and in a way that allows for the display of more moderate ideological persuasions. Figure 2.3 shows ADA scores for House members. These scores are meant to showcase liberal tendencies—in keeping with the goals of the ADA. We observe that most members possess near-perfect ratings—either at or near zero or at or near 100 percent. There is almost no one in the middle of the space. Figure 2.4, by comparison, shows NOMINATE scores for House members. While the NOMINATE scores also yield two "humps," the scores are not nearly as bunched together, and the medians of the two distributions are located far from the most extreme values. In short, there are far more members with NOMINATE scores near the middle of the space. Thus NOMINATE, by using nearly all roll call votes in a given Congress, allows members to be differentiated on a range of issues and avoids presenting a distribution of members' preferences that is artificially extreme.

Several types of NOMINATE scores exist. The most common NOMINATE score is a dynamic one that allows legislators from the same chamber (House or Senate) to be compared across time. Dynamic scores also allow individual legislators to move to the left or to the right based on changes in their voting behavior across time. Static scores, which provide a single ideological position for each legislator across time, allow individual legislators to be compared across chambers and across time.

Poole and Rosenthal have found that a single left-right (or liberal-conservative) NOMINATE dimension—often characterized as representing conflict over the role of government in the economy—correctly predicts a large majority of individual-level vote choices in Congress across time.[69] Often, however, a second NOMINATE dimension provides additional explanatory power. In other words, issues that do not always fit well on a basic liberal-conservative dimension—issues, for example, that divide each party—often require a second dimension. Across congressional history, such issues have involved slavery early in the nineteenth century, currency issues (gold versus silver) later in the nineteenth century, and civil rights during the mid–twentieth century. In recent decades, however, a new second dimension has not emerged. Instead, a single liberal-conservative dimension appears to encapsulate most political conflict in Congress.

In addition to providing individual-level information for members of Congress, NOMINATE scores can also be used to examine more macro-level congressional phenomena. For example, the median member of the Democratic and Republican parties can be identified by chamber in each Congress.

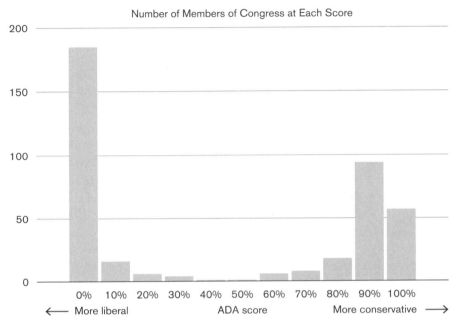

FIGURE 2.3 ADA Scores, 114th House (2015–17)

Number of Members of Congress at Each Score

← More liberal   ADA score   More conservative →

ADA scores for 2015 and 2016 obtained from "2015 Congressional Voting Record" and "2016 Congressional Voting Record." Americans for Democratic Action, https://adaction.org/wpcontent/uploads/2017/11/2015 .pdf and https://adaction.org/wpcontent/uploads/2018/02/2016.pdf (accessed 8/14/18).

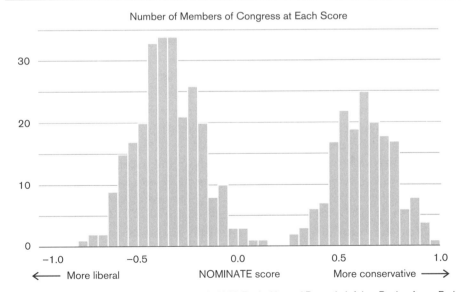

FIGURE 2.4 NOMINATE Scores, 114th House (2015–17)

Number of Members of Congress at Each Score

← More liberal   NOMINATE score   More conservative →

NOMINATE scores obtained from Jeffrey B. Lewis, Keith Poole, Howard Rosenthal, Adam Boche, Aaron Rudkin, and Luke Sonnet. 2017. *Voteview: Congressional Roll-Call Votes Database*, https://voteview.com/.

This provides a way to assess the relationship between ideology and partisanship over time.[70] And the difference between the median Democrat and the median Republican can be used as a measure of polarization in each congressional chamber.

We will use NOMINATE throughout this book to examine how Congress behaves. So bookmark this explanation, as you will likely need to return to it again.

Critical Thinking

1. Imagine that three members of Congress—Mr. Smith, Ms. Jones, and Mr. King—vote on 10 roll calls that an interest group deems important for its mission. The 10 roll calls, members' votes, and the interest group's position on each roll call appear in the table below. A "yea" vote is cast in support of a legislative measure (encapsulated in a roll call, labeled RC), while a "nay" vote is cast in opposition.

	RC1	RC2	RC3	RC4	RC5	RC6	RC7	RC8	RC9	RC10
Mr. Smith	Yea	Yea	Nay	Yea	Nay	Yea	Nay	Nay	Yea	Nay
Ms. Jones	Nay	Yea	Nay	Nay	Yea	Yea	Nay	Yea	Nay	Yea
Mr. King	Yea	Nay	Yea	Yea	Nay	Nay	Yea	Nay	Yea	Yea
Interest-Group Position	Yea	Nay	Nay	Yea	Yea	Yea	Nay	Nay	Nay	Nay

Calculate a pro-interest-group rating for each of the three members of Congress.

2. Imagine that a committee in Congress is made of 10 members: 5 Democrats and 5 Republicans. The first-dimension NOMINATE scores for the 10 members of Congress (labeled MC1 through MC10), along with their party affiliations (D = Democrat, R = Republican), appear in the table below.

	MC1	MC2	MC3	MC4	MC4	MC5	MC6	MC7	MC8	MC9	MC10
Party Affiliation	D	D	D	D	D	R	R	R	R	R	R
NOMINATE Score	-0.7	-0.1	-0.3	-0.5	-0.2	0.2	0.8	0.5	0.4	0.6	0.7

Line up the members from left to right along a single dimension and identify

    a. which member of Congress is the Democratic median on the committee,

    b. which member of Congress is the Republican median on the committee, and

    c. the degree (or amount) of partisan polarization that exists on the committee.

3. While roll call votes provide many benefits as a means of studying legislators' preferences systematically across chambers and across time, what might be some of their limitations? How might these limitations potentially affect our analyses?

CONCLUSION

The role that Congress plays in governing and representation in our separated system has changed over time. When the Constitution was drafted, the Framers viewed Congress as the chief institution in the federal system. Congress was the lawmaker—the representative body of the people—and would govern based on what representatives and senators decided in their deliberations and eventual vote choices. The other institutions in our federal system—the president and the courts—would play a lesser role. Both would provide some checks and balances, thereby allowing a system of separate powers to exist. But Congress was intended to be the linchpin—the engine that drove the republic.

The first period of American congressional history reflected the Founders' aspirations. While the federal government was limited in the antebellum era, Congress largely determined the major policies of the day. Although ambitious presidents existed during this era, the presidency was underdeveloped as an institution, and the federal bureaucracy was in its infancy. And the federal courts were only beginning to evolve, with the Supreme Court only "discovering" the power of judicial review in the early 1800s.

The second period of American congressional history, from the Civil War through the early 1930s, saw a slight shift. Congress was still paramount in the federal system, but the presidency and courts were beginning to develop as rivals. As the presidency and courts started to institutionalize, they developed the capacity to better engage with policy and act as foils to congressional policy-making authority. This evolution became increasingly clear in the third period of congressional history, as the "institutional presidency" emerged and the scope of presidential power and authority expanded decade by decade. A more activist Supreme Court also became more willing to decide policy matters that Congress was not able or willing to address.

As we turn our attention to contemporary American politics, we observe that Congress is hampered by polarization and the accompanying policy gridlock, which has only incentivized the president and the courts to look for ways to expand their authority. This status quo is entering a new phase with the election of President Trump, who appears unwilling to be constrained by the prevailing norms and institutional roles of our federal system. Should collective action and collective will fail to rein in a more aggressive president, Congress's authority will be further reduced in the constitutional order.

Discussion Questions

1. In designing the Constitution, the Framers considered the Congress to be the most important institution in the new federal government. And, indeed, Congress dominated the federal government throughout much of American history. But today, that is not necessarily the case. Should we be troubled by this change? Or have other considerations emerged over time that require the president and courts to play a more meaningful role?

2. The number of citizens that House members (in their districts) and senators (in their states) represent has increased over time. What does this change imply about the quality of representation today? Is it necessarily worse than in the past, or have other conditions changed to make it easier for members of Congress to connect with constituents?

3. A major theme in this chapter is the growing partisan polarization in Congress over the last few decades. While this polarization presents a problem for Congress's ability to govern—and creates opportunities for the president and the courts to exert policy-making authority—how should we think about polarization in the context of representation? Is it possible that greater polarization reflects successful representation of constituency interests? Why or why not?

4. As the "Then and Now" section describes, postelection lame-duck sessions have become a common part of contemporary politics, in part because party leaders have come to believe that these sessions are the best time to hold necessary but politically difficult votes. But is it worth trading representation for better governing? Or are the dangers of undemocratic and possibly even corrupt policy outcomes too great?

5. In recent years, the Senate has eliminated the use of the filibuster in certain contexts—first in the consideration of executive appointments below the Supreme Court level and, more recently, on Supreme Court appointments themselves. Should the Senate do away with the filibuster on standard policy matters? Why or why not? How would completely eliminating the filibuster affect how Congress governs?

3

Representation

Ever since the Affordable Care Act (or "Obamacare") was adopted in 2010, Republican Party leaders have promised their constituents—especially party activists and important campaign donors—that they would repeal it. During the later years of the Obama administration, this promise led to numerous repeal efforts, though all proved to be fruitless because the Democrats controlled either the Senate or the presidency. Nonetheless, these failed repeal efforts were symbolic, as they allowed Republican Party leaders to communicate to their constituents that they were listening to their concerns and were trying, and that they were determined to succeed.

The elections of 2016 changed the game. When the electoral dust had settled, the Republicans found that they would control all levers of the federal government: the House, the Senate, and the presidency. President-elect Trump actively supported repealing Obamacare, so Republican leaders in Congress were suddenly on the spot—future fundraising and electoral success for the party would mean delivering on past promises. This pressure filtered down to the Republican membership in both chambers. Taking anti-Obamacare positions during roll calls that were not ultimately going to change policy was a thing of the past; a real opportunity to repeal the law was at hand.

Amid the congressional push to repeal Obamacare in early 2017, many constituents gathered outside their representatives' district offices, and inside town hall meetings, to voice their support for the existing law and opposition to the repeal efforts.

However, Republican lawmakers were in for a rude awakening as the 115th Congress (2017–19) convened. Repeal efforts stalled as public pressure to preserve Obamacare mounted. In town halls (events that allow citizens to gather and engage directly with public officials), Republican members of Congress were excoriated for their attempts (and continued plans) to roll back Obamacare. In Chico, California, one constituent told Representative Doug LaMalfa, "I hope you suffer the same painful fate as those millions that you have voted to remove health care from. May you die in pain."[1] In Idaho, Representative Raul Labrador was angrily denounced by constituents after he claimed, "Nobody dies because they don't have access to health care."[2] And in Plattsburgh, New York, Representative Elise Stefanik was greeted with chants of "shame, shame, shame" for her support of GOP repeal attempts.[3]

As Republican leaders persisted in their attempts to roll back Obamacare during the spring and summer of 2017, GOP lawmakers adopted different approaches to facing their constituents. Some still participated in town halls, while others avoided them altogether.[4] Those who continued to hold town halls made greater efforts to control them. Some Republican lawmakers, for example, claimed that "paid liberal protesters" from out of town were descending on town halls to cause trouble. While there was little evidence to support these claims, some legislators responded by holding lotteries for seat assignments or checking IDs to validate home addresses.[5] After many fits and starts, Republican House leaders were able to coordinate enough of the party's rank and file to repeal Obamacare; however, Republican Senate leaders fell one vote short.

The health care issue and the attempt to repeal Obamacare make clear that a lawmaker's job is often difficult. For many members of Congress, representing constituent interests and governing are not always easy or compatible, especially regarding policy matters that are both important and controversial. With respect to health care, rolling back Obamacare was important for the Republican Party in general. The party needed to maintain its collective promises over the previous years and show that it could govern when given the opportunity. But rolling back Obamacare was detrimental to some GOP members, who faced a significant number of constituents who (now understanding that policy change was actually a possiblility) were not in favor of the repeal.

While the challenges of representation in particular cases can be instructive, we will also address more fundamental questions in this chapter. For example, what does it mean to "represent" someone? Do members of Congress always follow what (some) constituents want? Or do they sometimes use their own expertise and experience to make decisions? Another question involves who lawmakers' constituents actually are. Do members of Congress think about everyone in their district or state? Or do they (sometimes) focus only on those individuals who will be important for their reelection efforts? And what if other political actors—party leaders, for example—pressure members of Congress to act in a certain way that might be contrary to what some in their district or state want? How do members of Congress balance these pressures while keeping in mind that they are electorally accountable to constituents back home?

THE BASICS OF REPRESENTATION

As we learned in Chapter 1, the Framers of the Constitution established a system of *representative government* at the federal level. This means that citizens do not make decisions on policy directly. That kind of system is referred to as *direct democracy*, and it is ill suited for solving the many complex problems that a large and diverse republic often faces. Instead, citizens in the United States choose political agents in regular elections to represent them—that is, to act on their behalf. These political agents are thus known as *representatives*. They are selected from geographic units—states for senators and districts for House members—and assemble in Congress to perform their roles as federal legislators.

The size of Congress has increased substantially over time. The First Federal Congress was composed of only 90 members—26 senators (two from each of 13 states) and 64 House members (distributed based on population across the states). As new states were added to the nation, the size of both the Senate and House grew. Today, Congress is made up of 535 legislators from 50 states: 100 senators and 435 House members.

A particular Congress assembles for two years, in between the November elections that occur in every even-numbered year. The First Congress convened in 1789, and the opening of each subsequent Congress has taken place in every odd-numbered year. The 116th Congress, following the midterm elections in November 2018, convened in January of 2019. Every House seat and one-third of Senate seats are up for election every two years, with senators composed of three classes (with staggered elections across six years).

Article I of the Constitution established the requirements for serving in Congress. To serve in the House, an individual must be at least 25 years of age and a citizen of the United States for at least 7 years at the time of election. To serve in the Senate, an individual must be at least 30 years of age and a citizen of the United States for at least 9 years at the time of election. In both cases, an individual must be an inhabitant of the state in which he or she is chosen.

IS CONGRESS REPRESENTATIVE OF THE NATION?

Do members of Congress resemble the citizens of the United States? In other words, is the membership of Congress broadly representative of the rich diversity that exists in the nation? The answer is essentially "no." On most dimensions, the membership of Congress does not closely resemble the U.S. population. Table 3.1 provides a breakdown of some important demographic characteristics, comparing members of the 116th Congress to the U.S. population as a whole (based on data from the 2010 U.S. Census).

First, Congress is considerably older than the nation as a whole. In relation to the median age in the United States, the median senator is more than 25 years older and the median House member is more than 20 years older. Second, Congress is considerably more educated than the nation as a whole. All senators possess a bachelor's (four-year college) degree, and nearly all House members do as well—as compared to just over a quarter of the U.S. population.[6] Third, nearly all members of both the House and Senate are affiliated with a particular religion, while just over three-quarters of the U.S. population is religiously affiliated. Of those members of Congress who claim an affiliation, more than 9 in 10 are Christians.[7] This percentage is similar to the U.S. population. Fourth, Congress is

TABLE 3.1 Does Today's Congress "Look Like America?"			
	House	Senate	U.S. Population
Age (median)	58	64	37
Female (%)	23	25	51
Bachelor's degree (%)	94	100	30
Religious (%)	97	96	76
% of religious who are Christian	92	91	93
African American (%)	12	3	13
Hispanic American (%)	9	5	16
Asian American (%)	2	3	5

Based on data from *Vital Statistics on Congress*, Brookings Institution. www.brookings.edu/multi-chapter
-report/vital-statistics-on-congress; "Representatives and Senators: Trends in Member Characteristics Since
1945." Congressional Research Service, January 27, 2014. www.everycrsreport.com; "Membership of the
115th Congress: A Profile." Congressional Research Service, July 12, 2017. www.everycrsreport.com; Abigail
Geiger and John Gramlich. February 2, 2017. "The Changing Face of Congress in 5 Charts." Pew Research
Center, www.pewresearch.org (all accessed 5/15/18). Data for 2019 calculated by the authors.

considerably more male and whiter than the nation as a whole. While women
make up slightly more than half of the U.S. population, they only comprise
about a fifth of Congress. And the percentages of African Americans, Latinos,
and Asian Americans in both chambers lag the respective national percentages.

This snapshot of the 116th Congress, however, does not tell the whole story.
While the membership of Congress may not reflect the U.S. population, the
membership is more reflective than in the past. Diversity has been on the rise,
especially over the last 25 years. Figures 3.1 and 3.2 illustrate this increased diversity. Since the 102nd Congress (1991–93), the number of women in Congress has
more than quadrupled. During the same time, the number of Latino members
has nearly quadrupled, the number of Asian American members has more than
tripled, and the number of African American members has more than doubled.
Thus while the current (116th) Congress ranks 76th out of 193 countries in terms
of women's parliamentary representation, and underrepresents key ethnic and
racial minorities, the trends are positive toward a Congress that more closely
resembles the nation, at least on these dimensions.[8] The 116th Congress, in fact,
counts the most female members and is the most racially diverse in the nation's
history.[9]

At the same time, these trends are not guarantees. For example, after a big jump
in the number of African Americans in Congress following the 1992 elections,
the overall count has risen only slightly since, with some intermittent declines
(the most recent of which took place in 2008). In addition, the diversity gains

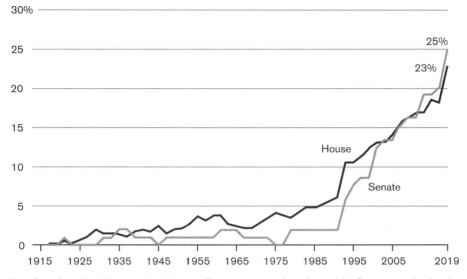

FIGURE 3.1   Women in Congress

Note: Data do not include nonvoting delegates. Figures represent the makeup of the Congress on the first day of the session.
Abigail Geiger and John Gramlich. February 2, 2017. "The Changing Face of Congress in 5 Charts." Pew Research Center, www.pewresearch.org (accessed 5/15/18). Data for 2019 collected by the authors.

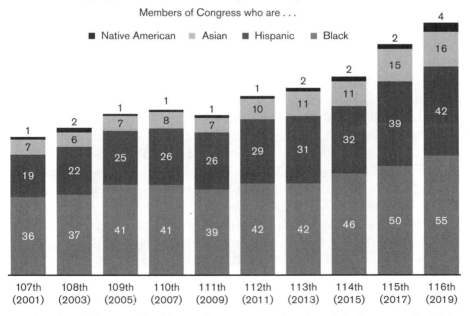

FIGURE 3.2   Growing Racial and Ethnic Diversity in Congress

Note: Data do not include nonvoting delegates. Figures represent the makeup of the Congress on the first day of the session. The category of "Asian" includes Pacific Islanders. For the 115th Congress, Sen. Kamala Harris is included in both the black and Asian categories, and Rep. Adriano Espaillat is included in both the Hispanic and black categories.
Abigail Geiger and John Gramlich. February 2, 2017. "The Changing Face of Congress in 5 Charts." Pew Research Center, www.pewresearch.org (accessed 5/15/18). Data for 2019 calculated by the authors.

in Congress are very lopsided in terms of party, with the Democrats disproportionately leading the way. In the 116th Congress, 85 percent of women, 96.4 percent of African Americans, 88 percent of Latinos, and 100 percent of Asian Americans were Democrats.

CHARACTERIZING REPRESENTATION

As we noted in Chapter 1, our federal system of government is constructed around the notion of a constituency-representative linkage. Citizens (or constituents) select agents (or representatives) to serve their interests in Congress. Constituents evaluate how well representatives perform in office and make their judgments known in regular elections. Accountability is thus built into the system via this electoral connection. Representatives are either rewarded for their performance and given another term, or punished and replaced by someone else.

But what does it mean to act on citizens' behalf or serve their interests? In short, what does it mean for a member of Congress to represent his constituents? Recall from Chapter 1 that representation has often been characterized in two ways: (1) delegate based or (2) trustee based. An elected representative takes on a *delegate* role by assessing where his constituents stand on issues and supporting those preferences through a variety of actions, such as votes, speeches, and bill introductions. A representative as delegate, therefore, sees himself as channeling the wishes of his constituents. This was the mode of representation envisioned by James Madison, as argued in the Federalist Papers. However, an elected representative who takes on a *trustee* role acts very differently, taking actions that she believes are in the best interests of her constituents, even if such actions are at odds with their stated preferences. For example, a representative as trustee may believe that her expertise and experience require her to support legislation or vote in a way that runs counter to what her constituents say that they want. This was the mode of representation envisioned by Edmund Burke, a conservative thinker of the late eighteenth century.

In reality, no member of Congress acts as a "perfect delegate" or a "perfect trustee." Whether a representative behaves more like a delegate or trustee often comes down to various factors. If constituents—or *some* constituents—care deeply about an issue, a representative has an incentive to satisfy their wishes. Political scientist R. Douglas Arnold famously referred to such constituents as "attentive publics."[10] On highly salient issues, such as gun rights and abortion rights, groups of citizens will care deeply about public policy and follow relevant decision making in Congress very closely. Legislators often respond to such attentive publics—and represent their stated preferences—because they are more likely to organize politically, contribute time and money to campaigns, and vote in elections. On the other hand, Congress deals with many issues that are not especially salient to groups of citizens, or that constituents by and large do not know much about, and thus legislators are freer to act as trustees. Indeed, if constituents lack information on a complex issue that is on the legislative agenda, and thus do not necessarily possess true preferences, members of Congress must step in and represent them by relying on their own expertise or experience, or turning to others for advice.[11]

HOW DO MEMBERS OF CONGRESS REPRESENT CONSTITUENTS?

There are a number of ways that members of Congress can actively show that they are performing their roles as representatives. These include legislating (both voting on and crafting legislation), constituency service, and speeches and personal interactions.

Legislating

Perhaps the clearest way that a member of Congress represents his constituents is through day-to-day activities in the legislative process. Members of Congress are often assessed via the end goal of the legislative process itself—the actual production of a new law. Each Congress adopts hundreds of new laws, some of which are major pieces of legislation. Constituents may judge a member of Congress on what bills he voted for that went on to become law. This is especially true of bills on highly salient issues, which are followed closely by one or more attentive publics. The vote to adopt Obamacare and later votes to repeal the law are examples of highly salient issues followed closely by attentive publics.

Yet a vote by a member of Congress often involves more than simply following constituents' interests. For example, party leaders in Congress (as in the Obamacare example discussed earlier in this chapter) may pressure lawmakers to vote a certain way in order to expedite the party agenda. And such pressure may take the form of rewards or punishments. For example, when Tom DeLay was the Republican majority leader in the House, he was a master of getting the Republican rank and file to vote for the party's policies by promising to distribute money to them for their reelection campaigns via his political action committee (a reward) or threatening to run a primary challenger against them (a punishment).[12]

The president may also try to influence a lawmaker's vote, in combination with or separate from congressional party leaders. President Lyndon Johnson was famous for meeting with members of Congress in person and browbeating them into supporting his position—which became known as the "Johnson treatment." More recently, when it looks like a vote will be close, the president will often pick up the phone and call wavering members, with the goal of persuading them. For example, in 2010, prior to the final vote on the Affordable Care Act in the House, when the outcome was far from certain, President Obama called Democrats who were undecided and asked why they "were not being part of the team."[13]

Interest groups, which may or may not formally be constituents, will also often pressure members on votes that they care about, with implicit promises of more campaign donations down the line or threats of future donations being cut off or distributed to election challengers. The National Rifle Association, for example, has been very active in lobbying members to preserve gun rights, and it distributes considerable sums of money—almost $52 million during the 2016 election cycle—to attempt to influence congressional legislation and elections.[14] Finally, other members of Congress sometimes lobby their fellow lawmakers on issues that they care about, providing information in an attempt to influence their vote.

Thus, for all of these reasons, the act of voting by a member of Congress often involves more than the simple constituency-representative linkage would imply. Many forces are often in play, with some more powerful or relevant than others.

Constituents may also judge a member of Congress on the role that she played in crafting legislation that went on to become law (and sometimes a "landmark law"). Constituents may look at the committee that she sits on—and the work the committee did in navigating the bill through the legislative process—or the effort that she expended to craft and sponsor new legislation. A member of Congress who has a more active role in the production of legislation via committee work and bill sponsorship will often have a stronger claim to being an effective representative.[15] An individual vote, after all, is rarely pivotal in determining whether a bill succeeds in becoming a law.

Of course, while working to produce new legislation is a typical way that members of Congress seek to fulfill their roles as representatives, *preventing* new policy from being adopted is also common. Sometimes, this decision—whether to produce or to prevent—comes down to whether a member is in the majority or the minority. Majority parties are much better positioned to get new legislation passed. Minority parties, on the other hand, must work mostly to block policies that run contrary to their constituents' wishes from being adopted. Thus how a member of Congress spends his legislative time will be a function, at least in part, of whether his party is in power or not. But there are exceptions. Recently, a conservative movement (associated with the Tea Party) has arisen to

President Lyndon Johnson was known for his aggressive, intimidating efforts to persuade members of Congress to support his issue positions.

oppose the expansion of—as well as to roll back—the size of the federal government. In the House, the Freedom Caucus has emerged to encapsulate this conservative sentiment. This group of conservative Republicans has actively sought to represent their constituents by refusing to go along with their majority-party leaders on a number of issues, which until recently would have been viewed as routine aspects of governing—for example, funding the Department of Homeland Security and granting the president the authority to negotiate international trade deals.

Constituency Service

Apart from the standard legislative process, a member of Congress has other ways to serve as a representative. One common way is through constituency service, also known as *casework*.[16] This refers to the various tasks that a member of Congress can perform to fix problems for constituents and otherwise satisfy their requests, often by contacting the appropriate federal agency. These tasks may seem minor—helping to locate a lost Social Security check, identifying the right form(s) to fill out to receive certain federal benefits, and writing a letter of recommendation for a child's college admission, for example—but they are important to constituents. And by dutifully providing such assistance, a member of Congress can build a reputation as a responsive representative. Such a reputation can go a long way toward helping a legislator be successful and get reelected. During his time in Congress, former three-term senator Al D'Amato (R-NY) was known as "Senator Pothole," for his intense focus on constituency service. And he took great pride in the nickname: "It means you're attentive and you're there and available. And that pothole may be a matter of life or death for the person whose needs you are addressing. To them, that's not a pothole; that is making a difference in their lives."[17]

Members of Congress typically rely on their office staff to perform casework. These needs are built into the modern congressional system, but this phenomenon is relatively new. During much of the nineteenth century and into the twentieth century, members of Congress did their jobs without official help. There was no office and no public staff for the average member. (Only committee chairs were provided with an office and a staff person, which helps explain the proliferation of committees, some of which never actually met, after the Civil War.) If a certain task was required, the average member did it himself. And if he needed assistance, he generally paid for it out of pocket. Beginning in the twentieth century, and formalized and expanded in the Legislative Reorganization Act of 1946, members of Congress were provided with allowances, known as general expense accounts, to help them do their jobs.[18]

In the House, Member Representational Allowances (MRAs) can be used for all official expenses, such as hiring personnel, renting office space and purchasing equipment, and covering travel and mail costs. The average MRA for a House member in 2017, per initial authorization, was $1.315 million. From this account, House members can hire no more than 18 full-time and 4 part-time personal staff members. In the Senate, a similar allowance exists in the form of Senator Official Personnel and Office Expense Accounts (SOPOEAs). The average SOPOEA, per fiscal year 2017 legislative branch appropriation, was just over $3.3 million. SOPOEAs vary more than do MRAs, however, as a senator faces no restrictions on the number of personnel he or she may employ, and the size of the administrative/clerical assistance and office expense components are based on the population of his or her state. So, in 2017, SOPOEAs ranged from just over $3 million to more than $4.8 million.

Constituency service has become increasingly important to members of Congress over time. Part of this is demand driven. The needs and requests of constituents are ever increasing, and their ability to communicate those needs and requests to their congressional representatives has been made ever easier in the Internet age. But part is also supply driven. As party machines have disappeared and parties as organizations have grown weaker, more of the work of supplying services to constituents has fallen to individual members of Congress and their

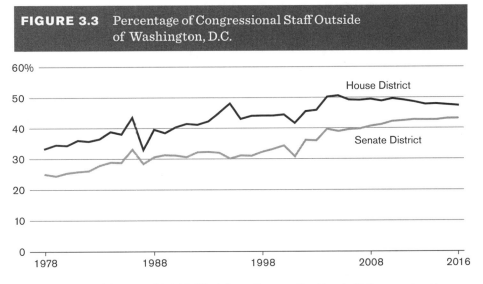

FIGURE 3.3 Percentage of Congressional Staff Outside of Washington, D.C.

Based on data from Table 5-3 and 5-4, *Vital Statistics on Congress*. Brookings Institution, www.brookings .edu/multi-chapter-report/vital-statistics-on-congress (accessed 5/15/18).

staffs. Thus more and more of lawmakers' personal allowances have been devoted to performing constituency service.

Lawmakers have both a Washington, D.C., office and a set of district or state offices. Personnel employed in the D.C. office include chiefs of staff, legislative assistants, and press aides. They perform the day-to-day legislative functions in support of lawmakers, providing advice, drafting legislation, researching policy, writing speeches, and communicating with other member offices. Personnel employed in district or state offices are focused on constituency service; lawmakers place caseworkers "at home" to be closer to and thus better serve constituents. As Figure 3.3 illustrates, the percentage of congressional staff located outside of D.C. has grown over time. In 1978, only a quarter of Senate staff was located in state offices; by 2016, this figure had grown to over 43 percent. While the increase for the House has not been as dramatic, it has followed a similar pattern. In 1978, one-third of House staff was located in district offices. By 2016, that figure was over 47 percent (and in fact exceeded 50 percent in the mid-2000s).

Speeches and Personal Interactions

Legislators also routinely give speeches on the floor of Congress and at events back in their states and districts. These speeches might be short (and take the form of policy statements) or long, and they can be tailored to the composition of the audience. A member of Congress may speak on the same policy topic to different groups, for example, but focus on entirely different components depending on the needs, sentiments, or demographics of the targeted group.[19] On the topic of national health care, for example, a member of Congress might focus on the need to preserve Medicare when speaking to a group of senior citizens but might focus instead on the importance of maintaining a universal mandate when speaking to a group of young voters. Policies, and their effects, are often complex, and a successful legislator is able to identify how his support for or opposition to them matches the preferences of a range of his constituents.

Beyond speeches, legislators also interact with constituents on a more personal level back home. Shaking hands, kissing babies, and small talk with constituents at fundraising and campaign events are one example. Meetings with important donors and interest groups are another. And then there are town hall meetings, which are often more policy focused than campaign events, and sometimes put members of Congress on the spot to clarify their positions on emerging policies, explain complex legislation, or defend their votes on contentious issues. The Obamacare town halls discussed at the start of this chapter—where Republicans faced hostile audiences opposed to repeal efforts—offer one example. More recently, in February 2018, after 17 people were shot and killed at a high school in Parkland, Florida, Republican senator Marco Rubio (FL) faced grief-stricken parents and students who challenged him on his past and future positions on gun regulations.[20]

Regardless of the context, just as lawmakers have located more of their staff back in their districts or states, they have also spent more of their own time back home. As pressure to interact personally with constituents has increased, the number of congressional workdays in a year has declined. Members typically arrive in Washington on Tuesday, in time for evening votes, and stay through Thursday afternoon, after which they fly back to their districts or states. As a result, the modern Congress has been called the "Tuesday-to-Thursday Club" (or, more pejoratively, the "Part-Time Congress").[21] This Tuesday–Thursday arrangement allows members of Congress maximum time to interact with constituents back home. But this timetable also affects how congressional proceedings are conducted. Leaders pack more into a tighter schedule. With less time for votes, for example, more omnibus bills—which package together several legislative measures that might be on diverse topics—are used. Only one full day, Wednesday, is devoted to important legislative matters such as committee hearings and bill markups. Thus the realities of modern representative life clearly affect the way that Congress governs today.

After the shooting at Marjory Stoneman Douglas High School in February 2018, students and other constituents challenged Senator Marco Rubio (R-FL, right) on his positions on gun control at a town hall meeting sponsored by CNN.

ORGANIZING AND COMMUNICATING REPRESENTATIONAL ACTIVITIES

Political scientist David Mayhew famously detailed a scheme for organizing the various representational activities of members of Congress.[22] For Mayhew, all such activities should be interpreted through the lens of legislators desiring and seeking reelection, and they fall into one of three categories.

The first category is *credit claiming*. Here the member of Congress takes responsibility for producing something positive for a constituent. Casework falls within this category, as a legislator can credibly make the case for providing the service: she (with the help of her staff) locates the lost Social Security check, identifies the correct form(s) to fill out, and writes the letter of recommendation. Claiming credit for a policy is harder. A legislator may argue that he voted for a piece of legislation, but his vote is only one of many that are needed for its passage. Instead, being on the committee that was responsible for crafting the legislation is a stronger signal that a legislator played a vital role in the policy-making process. And for members of both the House and Senate, tailoring committee assignments to the needs of their constituencies has been a standard and important practice in the modern congressional era.[23] For example, members who represent rural constituencies with significant farming interests gravitate toward the agriculture committees in both chambers, whereas members who represent large urban areas seek spots on the small business committees.

The second category is *position taking*. This category is less about producing something tangible for constituents, such as casework or policy, and more about providing symbolic support. Position taking would include making a speech favoring or opposing a policy, the direction of which is consistent with constituent preferences. A vote can also be an example of position taking. While a single vote does not usually determine whether a policy succeeds or not—almost no bills pass or fail by a single vote—it does place the member of Congress on the record, and she can accurately state that she supported or opposed a piece of legislation based on constituent preferences. Position taking is often more important for members of the minority party in Congress. Because the minority party does not control the legislative agenda and thus is rarely in a position to make policy, the minority party's members must focus on representing constituents through speeches and votes that are often in opposition to the majority's policy initiatives. In this way, they signal that they are "fighting the good fight" by working to keep the current policy in place and preventing the majority from shifting policy away from what their constituents prefer.

The third category, *advertising*, is more general. Here a member of Congress focuses on attributes rather than activities—it is more about who he is rather than what he has done. For example, a member may focus on his experience in office (how long he has served on important committees or what leadership positions in his party he has held) or on personal qualities (being hardworking and possessing integrity and competence). A member of Congress often turns to advertising when interacting with constituents before elections. At its core, advertising is about building trust. There will be many occasions when a member of Congress must make judgments on policy matters—and thus serve as a trustee—and advertising is about making clear to constituents that he is qualified to make them and can be relied on.

How do members communicate these representational activities to constituents? Stated differently, how do a member's credit claiming, position taking, and advertising efforts reach the average constituent back home? While members of Congress can sometimes communicate with constituents face-to-face, they typically use some form of media as a vehicle. In the past, the near-exclusive media source was the U.S. mail. Members of Congress, from the First Congress, have had the ability (subject to various caps) to reach constituents through the mail at no cost to themselves. This ability is known as the *franking privilege*. In lieu of a stamp, the member simply affixes his signature ("the frank") to a piece of mail, and the U.S. Postal Service delivers it. All members send a general newsletter to constituents, outlining their positions on votes, policy accomplishments, and general stances on issues of the day. These newsletters might include photos of the particular benefits that a member was able to secure for her constituents, such as a new post office, bridge, or other public works project. Members also use special mailings to target particular constituencies. Sometimes the mailing includes an opinion poll to allow constituents to weigh in on important policy matters.

In recent years, the means by which members of Congress communicate with constituents has expanded beyond "snail mail." They now actively use the Internet. All members have personal Web pages that provide constituents with a wealth of information, including biographical sketches, the committees on which they serve, policy positions, and key votes. Many members post videos that provide snippets from recent speeches or television appearances, and they also make their newsletters available electronically. Members rely heavily on social media, as all House members and senators now have Facebook and Twitter accounts, which staff—and often members themselves—maintain and update on a daily basis.

Members of Congress also care about having their accomplishments, positions, and votes covered in the traditional newspaper and television media, and they generally hire one or more press aides to keep local media outlets up to date. Local media typically do not have the budgets or resources to intensively cover the activities of their members of Congress, so they often welcome the information that press aides provide, even while recognizing that it is exclusively positive and self-serving. The House and Senate, as institutions, also provide television and radio technology for their members, which create easy ways to uplink via satellite to local stations and provide informational content. These communications to local newspapers and radio stations—expedited by technology and staff provided by congressional appropriations—are a tremendous electoral boon to members of Congress and serve as a major component of the *incumbency advantage* (covered in Chapter 4).

WHO ARE A MEMBER'S CONSTITUENTS?

We have been discussing constituents throughout this chapter, but who exactly are they? Technically speaking, a member's constituents are the citizens in the geographic unit that she represents. For a House member, this would be everyone in her congressional district. For a senator, this would be everyone in her state. However, defining a constituency as a member's geographic unit is only a starting point. The true nature of congressional representation is more complex and revealing.

Fenno's Concentric Circles

Political scientist Richard Fenno has argued that a member of Congress "sees" different constituencies, depending on his needs and situation. Fenno conceived of these different constituencies as a set of concentric circles—circles within circles—to indicate both size and proximity to a member on a personal level (see Figure 3.4).

The largest circle is the *geographic constituency* just discussed. On the most basic level, a member's geographic constituency is everyone in his district or state. In more practical—or political—terms, a member of Congress might consider his geographic constituency to be the full set of *voters* in his district or state. Within this circle, there are three others. The next-largest circle is the *reelection constituency*, the portion of the geographic constituency composed of those voters who are likely to support the member of Congress in the next election. While legislators technically represent their entire geographic unit, they rely on sub-constituencies within their districts or states for reelection.[24] In contemporary politics, for example, urban areas tend to vote Democratic, while suburban and rural areas often lean Republican. And even when legislators are of the same party and represent the same geographic constituency, as can happen with a unified party delegation in the Senate, they often build different support networks and represent different groups. As political scientist Wendy Schiller notes, same-party senators can be thought of as both "partners" and "rivals," as they tend to assert control and represent constituencies in distinct areas of the state.[25]

The next-largest circle is the *primary constituency*, which represents that portion of the reelection constituency that actively supports the member of Congress. These voters are typically strong party identifiers. They will often contribute money to the member's campaign and advertise their allegiance with bumper stickers and yard signs, and sometimes they volunteer their time to work for the campaign itself. They also can be counted on to participate in the member's primary election and thus actively support her renomination. Finally, the smallest circle is the *personal constituency*, which represents the member's personal friends, closest advisors, and biggest donors. These are the people whom she trusts the most, relying on them for financial and moral support, as well as critical political advice. They are her "firewall" against the outside world.

Summarizing Fenno's characterization of constituencies, political scientists John Aldrich and Kenneth Shepsle write, "While a geographic constituency is *assigned* a legislator as a matter of constitutional practice, a legislator's 'constituency'

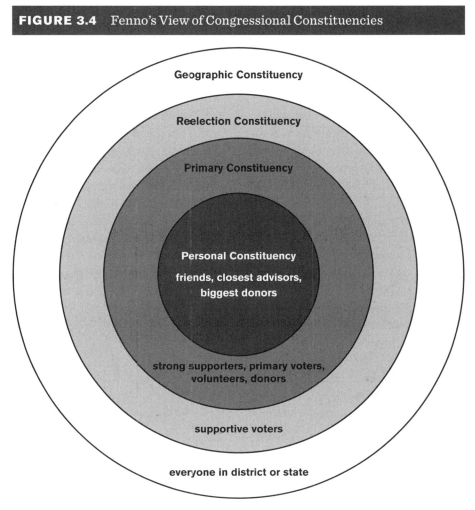

FIGURE 3.4 Fenno's View of Congressional Constituencies

Geographic Constituency

Reelection Constituency

Primary Constituency

Personal Constituency

friends, closest advisors, biggest donors

strong supporters, primary voters, volunteers, donors

supportive voters

everyone in district or state

Based on Richard F. Fenno, *Home Style: House Members in Their Districts* (Boston: Little, Brown, 1978).

is *chosen*."[26] Which of the various constituencies a member of Congress focuses on typically depends on the issue or problem at hand. For example, if a member faces a serious challenger within his party, he will pay special attention to his primary constituency. And if he is successful in beating back that primary challenge, he will then work on mending fences within the party and by doing so expand his focus to his reelection constituency. Alternatively, if a House member finds that his congressional district has been redrawn after a decennial census, he will focus on his geographic constituency in order to learn the range of voters that he now represents. And throughout it all, a member will lean on his personal constituency for advice and support.

Recently, political scientist Kristina Miler (2010) has built on Fenno's work by delving more deeply into the representational perceptions of members of Congress.[27] Miler elaborates a theory for why legislators "see" different sub-constituencies when they consider their geographic units. Miler argues that members of Congress have limited time, resources, and capabilities, and thus (rationally) they pay attention to some subconstituencies more than others. Relying on work in psychology, she argues that members of Congress use "cognitive shortcuts" to determine which subconstituencies to focus on. Principally, they will use information that is readily accessible to identify certain subconstituencies and not others. Those subconstituencies that are resource rich or highly active politically will have the best chance to get on members' radar. These cognitive shortcuts create a subsequent bias in how members of Congress vote, what types of committees they serve on, and what bills they sponsor. Ultimately, Miler's findings are somewhat depressing: members of Congress, concerned about reelection, will be most likely to see and respond to money and attentiveness. Poorer constituents and those who do not have the time or desire to be politically active are, by comparison, largely ignored.

THEN AND NOW
THE SHIFTING COMPOSITION OF THE GEOGRAPHIC CONSTITUENCY

As noted, a member's geographic constituency can be thought of as the total population in his district or state. But the meaning of "geographic constituency" has in fact changed over time. Here we discuss how the composition of a member's geographic constituency has evolved since the Founding, based on changing politics, perceptions, and values.

In the Constitution (Article I, Section 2, Clause 3), the nature of the geographic constituency was most closely tied to representation in the House of Representatives (and electoral college) and the allocation of House seats by state. To establish a formula for distributing said representation, the Framers wrote,

> Representatives . . . shall be apportioned among the several States . . . according to their respective Numbers, which shall be determined by adding to the whole Number of free Persons, including those bound to Service for a Term of Years, and excluding Indians not taxed, three-fifths of all other Persons.

The key provision here was the "three-fifths of all other persons," as the South had a significant population of African American slaves who were considered property and not people. To account for the slave population, the Framers reached a compromise and wrote it into the Constitution. They decided to count each slave as three-fifths of a person for the purpose of determining how many House seats each state would receive. The "Three-Fifths Compromise" would remain in effect until the Civil War, and it would finally be repealed by Section 2 of the Fourteenth Amendment (1868).[28]

But if we think of a member's geographic constituency not as the total population within a state or district ("their respective Numbers" per the Framers), but rather as the set of eligible voters—because this is often the view held by members themselves and is the basis of electoral accountability—the accounting becomes even more complex. Viewed in this way, changes to a member's geographic constituency have tracked closely to the right to vote in federal elections.

Before the Revolution, voting rights were quite limited, as suffrage was stringently guarded. Members of the upper class ran the political system, and they were not willing to risk the social order by sharing power. Voting was seen as the province of the "independent and virtuous," which was interpreted to mean white Protestant men who owned property. As a result, the percentage of the population that could vote was quite small.

After the Revolution, the system began to open up. First to go was the property restriction, as "gainful employment" became the new standard for voting rights. Pressure for greater participation increased in the 1820s and 1830s as the Democratic Party, led by Andrew Jackson, sought to build a coalition that included the common (white) man. The Whigs, on the other hand, represented the elite in society and thus sought to keep the voting-eligible population small. After more than a decade of conflict, "Jacksonian democracy" triumphed and universal suffrage for all white men became a reality.

These suffrage gains were made outside of the constitutional structure. In fact, the original Constitution (including the Bill of Rights, or the first 10 amendments) had nothing to say about who could vote. The closest provision was found in Article I, Section 4, wherein the power to determine the "times, places, and manner of holding elections" was granted to states, with the times and manner subject to federal regulation.

Voting rights would begin to find a home in the Constitution following the Civil War, during the Reconstruction era. Adopted in 1870, the Fifteenth Amendment stipulated, "The right of citizens of the United States to vote shall not be denied or abridged by the United States or by any State on account of race, color, or previous condition of servitude." The Fifteenth Amendment had the effect of providing universal suffrage for African American men (many of whom had previously been slaves),[29] and thus the voting-eligible population expanded to include all male citizens generally. This expansion in members' geographic constituencies had the greatest effect in the South. The Republican Party—thanks to the votes of former slaves—was able to make considerable inroads in the former Confederacy and thus (for a time) evolve into a true national party.

The voting rights provided in the Fifteenth Amendment were *negative* rights. That is, particular conditions for the *denial* of rights were stipulated and prohibited, which meant that other conditions (which were *not* stipulated and prohibited) could potentially be used to deny some citizens' voting rights. In time, the former slaveholding elite (represented by the Democratic Party) returned to power in the southern states and enacted legal provisions to disenfranchise African American voters. Examples included *poll taxes* (a dollar amount that a citizen must pay before registering to vote) and *literacy tests* (educational requirements that a citizen needs to meet before registering to vote). Because these initiatives were not based strictly on race, but rather on wealth and education, and thus class, they sometimes also disenfranchised poor, uneducated white voters. Thus allowances were often made to keep lower-class whites on the voting rolls—namely, *grandfather clauses*, which waived poll taxes and literacy tests if an individual's grandfather had possessed the right to vote.

For the first two decades of the twentieth century, a southern member of Congress thus considered his geographic constituency to be the *white male* population in his district or state (thus hearkening back to the pre–Civil War era)—and voted accordingly. However, in 1920, the Nineteenth Amendment was adopted, providing universal suffrage for women. The Nineteenth Amendment expanded the voting-eligible population, both in the South (to include white men and white women) and the North (to include men and women of any color). As a result of the Nineteenth Amendment, members of Congress saw their geographic constituencies effectively double in size.

Because of the disenfranchisement of African Americans, the South became a one-party (Democratic) state for more than a half-century. Beginning in the 1950s, however, the African American civil rights movement began to gain momentum, and liberal northern Democrats in Congress began to push for change. In the 1960s, suffrage restrictions against African Americans were rolled back considerably. For example, the Twenty-Fourth Amendment (1964) prohibited poll taxes, and the Voting Rights Act of 1965 outlawed literacy tests. As a result, by the late 1960s, African Americans in the South were beginning to register in high numbers, and over the next two decades, congressional candidates in the South—some grudgingly—began viewing their geographic constituencies as including both whites and African Americans. By the 1980s, the enfranchisement of African Americans had shifted the partisan dynamics in the South noticeably, as conservative whites found a home in the Republican Party while African Americans and liberal/moderate whites associated with the Democratic Party.[30]

The last major change to federal voting rights occurred in 1971, with the adoption of the Twenty-Sixth Amendment, which established 18 years as the national voting age. Prior to the Twenty-Sixth Amendment, states could set the voting age, and many selected 21 years. With the advent of the Vietnam draft, wherein 18-year-olds were being sent to Southeast Asia to fight for their country, pressure mounted at home to give similarly aged citizens a direct say in political matters. Thus the Twenty-Sixth Amendment further expanded the voting-eligible population and with it members' geographic constituencies.

Within established federal guidelines, states may restrict or expand voting rights. The disenfranchisement of African Americans in the South via poll taxes and literacy tests, as described earlier, is an example from the past. In recent years, some states have sought to restrict voting rights by attempting to require valid identification to register and/or vote, while other states have sought to expand voting rights by eliminating suffrage restrictions on former felons. Partisan motivations have driven these attempts, and the goal is to gain an electoral advantage. For example, Republicans in North Carolina have pushed to enact voter identification laws, and Democrats in Virginia have worked to roll back felon disfranchisement laws. These are contemporary examples of the parties trying, in a strategic way, to expand or limit the size and composition of geographical constituencies for their own benefit.

While these recent attempts by states to restrict or expand the voting-eligible population have been controversial, their effects have occurred at the margins. That is, small groups of voters (or potential voters) have been affected. This is not to say that these changes were unimportant. Marginal changes in the size and composition of geographic constituencies can sometimes mean the difference between winning and losing an election. And in an era when both parties believe they have a chance to win majority control of Congress every election cycle, these marginal changes might have huge consequences.

Critical Thinking

1. Once disenfranchisement efforts (such as poll taxes and literacy tests) helped create a one-party Democratic state in the South by effectively driving the Republican Party in the region out of existence, did southern Democrats in Congress still have an incentive to represent their constituents? Why or why not?

2. Which voter enfranchisement effort had a bigger effect on American politics: the Nineteenth Amendment or the Voting Rights Act of 1965? Explain.

3. Are there legitimate reasons why states might restrict some adult citizens' right to vote? For example, do you believe that felons or ex-felons should have a right to vote? Why or why not?

Beyond Concentric Circles

Fenno's characterization of constituency as a set of concentric circles helps us understand the complex nature of congressional representation. But these circles do not, by themselves, capture everything about the congressional representational experience. Political scientists often conceive of congressional representation in other ways. We discuss three such ways in the following sections: national representation, substantive representation, and descriptive representation.

NATIONAL REPRESENTATION   Although the conception of geographic boundaries makes sense in terms of congressional representation, both in terms of identifying the full set of voters and establishing a clear accountability mechanism for a member of Congress, it also has its limitations. While acknowledging the geographic nature of the constituency-representative linkage, some members of Congress think and act on a more national scale. These members often serve on the most powerful congressional committees, and they use their influence to design national policy and compete with the president for national authority.[31]

The Armed Services Committee in the Senate is one such case. Senators on the Armed Services Committee often vie with the president to establish policy and generate political responses on matters of national security. This interbranch competition would include responding to threats made against the United States and its citizens—a governing focus that extends far beyond the needs of any one congressional district or state. For example, in recent years, as Armed Services chairman, John McCain (R-AZ), used his position to compete actively with the Obama and Trump administrations—first pushing Obama to take a stronger stance against worldwide threats, especially those made by proponents of "radical Islam," and more recently criticizing Trump as poorly informed and impulsive while stating that Congress would not play a subordinate role on important policy matters or refrain from checking the power of the president when necessary.[32]

Senator John McCain (R-AZ), as chairman of the Senate Armed Services Committee, used his position to attempt to direct foreign policy on a national scale.

Another factor that leads certain members to think and act more on a national scale is higher ambition. Some members of Congress want to be president and thus push their way onto the national stage more than others in order to build a reputation that extends beyond the geographic constituency of their district or state. Overall, senators are more likely to be national representatives than House members because they already have experience building electoral coalitions on a broader (state versus district) scale. Senators who serve on powerful committees with a national focus have a further advantage. John McCain, for example, ran for president twice (in 2000 and 2008) and was the Republican nominee in 2008. Likewise, recent Democratic presidential nominees Hillary Clinton (2016), Barack Obama (2012 and 2008), and John Kerry (2004) were all sitting senators and served on the important Foreign Relations Committee. While House members have a harder time building a national constituency than senators do, some are able to accomplish that goal. One recent example is Paul Ryan (R-WI), who had served as the chair of the House Ways and Means and Budget Committees and Speaker of the House. Ryan has not run for president, but he has been part of a presidential election ticket (as Mitt Romney's vice presidential running mate in 2012) and is widely believed to desire the nation's top office (despite his recent retirement from the House).

SUBSTANTIVE REPRESENTATION   Another way to think about representation is to focus on the underlying substance of the representation, where "substance" reflects issue or policy content. Here the question might be, how well do the legislator's issues or policy positions correspond to what her constituents want? The term scholars often use to describe this correspondence is *policy congruence*.

Policy congruence can take various forms. One form is public statements—as in speeches made on the floor of Congress or elsewhere—and the degree to which such statements reflect the positions held by constituents. Such statements are relatively low cost, however, and thus mostly symbolic. Another form is the introduction of policies themselves. This form is more significant, as it is higher cost and involves actions—the crafting of legislation—rather than statements. Congruence, in this case, can be assessed by how well the bills that a member of Congress sponsors reflect the policy preferences of constituents.[33] Finally, perhaps the most common form is roll call votes themselves. The House and Senate, as legislative bodies, vote on hundreds of issues each term, from the small or symbolic (on resolutions) to the large and consequential (on major policy initiatives), and members stake out positions through their individual roll call votes. Constituents can track those votes to determine how well (and closely) their member of Congress is acting on their behalf.

The number of African American and Latina women in Congress has increased significantly in recent years. Here, John Lewis (left, D-GA) and Marcia Fudge (center, D-OH) hold a press conference with other members of the Congressional Black Caucus.

Vote-based policy congruence can itself take various forms. For example, some constituents are *single-issue voters*, and their support of or opposition to a legislator's reelection will depend on how he voted on legislation that dealt with that issue. In contemporary politics, issues that draw the exclusive attention of some constituents are typically polarizing, such as abortion and gun control.[34] Other constituents care about a range of issues or whether a member of Congress is voting in a suitably liberal or conservative direction. In this case, we can assess policy congruence by examining how a legislator votes on a number of roll calls, which can range from a handful of votes, to a few dozen, to perhaps all votes in a given Congress.

DESCRIPTIVE REPRESENTATION   Still another way to think about representation is to focus on the underlying qualities of the representatives themselves. We can think of descriptive representation in pure demographic terms: Does the representative "look like" his constituents? The answer might be predicated on background. For example, is the legislator a Catholic? Does he have a college degree? Is he a lawyer or business owner? More often, descriptive representation involves something that is immutable. Is the legislator African American? Latino? A woman? Thus to be represented by someone descriptively requires a *congruence of qualities* rather than a *congruence of substance*.

Many scholars argue that descriptive representation leads to better substantive representation. Most of this research has focused on African Americans, investigating whether African American Democrats in Congress do a better job of representing the interests of African American constituents than do white Democrats in Congress. The chief means of conducting this investigation has been to study how the different members of Congress vote. And most of these roll call–based studies find a significant relationship between descriptive and substantive representation: African American members of Congress represent African American constituents better than do white members.[35] The literature on Latinos is less developed, but the existing work suggests that there is also a link between descriptive and substantive representation: Latino members of Congress represent Latino constituents better than do white members.[36]

When we dig deeper, we find evidence that descriptive representation often manifests itself before votes are taken. That is, descriptive characteristics are a significant predictor of the kinds of bills a member introduces. For example, African American Democrats in Congress are more likely to introduce legislation that is important to African American constituents than are white Democrats.[37] And the pre-floor stage is where clear differences occur by gender, as a number of studies find that female members of Congress are significantly more likely to sponsor legislation on "women's issues," such as gender equity, child care, abortion, and employee flex time, than are male members of Congress.[38]

A more theoretical literature delves into the connection between descriptive and substantive representation. Some research in this vein suggests that low-cost (or symbolic) substantive representation by African American members of Congress provides a crucial benefit for their African American constituents. While awarding Rosa Parks a congressional medal or ensuring that Dr. Martin Luther King, Jr.'s birthday becomes a national holiday may not be commensurate with generating new policy, such symbolic initiatives are important. As political scientist Katherine Tate argues, they provide "voice and recognition" for African Americans, which is a "vital currency" in the "marketplace of ideas and ideologies."[39] Other research suggests that "shared fate," or common experiences related to the descriptive characteristic, leads members of Congress to better understand what their descriptive group needs and craft legislation to meet those needs.[40] For instance, growing up black in America creates a personal experience vis-à-vis discrimination in its many forms. An African American member of Congress, therefore, possesses an advantage in crafting legislation to combat discrimination because he may have faced instances of such discrimination in the past, and as an elected representative, he desires to pursue antidiscrimination legislation.

Recently, a creative study examined the causal power of common experience in affecting the behavior of members of Congress. Economist Ebonya Washington examined how male legislators voted on women's health issues before and after they became fathers to baby girls. Her expectation was that if shared fate mattered, male members of Congress with new daughters would be more likely to vote for policies that promoted women's health than all other male members of Congress would. And in fact, this effect is what she found, particularly on issues involving reproductive rights.[41]

HOW WE STUDY
MEASURING REPRESENTATION

The theoretical concepts inherent in congressional representation are straightforward: members of Congress will, to some degree and at some times, act in accordance with their constituents' wishes, either broadly or narrowly defined. Elections provide the accountability mechanism; if legislators deviate from representative behavior, they risk being voted out of office and replaced by someone constituents believe will do a better job of acting on their behalf.

Measuring representation—determining if members of Congress are in fact acting according to constituents' wishes—has been more challenging for political scientists. The most common attempt to measure representation has occurred at the geographic level. Studies have examined whether members of Congress vote in ways that are congruent with broad interests in districts or states. Often, such attempts have taken the form of statistical analyses, where data across members and across time are collected. The researcher then assesses whether a significant correlation exists between members' roll call votes and constituents' interests (measured with economic, demographic, or survey data).[42] If a significant correlation exists, then we can argue that policy congruence is occurring. One difficulty is establishing that the correlation is actually capturing a causal relationship.[43] For example, it could be that members of Congress are voting in accordance with constituent interests, consistent with the accountability mechanism underlying the representative-constituency linkage. That would be a causal relationship: members are voting for what constituents want in order to maximize their chances of reelection (and for fear of being voted out of office if they shirk constituents' concerns). However, it could also be that members of Congress simply share the same preferences as their constituencies. In that case, legislators are just voting for what they personally want or believe to be the best policies. Policy congruence would thus be accidental and not driven by any accountability concerns. Recent research has focused on tackling this thorny problem of establishing policy congruence as a true causal relationship.[44]

Measuring representation more narrowly than at the geographic level has been challenging because variables used to measure constituent interests for members of Congress are collected by geographic boundaries. If census data are used, for example, the underlying geographic unit will be the county. And county-level data can then be aggregated up to the district and state levels. The other concentric circles at the heart of Fenno's conception of representation do not follow geographic boundaries neatly. Reelection and primary constituencies, for example, are embedded within geographic units, but so are those voters who are not part of either constituency and will not be supporting the member in his reelection efforts. Determining whether a member of Congress acts in accordance with such subgeographic constituencies does not naturally lend itself to the same broad statistical approach.

Fenno approached the study of the subgeographic constituencies in a wholly different way. Instead of analyzing quantitative data, Fenno embedded himself in the reelection campaigns of various members of Congress, following them around to different events with different constituents and talking with them about their motivations and strategies. He referred to this qualitative approach as "soaking and poking."[45] Such a case-by-case approach yields inherently anecdotal evidence; however, Fenno argued that it could also generate evidence of individual causal relationships. In particular, he believed that legislators were "goal seeking [but also] . . . situation interpreting."[46] That is, members of

Congress developed "home styles," or strategic ways of presenting themselves and their accomplishments to constituents. For example, a member wants to get reelected, so she assesses how a key set of constituents would react to certain policy positions, and then she offers such policy positions in their presence while at a fundraiser or in a speech.[47] This logical chain would provide some evidence that electoral accountability is driving a member of Congress to adopt certain policy positions. While this sort of evidence, based on intensive participant observation, might not satisfy the requirements of scholars doing statistical research on large data sets, Fenno believed it might be the best that scholars could achieve in the study of subgeographic constituencies.

Fenno's work on congressional home styles began in the late 1970s, and the soaking-and-poking approach was considered the gold standard for the scholarly investigation of subgeographic constituencies for almost four decades. Recently, political scientist Justin Grimmer leveraged data and statistical advances to provide a more systematic way of studying how members of Congress present themselves to constituents.[48] Grimmer focused on the Senate and examined more than 64,000 press releases that were issued from senators' offices between 2005 and 2007. Applying computational techniques to the text of these press releases, Grimmer was able to study which issues senators emphasize, why they emphasize these issues, and how their choices matter for representation. After crunching the data, Grimmer concluded that senators pursue two basic styles of presentation. The first is an issue-oriented style in which they engage in debates on national issues. This style is most often used by senators who are ideologically well aligned with constituents. The second is an appropriator style in which they focus on claiming credit for "bringing home the bacon" to the state. This style is most often used by senators who are not ideologically well aligned with constituents. Many senators pursue a mixed style, focusing sometimes on issues and sometimes on their particular accomplishments.

Moving beyond Fenno's concentric circles, policy congruence connected to the concerns of particular groups is also a topic of considerable study. Interest groups often select a set of roll call votes from the congressional agenda to assess how well members of Congress support the issues and policies that they care about. Two well-known interest groups are the Americans for Democratic Action (ADA) and the Leadership Council on Civil Rights (LCCR). The ADA selects votes related to the broad topic of "political liberalism," while the LCCR chooses a narrower set of votes related to "civil rights." With these votes in hand, the ADA and LCCR identify how a member of Congress should vote (either "yea" or "nay" roll call by roll call) and construct a "support score" based on this set of votes.

As we discussed in Chapter 2, political scientists routinely use these scores as measures of members' preferences in statistical analyses. For example, ADA

TABLE 3.2 Legislative Support Scores, 114th Congress (2015–17)

	ADA Scores		LCCR Scores	
	House	Senate	House	Senate
All members	39.4%	44.2%	44.5%	49.9%
Democrats	88.2	89.8	97.1	96.9
Republicans	2.5	5.9	4.4	9.9

0% = perfectly conservative; 100% = perfectly liberal

"The Leadership Conference on Civil and Human Rights Voting Record: 114th Congress, October 2016." http://civilrightsdocs.info/pdf/voting-record/Voting-Record-October2016.pdf; "2016 Congressional Voting Record." Americans for Democratic Action, https://adaction.org/wp-content/uploads/2018/02/2016.pdf (all accessed 5/15/18).

scores measure members' preferences on a general liberalism dimension, ranging from not at all liberal (a.k.a. perfectly conservative) to perfectly liberal.[49] LCCR scores also measure members' preferences on a liberalism dimension, but a more specific one related to the concerns of racial and ethnic minorities.[50] LCCR scores range from strongly anti-minority to strongly pro-minority.

ADA scores and LCCR scores for the 114th Congress (2015–17) appear in Table 3.2. The scores are broken down by party and chamber. The ADA scores are based on 40 roll calls in each chamber, while the LCCR scores are based on 22 roll calls in the House and 21 in the Senate. Each set of scores reflects averages. So, for instance, the average ADA support score in the entire House was 39.4. Stated another way, the average House member voted for—that is, supported—the ADA's position 39.4 percent of the time.

When we consider the two sets of support scores by party, we find huge differences. Democrats voted much more in keeping with basic policy liberalism (as measured by the ADA) and pro–civil rights positions (as measured by the LCCR). The average Democratic score was nearly 90 percent in the House and more than 95 percent in the Senate (on both ADA and LCCR). The average Republican score was below 10 percent (on both ADA and LCCR) in both chambers.

Although these scores can illuminate the differences between the parties, we need to be mindful of artificial extremism (see Chapter 2). While interest groups choose roll calls that relate to their governing mission and values, the roll calls themselves are often on controversial, high-profile issues that typically divide the parties on their own core beliefs. Thus the scores help identify "heroes" (members who vote *for* the group's position on every roll call) and "zeroes" (members who vote *against* the group's position on every roll call).[51] Identifying these extreme legislators is one way that groups try to lobby legislators indirectly—using both rewards (showcasing their names on a "heroes list") and punishments (showcasing their names on a "zeroes list").[52]

Thus while interest-group scores can be useful in studying representation, they should also be used with caution. The limitations of interest-group scores explain why scholars have increasingly turned to measures that incorporate all (or nearly all) roll call votes, such as Poole and Rosenthal's NOMINATE scores, to create ideology measures for members of Congress (see "How We Study," Chapter 2). However, while measures such as NOMINATE better differentiate members within party and limit the artificial extremism problem, they incorporate votes on all kinds of things—procedures, amendments, and policies— and thus cannot be easily framed as measuring specific issue areas.

Critical Thinking

1. We have noted some of the methodological difficulties in establishing policy congruence between members of Congress and their constituents. How might redistricting—in which a House member's district is redrawn, with some new areas (usually counties) added and some old areas dropped— provide an opportunity to assess policy congruence? Speculate.
2. Will a member of Congress's "home style" change over time? Or does she establish such a home style when she first arrives in Congress and stick with it throughout her career? Explain.
3. Sometimes a member of Congress will switch parties—from Democrat to Republican or vice versa. When this happens, will his ADA score or LCCR score change? Why or why not?

COLLECTIVE REPRESENTATION

Our discussion of representation to this point has focused on the connection between individual members of Congress and their constituents. But there is another kind of representation that is also important. *Collective representation* is the connection between Congress as a whole and the American public. Stated differently, assessing collective representation means determining whether, and how well, Congress as an institution represents the preferences of the nation.

Is Congress reflective of the American public? The study of collective representation proceeds differently than similar examinations of individual-level representation. A useful place to start is citizens' perceptions of how well

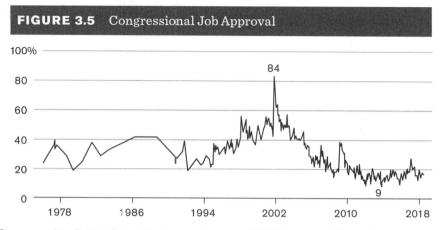

FIGURE 3.5   Congressional Job Approval

"Congress and the Public." Gallup, http://news.gallup.com/poll/1600/congress-public.aspx (accessed 8/15/18).

Congress is doing its job versus how well they believe their individual member of Congress is doing his job. This macro versus micro distinction is, in fact, quite telling.

To make this collective versus individual comparison, we use congressional job approval data collected across time by Gallup, a long-standing U.S. polling firm. Gallup asks a random sample of Americans at regular intervals two questions: (1) Do you approve of the way Congress is handling its job? and (2) do you approve or disapprove of the way the representative from your congressional district is handling his job? From these responses, we can assess whether citizens view the collective performance of Congress differently from how they view the individual performance of their particular House member.

Figure 3.5 presents congressional job approval data from the mid-1970s to the present. Until the early 1990s, around 35 to 40 percent of Americans approved of the way Congress was doing its job. This figure dipped to 25 to 30 percent through the mid-1990s and then gradually crept up through the mid-2000s to the 50 to 55 percent level, with a huge spike (84 percent) right after the 9/11 terrorist attacks. Congressional approval numbers declined significantly during George W. Bush's second term in office (as the war effort in Afghanistan and Iraq stagnated), bounced back during Barack Obama's first term in office (when Obamacare was adopted), then sank again, and has largely leveled off in the teens ever since. A low point was reached in November 2013, when congressional job approval was 9 percent.

These data suggest that very few Americans in recent years approve of the job that Congress as an institution is doing. How does this assessment compare to how Americans evaluate the job performance of their individual member of

Congress? While Gallup has asked about individual member job approval more sporadically over time, the data in Figure 3.6 are still illuminating: Americans view their individual House member's performance quite differently from how they view Congress as a whole.[53] Even as congressional job approval bottomed out at 9 percent in late 2013, around 45 percent of Americans judged their individual member of Congress favorably. And by late 2014, while congressional job approval was still only 14 percent, around 55 percent of Americans felt that their individual member of Congress was performing well.

Thus while Americans in recent years have been quite negative about how Congress as a whole has performed, they are considerably more positive in how they view their individual House member. In fact, a majority of Americans believe their individual member of Congress is doing a good job.[54]

There are many reasons why few Americans view congressional job performance in a positive light. For example, some scholars have suggested that Americans use different criteria to judge Congress as a whole as opposed to individual members: Congress is evaluated based on domestic and foreign policy produced, while individual members are evaluated on constituency service (or casework).[55] And, in recent years, it has become common to view Congress as dysfunctional, or the "broken branch," because of its high degree of partisan rancor and polarization, which has led to gridlock even on traditionally simple governing responsibilities (see Chapter 8).[56] At the same time, individual members have maintained or enhanced their constituency service efforts.

However, more fundamentally, the question is, does Congress as a whole respond to what Americans say they want? In fact, according to political scientists

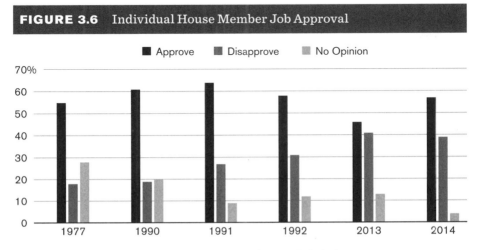

FIGURE 3.6   Individual House Member Job Approval

■ Approve   ■ Disapprove   ■ No Opinion

"Congress and the Public." Gallup, http://news.gallup.com (accessed 5/15/18).

who study collective representation, the answer is mostly "yes." The work of political scientist James Stimson and his coauthors is the gold standard for research on collective representation.[57] Stimson constructs an aggregate measure of public opinion over time, which he characterizes as "public mood," or Americans' desire for liberal or conservative policy. He then examines whether policy decisions in the House and Senate (using interest-group ratings and roll call votes) track the public mood. In this way, he asks whether congressional decisions reflect what the public wants and whether Congress changes in response to changes in public mood. Stimson finds that both the House and Senate are responsive to changes in public mood, with the House responding more quickly to short-term changes and the Senate responding a bit more slowly. Some of this responsiveness is due to sitting members of Congress "rationally anticipating" trends in public opinion and adjusting their voting behavior accordingly, but much of it is a function of membership turnover in Congress. That is, newly elected members of Congress will often reflect the most recent trends in public opinion better than the members they replace, and they help move Congress as a whole in the direction of that opinion. This latter finding highlights the power of elections and the degree to which accountability to the public is an important component of the representative-constituency linkage.

CONCLUSION

We opened this chapter with a description of how Republican members of Congress faced constituent anger and outrage over their party's goal of repealing Obamacare. This example is important for a couple of reasons. First, representing and governing do not always go hand in hand easily and simply. Major policy change will undoubtedly make some constituents unhappy—or benefit some more than others—and members of Congress will face the ire of those on the losing end as a result. Second, the definition of a "constituent" is somewhat fluid. Most of the citizens who attended the GOP town halls in the spring and summer of 2017 were residents of the members' districts or states, so they were in fact geographic constituents. But many—and likely most—of them were not Republican voters, and thus they were not considered to be part of the members' reelection constituencies. For Republican members of Congress, representing the interests of these constituents who did not vote for them, and probably would not vote for them in the future, was not a winning strategy. In the short term, a hostile audience meant that Republican lawmakers had to accept being yelled at in town halls. But in the long term, they hoped that their supporters—members of their reelection constituencies—would approve of their actions in Congress, turn out to vote, and reelect them.

While the Obamacare example suggests that members of Congress sometimes behave contrary to what some people in their districts or states want, most political science research finds that democratic accountability underlies representative government. That is, regular elections force members of Congress to provide representation for at least a majority of their geographic constituents through a variety of mechanisms such as roll call voting, bill introduction, and casework. If a member shirks these representational activities, he risks being voted out of office. And, on a macro level, the evidence suggests that aggregate decision making in Congress follows aggregate public opinion in the nation. As the public's "policy mood" shifts left or right, House and Senate decisions follow in due course.

This is not to say that our representational system is perfect. Congress does not "look like" the American public. Women and minorities are underrepresented in both the House and Senate relative to the U.S. population. And congressional job-approval figures are embarrassingly low, as the vast majority of Americans are unhappy with the institution's performance. And while the trend has been toward more-equitable representation in Congress, as the percentages of women and minorities have increased substantially in the last quarter century, there is less hope that Congress's job approval numbers will change for the better. Why?

The answer lies in how representation and governing play out in contemporary American politics. The high degree of polarization that exists in Congress today makes representation and governing nearly incompatible. A wide gulf exists between Republicans and Democrats on most policy issues, reflecting similar trends in American society. Members of Congress can serve their constituents' needs even as the stark differences between the parties leave little chance of finding compromise policy positions that can produce clear congressional majorities. And passing legislation with only majority-party votes is not easy. The schism within the Republican Party in recent years is a case in point. More populist Republicans (for example, those who associate with the anti-government Tea Party or the House Freedom Caucus) often refuse to do what used to be considered "basic legislating." As a result, many individual members successfully represent their constituents, while Congress as a whole produces few policies of importance. Other institutions—the presidency, bureaucracy, and courts—then step in to fill the policy void, and the public rates Congress's job performance as dismal.

Can this situation change? Can we reach a point where the public approves of the performance of their member of Congress *and* the performance of Congress as a whole? For this to occur, polarization in Congress would need to decrease, creating more opportunities for compromise. Moreover, populist tendencies in the congressional Republican Party (and in the Democratic Party, should they return to majority status) would need to be eliminated, which would allow an active and coherent majority agenda. Neither of these outcomes appears likely, at least in the short term. Rather, more of the same looms on the horizon.

Discussion Questions

1. If a member of Congress believes an issue that a majority of his constituents supports is actually bad for them—or inconsistent with their interests—what should he do? In this case, what does representing them entail?
2. If a House member from New York City runs for and is elected to the Senate from New York State, will her reelection constituency change? Why or why not? Will her personal constituency change?
3. How has the Internet age affected the representational abilities of a member of Congress? Are constituents today—compared to constituents in the pre-Internet era—more able or less able to hold members of Congress accountable? Explain.
4. Should the proportion of women, African Americans, and other minorities in Congress mirror their respective proportions in the U.S. population? If all structural barriers that these groups face are eliminated, will we see over time the proportions converge? Why or why not?
5. Americans do not like Congress, but they generally like their representatives (their House member and senators). Does this disconnect indicate that citizens are not rational or that they are being fooled or manipulated in some way (or both)? Explain.

4

Elections

By all accounts, Eric Cantor's congressional future in 2014 was bright. Cantor, a Republican who represented Virginia's Seventh Congressional District, was first elected to the House of Representatives in 2000. He became the minority whip in 2009, and after the Republicans retook majority control of the House in the 2010 midterms, they elected him majority leader the following year. After serving under House Speaker John Boehner (R-OH) for several years, Cantor was the odds-on favorite to succeed him.

Then David Brat, a largely unknown college professor who ran an underfunded campaign, defeated Cantor in the 2014 primary election for his House seat. In the aftermath of Cantor's loss, the media lurched about for explanations. With time, it became clear that Cantor failed to win for a variety of reasons. He ran a poor campaign, did not do a good job servicing his constituents' needs, devoted too much of his time to climbing the career ladder in Washington, and was increasingly out of step ideologically with his district.

The last factor may have had the biggest effect. The populist, anti-government Tea Party movement began in 2009 and swept the country. In Virginia, Cantor was largely blind to this movement; he could not see that it might cost him electorally. But his district was changing—partly based on the Tea Party movement

Representative Eric Cantor (R-VA) is one among a small group of incumbent congressional representatives who have lost their reelection bids. Cantor fell victim to a surprisingly successful campaign by Tea Party–backed candidate David Brat.

and partly because of a 2012 redistricting that made his district more Republican. These two factors interacted and helped create the perfect storm for his defeat in 2014.

The defeat of a powerful congressional incumbent is unusual, but the Cantor case was exceptional.[1] Never had a sitting majority leader been defeated in a congressional primary. But even when "regular" incumbents are defeated, such as Senator Bob Barr (R-UT) in 2010 (also by a populist Tea Party candidate), the event is big news because reelection rates for members of Congress—both in the House and the Senate—are very high. Congressional incumbents build long careers in the institution, and they often have little trouble achieving reelection if they decide to seek it.

In this chapter, we learn why reelection rates for members of Congress have been so high. We also discuss the institutional foundations of congressional elections, the rise of congressional careerism, and the role of ambition in the decision to seek election to Congress. Finally, we examine why incumbents sometimes (but rarely) lose, and we note that when a congressional seat turns over, it is typically because a member of Congress retires rather than runs for reelection and loses. We conclude by noting some data trends that suggest that the value of incumbency might be eroding, thanks to the increasing nationalization of politics in the early twenty-first century.

SOME BASICS OF CONGRESSIONAL ELECTIONS

Elections are at the heart of our representative democracy. As noted in Chapter 3, an electoral connection links citizens and their representatives in Congress. Citizens use elections both to choose who will serve their interests in Congress and to evaluate their representatives' performance. Citizens either reward members for doing a good job and grant them another term in office, or they punish them for not performing well enough and replace them with someone else. Elections thus serve as an accountability mechanism, a way for citizens every two years (or six years in the case of senators) to ensure that their representatives are behaving as faithful agents.

Congressional elections occur on Federal Election Day, the first Tuesday after the first Monday in November in even-numbered years. Sometimes congressional elections overlap with presidential elections (during presidential election years), and sometimes they do not (during midterm election years). All House seats and about one-third of Senate seats are up for election every two years, with senators composed of three classes (with staggered elections across six years).

The contemporary Congress is a professional legislature, composed mostly of individuals who desire a lengthy congressional career. Most incumbent members of Congress seek reelection—on average, 82 percent in the Senate and 92 percent in the House in the post–World War II era—and most of them win their races. There are differences between the House and Senate, however. Figure 4.1 illustrates these differences, tracking the percentage of incumbents seeking reelection who win. On average, House incumbents seek reelection, and win, at a higher rate than Senate incumbents. Moreover, there is much less year-to-year variation in the House than in the Senate.

While differences between the chambers do exist, the bottom line is essentially the same: once elected, incumbents typically seek another term in office, and they usually succeed. As a result, incumbents in the modern era have built substantial careers in Congress. The average years of service for members of the House and Senate since the early 1950s is 10.7 in both chambers. In the current (116th) Congress, the average for representatives and senators is 10.7 and 10.1 years, respectively.[2] So, in effect, once elected to Congress, a member can expect to serve (on average) for at least a decade. Initial electoral success breeds considerably more electoral success.

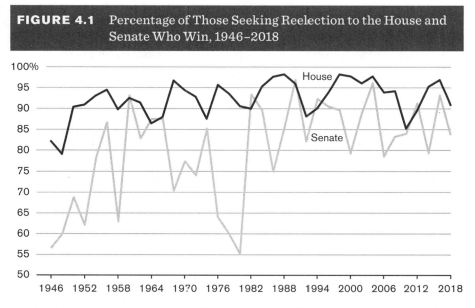

FIGURE 4.1 Percentage of Those Seeking Reelection to the House and Senate Who Win, 1946–2018

Based on data from Tables 2-7 and 2-8, *Vital Statistics on Congress*. Brookings Institution, www.brookings .edu/multi-chapter-report/vital-statistics-on-congress (accessed 12/18/18).

THE INSTITUTIONAL FOUNDATIONS OF CONGRESSIONAL ELECTIONS

Understanding how the modern electoral environment has developed—wherein careerism is a goal and incumbency is a powerful factor in achieving that goal— requires an understanding of factors both internal and external to Congress. One important factor is the institutional context, meaning the constitutional foundation for congressional elections and the relevant federal and state laws and processes.

The Constitution

While the Framers said almost nothing in the Constitution about who may vote in congressional elections, they did specify considerably more about the electoral process. As noted in Chapter 3, the Constitution specifies age, citizenship, and residency requirements for individuals wishing to be House members or senators. It also specifies that Senate representation is based on equality, with each state having two senators. House representation is based on population, with more-populous states receiving more representatives.[3]

In terms of elections, the Constitution stipulates, "The Times, Places, and Manner of holding Elections of Senators and Representatives, shall be prescribed in each State by the Legislature thereof; but the Congress may at any time by Law make or alter such Regulations" (Article I, Section 4, Clause 1). And while states have largely determined when, where, and how congressional elections have been held, Congress has stepped in occasionally to make regulations (as we discuss next). The Constitution also stipulates, "Each House shall be the Judge of the Elections, Returns and Qualifications of its own Members" (Article 1, Section 5, Clause 1). Thus if the results of a House or Senate election are disputed, the members of the relevant chamber decide who was duly elected and has a right to the seat. Stated differently, the Constitution establishes the House and Senate as the final arbiters of the election of their own members. In the decades after the Civil War, disputed election cases were quite numerous, and partisan motives often came into play when the House and Senate memberships determined who would be seated (see "Then and Now: Disputed Elections in the House of Representatives" in this chapter).

After the initial constitutional formulation, additional amendments affected the congressional electoral process indirectly. As noted in Chapter 3, liberalization of suffrage requirements occurred with the Fifteenth Amendment (voting could not be denied on account of race, color, or previous condition of servitude), the Nineteenth Amendment (voting could not be denied on account of sex), the Twenty-Fourth Amendment (voting could not be denied for failure to pay a poll tax or other tax), and the Twenty-Sixth Amendment (voting could not be denied on account of age, if citizens are 18 years or older). Each of these amendments had the effect of increasing the number of eligible voters in congressional elections.

One amendment had a direct effect on the congressional election process: the Seventeenth Amendment altered the method by which senators were elected. Under the original constitutional design, the people elected House members directly, while the state legislature elected senators directly (and thus senators were elected indirectly by the people). The Framers considered this stipulation to be a compromise, whereby popular democracy and high responsiveness to the people would characterize the House, while deliberate and dispassionate decision making by professional politicians insulated from momentary (and potentially radical) shifts in public opinion would characterize the Senate.

This initial constitutional design governed House and Senate elections for more than a century. By the late nineteenth century, however, the progressive movement was in full swing, and reformers sought to bring government in all its forms closer to the people. In addition to making the Senate more directly reflect the popular will, reformers sought to fix problems that had emerged with the indirect election system. In particular, the immediate motivations for the Seventeenth Amendment, which was ratified in 1913 and established the direct election of senators by the state citizenry,[4] were to limit corruption in the electoral process (by making influence more costly) and to avoid seat vacancies that resulted from deadlocked state legislatures.[5] Progressive media outlets contended that wealthy interests had effectively bought control of the Senate by buying a key group of state legislators. Direct election would make such vote buying considerably less efficient, as buying pivotal groups of voters in an entire state would be incredibly expensive. In addition, states sometimes went without Senate representation because of deadlocked state legislative elections. As political scientists Wendy Schiller and Charles Stewart note, "Deadlocks happened at least fourteen times in the decade and a half starting in 1891." Direct election would eliminate these deadlocks and the resulting seat vacancies.[6]

THEN AND NOW
DISPUTED ELECTIONS IN THE HOUSE OF REPRESENTATIVES

How often has the Article 1, Section 5, power been invoked? That is, how often has the House of Representatives decided the rightful occupant of a congressional seat in a disputed election case?[7] Over the House's history, there have been 610 disputed election cases, or an average of over 5 per Congress.[8]

Disputed election cases have been concentrated in particular periods. While the number of cases was low prior to the Civil War and during most of the twentieth century (and beyond), most disputed election cases occurred in the latter part of the nineteenth century—after the Civil War and during Reconstruction and the Gilded Age. The high of 38 cases occurred in the 54th Congress (1895–97).

A focus strictly on cases can be potentially deceiving, however. Some cases dealt with multiple elections (and seats), and the number of House seats in a given Congress differed over time, until it finally settled at 435 in the early twentieth century. A different way to assess the importance of the disputed election procedure is to calculate the percentage of House seats disputed in each Congress (Figure 4.2).

In three different Congresses, more than 10 percent of House seats were disputed, with a high of 11.5 percent in the 41st Congress (1869–71). In recent years, this percentage has dropped off considerably. In the last century, the per Congress average has been less than 1 percent, and many Congresses have seen no disputed election cases at all.

Why were a lot of House seats disputed in the late nineteenth century? Many of these cases stemmed from the loser of an election accusing the winner or his

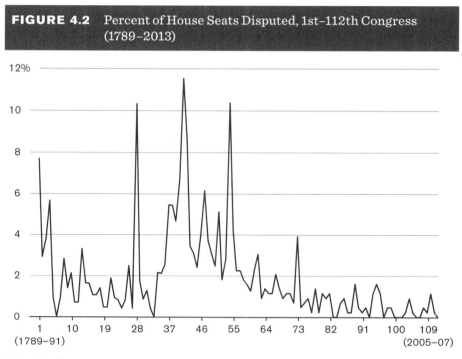

FIGURE 4.2 Percent of House Seats Disputed, 1st–112th Congress (1789–2013)

Jeffery A. Jenkins. 2004. "Partisanship and Contested Election Cases in the House of Representatives, 1789–2002." *Studies in American Political Development* 18: 112–35; data updated by authors through 2013.

campaign of criminal behavior. Such charges included bribery of voters and/or election officials, illegal alteration of ballots, and fraudulent certification of election results. A significant number of cases also involved insufficient provision of polling places, voting by persons not properly registered, improper treatment of ballot boxes, and improper counting of ballots.

In the late nineteenth century, the major parties were evenly matched at the national level, so a swing of a few seats from election to election could matter for majority control. Republicans brought most of the disputed election cases, stemming from elections mostly in the South. Republicans held that Democrats were using whatever means necessary to prevent African Americans—who had been granted citizenship and voting rights after the Civil War—from participating fully in elections and selecting representatives who would serve their interests in Congress. With control of the House hanging in the balance, Republican leaders could not afford to allow the South to slip away completely, even as Reconstruction came to an end in 1877 and the Democrats returned to power throughout the region. As a result, the Republicans actively encouraged disputed election cases as a way to maintain a partisan foothold in the South and to fight back against Democrats' electoral shenanigans.

Table 4.1 documents seat changes resulting from disputed election cases in the House from Reconstruction through the early twentieth century. The Republicans were the majority party during most of this period, but with slim margins toward the end of the nineteenth century. The "additions" in the table represent "flips" in the partisan control of seats. That is, based on Article 1, Section 5, the House decided to unseat the ostensible winner of the election (the individual with the most votes based on the count) and award the seat to the loser instead, based on evidence of fraud or other irregularities. In most of the cases, the majority party awarded seats to *their* members and unseated members of the *other* party. The Republicans were aggressive in these efforts, adding as many as 10 seats in a given Congress (the 41st). While some of these seat additions came outside of the South, most were in former Confederate states or other former slave states.

By the turn of the twentieth century, however, Republican efforts to flip seats had largely come to an end. The 1894–96 elections had created a partisan realignment in the country, making the GOP dominant or competitive in every region outside of the South. As a result, the Republicans no longer needed representation in the South to maintain majority control of the House. Moreover, beginning in the 1890s, southern states began to make statutory and constitutional changes that would disenfranchise African Americans. These changes severely limited Republican representation in the South. Thus, the southern wing of the GOP largely disintegrated, and it would not reemerge in a meaningful way until the 1960s.

In the twentieth century, disputed election cases faded away, and the last time the House flipped a seat because of a disputed election was in 1984. Why have disputed election cases effectively disappeared? First, literacy rates increased, and media coverage (from radio and television) expanded. By the early twentieth century, the populace was better informed, which required party leaders to justify more effectively their reasons for pushing election disputes and thereby attempting to overrule the voters' will. Second, as noted earlier, the South, which had been the site of much disputed election activity, was no longer a partisan battleground. Once their disenfranchisement provisions were in place, the Democrats firmly controlled the South through the late twentieth century such that it was effectively a one-party region. Third, voting became secret with the advent of the Australian ballot, and voting technology improved, making it more difficult for outright fraud to enter congressional elections.

A question arises: Could members of a highly polarized Congress, where seat margins between the parties are very close, use claims of illegal voting to revive the use of disputed elections? Many states have pursued voter identification laws based (ostensibly) on this concern, with the goal of preventing noncitizens from corrupting the electoral process. But, so far, there have been no attempts in

TABLE 4.1	Seat Changes Resulting from Disputed Election Cases, 41st–61st Congress (1867–1911)

		MAJORITY PARTY ADDITIONS			MINORITY PARTY ADDITIONS		
Congress (Years)	Majority Party	Former Confederacy	Other Former Slave States	Non-South	Former Confederacy	Other Former Slave States	Non-South
40th (1867–69)	Republicans	0	1	1	0	0	0
41st (1869–71)	Republicans	5	0	5	0	0	0
42nd (1871–73)	Republicans	1	0	0	2	0	0
43rd (1873–75)	Republicans	1	1	0	3	1	0
44th (1875–77)	Democrats	2	0	2	0	0	0
45th (1877–79)	Democrats	2	0	3	0	0	0
46th (1879–81)	Democrats	1	0	0	1	0	0
47th (1881–83)	Republicans	5	1	0	0	0	1
48th (1883–85)	Democrats	2	0	4	2	0	0
49th (1885–87)	Democrats	0	0	1	0	0	0
50th (1887–89)	Democrats	0	0	0	0	0	0
51st (1889–91)	Republicans	5	3	0	0	0	0
52nd (1891–93)	Democrats	0	0	1	0	0	0
53rd (1893–95)	Democrats	0	1	2	0	0	0
54th (1895–97)	Republicans	4	2	3	0	0	0
55th (1897–99)	Republicans	3	0	0	0	0	0
56th (1899–1901)	Republicans	3	0	0	0	0	0
57th (1901–03)	Republicans	0	2	0	0	0	0
58th (1903–05)	Republicans	0	0	2	0	0	0
59th (1905–07)	Republicans	0	1	0	0	0	0
60th (1907–09)	Republicans	0	0	0	0	0	0
61st (1909–11)	Republicans	0	0	0	0	0	0

Congress to begin actively using the disputed election procedure. However, given the hyper-partisanship that exists in Congress today, disputed elections could return. For example, if the Republicans are unwilling to allow a Democratic president to fill a vacancy on the Supreme Court, as the GOP Senate majority did when President Obama nominated Merrick Garland in 2016, following Antonin Scalia's death (see Chapter 11), just about any strategy seems to be in play.

Critical Thinking

1. If the Democrats were using fraud and intimidation to restrict African American voting in the South during and after Reconstruction, were the Republicans in the House justified in "flipping" seats via disputed election cases? Why or why not?

2. While the Constitution states, "Each House shall be the Judge of the Elections, Returns and Qualifcations of its own Members," if an election dispute for a House or Senate seat were to occur today, do you think the relevant chamber should have the power to decide the outcome? Or would you rather that a federal court handle the case?

3. If a serious election dispute were to occur today and require the House or Senate to sit in judgment and decide the outcome, what issues do you think would be in play? What sorts of things might the ostensible loser of the election cite as to why the result was illegitimate or tainted?

Federal Law

Federal law affects the congressional election process in various ways. We discuss three such ways here: the regulation of elections, apportionment, and campaign finance.

REGULATION OF ELECTIONS   As noted previously, the Constitution grants the primary responsibility for deciding the times, places, and manner of holding congressional elections to the states but allows Congress the discretion to intervene in the process via federal law. Congress has intervened sparingly over time, but such efforts have had a significant effect on congressional elections.

For example, federal law has affected how states elect their representatives.[9] The Constitution specifies that House members "shall be apportioned among the several States . . . according to their respective Numbers" and that "the number of Representatives shall not exceed one for every thirty Thousand" (Article I, Section 2, Clause 3).[10] But the Constitution does not specify how that apportionment should occur or which geographic unit to use. From the First Congress, the typical unit was a district: a compilation of whole counties that add up to the minimum population necessary for a representative.[11] And while most districts were *single-member* districts, in which citizens elected one representative, others were multi-member districts, in which citizens elected more than one representative. In addition, some states elected their House members by *general ticket*, with the entire state acting as a single district. If a state was entitled to six House members, for example, all citizens in the state would get to vote for six candidates, and the six individuals with the highest vote totals would be elected.

By the early nineteenth century, many political observers had recognized that single-member districts provided the fairest way to elect representatives. Multi-member districts and general ticket systems made it easy to elect multiple candidates, and even an entire House delegation, of a single party if the geographic area was sufficiently partisan. As a result, in 1842, Congress passed an apportionment act with a provision that mandated the use of single-member districts. While this provision had the effect of eliminating multi-member districts, general ticket systems continued to be used sparingly for more than a century.[12] Finally, in 1967, Congress passed a stand-alone law that prohibited anything other than single-member districts. In large part, Congress passed this law based on fears that the southern states might adopt general ticket systems in the wake of the Voting Rights Act of 1965, with the goal of diluting the voting power of newly enfranchised African Americans.

Federal law has also affected elections by specifying when states elect their representatives. While the Constitution stipulated that "the House of Representatives shall be composed of Members chosen every second year by the People of the several states" (Article I, Section 2, Clause 1), exactly *when* during the year was never stated. As a result, initially each state chose its own Election Day, and over the course of an election cycle for a given Congress, 18 months could separate the first state election and the last state election. Congress rectified these timing discrepancies in stages. In 1845, Congress established the first Tuesday after the first Monday in November as the date for choosing presidential electors.[13] In 1872, as part of a new apportionment act, Congress mandated that congressional elections match up with presidential elections. And while the various states did not succeed in fully aligning their elections for another decade, the 1872 act established a single Federal Election Day.[14] After the adoption of the Seventeenth Amendment, Senate elections would also be held on this date.

A final example of federal involvement in congressional elections concerns the method of electing representatives.[15] In the nation's early years, voting was often conducted by voice in public. This system was due, in large part, to high illiteracy rates. Over time, most states adopted some form of written or printed ballot, which the political parties handled themselves. In 1871, Congress codified this trend by mandating that all votes in House elections make use of written or printed ballot, with any voice votes being thrown out.[16] In 1899, Congress acknowledged the advances in vote-counting technology and allowed voting machines to be used in House elections. Congress would not legislate on voting technology again until the Help America Vote Act (HAVA) in 2002, which it adopted in the wake of the disputed and controversial Bush-Gore presidential election in 2000. HAVA sought to establish minimum standards for election administration across the states, mandating that all states and localities upgrade their election procedures, including their voting machines, registration processes, and training of poll workers.

APPORTIONMENT As noted earlier, the Constitution specified that apportionment of the House among the states was to be based on population. An initial enumeration of 65 seats distributed across 13 states was made, with the "actual Enumeration" to be made "within three Years after the first Meeting of the Congress of the United States, and within every subsequent Term of ten Years, in such Manner as they shall by Law Direct" (Article I, Section 2, Clause 3). A national census would be conducted every 10 years ("decennially") to arrive at the population for the individual states—"the whole Number of free Persons, including those bound to Service for a Term of Years, and excluding Indians not taxed, three fifths of all other persons."[17] The "three-fifths clause," a compromise made at the Constitutional Convention, allowed slaveholders to count three-fifths of slaves as "other persons" for purposes of representation in the House and the electoral college.

Over time, there have been 23 national censuses and 22 congressional apportionments (a new apportionment did not follow the 1920 census because urban and rural representatives could not agree on a plan).[18] As Table 4.2 indicates, the size of the House increased substantially across the first 13 apportionments (and censuses)—declining just once as a result of the 1842 act—until it was capped at 435 members in 1911.

Underlying these enumerations was the question of what method of apportionment to use.[19] That is, when determining how many representatives a state will receive, a simple procedure is to divide the state population by the total U.S. population. The result will report a whole number and a fractional remainder (a decimal). Different apportionment methods handle those fractional remainders differently. One method, developed by Thomas Jefferson, simply drops the remainder, regardless of the size, and then awards the whole number to a state. The Jefferson method was used for the first five apportionments. Another method, developed by Daniel Webster, rounds the remainder to the nearest whole number. This method was used after the 1850 census and in a slightly revised form after the 1900, 1910, and 1930 censuses. Another method, first developed by Alexander Hamilton, starts with a predetermined number of representatives (or House size) and rounds up the largest fractional remainders until that number is reached. This method was used for the last five apportionments of the nineteenth century. Finally, the current method in use, developed by Joseph Hill (a statistician for the Bureau of the

TABLE 4.2 Congressional Apportionment over Time

Act of	House Size	Method Used	Population of United States	Based on Census of
1792	105	Jefferson	3,929,326	1790
1802	142	Jefferson	5,308,483	1800
1812	182	Jefferson	7,239,881	1810
1822	213	Jefferson	9,638,453	1820
1832	240	Jefferson	12,866,020	1830
1842	223	Webster	17,069,453	1840
1852	234	Hamilton	23,191,876	1850
1862	241	Hamilton	31,443,321	1860
1872	292	Hamilton	39,818,449	1870
1882	325	Hamilton	50,189,209	1880
1891	356	Hamilton	62,947,714	1890
1901	386	Webster	76,212,168	1900
1911	435	Webster	92,228,496	1910
—	—	—	106,021,537	1920
1929	435	Webster	122,775,046	1930
1940/41	435	Huntington-Hill	132,164,569	1940
—	435	Huntington-Hill	150,697,361	1950
—	435	Huntington-Hill	179,323,175	1960
—	435	Huntington-Hill	203,302,031	1970
—	435	Huntington-Hill	226,545,805	1980
—	435	Huntington-Hill	248,709,873	1990
—	435	Huntington-Hill	281,421,906	2000
—	435	Huntington-Hill	308,745,538	2010

Census) and Edward Huntington (a mathematician at Harvard), is a modified version of the Webster method, but it uses a slightly different rounding method.

Fierce battles were waged in Congress over the various methods, even though the distribution of representatives to the various states differed only slightly. Often the method selected was based on the political party in power and whether that party reliably controlled the states that would receive more representation under that method. Eventually, at the urging of Congress, a committee of mathematicians studied the question to determine which method was the fairest from a mathematical perspective. They settled on the Huntington-Hill method. Congress quickly adopted it in 1940, and the following year it made reapportionment of the House's 435 seats automatic following each census with the Huntington-Hill method designated as permanent.

CAMPAIGN FINANCE   The financing of congressional election campaigns has been an issue of great importance since the early 1970s. The issue itself is far older, however. Throughout the nineteenth century, congressional candidates and their parties relied on the recipients of patronage appointments for money. Such recipients were expected to contribute a portion of their salaries to the party, to be used to support its electoral candidates. As progressives attacked the patronage system after the Civil War, and as civil service reforms were eventually passed in the 1880s, the parties shifted to big-money donors, often bankers and wealthy industrialists. Progressives responded by continuing their assault on campaign finance. As noted earlier, fears that special interests were "buying" state legislatures and U.S. senators led to the adoption of the Seventeenth Amendment in 1913. Eventually, Congress passed several campaign finance laws in the early twentieth century: the Tillman Act in 1907, which prohibited corporate contributions in national campaigns, and the Federal Corrupt Practices Acts of 1911 and 1925, which set campaign spending limits in House and Senate campaigns. No enforcement mechanisms were created to regulate the reporting of contributions and force compliance, however, so these laws were mostly ignored.

Almost a half century passed before the passage of the Federal Election Campaign Act (FECA) of 1971. The initial FECA created more-stringent disclosure requirements for campaign contributions in federal campaigns. But like the early twentieth-century laws, the initial FECA did not create or employ a serious enforcement mechanism. This lack of enforcement changed with the first amendment to FECA in 1974. Passed in the aftermath of the Watergate scandal and the revelation of significant campaign finance violations in the presidential election of 1972, the FECA Amendment of 1974 set limits on campaign contributions by individuals, political parties, and political action committees (PACs). Corporations had set up the first PAC organizations earlier in the century to channel contributions and sidestep the Tillman Act provisions. The FECA Amendment of 1974 also established spending limits, and, perhaps most important, created the Federal Election Commission (FEC) to enforce the law. FECA was quickly challenged in the federal courts, which led to the *Buckley v. Valeo* (1976) Supreme Court case and decision. The Court affirmed the contribution restrictions under FECA but struck down spending limits in general.

Because FECA did not prohibit corporations, labor unions, and membership organizations from creating PACs, and because PACs were allowed to contribute more to campaigns than individuals, the number of PACs nearly tripled between 1978 and 2016. Total contributions from PACs to congressional candidates more than tripled (adjusted for inflation) over the same time span.[20] In addition, a 1979 amendment to FECA allowed political parties to receive unlimited "soft-money" contributions—donations that could be used for the benefit of a party's electoral goals but could not be directed to specific candidates. The 1979 amendment led to an explosion in contributions. As Figure 4.3 indicates, the amount of soft money contributed to the parties more than quadrupled between 1992 and 2002.[21] FECA did not regulate soft-money contributions, which allowed wealthy donors, PACs, and the parties themselves to push the limit on how the contributions were used.

After several election cycles, many observers came to realize that the lack of soft-money limits was undermining FECA's effectiveness. As a result, new reforms were sought. Eventually, in 2002, a coalition of Republicans and Democrats in Congress passed the Bipartisan Campaign Reform Act (BCRA). The

FIGURE 4.3   Soft-Money Contributions to National Party Committees, 1992–2002

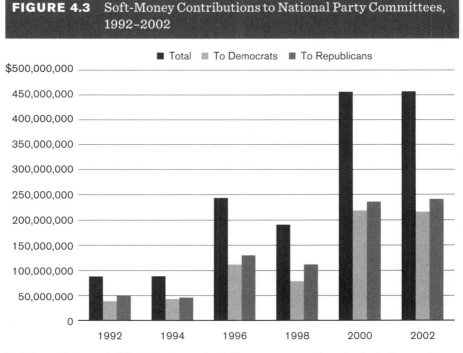

"Soft Money Backgrounder." Center for Responsive Politics, www.opensecrets.org/parties/softsource.php (accessed 5/16/18).

BCRA, otherwise known as "McCain-Feingold" after the two legislative sponsors, Senator John McCain (R-AZ) and Representative Russell Feingold (D-WI), eliminated soft-money contributions to political parties, raised individual contribution ("hard-money") limits, and placed restrictions on "electioneering communications" broadcast ads (especially by corporations and unions).

Reformers initially saw the BCRA as a victory, especially after it largely withstood a special-interest challenge before the Supreme Court in *McConnell v. Federal Election Commission* (2003). However, big-money interests quickly devised a work-around, establishing "527 organizations"—issue advocacy groups, named for their position in the federal tax code, that do not expressly support or oppose specific candidates. The BCRA did not regulate 527 organizations, which meant there were no limits on who could contribute, no caps on overall contributions, and no spending limits. In addition, attempts after 2003 to bring 527 organizations under the BCRA umbrella failed. More recently, in *Citizens United v. Federal Election Commission* (2010), the Supreme Court (in a 5–4 decision) held that, based on the free speech clause of the First Amendment, the government could not prohibit corporations, labor unions, and other membership organizations from making independent expenditures for electioneering communications. Two months later, the U.S. Court of Appeals for the D.C. Circuit in *SpeechNOW.org v. Federal Election Commission* used the *Citizens United* decision to deny Congress the ability to restrict the aforementioned organizations' ability to make independent expenditures. This decision led to the creation of "independent expenditure PACs," also called "super PACs."

The two court decisions in 2010 had a major effect. Through their super PACs, corporations, labor unions, and other membership organizations can now participate fully, with no contribution or spending limits, in congressional elections. Money in politics is thus at an all-time high and increasing. And, for now, Congress has few options to prevent further growth.

State Law

State law has perhaps the most pervasive influence on congressional elections. Its effects are felt in numerous ways at different points in the process.

ELECTION AND BALLOT LAWS   As noted previously, the Constitution gives states authority as to when, where, and how they will hold congressional elections, subject to any federal action. And for much of American history, states were given free rein. For example, during the Jim Crow era, southern states used a variety of techniques, including poll taxes and literacy tests, to disenfranchise African Americans. Many of these state-level restrictions on voting were swept away with time. The most significant remaining restriction involves felon disenfranchisement. Only two states, Maine and Vermont, provide unrestricted voting rights for current felons. Most states lift felon-voting restrictions after parole, probation, or release, although some states require felons to submit a formal petition to the court for the restoration of voting rights or a pardon from the governor, either of which might be denied. Two states—Iowa and Kentucky—never restore voting rights to people with felony convictions.[22]

In recent years, a new form of voter disenfranchisement has emerged: voter identification laws. Voter ID laws request or require voters to show a form of identification at the polls. Some of the laws require a photo ID (such as a driver's license), while others allow an ID that indicates a formal residence (for example, a bank statement). If a voter does not have the required identification, states handle the next step differently. Some states are not strict; they allow the voter to sign an affidavit of identity or allow a poll worker to vouch for the individual. Other states are strict and permit voting only on a provisional ballot. For the vote to be counted, the voter must take additional action (such as presenting required ID at an election office) after Election Day.

As Figure 4.4 indicates, the number of states with voter ID laws has increased substantially in the twenty-first century.[23] In 2000, only 14 states had such laws. In 2018, there were 34 states that had voter ID laws in place. Why the increase? Democrats contend that Republican state governments have passed the new laws to decrease voting by the people who are most likely to be affected by such ID requirements and who would likely vote Democratic: the poor and minorities. Republicans have countered that such laws are meant to maintain election integrity and help eliminate illegal voting. Most experts, however, believe that there is little evidence to suggest that illegal voting—principally voting by noncitizens—is large or widespread.[24] These arguments aside, battles over voter ID laws and voter fraud have moved to the courts, and Pennsylvania and Virginia have struck them down as unconstitutional. In other cases, states have been forced to make their existing laws less strict. More court cases are on the horizon, and partisan battles over voter identification are likely to continue.

Meanwhile, several states have made it easier for citizens to vote by allowing them to cast their votes early. That is, while Congress established a single Federal Election Day for congressional (and presidential) elections, 38 states have passed laws to allow citizens to vote prior to that date. Such early voting is also known as "no-excuse voting," because voters do not need to explain why they are unable to vote on Election Day.[25] Early voting periods vary by state, ranging from 4 to 45 days before the election, with the average around 19 days. Some states also allow early voting on weekends. In addition, all states allow absentee voting and will mail an absentee ballot to voters who request one—although in 19 states, voters must explain why they need an absentee

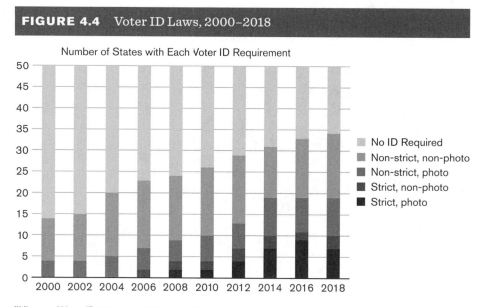

FIGURE 4.4   Voter ID Laws, 2000–2018

Number of States with Each Voter ID Requirement

No ID Required
Non-strict, non-photo
Non-strict, photo
Strict, non-photo
Strict, photo

"History of Voter ID 2000–2016." National Conference of State Legislatures, www.ncsl.org/research
/elections-and-campaigns/voter-id-history.aspx; "Voter ID Requirements." www.ncsl.org/research/elections
-and-campaigns/voter-id.aspx (accessed 12/14/18).

ballot (and cannot vote in person on Election Day). These pre-Election Day
state laws have been meaningful. Political scientist Michael McDonald has
reported that in 2018, more than 39 million votes were cast before the official
Federal Election Day.[26]

Finally, states control the format of the ballots and the technology (voting
machines) used. This was not always the case. During much of the nineteenth
century, parties managed the balloting process. Party workers stood outside the
polls with stacks of party ballots (lists of party candidates by office) and handed
them out to voters. The party ballots listed *only* that party's candidates, and the
ballots were often color coded. Voting was therefore public (not secret) as voters
placed their color-coded ballots in a clearly observable ballot box, which made
the entire voting process subject to manipulation. In the late nineteenth century,
progressives sought to clean up the process, and ballot management slowly
shifted to state governments. Between 1888 and 1910, nearly every state
adopted the Australian ballot (see Chapter 2).[27] The Australian ballot itself can
be organized in different ways. For example, with a party-bloc ballot, candidates
are listed by party, and with an office bloc ballot, candidates are listed by office.
Ballots can also take different forms. The infamous "butterfly ballot," which was
at the heart of the voting controversy in Palm Beach County, Florida, in the
2000 presidential election, is one example of an office bloc ballot.

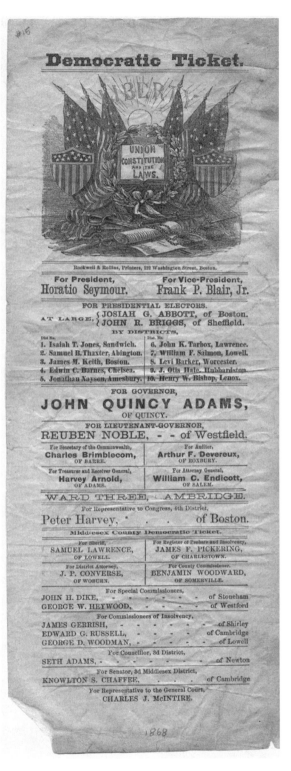

Party ballots, like this 1868 ballot that listed all the Democratic candidates for office, were common throughout the nineteenth century.

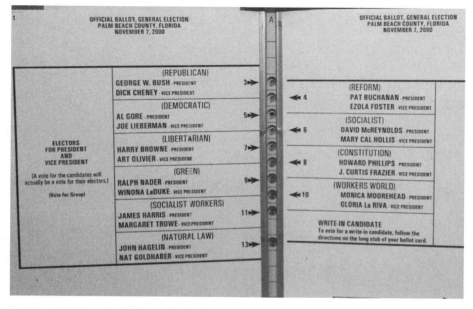

Florida's ballot from the 2000 presidential election is an example of an office bloc ballot. This ballot reportedly confused some voters, causing them to inadvertently vote for Pat Buchanan instead of Al Gore.

REDISTRICTING While the Constitution and federal law govern the apportionment of congressional districts, the states control the drawing of congressional district lines. And, in most states, the state legislatures manage the line-drawing (or "redistricting") process. That said, federal guidelines and court rulings over the years have constrained states by requiring congressional districts to have certain features or identifying desirable qualities. These include:

1. Compactness (minimize, to the extent possible, the geographic space or volume within a district, to allow better and more efficient constituent-representative relations)
2. Contiguity (ensure that the geographic space within a district is connected)
3. Equal population (conform to the "one person, one vote" principle; ensure that votes are worth the same amount across districts)
4. Preservation of existing political communities (attempt to keep together existing political boundaries such as cities and counties; attempt to keep together demographic communities based on race, ethnicity, or religion)
5. Partisan fairness (percentage of votes for a party in a state should translate roughly into the same percentage of seats in Congress)
6. Racial fairness (prevent the dilution of minority voting power)

The *Wesberry v. Sanders* (1964) Supreme Court case established the equal population criterion. Prior to that time, *malapportionment* was a problem. That is, some districts in a state were considerably uneven in terms of population. As a result, the votes of citizens in a low-population district were worth more than the votes of citizens in a high-population district. Malapportionment typically favored rural districts/voters at the expense of urban districts/voters.

The compactness criterion is often violated when line-drawing produces a greatly misshapen district or *gerrymander*. (These districts are named after Elbridge Gerry, the early nineteenth-century governor of Massachusetts, who drew a state senate district that looked like a salamander as a way to connect distant sets of Federalist voters.) Gerrymanders are created for specific political purposes. The earliest, like Gerry's, were constructed to create as many majority-party-controlled districts as possible (conflicting with the partisan fairness criterion). Partisan gerrymandering has been common ever since. Often it means packing as many voters of the other party as possible into a small number of districts to dilute their voting power. Sometimes, it means breaking apart (or "cracking") an existing district controlled by the other party and forcing the incumbent to win in a tougher electoral environment.

While redistricting in the modern era has tended to follow a decennial census, things were very different in the rough-and-tumble partisan era of the late nineteenth century, when new district lines were typically drawn every time majority control of a state legislature switched. As political scientist Erik Engstrom found, at least one state undertook a new redistricting in every year between 1870 and 1900.[28] While such raw partisan activity was deemed acceptable at the time, similar attempts today have drawn considerable attention and have been roundly criticized. One of the best-known cases occurred in Texas in 2002, when the Republicans won majority control of the state legislature for the first time since Reconstruction. At the behest of U.S. House Majority Leader Tom DeLay, the Republican state legislative majority in 2003 attempted to redraw district lines a year after the former Democratic majority did the same thing. Despite considerable political spectacle and media attention, the Texas Republicans were successful, and their efforts largely held up when challenged in court. As a result, the Texas delegation in the U.S. House flipped—from 17–15 Democrat after the 2002 elections to 21–11 Republican after the 2004 elections.

While the Republicans scored a victory, they did not emerge unscathed. Because of his fundraising efforts in support of the redistricting, DeLay was eventually charged with felony campaign finance violations and later convicted.[29] The Republican Party, as a whole, received a public-relations black eye. As a result, party leaders have generally become more reticent about pursuing a DeLay-like redistricting strategy.

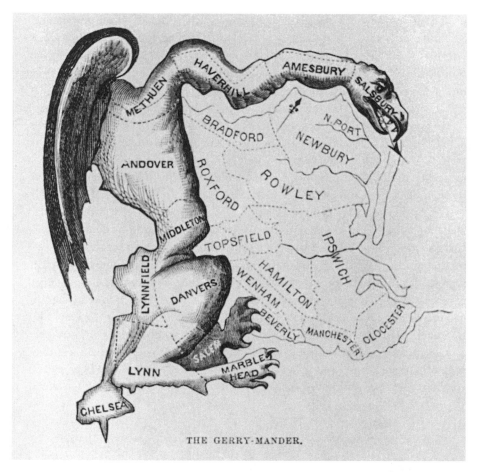

THE GERRY-MANDER.

The strangely shaped district drawn by Governor Elbridge Gerry inspired the term "gerrymander."

Gerrymandering can achieve more than just partisan benefit. For example, in recent years, bipartisan gerrymanders have been pursued to protect incumbents of *both* parties. A bipartisan gerrymander is a compromise between the parties. It limits competitiveness (and thereby uncertainty) in the electoral process, with the goal of maintaining the partisan status quo in a state. Bipartisan gerrymanders increased after the 2000 redistricting process. Political scientist Anthony McGann and his coauthors identify three post-2000 redistricting states with typical bipartisan gerrymanders: Illinois, Mississippi, and Wisconsin. However, only New Jersey engaged in bipartisan gerrymandering after the 2010 redistricting.[30]

Gerrymandering has also been used to produce more-descriptive representation for racial groups. Following the 1990 federal census, the Justice Department used Section 4 of the Voting Rights Act to require states to maximize the number of *majority-minority districts* in which a majority of constituents are nonwhite. Recall that the Voting Rights Act required several states (mostly in the South) that historically discriminated against African Americans to get *preclearance* (advance approval) before making changes in election laws to ensure that those changes would not harm racial minorities. As a result, many oddly shaped districts were created. Perhaps the most famous is that of Rep. Luis Gutiérrez (D-IL) in the Chicagoland area. The image that follows illustrates the 4th District in Illinois. As the image shows, two largely Latino communities were connected in a winding way, which has led some to call the district "earmuffs" because of its appearance.[31]

Oddly shaped districts notwithstanding, the desired effect was produced: after the 1992 elections, the number of African American representatives in Congress increased from 28 to 38, and the number of Latino representatives increased from 10 to 17.[32] But there was an unexpected consequence. Creating majority-minority districts in the South led to some districts becoming *whiter*, resulting in Republican victories in those districts and thus producing significant gains for the GOP throughout the South. As political scientist David Lublin stated, "For many of the moderate to conservative politicians who traditionally dominated southern politics, racial redistricting provided a real incentive to seek office as a Republican instead of a Democrat."[33] These Republican gains in the South were critical in helping the GOP become the majority party in the

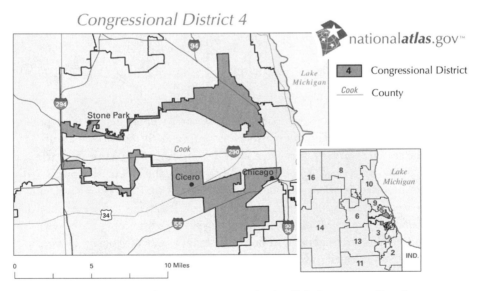

Illinois's Fourth Congressional District unites two predominantly Latino communities along a highway, giving it its "earmuff" shape.

House in 1994. Thus an effort to provide more-descriptive representation for minorities led to a situation in which they received less substantive representation (as the Democrats lost control of the House and the ability to shape the legislative agenda).

Not long after the 1992 elections, racial gerrymandering was challenged in a series of Supreme Court cases—pursuant to the equal protection clause of the Fourteenth Amendment—and the process was greatly restricted. Race could be considered in a redistricting effort (even in the pursuit of a partisan gerrymander), but it could not be the predominant factor.[34]

While racial gerrymanders have been challenged successfully in the courts, partisan gerrymanders have not. In 1986, the Supreme Court ruled that a partisan gerrymander could in theory violate the equal protection clause, but it could not agree on a standard to follow.[35] The Court revisited the issue in 2004, and again could not establish a clear constitutional standard to evaluate claims of partisan gerrymandering.[36] Recently, in June 2018 the Court considered the issue once again, based on the Federal District Court decision in *Gill v. Whitford* (2016), which used the "efficiency gap"—the difference in the two parties' wasted votes (or votes that do not help to elect a candidate) divided by the total number of votes—to hold that a partisan gerrymander in Wisconsin violated aspects of the First Amendment (freedom of association clause) and Fourteenth Amendment (equal protection clause).[37] In the end, the Court made no ruling on the question of partisan gerrymandering, sending the case back to the Federal District Court on a technical matter.[38] It is very likely that the issue will reemerge in the future in this or another case.

PRIMARY ELECTIONS States can also influence congressional elections through partisan nominations—that is, how candidates for each party get on the general election ballot. All states allow voters to select the party nominees for congressional office in primary elections. But this was not always the case. And different states have adopted very different forms of primary elections, which affect the types of party nominees who are chosen.

Like the rise of the Australian (secret) ballot, primary elections were a progressive reform adopted in the early twentieth century. Before then, the parties controlled the congressional nominating system, and party nominations were indirect; voters would choose delegates to local and state party conventions, and those delegates would choose the party's congressional nominees. Progressive reformers sought to eliminate the party convention system and replace it with a system in which voters select party nominees directly. They were successful, and the "direct primary" was created. An election would be held wholly within a party, only partisan candidates would be considered, and voters would choose directly among them. The winner of a party's primary election would be the party's candidate in the subsequent general election to Congress. This reform weakened party power generally, as party leaders lost control of the candidate-selection process. But the reform also helped heal internal divisions within the parties. Party factions that lost out under the indirect nominating system—and sometimes accused party leaders of playing favorites and rigging the system against them—were more willing to accept the voters' decisions in primary elections.[39]

Over time, primary elections have evolved, and some clear types now exist (Figure 4.5).[40] The main distinguishing criterion involves who is allowed to vote in a party's primary. *Closed primaries* restrict participation to only those voters who affiliate (register) with that party prior to the election. They are used in 10 states. *Semiclosed primaries* allow affiliated voters and independents (or unaffiliated voters) to participate. They are used in 12 states. *Open primaries* have no party registration requirement and thus allow voters of any partisan affiliation (as well as independents) to vote in any party's primary (but only a *single* primary). They are found in 21 states. Alaska, Alabama, Oklahoma, and South Dakota have dual systems, with one party using one primary system and the other party using a different primary system. California and Washington state have a *top-two primary* (otherwise known as a *jungle primary*), in which all candidates regardless of party affiliation are placed on the same primary ballot, all voters get to participate regardless of party affiliation, and the top-two finishers (regardless of party affiliation) are then placed on the general election ballot. Finally, Louisiana has a *blanket primary*, where voters get to participate in *both* primaries (Republican and Democrat), and the top-two party finishers are placed on the general election ballot. These different types of primaries exert different influences on nominee selection.

Of the two main primary types, the closed primary gives party leaders the strongest hand in controlling the context and process. Thus the eventual party nominees are more likely to be members of the party establishment. The open primary, by comparison, leaves party leaders much weaker. As a result, mavericks and individuals with cross-party appeal have a better chance of being nominated. And in terms of the nomination itself, 40 of 50 states determine a winner based on plurality rule—that is, the candidate with the largest number of votes receives the nomination. But in 10 states, eight of which are in the South, a majority is required. Thus if the top vote-getter in the initial primary election receives only a plurality of votes, a runoff is triggered, and the process continues until a majority winner emerges.

Finally, primary elections are different from general elections in two important ways. First, turnout in primaries is considerably smaller than turnout in general elections. In recent years, primary election turnout has been one-half

FIGURE 4.5   Primary Types by Party

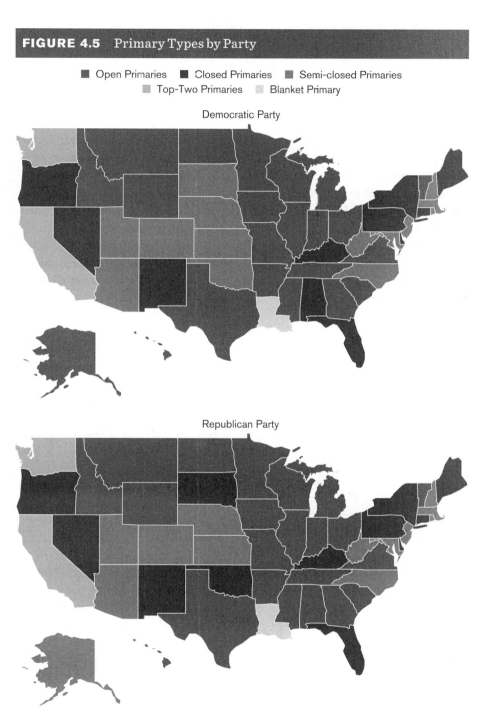

■ Open Primaries   ■ Closed Primaries   ■ Semi-closed Primaries
■ Top-Two Primaries   ■ Blanket Primary

Democratic Party

Republican Party

Data from "Primaries." FairVote.org, www.fairvote.org/primaries#congressional_primary_type_by_state (accessed 5/16/18).

to one-third of turnout in general elections. Second, the voters in primary elections tend to be more partisan, more ideological, more politically aware, better educated, and wealthier. As a result, voter distributions are skewed to the left in Democratic primaries and to the right in Republican primaries, which gives each party's candidates the incentive to appeal to more extreme interests in that party.

How often are incumbents defeated in primaries relative to general elections? Figure 4.6 provides the answer by chamber in the modern era, illustrating the percentage of defeated incumbents who lose in primaries.

There is a lot of variation in both the House data and the Senate data. The House data fluctuate less, and there is always at least one case in every election year of an incumbent losing in a primary. The Senate data show seven cases in which half or more of defeated incumbents lost in the primaries, but also 17 cases in which no defeated incumbents lost in the primaries. Overall, though, data on the House and the Senate tell a similar story. From 1946 to 2018, on average, around 22.6 percent of defeated incumbents in the House and 18.3 percent in the Senate lost in the primaries.[41]

FIGURE 4.6 Percentage of Defeated Incumbents Who Lose in the Primaries

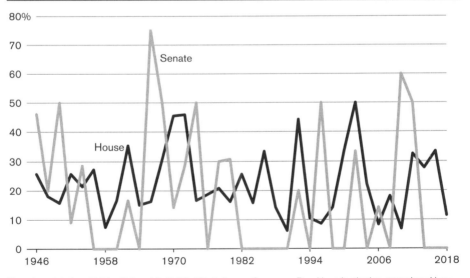

Based on data from Tables 2-7 and 2–8, *Vital Statistics on Congress*. Brookings Institution, www.brookings.edu/multi-chapter-report/vital-statistics-on-congress (accessed 12/18/18).

WHO SEEKS ELECTION TO CONGRESS?

Now that we have laid out the institutional foundations of congressional elections, we can begin to explore more-specific questions about individual factors that help shape the modern electoral environment. To begin, we ask a basic question: Who seeks election to Congress?

The Rise of Congressional Careerism and the Electoral Connection

In the nation's first 100 years, individuals who served in Congress did not see Congress as a final destination or a place that they expected to stay for an extended period of time.[42] During this period, the parties controlled the electoral process. They determined the design and distribution of the ballots, and largely chose the nominees. As a result, a political aspirant's career track was different than it is in the modern age. A career in politics meant a career in the party, not a career in any one political institution (such as Congress). Often, political aspirants in the nineteenth century pursued a leapfrog strategy in building a political career, with a seat in Congress representing just one stop along the way. For example, an individual often moved from a state legislature to Congress and then back again. That same individual would also sometimes seek a governorship or judgeship. Access to these latter positions often hinged on how he performed in Congress, as party leaders back home kept a close eye on Washington politics. Moreover, the parties, which cared about keeping congressional seats under their control, often formally dictated that a career in Congress was not possible. Some state parties adopted strict rules of *rotation in office*, whereby individuals were allowed to serve only a single term in Congress. Rotation in office allowed party leaders to provide congressional experience to a wider set of party politicians and to use a congressional seat as a reward for those who served the party especially well. To choose one notable example, Abraham Lincoln was affected by rotation in office, as Whig rules in Illinois restricted him to a single term in the House of Representatives.[43]

By the late nineteenth century, parties began to lose control of the electoral process. Progressive reformers took ballot design and distribution away from party leaders and turned them over to the state governments. The Australian ballot provided secrecy and limited party leaders' ability to observe and control voters' choices. Party nominations also changed as primary elections replaced party conventions. Primary elections allowed candidates to appeal directly to voters, without a party apparatus (such as the convention system) screening candidates and influencing the process. This Progressive Era democratization of the electoral process affected politicians' career decisions. By the end of the nineteenth century, voters had the ability to punish or reward candidates individually. And if members of Congress wanted to stay in office, they now had a greater incentive to be responsive to voters' needs. The Australian ballot and the party primary thus firmed up the constituency-representative linkage by increasing accountability. The electoral connection as we know it in contemporary politics had emerged.

By the turn of the twentieth century, members of Congress increasingly wanted to build a career in Congress. Prior to the Civil War, the majority of governmental activity was at the state and local level.[44] For someone interested in building a political career, then, the action was at the subnational level. After the Civil War, the federal government expanded considerably as more significant governmental activity began occurring at the national level. The action was increasingly in Washington. Moreover, by the early twentieth century, salaries for members of Congress were better because the value of the position was changing. And as the nation's political economy expanded, outside financial opportunities for members of Congress also multiplied.[45]

Most scholars agree that the emergence of congressional careerism can be traced back to the height of the Progressive Era. As David Brady and his coauthors note, "After 1900, the number of freshman House members sharply declined and the average years of incumbent service grew dramatically. . . . [B]y 1920 the House had been transformed from a body of amateur members to a modern legislature of professional politicians with established careers in Washington."[46]

However, the notion that Congress was at one time full of gentleman farmers and local merchants who dutifully performed their service in Washington before returning to their chosen vocations is inaccurate. Those who have served in Congress have always been careerists. But prior to the turn of the twentieth century, such careerism was primarily party focused and not Congress focused.[47]

Ambition and Strategic Choice

At the heart of the contemporary electoral connection is the assumption that members of Congress are ambitious and strongly desire to be reelected.[48] In fact, in his famous book, *Congress: The Electoral Connection*, political scientist David Mayhew refers to members of Congress as "single-minded seekers of reelection."[49] This statement is too strong; Mayhew intended it as a simplification. Members of Congress care about other things, including career advancement within the institution and good public policy.[50] But it is fair to say that all other goals require them to meet the reelection goal first.

Ambition is also at the heart of challengers' decisions to seek election to Congress. Like congressional incumbents, challengers value the office for a host of reasons. But as the reelection-rate figures for members of Congress earlier in this chapter indicate, unseating an incumbent is a very difficult task. Thus, from the outset, a challenger must be a highly ambitious person, someone who is willing to assess the costs and rigor of a serious congressional campaign and devote a huge amount of time to the endeavor.

The decision to run for a seat in Congress is a strategic calculation for incumbents, for would-be challengers facing an incumbent, or individuals considering an open seat. A simple equation captures all the relevant elements.

$$E(U) = (P \cdot U) - C, \text{ where}$$

$E(U)$ = the expected utility of choosing to run for an office

P = the probability of winning in a race for an office

U = the utility associated with holding an office

C = the cost of running for an office

Utility means satisfaction. The decision to run, then, comes down to the value of $E(U)$. If the expected utility is positive, the person should choose to run. If the expected utility is negative, the person should choose not to run.

The variables in the "calculus of election" equation (P, U, and C) capture the attributes of the individual candidate and the strategic context. For example, for the typical incumbent seeking reelection, P will be very large. Incumbent members of Congress possess a host of advantages that give them a significant leg up in any election. (We discuss this "incumbency advantage," and its various sources, in the next section.) The typical challenger, facing the typical incumbent, will have little chance; hence, P for the typical challenger will be small.

The utility associated with holding a seat in Congress (U) is a subjective assessment. By definition, an ambitious person will value the seat highly. Typical incumbents have already experienced a stream of benefits by holding the office, so their assessment will be very high. The cost of running for the office (C) will also be a subjective assessment. Individuals running in their first election will incur a variety of costs, including opportunity costs (the benefits from other activities or opportunities that are foregone), campaign costs (including not only the funds themselves but also the efforts necessary to raise campaign funds), and personal costs (health costs associated with conducting a serious campaign and costs to family members for making all aspects of their lives public). Arguably, an incumbent faces lower costs for future races: with experience, campaigning becomes more efficient, personal costs can be better assessed and managed, and so on. In other words, start-up costs are extremely high, but if an individual is elected, subsequent costs are lower.

We can classify the individuals who run for Congress into two basic groups: amateurs and professionals. Amateurs are political novices, having never served in an elected office. They sometimes emerge, or are recruited, around an issue-based cause, and they often contest a seat held by a strong incumbent. Many amateurs are long-shot candidates who secure a nomination because the likelihood of unseating an incumbent is near zero. Because of their inexperience or naïveté, amateurs often seriously overestimate their likelihood of winning and greatly underestimate the costs associated with running a congressional campaign. And while long-shot amateurs occasionally beat the odds and win—as David Brat did in defeating Eric Cantor, as noted at the start of this chapter— some amateurs possess attributes that make them formidable candidates. These amateurs are highly visible and/or highly wealthy. They might be astronauts, actors, entertainers, athletes, war heroes, or business leaders.[51] Their "star" qualities make them more viable in the eyes of donors and voters, which increases their likelihood of making a serious electoral challenge.

In contrast, professionals are seasoned politicians. They have held political office before, and they understand the rigors of organizing and running a campaign, and the odds of beating an incumbent. They are significantly more strategic than amateurs, carefully studying the political climate and unemotionally calculating the costs and benefits of making a serious run for office.[52] Professionals avoid long-shot campaigns and consider entering a race only when the odds of winning are better: when an incumbent is vulnerable (because of a scandal, a shift in public mood, or a redrawn congressional distric) or if a seat is open (no incumbent is running). When they do choose to run against an incumbent, they are viewed as quality challengers, and media and campaign watchers will cover that congressional race closely in anticipation of a highly competitive election.

Professional politicians may choose not to enter a congressional race (either against an incumbent or for an open seat) because they currently hold an elected office and do not want to give it up for the chance of winning election to a higher office. To study this issue of "progressive ambition" more formally, we can rewrite the simple calculus of election equation as follows:

$$E(U_L) = P_L \cdot U_L - C_L$$
$$E(U_H) = P_H \cdot U_H - C_H$$

Here two sets of offices are considered: a lower office (designated by subscript L) and a higher office (designated by subscript H). A professional then considers the expected utility associated with running for each office and selects the one that is larger. In other words, if $E(U_L) > E(U_H)$, then the individual should run for the lower office. And vice versa.

In the context of the U.S. Congress, we might think of these equations in terms of seats in the House (lower office) and Senate (higher office). Usually, the safe bet for a House incumbent is to seek reelection rather than to make a run

Amateur candidates who run for congressional office are sometimes successful if they have pre-existing name recognition. John Glenn, one of the United States' first astronauts, won election to the Senate in 1974. Al Franken, a comedian known for his appearances on *Saturday Night Live*, won election to the Senate in 2008. Glenn retired after serving 24 years. Franken announced his retirement in 2017 upon allegations of sexual harassment.

for a Senate seat. Having been elected (at least once), House incumbents understand their district, have built a campaign and fundraising network, and (probably) will not face a strong challenger. By comparison, a bid for the Senate is considerably more uncertain. Even if the current Senate incumbent is vulnerable, House incumbents have to weigh a variety of considerations. Who else from the party might choose to run? How might their ability to raise funds in their district translate to the state more generally? Would they be able to build a larger and broader campaign staff in time? Do their ideological positions, which fit their district well, also have statewide appeal? At the same time, a Senate seat brings several benefits: more perks, greater media attention, a larger say in policy matters (being one of 100, rather than one of 435), and more stability (with a six-year term instead of a two-year term). A Senate seat also makes further progressive ambition—a run for the presidency—more likely.

Keep in mind that the earlier equations are based on rational calculation. Would-be candidates weigh the subjective costs and benefits of running for office, or two different offices, and make a purely analytic decision. They will run for a particular office if the expected utility is positive, or they will choose the higher expected utility between two offices. These models assume that all *potential* candidates consider running for office. But structural issues in American society may not align with that assumption. We might think of these structural issues in the context of two domains: gender and race. In terms of gender, political scientist Jennifer Lawless finds that women are significantly less likely than men to consider running for office—and then to run. She attributes this "gender gap" in political ambition to recruitment patterns (party leaders are less likely to seek out women as potential candidates) and gender differences in self-perception (women are less likely than men to see themselves as qualified to run). Lawless finds this gender gap not only when comparing men and women generally but also when comparing men and women *within* racial categories, uncovering significant differences between white men and white women, African American men and African American women, and Latino men and Latina women. Interestingly, Lawless does not find evidence of a similar "racial gap" in ambition among men: there are no significant differences in the political ambitions of white, African American, and Latino men.[53]

THE INCUMBENCY ADVANTAGE

As noted previously, incumbent members of Congress possess an advantage in elections. Figure 4.1 indicates that most incumbents who seek reelection are returned to Congress at very high rates. Why? What advantages do members of Congress possess when they seek reelection?

Institutional Advantages

As discussed in Chapter 3, incumbent members of Congress receive a personal allowance that they can use in a variety of ways to meet the needs of their districts or states. They can hire a personal staff to service the needs of their constituents (via casework) and to help members of Congress make a mark in the policy-making process (by drafting legislation). They can travel to their districts or states to meet with constituents, give speeches, and conduct fundraisers. They have the ability to contact constituents (or "advertise") free of charge through the U.S. mail, thus keeping their supporters aware of their representational activities. Given their position as sitting lawmakers, they are routinely in the news, and they can also use the wealth of communications technology in Congress to stay in touch with local media back home. Finally, the legislative process in Congress routinely allows incumbents to claim credit (via committee work) and take positions (via bill introduction, roll call voting, and floor speeches).

All of these institutional advantages allow members of Congress to become highly visible and to build significant name recognition in their districts or states. This visibility has been an important factor in explaining citizens' voting behavior in the post–World War II era.[54] Challengers do not possess these institutional luxuries and thus struggle to become known.

Money

When it comes to fundraising, incumbents have a huge advantage over challengers. Donors understand that, all else equal, incumbents who seek reelection are very likely to win. They want their campaign contributions to be meaningful, and they want to buy access to the person who holds the seat. The incumbent is simply a much better bet.

The cost of winning an election to the House or Senate has increased considerably over the last three decades. It was roughly twice as expensive to win a House and Senate seat in 2016 as it was in 1986 (controlling for inflation). Today, candidates spend around $1.5 million (on average) to win a House seat and around $10 million to win a Senate seat. Money is at a premium, and those who can raise it for their campaigns have the best shot at winning.

How does campaign spending differ between incumbents and challengers? Not surprisingly, incumbents spend much more, as Figures 4.7 and 4.8 show.

In 2016, average spending by House incumbents was around three times as large as average spending by challengers. This significant difference did not always exist. As Figure 4.7 shows, for the first few elections after FECA began to require congressional candidates to report expenditures in 1974, incumbents on average spent more than challengers, but the gap wasn't that large. A signifi-

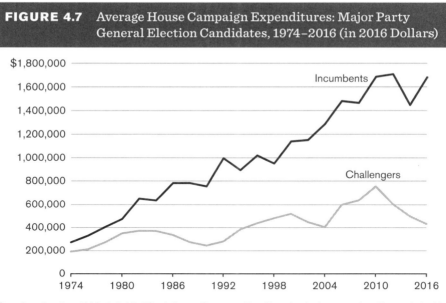

FIGURE 4.7 Average House Campaign Expenditures: Major Party General Election Candidates, 1974–2016 (in 2016 Dollars)

Based on data from Table 3-2, *Vital Statistics on Congress*. Brookings Institution, www.brookings.edu/multi-chapter-report/vital-statistics-on-congress (accessed 8/15/18).

cant widening occurred in the mid-1980s, and the size of the spending gap fluctuated over the next quarter century—with incumbent spending, on average, being about 2.5 times larger than challenger spending. Starting in 2012, however, the gap has increased each election year, with the 2016 gap being the largest in the time series.

Spending in Senate elections has fluctuated more than spending in House elections. As Figure 4.8 shows, average spending in the Senate in the mid- to late 1970s followed a pattern similar to that of spending in the House. Incumbents outspent challengers on average, but the gap was relatively small. A significant widening occurred in the 1980s and into the early 1990s, with incumbents spending twice as much as challengers. A narrowing then occurred from the late 1990s into the early 2000s. In 2014, a large gap emerged, and since then incumbent spending has outpaced challenger spending by a two to one margin.

Today, the amount of spending necessary to compete meaningfully with, and perhaps defeat, an incumbent is exorbitant. To have a reasonable chance, a challenger must close the fundraising gap considerably. For example, in the 13 House races in 2014 in which a challenger defeated an incumbent, the gap was much smaller ($3 million on average for incumbents, $2.13 million for challengers). The same was true for the five Senate races in 2014 in which a challenger defeated

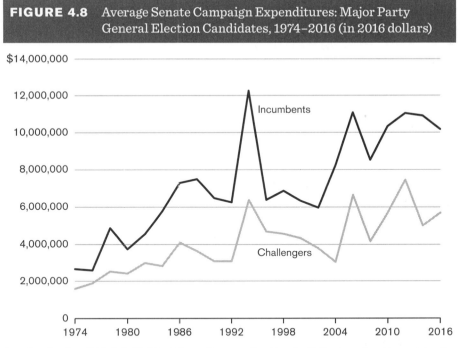

FIGURE 4.8 Average Senate Campaign Expenditures: Major Party
General Election Candidates, 1974–2016 (in 2016 dollars)

Based on data from Table 3-5, *Vital Statistics on Congress*. Brookings Institution, www.brookings.edu/multi
-chapter-report/vital-statistics-on-congress (accessed 8/15/18).

an incumbent ($17.07 million on average for incumbents, $12.05 million for
challengers).[55]

Overall, given the wealth of advantages that comes from incumbency,
attempting to match an incumbent's fundraising is difficult, and few challengers
try. Many would-be challengers are scared off by the financial hurdles they
would face if they attempted a serious run.

Legislative Redistricting

Following the *Wesberry v. Sanders* (1962) Supreme Court decision, legislative
redistricting has also been tied to the power of incumbency. Many scholars have
argued that an opportunity for political gain became apparent as a result of the
Court-ordered redistricting in the 1960s. Political scientists Gary Cox and
Jonathan Katz have shown that Democratic legislatures (and federal courts dominated by Democratic judges) in the 1960s reduced competition in congressional
elections significantly by packing Republicans into a small number of districts,

which gave Democrats a meaningful advantage in the remaining districts.[56] This redistricting solidified the Democrats' hold on the House, even as the civil rights movement was changing the political world around them.

Politically motivated redistricting has continued into the present day. In a recent study, political scientists Jamie Carson, Michael Crespin, and Ryan Williamson examined the effects of redistricting on electoral competition in the House from 1972 to 2012.[57] They compared the effects of redistricting efforts made by three different decision-makers: state legislatures, courts, and commissions. Like Cox and Katz, Carson and coauthors found that congressional districts that are redrawn by state legislatures (politicians) produce significantly less competitive elections (and are biased toward the interests of the parties in power) when compared to congressional districts that are redrawn by courts and commissions (more independent decision-makers). This difference is most pronounced since the early 1990s, as the parties have increasingly polarized and technological advances in line drawing (via computer software) have occurred.

HOW WE STUDY
THE INCUMBENCY ADVANTAGE

While identifying the factors that give congressional incumbents an advantage when they seek reelection is valuable, we also want to assess the importance of that advantage over time. Stated differently, we want to *measure* the incumbency advantage. We want to assess how much of an incumbent's vote total can be attributed to being an incumbent.

Political scientists have been studying the congressional incumbency advantage for 60 years.[58] They have developed many advanced statistical techniques to calculate the incumbency advantage, all building on two simple measures:

1. *The Sophomore Surge*: The electoral gain an incumbent achieves when running for reelection for the first time
2. *The Retirement Slump*: The electoral loss for a party when its incumbent member of Congress retires

Both the Sophomore Surge and the Retirement Slump are calculated relative to a partisan baseline, which is the "normal" partisanship in the district plus trends over time. The partisan baseline is estimated using open-seat elections, in which no incumbents run. The Sophomore Surge and Retirement Slump represent deviations from that partisan baseline. The Sophomore Surge is the change in the vote from an incumbent's initial election to his or her first reelection. The

Retirement Slump is the change in the vote from an incumbent's final reelection to his or her party's vote in the next election when it contests an open seat. The size of the Surge and Slump can then be considered the value of incumbency, where the Surge represents the bonus of incumbency and the Slump represents the loss of incumbency.

As Figure 4.9 illustrates, for the three decades spanning the 1970s through the 1990s, the Sophomore Surge and Retirement Slump measures tell a similar story, suggesting that that the size of the incumbency advantage was (on average) between 7 and 8 percentage points. In other words, the value of being an incumbent during those three decades—all the institutional advantages, the money-raising advantage, and the redistricting advantage—was worth 7 or 8 percentage points of the two-party vote. Viewed from the perspective of a challenger during that time, a 7 to 8 percentage-point advantage meant that incumbents had a large head start toward getting reelected even before the race began and votes were cast. The incumbency advantage was a huge hurdle for a challenger to overcome.

The 2000s saw a drop in the incumbency advantage, down to roughly 3 percentage points (based mostly on the Sophomore Surge measure).[59] The estimate

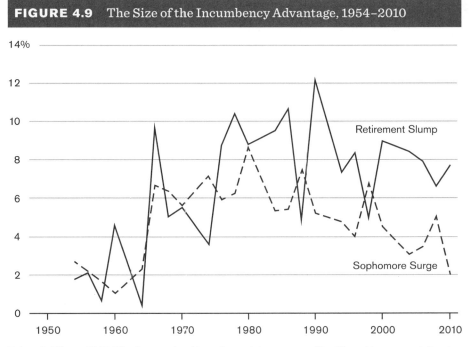

FIGURE 4.9   The Size of the Incumbency Advantage, 1954–2010

Robert S. Erikson. 2017. "The Congressional Incumbency Advantage over Sixty Years: Measurement, Trends, and Implications," in *Governing in a Polarized Era: Elections, Parties, and Political Representation in America*, ed. Alan S. Gerber and Eric Schickler, 80. New York: Cambridge University Press.

for 2010 is even smaller—only 2 percentage points (similar to the estimates from the 1950s and early 1960s). Why the drop? The best evidence suggests that the 1970s through 1990s might have been an unusual period; partisan identification was weak, and voters used other information (including name recognition, which helps incumbents) to make their choices. Partisanship has become much more important in recent years, and thus voters increasingly use it, rather than other information, when making their vote choices. We discuss this nationalization of politics in more detail below.

Critical Thinking

1. How is the incumbency advantage related to the Australian ballot? Do you think an incumbency advantage existed when the parties controlled the balloting process? Why or why not?
2. If a House incumbent decides to run for a Senate seat, will the incumbency advantage that she enjoyed in her district help her in the Senate election campaign? Why or why not?
3. Do you consider the Sophomore Surge or the Retirement Slump to be a better measure of the incumbency advantage? Why?

WHEN AND WHY DO INCUMBENTS LOSE?

Given the many advantages that incumbents possess, why do they sometimes lose? As we have noted, quality challengers, who generally represent the best hope against an entrenched incumbent, understand the structural challenges of taking on a sitting member of Congress. Thus there must be compelling reasons why experienced, quality challengers choose to oppose an incumbent.

National Tides

Sometimes the party in power is blamed for poor economic conditions or failure to govern at some acceptable level. In such cases, voters respond by disproportionately punishing members of Congress from that party who are running for reelection. If some incumbents are marginal—having narrowly won one or more recent elections—a partisan tide puts them at risk of being voted out of office.

Historically, House members from the president's party suffer losses in midterm elections. Generally, these midterm results are considered "corrections," as winning presidential candidates generally improve the election performance of

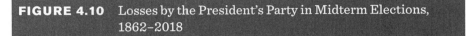

FIGURE 4.10 Losses by the President's Party in Midterm Elections, 1862–2018

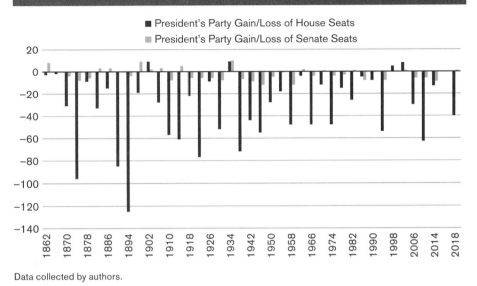

Data collected by authors.

all party members down the ticket in the year that the president is elected (which we call *presidential coattails*). Two years into a presidential administration, however, any "honeymoon" period has long passed, and presidential popularity declines as a result of presidents having to make any number of decisions, at least some of which will be unpopular. As a result, incumbent members of the president's party lose any presidential bump that they may have received two years earlier.

Figure 4.10 documents the midterm performance of the president's party in both the House and Senate since the Civil War. The negative effect is more pronounced in the House than in the Senate, in part because of the scale of potential loss; all House seats are up for reelection every two years, whereas only about one-third of Senate seats are. The negative effect in the House has spanned different eras in American history, with only four cases of a positive result for the president's party: 1902 (shortly after Theodore Roosevelt replaced William McKinley, following the latter's assassination), 1934 (the first election after Franklin Delano Roosevelt and the Democrats' realigning election victory of 1932), 1998 (following the government shutdown battles between congressional Republicans and President Clinton, for which the GOP was largely blamed), and 2002 (the first election after the 9/11 terror attacks, when the country rallied around President George W. Bush).

Scandals

Incumbents who are involved in a scandal take an electoral hit if they try to seek reelection. The average scandal-ridden incumbent who tries to remain in office can expect to see his or her vote total drop by 5 to 11 percentage points in the next election.[60] For incumbents who are somewhat marginal, this decline could be enough to cost them reelection. Political scientist Rodrigo Praino and his coauthors found that between 1976 and 2006, 25 percent of House incumbents who were involved in an ethics investigation were defeated in a primary or general election, compared to only 5 percent who were not being investigated.[61]

Redistricting

Elections following a redistricting can sometimes put an incumbent at risk. If the party in power changes, then a significant redistricting may occur. This redistricting could have the effect of protecting all incumbents, as we discussed previously. But if the redistricting is an aggressive partisan gerrymander, then it might result in the splitting of another party's incumbent's district. The incumbent may then face a new and uncertain electorate, with many of the new district's voters of the other party. A partisan gerrymander could also attempt to split two existing other-party districts and combine them into one, which could result in two other-party incumbents facing off against each other. For example, in 2012, Republicans redrew district lines in Pennsylvania and put two Democratic incumbents, Jason Altmire and Mark Critz, into the same House district.[62] Critz defeated Altmire in the Democratic primary and then lost the general election to Republican Keith Rothfus, allowing the GOP to pick up a seat.[63]

Shifting Intrapartisan Forces

Sometimes, the nature of an incumbent's party may change, leaving incumbents out of step with their primary constituency. Often, change in a district or state will be gradual and thus play out over a lengthy period, but sometimes an abrupt change occurs. For example, primary elections in the South in the middle of the twentieth century were typically conservative affairs. To win a Democratic primary, a candidate had to be reliably conservative, especially on issues of race and labor. However, the Voting Rights Act of 1965, which enfranchised African Americans and thereby diversified the southern Democratic electorate, changed all of that and forced a number of conservative southern Democrats from office. Many retired, some became Republicans, but some were defeated in primary elections by more moderate Democratic candidates.[64] More recently, as this chapter's opening story indicates, the Tea Party movement developed quickly after Barack Obama's presidential election in 2008 and has made life difficult for many establishment Republican incumbents. While Tea Party–backed candidates have made the greatest impact in open-seat elections (races in which no incumbents were running), they have scored some significant primary victories against GOP incumbents, with David Brat's defeat of Republican House Majority Leader Eric Cantor in 2014 being the most significant.

Retirements: The Hidden Story

While the previously mentioned factors help to explain why incumbents sometimes lose in their reelection bids, they also explain why some incumbents throw in the towel and decide not to seek reelection.[65] Not all retirements are strategic, of course. Some members retire for age or health reasons, or simply because they would like to pursue another line of work. And some retire because a different form of strategic behavior guides their choice: they intend to seek a higher office. But many anticipate a tough reelection battle, or a likely defeat, on the horizon, and they refrain from making the attempt. For example, in 2017, Senators Jeff Flake (R-AZ) and Bob Corker (R-TN), who both ran afoul of President Trump and were looking at serious primary challenges, retired.[66] Prior to the 2018 elections, 34 Republicans in the House—including Speaker Paul Ryan—announced that they would not seek reelection, likely fearing a Democratic tidal wave in November in response to the unpopularity of the Trump administration.[67]

Figure 4.11 illustrates how incumbents exit Congress, whether by choice (retirement) or by law (having been defeated in a primary or general election). Data are plotted by chamber, and the lines measure the percentage of exiting incumbents who leave office by choice (retirement). Both the House and Senate data display some variability, but the general trends show that, over time, a greater percentage of incumbents have left office via retirement. The only significant deviations have occurred in recent years, especially in 2010 and 2012, when a number of House incumbents who sought reelection were defeated.

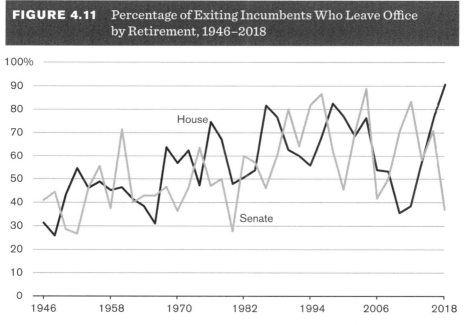

FIGURE 4.11 Percentage of Exiting Incumbents Who Leave Office by Retirement, 1946–2018

Based on data from Table 2-7 and Table 2-8, *Vital Statistics on Congress*. Brookings Institution, www
.brookings.edu/multi-chapter-report/vital-statistics-on-congress (accessed 12/18/18).

THE INCUMBENCY ADVANTAGE AND THE NATIONALIZATION OF POLITICS

As noted earlier, much of the research on elections in the modern era has focused on measuring the size of the incumbency advantage—how incumbents' institutional and money advantages translate to votes in elections. Most scholars find a large incumbency advantage in the last three decades of the twentieth century but a much smaller (and declining) advantage in the early twenty-first century. The latter finding serves as one basis for trying to understand the contemporary political era. Why has the incumbency advantage shrunk, and what does this shrinkage tell us about the dynamics of today's electoral politics?

Most scholars believe that a "nationalization" of electoral politics has occurred in recent years. In other words, voters are relying more and more on simple party cues to make their vote choices. They increasingly associate with a given party, and they vote for members of that party rather than base their votes on other factors such as incumbency. Political scientist Morris Fiorina sums up this

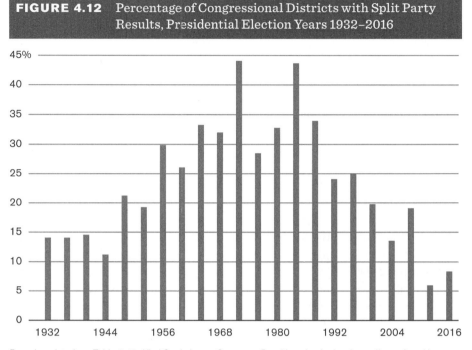

FIGURE 4.12 Percentage of Congressional Districts with Split Party Results, Presidential Election Years 1932–2016

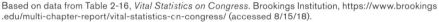

Based on data from Table 2-16, *Vital Statistics on Congress*. Brookings Institution, https://www.brookings.edu/multi-chapter-report/vital-statistics-cn-congress/ (accessed 8/15/18).

process of nationalization succinctly: "When elections are nationalized, people vote for the party, not the person. Candidates of the party at different levels of government win and lose together. Their fate is collective."[68]

As a result of nationalization, *split-ticket voting*—voting for one party's candidate for one office and the other party's candidate for another office—has decreased. Figure 4.12 reveals the percentage of House districts carried by a presidential candidate of one party and a House candidate of the other party. The percentage of split districts was routinely over 30 in the 1960s, 1970s, and 1980s. A drop to 25 percent occurred in the 1990s, and a further drop has occurred since then. The percentage has been under 20 since 2000, and a massive drop occurred in 2012, with only 6 percent of districts being split.

In the early 1950s, when much of the initial research on voting behavior was conducted, a relatively low percentage of congressional districts were split. For scholars studying voting behavior and congressional elections, that was the state of the electoral world. Over time, "de-nationalization" occurred as partisan identification weakened and ticket splitting increased. This trend led scholars in the 1970s and 1980s (and even in the early 1990s) to talk about "party decline" and even the demise of parties as we knew them. During this period, partisanship was a much weaker predictor of vote choice in national elections, and voters relied on other information, including the name recognition that comes with incumbency. Correspondingly, the 1970s and 1980s were the decades when the incumbency advantage was the strongest. Beginning in the 1990s, party became a much stronger predictor of vote choice in national elections, and it has grown to the point that today it overrides every other consideration.[69] District electorates now overwhelmingly vote straight party tickets, and the incumbency advantage has shrunk as a result.

What are the causes of nationalization? Scholars disagree. Some believe it is due mostly to shifts in the mass electorate: citizens have become more loyal to a given party. Ideology and party have become better aligned—"conservative" with Republican and "liberal" with Democrat. This alignment allows citizens to simply "pull a party lever" in the voting booth rather than spend time choosing candidates office by office.[70] Others argue that nationalization is mostly elite driven: party leaders in Congress have increasingly emphasized party loyalty as a requirement for members to advance in the chamber and to receive rewards. And leaders now devote a significant amount of resources to creating a single party message in advance of the next electoral cycle. As a result, elites have made "party" the overriding factor in the congressional environment, which includes elections.[71]

Which argument is correct? More research is needed to determine a definitive answer, but both are likely correct to some degree. Elite and mass politics are usually interdependent; the "causal arrow" (what leads to what?) rarely points in one direction. An important and related question is, will nationalization continue? Are there factors that might lead party and ideology to diverge once again? Or will incumbent politicians begin to reassert authority to create their own messages? Some believe that the rise of the House Freedom Caucus, an intra-congressional group of very conservative Republicans who have organized around issue positions and messages that diverge from the Republican leadership, is one example that an anti-partisan reassertion of authority is already under way. A similar splinter group within the Democratic Party has not yet formed, although populist tensions—associated with Bernie Sanders's failed bid for the Democratic presidential nomination in 2016—exist and could eventually produce a Freedom Caucus–like group on the left.

Finally, apart from eroding the incumbency advantage, what has the recent trend toward nationalized elections meant? Because politicians' fates are now intertwined, we have seen more "wave elections," where governing coalitions are swept in and out of power, as in 2006, 2010, 2014, and 2018. How should we evaluate these wave elections? On the one hand, waves can be viewed as good things, as the greater nationalization is forcing parties to be collectively responsible for ensuring that election promises—many of which are broad in scale and affect the nation as a whole—are converted into policy. On the other hand, regular elections and the ever-present possibility of new waves give parties little time to develop and implement their policy agenda fully. The policy-making process takes time, especially if well-thought-out and comprehensive policies are to be adopted. The continual possibility of wave elections makes the production of such good policies very difficult.[72]

CONCLUSION

The material in this chapter builds on the material in Chapter 3 on representation, fully documenting what political scientists call the congressional "electoral connection." Members of the House and Senate care about building a career in Congress. To show that they've been good representatives, they use a variety of institutional advantages to service their constituents' needs. In doing so, they hope to be reelected. Elections serve as the accountability mechanism in the constituency-representative linkage. Every two years (House) or every six years (Senate), constituents can evaluate how their representatives have performed and punish or reward them by voting them out of office or granting them another term.

And the evidence shows that constituents overwhelmingly reward incumbents. Reelection rates for incumbents in both the House and Senate are extremely high. It is very difficult for a challenger to unseat an incumbent. Challengers do not possess the institutional advantages that incumbents do, and they struggle to raise campaign funds to keep up with incumbents. When an incumbent does lose an election, it is usually to a quality challenger— someone who has held political office before and who enters a race strategically when the national or local conditions are right. Often, vulnerable incumbents will retire strategically rather than put themselves in a position to lose a reelection bid.

In recent years, however, there is some evidence that the electoral power of incumbency is waning. Various data point to increasing nationalization in politics as voters rely more heavily on party as a cue to guide their voting behavior. As a result, less emphasis is being placed on other sources of potential voting information, including candidate name recognition (which goes hand in hand with incumbency). Thus more straight party voting is occurring, and measures of the incumbency advantage are declining. Nationalization has led to more wave elections, in which governing coalitions come in and out of government in single swoops, enhancing partisan collective responsibility but also putting great pressure on the policy-making process.

Scholars and pundits will be watching these trends to see if they are temporary or more permanent. Whichever the case, it is clear that the current electoral environment is both dynamic and fluid, and upcoming elections will undoubtedly be both interesting and unpredictable.

Discussion Questions

1. Is it a good thing that, once elected to Congress, individuals in the modern era typically want to have a long congressional career? What are the pros and cons of a Congress made up of many members who have served for a long time?

2. Of the various primary election systems used in the United States—open, closed, semiclosed, jungle, and blanket—which one is the best? Why?

3. Has the increasing nationalization of congressional elections in recent years been—on the whole—a good thing or a bad thing? Explain.

4. Three potential candidates—Mr. Pink, Ms. Green, and Mr. Black—are considering a run for the House of Representatives in 2020. Based on the candidate-by-candidate data that follows, determine whether each of the potential candidates should run for a House seat. (Hint: refer to the discussion on page 131.)

    (a) *Mr. Pink*: Probability of winning=0.45, benefit of holding office=60 utils, cost of running=30 utils

    (b) *Ms. Green*: Probability of winning=0.3, benefit of holding office=100 utils, cost of running=25 utils

    (c) *Mr. Black*: Probability of winning=0.4, benefit of holding office=50 utils, cost of running=20 utils

5. Three House members—Rep. Wolf, Rep. Bird, and Rep. Deer—are considering a run for the Senate in 2020. Based on the candidate-by-candidate data that follows, determine whether each of these House members should run for election to the Senate or run for reelection to the House. (Hint: refer to the discussion on page 132.)

    (a) *Rep. Wolf*: Probability of winning reelection to the House=0.7, benefit of holding House seat = 20 utils, cost of running for reelection to the House = 10 utils; Probability of winning election to the Senate=0.5, benefit of holding Senate seat=60 utils, cost of running for election to the Senate: 25 utils

    (b) *Rep. Bird*: Probability of winning reelection to the House=0.8, benefit of holding House seat = 10 utils, cost of running for reelection to the

House=6 utils; Probability of winning election to the Senate=0.4, benefit of holding Senate seat = 70 utils, cost of running for election to the Senate: 25 utils

(c) *Rep. Deer*: Probability of winning reelection to the House=0.55, benefit of holding House seat=20 utils, cost of running for reelection to the House=5 utils; Probability of winning election to the Senate=0.5, benefit of holding Senate seat=40 utils, cost of running for election to the Senate: 15 utils

5

Committees

As the 2014 elections approached, nine House and Senate committee chairs announced their retirement from Congress. Among these retirees was Dave Camp (R-MI), the chair of the influential House Ways and Means Committee, whose announcement came only months after his Democratic counterpart on the Senate Finance Committee, Max Baucus (D-MT), stepped down from his chairmanship to become ambassador to China. Baucus's exit occurred shortly after Carl Levin's (D-MI) announcement that he would retire from his powerful perch as the chair of the Senate Armed Services Committee. Many other influential committee chairs followed suit. Just a few short years later, when Republicans controlled both chambers of Congress and the presidency, a slew of powerful chairmen again announced their retirement, including Bill Shuster (R-PA) of the House Transportation Committee, Bob Goodlatte (R-VA) of the House Judiciary Committee, Jeb Hensarling (R-TX) of the House Financial Services Committee, Bob Corker (R-TN) of the "Senate Foreign Relations Committee, and Orrin Hatch (R-UT) of the Senate Finance Committee. Some of these announcements came more than a year before the November 2018 elections.

Why would so many members of Congress voluntarily leave positions long considered among the most influential on Capitol Hill? One can point to idiosyncratic

Senator Orrin Hatch (R-UT), chairman of the Senate Finance Committee, announced his retirement in January 2018, after more than 40 years in the Senate.

reasons for each retirement, including age (Levin was 79 years old), bleak reelection outlook (Corker faced the real possibility of losing in the GOP primary), or dimmed prospects for the party retaining its majority after the next election (every House Republican in 2017–18). However, far more sitting chairs are stepping down from their posts than in the past. The position is just less attractive than it once was. As a result, the post holds less influence now than it did a generation ago. Committee chairs are term limited (although the party leadership occasionally grants waivers on those limits). Even some chairs who are not term limited headed for the exits. For example, in 2018, Marsha Blackburn (R-TN), chair of the House Budget Committee, left to run for senator, and Gregg Harper (R-MS), chair of the House Administration Committee, left with the common pronouncement that he wished to spend more time with his family.

Along with a limited tenure, chairs have less say over policy than they used to. The experience of Chairmen Camp and Baucus in late 2013 is a good example. As the deadline for a budget and tax cut extension agreement approached (called the "fiscal cliff" at the time), both Camp and Baucus were all but cut out of the deal making with the Obama administration, even though their committees were traditionally responsible for crafting tax legislation. The eventual package of tax and spending measures was ultimately the product of hasty negotiations between congressional leadership (the House Speaker and the Senate majority and minority leaders) and the White House. In the end, Camp and Baucus, as Ways and Means and Finance chairs, were relegated to cheerleading for a widely unpopular piece of legislation that passed largely as a result of the dire economic consequences that the nation (and lawmakers) would face if the proposal failed.

Tom Cole (R-OK), chair of the House Appropriations Transportation sub-committee, summarized the effect of this shift in policy-making authority from committees to party leaders. Speaking about compromise legislation that the House and Senate Appropriations Committees had drafted earlier in the year to fund government agencies, which was rejected by Speaker Boehner and his leadership team because of pushback from conservatives in their own caucus, Cole said, "You just see your work product thrown away . . . [Republican leaders are] more and more disconnected from the life of an average member, and a lot of them got there without having done much at the committee level."[1]

The flood of committee chairs leaving Congress has been attributed to exactly the phenomenon seen in the fiscal cliff negotiations. Committees were once the nucleus around which the policy world revolved. As the modern Congress was taking shape in the latter part of the nineteenth century, contemporaneous legislative scholars recognized the centrality of committees to the House and Senate's operations. As Woodrow Wilson famously noted in 1885, "Congress in session is Congress on public exhibition, whilst Congress in its committee-rooms is Congress at work."

Wilson's statement was no less true four generations later when the nation finally resolved to tackle the vexing problem of ensuring African American civil rights. While popular accounts often give sizable credit to President Lyndon Johnson, who certainly advocated for what became the Civil Rights Act of 1964, in reality, much of the policy-based heavy lifting was handled in congressional committees, notably the House Judiciary Committee chaired by Emanuel Celler (D-NY).[2] Moreover, other committees, like the House Rules Committee chaired by Howard W. Smith (D-VA) and the Senate Judiciary Committee chaired by James Eastland (D-MS), played a significant role in the process—in this case, in a negative way, by attempting to torpedo the bill. Put simply, the major civil rights legislation produced from the late 1950s through the late 1960s was the product of committee politics. And the most prominent congressional figures in the legislative narratives were often committee chairmen.

With the wave of recent chair departures, however, the vaunted role of committees in the lawmaking process appears to be diminishing. Is it true that committees are no longer able to provide the representation and governance functions that they once did? Do members no longer see committees as the place from which they can influence government resources to benefit their constituents? Have party leaders replaced committee chairs as the legislative actors responsible for crafting new policy proposals? In essence, how powerful are congressional committees today?

THE BASIC STRUCTURE OF COMMITTEE GOVERNMENT

Congress is a lawmaking body with many policy responsibilities. It is not hard to imagine the difficulties that Congress would experience if every one of its duties required the collective action of the entire membership. Committees are smaller structural units within the larger body that manage the workload in Congress and provide specialized expertise in particular policy areas. The committee system is designed to make the complex policy world that Congress deals with easier to manage. Committees concentrate responsibilities and allocate authority over particular issue areas to subunits of lawmakers who then carry out the legislature's basic functions before presenting policy decisions to the larger body. In the following sections, we discuss the variety of committees that exist in Congress and the feature that most distinguishes one committee from another: their jurisdiction.

Types of Committees

Congress is home to many types of committees: standing committees, subcommittees, select or special committees, joint committees, conference committees, and the Committee of the Whole.

Standing committees do the bulk of the legislative work in Congress. Standing committees are distinguished from other committee types by their legislative authority and permanence. They are the only committees that exist from one congressional term to the next, unless they are otherwise explicitly removed from the chamber rules describing their policy jurisdiction, and they have the right to receive and report bills to the wider chamber.[3]

Standing committees are almost always further divided into *subcommittees*, whose responsibilities encompass a portion of the committee's overall issue jurisdiction. The subdivision of labor on a committee often coincides with its major responsibilities. For example, the Foreign Affairs Committee in the House has regularly divided its subcommittees by regions of the world (for example, Asia and the Pacific, Middle East and North Africa, Western Hemisphere) along with a few topics of contemporary interest (including Terrorism, Nonproliferation, and Trade). A small number of standing committees in the House are not broken into subcommittees; these are panels that have more narrow and specific jurisdictions, such as the Ethics Committee, the Committee on House Administration, and the House Budget Committee. In the Senate, four committees operate without subcommittees: Budget, Rules and Administration, Small Business and Entrepreneurship, and Veterans' Affairs.

Select or special committees (such as the Senate Special Committee on Aging and the House Select Committee on Benghazi) generally do not have permanent status, nor do they typically have the authority to consider or report legislative proposals to their respective chambers. For example, the House committee investigating the 2012 attacks on the U.S. diplomatic compound in Benghazi was charged only with examining the circumstances surrounding the events and creating a report with policy recommendations. The House and Senate Select Committees on Intelligence have been the major exception in recent history, in that they are granted a certain degree of legislative authority and possess permanent status through respective chamber rules. Similarly, most *joint committees*, those composed of members both from the House and Senate, do not usually have legislative authority. These committees provide oversight of relatively minor matters such as the Government Printing Office or the Library of Congress.

Select committees, such as the House Select Committee on Benghazi, are convened to consider or report specific legislative proposals. Rep. Trey Gowdy (R-SC), chairman of that committee on Benghazi, summarized its findings to the press in June 2016.

Two other kinds of committees, while not permanent, often possess legislative authority: conference committees and the Committee of the Whole. The main purpose of *conference committees* is to reconcile differences in legislation passed by the two chambers on the same topic before that legislation moves on to consideration by the president. Like joint committees, conference committees are composed of members from both chambers, and they are commonly dominated by the members of the original committees of jurisdiction in the House and Senate. The conference committees exist only for consideration of a single piece of legislation and are dissolved when the job is done. The *Committee of the Whole (COW)* operates in the House and makes conducting legislative business easier. The COW is mostly a procedural device that allows the House to organize itself more easily (the COW's quorum requirement is 100 members, instead of a majority of the entire House) and handle bill amendments more quickly (by limiting debate). The COW became an important mechanism of majority party control in the late nineteenth century, when the minority would try to shut down House business by not responding to quorum calls. Positive decisions on amendments in the COW must inevitably be dealt with again in the whole House. However, amendments that are defeated in the COW are killed for good.

Committee Jurisdictions

Jurisdictions refer to the issue boundaries over which a committee is allowed to legislate. Until the mid–twentieth century, jurisdictions were, for the most part, not written into the formal chamber rules. Instead, they were mostly defined by the precedent of previous bill referrals. Jurisdictional ambiguities were inevitable and battles between committees over control of particular bills were common, especially as the number of committees grew considerably after the Civil War. The reforms instituted by the Legislative Reorganization Act of 1946 consolidated committees in both chambers, streamlining the sprawling committee system and defining clear issue jurisdictions in each chamber's legislative rules.

Rules of both the Senate and the House allocate control over specific issues areas and determine standing committee jurisdictions. The rules also clarify how bills are referred to committees. Sometimes the text defining a committee jurisdiction can be quite vague, and other times it can be quite precise. For example, the House Committee on Energy and Commerce is given the very specific jurisdiction of "generation and marketing of power (except by federally chartered or Federal regional power marketing authorities); reliability and interstate transmission of, and ratemaking for, all power; and siting of generation facilities (except the installation of interconnections between Government waterpower projects)." At the same time, it also has authority over the wide-ranging and vague concept of "interstate and foreign commerce generally." Long-time Energy and Commerce chair John Dingell (D-MI) had a photo of Earth taken from outer space on the wall of his Capitol Hill office; he used to point to it as the jurisdiction of the panel he chaired. Lawmakers would hear him say, "If it moves, it's energy, and if it doesn't, it's commerce."[4]

Are committee jurisdictions self-evident? Not necessarily. Consider the House Agriculture Committee. While the vast majority of its jurisdiction covers agricultural policy, as might be expected, the committee also controls the federal food stamp program created as part of President Johnson's antipoverty and Great Society programs. Rather than falling under the auspices of one of the various other committees with jurisdiction over aspects of federal welfare policy—such as Education and the Workforce, which has jurisdiction over school lunch programs, or Ways and Means, which has jurisdiction over a wide variety of Social Security programs such as Supplemental Security Income and Temporary Assistance for Needy Families—the food stamp program (now known as the Supplemental Nutrition Assistance Program) was given to the Agriculture Committee as part of a logroll arrangement between urban liberals and rural conservatives. When the food stamp program was created in 1964, liberals in Congress wanted to make it permanent but faced resistance from conservative Democrats who controlled several key committee chairs and were hostile to many of Johnson's Great Society efforts. At the same time, conservative Democrats and Republicans were looking for support on a controversial Farm Bill proposal that included important subsidies to rural constituencies. The result was a deal within the Agriculture Committee in which conservative support for the food stamp program was traded for liberal support for farm subsidies. And the Agriculture Committee maintained control of both programs.[5]

Why are committee jurisdictions important? Jurisdictions regulate which committees receive bills, so they effectively determine who has legislative authority for consideration of specific issue areas. The "textbook view" of congressional lawmaking holds that a bill, once introduced, must be referred to an appropriate committee in the same chamber, per the relevant chamber rule(s). The House Speaker and Senate majority leader handle bill referral, but the formal task is carried out via their chamber's parliamentarian based on the match between the bill's subject matter and the jurisdiction of the appropriate committee. For example, when a bill is introduced directing that unclaimed money recovered at airport security checkpoints go to nonprofit organizations that provide respite for members of the armed forces and their families, the bill would be referred to the Homeland Security Committee because of its stated jurisdiction over the Transportation Security Administration. Internal committee rules then govern the additional referral of a bill to the appropriate subcommittee, in this case the Subcommittee on Transportation Security.

For the most part, the referral of bills to committees is routine, thanks to detailed jurisdictional language and long-standing, referral-based precedent.

Nevertheless, vagaries in jurisdictions and bill subject matter provide openings for lawmakers to manipulate the bill referral process so that legislation is directed toward a more desirable venue for deliberation. In 2005, shortly after a controversial Supreme Court decision affirming the right of state and local governments to seize property from landowners for private development deemed to be in the community interest (*Kelo v. City of New London*), Rep. Henry Bonilla (R-TX) introduced legislation that would deny federal funding to any state or local government that engaged in this form of "eminent domain." While the subject of eminent domain fell largely under the jurisdiction of the Judiciary Committee, Bonilla knew that Judiciary chair James Sensenbrenner (R-WI) would not be receptive to this heavy-handed approach. Bonilla, therefore, wrote his bill in such a way that placed it under the control of the House Agriculture Committee and its more receptive chairman, Bob Goodlatte (R-VA).[6]

In an effort to leverage the expertise of multiple committees in legislative matters that span jurisdictions, and as means of placating growing jurisdictional disputes between powerful committee chairs, the House adopted a rules change in 1974 that allowed for the referral of bills to more than one committee—either jointly, split into pieces, or sequentially. Between the mid-1970s and mid-1990s, about 15 to 20 percent of bills were referred to multiple committees, but that percentage was even higher for important legislation.[7] Committee members have a great interest in handling meaningful legislation that has a high likelihood of floor consideration and eventual adoption. So from a participatory perspective, members welcomed having more input on important business. However, multiple referrals came with a cost. Committee power deteriorated as chamber leaders exercised their ability to move legislation forward without the actions of one particular committee. Leaders also used multiple referrals to skirt the influence of uncooperative committees.[8] In addition, the greater number of committees involved in the crafting of legislation resulted in greater opportunities for obstruction of legislation before it could even reach the point of wider consideration by the entire chamber.[9]

A contemporary example of the multiple referral process was the complicated Obama initiative to overhaul health insurance in the United States, which eventually became the Affordable Care Act. The bill was considered by five different committees in the House and Senate, according to the provisions in the legislation that matched their jurisdictions. For example, the House Ways and Means Committee considered the taxation and Medicare portions of the bill. The House Education and Labor Committee considered aspects of the law that affected worker issues and eligibility for subsidies related to employment.[10]

Multiple referral also exists in the Senate, but it is rarely used. Because the Senate does not have a germaneness rule, amendments of any kind can be tacked onto pending legislation, which gives senators the opportunity to consider legislation in a wide range of contexts. When bills are referred to multiple committees in the Senate, they are usually the result of a unanimous consent agreement (UCA; see Chapter 7). Thus the relevant stakeholders typically have been consulted in advance to ensure the UCA is accepted.[11]

Because committee jurisdictions delineate the parameters of issue authority, it should not be surprising that tension exists over where jurisdictional boundaries begin and end. Perhaps no battles on Capitol Hill are more fiercely fought than those over committees' jurisdictional boundaries. Walter Oleszek, a long-time observer of congressional operations and a veteran staff member of jurisdictional reform efforts, once recalled that the tumult over jurisdictional changes in the early 1970s was far more contentious than disagreements among lawmakers over the Vietnam War.[12]

Congressional researchers have taken a keen interest in the topic of jurisdictions as a way to deepen our understanding of how committees interact and how this interaction influences policy deliberations. One study finds that jurisdictional change is part of a concerted effort by committees to extend their reach through the bill referral process. According to the study, committees craft legislative language to increase the likelihood that a bill on a topic of interest will be referred to a specific committee. Eventually, committees try to use chamber rules to codify their formal jurisdictional control over an issue area.[13]

In recent years, for example, cybersecurity matters have generated jurisdictional competition between committees. In the wake of significant security breaches of consumer data at companies such as Target, Home Depot, and Walmart, several House committees introduced legislation that would require the sharing of cyberthreat information between the private sector and government agencies (House Intelligence Committee), create federal information security programs (House Oversight and Government Reform Committee), require government agencies to develop cybersecurity research and development plans, and expand interagency development efforts for advanced computer networking and security (House Science Committee)—and these are just the House committees.[14] During the 113th Congress (2013–14), the Senate Commerce, Intelligence, Banking, and Homeland Security Committees all introduced legislation or held hearings on the issue of cybersecurity.[15] In the end, none of these proposals were enacted into law. Senator Jay Rockefeller (D-WV), chair of the Senate Commerce Committee, laid the blame for inaction squarely on the jurisdictional turf battles between committees.[16]

The process of granting one committee jurisdictional authority over a policy area extends beyond mere power grabs, however. Research has shown that when lawmakers codify jurisdictional changes in chamber rules, those changes are usually intended to promote efficiency (by combining similar policy areas as a means of using developed expertise) and to rationalize policy oversight through consolidation of legislative responsibility.[17] For instance, in 1999,

Congress significantly reconfigured regulation of the financial services industry by eliminating the barriers between banks and securities and insurance companies. The new law expanded market opportunities for banks in the United States, but it also made it more difficult for government regulators to oversee the institutions' functions and behaviors. Two years later, as a way of rationalizing committee jurisdictions and improving oversight and governance of the financial services industry, as well as solving a nasty turf battle between two Republicans vying for the chairmanship of the House Energy and Commerce Committee, the Republican leadership consolidated the jurisdictions of securities and insurance industry regulation with the committee that already controlled bank regulation. The result was the newly reconfigured House Financial Services Committee.[18]

THEN AND NOW
THE EVOLUTION OF COMMITTEES

The notion of granting authority to a subgroup of lawmakers to craft legislative proposals before consideration by the entire House or Senate took some time to develop (see the related discussion in Chapter 2). The initial formation of committees in both the House and Senate was an outgrowth of the system that existed in the Continental Congress. Legislation was first considered by the entire membership of each chamber before being sent to a select committee appointed specifically to iron out the details of a given bill. To handle recurring business and to build greater issue expertise, lawmakers in the House quickly turned to standing committees. The growth of the standing committee system began with a committee on elections (1789), followed by more policy-oriented committees such as the Interstate and Foreign Commerce Committee (1795) and the Ways and Means Committee (1802), both of which still exist in more or less the same form today. As the new century progressed, Congress created the following committees: Public Lands (1805), Post Offices and Postal Roads (1808), Judiciary (1813), Agriculture (1820), Indian Affairs (1821), and Military Affairs (1822). The Senate was slower to transition from a system of select committees to a system of standing committees, finally making a wholesale shift in the early 1820s.[19] Ultimately, the expansion of standing committees allowed Congress to build a measure of autonomy in the larger political system. That is, Congress developed an informational capacity that allowed it to craft legislation independent of direction from the president or input from executive branch agencies.

After the Civil War, the makeup of Congress and its committee system changed dramatically. Lawmakers increasingly saw service in Congress as a long-term career choice, foregoing the typical strategy of moving back and forth from state to national office within the prevailing party structure. At the same time, around the turn of the century, Progressive Era reforms such as the Australian ballot and the direct primary were eroding the parties' control over elections and creating a more direct link between members and the citizens they represented. As a result, members felt increasing pressure to service the needs of voters back home. Because committees had the ability to regulate and promote policies that were important to the needs of particular districts or states, members came to view seats on committees as a mechanism by which they could claim credit for generating policy benefits and thereby satisfy their constituents' demands and their own career aspirations.[20] Thus a variety of committees oriented toward constituency service were created during this time: Mines and Mining and Pacific Railroads (both created in 1865), Levees and Improvements of the Mississippi River (1875), Rivers and Harbors (1883), Merchant Marine and Fisheries (1887), Irrigation and Reclamation and Civil Service (both created in 1893), Roads (1913), and Flood Control (1916). These were also among the most popular committees with lawmakers, with Rivers and Harbors ranking as one of the most attractive destinations between 1889–1947.[21]

During this same period, Congress saw an enormous expansion in the number of seats on committees. The largest growth took place on panels with appropriating authority over the federal budget; many of these committees, such as Agriculture and Post Office, were able to funnel benefits directly to constituents. Moreover, the concept of a *property right* to one's committee assignment (that is, a norm entitling a lawmaker to maintain his seat on a committee from one congressional term to the next) was solidified during this period. In the 1870s, only about a third of lawmakers returned to their previous term's committee assignments. By the 1910s, this percentage had risen above 50 percent.[22] While this right was never codified in chamber or party rules, the norm that returning members could retain their previous committee assignments (if desired) was rarely violated.

The transition to the textbook committee-oriented Congress was inaugurated by the adoption of legislative reforms just after World War II. The most notable changes, previously mentioned, were the consolidation of committees and the construction of formal committee jurisdiction in both chambers. Along with these rearrangements came provisions for greater staff resources and a clear directive that committees stand watch over executive branch agencies. Equally notable, lawmakers rejected measures that would have shifted some control over the legislative agenda to party and chamber leaders, such as party caucus–based policy committees. They also abandoned other reforms as unworkable, including the creation of a joint House-Senate Committee on the Legislative Budget that would have set an overall ceiling for federal spending each year (a precursor to the modern-day Budget Committee in Congress). The outcome of the reform period in the mid–twentieth century was the dominance of congressional committee chairs over policy matters under their control—what we refer to as the textbook period. As we see in this chapter, the era of authoritarian committee chairs and committee domination of the policy-making process has given way to one that is controlled more tightly by party leadership.

Critical Thinking

1. How does the role of committees in the formulation of policy proposals in the modern era differ from their role in the earliest days of Congress?
2. What fueled the expansion in the number of congressional committees from the late nineteenth century through the mid–twentieth century?
3. Does Congress still have the need occasionally to create select committees? What purpose might a select committee serve in the modern era?

COMMITTEE SEAT ASSIGNMENTS AND COMMITTEE CHAIRS

The attractiveness of seats on particular committees has long been viewed as an indication of their power and influence. Before we unpack the meaning and trends of committee composition, however, we must first understand how the assignment process works.

In both the House and Senate, parties control the committee assignment process. Specifically, the majority party in both chambers is able to determine the number of committee slots for both itself and the minority party by virtue of controlling more votes when adopting chamber-organizing rules. As a result, the majority party nearly always grants itself the lion's share of committee slots, sometimes based on the ratio of majority to minority party members in the chamber and sometimes in far greater proportion (see Tables 5.1 and 5.2). The particular ratio often reflects the majority party's desire to influence a committee's agenda. Compare, for example, the majority-minority ratios on the House Veterans' Affairs Committee and the House Rules Committee. The Veterans' Affairs panel rarely deals with matters that are vital to either party's political agenda, but it is responsible for issues important to veterans, who comprise a key cross-partisan population. As a result, it has a ratio of Democrats to Republicans (14:10) that approximates the overall chamber composition. The Rules Committee, in contrast, determines whether and how bills are considered on the House floor. As a result, Rules is considered to be an "arm of the party leadership,"[23] and thus is controlled by a Democratic supermajority.

TABLE 5.1 Senate Standing Committees, 116th Congress (2019–21)

Committee (# of members)	Majority Seats	Minority Seats	Chairperson
Agriculture (20)	55%	45%	Pat Roberts (R-KS)
Appropriations (31)	52	48	Richard Shelby (R-AL)
Armed Services (27)	52	48	James Inhofe (R-OK)
Banking, Housing, and Urban Affairs (25)	52	48	Mike Crapo (R-ID)
Budget (21)	52	48	Mike Enzi (R-WY)
Commerce, Science, and Transportation (26)	54	46	Roger Wicker (R-MS)
Energy and Natural Resources (20)	55	45	Lisa Murkowski (R-AK)
Environment and Public Works (21)	52	48	John Barrasso (R-WY)
Finance (28)	54	46	Chuck Grassley (R-IA)
Foreign Relations (22)	55	45	James Risch (R-ID)
Health, Education, Labor, and Pensions (23)	52	48	Lamar Alexander (R-TN)
Homeland Security and Governmental Affairs (14)	57	43	Ron Johnson (R-WI)
Judiciary (22)	55	45	Lindsey Graham (R-SC)
Rules and Administration (19)	53	47	Roy Blunt (R-MO)
Small Business and Entrepreneurship (19)	53	47	Marco Rubio (R-FL)
Veterans' Affairs (17)	53	47	Johnny Isakson (R-GA)
Select Intelligence (19)	53	47	Richard Burr (R-NC)
Total Senate Seats	53	45 (2 independents caucus with Democrats)	

"Committee Membership List." U.S. Senate, www.senate.gov/general/committee_membership/committee _memberships_SLIN.htm (accessed 1/17/19).

In the House, members are prohibited from serving on more than two standing committees (though exceptions to this rule are routine when a member has a less desirable assignment, such as the Small Business Committee). In the Senate, however, because of the much smaller membership, lawmakers may serve on up to four standing committees. In addition, parties in both chambers divide the list of committees into groups based on their importance, influence, and workload. This classification places further restrictions on committee membership. For example, both Democrats and Republicans in the House consider Appro-

TABLE 5.2 House of Representatives Standing Committees, 116th Congress (2019–21)

Committee (# of members)*	Majority Seats*	Minority Seats*	Chairperson
Agriculture (46)	57%	43%	Collin Peterson (D-MN)
Appropriations (52)	58	42	Nita Lowey (D-NY)
Armed Services (61)	54	46	Adam Smith (D-WA)
Budget (36)	61	39	John Yarmuth (D-KY)
Education and the Workforce (40)	58	42	Robert Scott (D-VA)
Energy and Commerce (55)	56	44	Frank Pallone (D-NJ)
Ethics (10)	50	50	Ted Deutch (D-FL)
Financial Services (60)	57	43	Maxine Waters (D-CA)
Foreign Affairs (47)	55	45	Eliot Engel (D-NY)
Homeland Security (30)	60	40	Bennie Thompson (D-MS)
House Administration (9)	67	33	Zoe Lofgren (D-CA)
Judiciary (41)	58	42	Jerrold Nadler (D-NY)
Natural Resources (43)	58	42	Raúl Grijalva (D-AZ)
Oversight and Government Reform (42)	56	44	Elijah Cummings (D-MD)
Rules (13)	69	31	Jim McGovern (D-MA)
Science, Space, and Technology (39)	55	45	Eddie Johnson (D-TX)
Small Business (23)	61	39	Nydia Velázquez (D-NY)
Transportation and Infrastructure (61)	56	44	Peter DeFazio (D-OR)
Veterans' Affairs (24)	58	42	Mark Takano (D-CA)
Ways and Means (40)	60	40	Richard Neal (D-MA)
Intelligence (22)	59	41	Adam Schiff (D-CA)
Total House Seats	235	199 (1 vacancy)	

"Official List of Standing Committees and Subcommittees." U.S. House, http://clerk.house.gov/committee_info/index.aspx (accessed 12/14/18).
* Data for committee size and partisan breakdown is based on the 115th Congress. Data for the 116th Congress was not available at the time of publication.

priations, Rules, Ways and Means, Energy and Commerce, and Financial Services to be exclusive committees, and, therefore, members of those panels generally do not serve on any other committees.

Senate committees also have varying levels of power and desirability, and thus a different set of guidelines regarding committee seat assignment. When Lyndon Johnson became Senate majority leader in 1953, he established a method for allocating committee assignments known as the *Johnson Rule*, which both parties now use. Committees are separated into tiered categories: major (or exclusive) committees in category A, midlevel committees in category B, and minor committees in category C. Every senator must be assigned to a major (category A) committee before any senator can be assigned to a second major committee. (Like their House counterparts, Democrats and Republicans in the Senate have a few very exclusive committees—Appropriations, Armed Services, and Finance for the Democrats; Republicans add Foreign Relations to this list). After that, each senator can select one mid-level (category B) committee and then one minor (category C) committee.

As noted earlier, lawmakers usually have a property right to their existing seat from one term to the next. That is, assuming no major reduction in committee positions (which occurs when the majority party in one Congress loses its majority during election to the next Congress), incumbent lawmakers wishing to return to their previous term's committee assignments normally can do so. This norm does not exist in the rules of either chamber or their party caucuses, but violations of committee property rights have been fairly rare in the post–World War II era. They occurred more frequently under the Republican-controlled Houses of Newt Gingrich and John Boehner, however, especially when members were not viewed as sufficiently loyal to the party and its agenda.

Committee vacancies do occur, of course, because of committee expansion, retirements, and members transferring from one committee to another. Filling those vacancies is an important task fraught with political complications and wider implications for representation and governance. To fill open committee seats, Democrats and Republicans in both chambers have caucus-based committees that consider rank-ordered requests from incoming freshmen and incumbents seeking transfers from one panel to another. These "steering committees," as they are commonly known, are typically composed of party leaders, important committee chairs/ranking members, and regional representatives. (The minority party member of a committee who possesses the most seniority is called the *ranking minority member* and serves as the leader of the minority on the committee.)

A wide range of member and caucus needs determines whether an initial assignment or transfer is granted. These include the member's ideology and party loyalty, along with partisan political priorities. Unquestionably, lawmakers' constituency needs are critical in determining their best fit on committees. Accordingly, the Agriculture Committee is filled with lawmakers from districts heavily reliant on farming, the Natural Resources panel is usually chock full of members from the West, and the Financial Services Committee usually has a disproportionate number of representatives hailing from the Northeast. In recent years, a few new trends have crept into the committee assignment process. For example, both Democrats and Republicans have used some vacant spots on powerful committees as a way to shore up the reelection prospects of lawmakers who are vulnerable.[24] House Democratic leaders have also emphasized greater diversity in committee composition, allocating seats as a way to broaden a committee's regional, ethnic, gender, and generational makeup. Alternatively, House Republican leaders have distributed seats as a way of maintaining ideological control of the party, granting plum assignments to members in the conservative mainstream rather than to often-uncooperative Freedom Caucus members.

Once each party's steering committee names the members of the various committees, the slate goes before the entire caucus for a vote. It is then subject to ratification (majority vote) by the entire chamber, where it is usually approved without controversy.

Committee Assignments and Attractiveness

The movement of representatives and senators between panels can signal the attractiveness of certain committee assignments and how that attractiveness changes over time. Tim Groseclose and Charles Stewart's study of committee value is based on the observation that members of Congress will seek a transfer only if the eventual destination (the committee assignment sought) is more attractive than the starting point (the current committee assignment).[25] Based on this "trading up" assumption, they have generated "scores," and, subsequently, a ranking for all committees across time. Table 5.3 shows the change in committee seat value from the late 1970s to the early 2010s, with the period divided at 1995, the year in which the Republicans regained majority control of Congress after many years in the minority. This year also serves as a good substantive break, as 1995 is generally seen as the year in which party control of the legislative agenda and committee system tightened considerably.

The Groseclose-Stewart measure of committee value shows few dramatic shake-ups among the top committees in either chamber. In the House, Ways and Means, Energy and Commerce, Appropriations, and Rules remain the four most highly valued committees. However, the Rules Committee suffered a moderate drop in its relative value after the Republican takeover, likely because GOP leaders sought to centralize control of the chamber agenda, which eroded the Rules Committee's autonomy in moving bills from committee deliberations to chamber consideration. Such autonomy had long been attractive to lawmakers, but once curtailed under the Republicans, the Rules Committee became a slightly less attractive destination for assignment.

On the Senate side, there has been almost no movement among the top three committees: Finance, Appropriations, and Rules and Administration. However, Foreign Affairs, which used to be a very popular policy committee,

TABLE 5.3 Relative Value of Congressional Committees, 96th–112th Congress (1979–2013)

House

	96th–103rd Congress (1979–95)	104th–112th Congress (1995–2013)
More Sought After	Rules	Ways and Means
	Ways and Means	Energy and Commerce
	Appropriations	Appropriations
	Energy and Commerce	Rules
	Armed Services	Foreign Affairs
	House Administration	Financial Services
	Foreign Affairs	Armed Services
	Post Office and Civil Service	Judiciary
	Judiciary	Ethics
	Budget	House Administration
	Natural Resources	Budget
	Ethics	Transportation and Infrastructure
	Merchant Marine and Fisheries	Natural Resources
	D.C.	Oversight and Government Reform
	Financial Services	Education and the Workforce
	Education and the Workforce	Agriculture
	Veterans' Affairs	Veterans' Affairs
	Transportation and Infrastructure	Science, Space, and Technology
	Science, Space, and Technology	Homeland Security
	Small Business	Small Business
	Oversight and Government Reform	
Less Sought After	Agriculture	

Senate

	96th–103rd Congress (1979–95)	104th–112th Congress (1995–2013)
	Finance	Finance
	Rules and Administration	Appropriations
	Appropriations	Rules and Administration
	Foreign Relations	Armed Services
	Veterans' Affairs	Commerce, Science, and Transportation
	Armed Services	Judiciary
	Energy and Natural Resources	Homeland Security and Government Affairs
	Budget	Budget
	Small Business	Veterans' Affairs
	Homeland Security and Government Affairs	Foreign Relations
	Banking, Housing, and Urban Affairs	Environment and Public Works
	Agriculture, Nutrition, and Forestry	Agriculture, Nutrition, and Forestry
	Judiciary	Energy and Natural Resources
	Environment and Public Works	Banking, Housing, and Urban Affairs
	Commerce, Science, and Transportation	Small Business

Left axis (top): More Sought After — Less Sought After (bottom)

From Charles Stewart III. April 6, 2012. "The Value of Committee Assignments in Congress since 1994." Midwest Political Science Association, M T Political Science Department Research Paper 2012–07. Available at SSRN: https://ssrn.com/abstract=2035632 (accessed 6/1/18).

fell dramatically, from the fourth slot to the eleventh. Other broad policy-focused panels fared better during this period, notably the Judiciary Committee and the reformed Governmental Affairs Committee with its expanded jurisdiction to include Homeland Security matters.

From the perspective of distributive politics and the ability to provide for constituents, the "money" committees, which dole out funds from the federal Treasury (Appropriations in both chambers) and control tax policy (Ways and Means in the House, Finance in the Senate), are always among the most popular with lawmakers, as one of Congress's key functions is controlling the federal purse strings. In addition, three more-narrow constituency-based committees have seen a significant increase in attractiveness: Agriculture and Transportation in the House and Commerce, Science, and Transportation in the Senate.

Finally, the House Financial Services Committee has become more attractive over time because of a combination of factors related to its expanded governing role. Recall the jurisdictional rearrangement that resulted from legislative changes in the financial industry in the early 2000s (discussed earlier in this chapter). In addition, in 2008, as the financial industry was facing near-calamity amid the Great Recession, the committee was again at the center of key governing decisions and eventually became the venue for a new set of sweeping financial regulations, known as the Dodd-Frank Wall Street Reform and Consumer Protection Act, which were enacted in 2010. The consequence was not only a broadly more powerful committee but also one with expanded authority over a very deep-pocketed constituency. When it comes to campaign contributions, Financial Services is often second only to the tax committee (Ways and Means) for its members' haul.

The Evolution of Committee Chair Appointments

Over the decades, the rules governing the selection and retention of committee chairs have evolved dramatically, transforming what used to be a considered a seniority property right into an intrapartisan electoral competition. Throughout much of the twentieth century, the position of committee chair in the House was granted to the majority party member with the longest continuous service on the committee. This norm, known as the "seniority system," governed committee hierarchy and resulted in southern Democrats controlling many of the top spots.[26] As a result, the most conservative subset of Democratic lawmakers controlled key policy-making areas during this time. While important in the Senate, committee chair positions were not coveted nearly as much as they were in the House, because the Senate agenda is much more open. Substantive amendments in the Senate, for example, need not be germane to the policy being considered, and rules to restrict or eliminate amendments do not exist, giving committees considerably less control over the course and content of policy.

As the Democratic Caucus shifted to the left in the 1960s, a backlash occurred against the domineering control by conservative chairs. Over the next decade, the Democratic Caucus and the House as a whole adopted a series of democratizing reforms, one of which partially undermined the seniority system by altering the rules regarding selection and retention of committee chairs. Democrats eventually required committee chair candidates to stand for a secret ballot vote of the entire party caucus. In 1975, the Democratic Caucus, bolstered by a sizable freshman class of liberal lawmakers (the "Watergate Babies"), unseated three long-standing committee chairs whose conservative and heavy-handed decisions had rankled the sensibilities of the emboldened liberals.[27]

Table 5.4 shows the number of House seniority violations for committee chairs from 1975 to 2010. The high number of seniority violations in the 94th Congress supports the post-Watergate narrative of liberals flexing their muscles. Over the next two decades, however, the House Democratic Caucus rarely violated the seniority norm. This situation changed when the Republicans took control of the House following the 1994 elections, instituting a number of changes that had far-reaching effects on chair autonomy. As part of the Republican Revolution, Speaker Newt Gingrich handpicked most of the committee chairs, and though he did not entirely ignore committee seniority, he bypassed high-ranking members on several key committees (Appropriations, Energy and Commerce, and Judiciary) and selected instead individuals who were more ideologically reliable, politically skilled, and energetic.[28]

Perhaps just as important, the Republicans instituted chair term limits, which would significantly affect long-term committee operations in the House and seniority violations. Specifically, the GOP changed its caucus rules such that lawmakers could serve only three congressional terms as committee chair before they were rotated out of the position. Looking again at Table 5.4, we see few seniority violations again until the 107th Congress, three terms after the Republicans took control of the House. At that point, we begin to see a sharp rise in seniority violations, particularly those involving chairs. When the Democrats regained control of the House in the 110th Congress, seniority violations for committee chairs tapered off, although there have been several seniority violations for the position of ranking minority member on the GOP side.

One result of the new chair term limits is lawmakers now actively campaign among their colleagues for chair positions, which has changed the dynamic of chair positions themselves.[29] For example, Jerry Lewis, a long-serving Republican from California, along with two rivals, engaged in an extensive campaign in 2004 to become the chair of the House Appropriations Committee following

TABLE 5.4   Congressional Committee Seniority Violations,
94th–111th Congress (1975–2010)

Congress (year)	Chair Seniority Violations
94th (1975–77)	7
95th (1977–79)	0
96th (1979–81)	3
97th (1981–83)	0
98th (1983–85)	0
99th (1985–87)	2
100th (1987–89)	1
101st (1989–91)	0
102nd (1991–93)	4
103rd (1993–95)	3
104th (1995–97)	5
105th (1997–99)	1
106th (1999–2001)	0
107th (2001–03)	7
108th (2003–05)	5
109th (2005–07)	8
110th (2007–09)	1
111th (2009–11)	1

Data are from Russell Renka and Daniel Ponder, http://cstl-cla.semo.edu/rdrenka/Renka_papers/seniority
_cases.htm (accessed 6/1/18).

the end of the six-year term of its chair, C. W. Bill Young of Florida. Lewis not
only had to impress the GOP leadership with his management skills on one of
the House's most powerful committees, he also needed to demonstrate his commitment to national party principles of limited government. Most of all, Lewis
had long outperformed his rivals in his efforts to increase the Republicans'
House majority. Leadership PACs (campaign finance committees maintained by
lawmakers to help fund their co-partisans' election efforts) have been an important outgrowth of recent changes in congressional structure and partisanship. In
the election cycle immediately prior to his selection as Appropriations chair,
Lewis brought in more than $1.35 million to the campaigns of GOP House candi-

dates.[30] In the new world of chair term limits, then, leadership ambition goes hand in hand with fundraising ability.

THE TEXTBOOK COMMITTEE SYSTEM

Committees are deeply embedded in the textbook view of how a bill becomes law and how Congress operates. This perspective on the regular order of congressional operations has existed for many decades, and it assumes a variety of duties for committees at several critical stages of the governing process: policy formulation and deliberation, reconciliation of differences between the two chambers, and oversight of the executive branch's implementation of the laws. Here we review the textbook notion of committee duties and provide an updated perspective on the status of each.

Policy Formulation and Committee Deliberation

Policy formulation and deliberation is generally considered the core role of committees. As described earlier, governing is one of Congress's fundamental responsibilities, and the committee system has long been the structure for achieving it.

Committees formulate policy in both positive and negative ways. *Positive* or *proposal authority* occurs when committees introduce legislation, with the hope of getting legislation onto the agenda and to the final passage stage. Positive authority is important, but it does not guarantee legislative success. Indeed, legislation will face a series of roadblocks along the way.

Once a member of Congress introduces legislation it is referred to a committee in accordance with its topic. Lawmakers will often introduce legislation aimed at their own committee's jurisdiction. After referral, further action is not guaranteed. In fact, most bills die at the committee stage. In the last two decades, only 10 to 20 percent of bills introduced in Congress have navigated the legislative gauntlet to become law.[31] For example, in the 114th Congress (2015–17), there were 6,634 bills introduced in the House, and only 896 passed the chamber. Similarly, of the 3,589 Senate bills introduced, only 427 passed the entire Senate. In the end, a total of 329 public laws were enacted that term—passed by both chambers and signed into law.[32] On top of that, a fairly sizable proportion of laws in any term (about 45 percent) are either commemorative or of minor importance.[33]

At the committee level, and in accordance with the bill's substantive content, action typically begins with a further referral to a subcommittee, where consideration usually takes the form of hearings and then an eventual markup session. Hearings, in which members of Congress and other interested parties meet in a hybrid court/forum-style environment to discuss the pros and cons of the legislation, are the most public way that committees engage in lawmaking and governance. While hearings are sometimes held to address a specific piece of legislation, they can also revolve around a general issue of government concern or oversight of an executive branch agency (as discussed below).

Members of Congress use hearings for three primary purposes: (1) to generate information and opinions about the merits or pitfalls of a given legislative proposal, (2) to oversee the actions of an executive branch agency or program (see Chapter 10), or (3, specific to the Senate) to provide advice and consent with regard to treaties and presidential appointments (see Chapter 9). Within these broad purposes, hearings may also be used to satisfy a number of other aims. Hearings may help with the practical functions of lawmaking, such as helping to determine if a new law is warranted in the first place, garnering publicity for a policy matter (or a particular perspective on that issue), assessing the intensity of congressional support for a bill or amendment, or protecting jurisdictional boundaries (or asserting the committee's jurisdictional reach). Hearings may also address members' political concerns, by providing a platform for external actors to air their position, establishing a public record of scrutiny on an issue and thus building the committee members' reputations, or simply providing a venue for partisan bomb throwing.

Various chamber rules govern the format and procedures of committee hearings, including quorum minimums, witness duties, and public accessibility to the proceedings. Nevertheless, committee and subcommittee chairs exercise a great deal of discretion in deciding what bills get hearings, when those hearings occur, and how they are to be carried out. Chairs exercise the most discretion in dealing with the privileges of the minority party. When hearings exhibit a partisan division, chairs have been known to prevent particular witnesses from testifying, to schedule hearings when most lawmakers are out of town, and to end hearings abruptly. For example, in 2014, during a heated and partisan House Committee on Oversight and Government Reform hearing on Internal Revenue Service scrutiny of Tea Party groups, Chairman Darrell Issa (R-CA) cut off the microphone and ended the meeting before the ranking minority member, Rep. Elijah Cummings (D-MD), had a chance to speak.[34]

Another crucial part of a committee's responsibility in advancing legislation is the markup of bills. Markup sessions occur after hearings and other information gathering, and involve the more formal debate and amending of legislation. At this point, committee members, usually led by the chair, choose the legislative vehicle (the particular bill) that will move the policy matter forward to the entire chamber. It is extremely rare for the chosen bill to have been offered by a

Committees spend much of their time in bill markup sessions. Here, the House Ways and Means Committee meets to mark up the Tax Cuts and Jobs Act in November 2017.

noncommittee member, and by far the most common bill at this stage is the *chair's mark*, a bill introduced by the chair (sometimes just before markup) that contains her perspective on what should be included in the legislation.

During the markup, members synthesize the information they compiled and hash out a bill's details. Markup sessions are generally less formal affairs than hearings or floor debate (although the norms of each committee vary), but in general, members negotiate the details of legislation, trade support for key amendments, and eventually build coalitions necessary for success when the bill is considered on the chamber floor. During markup, opponents of the bill attempt to tack on amendments to complicate legislation or make the language unacceptable to a majority of the wider chamber. Because it can be very difficult to remove language from a reported bill, committee members have been known to engage in delaying tactics or obstructive behavior tc prevent bills they oppose from moving on to the chamber for further consideration.

During the public period of hearings and markup, committees are heavily engaged in activities often unobservable by voters or the media. These activities run the gamut from gathering information from stakeholders (affected constituents, lobbyists, and governmental/bureaucratic actors), to interviewing potential witnesses, composing questions for hearings, following up with witnesses regarding matters that arose during testimony, securing legislative cosponsors, and building consensus among key decision-makers (including other committee members, critical leaders in the chamber or across the Capitol, outside groups, and perhaps White House officials) to craft a viable bill.

While lawmakers are the public face of working committees, the professional committee staff carries out much of the behind-the-scenes activity. Committees can have sizable staff operations, with the number varying with the policy scope and culture of a particular panel. Staff size ranges from 20 to 30 on the House Small Business or Veterans' Affairs Committee, to 150 to 200 on the House Appropriations Committee. Committee staff members are generally older, more experienced, and better paid than the staff who serve in individual lawmakers' offices. As a practical matter, they serve as the eyes, ears, and, in some cases, the brain trust for the committee and its chair. They possess much of the historical policy knowledge and continuity, often having been involved in many prior rounds of policy formulation and legislative battles. Committee staff members hold both formal and informal discussions with rank-and-file committee members and minority party lawmakers (and their staff) to discern priorities and the committee's latitude regarding the content of legislative proposals. They gather intelligence regarding lawmakers' strongly held preferences on particular aspects of policy, warning of potential problems as bills develop and move through committee consideration and on to floor consideration. Ultimately, the committee staff translates lawmakers' policy preferences and priorities into workable bill language.[35]

Finally, once the committee has completed its work on a bill, it votes to report it to the wider chamber. (A committee almost always reports out a bill favorably, though some bills have been reported out without the committee's endorsement.) Accompanying the bill is an official committee report, which provides background information and justification for the legislative language used. In some cases, a committee report later serves as an important part of the legislative history, particularly when courts are trying to discern lawmaker intent. (See Chapter 11.)

UPDATING POLICY While the power granted to committees to place preferred legislation onto the congressional agenda would seem to be quite extensive, that power is perhaps most frequently exercised as part of their exclusive authority to formulate and update laws. For many decades, committees have been charged with the responsibility to renew or "reauthorize" legislation for specific government departments, which ultimately makes committees quite powerful. This broad power is perhaps best exemplified by the annual defense reauthorization, controlled by the House and Senate Armed Services Committees. Usually, these two panels wrap nearly all defense-related legislative activity into one annual bill. The defense authorization often includes matters as wide-ranging as funding for new weapons systems to policy regarding how the military deals with sexual assault to whether or not detainees remain at the detention center at Guantánamo Bay.

The system of policy authorizations allows committees' members, particularly committee leaders, to bring their legislative ideas to the floor with the designation of "must pass." Why the sense of urgency? Failure to pass an extension of the existing authorizing statute can result in popular and vital programs and agencies losing their operating authority. For example, in the summer of 2011, amid partisan wrangling over a deficit-reduction package, the House and Senate Transportation Committees were unable to agree on the terms of a short-term extension of the authorization for the Federal Aviation Administration (FAA). While such stopgap measures normally do not include any new legislative language to change existing programs and usually extend existing funding levels until a longer-term reauthorization can be completed, House Transportation Chair John Mica (R-FL) included language to cut subsidies for small airports, and Democrats in the House and Senate balked. The partial shutdown of the agency, which lasted two weeks, resulted in the furlough of several thousand nonessential FAA employees (not air traffic controllers) and halted much-needed construction projects at airports across the country.[36] A temporary authorization was eventually passed to bring the agency back to full force, and Congress approved a long-term authorization, including the small airport funding, in February of 2012.

BLOCKING POLICY Committees also possess *negative* or *gatekeeping authority*, which they use to prevent unwanted legislative proposals from gaining traction. Negative authority is derived from several organizational rules: (1) adherence to committee jurisdictions and their exclusivity with respect to policy property rights, (2) requirements that bills be referred to committees once introduced, and (3) a germaneness clause (in the House) preventing unrelated measures from being attached to bills. Committees thus can serve as a choke point for the movement of legislative proposals within their purview. Committee members, particularly committee leaders, can kill legislation simply by failing to act on bills or amendments (beyond what is required in chamber rules). This is the fate of the vast majority of bills introduced in Congress each term. One of the more infamous examples of this conscious neglect occurred in the late 1950s and early 1960s, when the House Rules Committee, led by avowed segregationist Howard W. Smith of Virginia, refused to permit early versions of the Civil Rights Act from receiving floor consideration.

This ability to kill legislative proposals is often used as a raw expression of representational power. For instance, the House and Senate Agriculture Committees have used their exclusive control over the Farm Bill, a once-every-five-years statute that sets federal policy regarding the Department of Agriculture and farm programs, to prevent any elimination or serious restructuring of the rules regarding federal government subsidies to farmers. (As we discuss later in this chapter, lawmakers from constituencies that are completely dependent on their farm economies dominate the agriculture committees.)

Senate committees operate somewhat differently. While Senate committees have the same proposal function with respect to legislation authorizing government programs and agencies, they do not have the House committees' ability to prevent unwanted legislation from receiving floor consideration. Because of the germaneness clause in the House—"no motion or proposition on a subject different from that under consideration shall be admitted under color of amendment"—a committee retains exclusive control over policy that falls within its jurisdiction. In the Senate, no such germaneness rule exists, and members can compete with committees on policy by proposing legislation via a nongermane amendment. For example, in 2009, a federal court banned guns in national parks. House Republicans attempted to reverse this ruling by placing new language in that year's omnibus public lands bill. Their goal was to codify the rights of individuals to carry concealed weapons on federal lands. The amendment was rejected by the House Natural Resources Committee and then turned back by the House Rules Committee during its crafting of a rule for floor debate.[37] However, later that year, Senator Tom Coburn (R-OK) successfully attached similar language to a measure imposing new restrictions on credit card companies. The credit card bill was strongly supported by the Obama administration, which very much wanted it to be completed before the impending Memorial Day break, and the gun amendment was passed and signed into law.[38]

In addition, once a House committee's bill reaches the floor, it can be protected by a *special rule* granted by the Rules Committee. Special rules typically limit or restrict amendments that can be offered, with the *closed rule* (no amendments) being the most prohibitive. The Rules and Administration Committee in the Senate does not possess a similar special-rules-making authority, further limiting a Senate committee's agenda control.

House/Senate Reconciliation: Conference Committees

Committee members, who are policy experts and architects of an original legislative proposal, also play another key role: negotiating any differences that might remain between House and Senate versions of legislation. Traditionally, when the House and Senate pass differing bills on the same legislative matter, a *conference committee*—a joint House-Senate Committee—negotiates the differences.

Conferees, the House and Senate members assigned to the conference committee, come mostly from the original committees of jurisdiction. This additional duty of conferees gives committee members a great degree of authority over the final legislation, as their compromise is almost always brought back to their respective chambers for a "take-it-or-leave-it" vote (no amendments allowed). Thus any changes made on the chamber floors after initial committee consideration and report of the bill can be reversed by the originating committee later in the conference negotiations. This ability to undo floor decisions after the fact effectively gives conference committees a final veto over legislation, which can be a tremendous source of power.[39]

For instance, in late 2013/early 2014, a conference committee composed mostly of members from the House and Senate Agriculture Committees negotiated a compromise on a five-year deal to reauthorize farm programs (the previously mentioned Farm Bill). In what turned out to be a surprisingly contentious fight, conferees, in conjunction with some chamber leaders, were able to fend off attempts to end all farm subsidy programs and to institute deep cuts in food stamp programs that were part of the House legislation. Such significant changes to existing U.S. Department of Agriculture programs would have had severe consequences for committee members' constituencies and their supportive interest groups.

Oversight of the Executive Branch

In addition to their legislative duties, committees are central players in the separation-of-powers responsibilities of Congress via their oversight of executive branch agencies. Such oversight takes the form of monitoring, adjusting, and updating the actions and administrative duties of federal agencies. Former House Committee on Oversight and Government Reform chairman Henry Waxman (D-CA) contended that congressional oversight of the executive branch may be "just as important, if not more important, than legislation."[40]

Committees perform oversight in a number of ways. The most visible form of oversight is public hearings. For instance, in the spring of 2014, after revelations of mismanagement at the Department of Veterans Affairs (VA), the House and Senate Veterans' Affairs Committees held a set of hearings focused on delays in the provision of health care to veterans and the falsification of associated documents. As a result, Secretary of Veterans Affairs Eric Shinseki was fired (along with a number of other top department officials) and new legislation intended to fix some of the more glaring problems in an underfunded, understaffed, and mismanaged agency was passed.[41] The overall frequency of oversight hearings increased considerably in the House in the late 1960s. From the end of World War II through the late 1960s, the House averaged about 120 days of oversight hearings per year across all its committees. However, from that point forward, the average has increased dramatically to about 550 oversight hearing days, in some years reaching close to 1,000.

Despite the media attention garnered by high-profile investigations, the bulk of federal agency oversight by committees occurs through normal hearings and other legislative efforts as part of the regularly scheduled reauthorization of agencies and programs. Committees also often require agencies, through language in authorizing or appropriating statutes, to report details about their activities for approval or consideration. For example, the VA must submit any new lease that amounts to more than $1 million annually to the two Appropriations Committees in Congress for approval prior to the allocation of funds.

While standing committees perform most of Congress's oversight and investigation functions, lawmakers sometimes create special committees for a high-profile investigation of the president (the Special Whitewater Committee to investigate the Clintons' private investments) or a specific federal department or agency (House Select Committee on Benghazi to investigate the State Department's handling of the attack on the U.S. Consulate in Libya in 2012).[42] Another variant involves investigating illegal or problematic activities within and outside of government, such as the prominent anticommunist investigations in 1953 led by Senator Joseph McCarthy (R-WI) in his position as chair of the Senate Committee on Government Operations. More recently, in 2008 the House Committee on Oversight and Government Reform engaged in an investigation of steroid use in Major League Baseball, which landed superstar pitcher Roger Clemens in court facing perjury charges after telling Congress he had not used banned substances.

ARE COMMITTEES STILL RELEVANT?

Recent years have seen an increase in partisan influence in Congress, and this has affected the world and work of committees. The committee system was once relatively autonomous, and partisanship and ideology were just a part of the mix of influences on members, along with constituency needs, policy expertise, and political ambition. Today, however, the dominance of partisan agendas pervades nearly all committee activities. As a result, the nature of committee work has changed. These changes have limited committees' governance and representation functions while highlighting their separation-of-powers role. The changes have also had a broader effect of diminishing committees' role in the legislative process, which raises an important question: Has the vaunted position of committees been lost? Are committees no longer central to governance?

The shift away from the textbook functioning of committees has been more tectonic than tidal wave. It began in the late 1960s and early 1970s, as the Democratic Caucus became increasingly populated by liberals who were unhappy with the iron-fisted control of committees by more conservative and senior members.

As noted earlier, the committee reforms of the early 1970s shifted control of committee agendas and operations away from committee chairs in two opposite directions: toward a concentration of authority in party leadership (greater influence of party leaders over committee assignments) and a devolution of power down to junior members through an expansion of the subcommittee system. At the same time, Republican and Democratic Caucuses in both chambers were beginning their ideological sorting, resulting in greater policy polarization and increasing partisan battles over matters of governance. Eventually, in the 1980s, major legislation that had previously been the domain of committees was handled more often through negotiations between party leadership and the White House. This legislation included the crafting of Social Security reforms in 1983 and the Gramm-Rudman-Hollings deficit-reduction package in 1985.[43]

The decline of committee power continued into the early 1990s, particularly at the beginning of the Clinton presidency as the administration overplayed its hand in its efforts to overhaul health care policy. The White House's insistence on a costly and wholesale reorganization plan for national health coverage was politically unworkable, and it led the many House and Senate committees who had devoted considerable time and resources to the effort to lose credibility. In the end, the failure of the Clinton health care initiative contributed significantly to the Democrats' losing majority control in both chambers in the 1994 elections.

Leading the Republican sweep that year was House Speaker-to-be Newt Gingrich (R-GA), whose ambitious legislative agenda, the Contract with America, included ten policy proposals planned for consideration during the first 100 days of the term. Gingrich's unorthodox approach consisted of a policy agenda defined and developed outside the regular channels of committee authority, jurisdictional boundaries, and expertise. Political scientist Barbara Sinclair believes that this approach ushered in a new era of weakened congressional committee power and greater reliance on entities outside the normal power arrangements in Congress.[44]

Over the succeeding years, both Republican and Democratic leaders employed mechanisms outside the traditional committee system for policy making and governance. In particular, Gingrich was fond of the use of task forces (small groups of handpicked GOP lawmakers assembled on an ad hoc basis to consider and propose one specific piece of legislation[45]) to complete legislative action in a manner that was more tightly controlled by the Speaker and his small inner circle of trusted partisans. More than a dozen such task forces were created at the start of 1995. Several were run by Majority Leader Dick Armey (TX) and focused on items in the Contract (such as regulatory reform, term limits, and welfare). Others were structured around Gingrich's personal priorities, including health care, gun rights, minority outreach, and immigration, and were intended to be more permanent.[46]

While task forces fell out of favor following Gingrich's departure as Speaker,[47] the use of other mechanisms to formulate and shepherd policy proposals through the legislative process, and thus circumvent the traditional authority and expertise of committees, persists. A recent study by Sinclair reports that committees are notably less involved in basic policy formulation and deliberation, and that this trend has accelerated in the last few decades. Sinclair's data on major legislation reveal that normal committee procedures were bypassed rarely (less than 10 percent of the time) in the 1960s and 1970s House and Senate. As Figure 5.1 shows, over the past two decades, regular committees of jurisdiction have been bypassed considerably more often—between 30 and 40 percent of the time. Similarly, postcommittee adjustment of bills (for example, floor amendments) was rare in the 1960s and 1970s, but the practice has increased dramatically, occurring in at least 40 percent of cases in the last few congressional terms.[48]

Yet the story of reduced committee influence in governance is not as simple as Sinclair's data might suggest. Some observers have suggested that the work of the House and Senate Appropriations committees exemplifies the dysfunction that defines current Washington politics. Textbook budget procedure tells us that these committees (or, more accurately, the various Appropriations subcommittees) must produce annual appropriations bills for the 13 different categories of discretionary spending in the federal budget (including agriculture, commerce/justice/science, energy and water, etc.). Otherwise, the associated government agencies and programs cannot spend any money. And it does seem that standard budgetary procedures are increasingly ignored, as it has become more common for federal agencies to be funded through omnibus appropriations (in which numerous appropriations bills are lumped together and adopted as a package) or simply maintained through continuing resolutions that extend the previous year's funding for an agency, department, or group of departments for another period (sometimes a year, sometimes less). These practices do not allow for either inflationary adjustments to spending levels or much-needed changes in funding for critical agencies and departments given evolving circumstances.

Recent research by Nolan McCarty, however, suggests that the growth in omnibus appropriations has not necessarily meant a lack of participation by the Appropriations Committees in budgetary lawmaking. In fact, McCarty shows that while there have been periods over the last four decades in which the Appropriations subcommittees have struggled to complete their required spending bills (in the early 1980s and from 2011 to 2013), for the most part, they have been successful in fulfilling their legislative responsibilities (see Figure 5.2).[49] The trouble has come in either passing these measures on the cham-

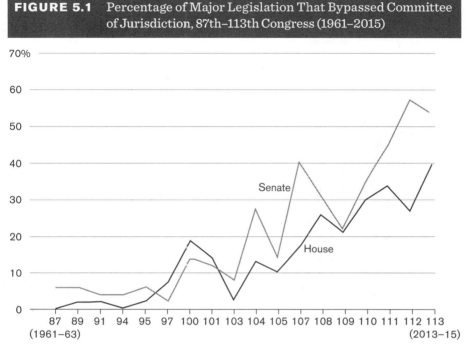

FIGURE 5.1 Percentage of Major Legislation That Bypassed Committee of Jurisdiction, 87th–113th Congress (1961–2015)

Barbara Sinclair. 2017. *Unorthodox Lawmaking: New Legislative Processes in the U.S. Congress*, 5th ed. Washington, DC: CQ Press.

ber floors or in coming to a cross-chamber agreement for specific bills. Nevertheless, the details of the Appropriations subcommittees' work have been included in the omnibus measures that are eventually adopted to keep government running.

On occasion, the contemporary Congress resorts to ad hoc committee structures to fulfill governing responsibilities when normal committee procedures are inadequate. In 2011, with Congress facing a deadline on increasing the federal debt limit (the statutory cap on the amount of financial debt the U.S. government can hold)—with defaulting on federal debt obligations and potential economic chaos being the price of failure—lawmakers hurriedly created the Joint Select Committee on Deficit Reduction, informally known at the time as the "Supercommittee." This bipartisan panel of House and Senate members was charged with accomplishing something no other committee would have been capable of doing: negotiating a meaningful agreement to reduce the federal budget by $1.2 trillion through budgetary cuts (normally under the purview of the Appropriations Committees) and increases in federal taxes (normally controlled

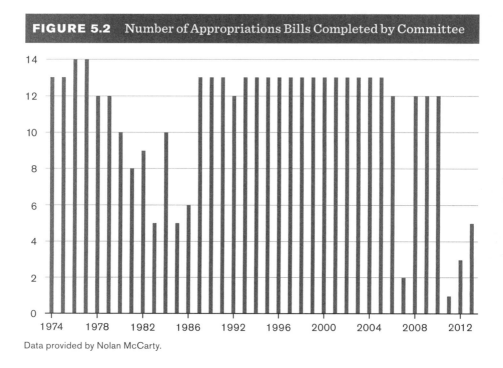

FIGURE 5.2 Number of Appropriations Bills Completed by Committee

Data provided by Nolan McCarty.

by the House Ways and Means and the Senate Finance Committees). Ultimately, the Supercommittee was unsuccessful in reaching an agreement by the deadline, and deep cuts in both defense and non-defense-related budgetary items, known as *sequestration*, was the result.

The Declining Influence of Conference Committees

As committees have seen their influence wane at the policy-development stage, they have been similarly impaired during interchamber negotiations. For example, in the early 1970s, the House and Senate relied on conference committees over 40 percent of the time to resolve their legislative differences and move bills on to final passage and the president's signature. Today, conference committees are rarely used (see also Chapter 7). This change is related to two phenomena. First, as already described, party leaders in both chambers have usurped more control over the policy-making agenda from standing committees. Second, lawmakers have increasingly worked to prevent the formation of conference committees on legislation they oppose. Prior to the mid-1990s, senators had never blocked a motion to form a conference committee. The first blocked motion came in 1994, when Republicans filibustered a conference motion on a largely Democratic campaign finance measure. Such tactics became commonplace over the next two decades.[50] For example, the government shutdown in 2013 occurred largely because lawmakers in both chambers refused to appoint members to a conference committee to negotiate interchamber differences in the budget bills.[51] Conservative lawmakers were particularly concerned that conferees would produce a take-it-or-leave-it compromise that would lead to more spending than they preferred.

In place of conference committees, the two chambers initially turned to *ping-ponging*: offering amendments to legislation being considered in each chamber until the two chamber bills align. However, in recent years, all forms of interchamber bargaining have declined dramatically, with less than a quarter of legislation involving any type of negotiations and conference committees engaged in less than 5 percent of all completed legislation.

Today, the chambers instead are simply accepting the language offered to them by their counterparts across the Capitol. This form of reconciliation accounts for 80 percent or more of legislation passed on to the president for his signature.[52] Occasionally, a chamber is backed into a corner and forced to accept the language of the other chamber due to lack of time. A good example is the 2009 extension of funds in the Cash for Clunkers program, a very popular economic stimulus measure that allowed owners of older gas-guzzling automobiles to trade them in for a voucher toward the purchase of a more fuel-efficient vehicle. Cash for Clunkers passed because the Senate had little choice but to adopt the House's language because the House had already adjourned for their August recess.[53]

The New Realities of Committee Oversight

While committee responsibilities have seemingly waned with regard to legislation, most evidence points in the opposite direction when it comes to committee oversight of executive branch activities. With the post-1994 Republican takeover of Congress came a series of rules changes in both chambers that expanded committees' oversight functions and responsibilities. Mandates included the creation of subcommittees devoted to oversight and requirements that committee reports include regulatory impact statements. As a result, oversight hearings today consume a larger proportion of committee time than in the past.[54] Tom Mann, congressional expert at the Brookings Institution, has argued that the rise of oversight "has been the most important change since the 2006 election in terms of relations between the Congress and the administration."[55]

As scholars began to study committee oversight in the post–World War II era, they initially found that the frequency of investigations of presidential administrations did not depend on whether government was divided or unified.[56] For example, the Senate Foreign Relations Committee, under the control of Senator William Fulbright (D-AR), for several years conducted hearings into both the Johnson and Nixon administrations' Southeast Asia policy and the conduct of the war in Vietnam. Missteps by the U.S. Secret Service, including lapses in security around the White House, prompted a largely bipartisan investigation by the House Committee on Oversight and Government Reform in 2014, including hearings just prior to the resignation of Julia Pierson, director of the Secret Service.

However, more recent and sophisticated statistical analyses have uncovered a surge in investigations into the executive branch when Congress is controlled by a party different from the president's.[57] Moreover, as congressional majorities have become more ideologically homogeneous (see Chapter 6), such committee oversight activity has increased in intensity.[58] For example, from 2011 to 2012, Rep. Darrell Issa, chair of the House Government Oversight and Reform Committee, held a series of hearings that investigated a botched operation by the Bureau of Alcohol, Tobacco, Firearms, and Explosives to track guns moving across the border to Mexico (which came to be known as Operation Fast and Furious). The hearings culminated in the first "contempt of Congress" citation

Congressional committee oversight activity is a crucial check on the executive branch and has increased recently, especially during periods of divided government. From 2011–12, Darrell Issa (R-CA) spearheaded an investigation into the executive branch's mishandling of efforts to track the movement of guns into Mexico. Attorney General Eric Holder, pictured here, testified in front of the committee and was issued a "contempt of Congress" citation for refusing to hand over certain documents.

for a standing attorney general when the administration refused to comply with the committee's subpoena for documents related to the operation.

HOW WE STUDY
COMMITTEES: THEORY AND EVIDENCE

For many years, scholars have believed that the only way to truly understand how Congress functions is to grasp the specific role that committees play as the key lawmaking structure within the legislature. Accordingly, scholars have developed different theories of how lawmakers have perceived committees and the purpose those committees served for them as representatives and for the legislature as a governing body. We present three different theories of congressional committees below: the distributive, informational, and partisan theories.

Distributive Theory

The distributive theory of legislative organization is often considered an integral part of the textbook view of committee functioning. Its proponents see Congress as an institutional means to provide for constituent interests and thus for lawmakers' reelection needs.[59] Committees are the structures that allow for a meaningful representative-constituency linkage. Because constituents' interests are geographically based, members must find a way to claim credit for policy achievements intended to satisfy those needs. The committee system is designed to fulfill this role. Members with a clear constituency stake in a particular realm of federal policy receive a seat on the committee with jurisdictional control of that issue, and they are allowed to serve on that committee indefinitely. As a result, when *pork-barrel* policies—legislation that directs federal spending to projects and programs in a particular lawmaker's constituency—are generated, committee members can legitimately claim to constituents that they had a hand in writing and producing the legislation. Similarly, they can make clear that they blocked any legislative efforts that might have harmed district interests.

For instance, Senator Mary Landrieu (D-LA), speaking about her newly acquired position as chair of the Senate Energy and Natural Resources Committee during her hotly contested 2014 reelection campaign, stated, "Now that I am the chair, and have this clout for the people of Louisiana, I'm running for reelection to use that on behalf of creating jobs, and hope, and opportunity here. Why would we want to throw this clout away when that committee is so important, so essential to economic growth of our state?"[60]

Distributive theory predicts that committee composition should follow constituency interests. That is, membership on the various committees should be based on the underlying economic demographics of the constituency. Committees should thus be composed of members who come from "high-demand" districts. For example, the Agriculture Committee should be composed of members from rural farm areas that have strong views on agricultural issues (subsidies, crop insurance, and so on).

A distributive approach to committee composition is predicated on "gains from trade," meaning that individuals—in this case, members of Congress—benefit from the ability to enter into voluntary trade agreements with other members of Congress. Issue jurisdictions are considered "turf" to be divided and allocated to committees based on geographic (economic) need. Committee members have agenda power to control policy making within their jurisdictions, and they use that power to provide benefits to their constituents. Members of Congress gravitate to committees that control issues of heightened interest to their districts and constituents. The committee system, then, is an "institutionalized logroll," whereby members trade rights and influence across committee areas, and members of each committee get what they need for reelection purposes. It is a live-and-let-live system; members control policy making on issues of importance to their constituents, and they let other members manage policy making on similar terms. The result is a committee system that is efficiently constructed for specific payouts in narrow policy areas, but it is not a system that generates a broader collective good.

Informational Theory

In the late 1980s and early 1990s, a theory based upon the informational role of committees emerged as an alternative to the distributive theory. Informational scholars consider congressional policy making to be more complex than the mere distribution of geographically based benefits. They believe that policy making requires a more nuanced understanding of policies and their consequences. Specifically, informational theory rests on the notion that a disjuncture exists between policies and outcomes. Members of Congress know what outcomes they want to achieve (like lower unemployment, better schools, or a cleaner environment), and they understand that they will be judged by constituents based on outcomes. However, given the complexities of the world, it is difficult for them to discern what specific policy language (for example, more government investment in building infrastructure, vouchers for private schools, punishments for polluters) will achieve the desired outcomes. Bridging the gap between policy and outcome requires information or policy expertise. But for members of Congress, obtaining policy expertise is costly. How can Congress be organized such that policy expertise—a collective good for the entire chamber—is achieved? Informational scholars answer this question by arguing that committees are not composed of lawmakers from high-demand districts, as in distributive theory, but rather are constructed as smaller versions (or microcosms) of the overall chamber. Thus committees represent the array of preferences of the entire membership. Therefore, committee members can be induced to (1) invest in expertise and (2) share that expertise with the rest of the chamber.

Thus, while informational scholars agree that members of Congress care deeply about reelection and thus seek to provide distributive benefits to constituents, they also believe that members organize Congress—specifically its committee system—to meet the informational needs of the overall membership. If committees can be constituted to represent the chamber's overall policy preferences, rather than being ideologically extreme, they can produce a public good—information regarding the connection between policies and outcomes—that is both widely shared and necessary for the production of good policy.

Partisan Theory

As Congress became increasingly partisan and polarized at the end of the twentieth century, scholars came to view committees as subordinate to parties. Partisan theory holds that Congress is organized primarily for the benefit of the majority party. Committees play a role in partisan theory only insofar as leaders can use committees to achieve partisan goals, with majority party members on committees using their gatekeeping power and proposal authority to promote majority party interests.

Partisan theories consider committee chairs to be agents of the majority party rather than autonomous actors (as in distributive theory) or operatives of the wider chamber (as in informational theory). Members receive committee chair appointments, in part, as rewards for party loyalty. For example, partisan theories hold that committee seniority, which in distributive theory is the primary criterion for chair appointments, can be bypassed if a member has not been sufficiently loyal to party leadership.

For some committees, nearly all major legislative activities reveal increased levels of partisanship. For example, evidence suggests that majority party leaders have taken greater control of the House Appropriations Committee over the last two decades. That is, while majority party members on the committee have preferences similar to those of their party as a whole, the actions of the committee are more in keeping with the wishes of the majority party leadership—and more likely to be opposed by the minority party. One of the first actions of the Gingrich

Congress in 1995 was to have Republican Appropriations Committee members sign a "letter of fidelity" to Gingrich and his agenda of budget cutting.[61] In recent years, floor amendments to appropriations bills largely come from the minority party, but they are far less likely to pass than those from the majority party.[62]

A stark example of partisan assertion of authority with regard to committee composition occurred in December 2012, just prior to the start of the 113th Congress. As the Republican Steering Committee was making its list of House GOP committee assignments, Speaker Boehner and his leadership team stripped four incumbent members from their assignments on the Financial Services, Budget, and Agriculture Committees. The Republican Steering Committee took this action after reviewing how often each lawmaker had voted with party leadership, with one ousted lawmaker told that his removal occurred because his "votes were not in lockstep with leadership."[63] All four lawmakers had opposed the GOP leadership's positions on important legislation, including critical budget votes.

The Theories in Practice

As these theoretical perspectives gained a foothold in the academic literature, scholars also searched for data that would allow them to test theoretical predictions. Proponents of each perspective had an underlying structural argument as to why committee composition would conform to the proffered theoretical view. For instance, the reelection-seeking, constituency-oriented lawmakers combined with the self-selection element of committee assignment requests—concepts that lie at the core of distributive theory—suggested that over time, lawmakers hailing from districts with far more than average interest in the committee's jurisdiction would dominate committees (at least those committees with a more narrow policy focus). Therefore, distributive theory would predict that high-demand committees would be composed of a disproportionate number of members who hailed from districts with excessive or concentrated need in the policy area under the panel's control. So, for example, the Agriculture Committee would be composed of many members from farming districts, the Armed Services Committee would be populated with lawmakers whose districts had large military installations, and so on.

Alternatively, informational and partisan theories are more concerned with lawmakers' overall ideological orientations than with their direct constituency interests. But the theories differ slightly in the membership on which they focus. Informational theory is concerned with the orientation of the entire committee relative to the chamber as whole, whereas partisan theory focuses only on the ideology of majority party members of the committee relative to the orientation of the chamber's majority caucus. Both theories, however, predict that (most) committees (or committee contingents) will be representative of the larger underlying body.

To analyze the ideological orientation of committees, we examine lawmakers' NOMINATE scores (as described in Chapter 2). By exploring the "central tendency" of a committee's ideology score, in this case its median score, and comparing it to a larger body, we can assess statistically whether or not the committee is representative of the parent body's policy sentiment. Therefore, to test the informational hypothesis, we compare the median NOMINATE score of each committee's membership against the chamber's entire membership to see if the scores are significantly different.[64] To evaluate the partisan theory, we compare the median NOMINATE score of the majority party contingent on each committee to that of the entire majority party caucus in the chamber.

In Table 5.5, we show the results of these tests for all standing committees in the House between the 106th Congress (1999–2000) and the 112th Congress (2011–12). Columns show the results of the informational theory tests (entire committee versus entire chamber) and the partisan theory tests (majority party committee members versus entire majority caucus) for each Congress. A cell with the letter C indicates that the committee (or majority contingent) is significantly more conservative than the chamber (or majority caucus) and is therefore not representative. The letter L indicates instead that there is a significant liberal bias. A blank cell indicates that the committee (or majority party contingent) is representative of the relevant, larger body.

Examining the committees' ideological orientations, we see very little evidence of unrepresentative panels, with the ideological outliers occurring repeatedly on just a few committees. For instance, in Republican-controlled Houses, the Judiciary Committee always appears to be a conservative outlier. In Democratic-controlled Houses, it is a liberal outlier. Why? Even among all Republicans, the majority caucus on Judiciary (during Republican terms) is significantly more conservative, and the same is true of the liberal orientation of Democratic members during Democratic terms. We see similar results for the informational tests when examining the Rules Committee. In Republican Houses, the Rules Committee is more conservative than the chamber; in Democratic Houses, it is more liberal than the chamber. Here, though, the explanation does not lie in overly extreme majority party contingents.

Beyond these two examples, there is only a scattering of other instances where the committee is more extreme in the informational tests. Ways and Means, Natural Resources, Small Business, and Education and Labor are all more conservative than the chamber in just one congressional term. There are, however, several instances where the analysis of the partisan makeup of committees

TABLE 5.5 House Committee Outlier Tests Using Ideology Scores for Members of Congress

Committee	106th Congress (1999–2000) Republican Info	Partisan	107th Congress (2001–02) Republican Info	Partisan	108th Congress (2003–04) Republican Info	Partisan
Agriculture						
Appropriations			L		L	
Armed Services						
Financial Services						
Budget		C				
Education and Workforce				C		
Energy and Commerce						
Foreign Affairs						
Government Operations		C				
Homeland Security	N/A	N/A				
House Administration						
Judiciary	C		C	C	C	C
Natural Resources			C			
Transportation		L				
Rules	C		C		C	
Space, Science, and Technology		C				
Small Business					C	
Ethics						
Veterans' Affairs						
Ways and Means	C					
Select Intelligence		L				

Data compiled by author with Adam Cayton.

109th Congress (2005–06) Republican		110th Congress (2007–08) Democrat		111th Congress (2009–10) Democrat		112th Congress (2011–12) Republican	
Info	**Partisan**	**Info**	**Partisan**	**Info**	**Partisan**	**Info**	**Partisan**
			C		C		
	L						L
			C		C		
							C
				C			
C	C	L	L	L	L	C	C
C		L		L	L	C	
			C				
					C		
			C		C		

offers other interesting findings. For instance, during nearly all Republican-controlled congresses, the GOP contingent on Appropriations is significantly more liberal than the Republican Caucus. Similarly, during Democratic-controlled Houses, the majority party contingents on the Agriculture, Armed Services, and Veterans' Affairs Committees are considerably more conservative than the Democratic Party Caucus as a whole. All told, the tests indicate that between 1999 and 2012, there is some evidence of outlier committees, but for the most part, there have been only a few.

Finally, we conduct similar tests for the distributive orientation of committees, but instead of using lawmakers' ideology as the measure of interest, we employ various measures of constituency characteristics that are relevant to each committee's jurisdiction. Again, we are trying to discern if committees are composed of lawmakers whose district needs are systematically higher than that of the overall chamber—and, therefore, the committee preferences are not likely to represent the chamber preferences. Because many committee jurisdictions are broad, and it is hard to pinpoint a single measure that would be a good indicator of constituency need for the committee's policy jurisdiction, we conduct these tests on only six committees, with the relevant constituency measure listed below the committee name (Table 5.6).

Four committees stand out as being consistently composed of lawmakers from high-demand districts. Agriculture is always dominated by members from farming districts (measured by the percent of the population employed in agriculture); the Armed Services Committee is dominated by members from districts with a heavy concentration of people employed in the military; Financial Services is almost always composed largely of lawmakers from districts with high employment in the financial and banking sectors; Veterans' Affairs is mostly made up of members with large numbers of veterans in their districts. The Transportation Committee showed only occasional instances in the later years where its membership was dominated by high-demand outliers as measured by employment in transportation and construction.

Looking at all the evidence presented in these tests, it is not possible to say that one theory best explains all the committees.[65] Clearly, some, but not all, committees seem to attract a disproportionate number of lawmakers whose districts are heavily invested in a committee's jurisdiction. Alternatively, there are some committees whose collective policy preferences, or those of the majority party contingents, frequently, but not always, align closely with those of the parent body. The theories help us understand what is happening in some instances and provide an ideal or stylized Congress by which to measure the reality of lawmaker behavior.

TABLE 5.6 House Committee Outlier Tests: Constituency Characteristics

	106th Congress (1999–2000)	107th Congress (2001–02)	108th Congress (2003–04)	109th Congress (2005–06)	110th Congress (2007–08)	111th Congress (2009–10)	112th Congress (2011–12)
Agriculture High percentage of constituents employed in agriculture	✓	✓	✓	✓	✓	✓	✓
Armed Services Large military workforce in district	✓	✓	✓	✓	✓	✓	✓
Financial Services High percentage employed in banking, finance, or real estate in district		✓	✓	✓	✓	✓	✓
Government Operations High percentage of civilians employed by federal government in district							
Transportation High percentage of constituents employed in transportation and construction in district					✓	✓	✓
Veterans' Affairs High percentage of military veterans in district	✓	✓	✓	✓	✓	✓	

Data compiled by author with the help of Adam Cayton.

Critical Thinking

1. What is the evidence for each of the three theories of legislative organization, and how strong/persuasive is it? Is each theory evaluated against both other theories?
2. What are the normative implications of each theory, vis-à-vis the policy-making process? That is, if each theory is correct in its conjectures, what should we expect to observe about policies produced from the respective committees? How does the expectation square with notions of representative government and democracy?
3. Can each theory be "right" to some degree? That is, are they mutually exclusive, or can they be complementary and together help build our understanding of congressional organization? If so, how?

CONCLUSION

During the middle part of the twentieth century, committees dominated policy making in Congress. The textbook view of the legislative process at midcentury held that governing power resided in committees, and parties did little more than assist committee chairs in coordinating policy outcomes. Today's view of committees is much different. Parties reemerged in the 1980s and 1990s as a driving force of congressional activity, usurping much of the independent power that had resided in committees. A "new" textbook view of the legislative process would place committees in a supporting role, no longer the lead actors in the congressional drama.

Yet to conclude that modern congressional committees are a shell of what they once were would paint an incomplete and perhaps misleading picture. In terms of governing, while parties do set the legislative agenda in today's Congress, committees are not cut out of the process entirely. The internal struggle for governing influence continues on a near daily basis.

The intense partisan conflict that is so frequently the centerpiece of contemporary congressional activity has in some ways enhanced the role of committees in legislative operations. Because of the frequency of divided government in the modern era, partisan conflict has often amounted to interbranch conflict. Because of their core responsibility for executive branch oversight, committees are central in the political tussle of today's separation-of-powers system. Hyper-partisanship has increasingly inserted itself in Congress's relationship with the president, and oversight and investigations of the presidential administration and its bureaucratic agencies have become a key part of interactions between the branches of the federal government.

Similarly, the era of intense partisan gridlock has made high-level legislative accomplishment increasingly difficult, resulting in less historic legislation being enacted.[66] As a result, the default of congressional lawmaking has been to maintain the governing status quo and renew expiring programs and laws. Thus legislative committees and their leaders have for the most part been able to keep the machinery of government functioning by reauthorizing existing programs and agencies.

Moreover, some genuine bipartisanship remains on a variety of committees. Partisan consensus still permeates governing on constituency service committees, and partisan conflict is only slightly higher on policy committees.[67] In 2015, after years of struggle to renew the expired No Child Left Behind Act (legislation governing a wide variety of Department of Education programs), the Republican chair of the Senate Committee on Health, Education Labor, and Pensions, Senator Lamar Alexander (TN), and his Democratic counterpart on the committee, ranking minority member Senator Patty Murray (WA), shepherded through Congress a compromise reauthorization that gave states and school districts more autonomy in using controversial math and reading assessments. The bipartisan agreement passed both chambers with overwhelming majorities of both parties. Stated simply, considerable policy work is still done in committee, and even in a strong party era, that work doesn't always reveal popular notions of deep partisan divisions.

Discussion Questions

1. Why are committee jurisdictional boundaries so important?
2. Committee members often see committee seat assignments as critical to their influence in Congress and their reelection strategies. Explain why this is the case.
3. What does it mean for a lawmaker to have "property rights" to a committee seat? Do you think this view of members having property rights is accurate?
4. How is it that committee seat assignments, and more particularly transfers between committees, can serve as a gauge of the "value" of specific committees?
5. With the increasing influence of party leaders and greater polarization between members of the two parties, the role of committees in determining the agenda of Congress and the specifics of major policy initiatives has changed considerably. Describe the ways in which committee involvement in congressional lawmaking has changed in the last few decades.

6

Parties

As 2017 was coming to an end, President Donald Trump and Republican majorities in Congress needed a policy victory. The first year of the Trump administration had come up short in terms of meeting important policy goals, despite the Republicans' unified control of government. The major policy initiative to that point—the repeal of the Affordable Care Act—had failed, and GOP leaders believed a significant policy success was important for the party as the end of the year neared. They settled on tax reform, which was a shared policy goal of the White House and congressional Republicans.

The bill was first introduced in the House in early November 2017. By early December, both chambers had passed separate bills. After some differences in the House and Senate bills were ironed out, the Tax Cuts and Job Act of 2017 was passed and signed by President Trump in late December 2017. The legislation (among other things) reduced tax rates for individuals and businesses, reduced the alternative minimum tax for individuals and eliminated it for corporations, and repealed the Affordable Care Act's individual mandate. While 12 Republicans in the House opposed the final bill, largely because it limited deductions for state and local taxes and mortgage interest, nearly all GOP lawmakers hung together to pass the legislation.[1] Per-

Paul Ryan (R-WI), then Speaker of the House, and other Republican members of Congress celebrate the passage of the Tax Cuts and Jobs Act. Despite months of debate, discussion, and political posturing, the Tax Cuts and Jobs Act passed without a single Democratic vote, reflecting the continuing partisan divide in today's Congress.

haps more telling, not a single Democrat in the House or Senate supported the bill. The Tax Cut and Jobs Act of 2017 was a wholly Republican policy initiative.[2]

The story of the GOP's tax reform is consistent with how policy making has been accomplished in Washington in recent years. Major policy change is often the by-product of partisan effort and initiative, rather than bipartisan coordination. This is especially true when one party enjoys unified control of government. For example, when the Democrats controlled the House, Senate, and presidency in 2010, the Affordable Care Act, the signature legislative achievement of the Obama administration, followed the same pattern as the Tax Cut and Jobs Act. That is, the Affordable Care Act was passed into law without a single Republican in the House or Senate voting for the measure.

Moreover, there is considerable evidence to support the belief that congressional actions today are the embodiment of larger partisan conflicts. Partisan polarization, or the ideological distance between the parties, is a distinguishing characteristic of the contemporary Congress. Presidents rail against congressional gridlock and partisan conflict; members of Congress run for reelection touting their political skills in navigating the partisanship on Capitol Hill; and political commentators and newspaper editorialists blame party leaders and their unwavering agendas for everything that ails Washington.

We live in a world in which partisan polarization in Congress is greater than at any time in modern history—and perhaps ever. For example, the *National Journal*, in 2014, reported that the ideological overlap between the Democrats and Republicans in the Senate was nonexistent. That is, no Senate Democrat was ideologically more conservative than any Senate Republican, and no Senate Republican was more liberal than any Senate Democrat. In the House, the story is much the same; only two Democrats were more conservative than anyone in the Republican conference, and only two Republicans were more liberal than any Democratic member.[3] In 2016, political scientist Keith Poole arrived at the same general conclusion, finding little partisan overlap between the two parties and describing the 114th Congress (2015–17) as "the most polarized Congress since the early 20th century."[4] Examining roll call outcomes in the House during the 114th Congress, we find that the percentage of votes in which a majority of Republicans opposed a majority of Democrats (commonly referred to as *party-unity votes*) was the highest of any Congress since World War II.[5]

However, this picture of Congress as consumed by partisan disagreement and gridlock is not the full story. Over the last few years, bipartisan majorities have produced major legislative accomplishments. For example, early in 2013, Congress enacted several significant policy changes: ending the tax cuts on the wealthiest Americans enacted by President George W. Bush, providing a massive aid package for northeastern communities damaged by Hurricane Sandy, and renewing the Violence Against Women Act. All were passed with at least some support from both parties. In 2015 and 2016, Congress made sweeping changes to the formula for Medicare payments to physicians that had been lingering for years (the so-called "doc fix"), passed new legislation to punish individuals engaged in human trafficking and to help victims, altered government surveillance programs, and overhauled regulations on toxic chemicals. All these laws were adopted with the overwhelming support of both parties in the House and (with the exception of surveillance) the Senate.

All in all, the effect that parties have in Congress is more complicated than we might assume. There are certainly plenty of activities on Capitol Hill that are fraught with partisan rancor and finger-pointing. And considerable evidence suggests that the congressional parties are more deeply divided than perhaps at any time since the Civil War. That said, circumstances and leadership efforts can bring large numbers of lawmakers on either side of the partisan aisle together to pass important legislation. This is true not only on high-profile matters but also on issues that typically divide Democrats and Republicans.

Partisanship structures how individual members of Congress behave, how collective decisions are made (or not) within a chamber, and how the branches of government are organized and relate to one another. Strong parties focus the legislative agenda, establish a hierarchy of leadership, and provide tools to construct majority coalitions to get things done. Yet facilitating governing can come at a cost. For party members, conforming to a strict party agenda and toeing the line on roll call votes can also mean compromising on constituent preferences. This important tension between governing and representation has defined much of Congress as it has evolved over time.

Thus the question that we ask in this chapter is: Should we consider parties to be *the* defining structure for the operation and organization of Congress today? Whereas committees were long seen as the dominant institution for defining power and policy making in Congress (see Chapter 5), parties seem to have largely supplanted them.

We begin the chapter by describing how parties arrange the structures and organizational activities of Congress both for the entire membership (for example, by writing and adopting the rules and organizing committees) and for their own members (for example, by electing their party leadership structure and providing electoral assistance for party candidates). We also note several informal party duties, such as coming up with a unified agenda, negotiating with an opposing party president, and overcoming collective-action problems. We then examine the different theories of why parties would structure institutional arrangements in Congress, emphasizing when, and to what degree, the majority party controls the legislative agenda. Next, we explore the polarization of the two parties, describing what it means, its historical development, and its causes. Finally, we discuss the changes in parties over the last few years—particularly fractionalization in the Republican Party—and how these changes have altered governing and representation in Congress.

PARTIES AND THE ORGANIZATION OF CONGRESS

Although political parties are not mentioned anywhere in the U.S. Constitution, their history as an organizing entity in Congress, as discussed in Chapter 2, dates back nearly to the Founding.[6] Since then, the role that parties play in the operations and organization of Congress has been codified both in the rules of each chamber and in the rules that the party caucus approves at the start of each congressional term.[7] In the following sections, we explore the formal role that parties play in electing chamber leaders, writing and adopting chamber rules, organizing committees, conducting the business of the chamber, whipping votes, and providing electoral assistance.

Electing Chamber Leaders

The parties' role in selecting chamber leadership is its most important formal duty. Chamber leaders are essentially party positions, meaning that, with the exception of the Speaker of the House and the president of the Senate, none of these positions are mentioned in the Constitution. Nevertheless, formal party positions, such as majority leader and minority leader, have a limited set of official duties as defined by the chamber rules. These chamber and party officers are critically important for organizing House and Senate business, as they decide who is permitted to speak on the floor, how the legislative agenda is structured, and how information is disseminated and controlled.

ELECTING THE SPEAKER   The election of the Speaker of the House occurs on the first day of each two-year congressional term. It is the first order of business once the House clerk calls the roll of members-elect. Prior to the formal opening of the legislative term, the majority caucus convenes, usually between the November elections and the end of the calendar year, to select its nominee for the speakership. After a quorum is established, the Speaker is then elected in the first recorded roll call taken by the whole chamber, which typically breaks down perfectly along party lines—with minority party members voting for the individual who will become minority leader.[8]

The Speaker is the only House leadership position that is elected by the entire chamber, and the vote is conducted in the open (not by secret ballot) so that all lawmakers—in particular the Speaker himself or herself—know if there are defections.[9] Consequently, multiple ballots for Speaker are rare. In fact, the last time a speakership race extended beyond a single ballot was in 1923, when eight ballots were necessary to produce a majority winner at a time when a significant internal division within the Republican majority existed. Since 1923, majority party defections on speakership votes have been quite uncommon—that is, until the last few years, when ultraconservatives within the Republican Party chafed at supporting the party nominee, John Boehner. In 2013, nine Republicans voted for someone other than Boehner; in 2015, that number increased to 25, the greatest number of party defections in a speakership election in nearly a century. While Boehner was elected Speaker each time, his constant and contentious battles with his conservative wing— now embodied in the House Freedom Caucus—wore him down and eventually led him to resign in late 2015.[10] More generally, these intraparty battles within the GOP perhaps foreshadow significant and lasting changes in the way Speakers are elected in the contemporary Congress and the operations of the body more generally.

ELECTING OTHER PARTY LEADERS The remaining party leadership structure in the House and Senate is determined in party caucus elections that traditionally occur in the weeks following the November general election. Table 6.1 provides an overview of the Republican and Democratic leadership in the 116th Congress.

In the House, the majority leader and majority whip—which have existed as formal leadership positions since the late nineteenth century—operate just below the Speaker in the party hierarchy. The members who hold these three positions, generally speaking, are the faces and voices of the majority party in the House. Below them are secondary leadership positions in the broader majority party organization.

In the Senate, there is no exact equivalent of the Speaker. The president of the Senate, per the stipulations of the Constitution, is the vice president of the United States. While the president of the Senate technically presides over the chamber's proceedings, the rules of the Senate give the holder of this position little authority—with the most important power being the ability to cast a tie-breaking vote when the chamber is deadlocked. In the vice president's absence, the Senate chooses a president pro tempore to preside. Like the president of the Senate, the president pro tempore has little authority, and in practice, junior senators typically preside over Senate proceedings to learn the rules.

The majority leader is actually the most powerful Senate leader. As in the House, the majority leader of the Senate is a partisan position. While powerful partisan leaders of the Senate have operated since the antebellum era, formal majority (and minority) leadership positions emerged only in the early twentieth century.[11] Below the majority leader in the party hierarchy are the majority whip (also known as the assistant majority leader) and a set of other leadership positions (similar to that of the House).

Occasionally, these leadership positions can be actively contested. For example, following the 1984 election, five senators initially sought to become majority leader. After four ballots, Bob Dole (R-KS) was elected majority leader by just three votes over Ted Stevens (R-AK).[12] Dole's election would help reshuffle lower-level positions in the Senate and reestablish moderate leadership within the governing Republican Party. And in February 2006, in the House majority leadership election to replace Tom DeLay (R-TX), who stepped down from the position after his indictment in late 2005, Boehner (R-OH) scored an upset victory over Roy Blunt (R-MO) on the second ballot (after Boehner, Blunt, and two others split the vote on the first ballot). Boehner had trailed Blunt, the acting majority leader (after DeLay's departure) and former majority whip, by

TABLE 6.1 Party Leadership, 116th Congress (2019–21)

HOUSE

Democratic Majority	
Speaker of the House	Nancy Pelosi (CA)
Majority Leader	Steny Hoyer (MD)
House Majority Whip	James Clyburn (SC)
Assistant Majority Leader	Ben Ray Luján (NM)
Caucus Chair	Hakeem Jeffries (NY)
Caucus Vice Chair	Katherine Clark (MA)
Campaign Committee Chair	Cheri Bustos (IL)
Steering and Policy Committee Co-Chairs	Rosa DeLauro (CT)
	Eric Salwell (CA)
	Barbara Lee (CA)
Policy and Communications Chair	David Cicilline (RI)

Republican Minority	
Minority Leader	Kevin McCarthy (CA)
Minority Whip	Steve Scalise (LA)
Conference Chair	Liz Cheney (WY)
Conference Vice Chair	Mark Walker (NC)
Conference Secretary	Jason Smith (MO)
Campaign Committee Chair	Tom Emmer (MN)
Policy Committee Chair	Gary Palmer (AL)

SENATE

Republican Majority	
Majority Leader	Mitch McConnell (KY)
Majority Whip	John Thune (SD)
Conference Chair	John Barrasso (WY)
Conference Vice Chair	Joni Ernst (IA)
Campaign Committee Chair	Todd Young (IN)
Policy Committee Chair	Roy Blunt (MO)

Democratic Minority	
Minority Leader	Charles Schumer (NY)
Minority Whip	Dick Durbin (IL)
Assistant Minority Leader	Patty Murray (WA)
Minority Chief Deputy Whip	Jeff Merkley (OR)
Caucus Chair	Charles Schumer (NY)
Policy Committee Chair	Debbie Stabenow (MI)
Caucus Vice Chairs	Mark Warner (VA)
	Elizabeth Warren (MA)
Caucus Secretary	Tammy Baldwin (IL)
Campaign Committee Chair	Catherine Cortez-Masto (NV)
Policy Committee Vice Chair	Joe Manchin (WV)
Outreach Chair	Bernie Sanders (VT)

In 2019, Nancy Pelosi (D-CA) was elected Speaker of the House. Following the 2018 elections, the new Democratic majority nominated Nancy Pelosi (D-CA, left) to be Speaker of the House, a position she also held from 2007 to 2011. Republicans also chose new leadership, nominating Kevin McCarthy (R-CA, right) to be House Minority Leader.

31 votes on the first ballot. Boehner was able to successfully coordinate all the non-Blunt votes on the second ballot, after the other two contestants dropped out.[13] Boehner would go on to become the leader of the House Republican Party in 2011 with his election as Speaker.

The choice of individuals to serve in leadership positions generally reflects the central tendency in the party. A recent study by political scientists Stephen Jessee and Neil Malhotra explored the ideological position of chamber leaders (speakers, majority and minority leaders, whips, and lower elected party officials). They found that candidates who win these positions are slightly more extreme ideologically than the median of the party caucus. That is, Democratic leaders are often slightly more liberal than the median of the Democratic caucus in their chamber, and Republican leaders tend to be slightly more conservative than the median of the GOP Caucus in the chamber.[14]

The choice of recent House leaders largely supports these findings. Nancy Pelosi has been the Democratic leader since she was elected minority leader in 2003; she became Speaker in 2007 before transitioning back to minority leader after the Democrats lost majority control in the 2010 elections. For much of that time, she has been slightly more liberal than the median of the Democratic Caucus. A similar story has been true on the Republican side of the aisle. Longtime GOP leader Boehner, who served as Speaker from 2011 to

2015 (and minority leader from 2007 to 2011), was largely reflective of the median of the Republican conference. When Boehner stepped down as Speaker in 2015, he was replaced by Paul Ryan, who was somewhat more conservative than Boehner, though not as far right as the most conservative House Republicans.

In recent decades, campaign contributions have increasingly been used to garner support in leadership elections.[15] Lawmakers with ambitions to win a leadership office often direct contributions from specially created political action committees, called *leadership PACs*, to potential supporters, with the hope of obtaining their support in a future intraparty campaign. For example, in the 2010 election cycle, Eric Cantor (R-VA), the minority whip, controlled the top leadership PAC in the House. Cantor was positioning himself to become majority leader should the Republicans win a majority of seats in that year's elections—which they did. The $1.7 million in contributions that Cantor distributed from his "Every Republican Is Crucial" (ERIC) PAC to GOP incumbents and candidates would earn him widespread support among party colleagues for the majority leader position after the election.[16]

Writing and Adopting the Chamber Rules

Prior to the start of each congressional term, the majority party in each chamber reviews the existing rules in the House and Senate. It then considers revisions, which span from the trivial (such as increasing the number of Congressional Gold Medals that can be awarded each year)[17] to the consequential (such as a reshuffling of committee jurisdictions). The majority party's authority to propose and (at least in the House) adopt changes to the rules derives mainly from its ability to control the agenda and keep its members aligned on key procedural votes at the opening of the term.[18]

One recent change in House rules that has had a substantial effect on chamber operations and politics is the adoption of term limits for committee chairs. Originally adopted by the new Republican majority in the 104th Congress (1995–97), the change restricted committee and subcommittee chairs to three consecutive terms before they had to step aside. Two years after Democrats regained control of the House, at the start of the 111th Congress (2009–11), they eliminated this rule. However, Republicans restored the rule at the start of the 112th Congress (2011–13), when they regained the majority.[19] Political scientist Molly Reynolds finds that the rules change has led Republican chairs, once their terms are up, to retire from the House at a significantly higher rate than other members—because they typically become less-effective legislators without the authority that comes from holding a chair.[20]

In order to avoid a Democratic filibuster of Neil Gorsuch (right), Senate Majority Leader Mitch McConnell (R-KY, left) and the Senate Republicans reinterpreted the rule to invoke cloture on Supreme Court nominees. Instead of 60 votes, only a simple majority would be necessary to confirm nominees, allowing Gorsuch to join the Supreme Court.

Rules changes in the Senate are slightly more complicated, as the chamber operates as a continuous body from one term to the next. (Recall that only one-third of Senate seats are up for election every two years, which means that a majority of senators remain in office during any election cycle.) Thus chamber rules in the Senate do not have to be readopted at the start of each Congress, as they do in the House. And because senators can filibuster—or refuse to end debate—in the Senate, changing the rules has generally required a supermajority of two-thirds (rather than the normal three-fifths for invoking cloture).[21] As a result, the Senate is more immune to external forces, such as majority party influence, which might lead to rules changes in the House.

Nonetheless, change does occur occasionally in the Senate. For example, in November 2013, a major revision to the cloture rule occurred. Frustrated by persistent Republican efforts to block votes on President Obama's judicial nominees, Democrats, led by Majority Leader Harry Reid (D-NV), reinterpreted the chamber's cloture rule as applied to executive branch and judicial appointments below the Supreme Court level. Dubbed the "nuclear option," the Democrats— on a 52–48 vote—declared that a simple majority, rather than a supermajority of

60 senators, was now required to end debate and bring a nomination to a vote.[22] Upon retaking majority control of the Senate following the 2014 elections, the Republicans did not reverse this change,[23] and evidence suggests that it had a positive effect on the number of President Obama's judicial nominees that were confirmed by the Senate.[24] However, after Republican Donald Trump was elected president in 2016, Majority Leader Mitch McConnell (R-KY) decided to up the ante. In April 2017, Senate Republicans, on a 52–48 vote, extended the nuclear option to Supreme Court nominees.[25] As a result, President Trump was able to nominate Neil Gorsuch to the Supreme Court as Antonin Scalia's (who had died more than a year earlier) replacement and advance the nomination by a simple majority vote.[26]

Organizing Committees

As discussed in Chapter 5, the parties have a great deal of responsibility in organizing committees, from the majority party determining the overall size of each committee and the proportion of seats allocated to the minority party, to deciding which of their own members will serve on which committees. Party leaders view certain committees as more critical for pursuing party priorities and therefore maintain tighter control over the membership of those committees.

Leaders typically use committee assignments and chairs to reward members who have been loyal to the party, particularly on committees that are critical to the fulfillment of the party agenda. For example, in 2013, when four Appropriations subcommittee chair positions opened up in the middle of the term because of unforeseen circumstances (a death and two resignations from the House), Republican leaders awarded these coveted positions to moderates who had long histories of demonstrated loyalty to the leadership. Earlier in 2013, in a controversial vote to raise the debt limit and avoid a government default, each of these lawmakers had bucked the GOP majority and voted in line with the leadership and, out of necessity, House Democrats to pass the legislation.[27]

Alternatively, party leaders have punished rogue lawmakers through their control over committee seats. For example, the extremely influential Rules Committee in the House, which plays the role of "legislative traffic cop," has long been seen as an arm of the majority party leadership, as it is responsible for carrying out the Speaker's agenda on important items as they pertain to floor activities. Consequently, the membership of the Rules Committee is tightly restricted to those party members most trusted by the Speaker. When Rules Committee members have been disloyal, they have lost their seats. A recent example occurred in January 2015, at the start of the 114th Congress. As mentioned previously, Speaker Boehner faced 25 Republican defection votes in his speakership election that year. These defections were not enough to derail Boehner's reelection, but they did reveal serious cracks in Republican Party discipline. Two of the dissenting GOP votes came from members of the Rules Committee: Daniel Webster and Rich Nugent, both of Florida. The two insurgents were soon thereafter relieved of their seats on the Rules Committee and replaced with more reliable supporters.[28] Moreover, Webster and Nugent became *personae non grata*, no longer receiving campaign support from the GOP establishment and unable to move legislation forward.[29]

Conducting Chamber Business

Party leaders also control *bill scheduling*, or floor consideration of legislation that has successfully navigated its way through the committee process. In the House, the Speaker, working with his leadership team, chooses the date that a bill will undergo debate (more on the stages of floor debate in Chapter 7). And the majority-controlled Rules Committee determines how the bill will be considered, in terms of both the time that will be allocated for debate and the types and number of amendments that will be allowed. In the Senate, the process is a little more complicated, but power still largely resides with the majority party, specifically with the majority leader. Although the majority leader has the privilege to seek recognition on the Senate floor before all other lawmakers, as a practical matter, most meaningful legislation is considered under a "unanimous consent agreement." This agreement is negotiated between the majority and minority leaders beforehand, and it acts much like a special rule in the House by structuring the terms of debate (more in Chapter 7).

Whipping Votes

"Whipping" emerged in the British House of Commons centuries ago. The term derives from the language of fox hunting. The "whippers-in" were individuals who kept the hounds from straying off. In the legislative context, whipping refers to the act of keeping members informed as well as persuading them to vote in a certain way. Whips emerged in Congress in the late nineteenth century. As the chambers increased in size, consistent and timely information flow between leaders and the rank and file became more important. The structure of the parties' whip system in each chamber has evolved over time. The chief whip of each party now has a complicated arrangement of assistant whips: chief deputy whips, deputy whips, at-large whips, and regional whips.[30]

The duties of the whip organizations have changed as Congress has developed. Today, whips are normally responsible for ensuring that sufficient numbers of party members are present when important business occurs, conducting informal polls or counts of votes prior to the consideration of major legislation on the floor, providing information on the details and timing of pending activities, tabulating summary information on current votes for busy lawmakers, and convincing members to stay loyal to party positions when such positions are declared.

In the mid-2000s, whip operations in the House, which were spearheaded by Tom DeLay (R-TX) and later Roy Blunt (R-MO), were at perhaps their most efficient. DeLay, known as "The Hammer," was especially forceful at getting Republican members to toe the line on issues important to the party leadership, and Blunt followed suit when he took over the position. This effectiveness was on display in the summer of 2005 during the final-passage vote on the Central American Free Trade Agreement (CAFTA), which was considered a GOP priority that year. With many Republican House members concerned that CAFTA could lead to significant job losses in their districts, Blunt (majority whip at the time) and DeLay (who had ascended to the position of majority leader) got to work in building a majority coalition. Over the course of nearly six months, they oversaw a wide-ranging whip operation that won over nearly 70 Republican votes. The whip network included a sizable number of corporate and trade association lobbyists, as well as former Bush administration officials, and it brokered side deals with individual lawmakers to secure votes. On the day of the final roll call, with the Republican majority seemingly short of votes, Blunt and DeLay pulled out all the stops. President Bush, Vice President Dick Cheney, and other high-ranking administration officials were brought in to visit with the GOP conference, and Republican leaders even postponed the final vote on a major transportation measure until after the CAFTA vote—as a signal to members that their individual highway projects could be threatened if CAFTA failed. Thanks to this extensive whipping, the measure passed just after midnight by a bare majority, 217–215.[31]

Providing Electoral Assistance

Each chamber's party caucus has its own campaign operation or "Hill committees" responsible for electing and reelecting party members. In the House, they are the Democratic Congressional Campaign Committee (DCCC) and the National Republican Congressional Committee (NRCC). Their Senate counterparts are the Democratic Senatorial Campaign Committee (DSCC) and the National Republican Senatorial Committee (NRSC). Duties for these Hill committees include recruiting candidates, courting donors, and distributing funds and resources. Resources are sometimes provided directly to campaign organizations, but more often than not, they are uncoordinated activities on behalf of a candidate's campaign, which allows them to avoid violating campaign finance laws.

These party campaign committees often raise and spend considerable amounts on television advertising in highly competitive races. For instance, the NRCC spent nearly $4 million on television ads supporting incumbent Rep. Mike Coffman (R-CO), whose suburban Denver district was considered one of the most vulnerable in the House in 2014. Not only had the district been drawn to balance voters aligned with both parties but Coffman was also being challenged by a former state legislator, Andrew Romanoff, who had good name recognition and ties to Democratic leaders across the country. The potential existed for Romanoff to raise a large amount of money and seriously challenge Coffman. And while the DCCC did its part by spending nearly $2 million on media for this race, it wasn't enough as Coffman, in the end, won a relatively easy victory.[32]

Conversely, as the election season progresses and the likely outcome of a given race crystallizes, the campaign committees withdraw their resources from hopeless campaigns. In 2010, as House Democrats sensed the coming wave of defeats for incumbents, many of whom had been swept into office during the previous two elections, the DCCC shifted its support away from candidates whose reelections were increasingly unlikely. This triage approach removed support for longtime incumbents, such as Earl Pomeroy, who had held his North Dakota seat since 1993, and relative newcomers, such as Betsy Markey, who was elected from a normally Republican seat in Colorado in 2008.[33] Similarly, by early October 2014, in Coffman's race (described above), polling numbers indicated that Romanoff was no longer within striking distance of the incumbent Republican. Consequently, the DCCC canceled more than a million dollars of ad buys it had planned to spend on Romanoff, mostly in the Denver media market.[34]

During the 2006 election cycle, Rep. Rahm Emanuel (D-IL) headed up the DCCC, and he made recruiting top-notch candidates a priority. Emanuel's efforts helped the Democrats retake majority control of the House with a 31-seat pickup for his party. Among his many recruits were two high-profile candidates: (1) Tammy Duckworth, a disabled Iraq war veteran, and (2) Heath Shuler, a former NFL quarterback.[35] Duckworth narrowly lost in an open-seat election in an Illinois district long held by Republicans; however, after serving in various appointed government positions, she went on to win election to the House in 2012. Four years later, she ran for and won election to the Senate. Shuler handily defeated an eight-term incumbent Republican in a reliably conservative North Carolina district; he eventually retired in 2012 after Republicans in the state legislature redrew the district to remove a good portion of the Democratic voters.

The funding for the campaign committees comes in part by collecting dues from current caucus members. That is, lawmakers are responsible for raising money on behalf of the campaign committees, which then use these funds to support the election (and reelection) efforts of other party members. The amount of these dues varies by the seniority, status, and electoral security of the lawmaker, but it is routinely in the hundreds of thousands of dollars.[36] The ability to raise considerable levels of money for the campaign committees is one way that members show their loyalty to the party and position themselves for advancement within the party hierarchy.

PARTIES AND THE CONGRESSIONAL AGENDA

Aside from their role in structuring the organization of and operations in Congress, parties also have a secondary role in articulating and expediting a governing agenda. This role entails a wide range of less-formal activities that seek to translate policy ideas into legislative outcomes.

Presenting the Party Agenda

When the president's party controls the majority in Congress, the president usually sets the legislative agenda (with some input from majority party leaders; see Chapter 9). The minority party leadership often presents a legislative vision—sometimes quite bold—to counter the party in power.[37] Here, legislative vision means formulating an alternative view of governing to attract voters in a coming election and to unify partisan lawmakers around particular policy objectives. When the president and Congress are from opposing parties, majority party leaders sometimes espouse a broad legislative vision, often national in scope, in contrast to the president's agenda.

Perhaps the best-known statement of legislative vision is the Republican Contract with America, which was formulated in 1994 (during the first midterm election of the Clinton presidency) by then–minority whip Newt Gingrich (R-GA) and then–conference chairman Dick Armey (R-TX). Rolled out in late September, the Contract was signed by 350 GOP House members and candidates, who pledged to support its provisions during the first 100 days of the coming congressional term—should they become the majority party. Provisions of the Contract included welfare and Social Security reform, tax cuts, crime prevention, and a constitutional amendment mandating a balanced federal budget. In truth, many voters were not aware of the Contract at the time of the election,[38] but it nonetheless became the primary agenda for lawmaking in the following term after the GOP's historic (and stunning) electoral victory. Ultimately, the Republican House leadership struggled to enact many of the Contract's provisions, with President Bill Clinton, the Republican-controlled Senate, and even some members of the GOP House majority acting as roadblocks. At the end of the 100 days, only relatively minor Contract provisions—applying federal labor laws to Congress and curbing unfunded federal mandates—had been signed into law.[39]

In the 2006 election, House and Senate Democrats sought to match the Republicans' 1994 success by crafting a "Six for '06" agenda. The Democrats planned to enact a number of agenda items in the first 100 hours of congressional deliberations, including a minimum-wage hike, student-loan reform, and strengthened national security. Democrats gained control of both chambers in the 2006 election, but they found legislating on the Six for '06 agenda to be difficult. Lawmakers did succeed in raising the minimum wage and implementing many of the recommendations of the 9/11 Commission, but President Bush vetoed changes to stem-cell policy, and other items (like fixing the Medicare prescription-drug program) were never completed.

Members of the minority party in Congress often find that their political agenda is defined by an external entity.[40] When minority party lawmakers have a co-partisan in the White House, as was the case for House Democrats throughout most of Obama's presidency, they are expected to support the president's policy priorities and positions. They deviate from supporting the president, however, when it suits their electoral needs and when it will not influence the outcome of a vote. When a congressional party is both in the minority in Congress and without presidential leadership, the agenda is often simply to oppose the majority and/or the president. For instance, journalist Robert Draper notes that after Obama's election victory in 2008, which unified the House, Senate, and presidency under the Democrats, conservative GOP leaders met to decide how to react. Many political observers believed that the Republicans' only recourse would be to accommodate Democratic policy priorities and negotiate for small concessions. Instead, GOP leaders chose to construct an agenda of united and unyielding opposition.[41] During the first two years of the Obama adminstration, Republicans voted as a bloc against all major Democratic initiatives, including the economic recovery package, Obamacare, and the overhaul of Wall Street regulations.

Negotiating with the President

Party leaders also work with the president on legislation. Because the Constitution provides the president with veto power, the lawmaking process involves more than just what happens on the House and Senate floors. For a measure to become law, the president must support it, or two-thirds of the membership of both chambers must be willing to override the president's veto. Policy making by veto override has happened in the past—most notably in the aftermath of the Civil War, when the Republican Congress repeatedly overrode President Andrew Johnson on Reconstruction policy—but it is rarer today. An override is easier to achieve when a party has two-thirds majorities in both the House and Senate—an infrequent scenario in the post–World War II era.

As a result, majority party leaders often need to negotiate with the president on important legislation. Such leaders could try to play "chicken" with the president, forcing him to accede to a policy measure by courting public opinion, but such pressure tactics are not always effective.[42] Finding common ground with the president is often the safer and more cost-effective strategy, especially because the majority has many policy goals and finite time to accomplish them.

Two recent examples of majority party leaders negotiating with the president highlight the benefits and costs of the separation-of-powers arrangement. The first (welfare reform in 1996) was successful, while the second (the "grand bargain" in budget negotiations in 2012) was not. The difference between these cases involved the ability of the key congressional leader to negotiate a settlement that both the president and his co-partisans in Congress could accept.

In the 104th Congress (1995–97), the Republicans controlled both the House and Senate for the first time in more than 40 years, and sought to enact a key provision of their Contract with America: an overhaul of the nation's welfare system. Within this policy area, there appeared to be room to work with President Clinton, who made welfare reform a key element of his election campaign in 1992. But the GOP's initial attempts to force a conservative policy change met with resistance. Clinton issued two vetoes, and Republicans did not have the votes to override them. As the 1996 election season neared, both congressional Republicans and Clinton sought to get a welfare reform bill passed. Speaker Gingrich worked behind the scenes with Clinton and his policy advisers to share information and adjust the legislation enough to keep congressional Republicans on board and get the president's signature.[43] Eventually, the Personal Responsibility and Work Opportunity Reconciliation Act of 1996 was adopted and successfully overhauled the existing welfare system. It established "welfare-to-work" provisions (limiting lifetime benefits to five years and requiring able-bodied adults to enter the workforce two years after receiving benefits), provided states with considerably more discretion over policy (through block grants), and tightened eligibility requirements for the federal food stamp program.

In the 112th Congress (2011–13), a divided Congress—Republicans controlled the House, and Democrats controlled the Senate—struggled to govern. In July 2011, concerns were raised about increasing the nation's debt limit by $2.4 trillion (which had an August deadline), with Tea Party–affiliated Republicans in the House balking. As worries about the United States defaulting on its debt obligations grew, Speaker Boehner and President Obama met privately in an attempt to negotiate a wide-ranging solution to the federal government's fiscal problems. Put simply, Boehner and Obama set out to craft a "grand bargain" that would "rewrite the tax code, roll back the cost of entitlements, and slash deficits."[44] Such an agreement would tentatively yield around $800 billion in revenue and significantly reduce various entitlement programs, such as Medicare, Medicaid, and Social Security.[45] Unlike the Gingrich-Clinton partnership in 1994, the Boehner-Obama pact in 2011 fell apart. In the end, while Gingrich was able to keep his Republican colleagues together on welfare reform, Boehner was not able to sell his economic deal to his co-partisans. Conservative Republicans in the House balked at the deal, and Boehner's second in command, Majority Leader Eric Cantor, would not support him. In many ways, Boehner was a victim of the ever-growing polarization in Congress, and his leadership failure prevented the successful negotiation of a historic agreement with the president.

Overcoming Collective-Action Problems

Since their emergence not long after the Founding of the republic, parties have served as a means by which like-minded lawmakers bring together all the necessary actors to overcome various obstacles in our complicated system of governing. In other words, parties are institutions that lawmakers use to coordinate behavior and overcome problems in acting collectively.

BUILDING COALITIONS AND A UNIFIED MESSAGE   One of the most important duties of congressional parties is building majority coalitions to support the party's agenda and pass legislation. Coalition building can involve a number of possible methods for corralling lawmakers, including promises of campaign support and resources, side deals on legislation, and pressure tactics.

Coalition building is most difficult when it involves high-profile and controversial legislation. During the Obama administration, no legislation required more deft coalition building than the Affordable Care Act. President Obama had repeatedly stated that he wanted major health care legislation to be a bipartisan effort, and that he sought to incorporate Republicans' input and perspective in the final package. However, as the months wore on, it became increasingly clear that President Obama and his party members would have to go it alone. This strategy was possible because Democrats had large majorities in both chambers of Congress—nearly an 80-seat majority in the House and 20 seats in the Senate. Perhaps most important, Senate Democrats had a filibuster-proof majority of 60 lawmakers until Senator Ted Kennedy (D-MA) died in late 2009 (and was replaced, in a surprising special election, by Republican Scott Brown).

With so much on the line, Democratic leaders needed to be attentive to the needs of wavering co-partisans who were facing resistance from their constituents. Building a supportive coalition required delicate negotiations and, in some cases, side deals with individual members to mollify constituent concerns. For example, two of the more moderate Democratic senators, Ben Nelson (NE) and Mary Landrieu (LA), both from Republican-leaning states, were granted what many considered to be special "payoffs" that involved increased federal funding intended to subsidize health care programs under Medicare (Nebraska) and Medicaid (Louisiana). Both Nelson and Landrieu claimed that they were not solely responsible for the increased funding and that it did not influence their votes. Nelson's "Cornhusker Kickback" was eventually removed from the version of the bill that passed in the House, but Landrieu's "Louisiana Purchase" was kept in.[46] In addition, a small but sizable group of antiabortion lawmakers in the House, led by Bart Stupak (D-MI), threatened to oppose the legislation unless it contained language that precluded federal funding for abortion. To win the support of these dissidents, President Obama issued an executive order making clear that existing limits on the federal funding of abortion would remain in place under the new health care law.[47]

BENDING RULES TO WIN VOTES Parties also manipulate legislative rules to win votes and enact policy. A high-profile example occurred in 2003, when the Republican leadership used its powers over the agenda to reform Medicare. Such a reform had been promised to senior citizens for years, and neither President Bush nor the Republican Congress wanted to face voters empty-handed in 2004. GOP leaders therefore proposed adding prescription-drug benefits to the established Medicare program. House Republicans were divided over the reform, however, with more conservative members troubled by the significant cost of the drug-benefit provision. This conservative opposition jeopardized the passage of the bill.

Republican leaders responded by using several tactics that eventually put the measure over the top by a single vote. National GOP leaders, including Vice President Cheney, intervened and lobbied for the bill. And congressional leaders tacked on provisions that were popular among some Republicans, including one to expand medical savings accounts and another to permit some importation of less-expensive drugs from Canada. Nevertheless, arm-twisting and favor trading would not be enough by themselves.

During the roll call on final passage, the Republican leadership was aware that they were short of votes. After the initial electronic vote tally suggested they would lose 214–218, GOP leaders responded by keeping the roll call open an additional 50 minutes (a typical roll call takes only 15 minutes to complete) until they could round up enough votes to secure passage. Eventually, one Republican was convinced to switch his "nay" vote to "present," while two others were pressured to switch their votes from "nay" to "yea." As a result, the Republicans eked out a 216–215 victory.[48] The Democrats cried foul, but the Republicans were the majority party and thus dictated how the rules would—or would not—be followed.[49]

In the summer of 2015, House Republican leaders used a similar tactic of holding open a late-night roll call longer than normal to secure enough votes to pass a reauthorization and overhaul of the No Child Left Behind Act. In this case, GOP leaders faced several defections by conservative members of the Freedom Caucus, and thus they needed extra time to twist the arms of a sufficient number of mainstream Republicans to produce a narrow victory.[50]

ENFORCING PARTY DISCIPLINE Party leaders have a variety of means to punish members who do not toe the line on important party matters and reward members who do. These means are often called carrots and sticks. A *carrot* is an incentive to support the party leadership. Carrots may be the promise of a good committee assignment or the increased likelihood of a bill important to a member's constituency being considered on the floor. A *stick* is just the opposite; it is the threat of something unpleasant. For example, an important committee assignment might be withheld, or a bill important to a member's constituency will not be pursued. Leaders recognize that such carrots and sticks are not limitless, and thus they use them sparingly and strategically, where they might have the greatest effect for the party.

Recently, majority party leadership has made use of sticks on what it considered to be litmus-test votes (such as a vote to support the party's speakership nominee) as well as less-visible actions. For instance, lawmakers who are part of their caucus's whip system have traditionally been required to support the party's position on important procedural votes. In June 2015, as GOP leaders sought to clear the way for a major international trade deal involving many Pacific Rim nations, a small band of Republicans in the House defected on a vote that would grant President Obama "fast-track" authority to negotiate the deal. Such authority would have prohibited Congress from amending the deal and thus lawmakers would have to either approve or reject it in its entirety. Among the defectors on this procedural vote were three members of the Republican whip system. Within days of their insurrection, Speaker Boehner announced that all three were relieved of their posts as deputy whips.[51]

Sticks also extend into the realm of direct electoral support. Recently, Rep. David Jolly (R-FL) drew the ire of Republican leaders, especially the NRCC. In 2014, Jolly won a special election for his Florida congressional district, thanks in part to $2.5 million raised on his behalf by the NRCC. Once reelected to his first full term in office, Jolly criticized the NRCC for requiring him (and other GOP lawmakers) to spend considerable time each day fundraising, and he sought to introduce legislation that would prevent members from directly soliciting campaign donations. In addition, Jolly worked with CBS (through its *60 Minutes* television news show) to sneak a hidden camera into the party's "call center" near the Capitol where members "dial for dollars."[52] The NRCC felt that Jolly, by attempting to position himself as a reformer in order to run for a Senate seat, was being actively disloyal to the party. As a result, when Jolly later reconsidered his Senate run and decided instead to seek reelection to the House, the NRCC struck back, refusing to pledge any further financial support and thus leaving him to twist in the wind.[53] Jolly would go on to lose a close election in 2016 to Democratic candidate (and former Florida governor) Charlie Crist.

TWO THEORIES OF PARTY INFLUENCE

Any theoretical understanding of political parties in Congress is built on the premise that lawmakers who share a partisan label also share a common electoral fate. That is, citizens with limited information about candidates—and limited time to invest in the political process—will often rely on simple cues (or "shortcuts") to arrive at a voting choice. One typical cue is partisan affiliation, which provides voters with quick hints about candidates' positions on the major issues of the day.

Party affiliation serves as an effective voting cue only if parties possess a significant degree of internal cohesion such that voters can easily associate parties with clear ideological positions. Therefore, a party's reputation, or brand, is a critical asset that must be built around perceived accomplishments and ideological unity.

One way to examine shared electoral fate is to focus on the majority party in Congress. For example, one study found that voters who approve of Congress's overall job performance are more likely to vote for majority party congressional candidates. This effect held regardless of which party controlled the presidency (that is, whether government was unified or divided) or how voters viewed the president. Conversely, voters who disapprove of Congress are less likely to vote for majority party congressional candidates.[54] Table 6.3 demonstrates this relationship by looking at the effect that general approval of Congress has on the collective electoral fate of the majority party in the House. Looking only at midterm elections, and thus removing any coattails effects that might occur with presidential candidates on the ballot, we see that in periods of particularly low approval for Congress, the majority party in the House suffers greater seat losses, which can sometimes translate into losing majority status.

TABLE 6.3   Congressional Approval Ratings and President's Party Seat Changes, 1974–2014

Year	President	House Majority	% Approve of Congress	Seat Gain/Loss in House for President's Party
2014	Democrat	Republican	20	−13
2010	Democrat	Democrat	21	−63
2006	Republican	Republican	26	−30
2002	Republican	Republican	50	+6
1998	Democrat	Republican	44	+5
1994	Democrat	Democrat	23	−53
1990	Republican	Democrat	26	−8
1986	Republican	Democrat	42	−5
1982	Republican	Democrat	29	−28
1978	Democrat	Democrat	29	−11
1974	Republican	Democrat	35	−43

Jeffrey M. Jones. August 12, 2014. "Congressional Job Approval Stays Near Historical Low." Gallup Poll, http://news.gallup.com/poll/174806/congressional-job-approval-stays-near-historical-low.aspx (accessed 5/21/18).

Once grounded in a foundation of shared electoral fate, party-based theories of Congress take two forms: (1) conditional party government theory and (2) party cartel theory.

Conditional Party Government Theory

Conditional party government (CPG) theory, most closely linked to research by political scientists John Aldrich and David Rohde, holds that party power waxes and wanes based on the existence of certain conditions.[55] That is, the majority party does not always behave as an organizing mechanism in Congress, but it is more likely to do so when (1) lawmakers from the majority party share the same ideological and policy goals, and (2) there is a wide gulf in the policy perspectives between the members of the majority party and the minority party. CPG advocates, therefore, believe that only at certain times are the parties so neatly divided that they will clearly seek different policies, and that the majority party will stake its electoral reputation on its unified agenda and governing ability.

When these primary conditions are met, members of the majority party will entrust their leadership with greater organizational authority and agenda-setting powers to help overcome the coordination problems inherent in a large and complex legislature. Under CPG, the goal is to exercise *positive agenda control*—that is, to get a bill onto the agenda, through the legislative process, and enacted into law.

The 111th Congress (2009–11), which was President Obama's first Congress after his initial election in 2008, represents a good example of CPG in operation. The Democrats controlled both chambers of Congress and the presidency; congressional Democrats were quite homogeneous in their policy preferences, and the Democrats controlled 60 seats in the Senate (until Senator Kennedy's death in August 2009), which provided them—if they voted as a bloc—with the ability to forestall any Republican attempts to filibuster. This constellation of factors allowed the Democrats to design an ambitious policy agenda and enact an assortment of landmark laws, such as the American Recovery and Reinvestment Act (an important economic stimulus package in the wake of the Great Recession), the Credit Card Accountability and Responsibility Disclosure Act (which provided consumers with a "credit card bill of rights"), the Matthew Shepard and James Byrd Jr. Hate Crimes Prevention Act (which expanded the definition of federal hate crimes to cover attacks based on gender, sexual orientation, and disability), and the Affordable Care Act.

By comparison, the 96th Congress (1979–81), which was President Jimmy Carter's second Congress, is a good example of CPG not being in operation. And this situation prevailed despite factors that were similar to President Obama's situation in the 111th Congress: the Democrats controlled both chambers of Congress and the presidency, and Democratic majorities in both the House and Senate were quite large. The Democrats in the 96th Congress, however, were not very homogeneous, with conservative and liberal factions often disagreeing on policy. And President Carter did not have a good working relationship with congressional leaders. Thus considerably fewer landmark laws were enacted.

Party Cartel Theory

Party cartel theory, which was developed by political scientists Gary Cox and Mathew McCubbins, offers a competing view of parties that differs from CPG in two ways.[56] First, while CPG theory is predicated on majority party power being conditional (that is, only achievable under certain circumstances), party cartel theory assumes that the majority party can control the agenda *unconditionally*, no matter the size or composition of the majority. Party cartel theory is based on the premise that majority party leaders in the House—that is, the

Speaker, the committee chairs, and the Rules Committee—act as a procedural team. Like a cartel in economics (a collection of businesses or countries that act together to influence the price of certain goods and services by controlling production and marketing), the majority party cartel in the House uses its procedural influence to set the legislative agenda for the benefit of majority party members (rather than the full membership). Setting the agenda, in this case, means screening out legislation that would adversely affect the majority party. That is, cartel leaders block bills from reaching the floor of the chamber that would, if passed, be opposed by a majority of majority party members. This *negative agenda control* represents the second way that party cartel theory differs from CPG theory: where CPG is about enhancing the party brand by pushing majority-preferred bills onto the agenda and enacting them into law, party cartel theory is about protecting the party brand by weeding out bills that divide the majority and thus keeping existing laws in place.

How might the screening-out process in party cartel theory work? There are several possibilities. The Speaker, for example, might use her power of recognition to avoid calling on members who she believes would offer motions or

House Speaker from 1999 to 2007, Dennis Hastert (R-IL) was famous for his informal rule that he would not bring any bill to the floor that was not favored by a majority of Republican House members. This "rule" was used by Speakers from both parties before and after Hastert's speakership.

amendments that would divide the majority. Committee chairs could use their intracommittee scheduling powers to bury legislation that would harm the majority. The Rules Committee could refuse to provide a rule to a bill that would run counter to the majority's interests. If these party actors are working in concert, then there are multiple barriers in place to protect the majority. If one barrier fails, other barriers pick up the slack.

In the contemporary era, this screening-out process has been embodied in the *Hastert Rule*, a principle of behavior named after former Speaker Dennis Hastert (R-IL). In 2003, Hastert remarked, "The job of the Speaker is not to expedite legislation that runs counter to the wishes of the majority of his majority. . . . I do not feel comfortable scheduling any controversial legislation unless I know we have the votes on our side first." There is considerable evidence that Gingrich, Hastert's predecessor in the Speaker's chair, also held fast to the same rule.[57]

From the perspective of party leaders, negative agenda control is critical for party success. If legislation that divides the party gets to the floor and passes, this will negatively affect voters' perceptions of the party as well as the majority party's ability to govern. It will also erode the informational value of the partisan label by confusing voters about what the party stands for. Both of these effects will damage the overall party brand.

HOW WE STUDY
NEGATIVE AGENDA CONTROL

What evidence can we find to assess whether the majority party exercises negative agenda control by removing items from the agenda that would pass over the opposition of a majority of the majority? In other words, can we measure how successfully the majority party controls the legislative agenda? In effect, we are looking for "the dog that didn't bark," an event that would have occurred if not for the majority party's ability to control the bills that progress through Congress.

Cox and McCubbins have argued that if the majority party is effective at exercising negative agenda control by virtue of its control of positions of power, then we should rarely observe instances in which the majority party is "rolled"—that is, where a majority of the majority party opposes a bill on the floor but the bill nonetheless passes. In addition, we should regularly observe instances in which the minority party is rolled, or a majority of the *minority* party opposing a bill on the floor but the bill nonetheless passing. This is because the minority party does not control positions of power (the speakership, the Rules Committee, and committee chairs) that can be used to block items from getting onto the agenda. Thus the minority party should be rolled considerably more often than the majority party.

To gather evidence for their conjectures, Cox and McCubbins examined final-passage votes in the House of Representatives across time. For each Congress, they calculated "roll rates" for the majority and minority parties. A roll rate is effectively a percentage that answers the question, How often did a majority of a given party vote to oppose a bill that ultimately went on to pass, relative to all final-passage votes? So, for example, if there were 125 final-passage votes in a given Congress, and in 25 of those cases, a majority of the party opposed the bill but it passed anyway, then the party's roll rate would be 20 percent.

Do the data support party cartel theory? Does the majority party really have a negative agenda control advantage? Figure 6.1 plots majority and minority party roll rates from the 45th through 112th Congresses. The evidence is striking, and it validates Cox and McCubbins's conjectures. Over the entire data series, the majority party was rolled on only 2.3 percent of final-passage votes. This compares to 32 percent for the minority party. Examined from a different perspective, the majority party is rolled, on average, once every 43 votes. By

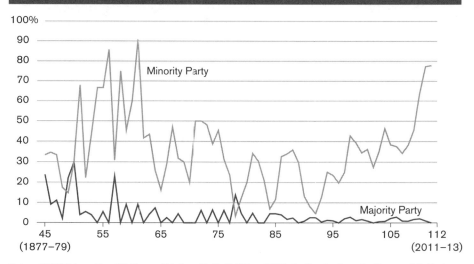

FIGURE 6.1 Party Roll Rates in the House of Representatives, 45th–112th Congress (1877–2013)

Data until 2005 from Gary W. Cox and Mathew D. McCubbins. 2005. *Setting the Agenda: Responsible Party Government in the U.S. House of Representatives*. Cambridge: Cambridge University Press. Data after 2005 was compiled by the authors.

comparison, the minority party is rolled, on average, once every three votes. Thus the incidence of final-passage votes that pass over the objections of the two parties is not random; the majority party is clearly in a superior position vis-à-vis being rolled. These results are consistent with the majority party operating like a cartel and setting the agenda to benefit the majority at the expense of the minority.

What about the Senate? While Cox and McCubbins developed party cartel theory with the U.S. House in mind, we can conduct a similar roll rate analysis on final-passage votes in the Senate. The expectation is that majority party influence should be weaker in the Senate because the House's institutional mechanisms for exercising negative agenda control are not present. Specifically, there is no Speaker, there is no Rules Committee, and committee chairs have less ability to prevent bills from receiving floor consideration. As a result, the minority party in the Senate should be less disadvantaged than the minority party in the House. Figure 6.2 confirms these expectations. The majority party roll rate in the Senate for the same set of Congresses is 3.6 percent. That number is low, but it is also more than 56 percent larger than in the House. Similarly, the minority party roll rate is lower in the Senate. The rate is 19.5 percent, which is 39 percent lower than in the House. Together, these results suggest that the majority party has a negative-agenda-setting advantage in the Senate, but a weaker one than in the House. *How*

FIGURE 6.2   Party Roll Rates in the Senate, 45th–112th Congress (1877–2013)

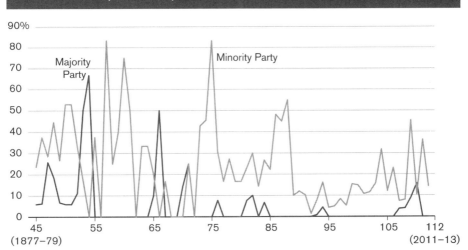

Data until 2005 from Gary W. Cox and Mathew D. McCubbins. 2005. *Setting the Agenda: Responsible Party Government in the U.S. House of Representatives.* Cambridge: Cambridge University Press. Data after 2005 was compiled by the authors.

the majority party in the Senate exercises such an advantage without the benefit of obvious institutional mechanisms to screen out bills is the subject of ongoing research in political science.

Critical Thinking

1. Are roll rates a good measure for empirically validating the party cartel theory? Why or why not?
2. While majority party roll rates in the House show little variation across time (they are always quite low), minority party roll rates fluctuate considerably. What factors might explain these fluctuations? Why would minority party roll rates sometimes be higher or lower?
3. Majority party roll rates are higher in the Senate than in the House, but they are still quite low overall—and much lower than minority party roll rates in the Senate. And yet the Senate lacks the institutional mechanisms that scholars believe are important in controlling the legislative agenda and protecting majority party interests. What, then, explains the low majority party roll rates in the Senate?

PARTY INFLUENCE VERSUS INDIVIDUAL PREFERENCES

While political scientists and pundits often point to the critical role that parties play in contemporary congressional politics, not everyone believes that parties significantly affect legislative organization and decision making. One critique of the "strong parties" perspectives, often associated with the work of political scientist Keith Krehbiel, holds that lawmakers' choices are based on their ideological preferences.[58] Put simply, Krehbiel argues that when we observe Democrats and Republicans being quite unified in their voting behavior in Congress, their votes may not be the result of party leaders pressuring them to toe the party line. Rather, lawmakers, like voters, could simply have, over time, sorted themselves better along ideological lines, with conservatives taking on the Republican label and liberals taking on the Democratic label. Thus when we observe Republicans and Democrats dividing neatly into "yea" and "nay" groups on a roll call vote, it could be that their ideological preferences are determining their vote choices, with party playing no independent role.

History provides some context. From the middle of the twentieth century through the 1970s, there was considerable overlap in the preferences of the two parties. While the Democrats were mostly a liberal party, and the Republicans were mostly a conservative party, members from the opposite ideological persuasion were also present in each party. Southern Democrats were very conservative—and made up a sizable portion of the caucus—and many northeastern Republicans were liberal. Beginning in the 1980s, the "big tent" nature of each party started to disappear as voters began to elect only Republicans from the conservative end of the spectrum and Democrats from the liberal end. During the 1980s, we also began to see an increase in partisan voting in Congress and the gradual emergence of gridlock on some important issues. Partisan voting and gridlock ramped up considerably in the mid-1990s with the Republicans' return to majority status in Congress, and reached even greater heights in the twenty-first century, first with the George W. Bush administration, and then with the Obama administration, and now with the Trump administration.

Because of the simultaneous sorting of Democrats and Republicans into homogeneous liberal and conservative groups, respectively, it becomes difficult to disentangle the source of the polarized voting behavior that we observe in Congress. Is it being driven mostly by party leaders' influence and organizational decisions? Or is it occurring naturally because members simply have very divergent policy preferences? Either view could be correct, and simply examining how Democrats and Republicans vote will not provide an answer.[59] And while there is anecdotal evidence of party being influential in Congress—like when party leaders hold open votes until they can pressure enough members at the margins to achieve the outcome that they want—more systematic evidence of party influence is considerably harder to come by.

The "parties or preferences" conundrum created a research agenda that spanned two decades. Political scientists designed creative analyses to separate party-based influence from preference-based influence. Examples included finding separate ways to measure members' preferences that did not rely on roll call votes, comparing how members voted in legislatures with and without parties, and looking for party influence on votes where pressure should be applied (votes where outcomes were close) versus where it shouldn't (votes where outcomes were lopsided).[60] None of these examples by themselves validated the independent effect of party influence, but together, they built an empirical case for party playing an independent role in structuring voting and organization in Congress. In short, scholars today believe that preferences definitely matter in how lawmakers behave in Congress. But most scholars also believe, based on a wide variety of evidence, that party influence also matters.

WHEN PARTY INFLUENCE BREAKS DOWN

While scholars debate whether party influence might be conditional (CPG) or unconditional (cartel), or how much influence parties actually have (Krehbiel and his critics), we can point to several cases where party influence clearly breaks down, either because a cross-party coalition emerges to compete for influence or because the internal homogeneity within the governing party disintegrates.

The Conservative Coalition

A good historical example of ideologically driven (as opposed to party-driven) influence is the "conservative coalition," which was a significant force in Congress from the late 1930s through the early 1980s. The conservative coalition was an alliance of southern Democrats and Republicans that formed as a reaction to Franklin Roosevelt's (and northern Democrats') attempt to expand New Deal policies, especially in the area of labor. After World War II, the coalition expanded its purview to resist the federal expansion of social-welfare programs more generally. Eventually, by the 1950s, the cross-party conservative alliance crept into matters of foreign policy and civil liberties.[61] By the early 1960s, the conservative coalition was a major influence in congressional lawmaking. In terms of measurement, a conservative coalition vote was one in which a majority of southern Democrats and a majority of Republicans opposed a majority of northern Democrats. As Figure 6.3 indicates, in some Congresses during the 1960s and into the 1970s, the conservative coalition was active on around a third of all roll call votes.[62]

Scholars disagree whether the conservative coalition simply acted as a voting bloc on the floor or was organized around a procedural agenda and thus operated as a different kind of cartel.[63] Regardless, the conservative coalition was powerful at midcentury and put its stamp on congressional policy making. Its ultimate influence was more negative than positive, blocking policy change that liberal northern Democrats sought rather than enacting new conservative policy.[64]

With the passage of the Voting Rights Act of 1965, the conservative coalition's reign began to crumble. As African Americans in the South were given voting rights and protections, the nature of party politics began to change. Liberal Democrats began having success in southern elections. To survive in the new political environment, conservative white Democrats either moderated their behavior or joined the emerging Republican Party in the South. By the mid-1980s, the realignment of the South had significantly played out: southern Democrats looked considerably more like northern Democrats, and a conservative Republican Party was now a force to be reckoned with. As a result, the split in the Democratic Party, brought about by the rise of the conservative coalition, had effectively ended.

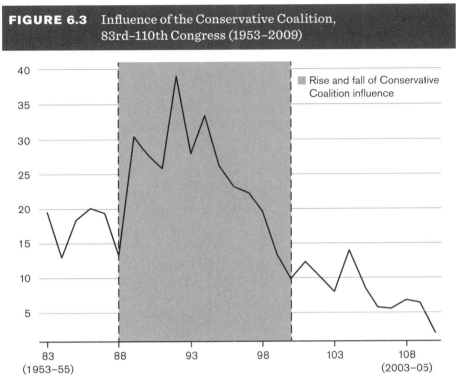

FIGURE 6.3   Influence of the Conservative Coalition, 83rd–110th Congress (1953–2009)

■ Rise and fall of Conservative Coalition influence

John Wilkerson and Barry Pump. 2011. "The Ties That Bind: Coalitions in Congress," in *The Oxford Handbook of the American Congress*, ed. by Eric Schickler and Frances Lee, 625. Oxford: Oxford University Press.

Divisions within the Republican Party: The Rise of the Tea Party

The contemporary Republican Party in Congress has experienced its own internal divisions over the last decade. Starting in the late 2000s, a segment of the Republican Party began to emerge that was particularly hostile toward increased government intervention in the economy; this emergence coincided with the financial crisis that resulted in the bailout programs for Wall Street, the housing market, and the auto industry (General Motors and Chrysler). This new wing of the Republican Party—voters and subsequently lawmakers—eventually coalesced into the "Tea Party" movement in 2009, largely in reaction first to the Obama administration's stimulus package during the recession and then to the enactment of Obamacare.[65]

The effect of this anti-establishment movement among Republican voters is present both at an electoral level and an institutional level. That is, it affects who wins elections and how Congress operates. On the electoral front, the issue involves primary challenges, or how the threat of a potentially more conservative challenger to Republican incumbents is influencing their behavior. While the rate of incumbent challenges in recent election cycles is somewhat higher in the Republican Party than in the Democratic Party, the overall rate has not changed significantly over time. What is different is the basis of the challenges—more are ideologically motivated. The 2010 through 2014 election cycles saw the most ideologically driven challenges of any election cycle since the early 1970s, and all these challenges were in the Republican Party.[66] Many of these primary challenges captured the attention of voters because they occurred during a period of little campaign activity and news, usually during the summer months, and some included high-profile candidates. Perhaps the most prominent of these challenges led to the 2014 ouster of House Majority Leader Cantor (R-VA), who lost his primary reelection to David Brat, a little-known and underfunded college professor who was backed by Tea Party organizations (see Chapter 4).[67]

The Tea Party movement took hold within Congress following the 2010 election when about 40 lawmakers, elected with the support of various Tea Party–affiliated groups, organized into a caucus in the House under the leadership of Michele Bachmann (R-MN). They opposed what they viewed as a bloated federal budget and were unwilling to increase statutory limits on the federal debt.[68] Their intransigence, along with a growing fear by more mainstream Republicans that they could face their own Tea Party challenge at home, resulted in several near misses on government shutdowns and federal government defaults. Eventually, in 2013, conservative Republicans, led by Tea Party–affiliated lawmakers, prevented a stopgap funding measure from passing Congress, in the hopes of defunding aspects of Obamacare. The two-week government shutdown also began to push dangerously close to another contentious increase in the federal debt limit. Eventually, GOP House leaders were forced to agree to a Senate-negotiated agreement that made almost no concessions to Tea Party demands. The agreement, like several other major last-minute deals Speaker Boehner was forced to make during his tenure, was passed by a majority of Democrats (in this instance, the entire Democratic Caucus) and a minority of Republican lawmakers (87 of 231) in the House.

After the 2014 election, in which the Republicans won majority control of the Senate, the splinter movement within the GOP reached a fever pitch. In the House, a new Tea Party–inspired caucus formed, the Freedom Caucus. Its goal was to coordinate lawmaking activities and pressure leadership to enact a more conservative agenda. The Freedom Caucus led a serious, but ultimately unsuccessful, insurgency against Boehner's speakership election at the start of the term. In response, Boehner immediately removed two of the rebel leaders from their plum positions on the Rules Committee. Later in 2015, Boehner pressured House Government Reform Chairman Jason Chaffetz (R-UT) to remove Mark

Attempts to unseat a sitting Speaker—like Mark Meadows's (R-NC) effort to replace John Boehner (R-OH)—are rare and always unsuccessful, but they reflect the often intense disagreements between factions within a party.

Meadows (a Freedom Caucus member) as a subcommittee chair after Meadows refused to support Boehner on an important procedural vote. Chaffetz, however, faced fierce opposition from Freedom Caucus members on the committee and ultimately allowed Meadows to keep his leadership post.[69] Later, emboldened by his victory, Meadows filed a petition to vacate the speakership—a move seen as a direct affront to Boehner's leadership. As a key budget deadline loomed in the fall of 2015—regarding funding to prevent another federal government shutdown, with Freedom Caucus members refusing to accede without a cut in funding to Planned Parenthood—Speaker Boehner decided that he'd had enough and announced his resignation. Freedom Caucus relations with Boehner's successor, House Speaker Ryan (R-WI), were better, though ideological tensions within the Republican Party were still high.

THEN AND NOW
PARTISAN POLARIZATION

In any discussion of the contemporary Congress, the term "polarization" immediately comes to mind, but the concept is more complicated than it first appears. Perhaps the best way to conceive of polarization is to think of Democratic and

Republican lawmakers distributed from left to right along a line, in keeping with the spatial model that we introduced in Chapter 2. Party polarization occurs when (a) parties are more internally cohesive on policy matters, and (b) each party's preferred policies are further and further apart.[70]

To measure polarization, which is fundamentally about the degree of ideological division between the parties, we must first measure the policy preferences of members of Congress so that we can compare the preferences of Democrats to those of Republicans. Where can we obtain such preference measures both across chambers and across time?

One option would be to have survey responses by members of Congress on a battery of questions, which can then be transformed into measures of preference. The problem is that such surveys exist only for the most recent Congresses, and even within such surveys, the number and types of questions to which members respond vary considerably.

Another option—the one that most scholars of Congress adopt—is to use NOMINATE scores, which we introduced in Chapter 2.[71] Developed by political scientists Keith Poole and Howard Rosenthal, NOMINATE scores are often considered measures of "revealed preference" because they are created from members' votes on roll calls. NOMINATE scores exist across chambers and across time (because roll calls are used in both the House and Senate, and have been used in every Congress back to the First Federal Congress), and thanks to innovations in the NOMINATE estimation procedure, scores can be compared by chamber across time. However, NOMINATE scores rely on the agenda items underlying the roll calls, which may not be a representative sample of the issues that are important (in a broader public sense) at a given point in time. For example, the majority party might set the agenda in such a way—by blocking some issues while allowing others—to make divisions between the parties appear to be more extreme than they really are. Nonetheless, NOMINATE scores represent the best method scholars have devised (so far) to compare the ideological positions of lawmakers across chambers and across time.

To assess the positions of the Democrats and Republicans in each chamber, Poole and Rosenthal calculate the mean (average) NOMINATE score for the total membership of each party. They consider the mean score to be a good measure of the "central tendency" of each party. Figure 6.4 provides a time series of the House and Senate Democratic and Republican means on the NOMINATE scale from 1879 until 2017. The first thing to note is the change in the average position of the two parties over time. While there has certainly been some variation in the average ideological position of House Democrats and Republicans, the distance between the two parties is what stands out. In recent years, there has been a wide gap between the average Democratic and Republican positions.

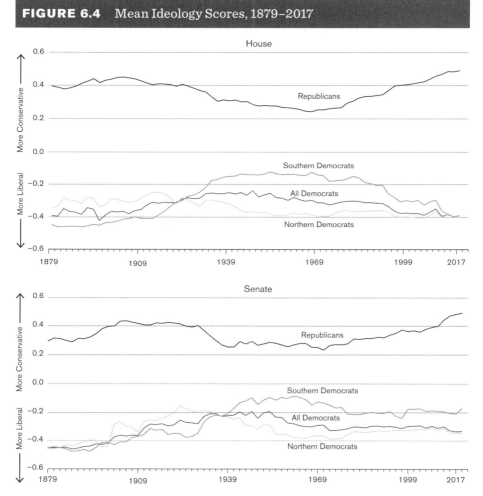

FIGURE 6.4   Mean Ideology Scores, 1879–2017

Jeff Lewis. March 11, 2018. "Party Means on the Liberal-Conservative dimensions over Time by Chamber." Voteview, voteview.com/articles/party_polarization (accessed 5/21/18).

That gap is similar to the division that existed between the parties in the late nineteenth and early twentieth centuries.

Interestingly, if we examine the middle of the twentieth century, from about the mid-1930s to the late 1960s, we see that the distance between the parties is not nearly as wide. To better understand this narrower gap, note that the Democrats who most closely align with Republicans in this period are from the South (mainly from the former Confederate states). This was a period of deep division within the Democratic Party, when southern Democrats and Republicans often voted together as a conservative coalition to limit liberal initiatives.[72] In the years following the re-enfranchisement of African American voters in the South via the Voting Rights Act of 1965, the policy positions of the two groups diverged. Over time, as the NOMINATE scores demonstrate, the ideological position of southern Democrats began to look more like the rest of the Democratic Party.

Poole and Rosenthal provide a direct measure of polarization by calculating the distance between the average Democrat and the average Republican. Figure 6.5 plots this distance for the 1879–2017 period, illustrating that the ideological division in both the House and Senate is wider now than it has been at any point in the last century and a half.

What explains this increasing polarization?[73] Rather than identify a single cause, scholars have suggested many contributing factors, both external (electoral driven) and internal (agenda related). Externally, in the decades following the passage of the Voting Rights Act in 1965, partisan realignment in the South meant that areas that had traditionally elected conservative Democrats were increasingly electing Republicans. Similarly, voters in the South and elsewhere were sorting themselves ideologically into more consistent party affiliation. More than ever before, conservatives are likely to identify as Republicans and liberals as Democrats. To some degree, this trend has also occurred geographically, as there is some evidence that citizens more frequently migrate to places where the dominant political views match their own. The result is that lawmakers more often represent homogeneous constituencies, with little pressure to demonstrate bipartisan policy views or behavior.

Two changes in the internal workings of Congress have also highlighted the differences between Democrats and Republicans. The first is a shift in the types of policies that Congress addresses. Specifically, Congress has focused more on economic issues than in the past, and these issues are more divided along partisan lines than many other issues, including more traditional moral issues. The second internal factor involves process. Congress must take votes on matters of organization and procedure to move legislative matters forward, and the number of such votes has increased substantially in recent decades. Procedural votes are more divisive on a partisan level for two related reasons: (1) They are more disconnected from policy content and thus harder for constituents to observe and understand, and (2) at the same time, party leaders, particularly in the majority party, see these procedural votes as vital to ensuring the smooth operation of the chamber and thus hold their members to vote the party line. Defections are often not tolerated.

Finally, it is worth noting that some scholars attribute increased partisanship to the choices made by party leadership. For example, Laurel Harbridge finds that Democratic and Republican leaders choose to highlight (and vote on) issues that are particularly divisive. Moreover, focusing on roll call votes emphasizes

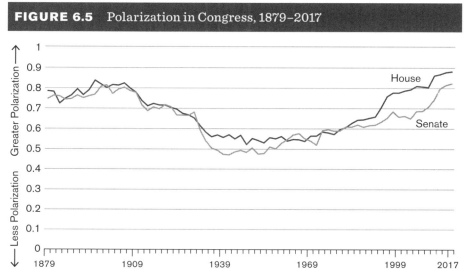

FIGURE 6.5 Polarization in Congress, 1879–2017

Jeff Lewis. March 11, 2018. "Party Means on the Liberal-Conservative Dimensions over Time by Chamber, Distance between Party Means." Voteview, voteview.com/articles/party_polarization (accessed 5/21/18).

these divisions. When Harbridge looks at the cosponsorship of bills, which takes place before party leaders set the agenda, she finds much less evidence of recent polarization.[74]

Critical Thinking

1. What are some pros and cons associated with using NOMINATE scores to measure polarization in Congress?
2. It has been suggested that polarization in Congress is increasingly driven by Republicans becoming more conservative. Do you think this trend will continue? Will Democrats become increasingly more liberal in the future? Why or why not?
3. During the 1980s and into the 1990s, based on NOMINATE scores, the House and Senate were about equally polarized. Over the last 25 years, the House has become considerably more polarized than the Senate. Why do you think this is so?

CONCLUSION

The standard scholarly perspective on how Congress operates has long placed parties in a highly privileged position. For the last several decades, political scientists have considered parties to be the chief analytic units for understanding how the legislative agenda is structured and policy change is produced in Congress. Whereas committees were once seen as the key lawmaking institution in Congress, parties have since commandeered that role. In recent decades, majority party priorities have largely defined the legislative agenda, and party leadership, for the most part, has designed the laws that are produced. Moreover, the majority party in each chamber, regardless of the partisan control across the Capitol or in the White House, has worked to ensure that budgeting is completed in a timely fashion and that vital government programs are reauthorized and updated.

While many elements of this perspective remain true today—the majority party clearly still dominates the legislative agenda, policy change still disproportionately benefits members of the majority, and partisan polarization still remains at an all-time high—we believe a process of change is underway. A growing number of lawmakers are less attached to traditional notions of what a party in Congress means and the responsibility that the majority has in ensuring that the institution fulfills its traditional governing duties.

Longtime observers of congressional affairs, Thomas Mann (of the left-of-center Brookings Institution) and Norman Ornstein (of the right-of-center American Enterprise Institute) assert that fundamental alterations in partisanship and growing polarization in recent years have been driven primarily by the Republican Party. As moderate members in each party began to disappear in the 1970s and 1980s, the Republicans became more extreme. (Recall Figure 6.4, which shows that the ideological shift as measured by NOMINATE scores is twice as large among Republicans as it is among Democrats.) This disproportionate shift by the Republicans was not just a function of changing policy preferences; it also involved changing tactics. Mann and Ornstein contend that the GOP has developed an ideologically based platform, and it has become scornful of compromise or legitimization of the political opposition.[75]

From the perspective of representation, the most conservative of the GOP conference, like those in the House who are affiliated with the Freedom Caucus, believe they are acting as faithful agents. They feel that their constituents want something different than the traditional notion of what it means to govern—they want government to do less, be smaller, and refrain from unnecessary intervention in many aspects of their lives. Freedom Caucus members are thus working to represent those smaller government interests by opposing the typical governing activities that scholars associate with legislative effectiveness.

This less traditional philosophy of representation has had implications for the Republican Party as a governing coalition. The independence of the Freedom Caucus made it difficult for the Republican majority to ensure that budgets are completed on time and that expiring programs are reauthorized. House Speaker Boehner, for example, found it difficult to build the necessary coalition for such critical votes as raising the debt ceiling and providing aid for victims of Hurricane Sandy. He had to build a cross-party coalition with Democrats on many of these high-profile votes to ensure their passage. These moves were strategic compromises during a period of divided government, but they incensed those Republicans who favored an oppositional posture toward the Democratic Obama administration. Eventually, Boehner's decisions to govern—in the traditional sense—led members of the Freedom Caucus to attempt to remove him from the speakership. Rather than allow a civil war to break out in the party, Boehner chose to resign as Speaker.

On the Senate side, Majority Leader McConnell (R-KY) presided over a more fluid and open lawmaking environment, but he too was compelled to collaborate with the Democrats to enact several important measures. His efforts in this regard exposed him to attacks from his right flank, led by Senator Ted Cruz (R-TX) and others. As a result, McConnell sometimes had to give in to their demands and schedule votes on conservative priorities (such as defunding Planned Parenthood), rather than continue to risk the far right's ire.

It is unclear whether such difficulties in governing by the parties will persist into the future. Pressures still exist on moderate and even establishment conservatives in the Republican Party, who continually face the threat of primary challenges from candidates aligned with the Tea Party/Freedom Caucus movement. Yet when extreme conservatives become lawmakers and prioritize independence over governing responsibilities, constituents are often not forgiving. In 2016, Freedom Caucus leader Tim Huelskamp (R-KS) lost in the GOP primary mainly because his resistance to traditional governing obligations prevented him from adequately representing the farming interests in his rural Kansas district. For example, he voted against reauthorization of the massive package of farm programs through the USDA, and his Freedom Caucus activities cost him his seat on the Agriculture Committee.[76] Ultimately, we do not know yet whether Huelskamp is the rule or the exception. As we move forward through the Trump era, it is still an open question whether traditional notions of partisan governing will reestablish themselves or not.

Discussion Questions

1. If more major legislation is being developed largely (or wholly) by one political party because of the intense polarization in Washington, what are some

of the possible consequences? What are the pros and cons of this approach to lawmaking?

2. Many commentators bemoan the high partisan polarization in Congress. But is polarization necessarily a bad thing? Can polarization be viewed in a positive light? Discuss.

3. For a member of Congress, to what extent does being a good party member potentially conflict with being a good representative of one's district or state? Why and when will a member of Congress sometimes be torn between her constituency and her party? Explain.

4. Scholars often talk about party leaders in Congress using various carrots and sticks to keep party members in line. But, in recent years, the Republican Speaker of the House has had a difficult time controlling members of the Freedom Caucus. Why? What factors have allowed Freedom Caucus members to actively, and often successfully, oppose the GOP leadership?

5. In recent years, the filibuster has been weakened in the Senate; executive appointments are now entirely governed by simple majority vote. If the filibuster is eventually eliminated on policy measures, what do you think will be the impact? How will the kinds of policies that Congress produces change, if at all?

7

Policy Making

In recent years, immigration has been one of the most complicated and thorny issues that Congress has faced. At the forefront of that debate has been the difficult matter of what to do about the "DREAMers," those individuals brought to the United States as children yet have no legal status to reside here. These young people face severe obstacles getting a college education and finding meaningful employment. While they can obtain a free public education through high school, the federal government (through a 1996 statute) actively discourages states from granting such individuals postsecondary education benefits. In addition, undocumented immigrants are unable to work legally in the United States.

In 2010, Congress came close to adopting a major reform to the DREAMers' legal status. As the year wound down, lawmakers were in a frenzy to complete legislative work on Capitol Hill. The November election had dealt the Democrats a harsh blow; they had lost their majority control of the House, and they were facing significant seat losses in the Senate. Consequently, the Democrats worked hard to pass important legislation in the lame-duck session, before the new Congress started in January. Laws adopted during the lame-duck session included a repeal of the military's controversial "Don't Ask, Don't Tell" policy regarding gay people serving in the military and an extension of the tax cuts

In 2010, the unique processes of the House of Representatives and the Senate led to differing results on the passage of significant immigration reform. While immigration is a particularly divisive issue nationwide, the differences between how the House and Senate make policy ultimately led to the bill's demise.

enacted under the George W. Bush administration. Over a quarter of the total laws enacted during that two-year congressional term were passed during the brief lame-duck session.

The Development, Relief, and Education for Alien Minors (DREAM) Act was another important piece of legislation up for consideration during the lame-duck session. This was because Congress had failed to produce a comprehensive immigration overhaul prior to the November election. For many years, versions of the DREAM Act had been introduced, but none of them had progressed very far. Now, proponents of the DREAM Act wanted to capitalize on the confluence of friendly conditions in the lame-duck session (while the Democrats still held power) and get a law passed.

With the clock ticking, Democratic leadership in the House took up the legis-lation in mid-December in an extraordinary and unexpected manner. Rather than advancing an existing House bill, none of which had even been considered in committee, the Democrats used a number of long-held practices and powers of the majority party to advance a new Senate version of the legislation that had been written to please moderate lawmakers in both parties. First, the House Rules Committee offered a resolution to replace an existing unrelated bill that

237

was moving through both chambers with the text of the Senate's DREAM Act. The resolution, which restricted the length of debate and provided no opportunity for any floor amendments, passed 211–208, with no Republican support. In opposing the legislation, Robert Goodlatte (R-VA) complained that the bill had been brought to the chamber floor with only a single day's notice and no opportunity for committee consideration or floor changes.[1] Just a few hours after the resolution was adopted, the bill passed 216–198, with Democrats attracting the support of only eight Republicans.

In the Senate, the Democrats had a 58-member majority, and several Republicans had previously introduced or voiced support for similar legislation. However, it did not look like the bill would pass. This was because the Senate, in recent decades, had come to require a supermajority—three-fifths of the chamber, or 60 votes—to enact any legislation of note. Even though Democratic leaders had made changes to the legislation to attract GOP support—such as a surcharge to apply for legal status, significant background checks, and a lengthy (10-year) waiting period to qualify for a green card—in the end, the bill fell victim to Senate rules. On December 18, when Majority Leader Harry Reid (D-NV) sought to end debate and move to a final vote on the bill, the measure failed, 55–41. While Democratic leaders were able to get the support of moderate Republicans Richard Lugar (IN) and Lisa Murkowski (AK), they lost the votes of some Democrats, including Max Baucus (MT), Kay Hagan (NC), Ben Nelson (NE), Mark Pryor (AR), and Jon Tester (MT). The DREAM Act died in that final effort to close off debate because the majority fell short of the 60-vote standard.

A year and a half later, in June 2012, with no prospect of Congress adopting new immigration legislation, President Barack Obama instructed the Department of Homeland Security to defer action on any deportation of qualified individuals for two years (subject to renewal) and to allow such immigrants to apply for employment authorization. The program, Deferred Action on Childhood Arrivals (DACA), became a prominent topic in both congressional and presidential politics. Notably, President Trump announced he would end the program if Congress did not act to reform it and other immigration policies to which he was opposed. Later in this chapter, we discuss how DACA recurred as a major agenda item in 2018 as moderate House Republicans tried to use a rarely employed legislative maneuver to press the issue forward.

These recent actions on immigration illustrate the many challenges facing members of Congress as they try to move legislation forward (or attempt to block it). In this chapter we look more closely at how the legislative process works, and how differences in House and Senate procedures affect the behavior and outcomes of the two chambers.

THE HOUSE AND SENATE: TWO VERY DIFFERENT ANIMALS

There is perhaps no part of the legislative process where the House and Senate differ more than in their lawmaking practices (or floor procedures) after committees have considered bills. The House is viewed as a majoritarian body whose large membership reflects the populace that it represents. With such a diversity of interests, achieving a reasonable consensus in the House is more often than not the equivalent of herding cats and requires a tight set of rules to ensure decisiveness. On the other side of the Capitol, the Senate is considered to be the more deliberative body. Its debate and accommodation practices make outcomes less certain.

In explaining how floor procedure works, we will highlight the differences between the two chambers. Some of these factors seem straightforward but nonetheless have an enormous impact on how the House and Senate operate. For example, we will examine how the different constituencies of the House and Senate, the size of each chamber, the length of terms of representatives and senators, and the minimum age of representatives and senators all affect how policy making differs in the two chambers.

These contrasts are based on distinctive principles of operation, one majoritarian (the House) and the other more egalitarian and contemplative (the Senate). We will also focus on how lawmakers, particularly party leaders, have in recent years used the distinctive nature of each chamber to engage in more extreme partisanship.

We will also discuss how the House and Senate have operated in past eras and how those operations have changed in recent years. For example, what is sometimes called "regular order" barely exists, if it exists at all, in the contemporary Congress. Consequently, Congress today is less able to exercise its functions as a governing body and participate as a coequal with the president in the oversight of executive agencies.

To appreciate the differences between the House and the Senate, we will start from the ground up, examining how the Framers intended the two chambers to be different. The House and Senate have evolved in ways that amplify those original differences. Then we will examine contemporary political conditions, particularly partisan polarization and what it means for the operations of the modern House and Senate.

The Roots of House and Senate Floor Procedure

In Article 1, Section 5, of the Constitution, the Framers gave each chamber the responsibility for designing its own internal rules and procedures: "Each House may determine the Rules of its Proceedings." The members of each chamber were left to decide how they would represent their various constituencies and govern the rapidly growing nation. Each chamber's ability to create its own set of rules might have resulted over time in two different groups of representatives developing quite different procedures. But the Framers did far more than just give the two chambers free rein over their internal organization. The Constitution provides different conceptualizations about these institutions that have shaped and influenced the differences in their operations.

The distinction was intentional according to James Madison: "[A]s the improbability of sinister combinations will be in proportion to the dissimilarity in the genius of the two bodies, it must be politic to distinguish them from each other by every circumstance which will consist with a due harmony in all proper measures, and with the genuine principles of republican government."[2]

We focus here on four main ways in which the constitutional design of the two chambers fundamentally affects and differentiates their operations: constituencies, size, length of service, and age. (See Chapters 1 and 2 for more detailed discussion of the origins of congressional design.)

CONSTITUENCIES   A central compromise that enabled the creation and adoption of the Constitution was the acceptance that one body—the House—would be determined by the size of the populace in the various states, while the other body would provide for equal representation of the states themselves. Popular election of representatives in the House meant close ties to the changing political winds within home constituencies. At the same time, the Framers gave state legislatures the power to select senators, thereby making senators beholden to another political body. (The Framers understood that the states would have to ratify the newly written Constitution, and it was likely that state legislators would be influential in, perhaps even critical to, that process.)

The Framers' goal was to remove popular pressure from the Senate's day-to-day operations and allow it to focus on lawmaking. While selection by state legislatures seemed like a good way to ensure state representation, a variety of problems emerged. Over the course of the nineteenth century, a number of state legislatures deadlocked in their selection process, resulting in no senator being sent to Washington. In fact, at one point, Delaware had so much trouble settling on a senator that it had no representation in the Senate for two years. Bribery and political corruption also found their way into the selection process, so that by the early part of the twentieth century, many states had already moved to a state referendum for selection of senators.

Even with the change to popular election of senators with the Seventeenth Amendment (added to the Constitution in 1913), the constituencies of the two chambers remained quite different. While senators no longer directly represented state legislatures, their constituencies (states) were typically more diverse than those of House members (districts).

SIZE The starkest difference between the House and Senate is the size of their membership. The size of each chamber is a direct manifestation of its unique representational arrangements. The Framers decided that the House of Representatives—the "people's house"—would expand with population growth. Starting with the first Congress (1789–90), the House had 65 members, but that number rapidly grew. Just two terms later (1793–94), the House had 105 members, and by 1823, it had over 200. By the turn of the twentieth century, the House included 357 lawmakers, and it reached its current statutorily capped size—435 lawmakers—by 1913.

Given that the Framers intended the Senate to represent the states, it would be smaller, but exactly how small was unclear. During constitutional debates, some delegates argued that one senator was too few because the state might risk representation in the case of the senator's absence or illness. Alternatively, too many senators would eliminate the Senate's distinctiveness and might allow the senators to avoid taking responsibility for their decisions and actions.[3] Small states feared that some variation on proportional representation would result in their being swamped in a majority-rule institution, so ultimately the delegates chose two senators per state. Even as the nation grew, this choice meant that the Senate would remain a significantly smaller body than the House. The Senate started with 26 members in 1789, and it took until 1835 to grow to over 50 senators. By the turn of the century, the Senate was at 90 lawmakers, and it was not until Hawaii and Alaska joined the union in 1961 that the Senate achieved its current size of 100 members.

LENGTH OF SERVICE The Framers also differentiated the two chambers in terms of the members' length of service. In keeping with the notion that representatives should be closely tied to their home districts, delegate Roger Sherman stated during the Convention, "Representatives ought to return home and mix with the people."[4] Delegates were concerned that lawmakers who did not face regular elections would become detached from their constituents' needs. Although some delegates suggested a one-year election cycle—a relatively common period of tenure in state legislatures at the time—it was ultimately determined that two years between elections would allow members to familiarize themselves with their districts; it was also acknowledged that frequent travel home would be time consuming. In addition, as Sherman pointed out, the many complexities of federal policy versus the issues of single states warranted a longer tenure in the Senate.[5]

Moreover, the Framers saw the Senate as the body that would provide leadership, stability, and a measure of independence from popular opinion. Consequently, delegates supported both longer terms and staggered elections (separating senators into three distinct classes). In emulation of the upper houses of several state legislatures, many of which had five-year or longer terms, delegates chose six-year terms for senators. These longer terms would further allow for a continuous body split evenly among the classes. That continuity of the Senate over time, the Framers believed, could provide for leadership in times of crisis.[6]

AGE   Finally, the Framers considered the matter of age. Initially, 21 years old was proposed for House representatives, but delegates raised it to 25 in response to George Mason's assertion that persons in the position of representing a sizable number of others should have gone beyond managing their own affairs to managing the "affairs of a great nation." At the time, Britain's prime minister was William Pitt. He was 24 years old.[7] The median age at that time was 16 years old, and over 65 percent of people in the United States were under the age of 25. The "senatorial trust," in contrast, was thought to require a "greater extent of information and stability of character," and as a result justified a minimum age of 30.[8]

Two Chambers, Two Governing Philosophies

The structural differences of the two chambers were intended both to assuage the demands of different interests—particularly small versus big states, North versus South, and stronger versus weaker central government—and to permit governance in fundamentally different ways. To think about how the rules and structural arrangements of the House and Senate evolved to where they are today, we consider the differences between what the two chambers were intended to achieve, and how they were to achieve it.

In the words of Madison, the Framers saw the House of Representatives as "the grand repository of the democratic principle of the government."[9] Madison felt that the House should be the locus of the new governing structure that "will derive its powers from the people of America."[10] Because of their direct representation of smaller constituencies amid shorter election cycles, House members would have "common interest . . . immediate dependence on, and an intimate sympathy with the people."[11] As the lower—or people's—chamber, the House was intended to translate constituents' interests at their most basic level into a relatively direct form of governance.

For this reason, the House of Representatives was the primary manager of the federal Treasury. Massachusetts's Elbridge Gerry stated that the House "was more immediately the representatives of the people, and it was a maxim that the people ought to hold the purse-strings."[12] As directed by the Constitution, all tax bills originate in the House. The Framers considered doing the same with spending (appropriations) bills too, potentially going as far as barring any amendments by the Senate.[13] In the end, the Constitution did not grant the House the sole power to introduce appropriations bills, but the House by tradition retains agenda-setting power over appropriations, usually offering its bill first.

While the House was intended to be responsive to the changing winds of the populace, the Senate was intended to counter the excesses of democracy. An often-recounted exchange between Thomas Jefferson and George Washington illuminates the relationship between the House and Senate. Jefferson asked Washington why he had consented to the creation of a second chamber, the Senate. Washington replied, "Why did you pour that coffee into your saucer?" "To cool it," said Jefferson. "Even so," said Washington, "we pour legislation into the senatorial saucer to cool it."[14] The Framers envisioned the House yielding to the "impulse of sudden and violent passions" of the populace and thus created a counterpart that would be free of these influences and possess greater firmness.[15] Thus the vast majority of legislation in the first decades of the republic originated with the House, with the Senate mostly reviewing and revising legislation formulated by the House. During the first year of the new Congress, the House originated and passed 26 bills. The Senate modified or rejected nearly all of them. The Senate originated only five bills in that same year.

In addition, the Framers endowed in this more elite body of lawmakers a greater say in the national interest via a set of quasi-executive functions. Specifically, they granted the Senate authority to confirm executive branch and judicial appointments, ratify treaties with foreign allies, and adjudicate impeachment charges against the president brought by the House of Representatives. As one observer noted, it was expected that the "Senate would serve as an advisory council to the President, but natural friction between the two, aggravated by the rise of the party system, made such a relationship impracticable. As time passed, the Senate was far more likely to try to manage the President than to advise him."[16] The vice president nominally presides over the chamber, although some delegates to the Constitutional Convention saw this role as a way of giving the vice president's position some purpose.

A perhaps less explicitly intended—but equally important—result of the design of the two lawmaking bodies was the *form* of their eventual decision-making. The House, with its representation of diverse, populace-based interests, was intended to be the chamber for decisive action. However, its size and inevitable growth meant that it would need to adopt procedures granting substantial powers to an agenda-setting entity. This entity would, no doubt, come at the cost of diminished power for individual lawmakers.[17] In short, it was evident that action in the House was going to involve majoritarianism. And, for much of its existence, particularly in the nineteenth century, that majority coalition was going to be partisan.

Within a few decades of its inception, the House saw its first powerful Speaker, Henry Clay (KY, 1811–25), who pushed the body to tackle more national policy issues and addressed the chamber's coordination problems by introducing more partisanship. Speaker Thomas Bracket Reed (R-ME), who served at the end of the nineteenth century, expanded the legislative authority of the majority party by reducing the minority's ability to use delaying tactics that then existed in the chamber rules. Speaker Joseph Cannon (R-IL) followed soon after Reed and exerted the same iron control over the chamber. But, in doing so, he faced a revolt from lawmakers. A bipartisan House coalition, led by progressive Republicans, dismantled the party-oriented control that Reed and Cannon had constructed and ushered in committee-based governing that typified the House for the better part of the twentieth century. The majoritarian coalition for much of the second half of the twentieth century, interestingly, was not always partisan. Sometimes, for example, a "conservative coalition" of southern Democrats and Republicans emerged on labor and union issues. It was not until the very end of the twentieth century that Speakers, particularly Newt Gingrich, began acting on behalf of more unified parties and reasserting centralized control of internal organization and the legislative agenda.

The operative word in the Senate's proceedings has always been deliberation, leading to its reputation as the "world's greatest deliberative body." The essence of that deliberation lies in the prerogative powers granted to individual lawmakers. Since the inception of the Senate, senators have often viewed themselves almost as "ambassadors of sovereign states." As such, senators have felt entitled to unlimited debate and the inherent right to consent to the major actions taken by the body. In addition, the Framers purposely gave senators long terms of service to breed familiarity within the body. Over time, that individual prerogative and the custom of deliberation became the most cherished traditions of the upper chamber.[18] As long-serving senator Lamar Alexander (R-TN) reflected, "The Senate, by its nature, is a place where consensus reigns and personal relationships are paramount . . . And that's not changed."[19]

Insecure Majorities

Given the inherent differences in the design of the House and Senate, it is not surprising that they developed in distinctive ways. To understand where the two chambers are today we need a brief refresher on some of the key electoral and partisan circumstances of recent years (many described elsewhere in this book; see especially Chapters 4 and 6).

First and foremost, partisan polarization has grown significantly in recent decades. Various factors have contributed to this growth. One factor has been the rise of "insecure majorities" in Congress. A generation ago, maintaining a majority in either chamber of Congress was not difficult. It is much less certain today.[20] The 1994 election was a turning point. Prior to that, the last time majority control in the House changed hands was after the 1952 election. For years after World War II, controlling majorities (mostly Democratic Party majorities) had a sizable advantage, averaging around 81 seats. Since the 1994 election, control of the House has switched parties four times. More important, the majority seat advantage has shrunk considerably to an average of 32 seats. Party leaders are more concerned today that their control of the chamber hangs on the results of each election cycle.

These partisan electoral fears have caused lawmakers, party officials, and voters to treat elections differently than they did in the past. Congressional districts have become less competitive in the general election because of a combination of two factors: (1) the U.S. population more extensively "sorting" itself into areas with homogeneous political leanings and (2) state-level parties more aggressively engaging in gerrymandering and drawing congressional district lines that produce solid partisan majorities. As a result, in a very large number of districts, there is little chance of a representative from the opposing party being elected. Thus a very large number of incumbent lawmakers hail from districts where they fear defeat more at the primary stage than in the general election. In addition, voters are more reluctant to split their tickets because they are increasingly aligned with a single party. All of these changes have increased the degree to which House and Senate elections have become nationalized (see Chapter 4 for more on the nationalization of elections).

These circumstances encourage more ideologically hardened behavior by members of Congress. In considering policy proposals (bills) on the floor of the House and Senate, lawmakers today dig more deeply into their ideological trenches than they have at any point in modern history. As a result, they find it more difficult to build coalitions to enact legislation from start to finish. Members of Congress are less likely to compromise, which is evident in their most publicly observable behavior: amendments offered and roll call votes on the floor. Failure to stand by ideological principles raises the prospect that lawmakers may face the wrath of their partisan base back home.

In short, behavior in the two chambers promotes the party agenda, not necessarily good governing. In the House, which is already a staunchly majoritarian institution, the minority party has little opportunity to shape legislation on the floor. In the Senate, traditionally a more egalitarian body, the majority party uses its prerogatives to prevent undesirable legislation from moving forward while its

The modern Congress is characterized by deep partisan divides, and parties are more likely to be unified when creating policies. The support for and against the Tax Cuts and Jobs Act, passed n December 2017, fell squarely along party lines, epitomized by the support of Senate Majority Leader Mitch McConnell (R-KY) and opposition of House Minority Leader Nancy Pelosi (D-CA).

leadership shapes the chamber agenda to avoid undesirable and potentially embarrassing votes.

Stages of Floor Consideration

Let us now examine several stages of the process of legislative consideration in the House and Senate. These stages reveal the differences in the functioning between the two chambers and help to explain the fate of much legislation in the contemporary Congress.

MOVING BILLS FROM COMMITTEE CONSIDERATION TO THE FLOOR   The process of moving bills from committee to chamber deliberations can occur in different ways. One might assume that legislation handled by committees would proceed to the floor in an orderly, chronological fashion. Indeed, this "calendar system" is one option. We discuss this system first and then move to a discussion of the less formal paths taken by consensual or privileged legislation and more controversial or higher-profile legislation.

CALENDARS   Each chamber has "calendars" on which bills are placed for consideration. The House has the *Union Calendar* for tax, authorization, and appropriations measures; the *House Calendar* for other public bills and resolutions; and the *Private Calendar* for measures affecting specific individuals. The Senate has a *Calendar of Business* for most legislation reported by committees, and it has the *Executive Calendar* for executive branch nominations and treaties. Some of these calendars specify that discussion of particular legislative matters should occur on particular days of the week.

However, if the chambers were to stick to a strict procession of bills as they trickle in from committees, most of the critical lawmaking that takes the longest to formulate—spending (appropriations), reauthorizations of major programs and agencies, new and transformative legislation—would fall to the back of the line and likely not get completed before the end of the congressional term. For that reason, both chambers have devised alternative means for scheduling legislation for wider floor consideration.

CONSENSUAL OR PRIVILEGED LEGISLATION The House of Representatives grants the Speaker significant authority for the scheduling of legislation. This authority, along with the Speaker's power to refer legislation to particular committees, is central to the modern powers of the office. Within this right, after consulting with the relevant committee(s), the Speaker may permit a member to make a motion that a bill pass under "suspension of the rules." This expedited procedure, meant for less controversial matters, severely limits debate (to 40 minutes) and prohibits the consideration of any amendments to the bill. The trade-off is that expedited bills require a two-thirds majority for adoption, thereby limiting this option to legislation with high levels of support and needing no further alteration. While such legislation is more often than not of little policy consequence (for example, the naming of post offices), the procedure can be used for more substantive legislation. In fact, recent years have seen an increase in legislation moving through the House under suspension of the rules, with nearly 750 bills using this process in the 114th Congress (2015–17). These bills included fairly substantial measures such as the Food and Drug Administration Reauthorization Act and legislation meant to curb the spread of the feared Zika virus.[21]

The Senate does not have a process identical to suspension, so it passes more trivial and consensual legislation by simple *unanimous consent agreements* (UCAs). We discuss more complicated UCAs next, but for now, suffice it to say that the majority leader, exercising his powers to schedule legislation in the Senate, can use the chamber's informality to dispose of many bills and executive nominations with a simple motion asking for unanimous consent to adopt. The majority leader does this with the cooperation of the other members (mainly the minority leader). Simple UCAs are often reserved for issues of relatively little importance and give tremendous latitude to the senators, permitting them to pass a package of noncontroversial bills all at once.

Importantly, the majority leader's privilege to decide the Senate's schedule or agenda is effectively derived from his right of first recognition to make a motion on the Senate floor. Interestingly, this privilege does not appear in the Constitution, any statute, or even the chamber rules. Rather, it exists through long-held precedent. By one count, the Senate has more than 1 million precedents that govern its operations.[22]

Finally, some legislative matters are considered "privileged" and may be called up for consideration on the floor of either chamber at almost any time without the need for special permission, agreements, or calendars. These matters include budget resolutions and appropriations legislation, ethics resolutions, veto messages from the president, reports from conference committees, and special rules regarding the consideration of bills in the House (discussed later in this chapter).

COMPLICATED OR MAJOR LEGISLATION   The House and Senate use different procedures to consider controversial and complicated bills, and these procedures reflect the inherent differences in how the chambers function.

The House is guided by a clear set of majoritarian procedures. Because a good portion of the chamber floor time would be otherwise occupied by bills considered in accordance with the House's various calendars, Speakers developed the concept of the "special rule" in the 1880s. Prior to that, legislation would usually be considered only as the chamber worked through its various calendars or by suspension of the rules. Speaker Reed made heavy use of the special rule as a means of deliberating important and pressing matters on the chamber floor in a timely fashion and within fairly restrictive limits on debate and amendment. In the modern era, the House Rules Committee has the power to draft special rules.

A special rule defines the terms and conditions of floor debate on a bill. It takes the form of a resolution and falls along a spectrum of restrictiveness that ranges from "open," permitting any germane amendment to be offered and debated on the House floor; to "modified" or "structured," providing for a limit on the specific amendments to be considered; to "closed," permitting no amendments to be offered on the reported bill. Open rules were more or less the norm until recently (more on this later in the chapter), but they came with the cost of potentially allowing lengthy floor consideration of a wide variety of amendments. Closed rules were traditionally common for tax bills; it was argued that such measures were too complex for the details to be formulated (and amended) beyond the expertise of the Ways and Means Committee members and its staff.

Special rules are likely to include another set of exceptions that are necessary to keep the chamber functioning: waivers on points of order to chamber rules. It is somewhat common for the procedures being employed or the actual bill language to violate existing House rules. For example, in recent years, Congress has often had trouble renewing programs and agencies whose authorization is about to expire. As a result, appropriations legislation commonly violates House Rule XXI, clause 2(a)(1), which prohibits appropriations for programs that have not been previously authorized. Consequently, special rules on appropriations bills often include a waiver on such points of order, thus permitting the consideration of such legislation without concern that the bill could be held up.[23] (We discuss unauthorized appropriations in more detail in Chapter 8.)

HOW WE STUDY
CONGRESSIONAL ORGANIZATION AND RESTRICTIVE RULES IN THE HOUSE

The increase in restrictive rules started in the second half of the twentieth century. Scholars of Congress became interested in what this trend revealed about the role of authorizing (legislative) committees in the House as well as the power of the governing majority to control outcomes in the chamber. By restricting what kinds of amendments can be offered once a bill reaches the chamber, special rules can either protect the work of the committee that originally crafted the bill, or leave the bill open to changes that may unravel agreements or alter the legislation's intended direction. Special rules thus are an opportunity for another entity to influence the shape of legislation after the issue-area specialists (the authorizing committee members) have had a crack at it. How those members treat such bills—as protected or unprotected—reveals how they view who should have the final say on legislation.

Recall that committees serve as providers of much-needed information about the quality and appropriateness of particular policy proposals. The argument goes as follows: as experts in a particular realm of federal policy, the committees work hard on shaping legislation so that Congress adopts the "best" policy. One way to encourage that effort is to assure the committees that their investment in gaining expertise and expending time and resources on new policy proposals will not be picked apart and undone by others, possibly nonspecialists, once the bill gets to the chamber floor. To assure committees and protect their work, the Rules Committee grants them restrictive rules that limit or prohibit the sort of amending that can take place. Use of restrictive rules, particularly for bills coming from committees seen as information specialists, signals both the importance of these committees' roles and what the House prioritizes when it makes policy: useful information.

Political scientist Keith Krehbiel studied the frequency of restrictive rules in the House of Representatives in the mid-1980s and found that they were often used to protect bills coming out of committees comprised of issue specialists and not from committees that were excessively partisan or ideologically extreme.[24] However, a follow-up study by political scientist Bryan Marshall, which examined many of the same factors but also included bills from a decade later (through the mid-1990s) did not find evidence to support the notion of protection for the legislative proposals coming from informational or specialist committees. In fact, there was much more evidence that the Rules Committee was providing restrictive rules to protect the bills from the most partisan committees.[25]

What changed over the course of 10 years that led scholars to find a more partisan tinge to the Rules Committee's use of restrictive rules? A lot. As noted in Chapter 6, the 1980s were the beginning of the era of excessive partisanship and polarization. This decade also saw a shift in the direction of many committees. Electoral changes and institutional reforms in Congress made in the 1970s had the effect of diminishing the autonomy of committees, and particularly their chairs. These changes placed committees more under the control of the party leadership and its pursuit of a partisan agenda. Consequently, the work of the Rules Committee became just a part of the grander strategy for an increasingly homogeneous and policy-focused majority party to achieve its legislative agenda.

As the political and electoral environment became increasingly more partisan, congressional actions came under greater scrutiny. As a result, members grew more uncomfortable with hard-to-explain votes on the chamber floor. To ensure that only the most partisan matters came up for a vote on the House floor, successive Speakers were under pressure from their majority-party colleagues to expand the use of restrictive rules. Figure 7.1 displays the progressive increase in the use of restrictive rules from around 15 percent in the mid-1970s, to 50 percent in the mid-1990s, to nearly 100 percent by the 2010s. Ironically, these increases have occurred despite the fact that each party declares its opposition to such restrictions when it is in the minority but perpetuates the trend when it becomes the majority.[26]

Critical Thinking

1. Restrictive rules in the House are often used to protect bills produced by committees from amendments on the floor. Is this limitation on chamber influence warranted, or should the entire membership of the House have a fair chance to amend all legislation?

2. Restrictive rules are one of the primary sources of control over the flow of legislation granted to the majority party in the House. Does the majority party have too much influence today (in contrast to a generation or two ago), or is it best to have a strongly majoritarian lawmaking body?

3. If polarization were to decrease in the future, would you expect the number of restrictive rules to decrease as well? Why or why not?

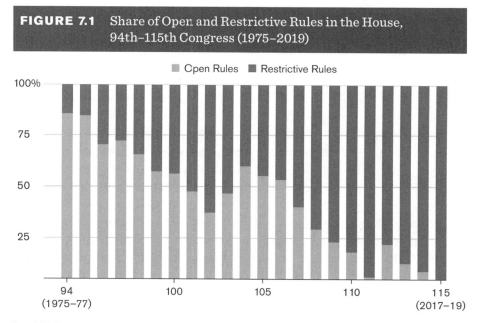

FIGURE 7.1   Share of Open and Restrictive Rules in the House, 94th–115th Congress (1975–2019)

Open Rules   Restrictive Rules

Donald R. Wolfensberger. "Share of Open/Restrictive Rules, U.S. House, 1975–2014." www.vox.com/polyarchy /2015/10/20/9570747/house-freedom-caucus-process-demands (accessed 6/14/18). Data for 2015–18 from Bipartisan Policy Center. "Special Rules Providing for the Original Consideration of Legislation in the House, 103rd–115th Congresses (1993–2018)." https://bipartisanpolicy.org/wp-content/uploads/2018/03 /BPC-House-Rules-Data-115th-.pdf (accessed 6/14/18).

Skirting Around Committees in the House

In general, there is considerable deference to committee jurisdictional authority, so lawmakers are hesitant to force a committee to relinquish a policy proposal that it has not fully considered and crafted into its desired form (that is, a fully reported bill). However, a committee will occasionally refuse to report out a bill even though there is sufficient support in the chamber to consider the matter. In the House, the membership can force the committee to act via a discharge petition, a procedure that extracts a bill from an unwilling committee and allows it to be considered by the chamber. A successful discharge petition requires the signature of an absolute majority of House members (218).

Filing a discharge petition is typically seen as hostile to the jurisdictional authority of a committee and its chair, and therefore lawmakers are often hesitant to do so. More often than not, representatives will take such action only when they consider the measure of the highest importance and believe that they have the support to gain the required signatures. Occasionally, discharge petitions are used in a largely futile effort by the minority party to call out majority obstruction. For example, in 2018, as the work of Special Counsel Robert Mueller investigating Russian collusion in the 2016 election generated speculation that President Trump might fire him, House Democrats introduced more than one discharge petition aimed at extracting legislation out of the Judiciary Committee to provide for judicial review of any such firing. The effort did not generate much support among the majority Republicans in the House.[27]

It is rare for the entire discharge process to play itself out. Often, filing a petition or even the threat of filing a petition is enough to induce the committee to act. Committees would rather keep control of the process by reporting out a bill on their own terms than relinquish control of the legislation to others. A recent study by political scientists Kathryn Pearson and Eric Schickler found that legislators who have less of a stake in the committee system (less seniority with fewer good committee assignments) and minority-party members are more likely to sign discharge petitions in the modern era.[28]

In the summer of 2018, the DACA issue (mentioned at the start of this chapter) reemerged as a very public battle within the House Republican majority. With election season heating up, moderate Republicans, particularly those facing reelection in districts where Democrat Hillary Clinton performed well during the 2016 presidential election, feared that their opponents would capitalize on the lack of progress on immigration. They were most concerned about the perception of DACA recipients losing their legal status. Knowing that they would receive widespread support among chamber Democrats, a group of Republican lawmakers rolled out a petition to discharge a bill from the Rules Committee that would provide legal protections for DACA recipients along with a number of border security measures. As the petition racked up signatures (including those of nearly every Democrat) and looked like it would gain a chamber majority, House GOP leaders began intense negotiations that also folded in the policy preferences of the more conservative Freedom Caucus. At around the same time, the Trump administration was cracking down on unauthorized crossing of the border with Mexico, based on a policy of "zero tolerance" issued by the Department of Justice. The practice of separating minor children entering the United States from their family members, including those applying for asylum, became national news.

Thanks to this attention, Republican moderates were able to leverage a floor vote for their immigration bill. However, their moderate bill (along with a more hardline Republican bill) failed to gain majority support in a full House vote.[29]

Debate and Amendments in the House

When considering consequential legislation, the first stage on the House floor is the adoption of the rule that the Rules Committee has crafted. To begin, the Speaker normally recognizes a majority-party member of the Rules Committee who then explains the special rule defining the potential limitations on debate and amendments. After no more than an hour's debate, the House votes to either adopt the rule and proceed to consideration of the bill or reject it and thus end consideration of it. While rejection is an opportunity to kill a bill before the chamber even gets started, it is uncommon for majority-party members to vote against a special rule. In essence, such an action would be seen as a rejection of the leadership's agenda.

Members of the majority party rarely defect from the leadership on procedural votes.[30] However, in recent years, defections have increased with the rise of the Tea Party and the Freedom Caucus in the Republican conference. Leaders do not look on such defections lightly, and a history of defections can be problematic for offending lawmakers in terms of receiving favors from the leadership. (In addition, in the modern era, it is uncommon for the Speaker to bring forward legislation that would not garner the support of the majority—usually the vast majority—of his own party. Recall, that this is commonly referred to as the Hastert Rule.)

After adopting the rule, the House proceeds to debate. Under its regular rules of procedure, sometimes called the "One-Hour Rule," the House restricts the length of debate, the order of votes, and the opportunity for amendments. However, this may not provide sufficient time for the House to consider many important and controversial bills. Thus, the House much more frequently uses the Committee of the Whole (COW), where the entire chamber acts as a committee for consideration of the bill. The rules under the COW allow for a smaller *quorum* size, or number of members that must be present to do business—100 members versus the typical 218 members for the House—and greater flexibility in debate and amending. Although the particulars are often specified in the special rule (that is, the resolution coming out of the Rules Committee), the COW procedure generally provides each member with five minutes of debate time on amendments, which is controlled by "floor managers," who are often the leaders on the bill's committee of jurisdiction (its chair or subcommittee chair and the associated ranking minority member).

Amendments are considered one at a time. *Germaneness*, the criterion used to limit debate and changes to only those items directly related to the subject of the bill at hand, is a much more severe restriction in the House than in the Senate. Usually the COW will consider amendments from the original committee of jurisdiction first and then others' recommendations—again, it all depends on the terms of the special rule. Ultimately, the House will likely vote on the amendments, but those adopted in the COW are simply *recommendations* for inclusion in the bill's final draft.

At the end of a bill's consideration, the COW will "rise and report," effectively no longer operating under the COW rules and returning to the formal House rules. It then proceeds to a formal vote. Often the House will officially include the recommended amendments, usually by simple voice vote, and then move to the final stages of passage. The final stages often entail an initial "motion to recommit" the bill to the originating committee, usually from a member of the minority party. This motion, if passed, would effectively kill the bill, although sometimes it includes a list of the changes the chamber would like to see. More often than not, bills that make it to this stage do not receive a positive vote on the recommittal motion, and thus the House proceeds to vote on adopting the bill.

Senate Floor and Unanimity: A Different Kind of Place

When it comes to consequential legislation, the Senate, thanks to its standing rules, is more permissive than the House. Rather than Senate leadership using majoritarian procedures, much of the power to determine the fate of bills in the Senate, in theory at least, resides in the hands of its individual members. The Senate is a body built on the collective experience and knowledge of its members and their autonomy to deliberate, compromise, and reach agreements without depending on party or coalition leadership for direction and coordination. Today, Senate procedure is organized through a combination of rules and precedents built over time around the rights and privileges of its individual members, who are all positioned to play a role in policy making.

Like the House, the Senate has developed a set of practices for its most important legislation so that it is not beholden to its prescribed calendar system. But because of its permissive rules of engagement and prerogative powers, the Senate has for most of its existence honored one critical difference: all senators at least tacitly acquiesce in proceeding to consideration of a matter at hand. This is the notion of *unanimous consent.*

In essence, a unanimous consent agreement (UCA) for consequential legislation allows the Senate to get around the strictures of chamber rules that would otherwise bog it down. Like UCAs on minor legislation, the more complex version requires the body to set aside a specific rule of procedure, or often many rules and precedents, to expedite its proceedings. UCAs are usually the result of a negotiation between the majority and minority leaders, often with input from the partisan leadership of the relevant committee(s). UCAs can be negotiated at any time, are sometimes directed at a specific amendment (limiting further amendments or time of debate), and can be adopted when the chamber is already considering the relevant legislation.

In many ways, UCAs are the Senate's version of special rules, defining the terms of debate on a bill. However, unlike the House, the Senate faces few rules that impinge on the prerogative powers of individual senators. There are no effective limits on debate in the Senate. (While there is a limit of two speeches per senator per question per legislative day, this rule is rarely enforced.) Therefore, the UCA can structure the time of debate, the necessary amendments, and the timing of a vote.

In the mid–nineteenth century, the Senate began to use UCAs to specify the date for a vote on a measure, which ultimately established the precedent for this type of formal agreement. Although UCAs acted mostly as gentleman's agreements for decades (and were violated frequently), in 1914, the Senate adopted the rule that these agreements "shall operate as the order of the Senate" and, importantly, could be altered only by another UCA. It was not until the 1950s that Lyndon Johnson (D-TX), the Democratic majority leader, began using the UCA to manage the entire legislative process: debate, amendments, time of vote, and so on.

In short, the UCA is a necessary informal modification that helps the chamber complete needed legislation and provides senators with a rough sense of the chamber's schedule, which helps them plan their own time. The critical difference from floor procedures in the House is the unanimity required in the Senate. Any senator can object (i.e., refuse to grant consent), in which case the body lacks an agreement regarding how it will proceed with consideration of a bill. The result is substantial individual power to hold up consideration of legislation. It is rare for the Senate majority leader to offer a UCA until all senators concerned have had an opportunity to inform their leaders that they find it acceptable. For example, Senator Rand Paul (R-KY) forced a very brief government shutdown in February 2018 when he initially refused to agree to a UCA on a spending bill, expressing his concern over lack of fiscal restraint.[31]

These prerogative powers mean that any senator can bring almost anything in the chamber to a halt. And the threat of such a stoppage is often enough to spur some accommodation. Bill sponsors who meet resistance usually try to resolve it in one of two ways: (1) they negotiate with the aggrieved lawmakers in an attempt to accommodate their demands, or (2) they accept that the chamber is at an impasse and move on to other important legislation that the Senate needs to consider.

In the mid-1970s the Senate, under Majority Leader Mike Mansfield (D-MT), developed the "track system" for considering legislation. The Senate, most often through agreement between the majority and minority leaders (although also possible through a UCAs), can continue considering important legislation during an effective filibuster. The track system permits the chamber to address critical or time-sensitive bills without grinding to a complete standstill over the opposition to a single bill. The consequence of the track system is twofold. First, the individual policy proposal is sacrificed in favor of the whole process and the body's governing ability. Second, being able to continue lawmaking by diverting the chamber around the legislative blockage lowers the cost of using the obstruction tactic and makes it more likely to occur and succeed.

We should note, however, that there is much for the Senate to do—meeting constitutional and statutory obligations, as well as responding to the demands of the public, interest groups, agencies, and the president—and relatively scarce time to complete its work. For this reason, delaying tactics are likely to be more effective at the end of a session, when there is a pressing need to complete tasks.

However, the need to complete important tasks can also serve as a motivator not to employ delaying tactics. As a practical matter, the Senate could not effectively function if it had to give in to the whims of every individual on every issue up for debate. As one long-time observer of the Senate noted, "The legislative process on the Senate floor reflects a balance between the rights guaranteed to Senators under the standing rules and the willingness of Senators to forego exercising some of these rights in order to expedite the conduct of business."[32] Ultimately, the success or failure of the Senate as a governing body depends on its members not exercising their prerogative powers in every instance or with every disagreement. To a much greater degree than the House, the Senate is built on compromise. Therefore, its functioning in many ways relies on its members' willingness to be accommodating.

Finally, a note about germaneness in the Senate: the Senate does not have the same restrictions that exist in the House, meaning that senators may offer practically *any* amendment to a bill being considered on the chamber floor (to the extent allowed by the relevant consent agreement).[33] As a practical matter, amendments can help to move forward a piece of legislation that has stalled at the committee stage or is otherwise difficult to advance. While the Senate has other means of getting around reluctant committees by using methods similar to the House's discharge petition, the far more common practice is to attach a bill as a nongermane amendment (otherwise known as a *rider*) to an existing bill.

WITHHOLDING CONSENT: FILIBUSTERS AND HOLDS   What, then, are the particulars on Senate obstruction? In recent years, lawmakers have been increasingly inclined to withhold their consent, thus implicitly threatening to extend debate on a bill. This withholding may result from something related to the bill itself, or it may be driven by a different matter entirely. There are two general versions of senators' refusal to acquiesce to unanimous consent: filibusters and holds.

The first form of obstruction, and the one more familiar to casual observers of Congress, is the formal filibuster. By definition, a *filibuster* is any tactic that blocks a measure on the Senate floor from coming to a vote, but often it takes the form of a single lawmaker's refusal to end debate by making a long, uninterrupted speech. The filibuster is possible for two reasons: chamber rules require the presiding officer to recognize all senators wishing to speak, and the Senate lacks any formal provision regarding the time limits on debate.

Once recognized, the senator may speak at length, without yielding the floor, but must remain standing and speak continuously. Senate precedent prohibits members from yielding the floor to each other. The Senate does not always observe the restriction on yielding the floor during the normal conduct of business, but this restriction is more likely to be insisted upon during the extended debate of a filibuster. In most cases, senators are not required to keep the debate germane to the topic at hand, so filibustering speeches may be very wide ranging, including the occasional reading of the phonebook or Dr. Seuss's *Green Eggs and Ham*.[34] Senate rules do permit the opportunity for other senators to ask questions during a filibuster. Of course, the Senate being the Senate, questions can take quite a bit of time to formulate and thus a friendly colleague may be able to provide a filibustering senator some relief with the articulation of a very long question.

The scheduling of filibusters is often intended to reduce disruptions to the Senate's normal functioning and to increase the cost of conducting the obstruction. However, scheduling can work to the filibustering senator's advantage. It is not unusual for filibusters to continue into the night or even overnight, often requiring cots to be brought to the Senate for members. Proponents of the

In 2013, Senator Ted Cruz (R-TX) spoke for 21 hours on the Senate floor, urging his colleagues to vote against funding the Affordable Care Act. While this filibuster did not change the outcome of the vote, it was a symbolic gesture in defiance of the bill.

measure must be able to maintain a quorum at any time. If there is no quorum, then the Senate must adjourn, providing some relief to those filibustering.

Perhaps the most well-known filibuster is the fictional filibuster conducted by Jimmy Stewart, who fights political corruption through his attention-grabbing 24 hours of continuous speech in Frank Capra's 1939 film *Mr. Smith Goes to Washington*. (The movie is worth watching.) The longest actual filibuster to date occurred in 1957 in Senator Strom Thurmond's (D-SC) 24-hour speech attempting to thwart the Civil Rights Act of 1957.

The more informal version of a filibuster—informal in that it is not specifically ensconced in chamber rules—is the "hold." By requesting a hold on a bill, senators express their opposition to the bill's proceeding to chamber consideration.[35] A hold implicitly states that a senator is registering his or her intention to object to any unanimous consent request for consideration of the measure. As a matter of practice, this maneuver, sometimes called the "silent filibuster," is recognized by the majority leader. The hold is derived from a very old courtesy extended to senators in the days of horse travel, when senators often needed time to return to Washington to cast their votes.[36]

The hold usually occurs on less salient legislation and may be intended only to ensure that the senator is informed that a matter will be coming up for debate. An unusual aspect of this obstruction tactic is that the holder's name is kept secret. Party leaders keep "hold lists" and never release them to the public. It is not unheard of for a senator to hold up Senate business—sometimes quite important action—in order to accomplish a completely different goal.[37] For example, Senator Richard Shelby (R-AL) put a hold on the confirmation process of at least 70 Obama nominees in a dispute over defense earmarks for his state. When this action was exposed in media accounts, Shelby relented on all but a few of the nominations.[38]

In 2007, the Senate passed a bill banning secret holds that last longer than six days. However, that new law did not put an end to the practice. To get around the ban, two or more senators can pass the hold back and forth in a "rolling hold" that keeps their names secret.

CLOTURE The Senate is not always held hostage to the preferences and desires of one uncooperative lawmaker. Rather, a supermajoritarian threshold allows the chamber to move beyond most blockages. For regular legislation, the threshold to limit debate (or invoke *cloture*) is three-fifths of the members, or 60 senators. A cloture petition can be filed with the signature of 16 members. On the second calendar day after the petition is filed a roll call vote on the cloture motion is triggered, and the motion is not debatable. If invoked, cloture does not completely terminate consideration of the matter, but it sets a limit of a maximum of 30 hours of additional debate. Under cloture, only germane amendments are in order.

This limit on debate in the Senate was not established until 1917. Initially, the threshold to invoke cloture was two-thirds (67 votes). In 1975, the Senate lowered the threshold to three-fifths (60 votes). This supermajority threshold is one of the primary means of reinforcing the notions of compromise and accommodation in the Senate. In most instances, the process of ending a filibuster necessitates concessions to the preferences of at least some of the more centrist members of the minority party. Only twice in the modern cloture era has a party had a large enough majority by itself to break a filibuster. Both times it was the Democrats, who had a supermajority of 61 members from 1975 to 1978 and 60 members for a few months in 2009. (See the story of the Obamacare vote in Chapter 1.)

Recently, the threshold to invoke cloture was lowered again—by precedent, not by a change to chamber rules. In 2013, the Democrats sought a change to address the Senate's unwillingness to approve President Obama's lower-court judicial nominees. Majority Leader Harry Reid (D-NV) thus lowered the necessary votes for cloture to a simple majority on votes for executive branch nominations and federal court nominations below the Supreme Court. This change was termed the "nuclear option" because it upended many years of Senate precedent. Just a few years later, the tables turned, and what was a Democratic-controlled Senate with a Democratic president (Obama) turned into a Republican-controlled Senate and a Republican president (Trump). The GOP played its only "nuclear" card in 2017 when it extended the simple-majority threshold to Supreme Court nominations. The Republicans used this change to confirm President Trump's nominee, Neil Gorsuch, to the Supreme Court. (The Senate still maintains the higher threshold of two-thirds for invoking cloture on changes to the Senate rules.)

As of now, the three-fifths threshold still stands on most legislation, upholding the Senate's long-held notions of deliberation and compromise. But one person's standard for accommodation is another's undemocratic decree—and this can be the same person, depending on the issue at hand. Senators who use the supermajoritarianism of the Senate when in the minority often complain when the tables have turned and they are in the majority—and a small group of legislators from the *other* party are thwarting their will. And, in many instances, minority-party members have little incentive to give a legislative "win" to the majority, particularly when they believe that the majority party will bear the blame for the failed legislation or the minority party will be rewarded for its obstruction.

THEN AND NOW
FILIBUSTERS AND CLOTURE

The use of the filibuster dates back to 1806, when the Senate eliminated the rule that allowed the "previous question" to be called to a vote. The elimination of this rule meant that the chamber had no majoritarian means of closing debate and was therefore reliant on unanimous consent to bring a matter to a final vote. Over time, the use of the filibuster has evolved considerably. Because filibusters (and other delaying tactics) come in different forms, identifying what is or is not a filibuster is no simple task. Recall that a filibuster is effectively the extension of normal Senate practices, in this case debate, to prevent legislation from moving forward. Senators may engage in such obstructionist tactics without specifically identifying the action as a filibuster. Therefore, until recently, there was no single list of Senate filibusters anywhere. Moreover, the intent to filibuster without actually engaging in it—the hold—can create the same outcome. Understanding the use of filibusters and trends over time requires some novel data-collection efforts.

The best-known catalog of filibuster activity, compiled by political scientist Gregory Koger, resulted from an extensive search through public mentions of filibusters, mostly in the media.[39] Based on this list, we observe that filibusters were relatively unheard of in the Senate in its early years. By the 1870s, about 20 bills faced a filibuster in the Senate, with many of these bills related to Reconstruction or civil rights issues. By the turn of the nineteenth century, the practice had tapered off considerably under increased public scrutiny of Washington lawmakers.

After the turn of the century, the use of filibusters remained rather low through the 1960s, with only a handful of measures facing this obstruction each congressional term. But within these low numbers were some intense legislative fights, particularly with respect to anti-lynching and civil rights legislation. Perhaps the most controversial filibuster of that era was attempted around what eventually became the Civil Rights Act of 1964. In the politically charged public debate over this landmark policy achievement, many feared the consequences if southern segregationist senators used a filibuster to kill the bill.

Filibusters have become much more common in the last few decades (Figure 7.2). Senate historian Donald Ritchie dates the increasing use of the filibuster to the Democrats in the late 1980s, when Majority Leader Robert Byrd (D-WV) used it to reassert the Democratic Party agenda after they regained a chamber majority in 1987 and faced a Republican president, Ronald Reagan, with a very different agenda.[40]

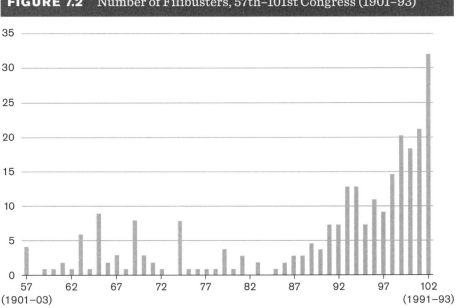

FIGURE 7.2 Number of Filibusters, 57th–101st Congress (1901–93)

Gregory Koger. 2010. *Filibustering: A Political History of Obstruction in the House and Senate.* Chicago: University of Chicago Press, p. 107.

Cloture motions provide another way to view obstructionist tactics in the Senate. Scholars debate what a count of cloture motions tells us. Multiple cloture motions can be filed on the same obstructed bill, and the majority can file cloture motions in anticipation of an obstruction that has not yet occurred. Nevertheless, because Senate leaders unquestionably prefer the certainty and structure of a UCA, the cloture motion becomes a necessity when a UCA is not possible. Thus, while not synonymous with obstruction, cloture motions indicate the degree to which the majority sees the need to move bills forward absent a UCA.[41]

Figure 7.3 shows the trend in cloture motions filed over the past several decades. The rapid increase is obvious through the 1980s and 1990s, but one of the most severe spikes in cloture motions occurred in the last two years of the Bush presidency (2007–08), after the Democrats took control of the Senate. (Note a second uptick after the Democrats exercised the nuclear option in 2013.) According to congressional expert Norman Ornstein, all the legislative initiatives considered in the Senate at that point were coming from Democrats, and the Republicans were trying to slow down or kill them. Republican filibuster

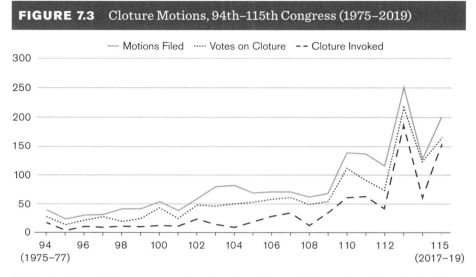

FIGURE 7.3 Cloture Motions, 94th–115th Congress (1975–2019)

—— Motions Filed ·········· Votes on Cloture – – Cloture Invoked

U.S. Senate. "Cloture Motions." www.senate.gov/pagelayout/reference/cloture_motions/clotureCounts.htm (accessed 12/14/18).

threats were "like throwing molasses in the road."[42] Democrats doubled the number of cloture motions, with one in five roll call votes that term aimed simply at cutting off debate.

What explains the increase in continuous debate/filibustering as a delaying tactic? A combination of factors likely contributes to this new normal in Senate procedure, which almost ensures that the 60-vote threshold is required to adopt any significant legislation. First, the Senate has far more on its agenda today than it ever has. These time pressures mean that delaying tactics can be very effective; as constructing a supermajority is not a simple task, it means that filibustering members will likely be granted concessions, otherwise the legislative proposal will be killed. Second, through the accepted use of holds and the multiple track system, Senate leaders have simplified the process of engaging in these delaying tactics, severely reducing their cost to the perpetrating lawmakers. Finally, in an era where public opinion is an effective part of a politician's tool kit, senators have discovered that they can gain considerable attention by engaging in a filibuster on an important issue.[43] Often, outside groups will reward senators for such obstructionist tactics on behalf of a particular cause, and sometimes that cause is themselves. Senator Ted Cruz (R-TX) in 2013 engaged in a 21-hour filibuster of a critical appropriations bill as a stunt to highlight opposition to Obamacare. His obstruction turned into several days of a government shutdown, which many of his conservative colleagues felt was unnecessary and futile. A year and a half later, Cruz announced his candidacy for the presidency.

Critical Thinking

1. Do opportunities for obstruction in the Senate, such as the filibuster or hold, provide senators with too much power to impede the progress of legislation? Or is it sufficient that a supermajority of senators can invoke cloture to overrule a small group of obstructionists?
2. We have seen a sharp increase in the use of cloture motions in the Senate in recent years. Is it best that the majority party now almost always seeks some degree of agreement from a small group of senators from the minority party?
3. How would the content of laws be different if the filibuster on policy proposals is eliminated? What effect does a 60-vote threshold have on the quality and content of legislation?

AMENDMENTS IN THE SENATE Once a bill reaches the Senate floor, it is open to amendments at any time, but the boundaries of the amending process are largely defined by UCAs (or potentially the germaneness provisions of a cloture motion). A bill can be amended in a variety of ways: changing the text of the bill (first-degree amendment), changing the text of an amendment (second-degree amendment), striking language from a bill, inserting new language into a bill, or replacing the entire text of a bill with new language. Recall that amendments are required to be germane to the bill only in certain circumstances (appropriations or budget measures, or under cloture or a restrictive UCA), so amendments in the Senate can severely change the intent of the legislation or tack on unrelated riders.

The Senate relies on a set of diagrams (like the one shown in Figure 7.4) that define the order in which amendments are offered and voted on. These diagrams, called *amendment trees*, vary with the type of amendments being considered. This process has developed over time into a set of precedents that often severely limit the number of amendments to a bill that is up for consideration. The cap is usually 11 amendments.

In the process of amending legislation, the Senate has begun to look much like the House, with majority leadership limiting the minority's involvement by restricting their amendments or precluding them altogether. Because the Senate majority leader has the right to be recognized before any other senator and can offer as many amendments as she or he wishes, it is possible for him to fill the entire amendment tree, thereby blocking anyone else from offering amendments.[44]

FIGURE 7.4 Sample Amendment Tree

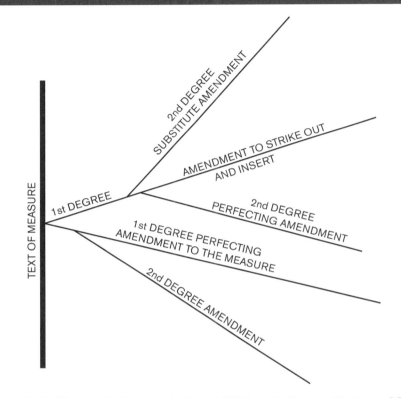

Christopher Davis. "The Amending Process in the Senate." CRS Report for Congress. Washington, DC: Congressional Research Service, September 16, 2015.

The majority leader might seek to control the amendment process for a number of reasons: to prevent a potentially controversial amendment from being offered, to gain bargaining leverage in pursuit of a UCA, or to move the bill along more quickly without any additions or changes. As Figure 7.5 shows, this approach to Senate agenda control gained considerable traction under Majority Leader Reid after the Democrats regained control of the chamber following the 2006 election.

In 2014, Reid filled the amendment tree on an unemployment insurance extension bill to prevent Republicans from using it as an opportunity to force votes repealing portions of the Affordable Care Act (Obamacare). Reid's amendments were simply filler, making mostly meaningless alterations to the bill, such as changing the enactment date by one day, then two days, and then three days. By all accounts, Mitch McConnell (R-KY), the majority leader after the

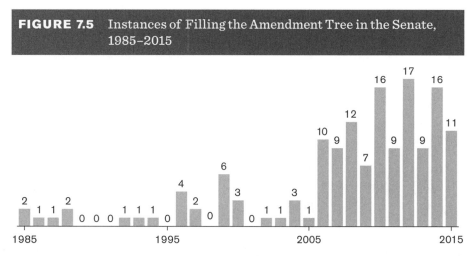

FIGURE 7.5 Instances of Filling the Amendment Tree in the Senate, 1985–2015

Congressional Research Service. September 28, 2015. "Instances in Which Opportunities for Floor Amendment Were Limited by the Senate Majority Leader or His Designee Filling or Partially Filling the Amendment Tree, 1985–2015." www.crs.gov (accessed 7/16/18).

Republicans took control of the Senate following the 2016 election, has continued using this tactic to take control of the Senate floor agenda.[45]

Reconciling Differences between Chambers

After the House and Senate have crafted their own versions of the same bill, they must reconcile those differences. Recall that the presentation clause of the U.S. Constitution includes the phrase "every Bill which shall have passed the House of Representatives and the Senate," which is interpreted to mean a bill passed *in identical form*. Reconciling the two versions of the bill can be a daunting task; when it comes to passing important legislation, the devil is often in the details. Nonetheless, the two chambers usually are able to bridge their divide and come up with mutually agreed upon language. About 97 percent of bills that pass both the House and Senate in one form or another eventually get enacted into law.

The textbook process for reconciling House and Senate differences has traditionally been the *conference committee* (see Chapter 5). This committee, usually composed of members of the originating House and Senate panels, negotiates the differences in the two chamber's versions of the same legislation after they have been passed. The committee's goal is to come up with a compromise. The negotiations are meant to be constrained to the "scope of differences," with the

Conference committees, like the one pictured here, were once essential to rendering identical legislation to pass in the House of Representatives and the Senate. Today, very few pieces of legislation are left to be decided on by conference committees.

committee bargaining only on those aspects where the House and Senate bills differ. But determining where that scope ends is often a difficult matter. If conferees must interpret this boundary broadly to reach an agreement, then so be it. Once an agreement is struck, the conferees are permitted to bring the bill back to their respective chambers as a conference report. They offer the conference report to their chamber as a "take-it-or-leave it" proposal, with no amendments or changes allowed.

For many years, it was generally believed that the higher the profile of the legislation, the more likely that House and Senate differences would be ironed out in a conference committee. However, recent decades have seen a disruption in the tactics used to reconcile House and Senate differences. Political scientist Josh Ryan examined all the possible avenues that the two chambers used, going back to the mid-1970s, to iron out their differences on legislation that was enacted (Figure 7.6). First and foremost, he found a severe drop-off in the percentage of successful bills that go to a conference committee. In the 1970s, over 40 percent of passed bills went to a conference committee, but by the first decade of the twenty-first century, this number was down to less than 5 percent. And it has dropped to just a handful (fewer than five bills) in each of the last four congressional terms.[46] In short, congressional leaders have decided to no longer leave the process of negotiating agreements across the two bodies to some other entity (committee members). Now, even with the most important legislation, conference committees are not part of the post-passage bargaining.

Moreover, the use of all forms of bargaining between the chambers has decreased. Occasionally, the two chambers engage in a more informal process of negotiations, trading amendments back and forth until the two versions of the bill look identical. The majority leadership often does this horse-trading, but sometimes prominent committee members are also involved. The use of this tactic has decreased, too, however, with only about 20 percent of successful bills using amendment trading.

Perhaps the most important part of Figure 7.6 is what is missing: give-and-take between the chambers. For the most part, in the end, one chamber simply

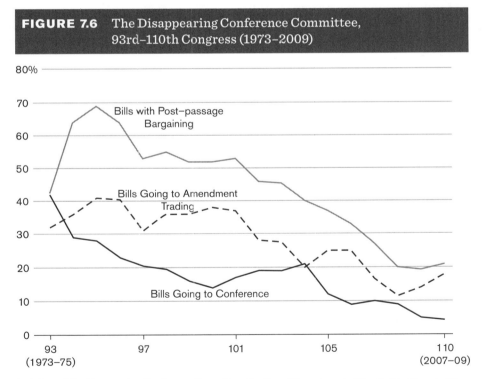

FIGURE 7.6 The Disappearing Conference Committee, 93rd–110th Congress (1973–2009)

Josh Ryan. "The Disappearing Conference Committee: The Use of Procedures by Minority Coalitions to Prevent Conferencing." *Congress & The Presidency* 38 (2011): 101–25.

adopts the other chamber's version of the bill with no conference and no horse-trading, just simple capitulation. Why? As the process of lawmaking in both chambers has become more fraught—with more partisan polarization and fewer lawmakers willing to give way on any ideological ground—extending the process of deliberation and bargaining makes reconciling differences more precarious. If a bill is going to make it through the legislative gauntlet, it may be that the chamber with the greatest challenges will often have to adopt the other chamber's bill simply to get something done.

CONCLUSION

This chapter has highlighted some of the major features of the postcommittee, policy-making practices in the House and Senate. The profound differences between the chambers emanate not only from the intent of the Framers, who purposely equipped them differently, but also from the evolution of the two bodies over more than two centuries. The House, with its more orderly structure, grants greater control to the majority party to direct the flow of legislation and advance its agenda. The Senate, in contrast, is more egalitarian in its design, providing a larger set of privileges to its members, who can influence Senate operations by obstructing legislation.

Recent political developments, particularly increased partisan polarization and more intense competition for majority control of both chambers, have created a new era of procedural politics in the House and Senate. In the House, the increase in partisanship tracks almost directly with the increase in restrictive rules for consideration of bills on the chamber floor. The majority-party leadership is keeping a tighter and tighter grip on what legislation looks like and what kinds of amendments the chamber can consider. The Senate has changed in somewhat different ways. While Senate majority leaders have slightly tightened their grip on floor amendments, the Senate has also experienced a very sharp increase in member independence through the use of obstructionist maneuvers. Although the Senate has always been a body governed by its members' privileges, the perpetual threat of a filibuster means that almost everything that goes through the Senate must now surpass the three-fifths threshold of support.

The evolution of the two chambers over the nation's history suggests that Congress's operations will continue to change with the times. Indeed, nearly every election in recent years has brought about significant surprises, with implications for the composition and incentives of members of Congress. We should expect further changes and continued evolution in the way policy is made in Congress.

Discussion Questions

1. In what ways did the Framers craft differences in the membership of the House and Senate? Were these distinctions effective in constructing law-making bodies with contrasting perspectives? Do the House and Senate today reflect the distinctions that the Framers intended?
2. How important was the adoption of the Seventeenth Amendment (providing for the direct election of senators) in shaping the behavior of senators and the operations of the Senate as a whole? In retrospect, was this a positive change?
3. Does the Senate majority leader's ability to restrict floor amendments (by filling the amendment tree) make the Senate operate too much like the House in terms of majority party control? Should this prerogative be restricted in any way?
4. What does the disappearance (for all practical purposes) of conference committees mean—if anything—for the quality and content of legislation?
5. Congressional policy making has always been hard, given separation of powers and checks and balances, and with greater polarization in recent years it seems to be getting only harder. Is this a cause for concern? What are the implications of an increasingly difficult policy-making process?

8

The Legislative Effectiveness of Congress and Its Members

During his reelection campaign in 1948, President Harry Truman continually railed against the "do-nothing" Republican Congress. He was determined to win reelection by campaigning against a Congress that he characterized as uncooperative and wary of supporting his policy agenda. The strategy worked. Truman won reelection, and the Democrats recaptured a majority of the seats in the House and the Senate. The moniker stuck, and the lawmakers who served that term would forever be known as members of the "Do-Nothing 80th Congress." Yet a close examination of the accomplishments of those two years does not reveal a legislature filled with slackers. The achievements of that Congress included statutes that authorized the Marshall Plan for reconstructing Europe after World War II, the Taft-Hartley Labor Management Relations Act to rein in trade unions, legislation to unify the armed services into the Department of Defense and create the Central Intelligence Agency, and adoption of critical economic and military aid to countries (such as Greece and Turkey) threatened by the Soviet Union. The 80th Congress (1947–49) also sent to the states for ratification a constitutional amendment limiting presidents to two terms.

In recent years, we have seen multiple government shutdowns and seemingly intractable partisanship in Congress. Does this mean that Congress, as a whole, is not doing its job effectively? What about individual members?

Unsurprisingly, presidents as well as members of Congress themselves have frequently used the perception of an unproductive and obstinate legislature to justify their own necessity in Washington—often saying, "Elect me, because I'll go to Washington to get things done!" (Interestingly, years later, many of the same lawmakers make a similar reference to the lack of progress in Washington as the justification for why they need to retire.) Recently, the phrase "Do-Nothing Congress" was resurrected to describe Congress during President Barack Obama's last term.[1] It had also been used to describe the prior 113th Congress (2013–15),[2] and in the term immediately preceding that, long-time Congress observer and scholar Norman Ornstein declared the 112th Congress (2011–13) the "Worst. Congress. Ever."[3] You get the picture. For a long time, journalists, commentators, scholars, and even lawmakers themselves have noted that Congress is incapable of fulfilling its role as the nation's central governing body.

But is Congress really that dysfunctional? On what criteria are such evaluations built? How do we measure whether Congress is doing its job? Certainly, it is easy to see how many bills Congress enacts, but is that number an accurate measure of effectiveness? It could be the case that lawmakers are filling their time with a great deal of legislative fluff—for example, commemorative and symbolic legislation—that does little to advance and adapt federal policy to evolving circumstances. Likewise, how do we know if individual lawmakers are effective at their job? And what does it even mean to be effective? The fact that representatives are in Washington does not necessarily mean they are making a difference serving their constituents or the nation as a whole. How can we measure congressional accomplishment at the individual level?

To tackle these questions, we divide this chapter into two sections: institutional and individual effectiveness in Congress. First, we focus on the macro view of Congress's governing responsibility. Accordingly, we conceive of "effectiveness" as the collective responsibility of Congress as a lawmaking body. Reflecting on the definition of governing presented in Chapter 1—the ability of Congress to keep the country and its government functioning in a competent manner—we ask, Is Congress meeting this obligation? The second part of the chapter explores the individual effectiveness of senators and representatives.

In most of the other chapters in this book, we have asked you to think about *how* Congress works. Here we ask, *Does* Congress work?

INSTITUTIONAL EFFECTIVENESS

To explore the effectiveness of Congress as a lawmaking and governing institution, we are essentially examining its performance over time. Interest in studying this aspect of Congress goes back for decades, and "performance" has mainly been defined as an analysis of its institutional operations, where the output or productivity of Congress is considered in categories such as lawmaking, oversight, and constituent service.[4] We analyze constituent service and congressional oversight elsewhere in this book (Chapters 3 and 10, respectively), so here we focus on lawmaking and governing performance. We concentrate on the range of activities Congress must perform to keep government operating and to meet its fiscal and statutory obligations. These activities include authorizations, annual budgets and appropriations, and monitoring of the federal debt. The primary question guiding our examination of congressional effectiveness is, How well does Congress meet its responsibilities in each of these categories?

Authorizations

Authorizing bills is one of the most important responsibilities of Congress. *Authorizations* establish or renew federal programs, agencies, policies, and other various projects, or they adjust the purpose or mission of an existing program or agency. In most instances, the authorization alone does not provide funding for

the programs and agencies it authorizes. Rather, *appropriations* legislation specifies the exact funding level of programs and agencies previously authorized,
granting agencies the authority to incur obligations and make payments out of
the federal Treasury. The goal of separating these two decisions is to ensure that
policy disagreements do not stand in the way of sustaining a program or agency's
funding.

Authorizations can be either short term (a matter of a few months or years) or
permanent (no statutory expiration date). In most cases, Congress enacts authorizations for a limited period—three to six years—but the authorization can be as
long as a quarter century or more. When legislation expires, appropriations or the
agency responsible for implementing a program are no longer legally authorized
to exist. According to congressional rules, when an authorization expires, funds
are not to be appropriated and agencies should cease their operations.

The use of short-term authorizations goes back to the Framers. Alexander
Hamilton argued in the *Federalist Papers* that such short-term legislation serves
as a "safeguard," allowing groups to "sound alarms" on policies they deem unfit.
While these short-term measures were used in the nation's early days, they only
became commonplace in the 1960s and 1970s.

Beyond the loftier goals of providing a periodic safeguard against problematic
statutes and allowing Congress to update existing programs and legislation according to changing circumstances, short-term authorizations were also attractive for
more practical political reasons. Forcing Congress to renew the authorization for
appropriations of many programs gives members of the authorizing committee
some control over the agencies within their purview. Without the requirement to
renew legislation that enables agencies and programs to exist, Congress's year-
to-year influence over executive branch departments would reside with the
Appropriations Committee members and their annual appropriations legislation.[5]

In addition, as the governing responsibilities of Congress ballooned in the
post–World War II period, using multiyear authorizations and staggering their
expiration dates provided a measure of control and predictability of the agenda
of House and Senate committees. Thus, except in cases of crisis, lawmakers
could put off stakeholders' persistent demands and proposals for policy changes
until the committee and its staff were prepared to consider the various aspects
of the relevant policy.[6] Some scholars have even argued that by forcing the
reconsideration of laws important to key corporate stakeholders (which often
have deep pockets and extensive government-relations operations), lawmakers
are simply "extracting rent" or ensuring a flow of campaign contributions from
these stakeholders, who wish to influence legislative decisions.[7] For example, the
Gallo family, long the owners of the largest winemaking company in the world,
became top contributors to the campaign committee of Senator Bob Dole (and
two of his sponsored foundations) in the 1980s and 1990s. The family's goal was

to protect a deferment in federal estate tax written specifically for them. This tax carve-out was continually up for review, and Dole had been the chair of the Senate Finance Committee (which is responsible for reviewing tax legislation) and eventually Senate minority leader.[8]

Placing so many government programs on short-term authorizations obligates future Congresses to update and renew them with some degree of regularity. In some instances, the laws contain a small number of expirations or a singular expiration that is critical to the existence of a program, such as the tax on the chemical and petroleum industries contained in the Comprehensive Environmental Response, Compensation, and Liability Act of 1980 (also known as Superfund), which provides federal authority over and funding for hazardous-waste cleanup. In other instances, sizable laws contain dozens or even hundreds of expiring provisions that fund a wide variety of programs (such as the Farm Bill or the Highway Bill) that have to be reauthorized every four to five years. In contrast, the massive Department of Defense authorization bill wraps up all the major matters regarding the department into one piece of legislation that needs to be authorized annually.

By one estimate, nearly a quarter of federal policy must undergo periodic reauthorization, making up an enormous proportion of the legislative work Congress performs.[9] With Congress needing to review hundreds of important laws that are set to expire each legislative term, the rate at which these laws are successfully renewed on time can serve as a good measurement of legislative productivity and accomplishment. If Congress is not renewing the authorizations for the plethora of federal programs, authorizing committees are abdicating their responsibility and putting governing on autopilot while new national and world issues, events, and circumstances emerge. When Congress is on autopilot, problematic programs can linger for years, wasting money and not fulfilling their original mission. Perhaps the poster child for this problem is the Endangered Species Act. Originally enacted in 1973 to prevent the extinction of and help in the recovery of endangered and threatened species, the law was last reauthorized in 1988, and its spending authority expired in 1992. Since then, the program has continued to exist simply through its annual appropriations, but difficulties and concerns with the law have racked up. Congress has only been able to enact very minor amendments to the law (mainly having to do with the Department of Defense), with no real substantive updates.

Why doesn't Congress reauthorize programs on time? The reasons can vary. Sometimes lawmakers are trying to avoid the controversy of the program or agency itself. For example, the Federal Election Commission—the agency that oversees the always-controversial laws governing campaign finance—has not seen its authorizing legislation renewed since 1980. The Endangered Species Act has made nearly no progress toward renewal in decades because lawmakers in the two parties have opposing goals. Republicans want to roll back the government's authority to restrict the actions of private citizens and landowners, while Democrats want to update the law's language and protections to better account for new scientific findings regarding climate change.

For other agencies and programs, Congress might not act on a reauthorization simply because the agency is doing its job well. The Civil Rights Commission, with its duties of promoting understanding and enforcement of U.S. civil rights laws, has been cited as an example of "if it ain't broke, don't fix it."[10]

Sometimes, reauthorization is a victim of the broader political environment on Capitol Hill. For example, in 2011, in the midst of the debt-ceiling crisis that gripped Washington that summer, the Federal Aviation Administration's (FAA) authorization expired. While the expired authorization went largely unnoticed, mainly because suspension of this relatively uncontroversial agency did not ultimately halt air travel, it did disrupt the FAA operations that are not directly related to air travel, such as the work of its construction contractors, for weeks. Lawmakers seemed to be more interested in scoring political points over the debt-ceiling crisis and taking their summer recess in July.

Figure 8.1 demonstrates Congress's growing problem with completing such authorizations. This figure accounts for the percentage of total discretionary

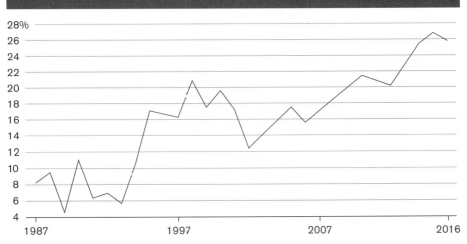

FIGURE 8.1 Percentage of Unauthorized Discretionary Spending, 1987–2016

Note: Data for years in which appropriations or defense authorization bills were not passed promptly are excluded from the graph.

Danny Vinik. February 3, 2016. "Meet Your Unauthorized Federal Government." *POLITICO*, www.politico.com /agenda/story/2016/02/government-agencies-programs-unauthorized-000036-000037 (accessed 6/19/18).

spending that Congress has had to appropriate without having a proper authorization enacted. As the figure shows, the percentage of federal spending that is unauthorized has increased significantly since the early 1990s.

At the same time, the percentage of laws enacted that include expiring provisions, and the average number of expiring provisions per law, have been decreasing. (See Figure 8.2.) This falling rate of expiring provisions in statutes is a result of Congress's increasing difficulty in passing regular authorizing laws. If Congress cannot enact authorizing legislation, it cannot enact laws that include provisions that will expire several years down the road.

What happens when Congress is unable to reauthorize a program or law? Government does not completely grind to a halt when one agency's authorization expires. If it is inclined to keep a program going, Congress can use a waiver in the appropriations to fund the program, even if it lacks an active authorization. It can also offer guidance to administrators through oversight hearings. This is what Congress has done for decades with the U.S. Fish and Wildlife Service and its administration of the Endangered Species Act. Is there any harm in that? Yes. The governance responsibility of Congress is not so easily fulfilled through such workarounds. For example, that short lapse in the FAA authorization

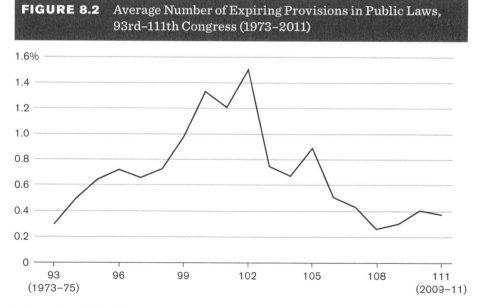

FIGURE 8.2 Average Number of Expiring Provisions in Public Laws, 93rd–111th Congress (1973–2011)

E. Scott Adler and Stefani Langehennig. 2016. "Tracking Statutory Reauthorizations: Creating a New Metric for Legislative Productivity." Paper prepared for the annual meeting of the American Political Science Association, Philadelphia, Pennsylvania.

(mentioned earlier) resulted in the temporary layoff of 4,000 FAA employees and halted construction across the country, affecting $2.5 billion in airport projects and 24,000 construction workers.[11]

Keeping the Lights On: The Congressional Budget and Appropriations Process

Among the most basic functions of Congress is its responsibility to approve spending for existing federal programs. It does so through a two-step process: budgeting (deciding the cap on overall spending) and appropriations (determining how much each individual program or agency can spend).

STEP 1: THE BUDGET   The word "budget" is often bandied about loosely when referring to how Congress spends money. To be exact, there are really three elements of the budget process: authorizing legislation (already discussed), the budget resolution, and appropriations legislation. Since authorizations generally entail multiyear planning, the annual budget process mostly consists of the budget and appropriations process.

For the better part of a century, the president has been mandated to start the budgetary process every year with a proposal for the entire federal budget. The federal budget incorporates the administration's estimates for revenues and expenditures in the coming year, its projections for several years going forward, and the president's budget request for each agency. You can think of this budget as the president's opening bid. The president is required to present this estimate in February. In addition to the budget provided by the president, federal agencies offer additional information to the committees in the form of a budget justification. (Table 8.1 shows a complete time line of the budget and appropriations process.)

Congress's response over the course of the next several weeks includes hearings by the budget committees in both the House and Senate, reports issued by the authorizing committees regarding their views of the proposed budget, and an important report from the Congressional Budget Office assessing the economy, along with revenue and expenditure projections.

By mid-April, the House and Senate are required to come up with their *concurrent resolution* on the overall budget for the coming year. (Because it is a resolution and not a public law, it does not require the president's signature.) Think of the concurrent resolution as a target overall ceiling on spending meant to constrain Congress's actions when it completes the appropriations bills. In recent years, it has not been uncommon for Congress not to be able to pass a budget resolution at all (as in fiscal years 1999, 2003, 2005, 2007, and 2011–15). While

TABLE 8.1 Budget and Appropriations Timeline	
Date	**Action**
First Monday in February	President submits budget to Congress.
February 15	Congressional Budget Office submits economic and budget outlook report to budget committees.
Six weeks after president submits budget	Committees submit views and estimates to budget committees.
April 1	Senate Budget Committee reports budget resolution.
April 15	Congress completes action on budget resolution.
May15	Annual appropriations bills may be considered in the House, even if action on budget resolution has not been completed.
June 10	House Appropriations Committee reports last annual appropriations bill.
June 15	Congress completes action on reconciliation legislation (if required by budget resolution).
June 30	House completes action on annual appropriations bills.
July 15	President submits midsession review of his budget to Congress.
October 1	Fiscal year begins.

Bill Heniff Jr. March 20, 2008. "The Congressional Budget Process Timetable." In CRS Report for Congress. Washington, DC: Congressional Research Service.

the average budget resolution is about a month late, some are considerably later. There are no real consequences for the budget being late, other than the absence of a coherent plan to guide the appropriations process. (For more details, see Table 8.2.)

STEP 2: APPROPRIATIONS While the budget resolution creates the context for overall spending, the appropriations bills allow the Treasury to make payments for a specific program or agency. Appropriations acts must be passed every year to provide funding for the continued operation of federal departments, agencies, and various government activities

The U.S. Constitution outlines the appropriations process in Article I, Section 9: "No money shall be drawn from the Treasury, but in Consequence of Appropriations made by Law." In effect, the Constitution declares that the process of spending money out of the Treasury is like any other statute enacted by the legislature. In laws passed over the years, Congress has reinforced this power

TABLE 8.2   Dates of Final Adoption of the Budget Resolution

Fiscal Year	Date Adopted	Fiscal Year	Date Adopted
1976	05-14-1975	1997	06-13-1996
1977	05-13-1976	1998	06-05-1997
1978	05-17-1977	1999	[none]
1979	05-17-1978	2000	04-15-1999
1980	05-24-1979	2001	04-13-2000
1981	06-12-1980	2002	05-10-2001
1982	05-21-1981	2003	[none]
1983	06-23-1982	2004	04-11-2003
1984	06-23-1983	2005	[none]
1985	10-01-1984	2006	04-28-2005
1986	08-01-1985	2007	[none]
1987	06-27-1986	2008	05-17-2007
1988	06-24-1987	2009	06-05-2008
1989	06-06-1988	2010	04-29-2009
1990	05-18-1989	2011	[none]
1991	10-09-1990	2012	[none]
1992	05-22-1991	2013	[none]
1993	05-21-1992	2014	[none]
1994	04-01-1993	2015	[none]
1995	05-12-1994	2016	05-05-2015
1996	06-29-1995	2017	01-13-2017

Bill Heniff Jr. November 16, 2015. "Congressional Budget Resolutions: Historical Information." In CRS Report for Congress. Washington, DC: Congressional Research Service.

of appropriation with other statutory provisions, including language stipulating that public funds may be used only for the purposes for which Congress appropriated the funds.

The appropriations process garners considerable attention because it serves as a flash point for battles between the two parties, between coalitions within Congress, and between governmental and nongovernmental stakeholders, but the appropriations process does not account for the majority of government expenses. An enormous proportion of federal spending is *mandatory* in that it must be incurred, and the only thing that could change that would be an act of Congress. These obligatory spending responsibilities include interest on the national debt, contractual obligations, and (most prominently) entitlement spending. *Entitlement* programs—including large government programs such as Social Security, Medicare, veterans' compensation, Medicaid, and Temporary Assistance for Needy Families (TANF)—are mandatory because they rely on formulas whereby anyone who meets certain criteria receives the benefit. *Discretionary spending* is, by definition, not mandatory. It covers the costs of executive branch agencies, congressional offices, and international programs.

Figure 8.3 shows the changes in the three major categories of federal spending since the early 1960s. As these data demonstrate, the ratio of discretionary/mandatory federal spending—and thus the degree to which congressional appropriators influence how government spends money—has changed dramati-

FIGURE 8.3 Percentage of Total Government Spending by Category, 1962–2017

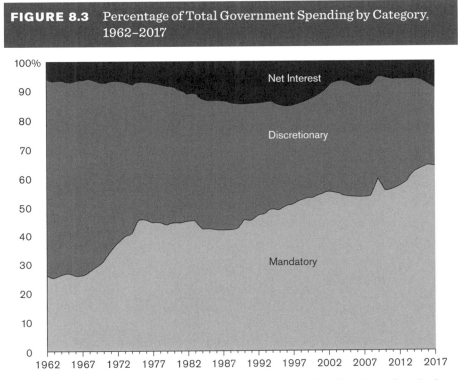

Austin, D. Andrew. November 26, 2014. "The Budget Control Act and Trends in Discretionary Spending." In CRS Report for Congress. Washington, DC: Congressional Research Service, Figure 1.

cally in the last few decades. As the federal government adopted new entitlement programs in the 1960s (such as Medicare and Medicaid) and as the large baby-boom generation reached retirement age, the cost of mandatory spending programs has increased from about one-third of total federal outlays to two-thirds.

How does Congress decide what to do with its third of the government's money? The process of congressional appropriating effectively begins in the House of Representatives, which is the first chamber to consider each appropriations bill. The Constitution grants the House the authority to originate revenue bills, and this privilege has historically been extended to include appropriations bills. However, rather than wait to consider the House appropriations bills, Senate appropriators have, in recent years, frequently considered their own version of appropriations bills simultaneously with their House counterparts. Starting in the second half of May, the various subcommittees of the House and Senate Appropriations Committees (Table 8.3) take action on the respective appropriations bills that coincide with their jurisdictions.

Members of Congress first consider appropriations bills in subcommittee. The first process includes hearings, bill drafting, mark up, and reporting. Appropriations hearings focus on the relevant agencies' budget justifications and often include the testimonies of agency officials. The subcommittee often solicits input from other members of Congress with respect to programmatic spending

TABLE 8.3 House Appropriations Subcommittees, 115th Congress (2017–19)
Agriculture, Rural Development, Food and Drug Administration, and related agencies
Commerce, Justice, Science, and related agencies
Defense
Energy and Water Development, and related agencies
Financial Services and General Government
Homeland Security
Interior, Environment, and related agencies
Labor, Health and Human Services, Education, and related agencies
Legislative Branch
Military Construction, Veterans Affairs, and related agencies
State, Foreign Operations, and related programs
Transportation, Housing and Urban Development, and related agencies

levels and instructions to be tied to appropriations language. Each individual appropriations bill is then reported to the full Appropriations Committee for consideration. The Appropriations Committee's subsequent report is brought to the entire chamber. Both House and Senate Appropriations Committees are expected to have completed their consideration of these bills by July, just prior to Congress's summer recess, so that early fall can be used for chamber consideration and reconciliation of differences in House and Senate versions. However, delays in this process, driven by the difficulty of resolving disputes over spending levels, have led to more frequent consolidation of the separate appropriations bills into large "omnibus" legislation.

After appropriations measures are reported by their respective chamber's committee, they are then considered on the House and Senate floors. This process, however, can be complicated by other factors. As we have seen by House and Senate rules, any program or agency needs an *authorization* from Congress, defining the terms of its existence and its budgetary cap before it can receive an appropriation. At the same time, however, lawmakers often cannot afford to have such programs simply go away because rules require authorization before the appropriation, as authorization often faces its own roadblocks. Accordingly, Congress will, as a matter of course, pass a *waiver* that allows funding to be enacted, even though the authorization is no longer in effect. Essentially, members of Congress are continuing a program or agency using the appropriations but without a proper authorization.

Once each individual appropriations measure is debated and adopted by the respective chambers, the "textbook" process will instruct the House and Senate to use conference committees to reconcile their differences. Recall from Chapter 7 that conferees for these panels are normally drawn from the members of the relevant committees of jurisdiction, in this case the Appropriations subcommittees.

As with many aspects of congressional operations, the traditional mechanisms of lawmaking and governance that reigned for years rarely apply in the contemporary period. Changes to the appropriations process are a good illustration of changes in congressional performance. In recent years, Congress has more often than not been incapable of passing all appropriations measures separately, and in many cases, it had to lump together all or several of the separate bills into an omnibus measure. Often, these omnibus measures include the full text of the separate appropriations measures as they were crafted by the individual subcommittees. Packaging the separate bills into one omnibus bill can smooth out negotiations between the chambers (or between Congress and the president) by providing more areas on which the relevant parties may give and take.[12]

Increasing polarization over the last few decades has resulted in a more dysfunctional appropriations process, with Congress getting fewer appropriations bills done on time.[13] When Congress is unable to complete appropriations legislation by the end of the fiscal year (October 1), it must pass a stopgap measure to provide funding for programs and agencies until regular appropriations can be finalized. This continuing appropriations act, commonly called a *continuing resolution (CR)*, provides for the uninterrupted operation of programs and agencies for which there is no current legal appropriation.

The use of CRs is commonplace in the modern Congress. Analyzing the use of CRs offers one indication of how successful the body is in completing its regular duties of federal budgeting. First, though, it is important to understand the distinction between full-year and temporary CRs. Temporary CRs are intended to buy Congress a few days, weeks, or months until it can complete and pass the regular appropriations. Thus such short-term CRs are usually an indication that lawmakers are close to a deal and simply need a little more time. Accordingly, these acts are often "clean" in that they generally fund programs at the same rate as the previous year's appropriation and do not add new legislation or start new programs.

However, when Congress has decided to abandon the regular appropriations process, largely because a new deal is either a distant prospect or completely infeasible, it will enact a full-year CR to cover funding for agencies until it can restart the process for the next year. In these circumstances, we are more likely to see changes to the funding rate of existing programs or even new legislative provisions (the equivalent of "authorizing" language). In effect, in these circumstances, the CR process supplants regular appropriations legislation. While legislative provisions are restricted in regular appropriations bills (although the restrictions are sometimes waived), these restrictions are more relaxed for CRs. As a result, meaningful legislation is sometimes included in these statutes. Most lawmakers usually consider this legislation to be *must pass*, which makes it easier to pass the CR. For example, the 1984 Comprehensive Crime Control Act— one of the most significant revisions of federal criminal statutes in nearly a century—was contained in a CR for fiscal year 1985. Interestingly, the use of CRs and omnibus appropriations—which are deviations from the normal procedures—have little meaningful effect on the overall budget surplus, total federal spending, or even the economy as a whole. In essence, it appears that lawmakers see these operations as the new normal.[14]

What are the trends with regard to Congress's use of CRs? Since fiscal year (FY) 1977, Congress has completed all the regular appropriations acts before the start of the fiscal year only four times—FY 1977, FY 1989, FY 1995, and FY 1997. The number and duration of CRs have varied considerably from year to year. In every year between 1978 and 1988, Congress used full-year CRs to cover at least one, and sometimes all, of the unpassed appropriations bills. In some recent years, lawmakers have used a considerable number of short-duration CRs (Figure 8.4). For instance, in 2001, Congress passed 21 CRs, averaging just

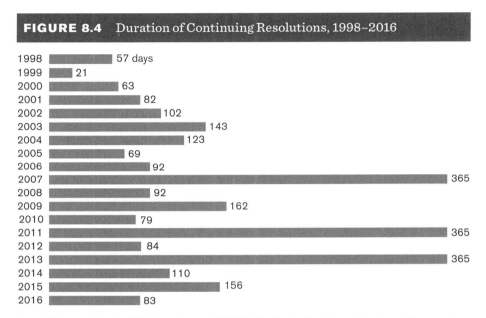

FIGURE 8.4 Duration of Continuing Resolutions, 1998–2016

1998	57 days
1999	21
2000	63
2001	82
2002	102
2003	143
2004	123
2005	69
2006	92
2007	365
2008	92
2009	162
2010	79
2011	365
2012	84
2013	365
2014	110
2015	156
2016	83

James Saturno and Jessica Tollestrup. January 14, 2016. "Continuing Resolutions: Overview of Components and Recent Practices." In CRS Report for Congress. Washington, DC: Congressional Research Service.

under four days per act. Full-year CRs covered all or nearly all required appropriations acts in FY 2007, 2011, and 2013.

FUNDING GAPS Sometimes, Congress is incapable of either enacting the required appropriations legislation or even the stopgap CRs. When this funding gap occurs, federal law bars the obligation or expenditure of federal funds, thus resulting in a shutdown of federal government activities. (Exceptions are made for the continuance of activities involving "the safety of human life or the protection of property.")

Since the late 1970s, funding gaps have occurred a number of times with varying degrees of effect on the functioning of the federal government (Table 8.4). The number and length of funding gaps provide a way to measure the successful functioning of Congress. For example, during the four years of Jimmy Carter's administration, several lengthy funding gaps occurred, resulting in many government shutdowns. During a number of these funding gaps, agencies curtailed some of their operations but continued to operate partially under expired funding.

Subsequently, in 1980 and 1981, the U.S. attorney general issued several opinions outlining the procedures to be taken by agencies to shut down their activities in the event of a funding gap. The result was more pressure on lawmakers to resolve their differences before a funding gap would affect citizens. Many of the funding gaps in the following 15 years were of short duration and

TABLE 8.4   Appropriations Funding Gaps since 1976

Year	Full days of gap(s)
1976	10
1977	12
	8
	8
1978	17
1979	11
1981	2
1982	1
	3
1983	3
1984	2
	1
1986	1
1987	1
1990	3
1995	5
	21
2013	16
2018	3

James Saturno. September 13, 2017. "Federal Funding Gaps: A Brief Overview." In CRS Report for Congress. Washington, DC: Congressional Research Service, with additional data collected by authors.

occurred over a weekend. Agencies were sometimes instructed not to shut down completely because a budget agreement among lawmakers seemed imminent.

Nevertheless, two of the longer shutdowns in recent memory included back-to-back funding gaps during the winter of 1995–96. The impasse was the result of a disagreement between President Bill Clinton and the Republican Congress over Medicare premium increases that were contained in the CR and a provision requiring the president to produce a balanced budget in seven years. President Clinton's veto of the CR resulted in the furlough of 800,000 federal workers. A funding gap in 2013 was caused primarily by a Democrat-controlled Senate that was unwilling to agree with a Republican-led House over the terms of the CR.

The use of continuing resolutions (CRs) to fund government activities can become controversial. In 2013, the government shut down over language Republicans wanted in the CR that would defund Obamacare. President Obama promised to veto any such resolution, leading to the stalemate.

At stake was language in the Republican bill that defunded programs that were part of the Affordable Care Act ("Obamacare"), resulting in a game of "chicken" between the two chambers with funding of the U.S. government at stake.

FEDERAL DEBT LIMIT Related to federal spending is the *gross federal debt*, or the total debt held by the federal government (including money owed to the public and obligations held within the government's own trust fund accounts—Social Security, Medicare, highways, and so on). Since the early part of the twentieth century, Congress has placed a limit on federal debt. As government spending increases, or as the economy lags and therefore tax revenues decrease, we frequently approach that limit. Given that the federal government runs annual deficits regularly—incoming receipts into the Treasury Department do not keep pace with the daily obligations of federal spending—Congress must authorize any increase in the debt limit to allow the government to continue to borrow and pay for its commitments. Without statutory approval for increasing debt, the federal government would effectively default on its obligations, which could include not paying Social Security benefits, the salaries of federal employees, and veterans' benefits.

In many ways, a default is an even more serious crisis than a government shutdown. In the case of a shutdown, government employees and contractors are not paid. But in a default, everyone to whom the government owes money is at risk of not being paid. The government is unable to make all mandatory payments, pay interest on its debt, or pay interest to U.S. bondholders around the world. While a default has never occurred, some believe that such an action would have a catastrophic effect on global financial markets and foreign economies owing to a ripple effect of skyrocketing interest rates, a plummeting value for the U.S. dollar, and likely worldwide financial crises as foreign governments divest their U.S. Treasury holdings.

Most members of Congress believe that an increase in the debt limit is must-pass legislation. Most often, the debt limit is raised with little disagreement among lawmakers or between parties. From 2008 to 2018, the debt ceiling has been raised 10 times, with four increases in 2008 and 2009 alone. Nevertheless, it is not hard to imagine that increases in the debt limit can become a battleground for larger disagreements on Capitol Hill and between Congress and the president regarding the federal budget and *fiscal policy* (that is, policies that affect federal taxing and spending).

Examining the process of raising the federal debt limit can help us assess congressional effectiveness. When federal debt comes close to the existing limit, the Treasury Department can temporarily reduce debt by taking extraordinary measures to handle its cash and debt-management responsibilities, including sophisticated accounting techniques and the shifting around of federal funds. Such actions might entail suspending payments into the retirement funds of federal government and postal employees. The Treasury Department taking these extraordinary steps to avoid an impending default is a sign of dysfunction in Congress.

In recent years, the Treasury Department has been compelled to take extraordinary measures during congressional debt-limit impasses in 1985, 1995–96, 2002 (twice), 2003, 2011, 2013, 2014, and 2015. For example, in 2011, an intense battle occurred between President Obama—allied with his Democratic majority in the Senate—and the Republican-controlled House of Representatives. While both sides had a vision for cutting the deficit, those visions were completely different and largely incompatible. Democrats wanted to end tax cuts that were instituted under President George W. Bush and cut defense spending, while Republicans wanted to turn Medicare into a voucher program, defund Obamacare, and impose other cuts in domestic spending. As the debt limit approached, and with no resolution in sight, Treasury Secretary Timothy Geithner engaged in several financial maneuvers to stave off a default on the debt. The reaction of financial and securities firms was exemplified by Standard & Poor's (a bond rating agency) lowering the rating on U.S. credit from AAA to AA+ in August 2011, causing a severe dip in U.S. stock markets. The ultimate agreement between President Obama and congressional Republicans raised the debt ceiling but put off the decision on deficit reduction until after the 2012 election.[15]

The increased number of such crises indicates the worsening difficulty Congress has experienced in finding common ground on fiscal policy. Interestingly, scholars have found that lawmakers' positions on debt-limit increases are less often driven by their ideological stance on government spending and more often driven by their party's stake in keeping the machinery of government operating. In particular, "the debt limit is generally a burden of those in power, meaning that majority parties and those controlling the presidency typically have to carry these bills. Meanwhile, the out party exploits these votes as an opportunity to denounce the performance of those responsible for governance."[16] In practice, members of Congress often take opposing positions when voting on increases in the debt limit depending on their party's governing status. They oppose the increase when they are in the minority, but with the full knowledge that the majority will have to vote together to increase the debt limit. Alternatively, they support it when they are in the majority or belong to the same party as the president. This phenomenon holds regardless of which party is in power, although the effect intensifies when one party has unified control of both chambers of Congress and the presidency.

By all the metrics we have examined thus far, it seems clear that Congress has had increasing difficulty in the last few decades fulfilling its governing responsibilities. From late or incomplete budgets, to appropriations bills enacted as a batch, to continual games of chicken on the debt ceiling, to the growing number of federal programs without an active authorization, Congress has demonstrated a wide array of dysfunction in its normal duties of overseeing the federal budget and keeping programs operating. But these examples also illustrate the variety of techniques and strategies that lawmakers can pursue to stave off pending disaster. We can conclude that as long as lawmakers have means at their disposal to get around the difficult and controversial decisions of governing, they will likely continue to kick the proverbial can down the road.

HOW WE STUDY
MAKING HISTORIC LEGISLATION

A loftier perspective on the legislative effectiveness of Congress could measure how well it steers the ship of government. As conditions arise and the needs and opinions of constituents evolve, Congress must adjust federal policy and, with some degree of regularity, redefine its role in society. Thus, rather than examining the year-to-year upkeep of government functions—renewing existing programs or ensuring their funding—a broader gauge of congressional performance is its ability to make major shifts in policy.

Whether members of Congress favor larger or smaller government or federal authority, they know that changing the size of government, moving it in different directions, or rescinding existing powers takes important new legislation. The decision by Congress and President Lyndon Johnson to widen the federal government's programs providing assistance for elderly, poor, and disabled Americans required a wide array of new legislation, including the Food Stamp Act of 1964, Social Security Amendments of 1965 (creating Medicare and Medicaid), and the Demonstration Cities and Metropolitan Development Act of 1966 (for urban renewal), among others. In 1996, when President Clinton and Congress decided to roll back the federal government's role in basic welfare programs, it passed the Personal Responsibility and Work Opportunity Reconciliation Act, which ended many direct payments from the federal government to impoverished individuals, limiting the time of eligibility for benefits and adding in a work requirement. This act is still considered one of the major legislative accomplishments of the Clinton presidency and the most profound welfare reform in a generation.

Many observers of Congress see the pace and extent of these landmark laws as a good way to gauge the body's ability to react to changing societal conditions, but questions remain: How do we study the output of landmark legislation? What distinguishes a run-of-the-mill law from one that should be considered of historic or landmark importance?

Perhaps the most important early work on these questions has been done by political scientist David Mayhew. Mayhew was interested in whether divided government (different parties controlling the presidency and one or both chambers of Congress) affects what legislation gets done. Mayhew's simple question was, Do congressional terms characterized by divided government experience significantly fewer landmark enactments than terms of unified government?

Mayhew wanted to answer this question by creating a list of landmark laws enacted during each two-year congressional term. To do so, he first examined annual end-of-the-congressional-session (year) wrap-up articles published by the *New York Times* and the *Washington Post*. These articles provide an assessment of the most significant legislation passed by Congress in the previous year by expert observers. Mayhew then wanted to capture the retrospective judgments of policy specialists on what laws should be considered historically significant. To do so, he relied on scholarly accounts of the development of a large number of specific policy areas over time.

The result of Mayhew's work was a term-by-term catalog of the landmark legislation enacted by Congress from the end of World War II until the present.[17] Aggregating the list of historic statutes by congressional term gives us an overview of Congress's ability to produce important legislation over time under different internal and external conditions (Figure 8.5).

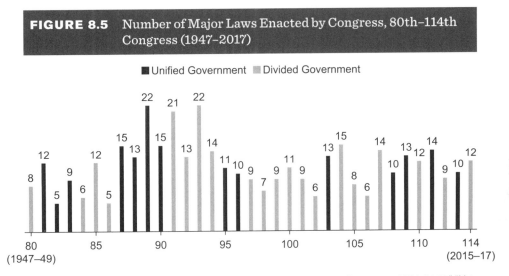

FIGURE 8.5 Number of Major Laws Enacted by Congress, 80th–114th Congress (1947–2017)

David Mayhew. "List of Important Enactments, 1947–1990," "List of Important Enactments 1991–2002," "List of Important Enactments 2003–2016," Datasets and Materials: Divided We Govern. http://campuspress.yale .edu/davidmayhew/datasets-divided-we-govern (accessed 7/5/18).

We see a few important trends. There is clearly a "bulge" in significant legislation throughout much of the 1960s and the early 1970s. This was a period of many profound legislative changes surrounding civil rights and the expansion of federal programs designed as part of President Johnson's Great Society initiative. Subsequently, there are ebbs and flows of legislation but no real sustained period of surges or slumps in lawmaking. Mayhew's measure shows that unified government does not contribute appreciably to any increase in landmark statutes. Other than the bulge of the Johnson/Richard Nixon era, periods of divided government (gray) do not show a significantly lower count of historic laws than periods of unified government (black).

In reaction to Mayhew's novel way of thinking of congressional accomplishment, other scholars undertook their own accounting of high-level lawmaking on Capitol Hill, often employing different primary-source information to denote "significant" or landmark legislation. For example, Howell et al. (2000) categorized all laws enacted in the postwar period into one of four levels of importance based on their coverage not just in the *New York Times* and the *Washington Post* but also in the large *Congressional Quarterly Almanac*, a 500- to 600-page yearly retrospective of all activity in Congress.[18] These researchers found that divided government *does* seem to have a depressing effect on the output of important legislation, and the lack of activity on landmark bills is apparently offset by more symbolic legislation. Alternatively, Joshua Clinton and John S. Lapinski, who measured significant legislation back to the 1870s, relied on the ratings of a more expansive set of experts, many of them from academia.[19] They too found that productivity is positively related to periods of unified governmental control.

While the number of historic laws passed is an important metric when evaluating legislative effectiveness, shouldn't effectiveness also be measured in terms of what the people actually want from Congress? In effect, some argue that the raw count of total important laws does not account for expectations of, or demand for, change in policy areas.

A few scholars have explored the question of the public's demands for policy. Of particular note is Sarah Binder's exploration of *legislative gridlock*. For her research, she created a list of legislative agenda items by congressional term—effectively, a measure of the expectations on Congress. She compiled this list based on the issues discussed in editorials in the *New York Times*. She used the level of the *Times*'s attention to an issue as an indicator of its salience among the public and political elites. Binder then examined whether Congress and the president took legislative action in that two-year congressional term to address each salient issue. The resulting gridlock score captures the percentage of agenda items left in limbo at the close of the Congress (Figure 8.6).[20]

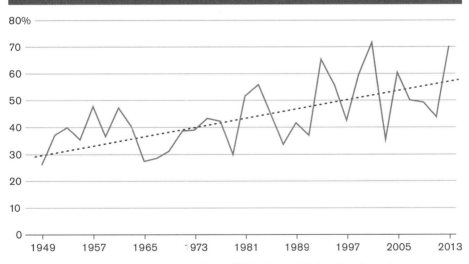

FIGURE 8.6 Percentage of Legislative Issues in Gridlock, 1949–2013

Sarah A. Binder. May 27, 2014. "Polarized We Govern?" Washington, DC: Brookings Institution, www .brookings.edu/research/papers/2014/05/27-polarized-we-govern-congress-legislative-gridlock-polarized -binder (accessed 7/5/18).

Binder's measure shows an overall increase in gridlock over time. Although not moving in a straight line, from 1947 to 2013, there has been a sizable increase in gridlocked policies or agenda items left in limbo at the end of a legislative term. Binder explains the trend in two ways. First, the shrinking of the ideological center and the related widening polarization of the two parties make it harder to create policy coalitions for the passage of agenda items, regardless of unified or divided partisan control of Congress and the presidency. Second, even controlling for party polarization, differences in the ideological positions of the two chambers also have a meaningful effect on gridlock. The further apart the median ideological position of the House and Senate (even factoring in divergent partisan majorities), the lower the probability that the two chambers can agree to adopt legislation addressing policy-agenda items.

The quantitative metrics we have discussed so far do not always satisfy the goal of capturing "accomplishment" or even what lawmakers are aiming to achieve. Political scientist Doug Arnold has expanded on this note of caution, asserting that there is a "liberal bias" in believing that successful governing or legislative performance should be judged by new laws, especially laws that are considered to have more impact on the redirection of governance.[21] Arnold argues that many, particularly those pursuing a shrinking of government, would prefer to judge Congress by the degree to which those policy goals are achieved. Perhaps such an evaluation can be conducted on the basis of a small number of laws and congressional actions that are part of the normal functioning of Congress—omnibus appropriations, budget reconciliations, and so on—or even extraordinary actions that do not result in any new legislation, such as a government shutdown or an instance of sequestration. Based on these criteria, recent Congresses could be judged as wildly successful.

Arnold's reservations notwithstanding, these broad measures of governing provide a closer look at congressional effectiveness. Lawmakers lately seem to be producing significant legislation at about the same rate that Congress has historically, although recent terms would not rank anywhere near the most productive Congresses in current memory. Although there is some dispute as to whether unified or divided government makes a difference, we can draw a similar conclusion as that gained from our examination of budgets, appropriations, and authorizations: Congress increasingly struggles to govern effectively.

Critical Thinking

1. At its most productive (in the 1960s and early 1970s), according to the work of Mayhew, Congress was producing 20–25 pieces of historic legislation in a two-year congressional term. In the last few decades, it rarely produces more than 10–15. Does its recent work seem sufficient, or would you call Congress underproductive?

2. Do you consider Binder's method of using *New York Times* editorials to construct a public agenda a good technique for creating a measure of demand for legislation? Does her gauge of gridlock conform with your perceptions of Congress's productivity?

3. Can you name historic legislation produced by Congress that you would consider liberal, conservative, or neither/both? Does Congress produce more historic legislation that is liberal or conservative? What effect do the conditions inside Congress and in the political climate overall have on the kind and amount of historic legislation passed?

INDIVIDUAL EFFECTIVENESS

Understanding effectiveness at the institutional level versus the individual level is comparable to contrasting congressional governance versus representation. Governing refers to the legislature making laws and conducting oversight in an effective manner. Representation, at least in part, means making legislation on behalf of the varied interests represented by the member of Congress. Here we examine how effective individual lawmakers are at performing their job of making laws.

Evaluating individual lawmakers' legislative effectiveness involves more than simply measuring who gets what done in Washington. When lawmakers campaign in their districts, they often justify their pursuit of power and policy on Capitol Hill with an emphasis on being legislatively effective.[22] Voters often cite effectiveness as a central reason for liking or disliking incumbent representatives.[23] Given that legislative effectiveness is integral to lawmakers' "home styles" (see Chapter 3) and how voters assess them, it is not surprising that scholars have created measures of effectiveness.

In gauging effectiveness, scholars have employed a variety of indicators. Some are relatively straightforward markers of the lawmaking process in Congress, such as a count of the total bills a representative authors or "sponsors" that are passed each term. Other measures of effectiveness construct more sophisticated metrics ranging from the proportion of bills introduced that are enacted to an even more complex score crafted from the combined progress of each bill that a lawmaker sponsors through the various hurdles of congressional deliberation (committee action, committee report, floor passage, and so on). While the means of measuring legislative accomplishment vary, they all aim to determine "the proven ability to advance a member's agenda items through the legislative process and into law."[24]

A primary goal of these analyses is to identify characteristics of individual members of Congress, or even circumstances surrounding these lawmakers, that contribute to more effective lawmaking. For decades, scholars have studied individual success—using "hit rates" or "batting averages"—to reveal the traits of lawmakers most associated with accomplishment.[25]

Scholars are interested in both inherent and acquired traits of lawmakers that are likely to lead to legislative success. Not surprisingly, a lawmaker who is a member of the majority party in either chamber—with its intrinsic control of the legislative agenda—possesses a sizable advantage when it comes to bill success. All things equal, if majority leaders need to choose between two identical bills, they will likely choose the one from a fellow majority party member over that of a minority party representative. In our era of hyperpartisanship and polarization, research along these lines has further discovered that loyalty to the majority party agenda and its leaders is rewarded with a greater degree of legislative success.[26]

Ideology, while often closely associated with partisanship, does seem to have a distinct effect on lawmaking effectiveness. In a study of lawmaking in the Senate—the chamber that is institutionally designed for consensual rather than majoritarian tendencies—researchers discovered that the body is more responsive to the policy proposals of ideologically moderate lawmakers. The bills of senators who hew toward the ideological center of the chamber are the bills most likely to advance through Senate passage.[27]

Tenure that lawmakers build over many years of service in Congress is also frequently associated with lawmaking accomplishment.[28] The advantages associated with senior lawmakers are likely a consequence of a number of factors, including long experience in navigating the legislative process, a reputation of expertise in an issue area, built-up networks of legislative partnerships, and acquired positions of institutional influence (such as party leadership positions and committee leadership).

Being a specialist within an issue area can give a lawmaker a degree of both credibility and knowledge that can be tremendously useful in propelling his or her legislative ideas forward. Specialization has been defined in different ways, including the degree to which a member's bills are focused within a small number of issue areas. Perhaps the most common indicator of specialization is committee membership. Committee seats provide lawmakers with access to information and institutional advantages that influence the legislative process in ways not possible otherwise. Committees have sizable and experienced staffs, and are privy to information provided from agencies, external policy experts, and affected groups and stakeholders as part of the regular deliberations for authorizing legislation and oversight. In addition, we have already noted the privileged position that committees frequently retain in setting the lawmaking agenda on matters within their jurisdictions.[29]

More than anyone else, committee leaders—committee and subcommittee chairs, and to a lesser degree the ranking minority members—are in a position of responsibility for ensuring that the panel's work gets done. Due to the prevalence of authorizing legislation that contains expirations, it is the committee leaders who nearly always take the lead in the effort to renew and update these laws. Thus legislative "success" is an imperative of their institutional position.[30]

Finally, some legislative effectiveness is attributed to lawmakers' entrepreneurial efforts to educate their colleagues about the advantages of proposed legislation and their efforts to build winning coalitions. Scholars have discovered that bills are more likely to pass when members give speeches in support of their bills on the chamber floor and when they seek cosponsors for their legislative proposals.[31]

Perhaps the most comprehensive effort to examine lawmaker effectiveness was undertaken by political scientists Craig Volden and Alan Wiseman, who took a broad view in measuring bill success, exploring effectiveness holistically. That is, they believed that lawmakers can be judged to be effective with measures that are more nuanced than total laws attributed or statutory batting averages. Volden and Wiseman contend that the ability to propel bills forward, even when those bills are not enacted into law, demonstrates a level of legislative acumen. Moreover, it is important to differentiate among commemorative/symbolic bills, more substantive bills, and proposals that are the most legislatively significant (that is, similar to Mayhew's historic statutes discussed earlier). Volden and Wiseman therefore accounted for the fraction of each member's bills that (1) are introduced, (2) receive action in committee, (3) receive action beyond committee, (4) pass the House, and (5) become law. Combining the progress of a lawmaker's bills and weighting in favor of the more significant one constitutes his or her legislative effectiveness score (LES).

Analyzing this score confirms that several factors are correlated with a representative's LES. Among these are circumstantial factors, such as being a member of the majority party, being more electorally safe, and being female. Electorally precarious members of Congress are likely to focus their efforts on activities that are more reelection oriented, such as fundraising and constituent contact, rather than bill activity. Alternatively, Volden and Wiseman found that female legislators adopt different strategies than male legislators, and legislative success comes in different ways depending on whether they are in the majority or minority parties. They contend that female members of Congress in the minority party tend to use consensus building and coalitions to strengthen the prospects of their legislative proposals. (Although, notably, Jennifer Lawless and Richard Fox do not find that female members of Congress are any more likely to build bipartisan coalitions than male lawmakers.[32]) Female representatives who belong to the majority party increase the perception of their legislative effectiveness, as measured by Volden and Wiseman, by introducing more bills. The latter strategy, however, has become less successful for succeeding in creating new laws in the more contentious and polarized modern Congress.[33]

Not surprisingly, committee membership is very influential in a lawmaker's LES. For example, acquiring a position of committee leadership (committee or subcommittee chair) accounts for an enormous amount of the difference in LES scores among members of Congress, as Figure 8.7 shows. For example, in the 113th Congress (2013–15), all of the 10 lawmakers in the House with the highest legislative effectiveness scores, and 20 of the top 25, were committee or subcommittee chairs. These included the chairs of Ways and Means (David Camp, R-MI), Appropriations (Hal Rogers, R-KY), and Judiciary (Bob Goodlatte, R-VA), as well as the subcommittee chairs Chris Smith (R-NJ) and Don Young (R-AK)—two former committee chairs and among the longest-serving members in the chamber. Somewhat surprisingly, Volden and Wiseman found that having a seat on a "power" committee (which they identify as the Appropriations,

Ways and Means is considered a "power committee" in the House, but simply sitting on the committee doesn't necessarily lead to greater legislative effectiveness. The committee's chair, Kevin Brady (R-TX, center) meeting here with fellow committee members Peter Roskam (R-IL, left) and Patrick Meehan (R-PA, right), however, is one of the most effective legislators in the House.

FIGURE 8.7 Average Legislative Effectiveness Score, by Seniority and Status

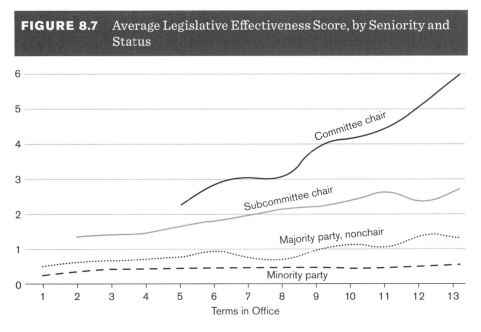

Note: Based on all lawmakers in the House from 1973 to 2014.

Craig Volden and Alan Wiseman. 2017. "Legislative Effectiveness and Representation," in *Congress Reconsidered*, 11th edition, ed. by Lawrence Dodd and Bruce Oppenheimer, 259–84. Washington, DC: Congressional Quarterly Press.

Rules, and Ways and Means Committees in the House), other than a leadership slot, often results in a lower LES. Rank-and-file members of these committees often focus all their legislative work on the supporting duties of these panel's bill responsibilities, while the sponsorship of the committees' critical bills is normally left to the committee leaders.

Finally, less tangible factors influence legislative success, including prior experience and some level of innate ability. Volden and Wiseman demonstrated that lawmakers more often than not enlarge their LES as they cultivate skills through experience over their years in Congress and as they learn to navigate the gauntlet of policy making. Even lawmaking experience in places other than Capitol Hill can prove effective in raising a member's LES score. Prior elective office in "professionalized" state legislatures (those that resemble Congress with regard to the number of staff, salary, and time in session) positively contributes to a member's effectiveness in Congress.[34] Finally, some lawmakers simply show more natural ability when they first arrive on Capitol Hill in executing the duties that propel their policy ideas. "Natural ability" can mean a number of intangibles, such as networking, hustle, hard work, luck, and the ability to read the political winds.

THEN AND NOW
INDIVIDUAL EFFECTIVENESS IN THE SENATE

Congress in the mid-twentieth century was a relatively different institution with different beliefs and norms than we see today. In no place is that difference more evident than the lawmaking activities and expectations of senators. If we observe senators' behavior with respect to policy deliberation and the formulation of new legislation in the decade just after World War II, and we then compare that behavior to how senators approach the institution and their role by the end of the twentieth century, we see a stark contrast in what constitutes an effective lawmaker in the Senate.

Donald Matthews's in-depth study dominates our image of the Senate in the 1940s and 1950s.[35] In particular, Matthews emphasizes that the chamber—a clubby, inward-looking body—regulated behavior through a set of "folkways" or norms required of its members. Among them were the belief that senators focused their work on a small number of issues directly related to their states' interests or committee assignments, that lawmakers prioritized work on legislating rather than seeking publicity, and that they adhered to a norm of reciprocity among the members so as to assist colleagues when feasible. Junior members were expected to spend a substantial amount of time serving in an apprenticeship role, gaining experience and knowledge of a small number of policy areas before they started seeking leadership roles in the Senate.

These norms had important implications for senators' participation and success in the legislative arena.[36] First-term senators in the 1950s were far less productive in sponsoring floor amendments (by half) than members who had served just one term longer, and they did the vast majority of their policy work solely within their assigned committees.[37] Ultimately, senators who adhered to institutional norms, such as deference to seniority, experienced greater legislative success.[38]

Yet there is not complete agreement that these norms entirely regulated Senate operations in the mid-twentieth century.[39] Scholars also note that the Senate had long tolerated a wide variety of institutional mavericks, who frequently operated and pursued leadership roles outside the boundaries of the body's behavior restrictions. These mavericks included Robert La Follette, Sr. (R-WI); Estes Kefauver (D-TN); and Robert Taft (R-OH).[40] Not the least of these institutional insurgents was Lyndon Johnson (D-TX), whose assent to Senate majority leader occurred quickly in the 1950s and who operated outside the body's norms of behavior on more than a few occasions.[41]

Through the 1960s and 1970s, demands on lawmakers shifted as the scope of federal government activities widened and the nature of elections changed.

Accordingly, many of the norms that had previously regulated senators' behavior began to fade. The politics of the 1960s undermined the restrictions that older folkways had imposed on junior members. In particular, the decade saw a growing set of liberal issues gain salience: civil rights, the women's movement, and opposition to the Vietnam War. In earlier decades, behavioral expectations within the upper chamber had limited the ability of younger, more liberal Democrats to redirect the work of committees, which had largely been under the influence of older and considerably more conservative Democrats, particularly from the South. By the 1960s, an ever-expanding national and local news media created both a demand and an opportunity for all senators to become policy leaders in a variety of issue areas beyond their committee assignments.[42] Consequently, less senior senators began to flout the norm of apprenticeship and take an active role in agenda setting and lawmaking.

The new approach to legislative involvement by all senators resulted in a number of changes to committee rules. The new rules expanded the number of assignments members could have to the most influential panels (thereby keeping senior lawmakers from monopolizing the power positions) and provided resources to allow junior lawmakers to hire additional staff to assist in their participation in committee legislative activities.[43]

The changes eliminated the clubbiness of the legislative body and led to the emergence of more individualistic lawmakers in the Senate (for more detail, see Chapter 7). In the early 1970s, senators were reporting that the expectation of apprenticeship by junior members no longer existed in any form. One junior Democratic senator interviewed at the time stated, "All the communications suggest 'get involved, offer amendments, make speeches. The Senate has changed, we're all equals, you should act accordingly.'"[44]

With larger staffs, more support by outside groups, and expanded opportunities for participation in legislative development, senators took it upon themselves to transform the body's operations. Today, junior members are not reticent about engaging in the tussle over controversial policies in committee and on the floor, offering a greater proportion of floor amendments than they used to. In addition, lawmaking has become more partisan, with members more freely choosing to filibuster or extend "holds" on nearly any legislation they oppose, which eventually led to a new three-fifths voting threshold for all meaningful legislation in the Senate (see Chapter 7).

Perhaps no group of lawmakers faced more resistance to their changing role in the modern Congress than female senators. As political scientist Michele Swers notes, until the early 1990s, there were very few female senators.[45] A major turning point was the confirmation hearing for Supreme Court Justice Clarence Thomas in 1991 when an all-male Judiciary Committee grilled Professor Anita

For decades, seniority dominated in Congress, leading to a "clubby" atmosphere and a lack of gender and racial diversity, especially in leadership positions, as seen in this image of the Senate Foreign Relations Committee in the 1950s (top). In 1992, four new women (bottom) were elected to the Senate—(from left) Susan Collins (R-ME), Patty Murray (D-WA), Olympia Snowe (R-ME), Carol Moseley-Braun (D-IL)—joining existing female senators Kay Bailey Hutchison (R-TX), Barbara Mikulski (D-MD), Dianne Feinstein (D-CA), and Mary Landrieu (D-LA). This "year of the woman" signaled that Congress was undergoing rapid change.

Hill regarding her allegations of sexual harassment while a subordinate to Thomas. The subsequent election year, widely referred to as the "Year of the Woman," brought four new female senators to the body.

However, Swers notes that it has taken a very long time for women to break down stereotyped perceptions that female lawmakers are interested only in traditional women's issues. While Swers notes that female senators unquestionably bring their unique life experiences to their lawmaking, many also go out of their way to establish expertise and policy influence in a wide range of issue areas. Moreover, the long-existing norm of senior senators dominating committee and party leadership selection was slow to change, which meant that it took many years for women senators to acquire positions of influence with respect to agenda formation and lawmaking.

Critical Thinking

1. Given what you have learned about the Senate in this chapter and the chapter on policy making (Chapter 7), do you prefer the Senate of the 1950s and 1960s, where newer members had to behave more like apprentices and seniority determined whose legislation advanced in the chamber?
2. As the Senate gains more diversity in terms of greater numbers of women, does this produce differences in how the institution operates?

CONCLUSION

Congress in the modern era is a lawmaking body that struggles to perform its job of governing. In nearly every responsibility, from creating budgets, to maintaining existing federal programs, to adapting government to changing world events, representatives and senators find it increasingly difficult to perform their collective duties as a lawmaking institution. Yet, at the same time, Congress has avoided some of the most potentially catastrophic governing failures, such as a breach in the debt limit.

Although labeling the contemporary Congress as a "do-nothing" Congress is probably unfair, the phrase does point to a vital concern of policy stakeholders and everyday citizens: in many of its governing responsibilities, Congress accomplishes only the bare minimum to keep federal programs and agencies operating. Lawmakers have always struggled to reach consensus on major policy changes, even when there is widespread demand from voters that something be done. Importantly, we have seen recently that even when the confluence of circumstances suggests a potentially unified set of institutions, lawmakers are not always on the same page legislatively. For example, in 2017, Republican President Donald Trump and two Republican-controlled chambers in Congress were not able to repeal Obamacare—one of the party's top priorities—but they were able to pass a massive tax reform.

Our exploration of congressional accomplishment and difficulties provides an opportunity for places to focus when seeking improvements in the institution's performance. Rather than simply demanding that members of Congress "do their job," it can be far more useful to provide specifics about which changes can make a difference in congressional operations. While there is certainly no unanimous agreement on reforms or institutional adjustments, there is also no lack of innovative thinking along these lines. Among the many suggested changes are linking lawmakers' pay to the adoption of budget and appropriations bills each term, increasing the number of required days members must work in Washington, limiting the number of years that appropriations can be granted to programs that do not have an active authorization, linking automatic increases in the debt ceiling to the levels required by adopted budgets, and requiring senators to attach their names publicly to a hold on legislation. None of these proposals is a panacea for all that troubles Congress, but each would provide a useful starting point for conversations about how to improve the work of Congress as a governing body. The first step, however, is for lawmakers to acknowledge Congress's deficiencies and begin the conversation about the areas of greatest need in changing the operations of lawmaking.

Discussion Questions

1. Congress and the executive branch have used a number of alternative means of operating in order to ensure the government meets its duties even when Congress does not meet its regular obligations (including continuing resolutions, Treasury taking extraordinary measures to avoid a default, etc.). Do you think that these exceptions allow Congress to shirk its responsibilities too easily?

2. Some critics of Congress have argued that there should be consequences for all members, such as withheld pay, when the body fails to meet its obligations (e.g., producing a budget on time, passing appropriations legislation, raising the debt ceiling). Should we hold these lawmakers personally accountable for the actions of the collective body? If so, is this the best means of doing that? Can you think of other ways to ensure that Congress meets its legislative obligations?

3. Of the measures offered for the performance of Congress as an institution (meeting budget deadlines, not breaching the debt limit, reauthorizing expiring programs, producing important legislation, etc.), which is the best way to gauge congressional accomplishment and why?

4. What criteria would you use to gauge whether an individual member of Congress was "effective" at performing his or her job? How does your current representative or senator rank on these metrics?

5. Would Congress be a more effective institution if it were more diverse (composed of a greater number of females, African Americans, Latinos, or other underrepresented minorities)? Why or why not?

9

Congress and the President

Reports of Russian meddling in the 2016 presidential election first began to emerge as early as September 2015. That's when the FBI alerted the Democratic National Committee (DNC) that Russian hackers had compromised a DNC computer.[1] U.S. intelligence agencies eventually determined that in addition to breaking into the DNC's computers, hackers affiliated with the Russian government had gained access to the e-mails of John Podesta, Hillary Clinton's campaign manager; released pro–Donald Trump propaganda online; posted stories designed to cast the Clinton campaign as beset by scandals; targeted voting systems in 21 states; and released information from the DNC hacks via third parties, including WikiLeaks. Most of the U.S. intelligence community concluded that Russia's goal was to help Trump defeat Clinton.[2]

During the election campaign, President Barack Obama and his administration pressured Russia to stop these activities. After the election, President Obama took a number of concrete and forceful actions, expelling 35 Russian diplomats, closing two Russian facilities on American soil that housed intelligence activity, and listing Russian companies and individuals that would be barred from doing business with the United States. The president's actions received bipartisan support from Congress, including support from respected Republican foreign policy

Donald J. Trump ✔
@realDonaldTrump

 Follow ⌄

Our relationship with Russia is at an all-time & very dangerous low. You can thank Congress, the same people that can't even give us HCare!

5:18 AM - 3 Aug 2017

Recently, Congress and President Trump have clashed over America's relationship with Russia. As these conflicts show, tensions between presidential and congressional power are inherent in the American political system.

experts such as Senators John McCain (R-AZ) and Lindsey Graham (R-SC).[3] Both of these senators called on Congress to impose additional and stronger sanctions on Russia, and they joined with Democratic Senate leaders Chuck Schumer (D-NY) and Jack Reed (D-RI) to issue a statement urging Republicans and Democrats in Congress to work together to protect future elections from such cyberattacks.[4]

This call to action carried extra weight because President Obama's action was an executive order, a type of presidential action that can easily be overturned by the next president. Furthermore, Obama's successor, Donald Trump, throughout the campaign had repeatedly praised Russia's strongman leader, Vladimir Putin. Trump also remained equivocal about the possibility of Russian involvement. During one of the presidential debates, for example, he opined that the DNC hacks "could be Russia, but it could also be China. It could also be lots of other people. It also could be somebody sitting on their bed that weighs 400 pounds."[5] Trump's skepticism continued after the election, perhaps because of a concern that Russia's tampering might cast doubt on the legitimacy of his election. Further adding to Congress's concerns, in the first year of President Trump's administration, reporters began to uncover numerous instances of members of the Trump campaign meeting, often secretively, with representatives of the Kremlin during the election.

In response to the mounting evidence of Russian tampering, combined with concerns about whether the new administration would be too soft on Russia and might even try to reverse sanctions, the Republican-led Congress held hearings about the extent of Russian meddling and the degree to which there had been communication, or even collusion, between members of the Trump campaign and Russia.[6] These hearings led to a bill that was passed by bipartisan majorities in both chambers, with resounding votes of 419–3 in the House and 98–2 in the Senate. This bill not only strengthened the Obama sanctions by putting them on a solid legislative footing; spurred by McCain and Graham, it also imposed new restrictions on exports to Russia, revoked U.S. visas, froze Russian assets, and imposed additional sanctions on Russia's energy and defense sectors. The bill also limited the president's power to weaken sanctions unilaterally, requiring him to get congressional approval before moving forward with any changes. According to journalists Peter Baker and Sophia Kishkovsky of the *New York Times*, the bill showed "deep skepticism among lawmakers in both parties about Mr. Trump's friendly approach to President Vladimir V. Putin of Russia and an effort to prevent Mr. Trump from letting the Kremlin off the hook" for tampering with the 2016 election.[7]

This bill presented a dilemma for President Trump. His administration had opposed the strengthening of sanctions and had lobbied against the provision that gave Congress the power to block presidential attempts to modify sanctions. At this point, the president had two options, neither of which was appealing. First, he could sign a bill that he disliked and had opposed, which would be embarrassing and might generate a strong reaction from Russia.[8] Second, he could veto it, in which case the bill's overwhelming support in Congress made it extremely likely that the veto would be overridden, leading to public embarrassment and loss of political capital. Although some in the administration suggested that he would sign it, Anthony Scaramucci, who served for a short time as the administration's communications director, indicated that President Trump might veto the bill and seek to negotiate a better deal with Congress.

Eventually, President Trump decided to sign the bill into law quietly and without ceremony, which is unusual given that it was one of the first major acts the 115th Congress (2017–19) passed. But Trump did not just sign the law. Instead, he called it "seriously flawed" and issued a statement offering his own (and his administration's) interpretation of the law. For starters, the statement asserted that aspects of the law—namely, those requiring the president to obtain congressional approval—were unconstitutional, potentially setting the stage for a future legal challenge. In addition, the statement said that President Trump would honor the waiting periods specified by the law—that is, the periods during which a presidential action on sanctions would not go into effect, pending approval by Congress.

Most important, while stating that the president would "give careful and respectful consideration to the preferences expressed by Congress," the statement also emphasized that he "will implement them in a manner consistent with the President's constitutional authority to conduct foreign relations."[9] In other words, the statement reminded Congress that the primary authority to negotiate with other countries resides with the president, indicating that he would do what he thought appropriate, regardless of what the law said.[10] Finally, President Trump emphasized that he, not Congress, should have the authority to make these decisions because "Congress could not even negotiate a health care bill after seven years of talking. . . . I built a truly great company worth many billions of dollars. . . . As President, I can make far better deals with foreign countries than Congress."[11]

The path that led to this law, and to President Trump's interpretation, illustrates several features of the often tense relationship between Congress and the president. For starters, it shows that Congress and the president frequently can be in conflict. In addition, it points to several of the tools that Congress can use to try to constrain the president: holding hearings, passing laws, issuing public statements, and overriding vetoes. And it shows some of the actions that presidents can take to achieve their goals, including issuing executive orders that have the force of law, acting unilaterally, vetoing laws, and offering statements that provide interpretations of laws they have signed.

Throughout this chapter, we explore these tactics to examine the ways in which the two branches interact. We begin by identifying the context in which we should consider the relationship between these two branches. Specifically, in assessing the relationship between Congress and the president, we need to recognize that the separation of their powers is not nearly as clean as it might initially seem, that the balance of power between the two branches has not remained the same throughout the nation's history, that each branch faces different incentives in terms of how it carries out its representation and governance functions, and that as a result each branch is constantly seeking to gain the upper hand over the other branch.

CONGRESS AND THE PRESIDENT IN THE CONSTITUTION

The Framers had a clear view of the relative importance of Congress, the presidency, and the courts. In the Constitution, they identified Congress as the primary branch of government, with the president serving a secondary role and the courts playing an even smaller role. Creating the position of president was a way to rectify one of the main weaknesses of the Articles of Confederation: the lack of executive power. In addition, the Framers recognized that the Constitution would need to endow the president with specific powers. Still, there is no question that they viewed Congress as the central and dominant power within the federal government (see also Chapter 2).[12]

In creating both a legislative and executive branch, the Framers sought to provide each with separate powers. Congress, as the first and most powerful branch, was given the power to legislate and thus to set policies for the new nation. As Article I, Section 1 of the Constitution spells out, "All legislative Powers . . . shall be vested in a Congress of the United States." Meanwhile, Article II, Section 3 assigned to the president the responsibility to "take Care that the Laws be faithfully executed." Thus the separation of powers between the two branches was well delineated: Congress would decide on and design policies, and the president (and the executive branch) would carry them out. Put even more simply, the Framers gave Congress legislative powers and the president administrative powers.

But is this separation really so clear? To begin with, Congress and the executive branch are not as separated or distinct as they may seem. The Constitution does primarily assign the president the task of executing laws passed by Congress, but it also provides the president with legislative powers. The process by which a bill becomes law, for example, is not complete until the president signs the bill into law, which means that the president is the main actor in the final stage of the legislative process. The president also can choose *not* to sign a bill, which potentially can stop it from becoming law. As we shall see, these powers can significantly affect the actions that Congress takes.

Just as the president plays a role in the legislative process, so too can Congress influence the activities of the executive branch. Congress can take numerous actions that affect the president's abilities to make policy, even in areas where the conventional wisdom holds that the president is the main actor. Overall, then, it is best to think of these two branches of government as having overlapping powers. Clearly, there is some separation of powers, but the existence of checks and balances provides for overlap and tempers the amount of separation. Thus the relationship between Congress and the president is best characterized as one of separate institutions that share powers.[13]

THEN AND NOW
THE RELATIVE POWER OF CONGRESS
AND THE PRESIDENT

The distribution of powers between the executive and legislative branches has changed dramatically over time. As already mentioned, the Framers planned for Congress to be the primary legislative actor and, more generally, the dominant actor in the federal government. Meanwhile, the president's powers were more limited and less well defined.[14] Yet over the course of nearly two and a half centuries, this power dynamic has evolved, with the balance of power moving toward the president at the expense of Congress.

In part, the president has gained power by playing a more active role in the legislative process. Throughout this chapter, we will explore the ways in which the president can do so, but here we can set the stage by examining one trend that illustrates the increased legislative role the president has played vis-à-vis Congress over time. Figure 9.1 shows the number of legislative requests presidents from George Washington to George W. Bush submitted to Congress— that is, the number of times the president submitted a formal request asking the House and Senate to address a policy. As the figure shows, the number of requests throughout the eighteenth and nineteenth centuries was generally low, although the number did steadily increase, rising from a few dozen per Congress in the first several Congresses to an average of 100 or so in the late 1800s. Starting at the end of World War II (79th Congress, 1945–47), however, the rate of

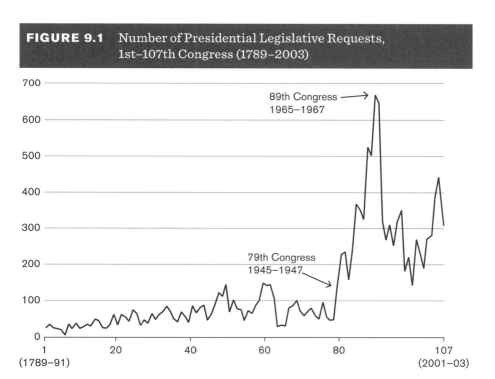

FIGURE 9.1 Number of Presidential Legislative Requests, 1st–107th Congress (1789–2003)

Jeffrey Cohen. 2012. *The President's Legislative Policy Agenda, 1789–2002*. New York: Cambridge University Press, 157.

requests per year exploded, reaching a peak of nearly 700 during the presidency of Lyndon B. Johnson (LBJ).

Other activities also show that the president has become much more involved in the legislative process than the Framers had envisioned. Presidential vetoes, which we explore in detail later in this chapter, were rare in the early years of the Republic, indicating that presidents almost never moved to strike down laws Congress had just passed. For perspective, presidents issued a total of 52 vetoes in the first 74 years of our nation's history, from 1787 to the start of the civil war. Franklin Delano Roosevelt (FDR), in contrast, issued an average of 53 vetoes *per year* during his presidency.[15]

By most measures, presidents played little role in the legislative process in the country's early years. There was a gradual increase in such activity by the end of the 1800s and then a more dramatic increase throughout the twentieth century. This level of presidential involvement in, and influence over, the legislative process continues today, to the point that Speaker Paul Ryan (R-WI), who occupied the most powerful position in Congress, openly acknowledged during the first two years of the Trump administration that he would not bring bills forward unless he knew the president was already on board. None of this, however, should be taken to mean that early presidents had no power. Indeed, recent research has demonstrated that early presidents in the early parts of the nineteenth century, including Jefferson, Madison, and Andrew Jackson, took strong actions—for example, procuring land to expand the nation's frontiers.[16] Rather, the point is that in the contested ground between the president and Congress, the pattern has been one of growing presidential power and increasing presidential involvement in the legislative process.

The result of the president's increased power has been a further blurring of the lines between the responsibilities of Congress and the president. It also has increased the frequency of the branches trying to influence each other, with Congress attempting to influence the president's actions and the president attempting to influence Congress's actions, to the point where one close observer of Congress has flipped the standard view by referring (with admitted hyperbole) to the "president as legislator and Congress as administrator."[17]

Critical Thinking

1. We tend to take it as a given that the Framers gave Congress great powers and described them in detail, while giving presidents more limited powers and describing them more vaguely. But why wouldn't they have sought to establish a system in which the powers of Congress and the president were balanced?

2. Figure 9.1 shows a dramatic increase in the number of presidential requests to Congress starting in the 1940s. Why would there have been this sudden increase at that time?

REPRESENTATION AND CONSTITUENCIES

Blurred lines, overlapping powers, and a tug-of-war over which branch has which powers might not matter so much if the president and members of Congress always shared the same perspectives. But they do not, mainly because of differences in the political foundations of the two branches. One of these differences is related to representation, which includes components related to election cycles and to constituencies. Regarding election cycles, the president's four-year term lies between the two-year term for representatives and the six-year term for senators. This difference in term length might not cause much of a difference on its own, but the more relevant issue is that most members of Congress regularly seek reelection and thus need to be accountable to their constituents for all the decisions they make. The Twenty-Second Amendment, meanwhile, restricts presidents to only one reelection, which orients them to take a much longer-term view of policy, especially in their second term.

Perhaps more important are the differences in constituencies. Because they are elected in a national contest, presidents are the only elected politicians in the United States who have a national constituency. To win reelection, they often need to continue catering to people in the states that supported them while trying to win over people in states that supported their opponent. Members of Congress face much different constituencies, with representatives elected within congressional districts and senators elected by states. An obvious difference here is size. Presidents represent all 326 million people in the United States, whereas the median state population is about 4.5 million, and the average population of a congressional district is well over 700,000. Thus the president will be concerned with the interests of a much larger and more heterogeneous population. To the extent that politicians are driven by their constituents' concerns, presidents will face a very different set of incentives than members of Congress.

The relationship between Congress and the president is thus far more complicated than a simple separation-of-powers story might imply. Although the relative balance of power between the two branches has shifted over time toward the president, exact boundaries are always subject to dispute, and each branch uses the tools at its disposal to affect or limit what the other branch can do. These disputes are therefore endemic to the system. That is, differences in the nature of representation and governance in each branch, and the incentives that these differences create, can produce and exacerbate conflicts between the two branches.

Keeping this context in mind, we can now explore several topics more deeply. We begin by looking more closely at the president's two main legislative powers that are outlined in the Constitution. We then examine the ways in which presidents can use these powers to try to influence Congress and how successful they are. And then we flip the view, looking at Congress's attempts and abilities to influence the president.

THE PRESIDENT AND THE LEGISLATIVE PROCESS

The presidential powers that the Constitution outlines deal primarily with the executive branch. As head of the executive branch, the president is charged with "faithfully executing the laws"—that is, with implementing and administering the laws that Congress passes. For example, when Congress passes laws related to agriculture, such as providing subsidies to farmers, the USDA makes sure that these subsidies are paid, and when Congress passes laws about tax policy, the Internal Revenue Service (IRS) ensures that the policies in these laws are implemented and followed. Similarly, Article II, Section 2 gives the president the power to ask cabinet members to submit their written opinions on "any Subject relating to the Duties of their respective Offices." It also spells out that the president "shall be Commander in Chief" of the military (which is located within the executive branch). These are purely executive powers that the president can carry out, by and large without needing any congressional action.[18]

As noted earlier, however, the powers of each branch do not fall neatly into one category, so in addition to listing the president's executive powers, the Constitution also provides the president with *legislative* powers—in other words, powers that allow the president to participate in the legislative process. Article II, Section 3, for example, gives the president the authority to "recommend to their [Congress's] Consideration such Measures as he shall judge necessary and expedient." It is unclear, however, exactly what it means for the president to "recommend" legislation to Congress. On one hand, it could imply that presidents, in conjunction with members of the Cabinet and other close advisors, could develop and write a law that one of their supporters in Congress can then introduce. This is the approach that President Bill Clinton took in 1993–94 when he and his administration created a health policy plan that he then sent to Congress for consideration. (Showing the weakness of such an approach, not only did this plan fail to become law but also Congress never even voted on it.) It is far more common for the president to exhort Congress to consider specific approaches to dealing with distinct policy areas, as we discuss in detail in the next section.

In contrast to its vagueness regarding the president's power to recommend legislation, the Constitution's description of the power to veto laws is much more specific. First, it's worth taking a step back to see how the Framers constructed and conceived of the veto. For a bill to become law, the Constitution stipulates that both chambers of Congress need to pass it. Next, it needs to be presented

Presidents routinely try to set the legislative agenda with Congress. In 1993–94 President Clinton pushed for major health care reform legislation, conceived by his administration and advisors, with little initial input from Congress. Many saw this approach as a mistake, as Congress never even voted on the legislation.

to the president. Article I, Section 7, states, "If he approve he shall sign it, but if not he shall return it" to the chamber in which it originated, with any objections spelled out. At that point, if two-thirds of the members of that chamber vote in favor of the bill, it will be sent to the other chamber, and if two-thirds of the members of that chamber approve it, then "it shall become a Law." Although the word *veto* never appears in Article I or anywhere else in the Constitution, this article describes the process by which a president can veto a bill.

The Framers clearly were attempting to strike a balance. Because presidents have veto power, Congress cannot pass a law on its own. But a president cannot simply kill a bill that the House and Senate have passed. Instead, the two chambers have the opportunity to reconsider the bill and can *override* the veto if two-thirds of the members in each chamber support it, in which case it will become law even without the president's signature. If both chambers pass a bill and send it to the president, who does not sign it but also does not send it back to Congress within 10 days and with specific objections, then the bill automatically becomes law. The Framers designed this rule to prevent presidents from ignoring bills that Congress passes and consigning them to limbo by neither signing nor vetoing them.

Another option has come to be known as a *pocket veto*. In this case, the president can prevent a bill from going into effect by just ignoring it, but *only* if Congress has sent the bill to the president when fewer than 10 days remain in the congressional session.[19] Just as the president cannot kill bills that Congress has passed by ignoring them, the possibility of a pocket veto prevents Congress from putting presidents in a position where they do not have enough time to consider and formally veto a law. That is, Congress cannot enact a law, send it to the president, and then immediately adjourn in order to avoid a veto.

There is some dispute about why the Framers created the veto. Some scholars argue that it was originally intended to protect the executive branch from Congress by giving the president a way to block bills that would encroach on presidential prerogatives. Others identify a more expansive justification, citing Madison's and Hamilton's views that the veto would provide another layer of protection against bad or improper laws.[20] What is not in doubt is that veto power allows—in fact, it requires—the president to be a part of the legislative process. As a result, Congress has to take the president's views into account when considering any legislation.

Before we move on to examine the ways in which presidents can use their power to recommend legislation and to veto legislation, it should be noted that presidents have other powers that are primarily executive but that also involve Congress (and in particular the Senate). First, as we discuss in more detail in Chapters 10 and 11, presidents can make appointments to government agencies and to the judicial branch. In each case, however, the president does so "by and with the Advice and Consent of the Senate" (Article II, Section 2). Thus presidents need the assent of the Senate to place their political appointees in executive branch agencies or on federal courts. Second, presidents have the power to negotiate with foreign powers but can finalize treaties only if "two thirds of the Senators present concur" (Article II, Section 2).[21]

How Do Presidents Try to Influence the Legislative Process?

The president's constitutional powers with regard to the legislative process can seem underwhelming. Yes, presidents can suggest legislation to Congress, but there is no assurance that Congress will heed those suggestions. Having the power to veto bills perhaps seems like a greater power. But viewed in stark (and ultimately simplistic) terms, the veto power merely means that presidents can give either a thumbs up or a thumbs down to any law that Congress has passed. Thus the ability to veto is certainly a measure of power, but at the same time, it makes the president's role seem purely reactive.

How, then, do we reconcile the idea that the president's constitutionally prescribed legislative powers can seem blunt, limited, or weak with the president's increasingly expanded powers, often at the expense of Congress, over time? One explanation is that presidents have a host of nonlegislative powers that they can use, which we explore in more detail next. Another explanation is that presidents can use a variety of tactics and approaches to expand the reach of their legislative powers. They use some of these powers to affect what Congress pays attention to, and they can use their veto power to shape legislation by threatening to block a bill unless it meets their approval.

To explore these powers in more depth, we proceed as follows. We begin by delving into the general ways in which presidents can use these powers, unpacking what it means to be able to suggest or veto legislation. Next, we turn to the tactics presidents can use when attempting to influence Congress, with an emphasis on three especially important tactics: bargaining, public appeals, and unilateral action. Essentially, this means that we consider why Congress would pay attention to what the president wants. It is important to note that initially we present these tactics uncritically. These are powers that presidents have, ones they clearly can (and do) avail themselves of. And they do so in the hope that these actions will be effective. But there is no guarantee that they actually will be. So after identifying and discussing them, separate from considering their effectiveness, we then investigate whether these tactics are successful.

HOW CAN PRESIDENTS USE THEIR LEGISLATIVE POWERS? The ability to suggest legislation might seem like a fairly weak power. However, because of the possibility of Congress ignoring them, presidents take actions that lend their suggestions more power and weight.

Presidents begin by deciding which issues to prioritize. President Ronald Reagan, for example, had a reputation for being especially disciplined in terms of focusing on a few key ideas he wanted to see implemented, such as his specific "four-part plan to increase economic growth and reduce deficits" outlined in his 1983 State of the Union address.[22] More recently, President Trump focused his energies on immigration and trade more so than other issues. When being interviewed, giving speeches, or interacting with the press, presidents aim to focus on their preferred issues, which in turn draws media attention to these issues. Clear statements of presidential priorities also enable other actors in the administration—cabinet secretaries, bureaucrats, the president's staff—to direct their energies accordingly. Such focus can resolve executive infighting and can better direct White House resources to where they will do the most good.[23]

Setting priorities allows presidents to seize the national policy initiative by influencing which issues Congress addresses and how it does so. In other words, by stating priorities, presidents attempt to *set the agenda* (see also Chapter 6). For example, several recent presidents, most notably Presidents Clinton, Obama, and Trump, placed reforming the complicated and inefficient U.S. health care system at the top of their agendas and asked Congress to address this issue.

After presidents have convinced Congress to place an issue on the agenda, they can frame, or define, the issue in specific ways. In the area of health care, for example, presidents might emphasize reducing the number of uninsured Americans, reducing health care costs, or improving overall health outcomes. Identifying and framing issues can subsequently shape press coverage and involve the public, which in turn generates pressure on Congress to address the issues.[24]

Just as the ability to prioritize some issues over others can lead to presidential influence over the congressional agenda, so too can presidents use their veto power to influence what Congress does. As Figure 9.2 shows, some presidents have used this tool often.

The power to veto can affect the legislative process in two ways. First, presidents can use it to block legislation that they dislike. Second, the possibility of a presidential veto affects *how* Congress addresses issues. Congress needs to be strategic and should attempt to anticipate whether a president is likely to veto a bill. And if Congress thinks the president is likely to do so, it can act to avoid a veto when drafting the bill.

This logic of *strategic anticipation* dramatically affects how Congress approaches the writing of bills. Consider, for example, a bill that provides for an increase in the minimum wage. Members of Congress might ideally prefer an increase of, say, 20 percent. They could simply write a bill specifying this increase, send it to the president, and see what happens. But they could also act more strategically by paying attention to any statements the president has made about what would constitute an appropriate increase, attempting to gauge the likelihood of a veto if they exceed the target the president has set, and so on. While they prefer an increase of 20 percent, they might be willing to settle for a 10 percent increase, and they would much prefer the 10 percent increase to the status quo (that is, no increase at all).

The president, meanwhile, has an equally strong incentive to act strategically. Suppose that, in the president's view, a 10 percent increase is ideal, but it's clear that a 20 percent increase is likely to pass both chambers. The president could wait for the 20 percent increase to pass both chambers and then veto it, but then the resulting policy (absent an override) would be the status quo level of the minimum wage rather than the president's preferred 10 percent increase. So the president instead can attempt to send signals to Congress that a 20 percent increase is out of the question, but a 10 percent increase is a possibility. From the perspective of both institutions, the current level of the minimum wage needs to be increased, but if both the president and Congress simply stick to their guns, no change will be made. This result would be a lose-lose situation, with neither side getting what it wants. Thus both sides will act strategically to obtain a better outcome, with the president sending signals that point to the desired 10 percent increase and Congress trying to produce something closer to

FIGURE 9.2　Presidential Vetoes

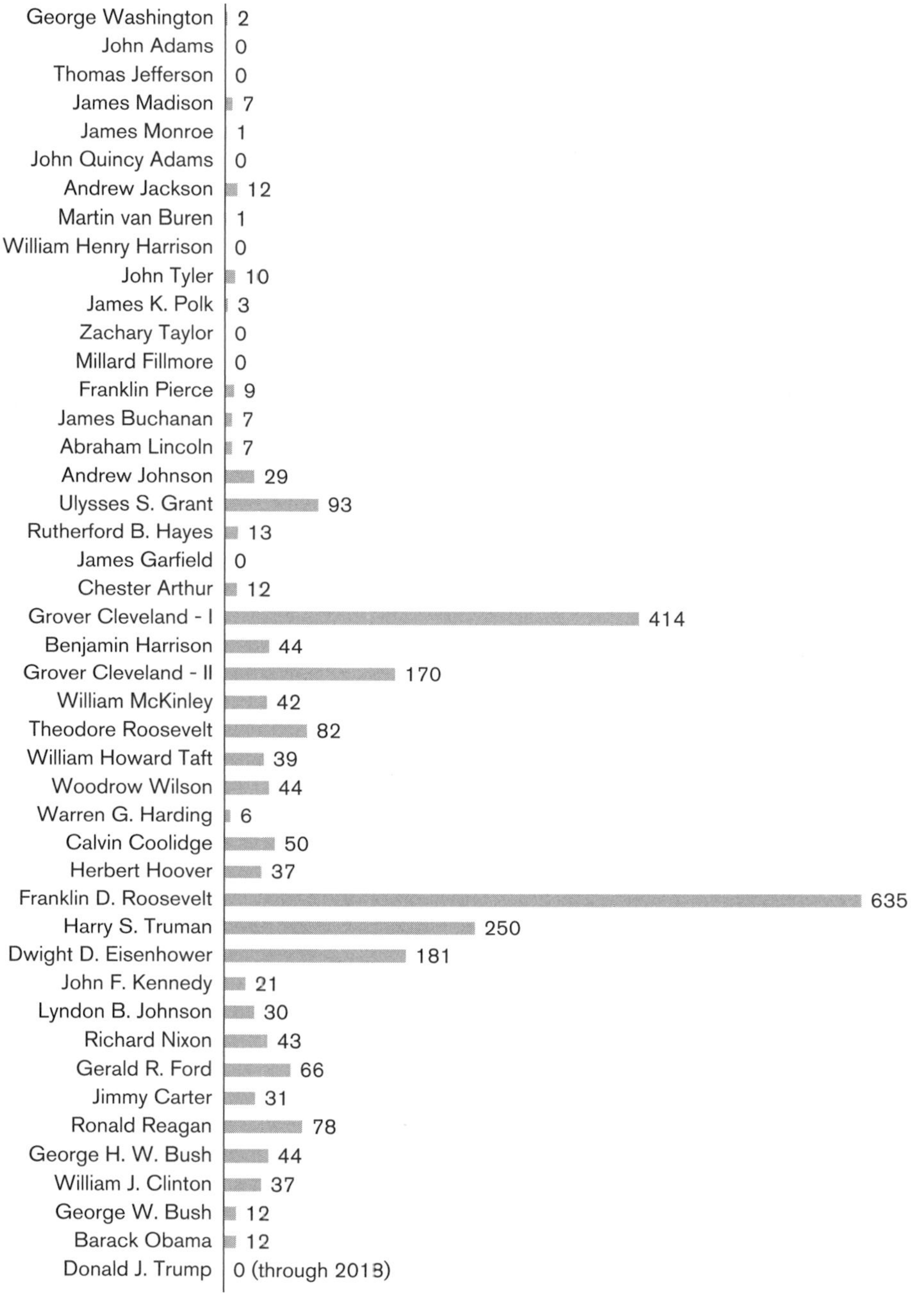

President	Vetoes
George Washington	2
John Adams	0
Thomas Jefferson	0
James Madison	7
James Monroe	1
John Quincy Adams	0
Andrew Jackson	12
Martin van Buren	1
William Henry Harrison	0
John Tyler	10
James K. Polk	3
Zachary Taylor	0
Millard Fillmore	0
Franklin Pierce	9
James Buchanan	7
Abraham Lincoln	7
Andrew Johnson	29
Ulysses S. Grant	93
Rutherford B. Hayes	13
James Garfield	0
Chester Arthur	12
Grover Cleveland - I	414
Benjamin Harrison	44
Grover Cleveland - II	170
William McKinley	42
Theodore Roosevelt	82
William Howard Taft	39
Woodrow Wilson	44
Warren G. Harding	6
Calvin Coolidge	50
Herbert Hoover	37
Franklin D. Roosevelt	635
Harry S. Truman	250
Dwight D. Eisenhower	181
John F. Kennedy	21
Lyndon B. Johnson	30
Richard Nixon	43
Gerald R. Ford	66
Jimmy Carter	31
Ronald Reagan	78
George H. W. Bush	44
William J. Clinton	37
George W. Bush	12
Barack Obama	12
Donald J. Trump	0 (through 2018)

John Woolley and Gerhard Peters. "Presidential Vetoes." The American Presidency Project. Santa Barbara, CA: University of California. http://www.presidency.ucsb.edu/data/vetoes.php (accessed 7/25/18).

a 20 percent increase. Which side will win? The extent to which presidents can use vetoes to shape legislation, and the extent to which they can set the legislative agenda or otherwise influence Congress, depends on their ability to draw on certain skills that we examine in the next section.

CONVINCING CONGRESS: BARGAINING, GOING PUBLIC, AND UNILATERAL ACTIONS   Perhaps the most famous line ever written by a political scientist about presidents, and about presidential power, is Richard Neustadt's dictum that "[p]residential power is the power to persuade."[25] Neustadt is pointing out that presidents are not kings; they cannot command. Instead, they need to *bargain* with other political actors. With respect to statutes, they need to convince members of Congress to take certain actions and not others. Neustadt writes, "The essence of a President's persuasive task, with congressmen and everybody else, is to induce them to believe that what he wants of them is what their own appraisal of their own responsibilities requires them to do in their interest, not his."[26]

Of course, the president's ability to bargain effectively and successfully is not absolute. Rather, it relies on a mixture of popularity, status, authority, and interpersonal skills. When presidents are more popular with the public, for example, they can use this popularity to get lawmakers to support their programs.[27]

Presidents also seek to elevate their status and authority in the eyes of Congress by claiming an *electoral mandate*, in which they move quickly to extend the political momentum generated by their election campaign into the governing arena. Usually, they do so by claiming that they ran for election on certain issues and their victory indicates that the public wants these issues addressed. Most presidential scholars give little credence to the idea that mandates actually exist; still, presidents regularly claim them.[28] LBJ, for example, pledged during his campaign to pursue civil rights and social welfare programs and then did so soon after taking office. Similarly, Reagan campaigned on reducing the role of government in the domestic arena and then immediately took steps in that direction upon taking office.[29] Claims of mandates do not always meet with such success, however. For example, George W. Bush's misreading of his 2004 electoral victory led him to pursue policies that had little public support, such as privatization of Social Security, immigration reform, and increasing troop levels in Iraq.[30]

When presidents have strong popular support, when they can claim electoral mandates to accomplish the tasks they highlighted during their campaigns, and when they are seen as formidable and authoritative, they are better able to persuade members of Congress to consider the issues they have deemed to be presidential priorities. Similarly, presidents or members of their administration will bargain with Congress over the *content* of legislation, pushing for changes that help ensure that the president will sign the bill into law, rather than veto it. During the presidency of George W. Bush, for example, Vice President Dick Cheney notified Congress that he planned to recommend that Bush veto a $288 billion appropriations bill for the military "unless lawmakers change it to take account of Defense Department objections."[31] More recently, the Trump administration used a "statement of administrative policy" to try to influence the content of the National Defense Authorization Act of 2018.[32] Specifically, President Trump indicated his opposition to provisions that would have prevented further base closures (which the military wants, but senators do not), limited the president's ability to determine military pay raises, and reduced housing subsidies for dual-career military families.[33] Presidents might not be able to get Congress to do exactly what they want, but through bargaining and negotiation, they often can secure at least some of what they want.

Bargaining usually involves negotiation, including direct attempts at persuasion (e.g., via meetings in the Oval Office, invitations to White House dinners, and one-on-one meetings) by the president. An alternative approach relies on the president's ability to speak directly to the American people in an attempt to rally their support. When presidents do this, they are *going public*, to use the term coined by Samuel Kernell.[34] They engage in this tactic in the belief that the public then can put pressure on members of Congress in a way

Presidents often try to influence the content of legislation through direct negotiation with key members of Congress. Here, President Trump meets with lawmakers to discuss details of legislation that would protect young undocumented immigrants brought to the United States by their parents.

that presidents cannot—that is, by threatening not to vote for a representative or senator who does not support the president's position, or promising to vote for those who do support the president.

When presidents go public, they are using what President Theodore Roosevelt famously referred to as the *bully pulpit*, where the word "bully" refers not to someone who relies on intimidation or force but rather an earlier sense of the word that conveyed excellence. Roosevelt saw the presidency as a bully pulpit because it was an outstanding position from which to promulgate his ideas and views.[35] Presidents can use this bully pulpit to try to prevent action, as when President Reagan, reacting to a proposed tax increase that Congress was considering, famously remarked, "I have my veto pen drawn and ready for any tax increase that Congress might even think of sending up. And I have only one thing to say to the tax increasers. Go ahead—make my day."[36] Or they can try to spur Congress to act, as President Trump did in July of 2017 when he told broadcaster Pat Robertson that he would be "very angry" with senators if they failed to pass a bill to kill Obamacare, adding that he was "sitting in the Oval Office with a pen in hand, waiting for our senators to give it to me. . . . It has to get passed. They have to do it. They have to get together and get it done."[37]

Presidents can go public in a variety of ways. Essentially, any use of travel or technology that allows presidents to reach outside of Washington, D.C., in order to stimulate pressure on members of Congress constitutes going public. They can hold televised press conferences or give addresses from the Oval Office. They can travel to give speeches in cities and states around the country, which, as Figure 9.3 shows, happens on a nearly daily basis over the course of a president's term. They can also tailor these speeches toward their particular goals at the moment, whether those goals concern setting the agenda, moving bills out of committee, or trying to secure votes.[38] More recently, although President Obama and his staff pioneered the use of social media to communicate with supporters, Trump has relied on social media—especially Twitter—to a much greater extent, and in unorthodox ways, to speak directly to his supporters (see p. 305).

In some respects, going public and bargaining can be seen as mutually exclusive strategies. Bargaining generally involves staying private—that is, conducting negotiations behind closed doors. In contrast, going public, as the name suggests, is a more visible strategy. Bargaining also tends to take place with a small handful of important members of Congress, especially those who have the power to make changes or those who will be most affected by a bill. Going public, on the other hand, is a much broader tactic, allowing the president to reach out to people across the country and thus, potentially, to influence a broader set of legislators.

For exactly these reasons, Kernell views going public as an alternative to bargaining, because it entails taking very public positions, which can then make bar-

FIGURE 9.3 Presidential Speeches over Time, 1961–2012

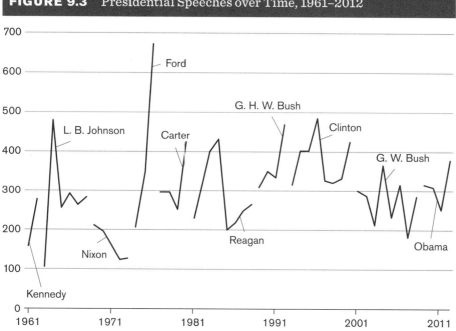

Ronald J. McGauvran and Matthew Eshbaugh-Soha. 2017. Presidential Speeches Amid a More Centralized and Unified Congress. *Congress & the Presidency* 44(1): 55–76.

gaining and compromise harder. Although the idea that going public runs counter to bargaining may be true in some cases, in other cases, the approaches could be complementary. Presidents could, for example, go public in order to shore up their bargaining position. A Speaker of the House who might not have been receptive to a president's views on, say, Medicare reforms or tax cuts, might suddenly become much more receptive if members of her party caucus are feeling pressure from their constituents because of the president's public appeals.

Why have recent presidents used the strategy of going public more frequently than their predecessors did? Kernell argues that going public is a more fitting strategy for modern presidents for three main reasons. First, the increasingly intense and contentious nature of politics in recent decades discourages quiet and considered bargaining, rewarding more public strategies instead. Second, reforms to the presidential nomination process have produced presidents who are more inclined toward and skilled at public relations. Third, the increased frequency of divided government, along with polarization, has made bargaining more difficult. When the two parties are ideologically distant from each other and one party controls the presidency while the other controls Congress, it is difficult for presidents to quietly convince members of Congress to compromise, as there may be few areas of agreement. In such cases, going public may be more effective in increasing pressure on those members of Congress.

In addition to bargaining and going public, presidents can threaten to use what has become known as *unilateral action*, which is an initiative that presidents can take on their own as the head of the executive branch. Although there are many types of unilateral actions, three stand out: executive orders, waivers, and signing statements.

EXECUTIVE ORDERS The most common and prominent form of unilateral action is when presidents issue executive orders, or related actions such as presidential memoranda and proclamations. *Executive orders* are presidential statements that provide agencies within the executive branch (e.g., the State Department, the Environmental Protection Agency) with instructions about what actions to take or what processes to follow. Upon taking office, for example, Trump issued Executive Order #13765, which directed the secretary of Health and Human Services, along with other agency leaders, to interpret any regulations related to the Affordable Care Act "as loosely as possible to minimize the financial burden on individuals, insurers, health care providers, and others."[39]

As Figure 9.4 shows, the use of executive orders began to increase dramatically during Theodore Roosevelt's presidency in the early years of the twentieth century, remained at a high level through FDR's presidency, and since then has settled at a lower level (although still higher than in the 1800s). Even at this lower

FIGURE 9.4 Executive Orders per Year, 1862–2012

Alexander Bolton and Sharece Thrower. 2016. "Legislative Capacity and Executive Unilateralism." *American Journal of Political Science* 60(3): 649–63, doi:10.1111/ajps.12190.

level, presidents in recent years have issued approximately 40 executive orders per year.[40] And in each of these cases, presidents have been able to change policy without securing congressional approval. Thus rather than bargaining directly with Congress, or speaking directly to voters who then will put pressure on Congress, presidents use executive orders to circumvent Congress entirely.

WAIVERS Presidents also can use *waivers* to change laws. For example, when Congress passes laws regarding, say, education or health care, these laws will contain provisions about how states are required to implement the law. But presidents can, if they so choose, offer states the opportunity to waive some of the requirements set out in these provisions. For instance, in the area of health care, states can request waivers to impose additional requirements (that is, requirements beyond what federal law demands) on their citizens who apply for Medicaid. In education, states or localities might seek exemptions from some of the requirements of the Every Student Succeeds Act (which replaced the No Child Left Behind law). Presidents choose when to initiate the waiver process. They offer states the opportunity to seek waivers; states then submit their proposed waivers; ultimately, presidents decide whether to grant the waiver that a state has proposed. As with executive orders, waivers provide presidents with the opportunity to change policy—this time at the state level—without needing to obtain cooperation from Congress.[41]

SIGNING STATEMENTS When Congress passes a bill, it submits the legislation to the president, who typically responds by signing it or vetoing it. But, especially in recent years, presidents have taken a different approach, signing the bill into law but adding a *signing statement* that explains how they will interpret various provisions within the law. One type of signing statement is the *constitutional signing statement*, which offers either constitutional objections to the bill or interprets the law in a way different from what Congress intended. However, signing statements need not be critical or limiting. In fact, as a recent study by Ian Ostrander and Joel Sievert showed, with the exception of the George W. Bush administration, the majority of signing statements issued by presidents have generally either praised the law or claimed credit for helping it pass.[42]

However, as Figure 9.5 shows, many signing statements *are* of the constitutional type, which means that they can offer an interpretation that is fundamentally at odds with Congress's intent. In such cases, presidents are effectively both signing the overall bill and implicitly vetoing part of it. In 2006, for example, Congress included a provision in an appropriations bill to restrict the U.S. military's use of torture during interrogations of enemy combatants. In signing the bill into law, President Bush attached a signing statement that essentially said that as commander in chief, he would construe this amendment to mean that the president

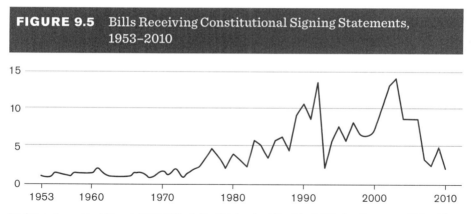

FIGURE 9.5 Bills Receiving Constitutional Signing Statements, 1953–2010

Ian Ostrander and Joel Sievert. 2013. "What's So Sinister about Presidential Signing Statements?" *Presidential Studies Quarterly* 43: 58–80. doi:10.1111/psq.12003.

had complete authority to decide what means of interrogation could be used, which in effect undercut the entire point of the provision. And as we saw at the start of this chapter, President Trump issued a signing statement that left open the possibility that he would ignore Congress's actions with respect to sanctions on Russia.

All of these types of unilateral action provide presidents with a way to act independently of Congress. Of course, there are limits to how and when these tactics can be used. Executive orders cannot be in direct conflict with existing laws; the president needs governors to agree to the terms of waivers; recent research has shown that many constitutional signing statements are about proper boundaries between the president and Congress rather than suggesting substantive changes to policy.[43] But each of these tactics allows presidents to act alone. When Congress failed to pass immigration reform during President Obama's time in office, for example, he turned to executive orders, which he used to order executive branch agencies to make changes to immigration policy.

Furthermore, by threatening to act unilaterally, presidents can put pressure on Congress. Thus, just as with the strategic anticipation that occurs with respect to the veto, where the House and Senate may change a bill in order to avoid a veto and obtain the president's signature, members of Congress will attempt to anticipate whether the president is likely to issue an executive order, signing statement, or waiver. More specifically, Congress will need to gauge whether the president's threat to use one of these unilateral actions is credible. If it is, representatives and senators may find it in their interest to compromise on the content of a bill, giving some concessions to the president, if doing so is likely to decrease the odds of a unilateral action that would, from their perspective, produce worse outcomes than the compromise.

Are Presidential Tactics Effective?

Do presidential pressure tactics work? That is, are presidents able to use these tactics to put their issues on the legislative agenda, to ensure that the content of bills is consistent with their preferences, and to alter policies when Congress is not compliant?

Agenda-setting is the first place to look for such evidence, and we begin by examining whether presidents are proactive in proposing agenda items. Evidence indicates that they are; although, we must keep in mind that presidents are just one of many actors jostling to influence the agenda. (Other actors include political parties, as discussed in Chapter 6, and interest groups, as discussed in Chapter 12.) Moreover, they are able to set the agenda across a range of issue areas, including health care, the environment, defense, crime, and the economy, and they have even greater influence in the area of international affairs.[44]

One of the most comprehensive studies of presidential attempts to influence the congressional agenda examined the *Public Papers of the President* for every president from Harry Truman through Bill Clinton.[45] These papers contain all the president's public communications, including those communications in

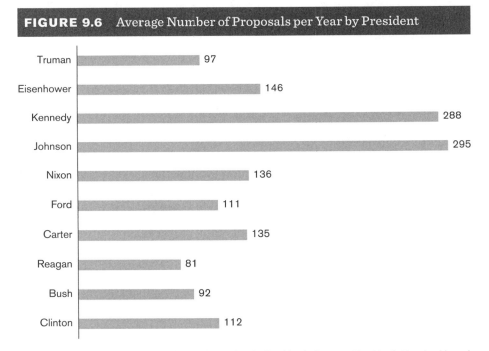

FIGURE 9.6   Average Number of Proposals per Year by President

Truman	97
Eisenhower	146
Kennedy	288
Johnson	295
Nixon	136
Ford	111
Carter	135
Reagan	81
Bush	92
Clinton	112

Based on data in Andrew Rudalevige. 2002. *Managing the President's Program: Presidential Leadership and Legislative Policy Formulation*, 72. Princeton, NJ: Princeton University Press.

which the president specifically makes legislative proposals and asks Congress to consider them. Two main points emerge from Figure 9.6, which shows the number of proposals each president made. First, there is considerable variation across presidents, with Kennedy and Johnson far more active than the others. Second, and just as important, all of these presidents, even those who were relatively less active, asked Congress to consider a large number of proposals. The average number of proposals per year for all presidents was 144 (just under three per week), but even if we exclude the two most proactive presidents, the others still submitted, on average, more than two proposals per week.

Based on our earlier discussion about the extent to which presidential power has increased over time, we might also expect that presidents of earlier eras were less likely to insert themselves into the legislative process, leaving that realm of governance to Congress. Scholar Jeffrey Cohen found precisely such a pattern. Using the *Public Papers* and a variety of other sources, he identified all legislative proposals that presidents have made over time.[46] His findings, which we saw earlier in Figure 9.1, provide evidence of a steady and gradual increase in presidential involvement from the nation's birth through the end of World War I and then a dramatic increase starting immediately after World War II. The large number of presidential policy initiatives indicates that presidential agenda-setting became institutionalized only in the second half of the twentieth century. In contrast, Lawrence H. Chamberlain's study of major legislation drafted between 1933 and 1940 found that most of it was formulated by Congress, or by Congress and the president working together, not by the White House alone.[47]

Not only do presidents make proposals, they often do so right after being inaugurated. In his book *The Strategic Presidency*, James P. Pfiffner stresses the need for presidents to move quickly and "strike when the iron is hot" to get Congress to consider their proposals.[48] Officials who have served in presidential administrations have confirmed the value of this approach, pointing to a straightforward reason: presidents are likely to encounter their most favorable political environment when they are first inaugurated. During this period, presidential approval tends to be highest, which aids them in their ability to bargain successfully with Congress. It is also a period when opposition in Congress might not yet have solidified. And as time moves on, Congress will begin to add additional items to the agenda. As an official in Jimmy Carter's administration put it, "It's definitely a race. The first months are the starting line. If you don't get off the blocks fast, you'll lose the race. Congress will come in first."[49]

Consistent with this view, George C. Edwards III and Andrew Barrett confirm that presidents propose more policy initiatives to the first Congress they work with than to the second.[50] This pattern could, of course, be contingent on other factors. For example, when partisan control of government is unified, the initiatives of both the president and Congress decline in the second half of the president's term, but when partisan control is divided, presidential initiatives decrease while congressional initiatives increase.[51] This "move quickly" approach also holds across terms. For example, political scientist Barbara Sinclair found that "presidents have been highly prominent agenda setters in their first Congress and less so later in their terms."[52]

Does Congress then take up the president's proposals? In other words, is the president able to set the congressional agenda in a meaningful way? Studies find that presidents in the second half of the twentieth century proposed approximately one-third of the significant bills that Congress considered. According to Mark Peterson, most of the major proposals the White House submits to Congress receive at least some consideration. In addition, nearly half of the minor proposals receive consideration.[53] Overall, one recent study concluded, "If there is a clear leader in the agenda stage of the policy process, it is the president."[54]

In short, by drawing attention to an issue, presidents can cause Congress to focus on that issue, provided that the president has strong approval ratings among the public. When the president mentions particular issue areas in a State of the Union address, Congress becomes increasingly likely to hold hearings on those same issues. The effect is relatively short-lived, however, which provides presidents with yet another incentive to move quickly. And the effect is weaker under divided government than unified government.[55]

The obvious next question is whether these proposals find success. Congress might, after all, just pay lip service to the president's ideas and favored policies. But it turns out that presidential proposals do fairly well once they reach Congress. Not surprisingly, presidents have trumpeted their success in this area. LBJ boasted that in the first two years after his election (1965 and 1966), he had a 91 percent success rate in Congress. Bill Clinton maintained that in his first two years in office, he worked with Congress to "substantially or partially accomplish" more than three-quarters of the issues on which he had campaigned.[56]

Of course, presidents are hardly unbiased evaluators of their own accomplishments. But independent studies confirm that once presidents place their items on the legislative agenda, these items tend to find success. The study mentioned earlier that relied on the *Presidential Papers* to identify legislative proposals ended up tracking a number of these proposals through Congress. In 29 percent of these cases, presidents received essentially everything they sought when they proposed a bill. In another 20 percent of proposals, presidents received the majority of what they sought, and in another 12 percent, they received some of what they sought. Taken together, presidents received some or all of what they wanted in more than 60 percent of the proposals that they suggested to Congress—not a perfect record, but a strong one. Presidents were especially likely to succeed when their ideology was similar to that of Congress, when the policy area was domestic, and when their approval ratings were high.[57]

In many cases, presidents engage in bargaining to achieve success, either in getting their items on the congressional agenda or in getting the items turned into laws. High approval ratings are one route by which presidents can attempt to increase their support among legislators, based on the idea that legislators are more likely to respond to appeals from presidents who are popular. These approval ratings do help presidents, but not on all issues. Instead, the effect of approval is conditional: higher levels of approval help presidents achieve greater success in Congress (as measured by a majority of the House voting to support the president's position) if the issue is salient but the public has not yet formed entrenched opinions about it.[58]

Going public provides another potential route by which presidents can attempt to improve their odds of legislative success. Some of the evidence that going public leads to legislative success is anecdotal. For example, during Reagan's first term in office, members of Congress spoke of their offices being "inundated with phone calls" after Reagan gave a televised speech promoting his proposed tax cuts. The speech was widely viewed as having secured the necessary support for Reagan's position.[59] It is just as easy to find instances in which the president's tactic of going public did not produce increased support. A historical example is Woodrow Wilson's push for the League of Nations. More recent examples include Bill Clinton's attempt to pass health care reform, George W. Bush's goal of privatizing Social Security, Barack Obama's push for immigration reform, and Donald Trump's use of Twitter to attempt to generate support for repealing the Affordable Care Act—none of which succeeded.

Systematic appraisals of the president's ability to influence public opinion have produced mixed findings. We might expect that the presidents regarded as great communicators—Ronald Reagan or Bill Clinton, for example—would be more successful at pulling public opinion toward their positions. Yet a careful evaluation of public opinion prior to major presidential addresses and after those addresses reveals that public opinion rarely changes in response to a president's public appeals, and when it does, the effect tends to be very short-lived.[60] This effect—or lack of effect—holds across a wide range of policy areas.

At the same time, there is some evidence that presidents' public appeals influence Congress. So, even if appeals do not significantly move public opinion, legislators might believe that they do. Budget data provide a useful way to examine the effect of public appeals from the president on congressional actions. Every year, the president sends a budget request, which recommends a certain level of funding, to Congress. Thus, in each year we know the previous level of funding, what the president requested for the current year, and what Congress passed in the current year. We can thus compare whether Congress authorized the additional amount that the president requested over the prior year's budget. If public appeals are successful, then we would expect that the level of change

Presidents often "go public" to influence legislation, but it's questionable if this tactic is effective. In the wake of the Sandy Hook school shootings, President Obama held several public events to press for stricter gun control. Ultimately Congress took little action on the issue, despite legislation introduced by Ted Cruz (R-TX) and Chuck Grassley (R-IA).

between last year's appropriation and this year's should be more likely to match what the president requested if the president made a public appeal on this topic. That is, if public appeals do matter, then there should be greater congruence between what the president asks Congress to do and what Congress eventually does.

An examination of televised presidential addresses shows that presidents make public appeals regarding budget items about two or three times per year.[61] Looking at these appeals in the context of appropriations requests and budgetary outlays produces a number of interesting findings. First, presidents are more likely to make public appeals on proposals that they know are popular. When the public's approval of a specific budget proposal—say, spending more money on defense—increases by 10 percent, presidents are 22 percent more likely to go public on that issue. Presidents also make public appeals more often on issues when they think such appeals will be effective. In other words, if they think they're likely to get their way anyway, they won't make an appeal, but if the only way for them to succeed is by making an appeal, they'll do so. Thus presidents are strategic about when they should appeal to the public. Most important, though, presidents do achieve greater success on budget matters when they decide to go public, with such appeals causing the change in appropriations from one year to the next to be 12 percent closer to what the president requested.[62]

Veto threats can also induce Congress to move policy toward the president's preferred position. In theory, Congress should have an incentive to anticipate a presidential veto and to make concessions that might avoid such a veto. And one recent study identified such an effect. Focusing on appropriations bills and explicit veto threats, it found that in 68 percent of cases where the president voiced opposition to legislation (but did not threaten a veto), Congress ended up moving the content of the bill closer to the president's preferences. But when the president explicitly threatened a veto, this percentage jumped up to 91 percent, indicating that such threats are far more powerful, and taken much more seriously, than milder statements of opposition.[63] Of course, presidents must be selective about issuing such threats, which would quickly lose their power if made too frequently or not backed up. But when used judiciously, veto threats provide another way for presidents to influence the content of congressional bills.

How the Political Context Affects Presidential Success in Congress

Three features of the political environment during a president's time in office can affect the president's ability to influence Congress: divided government, polarization, and war. Divided government is the most well-known constraint on the president. A president whose party controls Congress can rely on help from co-partisans within Congress in numerous ways—for example, they can introduce the president's proposals in Congress and then shepherd them through the legislative process. In contrast, a president faced with a Congress controlled by the opposing party can expect to encounter regular opposition, as this party will put its own issues on the agenda, oppose the president's bills in committee and on the floor, and fail to support the president's budget request.

A president's co-partisans are always more supportive than members of the opposition party. As Figure 9.7 shows, during the administration of George W. Bush between 2000 and 2008, the president received the support of, on average, about 80 percent of House Republicans on issues where he had taken a public position. Meanwhile, he received the support of only 25 to 30 percent of House Democrats on those issues. Furthermore, the gap in support between co-partisans and the opposing party has been increasing over time. Consequently, when the president's co-partisans in Congress outnumber members of the opposing party, which is the case during unified government, the president's policy proposals are more likely to receive support. This support during unified government, and the corresponding lack of support during divided government, suggests that presidents might be more likely to use unilateral actions during divided government. Interestingly, though, the evidence on this point is mixed. Although some studies find that presidents are more likely to use unilateral actions during divided government, others find that presidents use these tactics more often under unified government.[64]

The increase in legislative polarization—that is, the ideological distance between Republicans and Democrats in Congress—has been well documented

FIGURE 9.7 House Average Presidential Support, 1953–2009

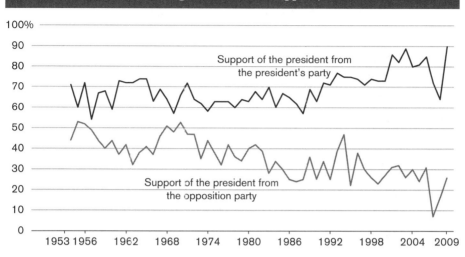

Bryan Marshall. 2012. "Congress and the Executive: Unilateralism and Legislative Bargaining," in *New Directions in Congressional Politics*, edited by Jamie L. Carson, 184. New York: Routledge.

(see Chapter 6). Polarization can combine with divided government to make life more difficult for presidents who try to influence Congress. If there is little ideological distance between the two parties, then divided government might not matter all that much, because presidents would be able to find plenty of ideological common ground with members of the opposing party. But the parties have grown further apart, and as Figure 9.7 shows, such common ground is scarce, which in turn affects the strategies that presidents use when dealing with Congress. For example, the use of veto threats has increased as the parties have become more polarized, but this increase in veto threats has been confined to periods of divided government.[65] At the same time, polarization might affect the president's strategy to go public. For going public to have a chance of succeeding, two key components are necessary: the president must first mobilize public opinion, and the public in turn must influence their representatives. With the large and growing divide between the parties, however, combined with fewer moderates and strong partisan loyalty, members have become less susceptible to "political breezes the president can stir up in their constituencies."[66]

The overall effect of polarization on presidential success in Congress, measured by Congressional Quarterly as the percentage of key votes in which the president takes a position and Congress votes to support that position, is also contingent on divided government. Figure 9.8 shows that in the 1960s and 1970s, when the parties were less polarized, presidents had more success under unified government than under divided government, but the differences were

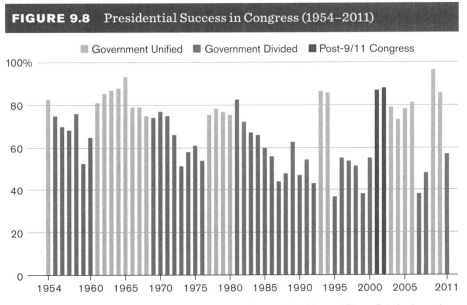

FIGURE 9.8 Presidential Success in Congress (1954–2011)

Government Unified Government Divided Post-9/11 Congress

Daniel Paul Franklin and Michael P. Fix. 2016. "The Best of Times and the Worst of Times: Polarization and Presidential Success in Congress." *Congress & the Presidency*, 43(3): 377–94.

not huge. More recently, however, and coinciding with increased levels of polarization, the gap is much larger. Polarization is thus making it harder for presidents to succeed in Congress under divided government.[67]

Finally, war affects the relationship between the president and Congress. During times of war, members of Congress become more deferential to presidents, not only on foreign but also domestic policies. During World War I and World War II, as well as in the post-9/11 period, individual members of Congress tended to shift away from their standard voting patterns and cast votes more in line with the president's views.[68] Thus a liberal member of Congress faced with a conservative president will vote more conservatively during wartime than in times of peace, while a conservative member of Congress faced with a liberal president will vote more liberally.

Presidents are especially dominant in foreign policy, where they operate more independently of Congress. Serving in the role of commander in chief, they are directly in charge of the armed forces and have the authority to order troop movements. They appoint ambassadors to other countries, and they alone have the power to negotiate with these other countries. In addition, presidents decide when to initiate treaties and trade agreements with other countries.

Congress can push back on some of these powers, but often with limited success. For example, the Senate has to approve treaties. In reality, however, treaties are rarely struck down; the Senate's vote in 2012 to prevent the United States from entering the United Nations Disabilities Convention (a treaty President Obama supported) offers a rare exception. The Senate can, however, block presidential treaties by just ignoring them and not taking any action, which has happened with dozens of treaties (e.g., the United Nations Law of the Sea).

Inaction provides Congress with another measure of power. But if presidents are concerned about either rejection or inaction, they can take a different tack and avoid the Senate entirely. They can pursue international goals via executive agreements, which are not subject to Senate approval, rather than via treaties, which are.[69] In fact, Obama effectively abandoned the Article II treaty process, submitting far fewer treaties to the Senate than any other modern president and winning a very low percentage of approvals when he did submit them. Instead, the Obama administration turned to executive agreements and political agreements to pursue a wide range of international policies, including the highly prominent Iran Nuclear Accord and the Paris Climate Agreement. In pursuing diplomatic goals through this means, President Obama effectively shut Congress out of the process. Obama's approach might have allowed him to avoid the Senate, but it also made it easier for his successor, Donald Trump, to withdraw from both agreements.

The push and pull between the president and Congress extends to war powers. According the War Powers Resolution, Congress, not the president, has the power to declare war. This resolution also restricts the president's ability to take military action. Still, presidents have found a number of creative ways to work around these restrictions—for example, by entering into hostilities with another country without calling it a war (which is what happened with both Korea in the 1950s and Vietnam in the 1960s). Congress can use its power of the purse to limit the president's ability to use the military, but Congress does not like to be in a position where it is seen as not supporting the troops. Overall, then, presidents clearly are more powerful in foreign affairs than in domestic affairs. This power allows presidents to react more quickly to crises, but it can be seriously problematic if a president is inexperienced, uninformed, or makes bad decisions in the arena of foreign policy. As this chapter's opening example explains, Congress was worried about President Trump's ability to act quickly with respect to lifting Russian sanctions, which is why it required congressional approval for those sanctions to be modified or lifted.

CONGRESSIONAL INFLUENCE ON THE PRESIDENT

The foregoing discussion leaves little doubt that presidents have the power to influence Congress, that they use that power in practice, and that their attempts to influence Congress are often successful. None of this, however, should be taken to imply that presidents can simply toy with Congress, or that they get what they want whenever they want, or that Congress is helpless in the face of presidential power. Although it has lost power to the president over time, Congress also has a variety of tools that it can use to counteract presidential activities.

Consider the president's interest in and ability to set the legislative agenda. Although we have seen that Congress often does address the president's policy proposals, it often does not. In fact, in as many as 25 percent of cases, Congress simply ignores the president's proposals and takes no action on them.[70] Furthermore, Congress can and does introduce its own proposals, regardless of whether these are issues the president wants to tackle, which is why the size of the agenda tends to increase under divided government.[71] And while presidents propose budgets, Congress, with its power of the purse, needs to pass them. Although we have seen that presidents can use public appeals regarding areas they care about to move the final budget numbers closer to their own preferences, the effect is rather small, and Congress often chooses to ignore the president's requests. Senator John McCain, for example, bluntly characterized Trump's first budget proposal as "inadequate" and "dead on arrival."[72] At the same time, Senate Majority Leader Mitch McConnell (R-KY) reminded everyone that Congress ultimately would decide what was in the budget: "The president's budget, as we all know, is a recommendation [that] will not be determinative in every respect."[73]

Vetoes provide presidents with a strong way to influence Congress. But Congress can override vetoes, and as Figure 9.9 shows, it takes advantage of this option on a fairly consistent basis. Furthermore, in some circumstances, Congress can use a president's veto threat against that president. In such cases, Congress passes a law not *despite* knowing that the president will veto it, but rather *because* members know that the president will veto it. This course of action might sound counterintuitive, but the underlying logic makes sense. For example, suppose that Congress wants to pass a bill, but the president has taken a position against the bill. If Congress has a strong sense that the public will disapprove of the president's veto, it might pass the bill and send it to the president, knowing that the resulting disapproval will then hurt the president politically, giving Congress greater leverage in dealing with other issues.[74]

A classic example of Congress playing this "blame game" occurred in 1992 when the Democratic leaders of the House and Senate worked together to pass a family-leave bill.[75] Notably, they did so knowing that President George H. W. Bush had promised to veto the specific version of the bill they were writing. Equally notable is that many observers believed that Bush was

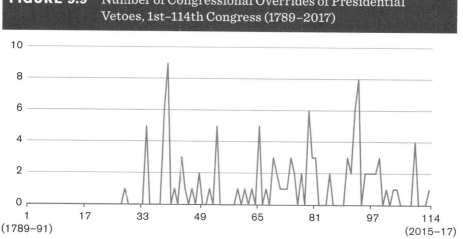

FIGURE 9.9 Number of Congressional Overrides of Presidential Vetoes, 1st–114th Congress (1789–2017)

John Woolley and Gerhard Peters. "Presidential Vetoes." The American Presidency Project. Santa Barbara, CA: University of California. www.presidency.ucsb.edu/data/vetoes.php (accessed 7/25/18).

open to a more moderate version of this bill. Yet Congress chose to go forward with its preferred version, knowing that Bush would veto it and that public opinion would turn against him, which is exactly what happened. More generally, vetoes are associated with drops in presidential approval, with the now familiar caveat that this relationship is especially likely to occur under divided government.

Congress also has tools it can use to counter the president's unilateral powers. Some of these take the form of passing new laws. For example, if Congress disapproves of a president's executive order, it can pass a new law that supersedes this order. It can do the same if it dislikes the way the president's agencies are implementing a law, or if it opposes the interpretation that the president sets out in a signing statement.[76] Such laws would, of course, be subject to a veto, so Congress often will attach provisions to must-pass legislation that act to constrain the executive. For example, Congress regularly includes *riders*—provisions that place limits on what agencies can do—in appropriations bills, because these bills must be signed into law in order to keep the government running. Here Congress hopes that even if the president does not like a specific rider, that rider won't be enough to spur a veto of the entire appropriations bill. Nonetheless, when faced with the possibility that Congress will include riders to limit presidential action, presidents often do threaten vetoes. These threats can be enough to force Congress to moderate the riders, bringing them closer to the president's preferred position.[77]

Congress doesn't need to pass laws to exert power.[78] One example of Congress exerting power without passing laws occurs with respect to signing statements. Because presidents can use signing statements to shape the ways in which agencies carry out legislative directives, and because the content of these statements can diverge from the legislative intent, Congress might find itself disagreeing with the signing statement. Passing a new law would be one option, but Congress has another option too: it can engage in more diligent and aggressive oversight of the agency's actions to pressure the agency into following its intent, rather than the president's. A recent study by Scott Ainsworth, Brian Harward, and Kenneth Moffett shows that Congress does just that. When presidents use signing statements to object to more provisions in laws, Congress (in particular, the congressional committees with responsibility for overseeing agencies) responds by engaging in more frequent oversight hearings.[79] As we will see in Chapter 10, these hearings can influence agencies and the actions they take.

HOW WE STUDY
CONGRESSIONAL INVESTIGATIONS

Congress has another useful arrow in its quiver: it can conduct investigations of the president. This approach shares some similarities with Congress's blame-game strategy, in that it is often done as publicly as possible, with the goal of turning public approval toward Congress and away from the president. Certainly, many investigations of presidents and their teams have legitimate and nonpolitical purposes. Republicans who led the many investigations of Secretary of State Hillary Clinton's actions related to the Benghazi tragedy (in which four American were killed in an attack on the American embassy there) undoubtedly wanted to know if Clinton had made specific mistakes and whether safeguards could be put in place in the future, just as Democrats who pushed for the investigations of Russian meddling in the 2016 presidential election and the Trump campaign's potential cooperation with the Russians wanted to know how to protect our country's elections from tampering by foreign adversaries. Yet there is also no doubt that investigations can weaken the president, or members of the president's team, politically. In unguarded moments, members of Congress have even acknowledged the political aims of investigations. For example, House Majority Leader Kevin McCarthy (R-CA) acknowledged that the hearings about the deaths of Americans in Benghazi were part of a strategy to make Hillary Clinton easier to defeat in an election: "Everybody thought Hillary Clinton was unbeatable, right? But we put

Congress can influence the actions of the president through its power to investigate executive branch activity. One of the most recent high-profile investigations was of the government's response to the terrorist attack on the U.S. Embassy in Benghazi, Libya. Secretary of State Hillary Clinton was brought before congressional committees multiple times for hearings on the matter.

together a Benghazi special committee, a select committee. What are her numbers today? Her numbers are dropping. Why? Because she's untrustable."[80]

As noted earlier, Congress has many other ways it can improve its position vis-à-vis the president: passing laws, overriding vetoes, voting against nominees, holding press conferences. Why does it sometimes turn to investigations to score political points? The most thorough and convincing analysis of investigations appears in Douglas Kriner and Eric Schickler's *Investigating the President*. To begin with, it is far easier to initiate and conduct investigations, which are entirely under Congress's control, than to pass laws, which requires the president's signature. Indeed, an investigation requires only the agreement of the majority party leaders and (usually) the chairs of the relevant committees. In addition, all Senate and House committees have subpoena power, which gives them great authority to compel witnesses to testify during investigations.

Moreover, claiming credit for investigations is easier than claiming credit for legislation. As Kriner and Schickler have observed, "Collective action problems may pose a less severe obstacle to investigative oversight activity than to legislative activity."[81] Furthermore, the members who lead investigations often receive favorable publicity, which means that they simultaneously benefit their party (by questioning the president) and improve their own reelection chances. Thus both individually and collectively, members of Congress have an incentive to investigate the president.

To determine the frequency of investigations and to assess their arguments, Kriner and Schickler drew upon data provided by Congressional Information Service (and later ProQuest) to identify hearings that "involved some official or entity within the executive branch" and that investigated misconduct or scandal. Figure 9.10, drawn from their study, shows their findings. The data show that not only does Congress have an incentive to investigate the president, but it does so frequently. From 1898 through 2014, Congress conducted 4,522 hearings aimed at investigating potential misconduct by the executive branch. Because many hearings occur across multiple days, this number of hearings corresponds to more than 11,900 days that Congress spent investigating the president, an average of more than 100 days per year.

Investigations thus are not rare events. Figure 9.10 shows peaks during the scandal-ridden presidencies of Warren Harding in the 1920s and Richard Nixon

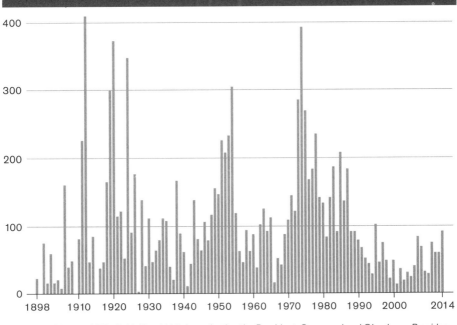

FIGURE 9.10 Days of Investigative Activity by Year, 1898–2014

Douglas L. Kriner and Eric Schickler. 2016. *Investigating the President: Congressional Checks on Presidential Power*, 36. Princeton, NJ: Princeton University Press.

in the 1970s, but the figure makes it clear that congressional investigations of the executive branch are a regular feature of the Washington, D.C., landscape. Kriner and Schickler's statistical tests support the conventional wisdom: investigations are more common when control of government is divided and polarization is high. Furthermore, these investigations are often damaging to the president. They attract media attention and raise the salience of the issue or action under investigation, sometimes trigger further legislative responses, often cause the president to change the course of policy preemptively, and can lead to a drop in the president's public approval. As Kriner and Schickler conclude, "Investigations systematically impose political costs on the president by diminishing his support among the public. . . . Even when it cannot legislatively compel the president to change course, Congress can raise the political costs of certain executive actions by alleging abuses of power and battling the president in the public sphere."[82]

Critical Thinking

1. Is there any way to distinguish congressional investigations of the president that are purely political from those that are not driven solely by political considerations?

2. The chapter notes that we often see more congressional investigations during scandal-ridden presidencies. But many investigations occur during relatively scandal-free presidencies, such as the Benghazi investigations during the Obama administration. What might explain why these investigations occur?

3. Kriner and Schickler find that investigations are more common under divided government than under unified government. Yet investigations also occur under unified government. Why might Congress investigate a president from its own party, knowing that such investigations might hurt the president's approval?

IMPEACHMENT The ultimate power Congress has over the president is the power of impeachment. According to Article II, Section 4 of the Constitution, the president (as well as other government officials) "shall be removed from Office on Impeachment for, and conviction of, Treason, Bribery, or other High Crimes and Misdemeanors." Although individual members of Congress often have raised the topic of impeachment, and sometimes even have taken steps to introduce articles of impeachment, no president has been impeached and then convicted. Both Andrew Johnson and Bill Clinton were impeached by the House of Representatives, but they were not convicted by the Senate; thus, they remained in office. The House had drawn up articles of impeachment for Richard Nixon, but he resigned in order to avoid his likely impeachment and conviction.

A complicating factor regarding impeachment is the unclear meaning of "other High Crimes and Misdemeanors." Legal standards do play a role in impeachment, but ultimately impeachment is a political decision, not a legal one; thus, Congress determines what constitutes a high crime or misdemeanor. The fact that a president has committed a criminal offense does not mean that Congress must impeach. Conversely, Congress can impeach a president even if the president did not commit a crime.

Given the uncertainty about the standards for impeachment, it is worth considering the Framers' views. Although the Framers recognized the necessity for a president to head the executive branch in the new constitutional system, they were deeply concerned about the pattern they had seen in previous regimes around the world and throughout time, in which persons heading governments had abused their powers. As one political observer has written, the Framers especially "worried that the enormous powers attendant to the office could be abused, that they could fall into the hands of an unfit incumbent, or that they could come under the influence of foreign powers."[83] Thus the Framers viewed impeachment as a potential remedy for cases in which presidents were unfit for office because they were not acting in the best interests of the United States and consequently were a threat to the Republic. Hamilton elaborated this view in *Federalist* 65, identifying impeachable offenses as those "that proceed from the misconduct of public men, or in other words from the abuse or violation of some public trust. They are of a nature which may with peculiar propriety be denominated political, as they relate chiefly to injuries done immediately to the society itself."[84] Impeachment is thus a drastic remedy that Congress should never consider lightly, but the Framers included it as a potentially necessary remedy for drastic situations.

CONCLUSION

When the Framers created the presidency, they had in mind democracies and republics of antiquity, many of which were eventually undermined by single leaders who became tyrants. Thus they recognized that a president, as the head of the new American system of government, could pose a serious threat to the new Republic's survival. At the same time, they also recognized the clear necessity of having a single person head the executive branch. The Framers' recent experiences with the Articles of Confederation had made it clear that without a president, the government would be undermined by its own potential impotence. Hence, they had a fine line to walk between giving the president too much power and not enough power. The appropriate equilibrium was hard to strike and then difficult to sustain, and this chapter shows how it has played out in practice.

Because the Framers created a system of checks and balances in which the president and Congress have overlapping powers, with the president having some legislative powers and Congress being able to influence the actions of the executive branch, tensions between Congress and the president are inevitable. Indeed, these tensions are built into the relationship and have been since the nation's founding. Because tension is the natural state, cooperation between the branches becomes a necessity in order to get things done. Cooperation does not mean that Congress and the president need to agree on everything. It simply means that they need to find ways to work together.

If tension is the primary characteristic of the relationship between the two branches, then a close second is the always-changing nature of this relationship. Each branch uses the tools at its disposal to attempt to gain an upper hand over the other branch, with the president relying on public appeals and the power of the veto, and Congress using investigations and control over its own agenda. Complete agreement over which issues to address and how to address them is unlikely to happen, even when one party controls both chambers. But each institution will react to the other's actions. Through this process of tension, change, and strategic behavior, politics plays out and policy is made.

Discussion Questions

1. This chapter argues that the balance of power between Congress and the president has shifted steadily toward the president over time. Is it possible for that trend to reverse? What would it take for that to happen?

2. Why do vetoes ever occur? After all, Congress and the president are in constant communication about each other's policy views. Why don't they just work out any differences in advance?

3. Are going public and bargaining complements or substitutes?

4. Many political observers contend that when presidents fail to get Congress to pass their programs, it is because they didn't work hard enough to convince the public of the value of their policy goals. Yet as we point out in this chapter, many studies find that presidents are unable to change public opinion. Given the bully pulpit, why are presidents so limited in influencing public opinion?

5. Some studies find that unilateral powers are used more commonly under divided government, but others do not. Why might presidents turn to unilateral actions when their party controls Congress (i.e., under unified government)?

10

Congress and the Bureaucracy

Government agencies rarely seek the spotlight. A high degree of attention from the public, interest groups, the media, and members of Congress rarely occurs when an agency is doing its job. Instead, such attention usually occurs when an agency has done something wrong—for example, when it is being singled out for incompetence, or, worse, when it is suspected of being at the heart of a political scandal.

This is exactly the unenviable position that the IRS, already consistently among the least popular of all government institutions, found itself in. In 2012 and 2013, it was accused of targeting conservative groups for intensive and unreasonable scrutiny. The situation first came to light when a number of nonprofit conservative interest groups began to complain of unfair treatment by the IRS. Specifically, these groups had applied for a specific legal status—known as 501(c)(4) status after the relevant portion of the Internal Revenue Code—that has several benefits. As long as they can certify that their organizations' primary purpose is *not* political (e.g., they are not endorsing specific candidates for office), then these groups are designated as tax-exempt organizations; they can engage in unlimited lobbying, and their donors can remain anonymous. Because the IRS needs to certify whether missions are nonpolitical, it frequently asks groups to submit a substantial amount of information about their activities. That part of the process is normal, and all groups

In 2012 and 2013, the IRS was accused of unfairly targeting conservative nonprofit groups for special scrutiny, and several IRS officials were brought before Congress for hearings. This scuffle shows the tensions that can arise between government agencies and a Congress that tries to exert control over them.

expect it. But conservative groups argued that they were being singled out and asked to provide an excessive amount of information, while liberal groups were not.

When conservative groups started to complain, members of Congress began to inquire about whether a pattern of bias existed. The head of the IRS, Douglas Shulman, a George W. Bush appointee who had carried over to the Barack Obama administration, stated unequivocally that the agency had not targeted conservative groups. IRS officials also noted that the increased scrutiny of groups applying for 501(c)(4) status was a natural result of a sudden and unexpectedly large increase in the number of such applications after 2010. Still, groups kept complaining, members of Congress kept inquiring, and the media kept investigating. Ultimately, these investigations revealed that the IRS had indeed been searching for groups with names that included words or phrases such as Tea Party, Patriots, and 9/12, all of which tend to be strongly associated with conservative groups, and subjecting these groups to extra scrutiny.[1]

In response to this revelation, Congress flew into action. High-level IRS bureaucrats were called before Congress for questioning, as were many former employees. The agency was asked to provide detailed answers to questions posed by members of Congress. In response to these questions, the agency produced 1.3 million pages of documents. Committees conducted more than 30 hearings and issued scathing reports.[2] And perhaps most important, Congress cut the agency's budget by approximately $1 billion over the next several years, making it hard for the agency to carry out its duties or to conduct additional investigations.

The aftershocks of this scandal continued to be felt for years. When the agency attempted to write new rules for dealing with applications for 501(c)(4) status, it immediately came under more criticism from Congress. In 2016, for example, the chair of the House Oversight and Government Reform Committee introduced legislation to impeach the head the IRS, John Koskinen, even though Koskinen had not been in charge of the IRS when the scandal occurred. Some members of Congress even supported a move that would have allowed them to reduce the salaries of specific bureaucrats to as little as $1.

The IRS scandal was notable for the amount of attention it generated. At the same time, the actions that Congress took in response to the scandal—hearings, investigations, subpoenas, budget cuts—are typical in terms of how Congress deals with agencies. In this chapter, we systematically assess how Congress attempts to influence agencies, not just in the case of scandals, but more generally. We begin by considering what agencies actually do and why Congress would even want to influence agencies. Then, after examining the factors that Congress takes into account when creating and staffing these agencies, we explain how Congress uses statutes, procedural constraints, budgets, and other means of oversight to try to influence agency activities.

WHAT DO AGENCIES DO?

As the first branch of government, Congress has vast authority over and responsibility for setting policy in the United States. Throughout this book, we have seen the many ways Congress can affect policy: through the committee system, which allows different members to specialize in different policy areas; through political parties, which choose to emphasize some policy areas and de-emphasize others when they control a chamber; and through the actions of individual representatives and senators, who focus their efforts on specific policy areas. Just as there is no doubt that Congress plays an active role in setting and influencing policy, there is also no doubt that government agencies create the vast majority of policies in the United States today. Modern American government is, in many respects, bureaucratic government.

Indeed, it is hard to think of a policy area in which government agencies do *not* play a key role in establishing policies. Perhaps when you wake up in the morning, you listen to the radio while drinking a cup of coffee and eating some cereal. Decisions from several government agencies influence all of those simple activities. The radio station to which you are listening can broadcast only because it has a license issued by the Federal Communications Commission (FCC); the Food and Drug Administration (FDA) designed the nutrition label on your box of cereal; the Federal Trade Commission makes sure that companies do not put any false claims about their product on the cereal box; the Consumer Product Safety Commission (CPSC) regulates the safety of your coffee maker. We could continue throughout the day. The car you drive or the bus you take to get to school, the wage you're paid at your job, the working conditions at that job, even the water you drink and the air you breathe—all of these involve policies set by government agencies.

Another way to consider the range of agency activity is to think about all the policies overseen by a single agency. Take, for example, the Department of Health and Human Services (HHS), which is one of the main agencies within the executive branch (and thus is under the president's direct control). Within HHS, there are units that have primary responsibility for setting policy in key programs, including Medicare, which provides health care and prescription drug benefits to more than 50 million senior citizens and disabled people. HHS also sets policy for Medicaid and the Children's Health Insurance Program, which provide health coverage to more than 70 million children and lower-income citizens. HHS units are also responsible for minimizing the health risks owing to exposure to hazardous substances; regulating the safety of food and the efficacy of drugs; providing health care for American Indians; conducting biomedical and health research, as well as research targeted toward improving the quality of health care; overseeing a host of additional programs that supervise mental health policies and address substance abuse issues; managing children's programs such as Head Start; tracking the spread of contagious diseases in the United States and abroad; and developing policies that outline how the United States should respond to outbreaks. And this list contains just a small number of the programs that fall under the auspices of this single agency. If we were to dig into any specific subagency or department within HHS—say, the Centers for Medicare & Medicaid Services or the Indian Health Service—we would find a wide range of additional programs, policies, and activities.

Some numbers help to provide additional perspective about the size and reach of government agencies. Table 10.1 provides information about the size, in terms of their budget and the number of employees, of cabinet-level agencies—that is, the major agencies located within the executive branch that are headed by people who report directly to the president. (We identify and discuss other types of government agencies later in this chapter.) The two agencies that receive the most funds are, perhaps not surprisingly, HHS (which, along with the Social Security Administration, is responsible for approximately one-quarter of all government spending, due largely to the high costs of Medicare and Social Security) and the Department of Defense (which has the most employees). But many other cabinet agencies have substantial numbers of employees, large budgets, or both. Some comparisons provide perspective in terms of agency spending. The Department of Energy and the Department of Housing and Urban Development (HUD) have budgets that roughly correspond to the budgets of the states of Georgia and Colorado, while the Departments of Education and Transportation are about the same size, in terms of budget, as the states of Oregon and Minnesota. Meanwhile, the Department of Veterans Affairs has a budget roughly equal to that of Texas and New Jersey combined![3]

TABLE 10.1   The Size of Cabinet Departments

Department	Number of Employees	Total Outlays, 2016 (in Billions of Dollars)
Defense	742,000	$516.2
Veterans Affairs	368,109	159.0
Homeland Security	188,844	46.4
Justice	115,424	35.0
Treasury	100,425	484.0
Agriculture	86,525	137.7
Health and Human Services	85,974	994.7
Interior	62,893	12.6
Transportation	54,697	69.7
Commerce	45,308	9.4
Labor	15,720	39.0
Environmental Protection Agency	15,325	7.5
Energy	15,040	24.6
State	12,890	27.7
Housing and Urban Development	8,063	25.7
Education	4,244	70.9

Data on budget outlays were compiled by InsideGov using estimated allocations of 2016 outlays from the Office of Management and Budget. These data were accessed at http://federal-budget.insidegov.com/stories/13371 /government-agencies-most-money on January 27, 2017. Data on the number of employees are from the Office of Management and Budget, except for the EPA and Department of Defense. These data were accessed at http://federal-agencies.insidegov.com/d/a/Cabinet-.-Level on January 27, 2017. Data for the EPA were taken from www.epa.gov/sites/production/files/2014-03/documents/fy15_bib.pdf (accessed 1/27/17). Data for the Department of Defense were taken from www.defense.gov/About (accessed 1/27/17).

Types of Agency Actions

Government agencies use a variety of approaches to carry out their responsibilities. In some instances, agencies act to *implement* laws that Congress and the president have created. In this type of agency activity, Congress passes a law, and then the agency carries out, or implements, that law. If, for example, Congress writes a law about health care for veterans that spells out exactly who qualifies as a veteran, then the Department of Veterans Affairs would simply need to look at the law when determining whether a person seeking health care through the department is eligible to receive it. If the person meets those qualifications, then he or she is eligible. In effect, then, Congress can prescribe exactly how policy should be applied, and agencies then carry out Congress's instructions.

Pure implementation accounts for some of what agencies do, but not a lot. In fact, a surprising amount of agency action involves agencies making judgments and decisions about how to carry out or interpret guidelines that Congress has set. In such cases, the law that Congress passes is not specific and detailed enough to tell the agency precisely what to do in every circumstance. Rather, the law sets out general principles and ideas that Congress wants the agency to follow; then the agency makes decisions about exactly what the law means and how to apply it.

Agencies can also carry out their duties through a process known as *adjudication*, in which an agency acts like a court, hearing two sides of a particular case and then deciding which side wins. Take, for example, the National Labor Relations Board (NLRB). Under the National Labor Relations Act (along with a series of amendments and other laws), the NLRB is charged with determining whether the rights of employees, employers, and unions have been violated. Because Congress obviously cannot foresee every particular issue or controversy that might arise among these three groups, it instead has passed laws that set out general guidelines governing employer-employee relations and has empowered the NLRB to hear cases that raise questions about whether, in a particular instance, someone has violated these guidelines. Thus an employee who believes that her employer has engaged in unfair labor practices can file charges and have her case heard in a trial-like setting, where the board will decide whether the employer's actions were consistent or inconsistent with existing statutes.[4]

Rule making is the most prominent and wide-ranging way in which agencies set policy. Unlike adjudication, in which case agencies act as pseudo-courts, in rule making, they act as pseudo-legislatures, making broad policy declarations that have the force of law. Agencies pursue these rules for a variety of reasons: because Congress has asked the agency (either directly or indirectly) to fill in details that the law has left out, because the underlying statute is unclear, or

The National Labor Relations Board weighs in on many issues related to employee-employer relations, including controversies involving unions. Here, NLRB officials leave a meeting focused on whether or not student athletes at Northwestern University will form a union.

because the agency views the topic as falling within its jurisdiction based on earlier legislation.

Two examples provide a sense of how agencies can act to provide more clarity to a law and to fill in details. One example comes from the Clean Water Act, which is the nation's primary law aimed at protecting the country's water from pollution and which states that its goal is "to restore and maintain the chemical, physical, and biological integrity of the Nation's waters." The law's mission might seem clear, but it turns out that this phrase, especially the part about the "Nation's waters," contains ambiguity. Is the law designed to protect only navigable waters, as it seems to indicate in some places?[5] Only waters that enter into the drinking supply? All waters? In response to this ambiguity, the Environmental Protection Agency (EPA), which Congress charged with carrying out the Clean Water Act, issued a rule in 2015 (the "Waters of the United States" rule) that extended the provisions of the law beyond navigable waters to upstream waters (for example, wetlands and headstreams), which can enter into and affect the integrity and cleanliness of navigable waters. Because Congress had not spelled out exactly which waters fall into the category of "the Nation's waters," the EPA did, even though Congress had not specifically asked the agency to do so. Thus, in this case, the agency used its powers to clarify the meaning of legislation and in so doing expanded the scope of waters covered by the law.[6]

A second example comes from the Affordable Care Act. When Congress wrote this law, it included a requirement that everyone either purchase health insurance or pay a penalty. The law also contained provisions that allowed for exemptions from this mandate (and from the penalty that normally would follow from ignoring it) for a variety of reasons, including religious concerns and situations in which obtaining coverage would create a hardship. But rather than spelling out exactly how these exemptions would work and who would qualify for them, the law then assigned to the secretary of HHS the task of determining precisely what constitutes a hardship. In response, the agency issued a detailed rule identifying who was eligible for an exemption and under what conditions.[7] The goal of this rule was to "ease implementation and help to ensure that the shared responsibility payment obligation applies only to the limited group of taxpayers who have ready access to affordable coverage but choose to spend a substantial period of time uninsured."[8] If the agency had not taken this action, then there would have been no standards for determining whether the hardship exemption applied. Eventually, Congress repealed this part of the law, as part of its 2017 tax cut law, but until that point, the agency determined who was exempt.

These rules related to the Clean Water Act and the Affordable Care Act are not rare examples of agencies engaging in policy making. Rather, they are the norm. To illustrate the volume of rule-making and other policy-making activities, we can turn to the *Federal Register*, in which agencies are required to publish their policy-making activities, including new rules that they are proposing, their solicitation of comments about such rules, and the final rules that they put forward and that, if implemented, will have the force of law. Figure 10.1 shows that agencies engage in a remarkable amount of policy-making activity, as reflected by the average 80,000 pages of the *Federal Register* that are filled by the text of these rules and other agency activities each year. In contrast, the laws passed annually by Congress fill only about 7,000 pages.[9]

The Decision to Delegate

On issue after issue, Congress writes laws and then turns the process over to agencies for implementation and interpretation. In some cases, implementation is straightforward, but in most cases, it is not. Thus, in these cases, Congress *delegates* policy-making responsibility to agencies. In doing so, Congress also ends up giving *discretion* to these agencies—discretion to determine the meaning of provisions in laws, to fill in gaps created by existing laws, and to create new policies.

Congress delegates to agencies and gives these agencies discretion for a variety of reasons. First, Congress simply lacks the time to deal with every policy issue in minute detail and to try to anticipate every future consideration that might arise, especially when taking into account that members of Congress are also spending time on running for reelection, engaging with constituents, meeting with the press, and so on. Because of time constraints (or perhaps because the

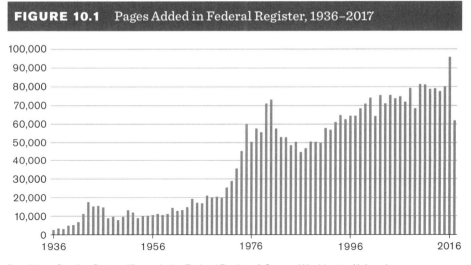

FIGURE 10.1   Pages Added in Federal Register, 1936–2017

Regulatory Studies Center. "Pages in the Federal Register." George Washington University, https://regulatorystudies.columbian.gwu.edu/sites/g/files/zaxdzs1866/f/downloads/Pages.JPG (accessed 9/12/18).

issue is controversial enough that they do not want to deal with it), members of Congress often have an incentive to delegate to agencies.

Perhaps more important, Congress often lacks the expertise necessary to write detailed laws—and expertise is exactly what agencies have. Consider laws about telecommunications. Congress knows far less about technical issues related to broadband, the Internet, satellites, and the broadcast spectrum than do the bureaucrats at the FCC who work on these issues every day. With respect to drug approvals, Congress knows much less than the scientists at the FDA. When writing laws about our nation's nuclear capacity and storage, Congress knows far less than the Department of Energy's employees. As a result, members of Congress know that delegating to agencies offers the possibility of producing policies that will be more informed, more predictable, and more flexible, as well as generally better than if they try to write detailed legislation themselves.

THE RISKS OF DELEGATION   In some ways, delegation sounds ideal for members of Congress—they get to hand off particularly complicated, time-consuming, or controversial issues to agencies that have both the expertise and the time to deal with them appropriately. But delegating can create a new problem: the agency's views on a policy might differ, in some cases substantially, from those of Congress. And because delegation is usually accompanied by some measure of discretion that allows agencies to use their expertise, it also provides the opportunity for agencies to act in ways different from what Congress would prefer. This is what we call a *principal-agent problem*, which occurs in any situation where one person or institution (here Congress) gives decisional authority to another (here an agency), but the agent then takes actions different from what the principal would like. Congress might, for example, delegate aspects of food safety to the USDA, only to find that the agency creates rules that are far stricter than Congress would have enacted if it had taken the time, and had the expertise, to write out detailed laws.

In some cases, Congress can try to avoid this potential problem by taking advantage of the federal structure of our political system. As political scientist Pamela Clouser McCann has shown, Congress has an alternative to delegating power to federal agencies: it can instead delegate to *state* agencies.[10] For example, if members of Congress suspect that they will not like new policies that the EPA is likely to create, they can instead delegate to state-level environmental agencies. McCann shows that members are especially likely to try to avoid the national agency, and turn to state agencies, when they are not from the same party as the president but are from the same party as their state's governor. Of course, in some ways, this practice just pushes the principal-agent problem down a level, but as McCann argues, members vote for moving policy making to the states when they trust that the state-created policies will be more in line with their own views (because of shared partisanship).

Still, in many cases, Congress needs to delegate, both because members do not have the time, expertise, or inclination to write laws and because policy needs to be carried out by national-level agencies. Because of the risk that delegation entails, an important question is whether Congress has the ability to influence what agencies do once it delegates to them. If so, then this ability helps Congress serve as the link that connects the preferences of voters to the actions of bureaucrats. That is, by monitoring agencies to make sure that their constituents' concerns are heard, Congress fulfills its representative role. If, on the other hand, Congress cannot influence what agencies do, the result is a potential problem from the standpoint of democratic theory, because the link between voters' preferences and agency actions might be severed.

Before examining the ways in which members of Congress might be able to influence agencies, we first need to consider a more fundamental question: Do members of Congress have an incentive to try to influence agencies? After all, it is not implausible to believe that members will be happy to pass policy-making authority along to agencies, because doing so frees up time they can spend on other activities (such as reelection campaigning), allows them to avoid making decisions on issues where they lack knowledge, and lets them sidestep making decisions on controversial issues where they are likely to be criticized no matter what action they take. But further consideration reveals that legislators actually *do* have incentives to keep tabs on agencies and to influence what agencies do. To begin with, agency policies will end up affecting citizens and groups within a representative's district or a senator's state. If the public ends up being unhappy with these policies, then they will complain to their senators and representatives, potentially holding them responsible. As a result, members of Congress have an incentive to make sure that agencies' actions and decisions will benefit their constituents, which means that monitoring the agencies helps the members perform their representative function.

In addition, legislators know that agencies are responsible for distributing federal money to districts, often deciding how much money should be distributed and which regions should get this money. For example, the Department of Justice distributes funds to support crime reduction programs, while the Department of Labor allocates money for job training and youth employment programs. Legislators further know that constituents value these sorts of programs, which means they have an incentive both to pressure agencies to send grant money to their districts and to make sure that constituents know that they had a hand in securing these funds. Rep. Stephanie Herseth Sandlin (D-SD), for example, claimed credit for obtaining $3 million for affordable housing in tribal communities, additional funds for highways in the Cheyenne River Indian Reservation, money to hire and retain 30 police officers, and financial support for a project designed to raise awareness of, and provide treatment for, methamphetamine addiction.[11]

In addition to fulfilling a purely representative function, members of Congress will monitor agencies to ensure that they are implementing and enacting policies that reflect the members' own policy preferences. In other words, oversight also helps the members fulfill their governing function. Members might actually prefer to make policy themselves, especially in areas they care about, but, as we mentioned, they might lack the time or expertise. Thus, when they delegate to an agency, they are not simply washing their hands of a policy area, but rather they are asking the agency to make the same decisions that they would make if they had more time or expertise. That is, Congress is asking the agency to serve as a faithful agent. Legislators want to monitor agencies to ensure that their preferences are reflected in agencies' policies.

Finally, members of Congress recognize that they are not the only elected politicians with an interest in the actions of bureaucracy. The president also has such an interest, and in the case of agencies that are located within the executive branch, the president can also exercise more direct control. The president's ability to exercise such control has increased, with the presidency as an institution gaining powers over time that enable occupants of the White House to keep closer tabs on agencies. From Congress's perspective, this isn't a problem when the president's views about what agencies should be doing align with Congress's views. However, when these preferences diverge, Congress will want to prevent agencies from moving closer to the president and farther from Congress. In these cases, Congress has attempted to counteract the innate advantage presidents have as head of the executive branch by enacting institutional reforms. For example, Congress gave itself more staff in the 1946 Legislative Reorganization Act in order to counter the growth in both executive agencies and the president's control over those agencies. Essentially, our separation-of-powers system gives Congress incentives to keep track of what agencies are doing and to try to prevent them from falling further into the president's orbit and away from the orbit of Congress.

Because they want to represent their constituents' interests, work toward their own policy goals, and win reelection, members of Congress clearly have an incentive to try to influence agencies. The members with the strongest incentives are those who sit on relevant committees. As noted in Chapter 5, committees in Congress have specific (and overlapping) policy jurisdictions, and members who sit on these committees specialize and gain expertise in those policy areas. Thus, if an agency is taking action on a specific policy, then members of committees with jurisdiction over that policy will pay special attention to the agency's actions. Members of the judiciary committees will have an incentive to look closely at the actions of the Department of Justice, members of the House Armed Services Committee will pay special attention to the activities of the Department of Defense, and so on.[12]

The Legislative Reorganization Act of 1946 also changed the internal structure of Congress so that committee jurisdictions lined up with agency jurisdictions, thereby facilitating the ability of committees to watch over and supervise these agencies.[13] Again, the ideas of representation and governance create incentives for members to pay attention to agencies, and in the case of committee members, these incentives are heightened. Representatives with strong policy interests in science and technology, for example, may choose to sit on the House Science, Space, and Technology Committee, where they will have the opportunity to oversee scientific research done by NASA, the Department of Energy, the EPA, and other agencies. Similarly, representatives who sit on the Homeland Security Committee will be able to fulfill their governance role by making sure that Congress's voice is heard on issues related to border security, cyberterrorism, and transportation security—all policy areas covered by the Department of Homeland Security.

Members of the majority party also have an incentive to watch over agencies, especially when the president is from the other party. A Democrat-controlled Congress facing a Republican president, for example, will want to watch closely the actions of the executive branch, because the president will attempt to direct agencies to take actions more in line with the president's own views than with those of Congress. Democrats in Congress will want to prevent those agencies from taking actions that they view as too far to the right. At the same time, Congress wants to signal that it has not simply abdicated control over policy to an agency, but instead wants to maintain its authority to govern.

Even when the same party controls Congress and the White House, members of the majority party have an incentive to watch over agencies closely. Here Congress's representation function stands out, because members of Congress will, for all of the reasons discussed earlier, want to make sure that agencies are taking actions that will help, and not hurt, their constituents. But the governance and policy functions also remain. For the former, legislators will not simply want to cede ground to the executive branch, preferring to maintain their institutional status. For the latter, legislators and presidents from the same party do not always agree on policies. During the 2016 presidential election, for example, Donald Trump announced his intention to create a deportation force by tripling the number of agents assigned to this task at the U.S. Immigration and Customs Enforcement agency. When asked about Trump's plan at a town hall meeting, however, House Speaker Paul Ryan stated unequivocally that Congress would not create such a force, as he saw no need for it.[14]

HOW CONGRESS CREATES AND STAFFS AGENCIES

Given that members of Congress—especially members of the relevant committees and the majority party—have an *incentive* to keep close tabs on government agencies, the question becomes whether they have the *ability* to do so. What actions can Congress take to attempt to influence agencies? What tools do they have to help constrain agencies and push them toward taking one set of actions rather than another?

Agency Location and Structure

One approach Congress can take has to do with an agency's location and its structure. *Location* refers to where, within the government, the agency exists. *Structure* refers to the way in which the agency is organized and the powers it is given. We will begin with location, because it is one of the first and most fundamental issues that Congress needs to decide when creating an agency.

Most (although not all) government agencies are created by acts of Congress. For example, Congress created the FCC in 1934 by passing the Federal Communications Act, the Occupational Safety and Health Administration (OSHA) in 1970 via the Occupational Safety and Health Act, and the Office of the Special Inspector General for the Troubled Asset Relief Program (SIGTARP) with the Emergency Economic Stabilization Act of 2008.[15] When creating agencies, Congress needs to decide whether to place them within the executive branch or to give them independent status by placing them outside the executive branch.[16] This decision can have dramatic implications for how the agency carries out its mission and how sensitive it is to political pressures.

Congress often locates agencies within the executive branch, which fits with the Constitution's conception of the responsibilities and duties of that branch (for example, that it should ensure that laws will "be faithfully executed"). The main executive branch agencies are the cabinet-level departments, as shown earlier in Table 10.1: the Department of Defense, the Department of State, the EPA, the Department of Energy, and so on. But there are also important units within those larger cabinet agencies, such as the National Highway Traffic Safety Administration within the Department of Transportation and OSHA within the Department of Labor.[17]

Sometimes, Congress creates these executive branch agencies in response to a new problem. For example, it created the Department of Homeland Security in 2002 in response to the 9/11 terrorist attacks. Other times, Congress can take an existing agency and convert it into a cabinet-level agency in order to give it more prestige and prominence, as it did in 1989 when it elevated the formerly independent Veterans Administration (VA) by making it the Department of Veterans Affairs. Often Congress creates these agencies by reorganizing existing parts of the federal government, which is what it did with the Department of Energy Organization Act in 1977.[18]

Placing agencies within the executive branch provides them with additional prestige and prominence. It allows Congress to respond to major issues (a policy-making role) and to respond to major constituencies (a representational role), such as when it elevated the VA, or when it created the Department of Education in 1980 to heighten attention to public school teachers and students. Placing agencies in the executive branch does come at a potential cost, however—one related to Congress's governing role: by putting agencies in the executive branch, Congress locates these agencies directly within the president's sphere of influence, as the heads of these agencies report directly to the president. This reporting structure can lead to conflict when the president's views differ from those of Congress.

Sometimes Congress chooses to place agencies outside of the executive branch. These independent agencies tend to be smaller than cabinet-level agencies and often focus on specific, rather than broader, issues. Sometimes, they focus on a particular industry, such as the Nuclear Regulatory Commission, which oversees nuclear power plants in the United States, or the Securities and Exchange Commission, which regulates stock exchanges and securities.

In addition to deciding whether an agency will be located within the executive branch (and if so, where), Congress also decides on the structure of the agency's leadership. Congress can, for example, decide that a single person will head an agency. Thus agencies such as the EPA or HUD have one person in charge. If the agency is in the executive branch, then that person reports directly to the president. Alternatively, Congress can create a multiperson board to head an agency. The FCC, for example, is governed by a five-member board, as is the Federal Trade Commission. Furthermore, Congress can also require that multimember boards have other features, such as partisan balance (e.g., no more than three of five seats can be filled by members of one party) or longer terms of service (e.g., members of the Federal Reserve serve for 14 years, ensuring that they can outlast any specific president and will be in place longer than most members of Congress).

The structure of agency leadership affects how independent the agency will be when making decisions. In agencies that are headed by a single person, Congress or the president can try to ensure that the secretary shares, and will act on, their policy views. In agencies headed by multimember boards, on the other hand, political influence is lessened by the need for members to work together, build coalitions, and reach agreements. Congress knows that if it wants to make an agency more independent and less sensitive to political pressure, it can place a multimember board at the head of the agency, which both slows down the agency's policy-making process and increases the likelihood that decisions will incorporate political compromises.

Congress can also specify the methods, or approaches, that agencies use to make decisions. Earlier we learned that two prominent types of agency activities are rule making, in which the agency creates policy in a manner similar to a legislature, and adjudication, in which the agency creates policy in a manner similar to a court. Rule making gives agencies considerably more authority to create policies that have far-ranging effects, whereas adjudication tends to be about more specific disputes (e.g., between business and labor, as discussed earlier). In addition, once finalized, rules can be difficult to overturn. Thus if Congress wants to limit an agency's powers, it can give the agency the ability to adjudicate but not to create rules, and if it wants to increase an agency's powers, it can do the reverse.

HOW WE STUDY
CONGRESSIONAL CREATION OF AGENCIES

The previous section outlines some of the decisions that legislators need to make when initially designing government agencies. It also identifies some reasons why Congress might make some decisions and not others. Congress might choose to place an agency outside of the executive branch, for example, if it wants to place some distance between the president and the agency. For example, Figure 10.2 shows that over a five-decade period starting in 1946, Congress frequently, but not always, chose to make new agencies independent rather than place them within the executive branch.[19] Similarly, it might give an agency a leadership structure that is less responsive to political pressure if it wants the agency to be able to act more autonomously.

Are there other factors that might affect Congress's decisions regarding an agency's location, leadership, and policy-making tools? And is there a way to test whether these factors systematically influence the ways in which Congress designs an agency? These are the questions that political scientists B. Dan Wood and John Bohte set out to explore.[20] They did so by constructing a theoretical argument to explain why Congress sometimes creates agency structures that make agencies more independent and then collecting data to assess whether these factors do indeed have the predicted effects.

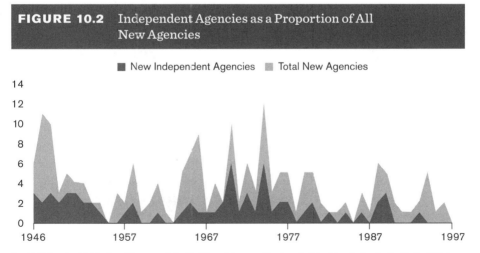

FIGURE 10.2 Independent Agencies as a Proportion of All New Agencies

■ New Independent Agencies ■ Total New Agencies

David E. Lewis. 2003. *Presidents and the Politics of Agency Design: Political Insulation in the United States Government Bureaucracy, 1946–1997*, 51, Figure 2.3. Stanford: Stanford University Press.

Their theoretical approach focuses on explaining why Congress sometimes chooses to give agencies more autonomy, which it can do by placing the agency outside of the executive branch, giving it a multimember board with partisan balance requirements and longer terms, and giving it rule-making authority. Here we focus on three of the main potential explanatory factors that they identified. The primary theoretical cause they identified centers on *policy disagreement* between Congress and the president. When Congress disagrees with the president, it worries that once legislation is passed, the president will use executive powers to move the agency away from what Congress wants and toward what the president wants. Thus, when conflict between Congress and the president is greater, Congress will act to increase the autonomy of agencies. To measure conflict, Wood and Bohte collected data on the number of presidential vetoes and veto overrides in each year, because vetoes and overrides increase when the two branches have conflicting policy views.

Second, they argue that *electoral turnover* might affect Congress's design decisions. If the majority party in Congress is confident that it will remain the majority for the foreseeable future, it may choose an agency design that is more open to political pressure, knowing that it can then take advantage of this structure to influence future agency actions. However, if it worries that it will lose control of Congress, it does not want to create a structure that the opposing party can take advantage of once it gains power. Hence, when it expects electoral turnover to be more likely, it should favor designs that give agencies more autonomy.

Third, Wood and Bohte consider how the strength of the majority party will affect Congress's decisions regarding agency design. According to their theory, when the majority party is stronger, it will prefer to create an agency that it can influence more easily and thus will desire a less autonomous agency. To assess party strength, Wood and Bohte relied on a measure that combines the size of the majority (relative to the size of the minority) and the cohesion of the majority.

The next step in their research involved testing whether these factors had the predicted effects. To do this, Wood and Bohte began by collecting data about the design of 141 agencies that Congress created over a 110-year period spanning the late 1800s to the late 1900s. For each agency, they read the legislation that Congress passed to create the agency, and they coded information about a variety of structural and locational features. Here we focus on three of their measures.

First, they found that in 51 cases, Congress created independent agencies, while in the remaining 90 cases, Congress placed the agency within the executive branch. Second, they coded each agency's leadership arrangements as being likely to facilitate either political responsiveness or agency autonomy, where more autonomous structures were those with multimember boards, partisan balance requirements, or terms longer than four years. In 61 cases, they classified agency leadership as autonomous; they classified the remaining agencies as politically responsive. Not surprisingly, they found substantial overlap between the location of an agency and its leadership structure, with all independent agencies coded as having an autonomous leadership structure. But leadership structures for agencies in the executive branch showed some variation, with 11 of those agencies having autonomous structures. Finally, they coded whether the law specifically gave the agency the power to enact rules. As we discussed earlier, rule-making power gives agencies greater autonomy, because it provides agencies with the authority to initiate policy change and makes such changes harder to overturn once finalized. Congress gave 62 agencies rule-making authority.[21]

Having collected all of this data, Wood and Bohte then tested whether Congress's conflict with the president, electoral turnover, and the strength of the majority party all had the expected effects. Their primary finding is that political conflict with the president does lead Congress to create more autonomous agencies. When Congress disagrees with the president, it is more likely to place agencies outside of the executive branch, to create autonomous leadership structures, and to give agencies rule-making authority. Thus, it is clear that Congress considers its relationship with the president when designing new agencies.

In addition, Wood and Bohte found that electoral turnover (or, more accurately, fear of electoral turnover) and the strength of the majority party affect structural and locational features. Stronger parties are less likely to place agencies outside of the executive branch or to create autonomous leadership structures atop the agency. Meanwhile, an increase in the likelihood of electoral turnover causes Congress to favor making agencies independent of the executive branch.

Critical Thinking

1. A potential criticism of Wood and Bohte's argument is that Congress might agree with the current president and as a result put a new agency in the executive branch, but then the next president might be from the opposing party, in which case Congress would have preferred the agency to be independent. When creating an agency, should Congress take into account the possibility that a president with whom it agrees could be replaced by one with whom it disagrees? How might it do this?

2. Congress always has the option of using oversight to react to an agency's decisions and actions. Given this power (discussed extensively in the second half of this chapter), why would it bother worrying about structural decisions?

3. Agencies cover an extremely wide range of policy areas. Would the charac-
    teristics of the policy area affect whether Congress wants to make the agency
    more (or less) independent? Explain your answer and provide examples.

Appointments

Structure and location are two tools that Congress can use to influence agencies. The nomination process is another. The president appoints approximately
4,000 people to serve in government agencies. Roughly 1,200 of these people
fill what are known as "PAS" positions, meaning that these positions require
presidential nomination and Senate confirmation.[22] For these 1,200 positions,
Congress—specifically the Senate—uses its constitutionally prescribed role to
exert influence over the nominee and the agency to which the nominee will, if
confirmed, be appointed.

The Senate's role in the appointment process occurs in three stages. First,
presidents often confer with Senate leaders before selecting a nominee. Presidents, especially those who are new to office, usually do not want to be drawn
into a fight with the Senate over nominees. Thus new presidents often seek the
advice of Senate leaders to determine whether a potential nominee is likely to
raise any red flags. Second, once the president nominates someone, senators
begin to consider that nominee. Some of this consideration takes place informally and behind the scenes, with nominees visiting senators in their offices and
responding to their questions. Other aspects of this stage are more formal and
more public; Senate hearings conducted by the relevant committee are the most
visible part of this process. Third, the full Senate conducts a vote.

It turns out that the Senate infrequently votes to reject a president's nominee. When it does so, the rejection is usually tied to a scandal having been
revealed during the confirmation process. From Jimmy Carter through Barack
Obama, presidents made 109 appointments to cabinet-level positions. Of these,
the Senate confirmed 103, a success rate of 94 percent.[23] Of the six who were
not confirmed, five withdrew. Thus even in a period in which polarization was
increasing, a period covering a span of six presidents, the Senate rejected only
1 out of 109 appointments. Indeed, in the history of the United States, the
Senate has formally rejected only nine nominees to cabinet positions. A similar
pattern holds for lower-level PAS positions, too, with one study finding that
from 1965 through 1994 the Senate confirmed more than 95 percent of presidential nominees.[24]

Why does the Senate approve such a high percentage of the president's
nominees? For starters, as we discussed, presidents often check to make sure

their nominees are not likely to encounter significant opposition. If they learn that prominent senators might oppose the nominee, they may choose not to go forward with that nominee. In addition, senators typically give presidents a good deal of leeway in filling key positions, confirming nominees who are not caught up in a scandal or hampered by a notable lack of qualifications.[25] In part, this tradition stems from a recognition that the president won the election and thus should be afforded deference in staffing the executive branch. Even among senators who are not members of the president's party, it reflects a view that the two parties are partners in a long-running game, where the out-party knows that it will at some time control the presidency and at that time will want members from the opposing party to support its president's nominees. Senator Brian Schatz (D-HI) expressed this view in 2017 when explaining why he voted for some of President Donald Trump's nominees: "The door swings both ways in Washington. . . . At some point we're going to want a Democratic president to [set] up a Cabinet. So we're trying to be reasonable when the nominees are reasonable."[26]

Finally, senators from the president's party are especially reticent to oppose a president's nominees, particularly if their opposition would endanger the nominee's chances. In 2017, for example, during the Senate Foreign Relations Committee's hearings, three Republican senators—John McCain (R-AZ), Lindsey Graham (R-SC), and Marco Rubio (R-FL)—expressed strong dissatisfaction with Rex Tillerson, who was Donald Trump's nominee to head the Department of State. Nonetheless, between the presumption that presidents should be allowed to choose their nominees and the inclination not to undercut a president of their own party, all three indicated that they would support Tillerson's nomination within the committee, allowing it to go forward to the full Senate with a narrow 11–10 majority.

The lack of rejections does not necessarily mean that the Senate's role is unimportant. As already noted, the president might have anticipated the Senate's reaction before submitting a nomination, which would mean that Senate influence took place early and out of the public eye. More important, the floor discussion of a nominee and especially the committee hearings provide senators with opportunities to extract promises from the nominees (for example, regarding future actions the nominee might take) and to make sure that the nominee knows the views of committee members. (The latter is especially important because, as we will see, committees play a key role in overseeing agencies.) Returning to the Senate Foreign Relations Committee's hearings for Secretary of State Tillerson, all three of the skeptical Republican senators—McCain, Graham, and Rubio—stressed to Tillerson that they favored a hard line toward Russia and countries with human rights abuses such as Saudi Arabia and the

"MORE OF KREMLIN'S OPPONENTS ARE ENDING UP DEAD"

MRS. SHAHEEN

Congress provides oversight of bureaucratic agencies through its confirmation of presidential appointments. Appointments can be contentious, but presidential appointees are usually confirmed. Republicans and Democrats (like New Hampshire senator Jeanne Shaheen, above) asked difficult questions of Donald Trump's first nominee for secretary of state, Rex Tillerson, about his business connections to the Russian government, but Tillerson was ultimately confirmed.

Philippines. They also pushed him to agree publicly that Russia constitutes a danger to the United States and that the United States should oppose Russian attempts to expand its spheres of influence.

Senators can also take actions to delay a president's nominee. Indeed, there has been an increase in the amount of time it takes the Senate to confirm a nominee (see Figure 10.3), leading some scholars to argue that this "malign neglect," whereby the Senate delays acting on a president's nominee, is a central feature of nominations today.[27] A longer delay can allow for questions to be raised about a nominee's qualifications, increase the opportunity for opposition to build and coalesce, and provide for additional time to uncover and investigate any potential scandals. Not surprisingly, studies have shown that delay increases when different parties control the presidency and the Senate.

Numerous other factors can also increase delay, as political scientist Ian Ostrander demonstrated in a recent article.[28] The Senate clearly acts more quickly on higher-level appointees than on lower-level appointees, as Table 10.2 shows. The Senate also takes more time when considering nominees to independent agencies, because these appointees often serve longer terms than appoin-

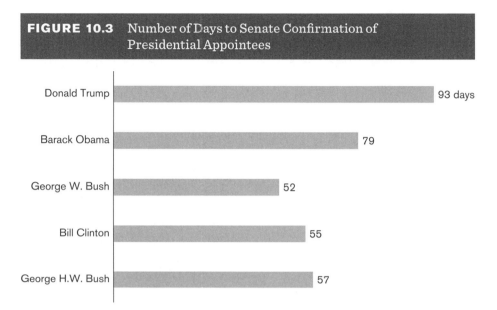

FIGURE 10.3 Number of Days to Senate Confirmation of Presidential Appointees

Partnership for Public Service. "Political Appointee Tracker." https://ourpublicservice.org/issues/presidential-transition/political-appointee-tracker.php (accessed 7/24/18).

TABLE 10.2 Delays in Presidential Appointments

Position by Tier	Average Delay (Days)
Cabinet Secretary and Attorney General	27
High-level nomination	96
Major IR Board/Commission member	137
Low-level nomination	133
Lowest-level/ Other nominations	108

Ian Ostrander. 2016. "The Logic of Collective Inaction: Senatorial Delay in Executive Nominations." *American Journal of Political Science* 60(4): 1067.

tees to executive branch agencies and because they generally cannot be removed from office as easily. In contrast, it tends to act more quickly during a president's first term—when many senators believe a stronger norm of deference is in place and when the president likely has greater popularity—than during a president's second term. Factors internal to the Senate also affect the length of delay. Most prominently, polarization within the Senate has significantly increased delays in confirmations. Clearly, though, a good part of the delay is due to increased conflict between Congress and the president.

The Senate is acting strategically when it delays consideration of the president's nominees. It is also acting within its rights, as there are no rules or even guidelines about how quickly the Senate needs to act; timing has been dictated by norms. Still, this issue of delay does raise concerns, as longer delays mean that agencies go for longer periods of time without being fully staffed. Two seats on the important Federal Reserve Board, for example, were left vacant during the last two years of Barack Obama's second term. Obama had nominated Allan Landon, the retired CEO of the Bank of Hawaii, and Kathryn Dominguez, a highly respected economist at the University of Michigan, to fill these positions in January and July (respectively) of 2015. Yet when the 114th Congress ended in January 2017, the Senate had not acted on either of these two nominees. As the *Economist* noted, such vacancies have the effect of weakening and "addling America's central bank," with potentially severe effects on America's monetary policy.[29]

Sometimes, the Senate leaves a position open specifically because it knows that doing so will cripple an agency. In 2006, for example, the Senate passed a law that converted the position of the director of the Bureau of Alcohol, Firearms, and Tobacco—the agency responsible for the enforcement of federal gun laws—to a PAS position, meaning that the Senate would get to weigh in on any presidential nominee to this position. In the ensuing years, the agency went five years without a confirmed director. Such vacancies are common throughout the bureaucracy, making it difficult for agencies to carry out their missions, which can in turn increase citizens' dissatisfaction with the performance of government.

At other times the majority party in the Senate has wanted to approve a nominee, only to be stymied by the minority party's opposition. These minorities would take advantage of the Senate's rules—most notably, the filibuster—to obstruct, or prevent, a vote on a president's nominees. In 2013, the majority-party Democrats in the Senate grew so frustrated with the frequency (and effectiveness) with which Senate Republicans were obstructing President Obama's nominees that they made use of a procedural maneuver, known as the *nuclear option*, to avoid the filibuster on such nominations. This move paved the way for the majority party to avoid obstruction of presidential nominees to agency positions and to the lower federal courts by allowing the majority to end a filibuster. It also led to a similar action in 2017 when the majority-party Republicans in the Senate voted to end filibusters on Supreme Court nominees in order to ensure the confirmation of Neil Gorsuch. Adoption of the nuclear option ensured a president's nominees would be voted on, assuming the nominee had majority support in the Senate, but it removed a powerful tool for the minority. Many senators lamented this change, in part because it decreased the incentive for presidents to select nominees with broad bipartisan appeal.[30]

Whether by discussing potential nominees with the president prior to an official nomination, using hearings to propound their views or to extract promises from nominees, delaying consideration of or obstructing a nominee, or (in rare cases) voting against a nominee, senators have multiple ways they can influence appointments. Notably, these appointments are not only for positions at the head of each agency but also reach deep into an agency's lower levels. For example, at the Department of Commerce, Senate confirmation is necessary for the appointment of not only the secretary of commerce but also for 20 other major positions within the agency, including the deputy secretary; the assistant secretaries of commerce for industry and analysis, enforcement and compliance, and environmental observations and prediction; and various undersecretary positions (for example, international trade and the National Oceanic and Atmospheric Administration).[31] Consequently, the Senate can use the confirmation process to affect who sits in positions of importance throughout an agency and to make sure those people know exactly where the Senate stands on key policy issues.

There are, however, limits to the Senate's ability to influence who occupies these positions of authority in agencies and to influence how the nominees will, if confirmed, approach issues. Once a nominee makes a promise to the committee, nothing prevents that nominee from breaking that promise after he or she is in office, other than the threat of being called back before the Senate committee. Congress can threaten impeachment, as it did in the aftermath of the IRS scandal discussed at the start of this chapter, but given that only one executive branch official in the nation's history has been impeached, such a threat rings hollow.

In addition, presidents can avoid the Senate. They can, for example, make interim appointments, which do not require Senate approval and in which temporary appointees can serve up to 210 days (and sometimes longer). The president can also choose to appoint people to related positions that do not require Senate approval. In late 2016, for example, President Donald Trump announced his intention to appoint Michael J. Flynn as his national security advisor, a position that falls within the Executive Office of the President and therefore does not require Senate confirmation. Flynn's combination of inflammatory remarks and his forced resignation as the head of the Defense Intelligence Agency (reportedly because of ineffective and chaotic managerial skills) would have made for a hard sell in the Republican-controlled Senate if he had instead been nominated for, say, the Department of Defense.[32] Instead, President Trump nominated the widely respected James Mattis for the PAS position of secretary of defense while ensuring that he would continue to get the advice he wanted from Flynn in the non-PAS position as National Security Agency (NSA) advisor.[33]

One additional presidential power derives directly from the Constitution: the power to make *recess appointments* to agencies. With this power, the president can wait until the Senate is in recess and then appoint someone, thereby avoiding the Senate entirely. This appointee is entitled to occupy that position until the end of the next Senate session, which can last up to one year. Here, too, the Senate is virtually powerless. In response to concerns about recess appointments by Presidents George W. Bush and Barack Obama, Senate majority leaders from the opposition party—Harry Reid in the former case and Mitch McConnell in the latter—kept the Senate in session more or less permanently, preventing the president from making a recess appointment.[34]

HOW CONGRESS INFLUENCES AGENCY ACTIONS

When Congress creates an agency, the decisions it makes about location and structure influence the agency's future actions and autonomy. Congress then can affect the staffing of the agency by using its constitutional power to confirm appointees who occupy positions throughout each agency. Once the agency is created, located, and staffed, Congress has other means it can use to influence the agency's actions. Some of these means of influence involve statutes, which Congress can use to instruct agencies about which actions to take (or not to take). Congress can also design procedures that guide agencies and affect which policies they are likely to enact. In addition, it can enact budgets that shape agency activities. Other actions Congress can take to influence agencies involve nonstatutory approaches, such as holding hearings, conducting investigations, and requiring reports.

Statutory Instructions

Congress can write laws to tell agencies exactly what to do. At times, these statutory instructions involve Congress delegating to agencies but removing, or at least limiting, discretion. For example, when writing the Affordable Care Act, Congress could have spelled out in detail exactly who qualified for a hardship exemption to the mandate and under what conditions. If Congress had provided these instructions, it still would have delegated responsibility for carrying out the policy to the agency, as people would have applied to the agency for an exemption. But such an approach would have removed any discretion or flexibility from the agency. Statutory instructions move an agency closer to a pure implementation role, where Congress tells an agency what to do and the agency then follows those instructions.

In other cases, Congress can use statutes to instruct an agency to take a specific action because the agency has done something that Congress disliked. In February of 2013, for example, the U.S. Postal Service announced that it was going to end Saturday mail delivery, a move it predicted would save up to

$2 billion per year.[35] Congress reacted swiftly by passing a law requiring the Postal Service to deliver mail six days a week.[36]

Of course, although Congress can attempt to pass laws that tell agencies what to do, these attempts are not always successful. But even unsuccessful attempts can influence agencies, as they indicate that the threat of legislation is real enough that agencies will then attempt to anticipate congressional action and think twice before taking actions Congress will object to.[37] In 2015, for example, the Consumer Financial Protection Bureau (CFPB), which Congress created in the aftermath of the financial crisis of 2007 and 2008, issued new rules that allowed it to regulate automobile loans based on its general authority to regulate loans. The House of Representatives responded by passing legislation, the Reforming CFPB Indirect Auto Financing Guidance Act, to overturn these rules and to curtail the CFPB's ability to regulate auto loans. The bill easily passed in the House with a vote of 332–96, with nearly all Republicans, along with 88 of 188 Democrats, voting in favor of the bill. Because the bill was never introduced in the Senate, it never became law. Still, the House legislation acted as a shot across the bow of the agency. And, notably, when the agency was asked about its fair lending priorities for 2017, it listed several other areas, such as mortgages, small businesses, and student loans—but not autos.[38]

Such attempted-but-failed laws can build momentum toward making changes in the future.[39] In 2013, it was revealed that the NSA had been collecting "metadata" on Americans' e-mails and phone calls that revealed who contacted whom, when the contact occurred, and the duration of phone calls (but did not contain information about the content of communications). The data collection was legal, as it had been authorized by Section 215 of the USA PATRIOT Act, which Congress passed and President George W. Bush signed into law in 2001. Supporters of this provision of the law argued that it helped to protect against terrorist acts, while opponents raised concerns about the violation of privacy and infringement on liberty.[40] In response to these revelations, a bipartisan group of legislators introduced legislation aimed at curtailing the agency's ability to collect such data. The bill eventually failed, but by a much narrower margin (217–205) than anyone expected. More important, it revealed the depth of opposition to the NSA's activities, began the process of building on and consolidating this opposition, and indicated that future success of a similar bill, if not guaranteed, was more likely than anyone had anticipated.[41] Indeed, in 2015, Congress allowed the NSA's authority to engage in such activities to expire.[42]

In addition to passing laws that limit agencies' discretion and telling these agencies what policies to put in place, Congress can use two other statutory tools to react to agency actions and rules. The first of these is the *legislative veto*, which allows Congress to stop an agency rule from going into effect. There are several variants of the legislative veto. Some require congressional approval; that is, the rule cannot go into effect until Congress approves it. Others rely on disapproval, where a rule goes into effect unless Congress votes to disapprove it.[43] Some legislative vetoes require both chambers of Congress to act for the veto to go into effect. For other vetoes, the action of only one chamber is necessary, and in some cases, the veto power is delegated to committees rather than to the full chamber.

By including legislative veto provisions in a law, Congress lays the groundwork for quickly and efficiently overturning an agency action without having to go through the full process of passing a new law. This quickness and efficiency, however, proved to be the downfall of the legislative veto. In the 1983 case of *Immigration and Naturalization Service v. Chadha*, the Supreme Court ruled that legislative vetoes were unconstitutional because they ran afoul of the constitutionally prescribed process by which new laws needed to be passed in the same form by both chambers and then presented to (and signed by) the president.[44]

Somewhat surprisingly, however, Congress has continued to include legislative vetoes in new laws. Prior to *Chadha*, Congress had written legislative veto provisions into law with increased frequency during the 1970s and early 1980s, after having rarely done so prior to 1970. But as political scientist Michael Berry notes, Congress has enacted more statutes containing legislative veto provision since the Court's ruling than it did in all the years prior to the ruling.[45] The courts have generally continued to find these post-*Chadha* legislative vetoes to be unconstitutional. But the ease of writing legislative veto provisions into a law, the ease of enacting a veto (compared to a standard law), the low likelihood that a court will strike down a particular provision, and the effect that the possibility of a veto might have on an agency (for example, by indicating that Congress will be watching the agency closely) all indicate that we will likely continue to see legislative veto provisions in laws for the foreseeable future.

Questions about the constitutionality of legislative vetoes produced another attempt by Congress to rein in agencies: the Congressional Review Act (CRA). This 1996 law, like the legislative veto, gave Congress the power to strike down an agency action, but it did so in a way that attempted to avoid the problems the Supreme Court had identified in its *Chadha* decision. According to the CRA, once an agency announces its intention to issue a final rule, that rule will not go into effect for 60 days, during which time Congress can take action—passing a resolution of disapproval by majority vote in each chamber and then getting it signed by the president—to stop the rule from going into effect.

The CRA provides an alternative to the legislative veto that is much more likely to pass constitutional muster. Initially, this tactic was little used. Out of more than 48,000 rules that agencies sent to Congress in the 12 years following the passage of the CRA, Congress struck down precisely one, a workplace safety rule about ergonomics proposed by OSHA in 2000.[46] But in the weeks after Donald Trump's inauguration in 2017, Congress rediscovered the power of the CRA, using it to strike down major rules that the Departments of Interior, Education, and Labor, as well as the Securities and Exchange Commission, the Social Security Administration, and others had finalized at the end of the Obama administration. Indeed, of the 19 pieces of legislation that President Trump signed into law during his first three months in office, more than half were congressional resolutions striking down Obama-era rules.[47]

Why this sudden increased usage of a tactic that had essentially been dormant for 20 years? The answer is that the conditions, with unified Republican control following a Democratic presidency, were exactly those under which this tool is most useful. When a final rule is proposed at the end of a presidential administration but has not yet gone into effect when the new president takes office, that new president is more likely to sign the resolution of disapproval than the previous president, who would most likely have protected the agency action by refusing to sign the resolution.

Procedural Constraints

Many statutes tell agencies exactly what they should or should not do. But Congress can also use a subtler statutory approach: putting constraints in place that guide agency actions. Congress does this by inserting various procedural provisions into laws, with the expectation that these provisions will steer an agency in one direction or another. The idea is that by telling the agency what procedures to follow, Congress can influence an agency without telling it exactly what to do. This approach allows Congress to get the public policy it wants while delegating to an agency with expertise in that area.

Congress can use a variety of procedural controls to influence an agency's actions.[48] It can require an agency to issue reports about its activities and to do so within a specific time frame. It can compel an agency to hold public hearings when it is about to develop a new policy, or to consult with specific groups when creating the policy. It can instruct agencies to follow certain procedures when creating new rules, procedures that might differ from those set out in the Administrative Procedure Act. And it can choose to either protect agencies from the courts or to open agency actions up to judicial review.

Procedural controls operate in two ways. First, they force agencies to expose their actions, making their policies more visible to the public and interested groups, as well as to members of Congress. Public hearings attract attention and allow opponents a chance to be heard, while requirements to issue regular reports help to ensure that senators and representatives know what agencies are up to. Second, these provisions can increase the likelihood of some policy outcomes while decreasing the likelihood of others. If, for example, a law instructs the EPA to meet with farmers when considering new policies having to do with the runoff of storm water from farms, it is more likely that the agency will hear about farmers' concerns and that any proposed rules will take these concerns into account. These legislative provisions do not dictate which actions agencies should take, but they can make agency actions more public and cause the agency to lean in one policy direction rather than another.

Because these provisions are enacted prior to the agency taking any action, rather than being written in response to specific actions, they are sometimes called *ex ante* controls, where *ex ante* is Latin for "before the event" (that is, these controls are put in place before agencies take actions). Some scholars have aptly characterized *ex ante* controls as *fire alarm oversight*. To draw out this analogy, consider the differences between how fire alarms work and how police patrols work. Fire alarms are placed at various locations, and when someone sees a fire that needs to be put out, he or she can pull the alarm. Once an alarm is pulled, the fire department springs into action, sending trucks and firefighters to put out the fire. This approach is much more efficient and effective than if fire trucks just drove around on patrol, looking for fires to put out.

Procedural provisions act like fire alarms. Congress puts them in place, via legislation, and then waits for them to be pulled, which in this context means that some person or persons—an interest group, concerned citizens, congressional staff members—can notify members of Congress about what the agency is doing. This notification, in turn, can spur members of Congress to take actions, such as introducing new laws, holding hearings, or conducting investigations that are designed to persuade or coerce the agency to change course. Provisions that require agencies have to issue reports, conduct public hearings, meet with certain interest groups, follow certain procedures, or meet certain deadlines all provide opportunities for interested parties to observe what agencies are doing and, if necessary, turn to Congress for corrective action. And although Congress can, and does, effectively use other tactics that resemble patrols, these fire alarm procedural provisions serve as useful early warning systems.

Budgets

In addition to putting policy instructions and procedural constraints into laws, Congress can use appropriations legislation, wherein it provides an agency with its yearly budget, to affect agency actions. To understand this tactic, recall that two types of statutes affect agencies. First, authorizing statutes give the agency the authority to carry out its duties. These statutes delegate policy-making responsibility to agencies and can place limits on an agency's discretion. Second, appropriations laws provide the agency with the money it needs to carry out the duties and responsibilities outlined in authorizing statutes.

Suppose, for example, that an authorizing statute gives an agency power to regulate a specific industry. As part of this power, the agency can monitor the activities of the businesses that it regulates. To do that, it needs funding to hire employees to carry out the monitoring, to conduct inspections, and so on. If Congress decides that an agency is being too aggressive in carrying out these functions, it can cut the agency's budget, leaving the agency with fewer funds to hire people or to pay the costs necessary to carry out investigations. This is exactly what happened in the years following the IRS scandal discussed in the introduction to this chapter. If, on the other hand, Congress likes what the agency is doing or wants the agency to be more proactive, it can increase the agency's budget. Budgets, therefore, can act as carrots or sticks.

There is an asymmetry between those two ways Congress uses budgets to influence agencies. Cutting an agency's funding sends signals to the agency about what Congress wants. But cutting an agency's funding not only sends a signal; it can also force an agency to reduce its activities by depriving it of the money it would need to carry out those activities. The EPA, for example, hires special agents to investigate "significant and egregious violations of environmental laws."[49] If Congress believes that the EPA is conducting too many of these investigations, or that such investigations represent governmental overreach, it can cut the agency's overall budget, or it could specifically cut funding for the salaries of these special agents, all in order to reduce the amount of this activity.

Increasing an agency's budget also sends a signal to an agency; in this case, it is a signal that Congress approves of the agency's activities. But the effects of such increases may be limited. A budget cut can force an agency to do less when it wants to do more, but an increase cannot force an agency to do more when it wants to do less. Still, although budget cuts are clearly the stronger tool, some studies have shown that agencies such as the FDA and the FCC change the level and frequency of their regulatory actions in response to both increases and decreases in budgets, as well as to recent patterns and changes in budgets.[50]

In addition to increases or decreases in an agency's budget, Congress has another power that it increasingly has used to influence agencies' actions. Appropriations bills differ from regular authorizing bills in that appropriations bills are must-pass bills, which means that Congress has to pass them in order to keep the government running (see Chapter 7). These important bills, along with some procedural protections that accompany them, provide members with a significant opportunity: they can attach *limitation riders* to these spending bills to place constraints on agency actions. These riders are provisions that Congress might not otherwise have passed separately, but because the appropriations bill must be passed (at least eventually), the president and other members of

Congress—even if they oppose these limitations—are unlikely to oppose the entire appropriations bill over a rider that constitutes an extremely minor part of the overall bill, especially because doing so could result in parts of the government being shut down.

It is not unusual for Congress to include 300 or more riders in each year's appropriations bills.[51] For example, an appropriations bill for the Departments of Commerce, Justice, and State in 2002 contained a limitation rider that prevented these agencies from using any funds to prepare for the implementation of the Kyoto Protocol, a major international treaty to address climate change that was being considered at the time. By using these riders, Congress can prevent agencies from taking actions—whether specific (as in the Kyoto Protocol example) or general (for example, prohibiting the agency from engaging in any rule making at all)—that members of Congress might disapprove of. Not surprisingly, Congress is especially likely to use limitation riders when the president is not from the majority party in Congress and when Appropriations Committee members have unfavorable views of the policies that likely would be produced in the absence of such riders.

Oversight Activities

Earlier, we learned about fire alarms, which Congress uses to ensure that it will be alerted when agencies start to take actions that members of Congress, or their constituents, disagree with. An alternative and more proactive form of influence falls under the heading of *police patrols*. Just as it sounds, this approach entails members of Congress actively going out and looking for potentially problematic agency actions. When Congress goes on patrol, it is engaging in *oversight*—that is, keeping an eye on the activities of agencies.[52] These oversight activities are sometimes called *ex post* controls because they consist of actions that Congress takes after agencies have created policies or have begun to engage in new policy-making episodes.

Oversight can take several forms. Some oversight is informal, with members of Congress and their staff communicating directly with agency officials, either to encourage the agency's activities or to register complaints.[53] Agency officials are especially likely to take these informal contacts seriously when they come from legislators who sit on relevant oversight committees, because the members of those committees are both more knowledgeable about the policy area and more likely to exert pressure on an agency, or when they come from the Committee on Oversight Government Reform, which has broad authority to review agencies. Thus officials at the USDA will pay far more attention to contacts from members of the agriculture committees in Congress, or from the Government Oversight Committee, than from other members of Congress.

An illustrative anecdote comes from a study, which we discuss in more detail next, by Jason MacDonald and Robert McGrath. A congressional staff member recounted how a constituent of one of the oversight committee members contacted the staffer about an FDA policy. More specifically, this constituent, who was a nurse, noticed that the FDA had approved a label for a particular drug, but that this label neglected to include a warning that the drug could have potentially deadly effects for patients who were already suffering from kidney disease, and people had died because of this omission. After some back and forth, the FDA agreed to change the label. This example shows both how agencies can be responsive to contacts from members of Congress (especially those who sit on oversight committees) and how members can engage in their representative function through oversight.

Many other instances of oversight are more formal. Congress can, for example, conduct audits of agencies. It can place *sunset provisions* in a law that cause the law to expire on a certain date. Knowing that the law will have to be reauthorized gives members of Congress a new chance to examine agency activities.[54] Congress can also issue reports that bring additional (and perhaps unwanted) attention to an agency. It can request that an agency's inspector general—a bureaucrat placed in an agency by Congress to conduct separate and independent investigations of agency actions—look into the propriety of actions by agency officials. In early 2017, for example, a bipartisan group of chairs and ranking minority members of a range of oversight committees asked the Department of Justice's inspector general to investigate whether FBI Director James Comey acted improperly in the investigation of Hillary Clinton's e-mails.[55] Some of these activities involve a mixture of *ex ante* and *ex post* controls. For example, sunset provisions are placed in laws *ex ante*, but are included in order to increase *ex post* activities. Inspectors general are appointed before they are needed, but they can also take part in ongoing investigations.

HEARINGS AND INVESTIGATIONS   By far, the two most prominent forms of oversight are hearings and investigations. These often work in tandem—Congress conducts hearings to facilitate investigations, and Congress conducts investigations that can lead to hearings. Hearings provide Congress an opportunity to bring agency officials to the Capitol, where members can shine a bright light on agency activities. If they like an agency policy and want to promote or defend it, hearings give them the chance to do so. But hearings (and investigations) also allow them to confront agency officials—very publicly—about whether their actions are subverting a law that delegated power to them, or are inconsistent with the preferences of current members of Congress. During these hearings, members can question whether agency officials have abused their powers. They can seek information on why agencies have prioritized some activities and policies at the expense of others, as well as how these agencies have spent their funding. And they can express their concerns about either specific agency actions or the general direction of agency policy making.

Do agency officials really need to worry about these hearings and investigations? After all, if Congress is as dysfunctional as many critics suggest, it might not be able to follow up on any threats that it makes at hearings or during investigations. Furthermore, structural changes in Congress have reduced its ability to engage in oversight. Indeed, two of the most respected observers of Congress, Thomas Mann and Norman Ornstein, have written that "executive agencies that once viewed Congress with at least some trepidation because of its oversight activities now tend to view Congress with contempt."[56]

It would be unfair and inaccurate, however, to paint all hearings as ineffective. Certainly, some hearings are simply cases of political grandstanding—opportunities for members to attract publicity, take positions, and claim credit. But hearings also allow members to carry out their representative function, ensuring that agency officials hear how proposed agency actions will affect members' constituents. Hearings also provide members of Congress with the opportunity to carry out their policy-making duties by showing that, despite having delegated powers to agencies, they have not abdicated their responsibilities. Similarly, hearings allow

As chairman of the House Energy and House Oversight Committees, Representative Henry Waxman (D-CA, center) was highly active in congressional investigations and hearings, which he used to push reluctant agencies to take important action on issues.

members to engage in their governing function by increasing the odds that their preferences have been taken into account in the policies that emerge from the executive branch. Indeed, as Rep. Henry Waxman (D-CA), who was one of the most active agency overseers in Congress in recent decades, stressed, a key result of hearings and investigations is that "[t]he ensuing pressure often forces the responsible party to take action."[57] The IRS example at the start of this chapter provides such an example: although Congress passed no new laws after conducting hearings, the agency did change some of its policies as a result.

THEN AND NOW
THE REALITY OF CONGRESSIONAL OVERSIGHT

A perception exists that Congress has little incentive to engage in proactive, police-patrol-style oversight activities, such as hearings and investigations.[58] And credible arguments can be made that fire alarm forms of influence are more effective and efficient.[59] But the evidence reveals that Congress carries out a great deal of police-patrol oversight. As political scientists Jason Mac-Donald and Robert McGrath have shown, for more than four decades, Congress has been quite active in terms of conducting oversight hearings, as measured by the number of days that Congress devotes to these types of hearings (Figure 10.4).[60]

Why was there such a dramatic increase in oversight hearings in the 1970s? Political scientist Joel Aberbach, in one of the first systematic studies of congressional oversight, attributed the change at this time to a series of inter-related factors.[61] Some of these were external to Congress. For example, the size of government, which had been increasing, jumped up even more in the 1970s, spurred in part by the creation of new agencies, including the EPA, OSHA, and CPSC. More generally, presidents had gained power relative to Congress over time, and oversight provided members with an opportunity to recapture some of that power. Internal factors also mattered: congressional reforms in the 1970s gave subcommittees more power to hold hearings, and members (and committees) also started to hire more staff, which gave them the ability to engage in more oversight. Finally, because of increasing deficits and concerns about high taxes, members found it harder to create and fund new programs and instead turned their attention to the functioning of existing programs.[62]

Other studies using slightly different measures have confirmed the finding that Congress regularly engages in police-patrol oversight. Political scientists

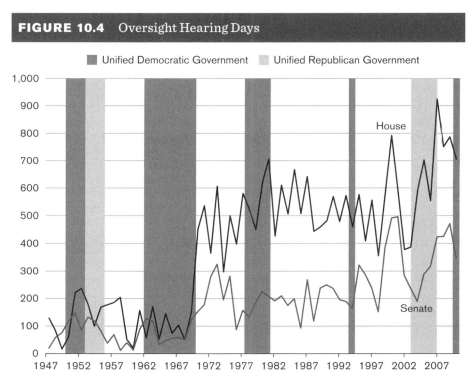

FIGURE 10.4 Oversight Hearing Days

The figure is adapted from Jason MacDonald and Robert J. McGrath. 2016. "Retrospective Congressional Oversight and the Dynamics of Legislative Influence over the Bureaucracy." *Legislative Studies Quarterly* 41 (4): 899–934.

Steven Balla and Christopher Deering carefully distinguished between hearings that Congress held in response to fire alarms being pulled and those that represented instances of routine, ongoing police-patrol oversight of agency activities.[63] They show that from the late 1970s through the 2000s, Congress engaged in a good deal of police-patrol oversight. In fact, although there was some variation across the committees they examined, all committees were far more likely to hold hearings of the police-patrol variety.

Finally, Figure 10.4 reveals not only evidence of a significant difference before and after 1970 but also shows significant variation year to year. MacDonald and McGrath provide a clever and convincing explanation for this variation. They start with the assumption that there will be more hearings under divided government because Congress is less likely to trust agencies under the control of an opposing-party president. And they find clear evidence that such an effect exists for divided government. But they also propose an explanation for why there are high levels of hearings and variation within periods of unified government, when we might reasonably expect to see fewer hearings.[64] MacDonald and McGrath argue that under unified government, congressional committees do have an incentive to engage in oversight, but of a different type: they engage in *retrospective oversight*, where they look back at actions the previous administration's agency had taken. The authors found that there are more hearings—even under unified government—when control of Congress and the presidency had been divided just before and when the opposition party had controlled the presidency for a longer period of time, giving agencies more opportunity to create new policies.

Critical Thinking

1. In terms of the effort that members need to exert, police-patrol oversight is costlier than fire-alarm oversight. Why don't members rely solely on fire alarms?
2. Given the increasing level of conflict and polarization in American politics, would you expect the number of oversight hearings to continue increasing?

CONCLUSION

The original design of the Constitution envisioned Congress as the primary policy maker in the U.S. system. Laws still originate in Congress, of course. But in terms of volume, there is no question that government agencies—both executive branch agencies and independent agencies—generate more policies. They do so because Congress has created these agencies and then delegated vast amounts of discretion to them. This leads to two questions. First, wouldn't it be better if Congress simply told agencies what to do, rather than giving them broad discretion to set policy? Second, given that agencies play such a significant policymaking role, has Congress lost influence?

The idea that Congress should simply tell agencies what to do certainly has some appeal. When Congress writes general laws that omit important details and then hands these laws off to agencies with instructions to fill in the missing parts, Congress could be considered derelict in its duty. This concern is potentially significant, especially if Congress does not take other actions to ensure that agencies are acting in ways consistent with Congress's preferences. At the same time, recall why Congress delegates: it does so because it does not have the time necessary to write detailed statutes that cover every eventuality, because it does not always have the expertise necessary to write good laws, and because delegating discretion to an agency can allow a law to be more flexible and more easily adjusted to changing times. When Congress chooses to micromanage, it loses many of the benefits of delegation, most notably the time and expertise that an agency can devote to an issue. Still, although Congress sometimes needs to give agencies discretion, at other times, it can write laws that limit discretion, usually by writing longer and more detailed statutes.[65]

As this chapter has explained, however, Congress does not necessarily abdicate its policy-making role when it empowers agencies to make policy. Certainly, delegation means that Congress has less power than when it makes policy itself. And a case can be made that presidents exert more control over agencies than Congress does.[66] Still, this chapter makes it clear that Congress has numerous tools that it can use to influence agencies and to pressure these agencies to act in certain ways. Congress's power starts with the creation and the staffing of the agency, both of which can increase the agency's receptiveness toward Congress. And it continues with Congress's ability to conduct investigations, threaten legislation, cut budgets, and hold hearings. Congress can use these tools to influence agencies even without passing new laws, which is what we saw in the case of the IRS, where the agency changed its practices toward conservative groups in deference to Congress's views, even though Congress did not pass a new law telling the agency what to do.

Interest groups play a central role in helping Congress fulfill its policy-making and governing roles with respect to agencies. These groups let members know whether they should support or oppose a president's nominees. They pay close attention to agency activities, ready to pull fire alarms to let members of Congress know when agencies are taking actions that the groups—and that members of Congress—dislike (as occurred with the IRS). And they can testify at hearings, make suggestions about budgets, and provide information for statutes. In Chapter 12, we explore in more detail the relationship between interest groups and Congress. First, however, we turn to the connection between Congress and the third branch of government: the courts.

Discussion Questions

1. What are the arguments in favor of Congress delegating policy-making authority to agencies? What are the arguments against delegation?
2. Why would agencies be especially responsive to members of congressional committees?
3. The number of representatives and senators has not increased for more than half a century. During that same time, however, the government bureaucracy has grown dramatically. Given this difference, is it possible for Congress to maintain any control over the bureaucracy? What could Congress do to increase its control?

4. If Congress is worried about the president's power over agencies, why wouldn't it just place all new agencies outside of the executive branch?

5. One argument against the 'nuclear option" is that it prevents the minority party from blocking a president's nominees. Should the minority party have this power? Why or why not?

11

Congress and the Courts

In February 2016, Supreme Court Justice Antonin Scalia joined a group of friends on a quail-hunting trip to Texas. Following dinner at the Cibolo Creek Ranch, Scalia said he was tired and went to his room. When he did not come down to join the group for breakfast the next morning, workers at the resort went to check on him. They found that Justice Scalia, at the time the longest-serving justice on the Court, had died during the night.

Scalia's unexpected death presented President Barack Obama with the opportunity to nominate a new justice. About one month later, Obama nominated Merrick Garland, who at the time was chief judge of the U.S. Court of Appeals for the District of Columbia, generally considered the second-most-powerful court in the country. Before Obama had even selected a nominee, however, Senate Majority Leader Mitch McConnell (R-KY) announced that the Senate would not consider any nominee whom Obama put forth. In McConnell's view, "[t]he American people should have a voice in the selection of their next Supreme Court Justice . . . [and] this vacancy should not be filled until we have a new president."[1] Then, and only then, he said, would the Senate consider a new nominee.

The ever-present tensions between Congress and the courts were on full display during the hearings on the nomination of Brett Kavanaugh to the Supreme Court. After responding to accusations of sexual assault, the Senate confirmed Kavanaugh 50–48—one of the narrowest margins in history.

McConnell's unprecedented tactic paid off when Donald Trump defeated Hillary Clinton, putting control over the nomination in the hands of the new Republican president and the Republican majority in the Senate. Trump nominated Judge Neil Gorsuch for the Court, and the Senate confirmed Gorsuch—albeit by the fairly close margin of 54–45. All Republican senators voted in favor of Gorsuch, while nearly all Democrats voted against.

Just over a year later, Justice Anthony Kennedy announced his retirement from the Court. Trump's nominee, Brett Kavanaugh, proved to be even more controversial, which was not unexpected. Justice Kennedy had been the swing vote—that is, the fifth vote in many cases decided by a 5–4 majority—which meant that replacing him with a more conservative jurist like Kavanaugh would likely pull the Court a good distance to the right, raising the possibility of a rightward shift in the Court's jurisprudence on issues like abortion, voting rights, free speech, and civil rights. Then, just as the Senate Judiciary Committee was getting ready to vote to move the confirmation to the Senate floor, Democrats on the committee revealed a serious allegation that Kavanaugh had committed sexual assault when he was a teenager, throwing the process into turmoil.

The committee invited Dr. Christine Blasey Ford, who had made this allegation, to testify. She did, and Kavanaugh responded with a passionate denial of the accusation and, in the eyes of some observers, a sharp partisan attack on Democrats. At this point it was unclear whether Kavanaugh had enough votes to win, given the Republicans' very narrow majority in the Senate and the fact that several senators from both parties were undecided due to the initial allegations and further questions about Kavanaugh's behavior that started to emerge. Just before the committee was set to vote, Jeff Flake (R-AZ)—who earlier that day had been confronted in a Senate elevator by two survivors of sexual assault— announced that he would not be able to support the nominee in the absence of further investigation by the FBI of allegations made against Kavanaugh. Other undecided senators agreed. After a one-week investigation that failed to shed much light on the situation, the Senate confirmed Kavanaugh by the narrowest of margins—50–48, the second closest margin of any successful nominee in the history of the Court, and once again almost entirely along partisan lines.

The conflicts between the president and the Senate over Scalia's seat, and within the Senate over Kavanaugh's nomination, were unusually contentious. But the unusual nature of these cases should not obscure a more general point: the politics of judicial nominations are nearly always contentious. This conflict is inevitable, for although courts are legal institutions, they are also political institutions. The federal courts issue tens of thousands of decisions per year, and thus they are prominent participants in the policy-making process.[2] In Scalia's last two years as a justice, for example, the Court issued decisions that struck down the EPA's rules requiring power plants to reduce emissions, recognized a national right to same-sex marriage, and upheld a portion of Obamacare.

Two main types of conflict involve Congress and the courts. The first type takes place between the Senate and the president over who gets to serve as judges and justices on the federal courts. Because of the courts' heavy involvement in setting policy and because of the limits on Congress's power to influence the courts' actions directly, the Senate has an incentive to pay close attention to who sits on the courts.

The second type of conflict centers on potential policy differences between Congress and the courts. Do these two institutions tend to agree on public policy? When they don't agree, is there anything Congress can do about it? After all, the courts are not subservient to Congress in the same way that executive agencies are subservient to the president (or to Congress); rather, Congress and the judicial branch are explicitly constitutional creations, each endowed with specific powers. But as we will explore next, Congress does have tools and tactics it can use to try to influence the courts.

The concepts of separation of powers, governing, and representation are central to the relationship between Congress and the courts. When Congress interacts with the courts, or engages with the president over who can serve on the courts, we are seeing the separation of powers at work. This separation of powers then results in a conflict over who has the right to govern. Can the Senate assert its right to influence presidential nominations to the courts, or does the president dominate this process? Can the House and Senate influence the actions taken by the courts, or are the courts able to act independently?

At the same time, Congress's activities surrounding the courts demonstrate its representation function. Republican senators who stated their refusal to vote for, or even meet with, Judge Garland, or found Kavanaugh's defense credible, were acting in part on their beliefs that their constituents would agree with their actions.[3] Similarly, members of Congress are driven to try to influence the courts by their goal of representing their constituents' wishes. These themes of separation of powers, the power to govern, and representation are found in nearly every interaction of Congress and the courts.

CONGRESS AND THE CREATION OF THE FEDERAL COURTS

Many of the Framers of the Constitution—including Alexander Hamilton and James Madison, two of the authors of the *Federalist Papers*—saw the lack of federal (i.e., national) courts under the Articles of Confederation as a serious weakness, one that the new Constitution would need to rectify. At the Constitutional Convention in 1787, there was general agreement on the need for federal courts, but there was disagreement about the form that these courts should take. Proponents of a stronger national government pushed for the creation of a Supreme Tribunal (i.e., Supreme Court) and also a series of inferior (i.e., lower) courts. Meanwhile, proponents of state power, who agreed on the need for a Supreme Tribunal, worried that the creation of inferior courts at the national level would be unnecessary (since state courts already could hear most cases) and would further shift power away from states and toward the national government.[4]

As with many issues that arose at the Constitutional Convention, the result was a compromise. Because nearly all participants agreed on the need for a Supreme Court, Article III of the Constitution explicitly creates one. But because Convention participants disagreed about the need for lower federal courts, the Constitution does not explicitly create such courts. It does, however, allow for the possibility of their creation in the future, with Article III, Section 1, providing for the creation of "such inferior Courts as the Congress may from time to time ordain and establish." In essence, the Framers kicked the can down the road.[5] By doing so, they added to Congress's powers, giving Congress the authority to create additional courts and establishing an important link between Congress and the courts.

Article III is surprisingly vague. The entire text of this article runs to only 369 words, approximately one-third the length of Article II, which deals with the presidency, and only one-sixth the length of Article I, which outlines the legislative branch. Given this lack of detail, it did not take Congress long to accept the invitation that Article III, Section I extends regarding the courts. In its first session, Congress quickly passed the Judiciary Act of 1789, which created two types of lower courts: circuit courts (also known as appellate courts) and district courts. In creating these courts—known as Article III courts, in recognition of the article that provided for their creation—Congress essentially added to the Constitution's skeletal details regarding the operation of the judicial branch and set out a structure for the federal judicial system that still exists.

THE STRUCTURE OF THE FEDERAL COURTS The Supreme Court sits atop the federal judicial hierarchy, given this privilege of place by the Constitution's designation that "the judicial Power of the United States, shall be vested in one supreme Court." Directly below the Supreme Court are the federal circuit (or appellate) courts. Below them are the federal district courts.

District courts function as trial courts. As a result, most cases enter into the federal court system through one of the 94 federal district courts that are spread across the United States.[6] In 2015, for example, district courts held 2,912 civil trials and 1,998 criminal trials, while also helping to settle hundreds of thousands more, numbers that have grown over time.[7] In these cases, the district court, presided over by a federal judge, hears evidence from both sides to reach a verdict. For example, in the 2014 case of *North Carolina v. League of Women Voters*, Judge Thomas D. Schroeder of the Middle District of North Carolina upheld provisions of a North Carolina voting law that limited early voting and ended same-day voter registration.[8]

There are 13 appellate courts. Eleven of these courts encompass specific states—for example, the Sixth Circuit Court of Appeals covers Michigan, Ohio, Kentucky, and Tennessee. The two other appellate courts are the D.C. Court of Appeals and the Court of Appeals for the Federal Circuit. Although cases can enter the federal court system directly at the level of appellate courts, the vast majority of cases that these circuit courts hear started out in the district courts.[9]

Finally, in rare cases, the Supreme Court exercises what the Constitution identifies as original jurisdiction. In these cases, the Court acts as a trial court and is the first court to hear a case.[10] For the most part, though, cases come to the Court through appellate jurisdiction, where someone who loses a case in an appeals court asks the Supreme Court to revisit the case and reconsider the decision. Such requests, however, are rarely granted. Indeed, in recent years, the Court's docket (the list of cases it agrees to hear each year) has been small and is getting smaller, partly because the Supreme Court gets to exercise discretion regarding whether it wants to hear a case. Congress specifically gave the Court this discretionary power in the Supreme Court Case Selections Act of 1988, and this power has decreased the number of cases the Court considers each year.

Exercising its discretion, the Court hears cases covering some of the most significant and controversial issues in American politics each year, from abortion (e.g., *Whole Woman's Health v. Hellerstedt*) to immigration (e.g., *Arizona v. United States*) to voting rights (e.g., *Shelby County v. Holder*). Many of the important cases that the Court hears derive directly from laws that Congress has passed. In 2007, for example, the Supreme Court heard *Gonzales v. Carhart*, which dealt with an abortion law Congress passed in 2003. That law, the Partial-Birth Abortion Ban Act, banned a specific kind of abortion procedure. Pro-choice groups sued in several states, and district courts in the Northern District of California, the Southern District of New York, and the District of Nebraska found the law unconstitutional. The federal government then appealed the district court rulings to several circuit courts and then to the Supreme Court. In the end, the Supreme Court upheld the law.

Another case involving a congressional statute occurred in 2013 when the Supreme Court ruled on the constitutionality of two provisions of the Voting Rights Act (VRA) in *Shelby County v. Holder*. Congress passed the VRA in 1965 to address racial discrimination in voting procedures. The law requires certain states and local governments to obtain permission (known as "preclearance") from the federal government before changing their voting laws. The goal was to ensure that any such changes do not negatively impact minority groups. One of those local governments, Shelby County, Alabama, sought to avoid the preclearance requirement, arguing that it was no longer necessary. A district court judge ruled that the preclearance provisions were constitutional, and the Court of Appeals for the DC Circuit affirmed that decision. The Supreme Court then heard the case and ultimately sided with Shelby County, ruling Section 5 of the VRA unconstitutional.

Appointments

The Framers strove to provide the judiciary with a strong measure of independence from the elected branches, reasoning that independence would allow judges to approach issues in a fair and impartial way.[11] One tactic the Framers adopted to increase the judiciary's independence was to give federal judges lifetime appointments. Participants at the Constitutional Convention made arguments both for and against this idea,[12] and even today it remains controversial.[13] The arguments on both sides were, and are, straightforward. If judges can be removed from office for making a decision that is unpopular with citizens, with members of Congress, or with the president, then they would not have the independence necessary to act impartially. On the other hand, if there is no possibility of removing a judge, then there would be nothing to stop him or her from behaving improperly, unethically, or illegally. To balance these competing concerns, Article III, Section 1, stipulates that federal judges "shall hold their Offices during good Behavior," which means that in the absence of misconduct, they keep their positions.

The Framers also sought to make the courts independent of the other branches by dividing the power over judicial appointments between Congress and the president.[14] Article II, Section 2, of the Constitution specifies that the president "shall nominate, and by and with the Advice and Consent of the Senate, shall appoint . . . Judges of the Supreme Court." Giving both branches a say in determining the appointment of judges decreases the likelihood that the courts will be subservient to either branch. Of course, it also means that conflict is endemic, as we saw in the clash between President Obama and the Senate over whether the Senate had an obligation to consider Garland's nomination. Sometimes, the president wins these disputes, but other times, the Senate does, which is what happened when Mitch McConnell's successful obstruction of Garland paved the way for President Donald Trump to nominate Neil Gorsuch, whom the Senate then confirmed.

The situation in the aftermath of Scalia's death was admittedly extreme, but there always has been, and always will be, conflict over judicial nominations. In recent decades, however, the level of conflict has increased, due in part to the greater prominence of the courts in policy making and in politics. This prominence, when combined with the life tenure that a judicial appointment affords, creates strong incentives for senators and the president to make sure that the "right" people end up serving on the courts. Furthermore, when the president and members of the Senate differ ideologically and disagree about policies, they do not want to let the other institution dominate the governing process.

THE DESIGN OF THE APPOINTMENT PROCESS   At first glance, the Constitution appears to be quite clear about the role that the Senate and president play in the appointment process. Article II, Section 2, states that the president "shall nominate, and, by and with the advice and consent of the Senate, shall appoint . . . judges of the Supreme Court." Three features of this provision stand out. First, the Constitution clearly prescribes a role for both the Senate and the president. Second, the president gets to take the lead in the process; if he does not act, there is no appointment for the Senate to consider. Third, the Senate's consent is a required part of the process. But although the Constitution provides for the Senate's role in the appointment process, it leaves the details of that role vague. What does it mean when it specifies that the Senate should give "advice"? And what should senators base their consent on? Policy preferences? Qualifications? Other factors?

It will come as no surprise that the wording of Article II, Section 2, was a compromise at the Constitutional Convention, one that followed two weeks of intense debate. Some participants in the Constitutional Convention, including Hamilton and James Wilson, favored assigning the appointment power predominantly, or even solely, to the executive. Others, including Madison and Benjamin Franklin, worried that such an approach would concentrate too much power within the executive branch.[15] The compromise ended up between these two positions, although closer to the Madison-Franklin position, assigning the primary and first-mover role to the president but giving the Senate a powerful check on this role. In the words of Gouverneur Morris, the presidential role would provide for "responsibility" while the Senate role would provide for "security."[16]

THE APPOINTMENT PROCESS TODAY The appointment process today plays out in multiple stages. The stages are roughly the same for the lower courts as for the Supreme Court, but there are some differences. We will first discuss the process in detail as it relates to the Supreme Court, and then we will discuss additional features that apply to lower-court appointments.

The process of appointing a justice to the Supreme Court begins with an opening on the Court owing to the death, retirement, or resignation of a sitting justice. Between 1869, when the size of the Court was set at nine justices, and 2018, when Justice Anthony Kennedy announced his retirement, there have been 75 vacancies on the Court. Thus vacancies occur approximately every other year, which means that a president serving a full four-year term can expect to have two opportunities on average to make an appointment. There is considerable variation, however. Some presidents, such as Jimmy Carter, had no opportunities to make an appointment. At the other end of the scale, William Taft appointed five justices during his four years in office.

Once a president learns of a vacancy, he or she consults with relevant advisors and, usually, prominent senators—including senators from any potential nominee's home states—before selecting a nominee. In the nation's early years, the president would then submit the nomination to the full Senate, but since 1870, presidents have submitted nominees' names to the Senate Judiciary Committee for initial consideration.[17] At this point, the Senate's formal role begins.[18] The Judiciary Committee sets out to investigate the nominee, to deliberate about his or her qualifications, and to send a recommendation to the full Senate. These duties have changed over time. Initially, the committee conducted its activities behind closed doors. It was only in the 1950s, with President Dwight Eisenhower's nomination of John M. Harlan, that the practice of having nominees testify before the committee became commonplace. And it was not until 1981, with President Ronald Reagan's nomination of Sandra Day O'Connor, that the committee allowed these hearings to be broadcast.

In most cases, a president's nominee for the Supreme Court is confirmed by the Senate. In 2016, however, Senate Majority Leader Mitch McConnell (R-KY) refused to even consider Merrick Garland, President Obama's choice to replace Antonin Scalia.

The Judiciary Committee's role in the process can be characterized primarily as informational. Members of the committee have the opportunity to question the nominee, with the goal of learning about his or her views on specific policy issues, judicial philosophy, and overall qualifications. The hearings also provide these members with a moment in the public eye, which in turn allows them to make their positions publicly known, to show that they are representing their constituents in this process, and to impress upon the nominee their views of specific cases and of the judicial role in the political process. The committee then votes on whether to report the nominee favorably to the full Senate, to report the nominee unfavorably, or to make no recommendation.[19] The hearings thus provide information about the nominee to the committee, to the full Senate, and to the public. They also provide information to the full Senate about the views of the committee members.

Once the Judiciary Committee submits its report, the full Senate begins its work. The majority leader schedules consideration of the nominee, which takes place in executive session. Senators who choose to take part in this stage, which consists of speeches and floor debate more generally, use it as an opportunity to state, for the public record, their reasons for supporting or opposing the nominee. Then when debate comes to a close, the Senate votes. In the past, many confirmation votes were voice votes, but since 1967, all have been roll call votes. If the vote is favorable, it is reported to the president, who signs the commission that officially seats the nominee on the Court.

CONFIRMATION VOTES In the vast majority of cases, the process described earlier results in the appointment of a new justice to the Supreme Court. Prior to President Trump's nomination of Gorsuch, presidents had made 161 nominations for positions on the Court. Of these, the Senate formally rejected only 11. In other words, in less than 7 percent of nominations did the Senate actually vote against confirming the president's nominee. This figure, while striking, overstates the president's success. In 11 cases, the president withdrew the nomination, while in another 15 cases—including Garland's nomination—the term ended before the Senate held a vote (although some of those nominees were later renominated and confirmed). Still, even taking all of these other instances into account, the Senate failed to confirm only 37 of the presidents' 161 nominations. Furthermore, nearly half of these were clustered during four nineteenth-century presidencies: John Tyler, Millard Fillmore, Ulysses S. Grant, and Grover Cleveland. Presidential success rates in the twentieth and twenty-first centuries have been high.

Why have presidents been so successful with their nominations? In part, their success has been due to the idea that the Senate, in the words of Senator Orrin Hatch (R-UT), "owes some deference to the president's qualified nominees."[20] Moreover, presidents have, by and large, chosen well-qualified nominees, especially in the past century or so. But a big part of presidents' success is due to their awareness of the Senate's power. Presidents seek to select a nominee whose appointment would shift the Court toward their own views. But the Constitution forces presidents to anticipate the Senate's reaction.[21]

Recall that the process consists of two stages. First, the president submits a nominee. Second, the Senate votes on the nominee. The Senate's vote might not provide much of a constraint when the Senate and president agree ideologically. However, when the Senate and president do not agree, the Senate can constrain the president. Of course, presidents are free to nominate whomever they want, but if they select a nominee who would shift the Court in a direction that the Senate dislikes, then the Senate is more likely to vote against confirmation. A rejection would be costly for the president in terms of a hit to the president's reputation, relationship with the Senate, and opportunity costs. Because presidents want to avoid these costs, they will take the Senate's view into account and choose a nominee who most closely shares their own views but who also will get confirmed by the Senate. Thus a positive confirmation vote from the Senate is not necessarily a sign of Senate surrender to the president's power to nominate. Rather, it could indicate the power that the Constitution bestows on the Senate in this process.

Anticipating a friendly Democratic Senate, President Obama was able to nominate liberal justices Sonia Sotomayor (left) and Elena Kagan (center), whom the Senate approved rather easily. When Republicans controlled the Senate, Obama nominated the more moderate Merrick Garland, whom the Senate refused to hold hearings on.

If the Senate plays this constraining role, we should expect to find two patterns. First, when the president and Senate are more distant, in terms of either partisanship or ideology, then we should find that the president takes longer to make a nomination, as the president is likely to spend more time consulting with Senate leaders to find out what they will accept. Second, we would expect presidents to choose nominees who share their views when they are unconstrained, but to select nominees who do not exactly share their views when they need to take the Senate into account. And, in general, those patterns have held: presidents do take longer to make nominations, and they moderate their choices, when they face a Senate that does not share their views. President Obama's nominations illustrate this latter point. The two nominations he made when Democrats controlled the Senate (Sonia Sotomayor and Elena Kagan) are generally viewed as being to the left of the nomination he made when Republicans controlled the Senate (Garland).

THEN AND NOW
CONFIRMATION VOTES

The Senate has shown a strong tendency to confirm presidential Supreme Court nominations, but this tendency masks variation across senators. For starters, even in positive confirmation votes, there are often senators who vote against confirmation. Furthermore, the tendency toward casting negative confirmation votes has increased markedly in recent decades. Table 11.1 demonstrates these patterns. If we look at all confirmation votes that senators cast on every nomination between 1937 and 2010, we see that about 14 percent of these votes were negative (that is, against the president's nominee). Prior to 1985, only about 9 percent of confirmation votes were negative, but this rate has nearly tripled since then, with nearly 25 percent of votes being negative. What explains this change?

Several factors stand out. Senators are more likely to vote for the nominees (1) if the president is popular, (2) if the president's party controls the Senate and the president is not in the last year of his or her term, and (3) when the senators' constituents and interest groups show support for the nominees.[22]

The most important factors that influence the likelihood of a senator voting to confirm a nominee, however, are the nominee's qualifications and ideology. The probability that a senator will vote to confirm a nominee goes up as the nominee becomes more qualified, which again provides the president an incentive to choose qualified nominees. In addition, senators are more likely to vote for nominees who share their ideologies and less likely to vote for those who are ideologically distant. As a result, the president has an incentive to take the Senate's ideology into account when selecting nominees. In addition, the *combination* of these factors is especially potent. That is, while senators are likely to vote for a qualified nominee,

TABLE 11.1	Frequency of Yes and No Confirmation Votes on Supreme Court Nominees	
	Yes	No
All nominations	3,454 (86.2%)	554 (13.8%)
Pre-1985	2,560 (90.7%)	262 (9.3%)
Post-1985	894 (75.4%)	292 (24.6%)

James B. Cottrill and Terri J. Peretti. 2013. 'The Partisan Dynamics of Supreme Court Confirmation Voting." *Justice System Journal* 34:1, 15–37.

TABLE 11.2 Frequency of Yes and No Confirmation Votes on Supreme Court Nominees by Party

		Yes	No
Pre-1985	Opposing-party senators	1,003 (84.1%)	190 (15.9%)
	Same-party senators	1,557 (95.6%)	72 (4.4%)
Post-1985	Opposing-party senators	289 (50.8%)	280 (49.2%)
	Same-party senators	605 (98.1%)	12 (1.9%)

and are likely to vote for a nominee who shares their ideology, they are even more likely to vote for a nominee who is both highly qualified and who shares their ideology.

Although these factors dominate the voting calculus of senators, the process has changed in two ways. First, the relative importance of ideology has grown over time. Whether this break occurred in 1987 with the Senate's high-profile rejection of Robert Bork, or in 1985 with a high number of negative votes against William Rehnquist's nomination to be chief justice, or at some earlier point, it's clear that there has been a change.

Second, the role of party has become increasingly prominent in Senate voting on Supreme Court nominations. A senator's vote is now more dependent than ever before on whether he or she is a member of the president's party,[23] as Table 11.2 makes clear. Prior to 1985, opposing-party senators were 3.6 times more likely to vote against a president's nominee than were senators from the president's party. Since 1985, opposing-party senators are now nearly 26 times more likely to do so.

Critical Thinking

1. Should senators consider a nominee's ideology during the confirmation process? Or should their decision be based on qualifications alone?
2. As noted in this chapter, Senator Hatch has argued that there should be a presumption of deference from senators toward a president's nominees. Would the Framers agree with Senator Hatch's view? Why or why not?
3. Why have opposing-party senators become so much more likely to oppose Supreme Court nominees?

THE LOWER COURTS Appointments to the lower courts proceed in a similar fashion to Supreme Court appointments, albeit at much lower levels of salience and public attention. As with the Supreme Court, the appointment process for lower courts begins with a vacancy. The president selects a nominee, and the Senate then has the authority to advise and consent. Within these basic stages, the lower-court process differs in a few key ways.

Unlike the Supreme Court, which is a true national court whose rulings cover the entire country, district and appellate courts are located in specific areas: the District Court for Northern Illinois, for example, or the Fifth Circuit Court of Appeals, which covers Texas, Louisiana, and Mississippi. When these courts reach a decision, their ruling generally holds only for that specific area. Thus a Fifth Circuit ruling covers only the three states just mentioned. Because these courts are located in specific states, and because their rulings hold only in those states, those states' senators have an especially strong incentive to weigh in on nominees and to provide advice about which nominees are likely to be acceptable. Furthermore, senators want their preferences over appointments in their states to be honored by other senators; a system of reciprocity has sprung up, with a norm of *senatorial courtesy* causing senators to defer to the wishes of the home-state senator.

To formalize this system, in the early part of the twentieth century, the Senate Judiciary Committee created the "blue slip" procedure, in which the committee would solicit the views of the home-state senators by sending them a blue slip of paper, asking for their opinion of a nominee. If these home-state senators approved of the nominee, the committee would proceed with its work. If not, the committee generally would defer to the individual senators and not consider the nominee. This system, of course, greatly empowers individual senators, with presidents needing to seek their consent before making a lower-court nomination.[24]

Until recently, a nomination to a federal court could be filibustered. Starting in 2013, however, there was a five-year period during which lower-court nominations could not be filibustered but Supreme Court nominations could. This prohibition on the filibuster for lower-court (and executive branch) nominations came about when Democrats voted to change Senate rules so that a filibuster for such nominations could be ended by a majority vote, rather than a three-fifths (cloture) vote, effectively eliminating the filibuster. Although Democrats implemented this so-called nuclear option, its roots with respect to judicial nominations reached back a decade, when Senate Majority Leader Bill Frist, frustrated by the delaying tactics Senate Democrats were using to block President George W. Bush's nominations, threatened to use this approach.[25] At that time, Democrats vowed to shut down the Senate if Frist proceeded, and the parties struck a deal to avoid filibusters in most cases.

The same issue arose again several years later, with all the partisan roles switched—now Senate Democrats were frustrated with Senate Republicans blocking President Obama's nominations. This time, however, the majority party carried through on the threat to use the nuclear option to eliminate filibusters on lower-court nominations, giving presidents a clearer path, if not necessarily an easy one, to getting their nominees through the Senate. Finally, the tables turned yet again in 2017 when Senate Republicans, worried about potential Democratic opposition to Gorsuch, eliminated the filibuster for Supreme Court nominations.

Relative Power of Congress and the Courts

With the power of appointment divided between Congress and the president, the Framers provided the courts with independence while allowing the other branches to check and balance them. But in truth, the Framers did not see much of a need for checks on the courts. Rather, they expected the courts to be, in the words of Hamilton, the "least dangerous branch."[26]

Over time, however—particularly throughout the course of the nineteenth century—the courts became more powerful. This growth in judicial power came about because of the actions and decisions of the courts, especially the Supreme Court. The Court's decision in *Marbury v. Madison* (1803) was particularly important.[27] Here Chief Justice John Marshall, writing for the Court, declared that a portion of the Judiciary Act of 1789—specifically, the portion that gave courts the power to issue writs of mandamus, which are essentially statements ordering other government institutions, including Congress and the president, to take specific actions—was inconsistent with the Constitution. By this action and logic, Marshall claimed the power of judicial review for the courts. That is, the decision established that the courts had the power to review the laws that Congress passed and to determine whether those statutes were constitutional.

In a series of additional landmark cases throughout the nineteenth century, the courts continued to increase their power as national policy makers.[28] As a result, by the end of the nineteenth century, the federal judiciary had traveled from its humble origins as the "least dangerous" branch to a position of power on a par with—if distinct from—Congress.

These nineteenth-century judicial actions led to what is now widely accepted as the division of labor between Congress and the courts. Congress's main power, in this view, is to legislate. Fulfilling both Congress's representative function and its governing function, the primary job of members of Congress is to represent their constituents during the lawmaking process and to produce laws that will govern the country. At that point, the courts can weigh in, determining whether congressionally enacted laws fall within the boundaries set by the Constitution.

When they do fall within these bounds, the courts allow the laws to remain in effect. When they fall outside the bounds of the Constitution, the courts can exercise the power of judicial review and deem these laws unconstitutional.

This view of the division of labor between Congress and the courts is largely correct, but Congress's own role in making the judiciary more powerful is often neglected. The courts did claim new powers early on, and they built on this momentum to become more active policy makers on the national stage. But Congress was not merely a passive bystander, watching while the courts accrued new powers, or objecting to these powers but unable to halt the judiciary's ascension. Instead, Congress has often preferred that the courts play a more active role in the governing and policy-making process, and has delegated such authority to the courts.

Congress at times prefers a more active judiciary, including one that can strike down congressional laws, for a variety of reasons. In some situations, Congress might not want to take the lead in setting policy. For example, Congress might want a certain policy to be enacted, but it is hesitant to take the lead because it worries about potential political consequences. Such a policy might occur in an area where it will be difficult to reach an agreement within or across the two legislative chambers. Or the policy action may be likely to have negative repercussions. Taking these realities into account, political scientist Mark Graber has noted that members of Congress often prefer judicial policy making, "both as a means of avoiding political responsibility for making tough decisions and as a means of pursuing controversial goals that they cannot publicly advance."[29] In addition, the majority party in Congress may be especially leery of taking actions that might jeopardize its status as the majority, and it is happy to let the judiciary take the lead on such issues, especially if the majority party believes its current hold on power is tenuous.[30]

Sometimes, Congress intentionally writes statutes in a way that opens the door to judicial activity. In such statutes, Congress crafts laws that are deliberately ambiguous, knowing that such an approach invites judges to step in and impose order on the ambiguity.[31] Congress might choose this course of action because the policy questions are difficult, or because legislators want to give the courts flexibility when considering different cases, because Congress wants to provide for additional oversight of executive agencies, or because it wants to break a stalemate. Sometimes, each faction within Congress thinks its best chance of policy success is to write a vague statute that the courts will interpret in a manner consistent with the faction's own views.[32] For these and other reasons, Congress often invites the courts to play a more prominent role in the policy-making process.

In short, the view that "Congress legislates, and the courts interpret" can be a useful shorthand description, but the reality is more complex. Initially, it was not clear that the courts had the power to interpret the constitutionality of laws.

After the courts asserted this power, they began to play a more central role in governing and policy making. In part, Congress acquiesced to this increased judicial role, but Congress also added to it. The relationship between Congress and the courts is thus a complex one that has evolved over time. Regardless of how the courts gained this power, Congress retains the ability to criticize, challenge, correct, and restrict the courts—a topic that we explore in the next section.

HOW CONGRESS AND THE COURTS INTERACT: RESPONSE AND ANTICIPATION

Given the changes over time in the power of the judicial branches, Congress now shares the national policy-making stage with the courts (and, as we discussed in Chapter 9, the executive branch). Congress retains its role as the originator of legislation, which helps it fulfill its governing function and allows members to pursue policies that represent their constituents' goals and desires. But the involvement of the courts in virtually every policy means that conflict between the two branches is frequent and often unavoidable.

Has the increased judicial role weakened Congress to the point where the courts now have the final say? Conventional wisdom holds that after Congress passes laws, the courts review these laws and decide which ones will be allowed to stand. In fact, the courts actually perform two distinct but related functions when they evaluate statutes. As discussed earlier, they can assess whether a statute is constitutional by considering whether it stays within the bounds created by the Constitution. They can also engage in *interpretation*, which means determining what a statute actually means. Statutes are often ambiguous, sometimes intentionally so. But the ambiguity might also be unintentional, the result of the complicated process by which laws are passed and the inability of legislators and congressional staffers to anticipate every situation or outcome that the law might encounter.

The case of Lilly Ledbetter provides a good example of the courts' power to interpret a statute and Congress's power to respond. Ledbetter, who worked for the Goodyear Tire and Rubber Company, filed suit against the company, arguing that she was paid less than men who held similar positions. After Ledbetter won some initial court victories, Goodyear appealed to the 11th Circuit. This court ruled against Ledbetter on statutory interpretation grounds: it held that, based on its reading of the Civil Rights Act of 1964, Ledbetter's complaint was filed outside of the window allowed for taking such action. Ledbetter had filed a complaint soon after learning about the discriminatory pay, but the court ruled that the time limit on complaints applied to when the discriminatory action took place and not

Supreme Court Justice Ruth Bader Ginsburg's strong dissent in *Ledbetter v. Goodyear Tire & Rubber Co.* encouraged Congress to eventually pass a law to restore protections against gender-based pay discrimination. Here, Lilly Ledbetter speaks at a rally for equal pay, with supporters and members of Congress, including Senator Hillary Clinton (D-NY, right), looking on.

to when an employee learned about it. Thus, the actions to which Ledbetter objected took place outside of the time period allowed by law.

A closely divided Supreme Court then agreed with the appellate court's ruling. In effect, the Court interpreted the earlier laws as follows: although discriminatory behavior was illegal, the behavior in question (in this case, Goodyear's decisions that might have led to differences in pay) took place too long before Ledbetter raised a complaint. Thus, she was not entitled to redress under the earlier statute. Justice Ruth Bader Ginsburg disagreed with this interpretation. In her dissent, she noted that companies would be able to get away with discriminatory actions if they could hide that discrimination just long enough to avoid the window for filing suit. She also directly invited Congress to fix this issue by clarifying that employees should be able to file complaints even against company actions that had not taken place recently but rather had occurred earlier in the employee's time with the company. After a couple of failed attempts, in 2009, the 111th Congress passed, and President Obama signed, the Lilly Ledbetter Fair Pay Act, which broadened the period during which complaints of workplace discrimination can be filed.

Given the courts' powers of judicial review and statutory interpretation, it is reasonable to ask whether the courts now dominate the policy-making process. If this process consists simply of Congress passing a law, followed by the courts determining whether the law should be struck down (that is, whether it is constitutional) or figuring out what the law means when applied to a specific situation, then it seems reasonable to conclude that Congress has been weakened, because the courts essentially have the power to say what a law means and whether it can be allowed to exist. Such a process would lead to significant normative concerns, too, because courts are staffed by unelected judges who have life tenure and might not have any incentive to respond to the desires of the public or its elected representatives.

There is little doubt that the balance of power between Congress and the courts has shifted in ways that the Framers neither intended nor anticipated. The crucial question is whether Congress has the ability to respond to or shape the actions of the courts. In other words, what tools does Congress have at its disposal to deal with the more powerful version of the courts it faces today?

Overrides

The most straightforward action that Congress can take when it disagrees with a judicial decision is to override that decision. The exact manner in which Congress overrides a judicial decision depends on the nature of the judicial action. For example, if the Supreme Court engages in judicial review and strikes down a statute on constitutional grounds, then Congress can overturn this decision only by passing a constitutional amendment. If the Court relies on statutory interpretation, as it did in the Lilly Ledbetter case, then Congress can override the Court's decision by passing another law.

A good example of the possibilities for overriding a Supreme Court constitutional decision can be found in the controversial area of campaign finance. In 2002, Congress passed the Bipartisan Campaign Reform Act (BCRA), also known as McCain-Feingold. Although this law covered a number of aspects of campaign finance, one key provision limited the ability of corporations, unions, and other groups to broadcast political advertisements close to an election. Specifically, the law prohibited these groups from paying for ads that were ostensibly about policy or political issues but that also named specific candidates, on the grounds that such ads were attempts to evade other limitations on campaign contributions. (See Chapter 12 for further discussion of this law and the court cases that followed.)

In 2010, the Supreme Court heard a case, *Citizens United v. Federal Election Commission*, that considered whether the prohibition in McCain-Feingold was constitutional.[33] In a 5–4 decision, the Court found that the provision was unconstitutional because it violated the First Amendment. Congress, the Court ruled, did not have the power to prevent corporations from making independent expenditures and engaging in "electioneering communications" in the period leading up to an election.

In the face of such a decision, where the Court has struck down all or part of a law as unconstitutional, what can Congress do? One option is to attempt to rewrite the law in a way that avoids the constitutional conflict or that ameliorates the effect of the decision in other ways. After *Citizens United*, members of Congress introduced bills that attempted to offset the significant advantages that the decision conferred upon corporations (for example, by providing for increased public funding for elections) or that required additional public disclosure of campaign spending by corporations. As another option, Congress could introduce a constitutional amendment designed to overturn the decision. In this case, the Court decision rested on the idea that corporations should be treated like regular people; thus, some politicians proposed an amendment that would eliminate or restrict this notion of "corporate personhood." In neither case—passing new laws or constitutional amendments—was Congress successful in counteracting the Court's decision.

To characterize the possibility of any proposed constitutional amendment succeeding as a long shot would be a severe understatement. Since the founding of the country, more than 11,000 constitutional amendments have been proposed.[34] But because of the difficulty of passing such amendments, which usually involves getting a supermajority of two-thirds of the members of each congressional chamber to agree to the amendment and then getting three-quarters of the states to ratify it, only 27 amendments have succeeded. And only seven of these amendments have been responses to judicial decisions.[35] Thus while Congress theoretically has the power to override the Court's constitutional decisions, in practice, its ability to do so is limited.

This is not to say that constitutional amendments as responses to Court actions never succeed. Consider the Sixteenth Amendment, which established the income tax. Congress previously had tried to shoehorn permanent income tax provisions into tariff legislation, but the courts struck down such attempts as unconstitutional. In response, Congress initiated the process of amending the Constitution to allow for such a tax. The amendment was passed by Congress in 1909 and adopted in 1913.

The saga of the BCRA, *Citizens United*, and the responses to the Court's decision illustrates both the possibilities and the limits of Congress's ability to respond to judicial declarations that laws are unconstitutional. Congress has much more power when it comes to addressing the judiciary's statutory interpretations. Consider a case where Congress passes a law, a federal court reaches a decision that provides an interpretation of part or all of the law, and members of Congress disagree with this interpretation. In such a case—for example, the Lilly Ledbetter case—Congress can respond by attempting to override the court's action. Unlike constitutional overrides, which require the support of supermajorities in each chamber and ratification by the states, an override of a statutory decision requires only a majority vote in each chamber. Once the president signs the bill that the two chambers have approved, the bill becomes law, and the decision is overridden.

In practice, a number of obstacles might prevent Congress from overriding a judicial interpretation of a statute. For starters, members of Congress might not even be aware of the court's decision. If they are aware of it, members might actually agree with the court's interpretation. But even if many members disagree with the court's interpretation, they might be blocked by other members who do not share their views. Committees might gatekeep legislation; party leaders might refer bills to unsympathetic committees or refuse to schedule bills for consideration; a committed minority in the Senate might engage in a filibuster. Even when members generally do agree that the court's action should be over-ridden, they might not agree, within a chamber, on which course of action to take, or the two chambers might not be able to reach agreement. In short, attempted overrides can fall prey to any of the general issues that can derail legislation in Congress.

Given all the challenges to enacting a meaningful congressional response, do the courts, in effect, have the final word on policy making? For a long time, the conventional wisdom among scholars and political observers held that the answer is "yes": they argued that members of Congress paid little attention to judicial decisions, and when the members did pay attention, they were unable to over-come the various obstacles that would prevent them from overturning these judicial decisions.[36] But then a number of political scientists and legal scholars started looking more closely at this issue and found something unexpected: in contrast to the conventional wisdom, Congress actually is highly aware of statu-tory decisions and ends up successfully overriding these decisions with surprising frequency.

A landmark study by legal scholar William Eskridge provided the first system-atic evidence regarding overrides. Eskridge looked at all reports written by congressional committees between 1967 and 1990 to see if they mentioned any judicial decisions that were affected by laws that the committee was consider-ing.[37] One of his primary findings was that the House Judiciary Committee, which has jurisdiction over legal issues, ended up scrutinizing between 44 and 65 judicial decisions per Congress, a surprisingly high number. He then examined whether responses to judicial decisions ended up being enacted into law. Again, the number was unexpectedly high. During the period he examined, Eskridge identified 187 laws containing provisions that overrode a total of 344 judicial decisions.

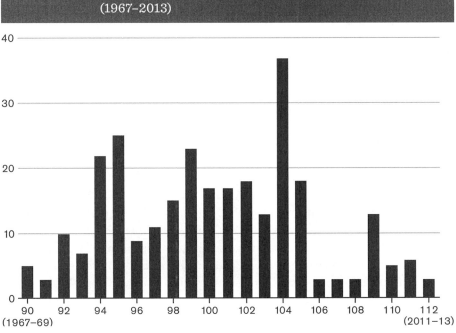

FIGURE 11.1 Number of Overrides by Congress, 90th–112th Congress (1967–2013)

Matthew R. Christiansen and William N. Eskridge Jr. 2014. "Congressional Overrides of Supreme Court Statutory Interpretation Decisions, 1967–2011." *Texas Law Review* 92: 1317.

An important question is whether the period Eskridge examined was an outlier, with Congress more attentive to judicial actions and more successful at overriding them in those years. Indeed, one later study, using Eskridge's methodology, showed that in the period following the initial study (post-1990), congressional overrides "fell off a cliff," with Congress overriding fewer than three judicial decisions per Congress.[38] Eskridge himself then updated his analysis using a more inclusive methodology. He found that the number of overrides actually *increased* in the 1990s, but then, as Figure 11.1 shows, decreased dramatically in the 2000s—most likely because of the increase in political polarization that has made the passage of any laws in Congress, and not just overrides, more difficult.[39]

Overall, the evidence indicates that Congress does indeed pay attention to judicial decisions and that it regularly overrides the courts' statutory decisions. The frequency with which it overrides these decisions does ebb and flow, but overrides occur with more regularity than many observers suspected (and far more frequently than in cases involving constitutional interpretations).

Pressure

In addition to its ability to pass laws that override judicial decisions, Congress can also use threats, or pressure, to get the courts to change their actions. The goal is not to reverse a particular judicial decision, but rather to send a shot across the bow, signaling congressional displeasure with recent judicial actions. In so doing, Congress can both assert its governing power by influencing the courts and curry favor with constituents.

Some of these tools are informal. Members of Congress can, for example, voice their displeasure with individual judicial rulings or groups of rulings. After the Court's ruling in *Burwell v. Hobby Lobby* (which ruled that for-profit corporations can be exempted from laws on religious grounds), Rep. Nancy Pelosi (D-CA) tweeted that "SCOTUS [the Supreme Court] took an outrageous step against women's rights, setting a dangerous precedent that permits corporations to choose which laws to obey." In response to *United States v. Windsor* and *Hollingsworth v. Perry*, which paved the way for marriage equality by overturning existing prohibitions on same-sex marriages, Rep. Michele Bachmann (R-MN) announced that the Court "undercut the people's representatives [and] the will of their constituencies."[40] Members of Congress can also voice their displeasure with the actions of specific judges. Rep. Peter DeFazio (D-OR), in response to the Court's *Citizens United v. FEC* ruling, announced, "I'm investigating articles of impeachment against Justice Roberts for perjuring during his Senate hearings, where he said he wouldn't be a judicial activist, and he wouldn't overturn precedents."[41]

Other tactics are more formal. Although they cannot vote to decrease judges' salaries, members of Congress can choose not to *increase* these salaries. And they can limit the amount of funding that gets allocated to the courts each year, which constrains the judges' ability to hire staff to help with their work. None of these actions truly threaten judicial independence, but they do make congressional displeasure clear to the courts and make the job of being a judge at least marginally less enjoyable.

The Structure and Operation of the Judicial Branch

In addition to these formal and informal tools of pressure, Congress can attempt to influence the structure and composition of the judicial branch. Because the Constitution is silent about the number of justices who should comprise the Supreme Court, it falls to Congress to determine this number by statute. Although the current size of nine justices has been in place since just after the Civil War, the Court has not always been this size.[42] In fact, the number of justices on the Court has ranged from a low of 5 in the early 1800s to a high of 10 during the Civil War.

Changes in the size of the Supreme Court in the 1860s illustrate the way Congress can use its powers to influence the Court based on political and strategic considerations. In 1863, the Republican Congress increased the size of the Court from 9 justices to 10, providing President Abraham Lincoln (also a Republican) with the opportunity to select an additional justice. Then, shortly after the end of the Civil War, the Republican-controlled Congress passed the Judicial Circuits Act of 1866. Part of this act reduced the number of justices on the Court from 10 to 7, with the reduction to come from not replacing departing justices. Congress's goal in making this change was clear: it was to prevent President Andrew Johnson—who acceded to the presidency after Lincoln's assassination and who was a Democrat, unlike his predecessor—from naming any new justices to the Court.

Similarly, as the Reconstruction era continued, Republicans in Congress increased the number of lower federal courts and their jurisdictions. They then worked to populate these courts with Republican-leaning judges with the goal of insulating the policies they had passed. Essentially, the GOP knew it would not be able to hold off the Democratic resurgence forever, so it sought to preserve its laws by stacking the courts.[43]

If the Civil War and its aftermath demonstrate how Congress can use its powers to change the size of the Court, then a well-known episode from the 1930s shows how Congress can use these powers to *block* change. During this decade, President Franklin D. Roosevelt (hereafter FDR) grew increasingly frustrated by the conservative Supreme Court's decisions that struck down aspects of his liberal New Deal plan. In response to these rulings, and based on the realization that none of the conservative justices who formed a majority on the Court had any intention of stepping down any time soon, FDR attempted to "pack" the Court by adding new justices who were more supportive of his New Deal programs. Although FDR had won a landslide victory only one year earlier, and his party (Democrats) controlled Congress, his plan died in the Senate, where the Judiciary Committee described it as "an invasion of judicial power such as has never been attempted in the country."[44]

Congress can also threaten to limit or eliminate life tenure for judges. Because the Constitution clearly states that federal judges have life tenure, Congress would need to pass a constitutional amendment to impose such limits. Indeed, members of Congress have introduced many such amendments to limit the number of years a justice can serve. But members also have introduced a large number of regular statutes designed to chip away at life tenure and otherwise alter who gets to serve on the Court and for how long. Proposals have included creating a means other than impeachment for the removal of justices, prescribing specific qualifications, and implementing mandatory retirement.

Recall that life tenure for judges is not absolute, but rather it is circumscribed. Thus Congress can also change the composition of the courts by impeaching, or threatening to impeach, federal judges. Several sections of the Constitution combine to provide guidance for how this process works. First, Article II, Section 4, states, "The President, Vice President and all civil Officers of the United States, shall be removed from Office on Impeachment for, and Conviction of, Treason, Bribery, or other High crimes and Misdemeanors." Second, Article I, Section 2, says, "The House of Representatives . . . shall have the sole Power of Impeachment," while Article I, Section 3, continues, "The Senate shall have the sole Power to try all Impeachments." In addition, as noted earlier, Article III, Section 1, provides that "judges, both of the supreme and inferior courts, shall hold their offices during good behaviour."

Taken together, these constitutional provisions have several implications. First, judges—like presidents and other officials—can be impeached. Second, although the word "impeachment" is sometimes used colloquially to mean "remove from office," in reality, impeachment is the first stage of the process, and an official is removed from office only if the House votes to impeach and the Senate follows this impeachment by voting to convict the judge. Third, the criteria for removing a judge are murky at best, as the Constitution spells out neither what constitutes "High crimes and Misdemeanors" nor what is meant by "good behaviour." Although there is no doubt that some impeachment hearings have been based purely on political grounds, in general, impeachment proceedings against judges, particularly those cases that reach the Senate, have been reserved for instances where judges behaved unethically or illegally.

Congress has used its impeachment power infrequently. Only once has a Supreme Court justice been impeached. In 1805, the House impeached Justice Samuel Chase for inappropriately engaging in partisan activity and allowing his partisan leanings to affect his rulings. The Senate, however, acquitted Chase of all charges.[45] The most recent removal of a federal judge took place in 2010, when the House impeached, and the Senate then convicted, Thomas Porteous Jr., a judge on the U.S. District Court for the Eastern District of Louisiana, for a wide range of improprieties.[46]

All told, the House has impeached 15 federal judges. Of these, the Senate has convicted eight. Spread out over more than 200 years and thousands of federal judges, these are obviously not large numbers. But the *threat* of impeachment is one that hovers over judges, as does the recognition that many impeachment cases have contained more than a hint of political maneuvering and political retribution.[47] In addition, between 1804 and 1989, the House "inquired into the conduct of at least seventy-eight judges over time" on suspicion of wrongdoing that could have led to the initiation of impeachment hearings, which works out to an inquiry every 2.4 years.[48] And informal suggestions that impeachment should be pursued occur far more frequently, such as when Rep. Louie Gohmert (R-TX) argued, "I think it's important to look at Justice Kagan for potential impeachment," because of her participation and vote upholding major provisions of Obamacare.[49]

Curbing the Courts

As we have seen, the textbook view—Congress passes a bill, the president signs it, then the courts have the opportunity to review it—is an incomplete description of the process, because it ignores Congress's ability to react to the judiciary's action. In addition, the textbook description presumes that the courts can always act. In reality, Congress can spell out when the courts can act and which cases the courts can hear. When Congress wants to, it can pass *court-curbing* bills, which are laws that limit the ability of the courts to act and that Congress uses to place pressure on the courts.[50]

Court curbing can take several forms. For example, bills that affect the composition of the courts are considered to be court curbing. So, too, are those bills that limit remedies that courts can prescribe in their decisions (for example, ruling out busing to deal with segregated schools). But the most prominent way Congress can try to curb the courts is by limiting their jurisdiction.[51] Members of Congress can attempt to define issues as occurring at the state level, rather than at the federal level, which would indicate that they fall outside of the federal courts' jurisdiction. Or they can be much more specific. In several sessions of Congress during the decade of the 2000s, for example, members introduced the Pledge Protection Act, which aimed to strip all federal courts of their jurisdiction to hear constitutional challenges to the Pledge of Allegiance. The pledge had recently been (and continues to be) the topic of several court cases, and some courts ruled that the inclusion of the phrase "under God" was unconstitutional because it violated the First Amendment. Although Congress did not pass the Pledge Protection Act, its introduction represented an attempt by members to prevent future courts from striking down the pledge by removing the courts' jurisdiction over this issue.

Members of Congress have introduced court-curbing bills regularly throughout history, but they have done so more frequently in certain periods, as Figure 11.2 shows. Not surprisingly, these periods are those in which the Court has tackled controversial issues in a way that raises the ire of members of Congress. For example, there was a large spike in such bills in the 1950s when the Warren Court issued a number of liberal decisions on highly controversial and divisive issues such as prayers in schools, school desegregation, and the rights of criminal defendants. In the aftermath of these decisions, over the next two decades, members of Congress introduced a number of bills designed to limit the Supreme Court's jurisdiction and to limit its ability to review laws for constitutionality.[52] It is important to recognize that although there are spikes or periods in which more of these bills are introduced, the introduction of bills aimed at curbing the courts has occurred frequently and regularly over time.

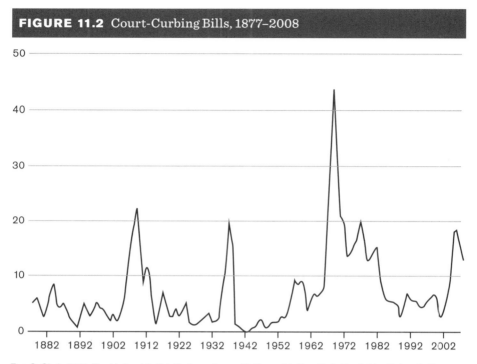

FIGURE 11.2 Court-Curbing Bills, 1877–2008

Tom S. Clark. 2011. *The Limits of Judicial Independence*, 43, Figure 2.1. New York: Cambridge University Press.

Do Judges Care about Congressional Actions?

Members of Congress clearly can and do introduce a variety of laws that pose threats to the judicial branch. They can threaten to remove jurisdiction from the courts. They can attempt to limit the judiciary's ability to conduct judicial review. They can change the size of the courts, threaten to impeach judges, or propose actions that would place limits on life tenure. They can refuse to raise judges' salaries, cut the judiciary's budget, or take to the airwaves or social media to castigate judges for specific decisions or for broader trends of judicial policy making.

The question that arises is, Why should judges care about any of these congressional actions? After all, federal judges have life tenure, and threats to remove them rarely succeed. Although changes to the size of the Supreme Court are hypothetically possible, the Court has remained the same size for nearly 150 years. Bills to limit the federal judiciary's ability to conduct judicial review or to limit its jurisdiction are frequently introduced but infrequently passed.

There are several reasons why judges might care about these congressional actions.[53] To begin with, many, perhaps even most, lower-court judges aspire to serve on a higher court, and to do so, they will need Senate approval. Avoiding controversy—or backing off when they receive signals from Congress that they are generating controversy—is a way to increase the odds of any future confirmations being successful. In addition, judges, like most other people, pay attention to what others say about them.

Perhaps more importantly, judges are concerned about the institutional legitimacy of the judiciary. Consider the members of the Supreme Court. They want to protect the Court's reputation and its prestige. Recalling Hamilton's point about the Court's dependence on other institutions of government—the executive branch to carry out its decisions and the legislative branch to provide funding—the Court does not want to be in a position where it regularly crosses the other branches, because doing so is likely to result in less efficacy (as well as less prestige) in the future. Furthermore, this institutional legitimacy helps the Court (and the judiciary more generally) to remain the most trusted of American national institutions in the eyes of the public. Evidence indicates that when the judicial branch is pulled into political fights, is seen as a political body more than a legal one, and exhibits lower levels of consensus, then its approval drops, which in turn makes it more susceptible to attacks from other institutions.[54]

Given that the courts do have an incentive to worry about threats from members of Congress, the next question is whether these threats make a difference in the courts' behavior. That is, do judges anticipate congressional threats and actions, and modify their own actions to avoid negative repercussions? Perhaps they do not need to be concerned about how Congress might react. After all, Congress often suffers from a decided lack of information about recent judicial rulings.[55] And even if Congress is aware of recent or upcoming judicial actions, it is far from clear that it will have the ability to act because of all the institutional and behavioral reasons discussed earlier (for example, the power of majority party leaders to keep issues off the agenda, the gatekeeping power of committee chairs, the multiple veto points that must be navigated to pass any law, and so on).

One way to approach this question is to investigate whether judges change their voting behavior when they hold views that contrast with those of Congress and the president. For example, is a justice who holds conservative views more likely to moderate these views when Congress and the president are more liberal? There are good theoretical reasons to expect this to be the case. Judges do not want to be overridden by Congress, because overrides can lead to a loss of personal and institutional prestige, and can produce policies they dislike. But what does research tell us?

Social scientists disagree about whether justices act differently depending on the ideological leanings of elected officials. One of the first and most prominent studies to examine this issue systematically found little evidence that individual justices moderate their views when faced with a Congress (and president) holding opposing views.[56] And while some studies of the votes of justices have found such an effect, many have not.[57]

At the same time, several studies have shown that justices are quite aware of the preferences of members of Congress and the president, and they take these preferences into account.[58] Other studies have taken a different approach. For example, instead of identifying whether individual justices modify their voting patterns when faced with a Congress that is ideologically distant, another study examined the data from the perspective of laws rather than justices' votes. That is, instead of asking whether the ideology of elected officials affects justices' votes, it examined whether the Court was more likely to overturn a statute that it disliked when it found itself in agreement with Congress and thus did not need to worry about negative reactions from Congress. The findings revealed that the conservative Rehnquist Court was unlikely to strike down acts passed by prior Democratic Congresses, at least while Congress remained under Democratic control. But after Republicans took control of Congress in 1994—which meant that the Court had less to fear in terms of negative responses from the majority party controlling each chamber—the Court became much more likely to overturn those earlier Democratic laws.

As noted earlier, Congress influences not only the way justices vote on a case but also what cases justices hear. Justices are far less likely to agree to hear constitutional cases in which there is a significant difference between their preferences over the outcomes of the cases and Congress's current preferences.[59] In addition, justices are likely to hear fewer cases overall when their views are out of step with those of Congress, because they are more likely to avoid controversial cases that might spur a strong, negative congressional reaction.[60]

Additional evidence for the influence of Congress, and whether it can exert subtle (or sometimes not-so-subtle) pressure on the courts, comes from a closer examination of the court-curbing bills discussed earlier. If the Supreme Court is concerned about institutional legitimacy, then it should be highly sensitive to signals that this legitimacy is being challenged. An examination of court-curbing bills reveals that the courts are, in fact, influenced by these congressional actions. Court-curbing bills indicate discontent with what the Court is doing, because members of Congress are more likely to introduce such measures when they and their constituents are dissatisfied with the Court's recent actions. When the Court observes these signals, it changes its ways. In particular, when it sees an increase in court-curbing bills, it becomes less likely to exercise its power of judicial review and to declare acts to be unconstitutional.[61]

When we look at congressional actions and judicial responses, a picture of the relationship between Congress and the courts starts to emerge. As we learned earlier, Congress does have the power to override judicial decisions, and it does so to a greater extent than most observers realize. But even when it does not directly override judicial decisions, it is not powerless. That is, a lack of overrides does not indicate acquiescence or surrender to the judicial branch. Much, but not all, evidence indicates that the courts take the preferences of Congress into account when issuing decisions.

HOW WE STUDY
THE INTERACTION OF CONGRESS
AND THE COURTS

Recent research has taken advantage of new statistical techniques to reassess the question of whether congressional preferences influence the votes of Supreme Court justices. One complication for political scientists who want to study the relationship between Congress and other branches has always been how to make comparisons when the political actors in these two branches cast votes on completely different sets of issues. A member of Congress might have a DW-NOMINATE score (see Chapter 2) of 0.45, but how does that score compare to a Supreme Court justice who casts a conservative vote 65 percent of the time?

To address this problem, scholars have developed new and innovative measures of ideology that are comparable across political institutions. One measure, Judicial Common Space scores, calculates ideology scores for Supreme Court justices based on their votes and then adjusts and converts these scores (known as Martin-Quinn scores, after the scholars who developed them) so that they are on the same scale as NOMINATE scores.

Another approach, developed by political scientist Michael Bailey and colleagues, starts with the observation that although members of Congress vote on a different set of issues than members of the Court, there are overlapping questions that can tell us what members of different institutions think about the same policy issues. For example, members of Congress often take public positions on Court cases, noting whether they agree or disagree with the Court's decision; they file briefs with the Court, urging the Court to vote in a certain way; and so on. Using these and other areas of overlap, Bailey has developed measures of ideology that place members of Congress and Supreme Court justices (as well as presidents) on the same ideological scale.

These scores allow us to see how the median ideology in Congress compares to the median ideology of the Court. Figure 11.3 illustrates how the ideologies of the median members of the Supreme Court, the House, and the Senate have varied over time, and how they compare. In some periods, such as the 1960s, Congress was more conservative than the Court. But since the mid-1970s, the Court has, with only a few exceptions, been more conservative than the two chambers of Congress.

With these scores in hand, Bailey and his colleague Forrest Maltzman were able to test whether justices exhibit different voting patterns when the Court's ideology differs from Congress's. To do this, they controlled for the extent to which justices allow legal factors (for example, adherence to precedent) to influence their votes, which is a factor that earlier studies of congressional influence had neglected.

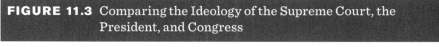

FIGURE 11.3 Comparing the Ideology of the Supreme Court, the President, and Congress

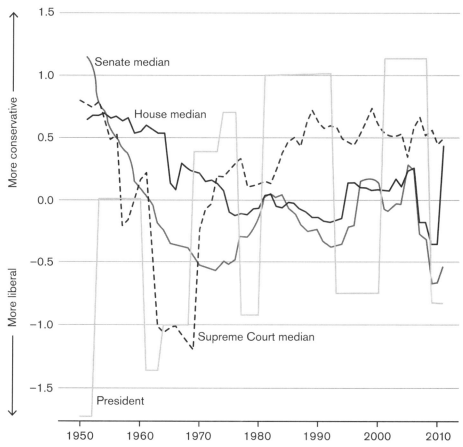

Michael A. Bailey. 2017. "Measuring Ideology of the Courts," in *Routledge Handbook of Judicial Behavior*, eds. Robert M. Howard and Kirk A. Randazzo, 72. New York: Routledge.

Bailey and Maltzman find that between 1950 and 2008, about half of the justices were likely to vote differently when their ideological beliefs differed from those of Congress. That is, conservative justices voted less conservatively when Congress was liberal, while liberal justices voted less liberally when Congress was more conservative. In addition, they found that justices also changed their voting patterns after major election shifts (e.g., elections that moved the ideological center of gravity in Congress and the president). Justices tend to move in the direction of this ideological shift, voting more liberally when the shift is in a liberal direction and more conservatively when the shift is in a conservative direction.[62]

Critical Thinking

1. Given that judges view themselves as legal actors, not as political actors, does it make sense to think of them having ideology scores?
2. When members of Congress take a position on a court case, is it reasonable to treat their positions as equivalent to having voted on that case?
3. Why might justices shift their voting behavior rightward after an election that puts Republicans in control of the elected branches, or leftward after an election that puts Democrats in control? Why might they not do so?

Congressional Anticipation and Judicial Review

Much of the previous section examined whether the courts anticipate congressional reactions. But anticipation can work both ways. Not only might the courts anticipate what Congress's reaction is likely to be, Congress also might attempt to anticipate what the courts are likely to do once an issue reaches the judiciary.

The current makeup of the Supreme Court has profound effects on congressional action. Before finalizing legislation, members of Congress often anticipate how the Court will interpret its laws. Right now, the Court consists of five conservative members and four liberal members.

Although legislators might not pay close attention to the nuances and details of judicial doctrines and recent judicial rulings, they do know that the courts can play a major role in the policy-making process. Thus Congress has every reason to expect the courts to be involved eventually in a policy area and to issue rulings that will affect laws that Congress has passed. Given this expectation, members of Congress frequently consider how the courts might interpret a law and, more importantly, how they might be able to influence that interpretation.

Sometimes, as we have discussed, laws may be intentionally ambiguous or contain contradictory language. But often Congress wants to make its intent as clear as possible, knowing that the courts may be called upon to assess and interpret laws. It turns out that there is much that Congress can do to influence the ways in which the courts view a law. For example, many judges, when trying to ascertain the meaning of a law, will turn to the law's legislative history. This history consists of a variety of sources of information that are not contained in the text of the law itself but that suggest what those who wrote the law and those who voted for it had in mind. Not all judges pay attention to this information, but many do.[63]

One source of legislative history is the record of discussions and debates on the floor of Congress. To influence future judicial interpretations of a law, members can use these floor statements to signal to the courts what the law means, in much the same way that a president might use a signing statement. This is a particularly effective technique if it comes from a prominent representative or senator—a party leader or a floor manager for the bill, for example. Committee reports constitute another prominent source of information about a bill. In these reports, the committees can explain, in standard English rather than the formal and legal language used in legislation, what certain provisions of the law mean, what goals the law is trying to accomplish, and the intentions of those who support the law.

Congress can take a number of other actions to communicate its intent to judges more clearly—for example, making the text of laws clearer, or having the floor manager identify which statements made on the floor should be taken as especially authoritative.[64] Again, it should be stressed that not all judges will pay attention to these materials. Justice Scalia, for example, was dismissive of the value of such materials. He instead adhered to an "originalist" approach, which holds that judges should look only at what the text of the law meant at the time it was written, not to other sources that document the law's path to creation.[65] But given that most judges rely, to some extent, on legislative history to aid in their interpretation of a law, Congress can significantly influence this interpretation by paying attention to these details.

Congress can also be strategic about future court behavior in another way: it can carefully construct laws so that they constrain what the courts may or may not do. Congress uses this approach when it writes a statute that delegates policy making and implementation authority to an executive or independent agency.

When agencies take these actions pursuant to the passage of laws, the courts are often called upon to assess whether the agency's action was consistent with the law, in much the same way that courts can assess whether a statute is consistent with the Constitution. This type of action, known as *administrative judicial review*, can have broad implications for policy, as it can either validate an agency action (as in *Chevron U.S.A., Inc. v. Natural Resources Defense Council*[66]) or strike it down (as in *Citizens to Preserve Overton Park v. Volpe*[67]).

Given that Congress knows that the courts are likely to hear cases that challenge agency actions, it has an incentive to structure how the courts can proceed. Specifically, it can insert distinct types of judicial review provisions into laws that will have the effect of increasing the courts' ability to review agency actions (thus opening the agency up to review) or decreasing this ability (thus protecting the agency from review).

Congress can use several types of provisions.[68] It can simply state that the courts may not review an agency action; it can specify that an agency action is reviewable; or it can allow review, but only within certain limits. If it chooses to allow review, then Congress can include other types of provisions that spell out how review should be conducted. It can put time limits on review, for example, and the shorter the time limits are, the less likely it is that an interested party will appeal an agency action to the courts. It can specify which courts can conduct this review. In doing so, it can broaden the opportunity for review by saying that review can be conducted by any district or appellate court, or it can identify a specific court as the only venue for review. It can specify who has standing—that is, who is or is not legally authorized to seek appeal of an agency's action. Perhaps most importantly, it can specify the scope of review, which tells the courts what approach they can take when assessing the agency's action, spelling out whether the courts have the authority to ignore the agency's findings of fact, or whether the courts must defer to the agency.

These provisions sound minor, but Congress can use them to dramatically affect the ways in which courts can review important regulatory actions. And although there has long been the perception that Congress rarely uses some of these provisions, especially the prohibition of review, it turns out that Congress uses them quite frequently. An assessment of 403 major laws that Congress passed between 1946 and 2010 (specifically, laws that delegate policy-making responsibility to agencies) found that in 35 percent of them, Congress specified whether the courts had the power to review or not.[69]

Congress can also use statutes to anticipate judicial action in another way: by increasing or decreasing the specificity of laws. If Congress wants to constrain the courts, it can write more detailed and specific laws. Congress might choose this route when it has clear policy preferences, because by spelling out in careful detail what a law is supposed to accomplish and how it should work, Congress can use statutes to constrain the discretion of any court that examines the law, helping to ensure that its policy preferences survive an encounter with the courts. In contrast, legislation that is unclear or ambiguous leaves judges less constrained and affords them the opportunity to incorporate their policy preferences into their decisions.[70]

CONCLUSION

The relationship between Congress and the courts has been described as a "continuing colloquy," one in which the two institutions are interacting and responding to each other on a regular basis, rather than a system in which the judiciary is completely dominant.[71] A close consideration of this relationship points to the accuracy of this description. Although in some respects, the courts might be seen as dominant (because they have the power to declare acts of Congress unconstitutional, which creates the high bar of a constitutional amendment if Congress wants to overturn that ruling), this view ignores the myriad ways in which Congress can, and does, influence the courts.

To begin with, Congress (more specifically the Senate) plays a significant role in determining who occupies seats on the federal courts. Whether it is the individual senators whose opinions the president considers when making lower-court appointments, or the broader set of senators whose votes are needed to confirm Supreme Court nominees, the Senate can influence the courts by influencing the president's choice of nominees. Once these judges and justices are in place, Congress is far from powerless. It can, and often does, override judicial statutory interpretation decisions. But it also has other ways of influencing the courts. In some cases, the mere threat of legislation is enough to cause the courts to shift their positions and vote differently, or to avoid hearing certain sorts of cases. And it can use other ways to pressure the courts.

None of this is to say that Congress dominates the courts. Far from it. Because of judicial independence, the courts often successfully take positions at odds with Congress. But it is also clear that Congress has a wide set of tools that it can use to attract the judiciary's attention. In effect, then, the result is a classic separation-of-powers situation in which the two branches sometimes work together and sometimes do not. In responding to and anticipating the actions of the courts, members of Congress are motivated by policy and representation concerns to exert influence on the courts, especially with the courts now playing such a prominent policy-making role. These concerns are consistent with the constitutional view of Congress as the first branch of government, because failure to monitor and weigh in on the court's behavior would be an abdication of Congress's governing role.

Discussion Questions

1. The Framers sought to make the courts independent by giving judges life tenure. What are the positive aspects of judges having life tenure? What are the negative aspects?
2. Should senators who oppose a president's nominees to serve on the courts be allowed to use the filibuster to prevent a vote on these nominations?
3. In what ways would the Framers be satisfied or dissatisfied with the current relationship between Congress and the courts?
4. What factors might explain why the number of congressional overrides of judicial decisions has dropped so dramatically since the mid-1990s?
5. Should Congress be allowed to curb the courts? Or does court curbing violate the spirit of checks and balances by giving Congress too much power?

12

Interest Groups

When Republicans won unified control over government following the 2016 elections, with majorities in the House and Senate to go along with Donald Trump in the White House, the party eagerly looked forward to enacting many of its main legislative priorities. Among these priorities, which included strengthening national security, cutting regulations, and reducing government spending, two stood out.[1] First, Republicans planned to enact a set of significant tax cuts centering on a significant reduction in the corporate tax rate, which Trump had touted as a key component of his platform. Second, the party aimed to make good on a promise it had been making for the past six years: to repeal the Affordable Care Act (ACA).

By the end of the first year of Republican control, only one of those goals had been achieved. In December 2017, Republican leaders from the House and Senate proudly watched as President Trump signed the Tax Cuts and Jobs Act of 2017 into law. In contrast, multiple attempts during the year to repeal the ACA ended in failure. A dramatic moment took place in July when Senator John McCain (R-AZ) moved to the center of the Senate chamber and gave a thumbs-down signal to express his vote against repealing some aspects of the ACA, an attempt known as "skinny repeal." Then, in September, McCain announced his

Though Republicans were able to pass the Tax Cut and Jobs Act in 2017, their repeated efforts to repeal and replace the ACA failed. Here, Senator John McCain (R-AZ) leaves the Senate chamber after dramatically voting "no" on the "skinny repeal" of the ACA. Did the pressure from interest groups influence the outcomes of these important bills?

opposition to a repeal attempt sponsored by his good friend Lindsey Graham (R-SC) and Representative Bill Cassidy (R-FL). In both cases, McCain's opposition, along with that of a small handful of other Republican senators, meant that the GOP would not be able to muster a majority of votes in favor of repeal.

Why did these two legislative attempts produce such contrasting outcomes? The answer cannot be found in differing levels of commitment to these two policy goals, as both were among the most prominent priorities the Republican Party had promised to tackle and achieve immediately after winning the election. It cannot be due to a lack of public support from the president; President Trump's "Contract with the American Voter" listed both tax cuts and repealing the ACA among his top-10 priorities. It also is unlikely that differences in public opinion mattered much. Although the tax-cut bill was slightly more popular among the public, the difference was rather small, with only about 24 percent of the republic favoring repeal of the ACA and only 30 percent favoring the tax-cut bill.[2] And it was not about procedural differences. When McCain announced his opposition to Graham's bill, he made it known that he was opposing it specifically because it had not followed regular order, meaning that the Senate Republican leaders had not let the bill be developed by expert committees, had not held informative hearings, had not allowed the Congressional Budget Office to provide a detailed analysis of the bill's effects, and had not allowed Democrats to participate in debating and writing the bill. Yet each of these claims also could have been made about the tax-cut bill.

On one important dimension, however, there was a significant difference: the positions taken by interest groups. With respect to the ACA, a quick look at interest-group positions reveals that the dominant feature of the political landscape surrounding repeal was interest-group opposition. Not all groups were opposed, but the groups that were opposed were numerous, prominent, and varied, and they included coalitions of groups that do not usually band together.

Table 12.1 lists the groups that took positions on the Graham-Cassidy attempt to repeal the ACA. A handful of conservative groups that traditionally align with Republicans did favor this repeal attempt. But most other groups opposed the repeal, including virtually every association in the country that focuses on the treatment of specific diseases (including the American Cancer Society), insurance companies (including Blue Cross Blue Shield), all major professional associations (including the American Medical Association), hospital associations, major nonprofits in the medical field (including Kaiser), and perhaps the nation's most powerful interest group, the AARP (formerly the American Association of Retired People). Even some prominent conservative groups, including the Heritage Action CEO and the Citizens Council for Health Freedom, opposed this bill, albeit for very different reasons. This pattern of resistance to the Graham-Cassidy bill mirrored the imbalance for repeal of the ACA overall. According to MapLight.org, which tracks interest-group position, a total of 76 organizations took public positions against repeal while only 13 organizations, from a much narrower swatch, favored repeal.[3]

Meanwhile, interest-group support for the tax-cut bill was much stronger, and opposition was less intense and less coordinated. Although some groups opposed the tax-cut bill, including AARP, most major corporations and business associations favored it.[4] In contrast to the ACA, when most of the relevant groups opposed repeal, the major beneficiaries of the tax cut bill—U.S. corporations—lined up in favor of enactment. The U.S. Chamber of Commerce, for example, took a strong position in favor of this law, as did the Business Roundtable.[5] The support of these groups came as little surprise. After all, cutting taxes has been a core foundation of the Republican Party's brand over the past several decades, and it is perhaps the single issue that most unites the disparate groups that comprise the party's coalition.[6] Thus, in contrast to the policy area of health care, in the area of taxes, there is a much tighter link between the party and these groups, which identify with the Republican Party overall but especially do so on the issue of tax cuts.

TABLE 12.1 Interest-Group Positions on the Graham-Cassidy Repeal of the Affordable Care Act

Opposed		In Favor
American Cancer Society	American Hospital Association	FreedomWorks
American Diabetes Association	America's Essential Hospitals	Americans for Prosperity
American Heart Association	American Medical Association	Tea Party Patriots
American Lung Association	American Psychiatric Association	Club for Growth
Arthritis Foundation	American Academy of Family Physicians	
Cystic Fibrosis Foundation	American Academy of Pediatrics	
ALS Foundation	American College of Physicians	
March of Dimes	American Congress of Obstetricians and Gynecologists	
Multiple Sclerosis Society	American Osteopathic Association	
AARP	Heritage Action CEO	
National Council for Behavioral Health	Citizens Council for Health Freedom	
Kaiser Family Foundation	Association for Community Affiliated Plans	
Blue Cross Blue Shield		

Compiled by authors from various sources. See, in particular, Paige Winfield Cunningham. September 20, 2017. "The Health 202: Everything You Need to Know About Who Stands Where on Graham-Cassidy." *Washington Post,* www.washingtonpost.com/news/powerpost/paloma/the-health-202/2017/09/20 /the-health-202-everything-you-need-to-know-about-who-stands-where-on-graham-cassidy /59c157fc30fb045176650d46/?utm_term=.2a1ae5373c9f (accessed 8/23/18); and Bruce Japsen. September 12, 2017. "Conservative Groups Oppose Graham-Cassidy Trumpcare Bill." *Forbes,* www.forbes .com/sites/brucejapsen/2017/09/12/even-conservatives-skeptical-about-cassidy-graham-trumpcare-bill /#6625ea277515 (accessed 8/23/18).

In addition, members of Congress frankly acknowledged that groups were putting heavy pressure on them to enact the tax-cut bill. Later in this chapter, we will see that interest groups have many ways of pressuring members that do not involve money. In the case of health care, for example, the AARP could have threatened to mobilize its massive membership against any legislator who supported repeal. But financial concerns certainly do exist. For example, in discussing the "flurry of lobbying from special interests" regarding this bill, Rep. Chris Collins (R-NY) acknowledged, "My donors are basically saying, 'Get it done or don't ever call me again.'"[7] Senator Graham voiced a similar concern about the likely reaction of groups and donors if the GOP failed to pass the tax-cut bill, noting that "financial contributions will stop."[8]

It is far too simplistic to ascribe the passage of the tax-cut bill and the defeat of the ACA repeal bills solely to the distribution and desires of interest groups. But we cannot ignore the stark differences in the interest-group context for these two bills. Interest groups might have affected the outcomes for these legislative attempts only at the margins; but as we have seen throughout this book, margins can be all-important in politics, especially in situations where passage or defeat is determined by a handful of votes.

Although the Tax Cut and Jobs Act was passed by Congress in 2017, it was relatively unpopular among Americans, especially after senators Lindsey Graham (R-SC), pictured here, and Chris Collins (R-NY) acknowledged that legislators were influenced by donors.

In addition to showing the potential power of interest groups, these two cases illustrate how the relationship between interest groups and Congress connects to two key concepts. Clearly, all of these groups—for example, the health groups opposing the repeal of the ACA and conservative groups supporting it— were representing individuals with a stake in the issue, and these groups turned to legislators so their concerns would be represented in Congress. Furthermore, to the extent that groups did influence the eventual outcomes, they were affecting Congress's governing function. Finally, although separation of powers issues were not central to the debates over these laws, this chapter will highlight the ways in which interest groups and lobbying provide insights into this theme as well.

INTEREST GROUPS IN THE UNITED STATES

Any discussion of interest groups in the United States needs to start with James Madison's observations about factions, particularly his statements in *Federalist 10*. In this document, Madison does not use the term "interest group," which had not yet come into fashion. But his definition of a *faction* as "a majority or a minority of the whole, who are united and actuated by some common impulse of passion, or of interest" certainly fits the current view of what an interest group is.[9]

Federalist 10 is rich with insights, two of which stand out.[10] The first is Madison's recognition that factions, or groups pursuing different interests, are inevitable in any society. Anywhere there is liberty, and anywhere people are free to form coalitions and act on their opinions, factions will form. In Madison's view, the inclination to band together with others sharing similar views to pursue common interests is "sown in the nature of man." Therefore, according to Madison, the designers of the new nation needed to recognize that groups or factions were inevitable. The question then becomes how to cope with the certainty that such groups will exist and how to prevent any particular group from dominating government at the expense of the remainder of the public.

Madison's second major insight centered on what he called the "mischiefs," or dangers, of factions.[11] One option for dealing with these mischiefs would be to outlaw factions. He quickly dismissed this option, noting that to prohibit factions would mean "destroying the liberty which is essential to [their] existence." Given the prominence of liberty in the formation of the new nation, this option was neither attractive nor feasible. The other option was to figure out how to control the effects of factions by decreasing the likelihood that any one group would be able to dominate government. Here Madison noted that a system of representation in government would provide one bulwark against domination by a group. The large size of the new nation would provide another. To these options he added, in *Federalist 51*, the importance of dividing and separating power across institutions, as well as giving institutions the power to check each other.[12] Together, the representative form of government, the large size of the nation, the separation of powers, and checks and balances would prevent any group, or faction, from dominating and imposing its favored policies on others.

Later in this chapter, we explore whether Madison's prediction that a well-designed representative government in a large country would prevent a group from dominating government and policy making has come to pass. That is, we explore whether interest groups in the United States are able to get what they want. First, however, we need to lay down some foundational ideas.

WHAT ARE INTEREST GROUPS?

What are the differences between *interest groups* and groups more generally? Overlapping or common interests are certainly a prominent reason why people join groups. But shared interests alone do not make a group an interest group. A local Little League team or a dance club certainly would qualify as a group, for example, but they are unlikely to be labeled interest groups because they do not mainly engage in political activity. However, if a group starts to engage in political activity—for example, a Little League team might push for public funding for a new baseball field—then it could indeed be considered an interest group. With these criteria in mind, we can define *interest groups* as associations of individuals or companies that become involved in politics to pursue a common interest by influencing policy, elections, or legislation.

Groups can engage in politics by actively seeking to influence the actions of public officials, including members of Congress, either by directly interacting with these officials or by trying to exert external pressures on them. This tactic, which we explore in detail throughout this chapter, is known as *lobbying*, and the groups that engage in it are called *lobbies*. These groups' right to lobby is enshrined in the Constitution, with the First Amendment providing people (and by extension groups) with the right to "petition the Government." The First Amendment therefore guarantees the public the right to make its views and preferences about policy known to its representatives in Congress.

Interest groups can be characterized in several ways. One straightforward method is to distinguish between those that exist primarily to seek economic benefits and those that focus mainly on noneconomic benefits. These categories can be subdivided further. For example, economic interest groups include corporations such as Alphabet, General Electric, Boeing, and AT&T; professional associations such as the American Medical Association and the National

Association of Realtors; labor groups such as the AFL-CIO; and a variety of business groups and trade associations. Economic interest groups can range from extremely large, prominent, and well-funded groups, including the U.S. Chamber of Commerce and the National Association of Manufacturers, to more specific and less well-known (although no less committed to their goals) groups, such as the Society for Protective Coatings and the Association of the Nonwoven Fabrics Industry. On the noneconomic side, some groups, such as the National Rifle Association (NRA) and the Brady Campaign to Prevent Gun Violence, focus on single issues. Others, such as Common Cause, are broader and characterize themselves as "public interest" groups (although almost all groups are careful to emphasize how their actions benefit the general public). All of these groups take actions in the political realm that are designed to further their goals, whether those goals are economic (for example, lower tax rates for corporations) or non-economic (for example, cleaner water or air).

Mentioning the names or types of groups that are involved in lobbying shows some of the variety of interests that exist. But to get a better sense of the enormous scope of lobbying, it helps to look at aggregate numbers. Figure 12.1 shows the number of lobbyists in Washington, D.C., along with the amount of money these organizations and individuals spent on lobbying between 1998 and 2017. Clearly, lobbies are omnipresent in national politics.

Despite, or perhaps because of, the omnipresence of interest groups in U.S. politics, it is not difficult to find negative views of these groups and their potential effects. In general, the American people take a dim view of interest groups, at least in the abstract. For example, when asked whether wealthy special interests have too much power and influence over elections, 80 percent of voters say that they do.[13] Nearly as many—69 percent—agree that Congress is too "focused on the needs of special interests."[14] In fact, when Americans were asked their opinions of the honesty and ethics of a set of 22 professions, lobbyists came in dead last, with only 5 percent of the public having a high or very high opinion of people in this profession, as opposed to a whopping 58 percent who hold a low or very low opinion. Notably, these data put lobbyists several notches below members of Congress (9 percent positive, 45 percent negative) and even below car salespeople (5 percent positive, 53 percent negative).[15]

These negative views cannot be attributed solely to the public being biased or uninformed. In fact, the public might not be wrong in suggesting that members of Congress pay more attention to special interests than to their overall constituents. Political scientist Kristina Miler has drawn on the discipline of psychology to explain people's low opinion of interest groups. She argues that even when legislators look out across the multiple constituencies in their districts in an attempt to perceive what they want, they end up seeing only a biased subset of those constituents. They do not set out to do so, of course; rather, because of

FIGURE 12.1 Total Spending on Lobbying and Number of Lobbyists in the United States, 1998–2017

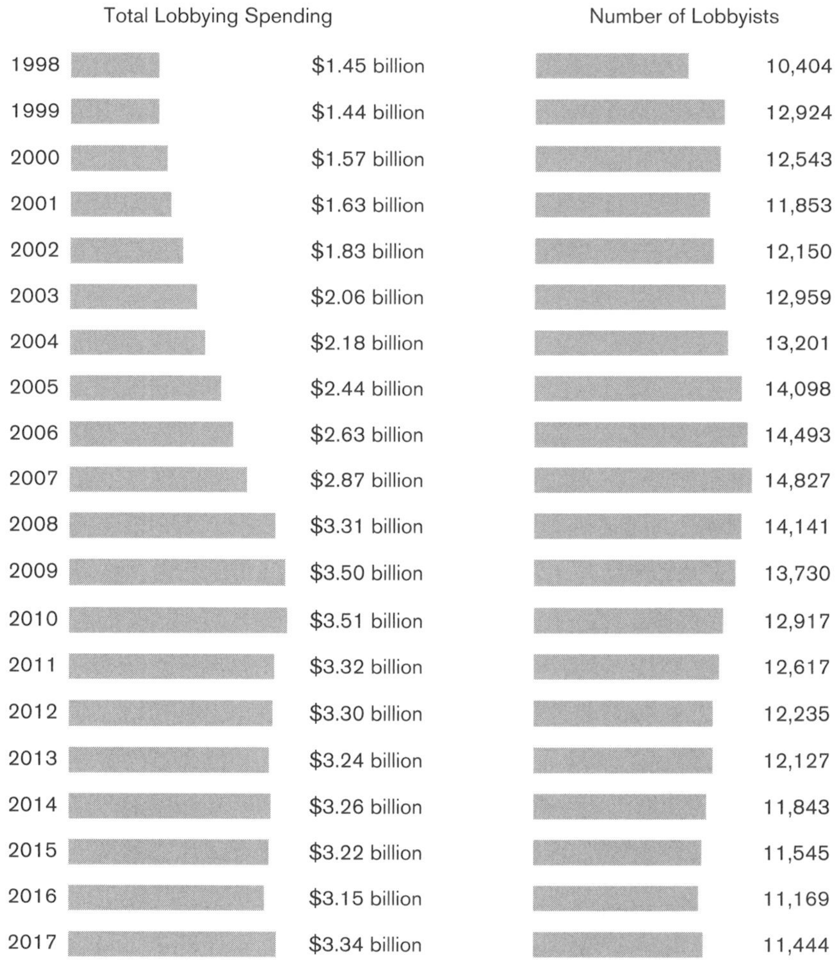

	Total Lobbying Spending	Number of Lobbyists
1998	$1.45 billion	10,404
1999	$1.44 billion	12,924
2000	$1.57 billion	12,543
2001	$1.63 billion	11,853
2002	$1.83 billion	12,150
2003	$2.06 billion	12,959
2004	$2.18 billion	13,201
2005	$2.44 billion	14,098
2006	$2.63 billion	14,493
2007	$2.87 billion	14,827
2008	$3.31 billion	14,141
2009	$3.50 billion	13,730
2010	$3.51 billion	12,917
2011	$3.32 billion	12,617
2012	$3.30 billion	12,235
2013	$3.24 billion	12,127
2014	$3.26 billion	11,843
2015	$3.22 billion	11,545
2016	$3.15 billion	11,169
2017	$3.34 billion	11,444

"Lobbying." Center for Responsive Politics, www.opensecrets.org/lobby (accessed 8/7/18).

time restrictions and other cognitive limitations, they rely on various shortcuts to determine what these constituents want. Not surprisingly, these shortcuts tend to favor the parts of their constituencies that are most visible, and the most visible consist of groups (and individuals) that have donated money and lobbied their offices. In other words, even a legislator who sets out to represent the entire district often ends up representing only the more active and richer groups within the district. Miler's analysis helps us understand why Representative

Collins (in our example earlier in this chapter) emphasized his concerns about major donors rather than the concerns of others in his district.

The idea that biases in the interest-group system lead to biased outcomes is far from new. More than five decades ago, E. E. Schattschneider issued one of the first and strongest broadsides against the pernicious effects of such groups, arguing that they tend to be heavily biased toward the interests of the upper classes. Current data show that this imbalance in the interest-group system, which is weighted toward wealthier business groups, continues to exist today. Table 12.2 lists the 10 organizations that spent the most money on lobbying Congress in 2017. A quick glance reveals that all are business-related groups, trade associations, or professional associations. None are groups that would primarily be considered broader public-interest groups.[16]

Identifying problems with, and complaints about, interest groups is a bit like shooting fish in a barrel: they're an easy target. Yet it's worth considering an alternative perspective. Because there are so many groups, because they spend so much money, and because the biggest spenders tend to be corporations and other economically motivated groups, it is tempting to assume that groups dominate the policy-making process. But this is an empirical question—that is, one that we can examine with data, a task to which we turn later in this chapter. In addition, it is worth keeping in mind that the Framers explicitly considered whether the Bill of Rights should protect the right to petition the government, which gives people and groups the right to press

TABLE 12.2 Top Spenders on Lobbying Congress, 2017

Lobbying Client	Total
U.S. Chamber of Commerce	$82,260,000
National Association of Realtors	$54,530,861
Business Roundtable	$27,380,000
Pharmaceutical Research and Manufacturers of America	$25,847,500
Blue Cross Blue Shield	$24,330,306
American Hospital Association	$22,094,214
American Medical Association	$21,535,000
AT&T Inc.	$19,717,000
Alphabet Inc.	$18,150,000
Boeing Co.	$16,740,000

"Top Spenders 2017." Center for Responsive Politics, OpenSecrets.org (accessed 8/23/18).

their concerns to the government—that is, to lobby. Other parts of the First Amendment were topics of debate, but the right to petition was quickly agreed on as an essential right.

Lobbying can also serve dual positive purposes for members of Congress. First, it can inform them about what their constituents want, which in turn potentially allows them to fulfill their representative function better. Second, lobbying can also provide information to representatives and senators about the details of specific policies: the main issues in the policy area, the proposed solutions, the potential effects of these solutions, and so on. Before he became president, Senator John F. Kennedy (D-MA) propounded exactly this view:

> Lobbyists are in many cases expert technicians and capable of explaining complex and difficult subjects in a clear, understandable fashion. They engage in personal discussions with Members of Congress in which they can explain in detail the reasons for positions they advocate. . . . Because our congressional representation is based on geographical boundaries, the lobbyists who speak for the various economic, commercial, and other functional interests of this country serve a very useful purpose and have assumed an important role in the legislative process.[17]

Furthermore, groups can provide a way for citizens to be heard by government when their views differ from those of their representatives and senators in Congress. Consider, for example, a gun-loving resident of San Francisco or an Alabaman who is pro-choice. These people are unlikely to have their views represented in Congress by their legislators, because a representative from San Francisco will almost certainly be in favor of gun control, while a senator from Alabama will almost certainly be pro-life. By joining a pro-gun-rights group or a pro-choice group, citizens benefit from these groups' lobbying efforts and thus see their views represented before Congress.

In addition, a dominant theory in political science, known as *pluralism*, holds that good policy results from the interplay of interest groups in the political system. Pluralists begin by arguing, like Madison, that groups are simply a fact of life and will turn to the government to pursue their goals. Pluralists argue that group activity will produce good policy. The arguments put forward to make this case are fairly nuanced, but generally they rely on the idea that because there will be so many groups, any individual group will rarely be unopposed. Instead, groups will be countered by other groups, and policy will spring from the interplay of all groups active in an area. Furthermore, no group will be powerful on all issues; some will be more powerful on some issues, while others are more powerful on others. That balance, combined with the likelihood that people will belong to various groups, prevents any single group from dominating across a variety of government activities.

Does pluralism accurately describe the realities of U.S. political life? Americans rail against "special interests," a label that in the abstract is almost always used pejoratively. And we've already seen that the interest-group system is more biased than pluralists assume. Yet what one citizen considers to be a "special interest," another citizen might consider to be a legitimate organization that works to represent his or her views to the government. For example, an advocate for gun control might view the NRA as a distasteful example of a special interest, one that uses its power to produce a set of policy outcomes that the gun-control advocate finds wrong, offensive, or both. Yet a gun-rights advocate may view the NRA through a completely different lens, seeing it as an organization that bravely stands up for the Second Amendment and pushes against those who seek to limit gun owners' rights. Whether an interest is considered negatively as a "special interest" or positively as a beneficial force is, like beauty, in the eye of the beholder.

Until now, we have been discussing interest groups in general, along with the idea that they will get involved in politics to pursue their interests. However, groups can use a variety of approaches to influence politics. They can attempt to influence who serves in Congress by affecting the outcomes of elections, and they can attempt to influence policy-making activities in the government overall and in Congress in particular.

INTEREST GROUPS AND CONGRESSIONAL ELECTIONS

Interest groups attempt to influence congressional elections for a straightforward reason: if their preferred candidates are elected, then the likelihood of favorable policy outcomes greatly increases. Supporters in Congress can help pass desirable new laws, keep favorable regulations in place, and prevent changes to existing policies that the interest group likes. To influence elections, and thereby achieve these goals, interest groups rely on three main tactics: mobilizing their members, contributing money, and providing information.

Groups commonly attempt to influence elections by mobilizing their members in support of or in opposition to particular candidates. For example, AARP informs its members which senators and representatives have been most supportive of senior citizens' issues. FreedomWorks urges its members to support candidates who favor less government involvement in the economy. These calls to action can have significant effects, motivating people to vote or to become engaged in other campaign activities.

Groups also attempt to influence elections by spending money to support some candidates and defeat others. Often, they make contributions directly to candidates and to political parties. In fact, groups have donated more than

AARP is one of the largest member groups in the country. It encourages senior citizens to vote for candidates who support reforms to Medicare and Social Security, among other issues.

$1 billion to candidates for congressional and presidential elections in recent campaigns. Incumbents and aspiring members of Congress use these direct contributions to finance their campaigns, pay for travel, organize events, pay for campaign staff, place advertisements on television and radio, and more. Given the exorbitant (and growing) cost of running for national office—on average, candidates for the House of Representatives spent just under $400,000 in the 2016 election, while candidates for the Senate spent $1.3 million—a high level of donations is necessary to run a competitive campaign.

Not all campaign contributions come from interest groups, however. Individuals can also make contributions to candidates' campaigns, as can political parties and other elected officials. But groups are extremely active in the area of campaign finance. In the 2016 election cycle, for example, the top-two contributors to federal elections, Comcast and AT&T, donated just under $11.5 million to campaigns. Other groups making major contributions included Blue Cross Blue Shield ($8.8 million), the International Brotherhood of Electrical Workers ($6.7 million), Microsoft ($6.5 million), and Alphabet Inc. (Google's parent company, $6.4 million).[18] Clearly, we're not talking about petty cash!

PACs—political action committees—are the primary means by which interest groups contribute to campaigns and candidates. PACs are created to raise and spend money in support of or opposition to political candidates. They are usually tied to interest groups, with PACs representing economic groups (in particular business and labor) and noneconomic groups (such as ideological groups), and they provide a way for these groups and their members to donate to campaigns. The NRA, for example, created the NRA Political Victory Fund in the 1970s to support the cause of gun rights through campaign contributions. Other PACs are associated with industries, such as the National Beer Wholesalers Association; professions, such as the National Air Traffic Controllers Association; and companies, such as Lockheed Martin.[19] Interestingly, although many people now think of PACs mainly in terms of corporations (such as those listed in Table 12.2), PACs formed in the 1930s as a way to get around bans that existed at the time on unions donating to candidates' political campaigns. It wasn't until the 1960s and 1970s, when the idea of a separate organization to provide donations became more fully accepted, that corporations started using PACs as a regular part of their involvement in politics. Thus what started as a union strategy ended up becoming a part of politics that is now dominated by corporations.

PACs are not entirely unlimited in what they can do, in how they can spend their money, and in how they can use their contributions. To begin with, all PACs must register with the Federal Election Commission (FEC) and provide that government agency with information about their activities. In addition, they face dollar limits. PACs can contribute only $5,000 per election per year to individual congressional candidates and only $15,000 to the national parties.[20]

The political landscape surrounding campaign contributions shifted dramatically with the *Citizens United v. FEC* case in 2010. In this decision, the Supreme Court ruled that the government cannot regulate or limit independent spending on behalf of a candidate for public office. Corporations, unions, and other groups still face limitations on direct contributions to candidates, but they can make contributions that support these candidates, provided they do not coordinate with the candidates. As a result, a group can now spend an unlimited amount of money on these noncoordinated activities, such as running ads in a member's district informing constituents about a scandal the member was involved in or the member's voting record on a particular issue. Furthermore, this spending does not need to be reported to the FEC, which makes it much more difficult to track. Nonetheless, the Center for Responsive Politics, a nonpartisan organization that tracks money in politics, has estimated the amount of independent spending that has taken place since *Citizens United*. As Figure 12.2 shows, this spending has dramatically increased in recent years.

These activities have led to the creation of a new type of organization. Super PACs are limited mainly in that they are prohibited from giving money directly to candidates and parties, but they are largely unlimited in their ability to spend money to support or defeat a candidate, provided they do not coordinate with

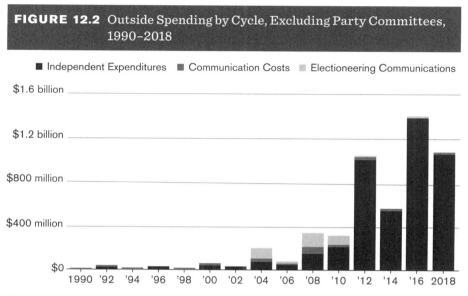

FIGURE 12.2 Outside Spending by Cycle, Excluding Party Committees, 1990–2018

■ Independent Expenditures ■ Communication Costs ■ Electioneering Communications

"Outside Spending." Center for Responsive Politics, www.opensecrets.org/outsidespending (accessed 12/14/18).

any candidates. Super PACs are deeply unpopular with the public, with 78 percent of survey respondents expressing the view that spending by super PACs should be limited by law and only 19 percent saying that such spending should not be limited.[21]

In addition to *Citizens United*, a second (and less well-known) 2010 case, *Speech-NOW.org v. Federal Elections Commission*, also had a significant effect on how money is spent in elections. In this case, the D.C. Circuit Court ruled against FEC limits on contributions from individuals to organizations, such as SpeechNOW, which pool these contributions and then spend them as independent expenditures. The court, basing its decision on the Supreme Court's *Citizens United* decision, ruled that such limits on both what individuals can give to SpeechNOW and what SpeechNOW can spend were unconstitutional, based on the First Amendment. This ruling has further increased the power of super PACs and has led to the rise of what is sometimes called "dark money," so labeled because those who donate this money can remain anonymous. Groups can form 501(c)(4) organizations, a designation the IRS gives to organizations specifically organized to promote social welfare. Although super PACs are required to disclose the names of their donors, 501(c)(4) organizations are not. Hence, these organizations provide a backdoor way to avoid disclosure requirements, because individuals can give unlimited amounts to 501(c)(4) organizations, and these organizations in turn can give money to super PACs.[22]

In addition to mobilizing voters or spending money on elections, either by contributing directly to candidates or by spending money indirectly to support those candidates, interest groups use another tactic to influence elections: they can provide information. Of course, spending is one way to provide information, as when a super PAC creates an advertisement to inform potential voters about a candidate's stances on particular issues. But groups can provide useful information even in the absence of sponsoring campaign ads. They also create *legislative scorecards* in which they identify members' specific votes on a variety of issues and then calculate a score of how well the member supports the group's positions, usually on a 0 to 100 scale, or with letter grades of A through F. The group then publicizes these scores by holding press conferences, posting information on the Internet, and mailing information about the scores to supporters.

The League of Conservation Voters (LCV), which has been creating these scorecards for decades, provides a useful example.[23] In each Congress, they identify a series of key votes that they can use to divide supporters from opponents, indicating whether a "yes" vote or a "no" vote constituted support for the environment. These votes are not chosen randomly; rather, they are chosen specifically to allow the group to identify legislators who share their views and those who do not. In 2016, for example, the Senate held a vote on whether to require providers of electricity and natural gas to meet targets for energy efficiency. It also voted on an amendment to limit the president's power to designate national monuments. In the former case, a "yes" vote was considered a pro-environment vote, while in the latter, a "no" vote was categorized the same way. Based on the votes that LCV used to compute its scorecards, Senators Brian Schatz (D-HI), Patty Murray (D-WA), and Cory Booker (D-NJ) earned scores of 100, indicating they took a pro-environment position on each issue identified by LCV. At the other end of the scale, Senators Bob Corker (R-TN), Ben Sasse (R-NE), Joni Ernst (R-IA), and Ted Cruz (R-TX) received scores of zero.

In what the organization calls its "signature program," each year LCV draws up a list of the "Dirty Dozen," borrowing from the classic film of the same name.[24] The goal is to draw attention to candidates who, in LCV's view, "consistently side against the environment."[25] The organization then touts which of these candidates were subsequently defeated in their campaigns for reelection. In 2014, for example, LCV bragged that it had helped to defeat 11 of the 12 Dirty Dozen candidates.[26]

Groups therefore can use strategies like scorecards not only to provide information to voters but also to issue threats to candidates. LCV makes it clear that it will publicize its scorecards, targeting specific members for defeat based in part on their scores. Another good example of an information-providing activity occurred in the battle over tax cuts at the end of 2017. The U.S. Chamber of Commerce, a pro-business interest group that ranks among the largest and most powerful interest groups in the United States, made clear its support for the tax

Organizations like the Chamber of Commerce and the AFL-CIO are powerful interest groups that can influence lawmakers and legislation. Here, Thomas Donahue (left), president of the Chamber of Commerce, and Richard Trumka (center), president of the AFL-CIO, meet with Senator Orrir Hatch (R-UT) before a hearing on U.S. trade policy.

cuts. It issued a public letter in which it not only stated its views about the benefits of these cuts but also made a not-so-veiled threat against senators who might vote against the bill. In short, the Chamber of Commerce put senators on notice that it would be using any votes related to the tax cuts in creating its legislative scorecard. The Chamber of Commerce boldfaced and underlined the relevant part so that senators would not miss it.[27]

Interest-group actions to publicize members' voting records, and thus to try to influence election outcomes, help us to see these activities in a new light. We know that the public sees interest groups as being overly powerful and as having too much influence on politics. But consider the actions of the U.S. Chamber of Commerce, LCV, or NRA. Gun-control activists might be furious about the purported power of the NRA; people concerned about the political power of business might cite the Chamber of Commerce as a case for placing limits on such groups, and small-business owners might be concerned about the pro-environment policies espoused by LCV. At the same time, there is no question that the NRA represents the views of many gun owners, that the Chamber of Commerce works on behalf of the owners of large businesses as well as many of the people who work there, and that environmentalists are delighted to have the

LCV highlighting which legislators do (or do not) share their views. In all of these cases, the groups are working to make sure that the people who get elected to office will represent their interests. PACs and super PACs play the same role.

LOBBYING

In addition to attempting to influence elections, interest groups engage in lobbying. But *why* do groups lobby Congress, *whom* do they lobby, and *what forms* does this lobbying take?

Why Lobby Congress?

At the most basic level, groups engage in lobbying to pursue their goals through politics. However, this simple statement buries some differences in what groups are trying to do. Lobbyists certainly try to get Congress to pass certain policies, although the popular myth that groups can simply "buy" the policies they want is almost certainly a dramatic overstatement of these groups' power.

Groups do not limit their activities to pushing for the creation of new policies. If they are satisfied with the current policies, groups often exert considerable pressure to *block* change. They're not always successful at doing so, but they have a built-in advantage over groups that are trying to effect change: those seeking change need to succeed at every stage of the legislative process, while those seeking to derail a bill have multiple opportunities to stop a bill, and they need to succeed at only one of these stages.[28]

Even when policies do change despite a group's efforts, that group might be able to forestall such changes for long periods of time. Frank Baumgartner and Bryan Jones have characterized a system in which policy remains stable for a long time before undergoing change as one of *punctuated equilibrium*. Prior to a change, policy tends to be very stable, and according to their argument, this stability is due in large part to the tactics that groups use to keep policy from changing. These tactics include lobbying members to frame policies in certain ways, preventing the consideration of new issues and perspectives, and ensuring that policy is decided in a venue that favors the group's goals.[29] Baumgartner and colleagues also point out one key reason that policy is often so difficult to change: a substantial number of powerful groups oppose such change. These groups not only lobby members to oppose changes to existing policies but also work to keep these potential changes off of the policy agenda, exercising what is sometimes called *negative agenda control* (see Chapters 5 and 6).[30]

Getting Congress to vote for change or preventing it from doing so are two key reasons that groups lobby Congress. In addition, groups lobby to change the content of a bill. Even if like-minded groups are confident that the bill will pass, it is often the case that parts of the bill can be improved. Therefore, groups might lobby members to make such changes. They might also push members to be active in shaping the legislation instead of sitting on the sidelines. As political scientist Richard Hall has documented, participation in Congress is rarely universal and never equal. Thus groups have an incentive to lobby more favorably inclined senators and representatives to be more actively involved in shaping a bill.[31]

Groups also might set their sights on policy making that takes place outside the legislative branch, particularly in the bureaucracy. In such cases, groups might observe actions that agencies are taking or planning to take and then enlist the aid of members of Congress to stop the agencies from acting or to pass legislation to overturn the agencies' actions. In 2017, a small nonprofit group named Fight for the Future used exactly this tactic to oppose the Federal Communications Commission's (FCC) decision to revoke net neutrality rules.[32] The group attempted to influence the FCC's decision directly by instigating a campaign to have supporters of net neutrality file comments against repeal with the FCC. At the same time, it lobbied members of Congress to pressure the FCC. With neither of these tactics successful, it turned to the next task: trying to convince Congress to write a law putting net neutrality rules back into effect. Other groups joined Fight for the Future, with the president of one of these other groups, Free Press, explicitly stating the groups' shared goal of pressuring Congress to lean on, and possibly overturn, the agency: "We want to raise the political costs on this issue. . . . We want members of Congress to think of this as a third-rail issue that they have to support or else they will suffer in their elections."

THEN AND NOW
THE INFLUENCE OF BUSINESS INTERESTS

Businesses have always been involved in politics for the same reason other interest groups have been involved: to pursue their goals. But we shouldn't assume that these goals have remained fixed over time. We know, for example, that today's businesses are heavily involved in attempts to change public policy. The examples of tax reform and health care discussed at the start of this chapter provide two recent and prominent instances in which businesses and their affiliated PACs attempted to influence the direction and content of public policy. Additional examples of issues important to business are easy to identify, ranging from agriculture to immigration to energy. But have businesses always been so proactive in attempting to change policy?

Surprisingly, the answer is no. There's no doubt that business have always been attentive to politics. But the nature of this attentiveness, as well as the type of activity it has produced, has changed markedly over time.[33] In the past, businesses dedicated their political efforts primarily to protecting the status quo. Their goal was to maintain existing policies that benefited them. In recent years, however, businesses have expended much more effort to change the status quo to produce more favorable policies.

This change went largely unnoticed, despite taking place in public view, until recent scholarship by Lee Drutman shined a spotlight on it.[34] Drutman illustrates this change through a brief case study of the Boeing Company, which, as one lobbyist pointed out to him, switched from playing defense (that is, protecting the status quo) 75 percent of the time in the 1970s and early 1980s to playing offense 75 percent of the time by the early 2000s. Along the way, the company expanded its staff of in-house lobbyists from just a few to 26 while also contracting with 28 outside lobbying firms, all to facilitate its change to a more proactive involvement with politics.

Boeing serves as a useful case study of what businesses and corporations were doing more generally. One lobbyist whom Drutman interviewed nicely captured this change: "I think twenty years ago, you had a Washington office to keep the government out of your business, and I think people have evolved to understand now that there are opportunities, partnerships with government. . . . We try to get out in front of issues."[35] Another put it even more succinctly: "It's gone from 'leave us alone' to 'let's work on this together.'"[36]

This change, from passive to proactive, took place over the course of several decades, at first moving gradually and then much more quickly. If we focus on the post–World War II years, we can easily understand why businesses were relatively passive: Washington, D.C., and politics in general, already had a strong pro-business tilt. The public largely shared this view, with the vast majority agreeing on the positive effects business had on society.[37] In this context, it is not surprising that a former president of General Motors, then serving in the Dwight Eisenhower administration, publicly stated, "What was good for the country was good for General Motors and vice versa." These positive views, along with routinely impressive economic growth at the time, gave business little incentive to shake things up. Indeed, perhaps the most respected study of lobbying in the era concluded that on many prominent issues, legislators were the target of almost no lobbying by business interests.[38]

The situation began to change in the 1960s and 1970s. First, social movements began to both spur and capitalize on Americans' growing distrust of all institutions, including political organizations and corporations. Second, during the Richard Nixon administration, a new series of government actions began to impose major restrictions on business. This set of actions, sometimes called *social regulation*, consisted of laws (for example, laws strengthening environmental protections, such as the National Environmental Protection Act) and the creation of regulatory agencies (for example, the Consumer Protection Safety Commission and the Occupational Safety and Health Administration). These agencies and actions reflected a change in political attitudes toward business, and they put new restrictions and regulatory hurdles in place, all of which constrained businesses' ability to act.

Initially, the reaction of business to these changes was muted—in part, as one lobbyist suggested to Drutman, because of the "general disdain for relations in Washington" among members of the business elite at the time.[39] But business leaders soon realized that the ground was shifting beneath their feet and that they needed to take action to prevent further losses. They started to be cognizant of their lack of political skill and influence, in addition to becoming aware of their need to influence national politics. It was during this period that the U.S. Chamber of Commerce began its transformation from a minor political player to a major political force, and the powerful Business Roundtable was formed.

More generally, the nation started to see the emergence of lobbying as a significant part of business activity. The number of firms with registered lobbyists in Washington, D.C., increased from 175 in 1971 to more than 2,400 a decade later, a fourteenfold increase. There were similarly large increases in related activities, including the creation of PACs, the amount of time executives spent on lobbying, and the number of companies that created internal units to address policy issues. And as Figure 12.3 shows, business lobbying—as measured by a combination of lobbying expenditures and increases in lobbying staff—continued to grow for the next few decades.

Business interest groups also changed their tactics. No longer content with the status quo, and no longer enjoying unconditional support from the public and politicians, businesses put their new employees, capabilities, and lobbyists to work—sometimes trying to prevent change, but much more frequently trying to enact new, and more favorable, policies. The election of Ronald Reagan, an ardently pro-business Republican, further emboldened them. Business began to use its newfound lobbying power to push, often successfully, for less regulation, lower tax rates, better trade policies, and other business-friendly policies. Thus, what started in the 1970s solidified in the 1980s.

Business involvement became fully entrenched in Washington politics in the 1990s and continued to grow. The fight over President Bill Clinton's health care plan was perhaps the first instance in which businesses not only lobbied for favorable policy changes but also formed coalitions in an attempt to increase their influence. In fact, one study showed that the number of health care companies engaged in lobbying in Washington, D.C., almost doubled from 1992 to 1994.[40] Success on a number of issues during this decade, including the passage of the Telecommunications Act of 1996 and the Medicare Modernization Act of 2003, further spurred business lobbying.

FIGURE 12.3 The Growth of Corporate Lobbying, 1981–2004

Lee Drutman. 2015. *The Business of America Is Lobbying: How Corporations Became Politicized and Politics Became More Corporate*, 67. New York: Oxford.

By the 2000s, the transformation was complete; the amount and nature of business lobbying had altogether changed since the 1950s. Once a minor presence on the Washington landscape, business was now heavily represented and attempted to exert influence on nearly all major policy issues. Even firms that only reluctantly entered politics initially, perhaps because of a specific issue, kept (and increased) their presence in the nation's capital. The change in the nature of involvement was just as dramatic. Once content mainly to protect the status quo, now business had become highly proactive in initiating contacts with politicians to effect significant policy changes.

CRITICAL THINKING

1. Why were businesses much less likely to have a presence in Washington, D.C., in the past? Was this a mistake on their part (i.e., would they have

benefited from a stronger presence)? If not, what has changed about politics that has made it more attractive or even necessary for them to be more active lobbyists?

2. Will the amount of business involvement in national politics continue to increase? What might it take for that level of involvement to flatten out or even decrease?

Whom to Lobby?

Given that groups have a variety of reasons to engage in lobbying, the next question to ask is, Whom do they lobby? Do they lobby members of Congress who disagree with them? Do they aim to influence those who already agree with them? Or do they take the middle ground, targeting members who are on the fence, neither strongly opposed to nor supportive of the group's position?

A case can be made for each of these options. Lobbying opponents is a straightforward proposition: these opponents do not agree with your group, so you lobby them to bring them around to your point of view. Although this strategy is direct, it is also risky. Members who are opposed to your group's position might already be entrenched in their views, having dug in to the point where it would be hard for them to take a different position, even if they come to see the merits of your case. Consequently, this approach has a low chance of success.

Alternatively, groups could lobby fence-sitters. These are legislators who have not yet taken a public position on a bill or issue, who are indifferent, who have equivocated about it, or who have sometimes favored and sometimes opposed your group. As with lobbying opponents, the goal is to persuade members to join your cause. The bar is lower in this case, as the fence-sitters have not already fully committed to an opposing position. Bringing them around to your position is therefore less costly than it is to lobby opponents.

Lobbying fence-sitters can be characterized as a strategy of *exchange*, in which groups give resources (for example, campaign donations) to a member in exchange for his or her support. Attempts to persuade fence-sitters can also be thought of in terms of *counteractive lobbying*, where the goal is still persuasion, but the motivation is slightly different. A group engages in counteractive lobbying when it worries that if it does *not* lobby these fence-sitters, opposing groups will, and they will be easy targets.

Finally, why might groups lobby their supporters? Time and money are scarce, and lobbying legislators who already support you might seem like a waste of these resources. Decades of observations by political scientists, however, show that lobbyists often do spend time and money lobbying their friends and supporters.[41] One potential explanation for this behavior is that groups might lobby friends to avoid losing the support of these legislators, perhaps because ignoring them would open them to lobbying from opposing groups. In other words, lobbying your supporters could be a form of counteractive lobbying.

A pathbreaking article by Richard Hall and Alan Deardorff provides a different theoretical explanation for the empirical observation that groups frequently lobby supporters.[42] Their starting point is the idea that the production of legislation is a costly endeavor. In addition, legislators have limited amounts of time and information, so even though they might care about multiple issues, they find it hard to become informed about all of these issues. As a result, they end up being uncertain about the outcomes that different policy choices might produce. Essentially, legislators are generalists who find it difficult to become deeply informed about various policies because of the competing demands on their time.

Groups, on the other hand, are specialists. A legislator might find it difficult, for example, to know exactly how changes in health policy are likely to affect doctor-patient relationships, but the American Medical Association is likely to be deeply informed about this issue. Because lobbyists are specialists, they can provide valuable and timely information to legislators, which means that, in Hall and Deardorff's view, they are engaged in lobbying as *legislative subsidy*. By providing legislators with valuable information, they are subsidizing legislators' knowledge—in essence, helping them free up time they can then use to participate in a range of policy-making activities: attending hearings, contributing to committee markups, offering amendments, and so on.[43] Lobbyists also enlist the aid of these members in lobbying other members. That is, a group can provide some legislators with helpful information, which those legislators can then use to attempt to persuade other senators and representatives to join their cause.

HOW WE STUDY
WHO LOBBIES WHOM?

As we have seen, groups might lobby their opponents, fence-sitters, or their supporters. But which of these approaches do groups take and under what conditions? This is the question that Marie Hojnacki and David C. Kimball examined in their perceptive article, "Organized Interests and the Decision of Whom to Lobby in Congress."[44] In approaching this topic, the authors started simply: they asked interest groups whom they lobbied. In analyzing the responses, they considered two related goals of all groups. First, groups want to increase the size of the coalition that supports them or, at a minimum, to maintain it. Second, they want to make sure that the content of the bill under consideration reflects their preferences and that the bill is likely to pass.

Given these goals, which legislators will lobbyists approach? Hojnacki and Kimball identified a series of factors that might determine the answer to this question, but two stand out. First, groups should be more likely to lobby legislators who share their views—in other words, supporters—because those legislators will be the ones they can count on to help maintain and build their coalition and who will invest the time and effort to shape legislation. Second, groups are more likely to lobby legislators who occupy institutional positions that provide them with greater ability to influence legislation and to reach out to their colleagues— namely, committee, subcommittee, and party leaders. In addition to these two main expectations, Hojnacki and Kimball also recognized that the question of whom to lobby might be affected by the group's level of resources, with wealthier groups potentially taking a different approach than those with fewer resources.

To examine whether groups target supporters and those in positions of power, Hojnacki and Kimball chose four policy areas—product liability, financial services, criminal justice reform, and grazing rights—and sent questionnaires to 648 groups that lobby on those issues.[45] One-third of those groups responded by indicating whether they had lobbied on those issues, and if so, which members of Congress they had lobbied. The data thus created a series of group-legislator pairs. Based on the answers to the questionnaire, the researchers identified whether lobbying took place within each pair. For example, the researchers examined whether the American Ranchers Association lobbied Representative Joe Barton (R-TX), or Representative Lucille Roybal-Allard (D-CA), or any other legislator. For each pair, the researchers also identified the group's level of resources and measured whether the group had a strong presence in the member's district (for example, a large number of constituents working in that field or a business located there). Finally, the researchers identified whether the legislator in each pair held an influential institutional position—namely, party leader, committee, or subcommittee chair—and whether he or she had previously indicated support for the group's positions (which the researchers determined by examining past votes in each specific policy area).

At this point Hojnacki and Kimball had all the information they needed to analyze why groups choose to lobby some legislators and not others. That is, they knew whether each lobbying organization lobbied each legislator; whether the group was resource rich or resource poor; whether the group had a strong presence in the legislator's district; whether the legislator held an influential position; and whether the legislator could be classified as a supporter, opponent, or in between. They then used this information to identify and explain groups' lobbying decisions.

TABLE 12.3 Whom to Lobby?

Legislator's Prior Position	Likelihood of Lobbying
Has supported the group	Most likely
Uncertain	Less likely
Has opposed the groups	Least likely

Adapted from Marie Hojnacki and David C. Kimball. 1998. "Organized Interests and the Decision of Whom to Lobby in Congress." *American Political Science Review* 92 (4): 775–90.

Table 12.3 summarizes their main findings. Most importantly, they found that groups are most likely to lobby supporters and least likely to lobby opponents, with fence-sitters in between. The data support the idea that groups turn to their supporters in Congress for help. The researchers also found that groups frequently focus their lobbying efforts on committee chairs, but not subcommittee chairs or party leaders.

Overall, these findings suggest that groups take the logical step of lobbying legislators who agree with them and who are in a position to help further their goals. However, this general conclusion masks some of the nuances of Hojnacki and Kimball's findings. For instance, groups were more likely to lobby a member of Congress if they had a strong presence in that member's district, even if that member was an opponent.[46] In addition, groups with more resources were more likely to lobby opponents and fence-sitters than groups with fewer resources, and resource-rich groups were less likely to bias their efforts toward committee chairs. These observations make intuitive sense: if a group had unlimited resources, then it would lobby all legislators. Taken together, these findings suggest that while groups do, on average, target their supporters, there are also times when they find it in their interest, and within their capabilities, to lobby fence-sitters and opponents.[47]

CRITICAL THINKING

1. Would we expect the type of lobbying—that is, whether groups lobby their friends, fence-sitters, or foes—to vary by policy area? If so, what types of policies might cause groups to focus on foes rather than fence-sitters, or fence-sitters rather than friends?
2. If you were a member of a group with limited resources, what might cause you to focus your lobbying efforts on fence-sitters rather than friends?
3. When might you expect legislators to be willing to change their position, based on lobbying from interest groups?

What Forms Does Lobbying Take?

We have now seen that groups lobby Congress for a variety of reasons: to change laws, to prevent change, to shape the content of bills, and to spur oversight of agencies. And we know that they lobby supporters most frequently, but also turn to fence-sitters and opponents when they can and when the conditions are right. What we have not addressed yet is how they actually go about lobbying legislators. That is, what forms does lobbying take?

INSIDE LOBBYING   Political scientists distinguish between *inside lobbying* and *outside lobbying.* Inside lobbying, also known as *direct lobbying*, involves groups approaching legislators and their staff to make requests. These requests are sometimes supplemented with donations (or promises of future donations) to a member's reelection campaign. Often, direct lobbying is hidden from view, occurring in legislators' offices rather than in a public forum. At times, though, it can take place in public, as when a committee chair invites a group to testify at a congressional hearing on behalf of a policy proposal. Inside lobbying also includes any activity in which groups invite legislators to participate in various activities where the group gets a chance to make its case. In the past, these activities frequently involved travel (perhaps to warm, sunny, and enticing places like Hawaii or the Bahamas) or centered on lavish meals, but congressional reforms passed in 2007 prohibited travel-based lobbying and placed restrictions on meals. Still, groups often find loopholes in these rules and regulations.

To engage in inside lobbying, groups either use an in-house employee or hire someone outside the group to lobby on their behalf. Lobbyists who are not in-house work as professional lobbyists, often as part of a broader lobbying firm or a legal firm with lobbying branches. Rather than representing a single client, external lobbyists might represent several groups at the same time.[48]

Some professional lobbyists are former employees of federal agencies, former staff for members of Congress, or former members of Congress. These lobbyists are sometimes called *revolvers* because they revolve in and out of government, often using their personal connections to acquire lucrative lobbying contracts. The phenomenon of former members of Congress moving into the lobbying world is not a new one, but it has increased dramatically in recent decades. As Figure 12.4 shows, in the 1970s, well under 10 percent of departing members of the House and Senate became lobbyists after retiring from Congress. By the 2010s, that rate increased dramatically to more than 30 percent for House retirees and more than 50 percent for Senate retirees.[49]

Studies have revealed that revolvers, who can credibly claim to have better access to current politicians than other lobbyists, are paid more than their colleagues and get better results for their clients.[50] In part, these revolvers produce

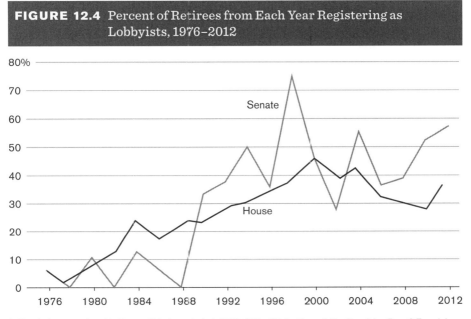

FIGURE 12.4 Percent of Retirees from Each Year Registering as Lobbyists, 1976–2012

Jeffrey L. Lazarus, Amy McKay, and Lindsey Herbel. 2016. "Who Walks through the Revolving Door? Examining the Lobbying Activity of Former Members of Congress." *Interest Groups and Advocacy* 5(1): 82–100.

better results because they are more actively involved with lobbying for bills that advance beyond the committee stage (and that therefore already have a greater chance of success). In addition, many other lobbyists are policy specialists, but revolvers tend to be more informed about the political strategies that can make or break a bill: how party leaders use negative agenda tactics, how a bill manager's marks are finalized, how party leaders negotiate unanimous consent agreements, when and how amendment trees get filled, and so on. Knowledge of political strategies overlaps with access to legislators, of course, but revolvers have taken part in these actions in the past and know from experience how they work.[51] Indeed, a disproportionate number of revolvers served as party leaders, committee chairs, or members of the powerful Appropriations or Ways and Means Committees during their time in Congress.[52]

The role of revolvers in lobbying raises a host of concerns. To begin with, because revolvers are often paid more and deliver better results (because of their political access), they have the potential to amplify representational disparities among interest groups. If only the wealthiest groups can afford to hire revolvers, the result is problematic for pluralism, because it means that only those groups with the most money can benefit from the best lobbyists. More generally, it raises the specter of current members of Congress (and staffers) thinking about the lucrative lobbying position they might pursue later, rather than their constituents' needs or the broader public interest.

Members of Congress also frequently become consultants in the lobbying world after leaving office. Former Speaker John Boehner followed this path. As reported at the time in the *Washington Post*, "Boehner will be a 'strategic adviser' at [lobbying firm Squire Patton Boggs]—a common designation for former legislators who take K Street jobs after leaving office but do not register to lobby. The firm said Boehner will not lobby Congress and will instead advise corporate clients on global business development."[53] The last sentence is key: if a former member does not register to lobby, then he or she technically is not in violation of "revolving door" laws (also known as "cooling-off periods"). Former members can be particularly well positioned to lobby current members of Congress because they have floor, dining, parking, and gym privileges. In fact, they may also receive commissions for lobbying even while receiving their congressional pensions.[54] Because of the potential for problems ranging from the appearance of impropriety to outright corruption, in 2007 Congress passed the Honest Leadership and Open Government Act, which lengthened the cooling-off period for former members. Although this act has helped to counter some of the potential problems associated with former legislators lobbying current legislators, some analysis has suggested that the act has merely driven lobbyists "underground" because they choose not to register.[55]

OUTSIDE LOBBYING In contrast to inside lobbying, outside lobbying is an indirect means of lobbying in which interest groups try to increase pressure on a legislator by getting the legislator's constituents involved in the issue. Outside lobbying can include a variety of tactics, such as getting constituents to make phone calls, send letters, and participate in town halls. Groups spur these activities by sponsoring protests, advertising on television or radio, conducting phone campaigns, sponsoring meetings, and using social media. The main goal of outside lobbying is to generate activity at the grassroots level to send a signal to a legislator about the strength or opposition to an issue among his or her constituents.

Sometimes, groups find it easy to send these signals, especially when the support or opposition in a district is latent and simply needs to be activated. But other times, it can be more difficult, with the costs of sending the desired signal rising whenever constituent support is harder to find. As a result, groups with broader bases of support are more likely to use this approach. For example, labor unions frequently engage in outside lobbying (sometimes by organizing protests), but corporations rarely do.

An insightful analysis by Ken Kollman confirms and explains this pattern. Kollman draws on a survey of interest groups to show that inside versus outside tactics tended to cluster by group type, with labor groups relying more on outside lobbying while businesses use inside lobbying. Among groups that rely on outside lobbying, labor unions and public interest groups employ a wider variety of outside tactics. More generally, groups find it easier to use outside lobbying when they have broad public support for their positions. For example, despite being a relatively small group with only 10 employees, the leaders of Fight for the Future (the group supportive of net neutrality rules) took advantage of the widespread public support for these rules—and their technological savvy—to get the public to make more than 800,000 calls to Congress and send 6.7 million e-mails to lawmakers.[56]

In contrast, groups with less popular or even more specialized goals see more advantage in outside lobbying. They try to follow the same playbook as groups with more popular goals, sending signals to legislators about support in their district, whether this support exists or not. This type of activity is sometimes referred to as *astroturf lobbying* to distinguish it from real *grassroots lobbying*. Fortunately, members of Congress usually can discern the true level of support in their districts. For example, an astroturf approach might consist of groups organizing haphazard call-ins in which constituents are ushered into a room where they can press a phone button that connects them with a member's office. At this point, they are supposed to state their support for the group's position, but the constituents often do not know what to say once they have a staffer on the line.

Although inside and outside lobbying are frequently considered separate tactics, they can and do work together. The NRA provides a good example. Although the group certainly engages in inside lobbying tactics, such as giving direct contributions to legislators, this aspect of the NRA's influence can be (and often is) overstated. In the 2016 election cycle, the NRA directly contributed $1.1 million to candidates for federal office (with 99 percent of that total going to Republican candidates). That may sound like a lot of money until you realize that candidates received a total of $1.7 *billion* in direct contributions overall, which makes the NRA contributions seem miniscule. Yet the group is regarded as exceptionally powerful on Capitol Hill. Why? For starters, it energetically engages in outside lobbying, working hard to keep its members informed and motivating them to vote and engage in other political activities, such as protests, based on their views about guns. As a result, the NRA then has more power when it engages in inside lobbying, as it can credibly point to its large and motivated membership.

Does Lobbying Work?

What do lobbyists get in return for the effort they put into lobbying? Many people assume that there is some sort of quid pro quo in which groups give legislators money and in return legislators give groups votes. Does such a quid pro quo exist? The answer to this question is somewhat complicated, but the evidence points to "no." Various studies have used sophisticated statistical techniques to look for evidence of such a relationship and have not found it.[57]

This finding, or, more appropriately, the lack of a finding, might be comforting to those worried about the influence of money on politics. But it is puzzling. Why wouldn't contributions lead to votes that are consistent with a group's goals? And why would a group continue to donate money to campaigns and to expend significant resources to lobby members if doing so doesn't produce the votes that it wants?

One possible explanation for the lack of a relationship between money and votes lies in the realities of outside lobbying. Studies of outside lobbying, as well as studies of group activity and influence overall, suggest that gaining influence with members of Congress is a more nuanced process than one based entirely on group resources. Some groups might not have as much money as others, but that does not mean they lack power and influence. For example, some groups achieve power by virtue of having a huge membership base. Although these groups might have smaller bank accounts, and therefore cannot afford higher-priced and more sophisticated lobbyists, they can still exercise plenty of influence. Vigorous outside lobbying can build on these groups' strength of numbers, allowing them to further their aims and counter the efforts of wealthier groups that make more donations.

Another explanation is that even if groups do not directly get votes in exchange for contributions, that doesn't mean they don't get anything. What they do get is *access*. Legislators are exceptionally busy, and it can be extremely difficult to get on their schedules. But given their essential need for cash to fund their campaigns, legislators make time to meet with groups that have made campaign contributions in the past and may do so again in the future. Few current or former members of Congress were as blunt about this relationship as Mick Mulvaney, a former representative from South Carolina. When later serving in the Trump administration as both the director of the Office of Management and Budget and an interim director of the Consumer Financial Protection Bureau, Mulvaney told a group of lobbyists, "We had a hierarchy in my office in Congress. If you're a lobbyist who never gave us money, I didn't talk to you. If you're a lobbyist who gave us money, I might talk to you."[58] These meetings are essential for groups, as they provide the opportunity to lobby legislators and to seek their support. In addition, as mentioned earlier, evidence suggests that revolvers (those who formerly served in Congress) are especially adept at gaining access.[59]

In short, even if money doesn't buy votes, it can lead to greater access. Access can then provide groups with the opportunity to make their case about provisions a particular bill should include, to explain why the legislator should spend time on a policy, and to provide information about the policy that the legislator

The NRA is a powerful organization not only in that it is able to make campaign contributions to candidates that support gun ownership but also because it mobilizes its members to protest stricter gun control.

can then pass along to colleagues. Beyond that, it is important to keep in mind that there is more to representation than just voting. Indeed, one of the fundamental decisions that legislators make, repeatedly, is whether to be involved in an issue at all.[60] That is, legislators can engage in a variety of *participatory* acts that consume their limited time. For instance, depending on their priorities, legislators can choose to focus more on particular issues by spending more time and legislative resources on ushering those bills through committee.

Along these lines, an innovative article by Richard Hall and Frank Wayman contends that to find influence, one must look at stages before the final floor outcome—that is, at stages where bills are developed, debated, and revised.[61] Given the importance of these earlier stages, which have dramatic effects on the shape and content of bills, lobbyists have an incentive to mobilize their supporters to act during these periods. Thus, lobbyists do not lobby or donate to change votes; rather, they do so to mobilize their supporters to participate in the earlier stages, when bills are first being formed. In analyzing PAC donations and participation, Hall and Wayman found that PAC contributions from particular groups were associated with greater committee activity by particular members.[62]

Another way to assess whether powerful groups get what they want is to look at *outcomes* rather than individual votes. Do groups with more resources get the policy outcomes they desire? Again, the conventional wisdom is that big money buys policy, with politicians in the pocket of rich interests. Media reports feed this perception, focusing on campaign contributions and the even larger amounts spent on lobbying, which confirms that groups are highly active, business interests are predominant, and large amounts of cash flow through the system.

The issue of whether more resources lead to favored outcomes is a particularly thorny one to unpack, but a team of talented researchers headed by political scientist Frank Baumgartner undertook a massive data-collection project designed to answer this question.[63] The researchers examined lobbying in the 1990s and 2000s, focusing on a set of policy issues that ranged from high-salience, high-conflict issues (for example, the attempt in the 1990s to normalize trade relations with China) to less prominent issues, such as efforts to promote American production of recreational marine craft (i.e., yachts).

They began by drawing a random sample of lobbyists who, based on the lobby disclosure reports that interest groups had filed, were involved in these issues. After identifying these groups, the researchers asked them to point out the most recent federal issue on which they had been active. This request helped to ensure that the results were likely to include most of the major issues during the years the researchers examined, as lobbyists were certain to have pressed their case on these issues. They then interviewed other groups and individuals active on these issues, asking them what policy goals they were seeking. Finally, they examined newspapers, political journals, and other sources to ascertain whether each group got what it wanted.

Overall, the researchers looked at 98 different issues where groups sought to change policy. In 58 of these cases, there was no change in policy; in 13 cases, there was marginal change; and in 27 cases, there was significant change. Surprisingly—at least from the perspective of the conventional wisdom—they found almost no relationship between a group's resources (measured in a variety of ways) and whether the group got what it wanted. As the researchers succinctly stated, their results "will disappoint those who assume that the wealthy interests can walk into the Washington offices of our elected officials and get what they demand." In other words, they found that neither money nor other resources appear to buy outcomes.[64] As Table 12.4 shows, there is virtually no correlation between whether a group has more resources and whether it gets the policy outcomes it wants, in either the current Congress or the following one. Whether spending more money through PACs or on lobbying, employing more former government officials as lobbyists ("covered officials"), having greater assets, or having more members in their group—none of these had much effect on getting the policy outcomes the group wanted.

The finding that groups with more resources do not have a major advantage in terms of changing policy may sound surprising, but perhaps it shouldn't. To

TABLE 12.4	Correlation between Resources and Outcomes	

How likely is the group with more of each resource to get the policy it wants?

Resource	In the Current Congress	In the Next Congress
PAC spending	Not at all	Not at all
Lobbying spending	Not at all	Not at all
Covered officials	Not at all	Very slightly
Association assets	Not at all	Not at all
Business assets	Very slightly	Not at all
Members	Not at all	Not at all

Adapted from Frank R. Baumgartner, Jeffrey M. Berry, Marie Hojnacki, David C. Kimball, and Beth L. Leech. 2009. *Lobbying and Policy Change: Who Wins, Who, Loses, and Why*, Table 10.3. Chicago: University of Chicago Press.

begin with, there usually are major groups on both sides of an issue, and only one side will win. Indeed, when resource-rich groups are unopposed, they are much more likely to win. Furthermore, lobbying rarely involves creating a new policy from scratch. Instead, it reflects an attempt to change policy in one direction or another, and the preferences of the more powerful group might already be baked into the existing policy. Finally, many issues never get raised in the first place. Indeed, keeping issues off the agenda might be the greatest power that groups can exert, and this power remains largely hidden from view.

In sum, the finding that powerful groups do not get their way when they seek policy change remains extremely important and counterintuitive. At the same time, however, we cannot say that groups overall do not affect congressional policy making.[65]

Limits on Lobbying

The continued presence of lobbyists, the vast sums of money spent on lobbying, the potential for influence, the perception of bias, and the possibility of corruption—all of these are potentially matters for concern. It is worth keeping in mind, however, that groups have an incentive to follow the rules and to provide accurate information to members of Congress. As one lobbyist noted, "As long as the members believe I'm honest and play straight with them, I'll have a chance to make my case."[66]

Given that politicians and groups both benefit from lobbying, and recognizing the potential for problems, it should come as no surprise that politicians and reformers have struggled to determine how to allow for lobbying and at the same time restrain it. As former senator Robert Byrd (D-WV) observed in 1987, "Congress has always had, and always will have, lobbyists and lobbying. We could not adequately consider our workload without them. . . . At the same time, the history of the institution demonstrates the need for eternal vigilance to ensure that lobbyists do not abuse their role."[67]

Outright bribery has long been illegal at both the state and national levels. A series of other laws have attempted more nuanced approaches to regulate the conduct of lobbying, usually by restricting lobbying activity (limits on gift giving, limits on campaign donations, cooling-off periods for revolvers) or by requiring disclosure of activities. Such laws include the Foreign Agents Registration Act of 1938, the Federal Regulation of Lobbying Act of 1946, the Federal Election Campaign Act of 1971, the Lobby Disclosure Act (LDA) of 1995, and the Honest Leadership and Open Government Act of 2007, among others.

Some aspects of these laws have been useful, but the courts have nullified other parts of them. For example, in *United States v. Harris* (1954), the courts overturned large portions of the original Regulation of Lobbying Act and left federal lobbying disclosure largely ineffective until the passage of the LDA in 1995. In addition, groups constantly seek and find loopholes. Some lobbyists, for example, might not register to avoid laws that apply only to registered lobbyists. As Figure 12.1 shows on p. 424, since peaking in 2007, the number of registered lobbyists has steadily declined, partly in response to limits that President Barack Obama placed on their involvement in the activities of federal agencies. That executive order was partially repealed in 2014. In addition, although contingent fees—in which a lobbyist is paid a bonus based on a particular outcome—are illegal in most states and are illegal for contractors bidding for federal projects, it remains legal to lobby Congress on a contingent basis.

We should also recognize that while groups make demands on legislators, the reverse is also true. In extreme circumstances, legislators can be just as guilty of excess and malfeasance as law-breaking lobbyists. In 1989, for example, anti-tax activist Grover Norquist formed a group to advise—or, more accurately, pressure—lobbying firms to hire Republican staffers and former members.[68] It is not clear how successful the group has been, but there are reports that congressional leaders in the late 1990s threatened to stall bills or withhold access if lobbying firms hired the wrong individuals.[69] In a related vein, the House ethics committee "formally admonished Tom DeLay (R-TX) in 1998 for pressuring the Electronics Industry Association *not* to hire former representative Dave McCurdy (D-OK) to run the organization, as DeLay instead wanted his former colleague Bill Paxon (R-NY) to get the job."[70] This arrangement is sometimes called "pay to play," because lobbyists have to do something (make a donation, hire someone, etc.) to gain political access.[71] In 2002, it was reported that

Norquist was compiling the political contributions records of hundreds of lobbyists in Washington, D.C., with the goal of using the list to control political access by ensuring that lobbyists made enough campaign donations to the right individuals.[72] It is not clear whether the project was anything more than just a list, but the Honest and Open Leadership Act of 2007 explicitly prevents members from trying to influence the hiring decisions of lobbying or other firms.

CONCLUSION

The presence of interest groups in the congressional process was foretold in the early days of our republic. The Framers knew groups would exist; the question was how to prevent them from dominating the political process. At the same time, it has long been recognized that despite this potential problem associated with the presence of groups in politics, there are also potential benefits.

These problems and benefits directly mirror two of the main themes of this book. The problem of undue group influence relates to the issue of governance. If we were to imagine an ideal version of the congressional process, one in which Congress performs its governing role in the most efficient and unbiased way possible, it would be a version in which well-informed members make policy decisions based on criteria that include efficiency, which policy proposals are best for their constituents, and which policy proposals are best for the nation as a whole. To the extent that groups interfere with any of these criteria, groups are exerting a negative influence on Congress's governing function.

That scenario portrays groups in a negative light. But it is not the only potential viewpoint. Groups also perform a necessary function, one that pluralists have long recognized: they help individuals who are members of those groups to be heard in Congress. On their own, these citizens might not be heard. Banding together, they are much more likely to be recognized. These groups thus represent individuals, and in doing so, they increase the likelihood that Congress will hear their voices. Thus groups can enhance Congress's representative function. Furthermore, they can do so by providing necessary information to congressional decision-makers.

Which scenario is true? The answer is almost certainly both. Ultimately, there is a trade-off, and the extent to which groups are either a negative force or a positive force depends on whether the observer places more weight on Congress's governing roles or its representative roles.

Discussion Questions

1. On balance, do the benefits of interest-group lobbying of Congress outweigh the costs?

2. The *Citizens United* and *SpeechNOW.org* cases have both led to increased campaign spending, much of which cannot be traced back to individual donors. Given that the public tends to disapprove of the amount of money spent on election campaigns, but members of Congress tend to benefit from this money, are there any circumstances under which Congress might act to limit the amount of money in elections?

3. The chapter mentions that groups such as the NRA and the LCV issue legislative scorecards, which show how members have voted on issues relevant to these groups. Because the public generally has low levels of information about politics, would we expect these scorecards to have any influence on how members of the public vote or on how members of Congress act? Might these scorecards be contributing to polarization?

4. Should Congress place stricter limits on the ability of representatives and senators to work as lobbyists after they retire? What would be the best arguments in favor of such limits? What would be the best arguments against them?

5. If lobbying does not tend to produce the outcomes that interest groups want, why do these groups continue to spend so much time, effort, and money on lobbying?

Appendix

PARTY CONTROL OF CONGRESS: 1789–2021

| | Unified Control of Government | | Divided Government |

Congress	Years	Senate			House			President
		Pro-Administration	Anti-Administration	Other	Pro-Administration	Anti-Administration	Other	
1	1789–91	18	8	—	37	28	—	George Washington
2	1791–93	16	13	—	39	30	—	Washington
3	1793–95	16	14	—	51	54	—	Washington
		Federalists	Jeffersonian Republicans	Other	Federalists	Jeffersonian Republicans	Other	
4	1795–97	21	11	—	47	59	—	Washington
5	1797–99	22	10	—	57	49	—	John Adams
6	1799–1801	22	10	—	60	46	—	Adams
7	1801–03	15	17	—	38	68	—	Thomas Jefferson
8	1803–05	9	25	—	39	103	—	Jefferson
9	1805–07	7	27	—	28	114	—	Jefferson
10	1807–09	6	28	—	26	116	—	Jefferson
11	1809–11	7	27	—	50	92	—	James Madison
12	1811–13	6	30	—	36	107	—	Madison
13	1813–15	8	28	—	68	114	—	Madison
14	1815–17	12	26	—	64	119	—	Madison
15	1817–19	12	30	—	39	146	—	James Monroe
16	1819–21	9	37	—	26	160	—	Monroe
17	1821–23	4	44	—	32	155	—	Monroe
		Adams-Clay Republicans	Jackson Republicans	Other	Adams-Clay Republicans	Jackson Republicans	Other	
18	1823–25	17	31	—	72	64	77	Monroe
19	1825–27	22	26	—	109	104	—	John Quincy Adams
20	1827–29	21	27	—	100	113	—	Quincy Adams
		Anti-Jacksons	Jacksons	Other	Anti-Jacksons	Jacksons	Other	
21	1829–31	23	25	—	72	136	5	Andrew Jackson
22	1831–33	22	24	2	66	126	21	Jackson

Congress	Years	Senate			House			President
23	1833–35	26	20	2	63	143	34	Jackson
24	1835–37	24	26	2	75	143	24	Jackson
		Democrats	Whigs	Other	Democrats	Whigs	Other	
25	1837–39	35	17	—	128	100	12	Martin Van Buren
26	1839–41	30	22	—	125	109	8	Van Buren
27	1841–43	22	29	—	98	142	2	William Henry Harrison/John Tyler
28	1843–45	23	29	—	147	72	4	Tyler
29	1845–47	34	22	—	142	79	6	James K. Polk
30	1847–49	38	21	1	110	116	4	Polk
31	1849–51	35	25	2	113	108	11	Zachary Taylor/ Millard Fillmore
32	1851–53	36	23	3	127	85	21	Fillmore
33	1853–55	38	22	2	157	71	6	Franklin Pierce
		Democrats	Oppositions	Other	Democrats	Oppositions	Other	
34	1855–57	39	21	2	83	100	51	Pierce
		Democrats	Republicans	Other	Democrats	Republicans	Other	
35	1857–59	41	20	5	132	90	15	James Buchanan
36	1859–61	38	26	2	83	116	39	Buchanan
37	1861–63	15	31	3	44	108	31	Abraham Lincoln
38	1863–65	10	33	9	72	85	27	Lincoln
39	1865–67	11	39	4	38	136	16	Lincoln/Andrew Johnson
40	1867–69	9	57	—	47	173	4	Johnson
41	1869–71	12	62	—	67	171	5	Ulysses S. Grant
42	1871–73	17	56	1	104	136	3	Grant
43	1873–75	19	47	7	88	199	5	Grant
44	1875–77	28	46	1	182	103	8	Grant
45	1877–79	35	40	1	155	136	2	Rutherford B. Hayes

(continued)

PARTY CONTROL OF CONGRESS: 1789–2021 *(continued)*

Congress	Years	Senate			House			President
		Democrats	Republicans	Other	Democrats	Republicans	Other	
46	1879–81	42	33	1	141	132	21	Hayes
47	1881–83	37	37	2	128	151	14	James A. Garfield/ Chester A. Arthur
48	1883–85	36	38	2	196	117	12	Arthur
49	1885–87	34	42	—	182	141	2	Grover Cleveland
50	1887–89	37	39	—	167	152	6	Cleveland
51	1889–91	37	51	—	152	179	1	Benjamin Harrison
52	1891–93	39	47	—	238	86	8	Harrison
53	1893–95	44	40	4	218	124	14	Cleveland
54	1895–97	40	44	6	93	254	10	Cleveland
55	1897–99	34	44	12	124	206	27	William McKinley
56	1899–1901	26	53	10	161	187	9	McKinley
57	1901–03	31	55	4	151	197	9	McKinley/Theodore Roosevelt
58	1903–05	33	57	—	178	208	—	T. Roosevelt
59	1905–07	33	57	—	136	250	—	T. Roosevelt
60	1907–09	31	61	—	164	222	—	T. Roosevelt
61	1909–11	32	61	—	172	219	—	William Howard Taft
62	1911–13	41	51	—	228	161	1	Taft
63	1913–15	51	44	1	291	127	17	Woodrow Wilson
64	1915–17	56	40	—	230	196	9	Wilson
65	1917–19	53	42	—	216	210	6	Wilson
66	1919–21	47	49	—	190	240	3	Wilson
67	1921–23	37	59	—	131	301	1	Warren G. Harding
68	1923–25	43	51	2	205	225	5	Calvin Coolidge
69	1925–27	39	56	1	183	247	4	Coolidge
70	1927–29	46	49	1	195	237	3	Coolidge
71	1929–31	39	56	1	167	267	1	Herbert Hoover

Congress	Years	Senate			House			President
		Democrats	Republicans	Other	Democrats	Republicans	Other	
72	1931–33	47	48	1	220	214	1	Hoover
73	1933–35	60	35	1	313	117	5	Franklin D. Roosevelt
74	1935–37	69	25	2	319	103	10	F.D. Roosevelt
75	1937–39	76	16	4	331	89	13	F.D. Roosevelt
76	1939–41	69	23	4	261	164	4	F.D. Roosevelt
77	1941–43	66	28	2	268	162	5	F.D. Roosevelt
78	1943–45	58	37	1	218	208	4	F.D. Roosevelt
79	1945–47	56	38	1	242	190	2	Harry S. Truman
80	1947–49	45	51	—	188	245	1	Truman
81	1949–51	54	42	—	263	171	1	Truman
82	1951–53	49	47	—	234	199	1	Truman
83	1953–55	47	48	1	211	221	1	Dwight D. Eisenhower
84	1955–57	48	47	1	232	203	—	Eisenhower
85	1957–59	49	47	—	233	200	—	Eisenhower
86	1959–61	65	35	—	284	153	—	Eisenhower
87	1961–63	65	35	—	263	174	—	John F. Kennedy
88	1963–65	67	35	—	258	177	—	Kennedy/Lyndon B. Johnson
89	1965–67	68	32	—	295	140	—	Johnson
90	1967–69	64	36	—	247	187	—	Johnson
91	1969–71	57	43	—	243	192	—	Richard M. Nixon
92	1971–73	54	44	2	254	180	—	Nixon
93	1973–75	56	42	2	239	192	1	Nixon/Gerald R. Ford
94	1975–77	60	37	2	291	144	—	Ford
95	1977–79	61	38	1	292	143	—	Jimmy Carter
96	1979–81	58	41	1	276	157	—	Carter
97	1981–83	46	53	1	243	192	—	Ronald Reagan

(continued)

PARTY CONTROL OF CONGRESS: 1789–2021 *(continued)*

Congress	Years	Senate			House			President
		Democrats	Republicans	Other	Democrats	Republicans	Other	
98	1983–85	45	55	—	267	168	—	Reagan
99	1985–87	47	53	—	252	183	—	Reagan
100	1987–89	55	45	—	258	177	—	Reagan
101	1989–91	55	45	—	260	175	—	George H.W. Bush
102	1991–93	57	43	—	268	166	1	Bush
103	1993–95	56	44	—	258	176	1	Bill Clinton
104	1995–97	47	53	—	204	230	1	Clinton
105	1997–99	45	55	—	207	227	1	Clinton
106	1999–2001	45	55	—	211	223	1	Clinton
*107	2001–03	50	49	1	210	222	3	George W. Bush
108	2003–05	48	51	1	205	229	1	Bush
109	2005–07	44	55	1	202	232	1	Bush
110	2007–09	49	49	2	233	202	—	Bush
111	2009–11	58	40	2	257	178	—	Barack Obama
112	2011–13	51	47	2	193	242	—	Obama
113	2013–15	53	45	2	200	233	—	Obama
114	2015–17	44	54	2	188	247	—	Obama
115	2017–19	47	51	2	193	236	—	Donald Trump
**116	2019–21	45	53	2	235	199	—	Trump

*The Republicans controlled the Senate in the 107th Congress, and thus had unified majority control of government until May 24, 2001, when Senator Jim Jeffords (VT) left the Republican Party to become an Independent and caucus with the Democrats. The Jeffords switch gave the Democrats organizational control of the Senate for the remainder of the Congress.
**One race in the House of Representatives was undecided as of January 4, 2019.

Endnotes

Chapter 1: Representation and Governing in a Separated System

1. For a list of reconciliation bills, see Molly E. Reynolds. 2018. "What If You Could Pick the Pivot? Budget Reconciliation and Pivotal Politics in the Contemporary Congress." *Journal of Politics*, https://doi.org/10.1086/697948.
2. Robert Saldin. 2010. "Healthcare Reform: A Prescription for the 2010 Republican Landslide?" *The Forum* 8(4), Article 10.
3. William Branigin. November 3, 2010. "Obama Reflects on 'Shellacking' in Midterm Elections." *Washington Post*.
4. Hanna F. Pitkin. 1967. *The Concept of Representation*. Berkeley, CA: University of California Press.
5. Alexander Hamilton, James Madison, and John Jay. 2012. *The Federalist Papers*. Edited by Richard Beeman. New York: Penguin Books. Hamilton wrote 51 of the essays, Madison 29, and Jay 5.
6. Hamilton, Madison, and Jay, *The Federalist Papers*, no. 10.
7. Robert A. Dahl. 2006. *A Preface to Democratic Theory, Expanded Edition*. Chicago, IL: University of Chicago Press; Christopher H. Achen and Larry M. Bartels. 2017. *Democracy for Realists: Why Elections Do Not Produce Responsive Government*. Princeton, NJ: Princeton University Press.
8. Hamilton, Madison, and Jay, *The Federalist Papers*, no. 51.
9. Hamilton, Madison, and Jay, *The Federalist Papers*, no. 51.
10. Among the historic New Deal legislation originating with Congress were the Federal Emergency Relief Act (1933), the Banking Act (1933; also known as the Glass-Steagall Act), the Tennessee Valley Authority Act (1933), and the National Labor Relations Act (also known as the Wagner Act, 1935). See Patrick J. Maney. 1998. *The Roosevelt Presence: The Life and Legacy of FDR*. Berkeley, CA: University of California Press.
11. To black men (Fifteenth Amendment in 1870), women (Nineteenth Amendment in 1920), and teenage voters (Twenty-Sixth Amendment in 1971).
12. For blacks (Twenty-Fourth Amendment in 1964 and Voting Rights Act in 1965), handicapped voters (Voting Accessibility for the Elderly and Handicapped Act of 1984 and the Americans with Disabilities Act of 1990), and the military (Uniformed and Overseas Citizens Absentee Voting Act of 1986).

13. The Hatch Act (1939), the National Voter Registration Act or "Motor Voter" Act (1993), and the Help Americans Vote Act (2002).

14. Through the Federal Election Campaign Act (1971 and amendments in 1974) and the Bipartisan Campaign Reform Act (2002), which invited action by the Supreme Court in the *Citizens United* decision.

15. Examples include the War Powers Act (1973) and the Congressional Budget and Impoundment Control Act (1974).

16. Thomas Kaplan and Alan Rappeport. December 19, 2017. "Republican Tax Bill Passes Senate in 51–48 Vote." *New York Times*, www.nytimes.com/2017/12/19/us/politics/tax-bill-vote-congress.html (accessed 5/29/18).

17. Scott Clement and Emily Guskin. December 13, 2017. "Exit Poll Results: How Different Groups Voted in Alabama." *Washington Post*, www.washingtonpost.com/graphics/2017/politics/alabama-exit-polls/?utm_term=.5fa108dfc5a8 (accessed 5/29/18).

18. Woodrow Wilson. [1885], 1981. *Congressional Government: A Study in American Politics*. Baltimore: Johns Hopkins University Press.

19. A roll call vote is one in which each member of Congress votes "yea" or "nay" when her name is called, so that the names of those voting on each side are recorded. The earliest statistical study of congressional roll call voting was Abbott Lawrence Lowell. 1902. *The Influence of Party upon Legislation in England and America*. American Historical Association.

20. Stuart Rice. 1928. *Quantitative Methods in Politics*. New York: Alfred A. Knopf.

21. Warren Miller and Donald Stokes. 1963. "Constituency Influence in Congress." *American Political Science Review* 57(1): 45–56.

22. Roger Davidson, David Kovenock, and Michael O'Leary. 1966. *Congress in Crisis: Politics and Congressional Reform*. Belmont, CA: Wadsworth Publishing.

23. Edward Tufte. 1975. "Determinants of the Outcomes of Midterm Congressional Elections." *American Political Science Review* 69(3): 812–26; Robert S. Erikson. 1971. "The Advantage of Incumbency in Congressional Elections." *Polity* 3(3): 395–405; Alan I. Abramowitz. 1980. "A Comparison of Voting for U.S. Senator and Representative in 1978." *American Political Science Review* 74(3): 633–40; Thomas Mann and Raymond E. Wolfinger. 1980. "Candidates and Parties in Congressional Elections." *American Political Science Review* 74(3): 617–32.

24. See such prominent works as the following: David Truman. 1959. *The Congressional Party*. New York: John Wiley; Barbara Sinclair. 1995. *Legislators, Leaders, and Lawmaking: The U.S. House of Representatives in the Postreform Era*. Baltimore: Johns Hopkins University Press; Barbara Sinclair. 2006. *Party Wars: Polarization and the Politics of National Policy Making*. Norman, OK: University of Oklahoma Press.

25. L. S. Shapley and Martin Shubik. 1954. "A Method for Evaluating the Distribution of Power in a Committee System." *American Political Science Review* 48(3): 787–92.

26. Duncan Black. 1958. *The Theory of Committees and Elections*. London: Cambridge University Press; Kenneth Shepsle and Barry Weingast. 1987. "The Institutional Foundations of Committee Power." *American Political Science Review* 81: 85–104; Barry Weingast and William Marshall. 1988. "The Industrial Organization of Congress; or, Why Legislatures, Like Firms, Are Not Organized as Markets." *Journal of Political Economy* 96(1): 132–63; Keith Krehbiel. 1987. "Why Are Congressional Committees Powerful?" *American Political Science Review* 81(3): 929–35; Keith Krehbiel. 1991. *Information and Legislative Organization*. Ann Arbor: University of Michigan; Gary Cox and Mathew McCubbins. 1993. *Legislative Leviathan: Party Government in the House*. Berkeley: University of California; Gary Cox and Mathew McCubbins. 2005. *Setting the Agenda: Responsible Party Government in the U.S. House of Representatives*. New York: Cambridge University Press; David Rohde. 1991. *Parties and Leaders in the Postreform House*. Chicago: University of Chicago;

Sarah Binder. 1997. *Minority Rights, Majority Rule: Partisanship and the Development of Congress*. New York: Cambridge University Press.

27. Keith Poole and Howard Rosenthal. 1991. "Patterns of Congressional Voting." *American Journal of Political Science* 35(1): 228–78; Keith Poole and Howard Rosenthal. 1997. *Congress: A Political-Economic History of Roll Call Voting*. New York: Oxford University Press.

28. Andrew Martin and Kevin Quinn. 2002. "Dynamic Ideal Point Estimation via Markov Chain Monte Carlo for the U.S. Supreme Court, 1953–1999." *Policy Analysis* 10(2): 134–53; Boris Shor and Nolan McCarty. 2011. "The Ideological Mapping of American Legislatures." *American Political Science Review* 105(3): 530–51; Nolan McCarty and Keith Poole. 1995. "Veto Power and Legislation: An Empirical Analysis of Executive and Legislative Bargaining from 1961 to 1986." *Journal of Law, Economics, and Organization* 11(2): 282–312; Michael Bailey and Kelly H. Chang. 2001. "Comparing Presidents, Senators, and Justices: Interinstitutional Preference Estimation." *Journal of Law, Economics, and Organization* 17(2): 477–506; Michael Bailey. 2007. "Comparable Preference Estimates across Time and Institutions for the Court, Congress, and Presidency." *American Journal of Political Science* 51(3): 433–48; Erik Voeten. 2000. "Clashes in the Assembly." *International Organization* 54(2): 185–215; Simon Hix, Abdul G. Noury, and Gérard Roland. 2007. *Democratic Politics in the European Parliament*. New York: Cambridge University Press; John B. Londregan. 2000. *Legislative Institutions and Ideology in Chile*. New York: Cambridge University Press.

29. Charles Clapp. 1963. *The Congressman: His Work as He Sees It*. Garden City, NY: Doubleday; Lewis Froman. 1963. *Congressmen and Their Constituencies*. Chicago: Rand McNally; David Mayhew. 1974. *Congress: The Electoral Connection*. New Haven: Yale University Press.

30. Among the most prominent names are David Mayhew, David Rohde, Ada Finifter, Bruce Oppenheimer, Barbara Sinclair, Steven Smith, Hanes Walton Jr., Rick Hall, Larry Evans, Forrest Maltzman, Frances Lee, and Jennifer Victor.

31. Richard Fenno. 1978. *Home Style: House Members in Their Districts*. Glenview, IL: Scott Foresman & Co.

32. Robert Peabody. 1976. *Leadership in Congress: Stability, Succession, and Change*. Boston, MA: Little, Brown; Randall Ripley. 1969. *Majority Party Leadership in Congress*. Boston, MA: Little, Brown; John Manley. 1970. *The Politics of Finance: The House Committee on Ways and Means*. Boston, MA: Little, Brown; Richard Fenno. 1996. *The Power of the Purse: Appropriations Politics in Congress*. Boston, MA: Little, Brown; Richard Fenno. 1973. *Congressmen in Committees*. Boston, MA: Little, Brown.

33. For example, Roger Davidson, Walter Oleszek, Larry Evans, Norman Ornstein, and Thomas Mann.

34. Frances Lee. 2009. *Beyond Ideology: Politics, Principles, and Partisanship in the U.S. Senate*. Chicago: University of Chicago Press.

35. Justin Grimmer. 2013. *Representational Style in Congress: What Legislators Say and Why It Matters*. New York: Cambridge University Press.

36. Nils Ringe, Jennifer Nicoll Victor, and Wendy K. Tam Cho. 2018. "Legislative Networks," in *The Oxford Handbook of Political Networks*, ed. by Jennifer Nicoll Victor, Alexander H. Montgomery, and Mark Lubell, 471–90. New York: Oxford University Press.

37. Adam Bonica. 2014. "Mapping the Ideological Marketplace." *American Journal of Political Science* 58: 367–86.

38. Solomon Messing, Patrick van Kessel, and Adam Hughes. December 18, 2017. "Sharing the News in a Polarized Congress." Washington, DC: Pew Research Center, www.people-press.org/2017/12/18/sharing-the-news-in-a-polarized-congress (accessed 6/8/18).

39. Scholars and individuals trained in advanced social science have begun to take a more active role in the public debate and supply of research-based insights on contemporary politics through such websites as the Monkey Cage, www.washingtonpost.com/news/monkey-cage/; the Upshot, www.nytimes.com/section/upshot; FiveThirtyEight, http://fivethirtyeight.com/; and Mischief of Factions, www.vox.com/mischiefs-of-faction.

Chapter 2: The Historical Development of Congress

1. On the problems of governing under the Articles, see Calvin Jillson and Rick K. Wilson. 1994. *Congressional Dynamics: Structure, Coordination, and Choice in the First American Congress, 1774–1789*. Stanford: Stanford University Press; George William Van Cleve. 2017. *We Have Not a Government: The Articles of Confederation and the Road to the Constitution*. Chicago: University of Chicago Press.
2. The literature on the Philadelphia Convention, and the events leading up to it, are voluminous. For a recent account, see Michael J. Klarman. 2016. *The Framers' Coup: The Making of the United States Constitution*. Oxford: Oxford University Press.
3. Joseph Cooper. 1970. *The Origins of the Standing Committees and the Development of the Modern House*. Houston: Rice University Studies.
4. See John H. Aldrich. 1995. *Why Parties? The Origin and Transformation of Party Politics in America*. Chicago: University of Chicago Press.
5. Henry Clay's leadership as Speaker of the House is explored in Gerald Gamm and Kenneth A. Shepsle. 1989. "Emergence of Legislative Institutions: Standing Committees in the House and Senate, 1810–1825." *Legislative Studies Quarterly* 14: 39–56; Jeffery A. Jenkins. 1998. "Property Rights and the Emergence of Standing Committee Dominance in the Nineteenth-Century House." *Legislative Studies Quarterly* 23: 493–519; Jeffery A. Jenkins and Charles H. Stewart III. 2002. "Order from Chaos: The Transformation of the Committee System in the House, 1816–1822," in *Party, Process, and Political Change in Congress: New Perspectives on the History of Congress*, eds. David W. Brady and Matthew D. McCubbins, 195–236. Stanford: Stanford University Press.
6. The best account of the politicking over the gag rule is William Lee Miller. 1996. *Arguing about Slavery: The Great Battle in the United States Congress*. New York: Knopf.
7. David Potter. 1976. *The Impending Crisis, 1848–1861*. New York: Harper.
8. Southern Whigs—without a serious alternative available—would eventually join the Democratic Party.
9. The best account of the emergence of the Republican Party is William E. Gienapp. 1987. *The Origins of the Republican Party, 1852–1856*. Oxford: Oxford University Press.
10. Secession occurred in two waves: the seven states of the Lower South were first (and they founded the Confederacy), and the four states of the Upper South followed later.
11. The politics of the proposed Thirteenth Amendment are documented in Daniel W. Crofts. 2016. *Lincoln and the Politics of Slavery: The Other Thirteenth Amendment and the Struggle to Save the Union*. Chapel Hill: University of North Carolina Press.
12. Ironically, the actual Thirteenth Amendment to the Constitution, which was adopted and ratified in 1865, abolished slavery.
13. A good, short history of Lincoln's interactions and relationship with the Republican-led Congress during the Civil War is William C. Harris. 2017. *Lincoln and Congress*. Carbondale: Southern Illinois University Press.
14. Bruce Tap. 1998. *Over Lincoln's Shoulder: The Committee on the Conduct of the War*. Lawrence: University Press of Kansas.
15. The Radicals' justification for the impeachment was based on Johnson's attempt to remove Attorney General Edwin Stanton (a fellow Radical) from office in opposition to the Tenure of Office Act (which the Radicals passed over Johnson's veto the previous year).

16. Michael Les Benedict. 1973. *The Impeachment and Trial of Andrew Johnson*. New York: W. W. Norton.

17. Eric Foner. 1988. *Reconstruction: America's Unfinished Revolution, 1863–1877*. New York: Harper & Row, 354–55.

18. The Compromise of 1877, as it became known, was an informal deal. The true elements of the compromise, and how much was explicitly agreed to by the parties involved, has been debated at length by historians. See C. Vann Woodward. 1951. *Reunion and Reaction: The Compromise of 1877 and the End of Reconstruction*. Boston, MA: Little, Brown; Allan Peskin. 1973. "Was There a Compromise of 1877?" *Journal of American History* 60: 63–75; Michael Les Benedict. 1980. "Southern Democrats in the Crisis of 1876–77: A Reconsideration of Reunion and Reaction." *Journal of Southern History* 46: 489–524.

19. In addition to disenfranchisement measures, Jim Crow laws also included measures to segregate the races in all public facilities.

20. See J. Morgan Kousser. 1974. *The Shaping of Southern Politics: Suffrage Restriction and the Establishment of the One-Party South, 1880–1910*. New Haven: Yale University Press; Michael Perman. 2001. *Struggle for Mastery: Disfranchisement in the South, 1888–1908*. Chapel Hill: University of North Carolina Press.

21. To combat Jim Crow, Republican members of Congress in the late nineteenth and early twentieth centuries occasionally offered bills to restrict southern representation in the House, per the "democratic form of government" guidelines of the Fourteenth Amendment. But these attempts were sporadic and, ultimately, unsuccessful.

22. Margaret Susan Thompson. 1985. *The Spider Web: Congress and Lobbying in the Age of Grant*. Ithaca, NY: Cornell University Press.

23. For example, several prominent members of Congress were implicated in the Crédit Mobilier scandal for taking bribes in the construction of the Union Pacific Railroad.

24. For more on the rise of congressional careerism, see Samuel Kernell. 1977. "Toward Understanding Nineteenth Century Congressional Careers: Ambition, Competition, and Rotation." *American Journal of Political Science* 21: 669–93; David Brady, Kara Buckley, and Douglas Rivers. 1999. "The Roots of Careerism in the U. S. House of Representatives." *Legislative Studies Quarterly* 24: 489–510.

25. The secret ballot was often referred to as the Australian ballot based on its earlier—and successful—implementation in that country. For more on the Australian ballot in the United States, see Jerrold G. Rusk. 1970. "The Effect of the Australian Ballot Reform on Split Ticket Voting: 1876–1908." *American Political Science Review* 64: 1220–38.

26. Jonathan N. Katz and Brian R. Sala. 1996. "Careerism, Committee Assignments, and the Electoral Connection." *American Political Science Review* 90: 21–33.

27. See Alan Ware. 2002. *The American Direct Primary: Party Institutionalization and Transformation in the North*. Cambridge: Cambridge University Press.

28. See Gary W. Cox and Mathew D. McCubbins. 2005. *Setting the Agenda: Responsible Party Government in the U.S. House of Representatives*. Cambridge: Cambridge University Press. For the best biography of Reed, see William A. Robinson. 1930. *Thomas B. Reed: Parliamentarian*. New York: Dodd, Mead.

29. See Lewis L. Gould. 2005. *The Most Exclusive Club: A History of the Modern United States Senate*. New York: Basic Books.

30. For a description of intra-Republican battles during the Theodore Roosevelt administration, see Michael Wolraich. 2014. *Unreasonable Men: Theodore Roosevelt and the Republican Rebels Who Created Progressive Politics*. New York: Palgrave Macmillan.

31. See Eric Schickler. 2001. *Disjointed Pluralism: Institutional Innovation and the Development of the U.S. Congress*. Princeton: Princeton University Press.

32. This informal arrangement was dubbed "the seniority system" and was a way for power to be disbursed within an institution that was still riven by regional (North-South) differences. For more on the seniority system in the House, see Nelson W. Polsby, Miriam Gallaher, and Barry Spencer Rundquist. 1969. "The Growth of the Seniority System in the U. S. House of Representatives." *American Political Science Review* 63: 787–807.

33. Matthew N. Green. 2002. "Institutional Change, Party Discipline, and the House Democratic Caucus, 1911–19." *Legislative Studies Quarterly* 27: 601–33.

34. The relevant legislation included the Federal Reserve Act (1913), the Federal Trade Commission Act (1914), the Clayton Antitrust Act (1914), and the Keating-Owen Child Labor Act (1916).

35. Sean Gailmard and Jeffery A. Jenkins. 2009. "Agency Problems, the 17th Amendment, and Representation in the Senate." *American Journal of Political Science* 53: 324–42.

36. Jeffery A. Jenkins and Charles Stewart III. 2013. *Fighting for the Speakership: The House and the Rise of Party Government.* Princeton: Princeton University Press.

37. Schickler, *Disjointed Pluralism.*

38. The one exception occurred for a brief period in the late 1950s and early 1960s when the House membership was increased to 437 after Hawaii and Alaska joined the Union.

39. For more on the politics of lame-duck sessions, see Jeffery A. Jenkins and Timothy P. Nokken. 2008. "Partisanship, the Electoral Connection, and Lame-Duck Sessions of Congress, 1877–2006." *Journal of Politics* 70: 450–65; Jeffery A. Jenkins and Timothy P. Nokken. 2008. "Legislative Shirking in the Pre-Twentieth Amendment Era: Presidential Influence, Party Power, and Lame-Duck Sessions of Congress, 1877–1933." *Studies in American Political Development* 22: 111–40.

40. As the First Congress held its initial meeting on March 4, 1789, March 4 (every two years thereafter) became the date that demarcated a new Congress in which new representatives and senators took office.

41. Craig Goodman and Timothy P. Nokken. 2004. "Lame-Duck Legislators and Consideration of the Ship Subsidy Bill of 1922." *American Politics Research.* 32: 465–89.

42. The Twentieth Amendment also changed the presidential inauguration date from March to January.

43. For more on Congress's activities during World War II, see Nancy Beck Young. 2013. *Why We Fight: Congress and the Politics of World War II.* Lawrence: University Press of Kansas.

44. Recent studies of these two landmark laws include Clay Risen. 2014. *The Bill of the Century: The Epic Battle for the Civil Rights Act.* New York: Bloomsbury; Gary May. 2013. *Bending toward Justice: The Voting Rights Act and the Transformation of American Democracy.* New York: Basic Books.

45. For more on LBJ's policy initiatives, and his relationship with Congress in achieving them, see Julian E. Zelizer. 2015. *The Fierce Urgency of Now: Lyndon Johnson, Congress, and the Battle for the Great Society.* New York: Penguin.

46. Examples of important environmental legislation included the Water Quality Act, the Environmental Quality Act, and amendments to the Clean Air Act. Examples of important transportation legislation included the Urban Mass Transit Assistance Act and the Rail Passenger Service Act (which created Amtrak). Examples of important nuclear arms limitation legislation included the US-USSR Antiballistic Missile Systems Treaty and the US-USSR Strategic Arms Limitation Act.

47. Examples included *Gideon v. Wainwright* (1963), which held that criminal defendants have a right to an attorney even if they cannot afford one; *Miranda v. Arizona* (1966), which held that prisoners must be advised of their rights—such as the right to remain silent—before being questioned by the police; and *Loving v. Virginia* (1967), which struck down state laws that prohibited interracial marriages.

48. The relevant legislation included the Economic Recovery Tax Act of 1981, the Fiscal 1984 Department of Defense Authorization, the Gramm-Rudman-Hollings Act (1985), and the Tax Reform Act of 1986).

49. See David W. Rohde. 1991. *Parties and Leaders in the Postreform House*. Chicago: University of Chicago Press.

50. See Barbara Sinclair. 2006. *Party Wars: Polarization and the Politics of National Policy Making*. Norman: University of Oklahoma Press, 190–91.

51. The relevant legislation included the Omnibus Budget Reconciliation Act of 1993, the Brady Handgun Prevention Act, the Violent Crime Control and Law Enforcement Act of 1994, the North American Free Trade Act (passed with Republican help), and the General Agreement on Tariff and Trade Act.

52. For a description of the specific reforms in the Contract with America, see John Micklethwait and Adrian Wooldridge. 2004. *The Right Nation: Conservative Power in America*. New York: Penguin.

53. The relationship between the Republican Congress and President Clinton is explored in Steven M. Gillon. 2008. *The Pact: Bill Clinton, Newt Gingrich, and the Rivalry that Defined a Generation*. New York: Oxford University Press.

54. The House voted 228–206 on perjury and 221–212 on obstruction of justice. The Senate voted 45–55 on perjury and 50–50 on obstruction of justice.

55. For a readable account of the 2000 election recount, see Jeffrey Toobin. 2001. *Too Close to Call: The Thirty-Six Day Battle to Decide the 2000 Election*. New York: Random House.

56. A caveat is that the 107th Senate flipped from Republican to Democrat after Senator Jim Jeffords (VT) switched from Republican to Independent and began caucusing with the Democrats in June of 2001.

57. Note that the authorizations of military force are still in effect, and they continue to be used to justify military actions.

58. This legislation, the Economic Growth and Tax Relief Reconciliation Act of 2001, in combination with legislation two years later, the Jobs and Growth Tax Relief Reconciliation Act of 2003, are together informally referred to as the "Bush tax cuts."

59. The relevant legislation included the Partial-Birth Abortion Ban Act of 2003 and the Medical Prescription Drug, Improvement, and Modernization Act of 2003.

60. "Table 6-7. Attempted and Successful Cloture Votes, 66th–114th Congress, 1919–2016." Brookings Institution, www.brookings.edu/wp-content/uploads/2017/01/vitalstats_ch6 _tbl7.pdf (accessed 5/7/18).

61. The 60-seat Democratic majority in the Senate was critical to passing a comprehensive health care bill. The Clinton-era Democrats did not enjoy this advantage.

62. Only the first of these three acts was adopted while the Democrats held 60 Senate seats.

63. Robert Draper. 2012. *Do Not Ask What Good We Do: Inside the U.S. House of Representatives*. New York: Free Press.

64. "Table 6-7. Attempted and Successful Cloture Votes, 66th–114th Congress, 1919–2016." Brookings Institution, www.brookings.edu/wp-content/uploads/2017/01/vitalstats_ch6 _tbl7.pdf (accessed 5/7/18). We discuss this attempt in more detail in Chapter 12.

65. Republicans in the House passed the American Health Care Act by a 217–213 vote, which would have repealed and replaced the Affordable Care Act. Republicans in the Senate sought to use the budget reconciliation process—and thus sidestep a Democratic filibuster—but could not secure the votes necessary for a repeal. The closest they got was a "skinny repeal"—a bare-bones bill that would have repealed the individual mandate in Obamacare—but it fell one vote short, 49–51 (a 50–50 tie would have made Vice President Mike Pence the tiebreaker, and he would have voted for it). Three Republican senators defected: Susan Collins (ME), Lisa Murkowski (AK), and John McCain (AZ).

66. The legislation was known as the Tax Cut and Jobs Act of 2017.

67. With the individual mandate eliminated, the requirement that individuals purchase health care is no more. As a result, the Congressional Budget Office has estimated that up to 13 million people—principally younger, healthier people—will likely opt out of insurance coverage. This would raise the premiums on the remaining (older, less healthy) pool, force further coverage drops, and potentially destabilize the insurance market. See www.cbo.gov/publication/53300.

68. James M. Snyder Jr. 1992. "Artificial Extremism in Interest Group Ratings." *Legislative Studies Quarterly* 17: 319–45.

69. For more on NOMINATE scores, see Keith T. Poole and Howard Rosenthal. 2007. *Ideology and Congress: Second, Revised Edition of Congress: A Political-Economic History of Roll Call Voting.* New Brunswick, NJ: Transaction Publishers.

70. The median is the middle number—or midpoint—in a sequence of numbers.

Chapter 3: Representation

1. David Weigel. August 11, 2017. "At Raucous Town Halls, Republicans Have Faced Another Round of Anger over Health Care." *Washington Post*, www.washingtonpost.com /powerpost/at-raucous-town-halls-republicans-have-faced-another-round-of-anger-over -health-care/2017/08/10/9d82cbbe-7de9-11e7-83c7-5bd5460f0d7e_story.html?utm _term=.c3c15071c1eb (accessed 5/14/18).

2. Elliot Smilowitz. May 6, 2017. "GOP Rep: 'Nobody Dies Because They Don't Have Access to Healthcare.'" TheHill.com, http://thehill.com/policy/healthcare/raul-labrador -town-hall-nobody-dies-access-to-healthcare-obamacare (accessed 5/14/18).

3. Zack Hirsch. May 9, 2017. "At Town Hall Meeting, Republican Lawmakers Get An Earful over Health Care." NPR.com, www.npr.org/2017/05/09/527533782/at-town-hall -meeting-republican-lawmaker-gets-an-earful (accessed 5/14/18).

4. Andrew Rafferty. July 10, 2017. "Republicans Continue to Skirt Town Halls with August Recess Looming." NBCNews.com, www.nbcnews.com/politics/politics-news/republicans -continue-skirt-town-halls-august-recess-looming-n781506 (accessed 5/14/18).

5. John Bowden. August 12, 2017. "GOP Lawmaker Holding 'Ticket Lottery' for Access to His Town Hall." TheHill.com, http://origin-nyi.thehill.com/homenews /house/346328-gop-lawmaker-holding-ticket-lottery-for-access-to-his-town-hall (accessed 5/14/18); Javier Panzar. February 24, 2017. "Rep. Steve Knight Will Ask Attendees at His Town Hall Next Week to Provide ID to Prove They Live in His District." *Los Angeles Times*, www.latimes.com/politics/essential/la-pol-ca-essential -politics-updates-rep-steve-knight-to-hold-town-hall-1487976322-htmlstory.html (accessed 5/14/18).

6. In addition, as political scientist Nicholas Carnes notes, members of Congress are much more likely to come from a white-collar (non-working-class) background. See Nicholas Carnes. 2013. *White-Collar Government: The Hidden Role of Class in Economic Policy Making.* Chicago: University of Chicago Press.

7. Drilling deeper, of those members of Congress who are Christian, roughly two-thirds are Protestant.

8. Inter-Parliamentary Union. April 1, 2018. "Women in National Parliaments." http:// archive.ipu.org/wmn-e/classif.htm (accessed 5/14/18).

9. See Colby Itkowitz. November 15, 2018. "Trickle-down Representation: Will the Most Diverse Congress Make Capitol Hill More Diverse?" *Washington Post*, www .washingtonpost.com/politics/2018/11/15/trickle-down-representation-will-most-diverse -congress-make-capitol-hill-more-diverse/?noredirect=on&utm_term=.fe82367cabf0; Beatrice Jin. November 23, 2018. "Congress's Incoming Class Is Younger, Bluer, and More

Diverse Than Ever. *Politico*, www.politico.com/interactives_116th-congress-freshman-younger-bluer-diverse (both accessed 12/18/18).

10. R. Douglas Arnold. 1990. *The Logic of Congressional Action*. New Haven: Yale University Press.

11. See John Kingdon. 1981. *Congressmen's Voting Decisions*. Revised Edition. Ann Arbor: University of Michigan Press.

12. Lou Dubose and Jan Reid. 2004. *The Hammer: Tom DeLay, God, Money, and the Rise of the Republican Congress*. New York: Public Affairs.

13. See Bob Cusack, Sarah Ferris, and Peter Sullivan. February 10, 2016. "The Chaotic Fight for ObamaCare." TheHill.com, http://thehill.com/policy/healthcare/268877-the-chaotic-fight-for-obamacare (accessed 5/14/18). In the Affordable Care Act example, Obama also brought wavering members to the White House for personal meetings.

14. Ryan Sit. February 22, 2018. "Here's Why the NRA Is So Powerful and Why Gun Control Advocates Have Reason for Hope." *Newsweek*, www.newsweek.com/nra-gun-control-parkland-florida-school-shooting-campaign-donations-813940 (accessed 5/14/18).

15. Craig Volden and Alan Wiseman. 2014. *Legislative Effectiveness in Congress: The Lawmakers*. Cambridge: Cambridge University Press.

16. For more on casework, see R. Eric Petersen and Sarah J. Eckman. January 3, 2017. "Casework in a Congressional Office: Background, Rules, Laws, and Resources." Congressional Research Service, https://fas.org/sgp/crs/misc/RL33209.pdf (accessed 5/14/18).

17. Quote is taken from interview by Craig Horowitz. April 6, 1998. "Al D'Amato: Senator Pothole, Proudly." *New York Magazine*, http://nymag.com/nymetro/news/people/features/2421/ (accessed 5/14/18).

18. See Ida A. Brudnick. September 27, 2017. "Members' Representational Allowance: History and Usage." Congressional Research Service, https://fas.org/sgp/crs/misc/R40962.pdf (accessed 5/14/18); Congressional Research Service. January 5, 2017. "Constituent Services: Overview and Resources." www.everycrsreport.com/files/20170105_R44726_1bace040086d26806d8ac843c25cda76789ad040.pdf (accessed 5/14/18); Congressional Research Service. July 14, 2016. "Congressional Salaries and Allowances: In Brief." www.everycrsreport.com/files/20160714_RL30064_3a67abc95bb84cd142c45373906cbd280d240b47.pdf (accessed 5/14/18).

19. See Richard F. Fenno Jr. 1977. "U.S. House Members in Their Constituencies: An Exploration." *American Political Science Review* 71: 883–917.

20. Alexander Burns and Patricia Mazzei. February 22, 2018. "Marco Rubio Finds Himself at Center of Gun Debate, Again." *New York Times*, www.nytimes.com/2018/02/22/us/marco-rubio-florida-nra.html (accessed 5/14/18).

21. Norman Ornstein. March 7, 2006. "Part-Time Congress." *Washington Post*, www.washingtonpost.com/wp-dyn/content/article/2006/03/06/AR2006030601611.html (accessed 5/14/18).

22. David R. Mayhew. 1974. *Congress: The Electoral Connection*. New Haven: Yale University Press.

23. Jonathan N. Katz and Brian R. Sala. 1996. "Careerism, Committee Assignments, and the Electoral Connection." *American Political Science Review* 90: 21–33.

24. Benjamin G. Bishin. 2009. *Tyranny of the Minority: The Subconstituency Politics Theory of Representation*. Philadelphia: Temple University Press.

25. Wendy J. Schiller. 2000. *Partners and Rivals: Representation in U.S. Senate Delegations*. Princeton: Princeton University Press.

26. John H. Aldrich and Kenneth A. Shepsle. 2000. "Explaining Institutional Change: Soaking, Poking, Institutional Choice in the U.S. Congress," in *Congress on Display, Congress at Work*, ed. William T. Bianco, 30. Ann Arbor: University of Michigan Press.

27. Kristina C. Miler. 2010. *Constituency Representation in Congress: The View from Capitol Hill*. Cambridge: Cambridge University Press.

28. Section 2 of the Fourteenth Amendment would also repeal the provision regarding indentured servants.

29. Slavery was prohibited in the Thirteenth Amendment, and the former slaves were provided with citizenship rights in the Fourteenth Amendment.

30. The increase in African American registration was met initially by an increase in white registration, which helped forestall change for almost a generation.

31. Recent work in political science has found that Congress, as a whole, can indeed play a meaningful role in checking presidential power and thereby represent the country as a whole in matters of national significance. This is most prevalent in international affairs. Scholars have found that the president is constrained in entering military conflicts abroad, in anticipation of pushback from Congress. See William G. Howell and Jon C. Pevehouse. 2007. *While Dangers Gather: Congressional Checks on Presidential War Powers.* Princeton: Princeton University Press. And once involved in a military conflict, the president limits the scope and length of U.S. involvement—once again, in anticipation of facing active resistance in Congress. See Douglas L. Kriner. 2010. *After the Rubicon: Congress, Presidents, and the Politics of Waging War.* Chicago: University of Chicago Press.

32. Laurie Kellman. January 20, 2015. "McCain Wages a New National Campaign, to Define His Legacy." Military.com, www.military.com/daily-news/2015/01/20/mccain-wages-a-new-national-campaign-to-define-his-legacy.html (accessed 5/14/18); Miranda Green. September 2, 2017. "McCain: Trump 'Poorly Informed,' Congress 'Not His Subordinates." CNN.com, www.cnn.com/2017/09/02/politics/mccain-regular-order-oped/index.html (accessed 5/14/18).

33. This differs from cosponsorship of legislation, which is more of a passive, symbolic act.

34. See Scott H. Ainsworth and Thad E. Hall. 2010. *Abortion Politics in Congress: Strategic Incrementalism and Policy Change.* Cambridge: Cambridge University Press; Robert J. Spitzer. 2017. *The Politics of Gun Control*, 7th ed. New York: Routledge.

35. This work is nicely summarized in John D. Griffin. 2014. "When and Why Minority Legislators Matter." *Annual Review of Political Science* 17: 327–36. An exception to this general result is found in Carol Swain. 1993. *Black Faces, Black Interests: The Representation of African Americans in Congress.* Cambridge: Harvard University Press.

36. See, for example, John D. Griffin and Brian P. Newman. 2007. "The Unequal Representation of Latinos and Whites." *Journal of Politics* 69: 1032–46.

37. David T. Canon. 1999. *Race, Redistricting, and Representation.* Chicago: University of Chicago Press.

38. See Michele L. Swers. 2002. *The Difference Women Make: The Policy Impact of Women in Congress.* Chicago: University of Chicago Press; Michele L. Swers. 2013. *Women in the Club: Gender and Policy Making in the Senate.* Chicago: University of Chicago Press.

39. Katherine Tate. 2004. *Black Faces in the Mirror: African Americans and Their Representatives in the U.S. Congress.* Princeton: Princeton University Press.

40. See John D. Griffin and Brian D. Newman. 2008. *Minority Report: Evaluating Political Equality in America.* Chicago: University of Chicago Press.

41. Ebonya L. Washington. 2008. "Female Socialization: How Daughters Affect Their Legislator Fathers' Voting on Women's Issues." *American Economic Review* 98: 311–32.

42. The class study here is Warren E. Miller and Donald E. Stokes. 1963. "Constituency Influence in Congress." *American Political Science Review* 57: 45–56.

43. See, for example, Christopher H. Achen. 1977. "Measuring Representation: Perils of the Correlation Coefficient." *American Journal of Political Science* 21: 805–15.

44. See, for example, Joshua D. Clinton. 2006. "Representation in Congress: Constituents and Roll Calls in the 106th House." *Journal of Politics* 68: 397–409; Joseph Bafumi and Michael Herron. 2010. "Leapfrog Representation and Extremism: A Study of

American Voters and Their Members in Congress." *American Political Science Review* 104: 519–42; Chris Tausanovitch and Christopher Warshaw. 2013. "Measuring Constituent Policy Preferences in Congress, State Legislatures, and Cities." *Journal of Politics* 75: 330–42.

45. This process is described in the introduction to Richard F. Fenno Jr. 1978. *Home Style: House Members in Their Districts* Boston: Little, Brown, xi–xvi. The term appears in Richard F. Fenno Jr. 1996. *Senators on the Campaign Trail: The Politics of Representation.* Norman: University of Oklahoma Press, 4.

46. Richard F. Fenno Jr. 1986. "Observation, Context, and Sequence in the Study of Politics." *American Political Science Review* 80: 3–15.

47. For members of Congress, another aspect of strategic presentation of self involves creating trust among constituents, which in turn provides them with more leeway to act as they wish in Washington. See Fenno, *Home Style*; William T. Bianco. 1994. *Trust: Representatives and Constituents.* Ann Arbor: University of Michigan Press.

48. Justin Grimmer. 2013. *Representational Style in Congress: What Legislators Say and Why It Matters.* Cambridge: Cambridge University Press.

49. The ADA chooses roll calls in keeping with its advocacy of "progressive stances on civil rights and liberties, social and economic justice, sensible foreign policy, and sustainable environmental policy." This leads to a set of votes on "a wide range of social and economic issues, both domestic and international." See "What is Americans for Democratic Action?" https://adaction.org/about/ (accessed 5/15/18).

50. The LCCR chooses roll calls in keeping with their legislative priorities, which are to work "toward the goal of a more open and just society" and "to ensure the proper enforcement of civil rights laws to unite us as a nation true to its promise of equal justice, equal opportunity, and mutual respect." See the Leadership Conference on Civil and Human Rights Voting Record, 114th Congress, October 2016, 2. For more on the composition and use of LCCR scores, see Daniel Q. Gillion. 2013. *The Political Power of Protest: Minority Activism and Shifts in Public Policy.* Cambridge: Cambridge University Press.

51. The heroes and zeroes categorization started with the ADA.

52. For example, the ADA's heroes list in the 114th Congress counted 24 House Democrats and 6 Senate Democrats, while the group's zeroes list tallied 140 House Republicans and 15 Senate Republicans. The LCCR's heroes list counted 124 House Democrats and 32 Senate Democrats, and the group s zeroes list tallied 144 House Republicans and 16 Senate Republicans.

53. Elizabeth Mendes. May 9, 2013. "Americans Down on Congress, OK with Own Representative." Gallup, http://news.gallup.com/poll/162362/americans-down-congress-own -representative.aspx (accessed 5/17/18).

54. This macro versus micro difference in performance evaluations is sometimes referred to as "Fenno's Paradox."

55. Glenn R. Parker and Roger H. Davidson. 1979. "Why Do Americans Love Their Congressman So Much More Than Their Congress?" *Legislative Studies Quarterly* 4: 53–61.

56. See Kenneth R. Mayer and David T. Cannon. 1999. *The Dysfunctional Congress: The Individual Roots of an Institutional Dilemma.* Boulder, CO: Westview; Thomas E. Mann and Norman J. Ornstein. 2006. *The Broken Branch: How Congress Is Failing America and How to Get It Back on Track.* Oxford: Oxford University Press.

57. James A. Stimson, Michael B. MacKuen, and Robert S. Erikson. 1995. "Dynamic Representation." American Political Science Review 89: 543–65; James A. Stimson. 1999. *Public Opinion in America: Moods, Cycles, and Swings,* 2nd ed. Boulder, CO: Westview; James A. Stimson. 2004. *Tides of Consent: How Public Opinion Shapes American Politics.* Cambridge: Cambridge University Press.

Chapter 4: Elections

1. See, for example, Lauren Cohen Bell, David Elliot Meyer, and Ronald Keith Gaddie. 2016. *Slingshot: The Defeat of Eric Cantor.* Washington: Congressional Quarterly Press.
2. Based on data from Tables 1-6 and 1-7, *Vital Statistics on Congress*, Brookings Institution, www.brookings.edu/multi-chapter-report/vital-statistics-on-congress (accessed 5/15/18). Averages calculated from the 83rd (1953–54) through 115th (2017–18) Congresses.
3. This was the "great compromise" between small and large states at the Constitutional Convention.
4. The Seventeenth Amendment also outlines a procedure for filling Senate vacancies—either via special election or by governor appointment (per the decision of the state legislature). Article I, Section 2, Clause 4 stipulates that House vacancies will be filled via a special election.
5. Wendy Schiller and Charles Stewart III. 2015. *Electing the Senate: Indirect Democracy before the Seventeenth Amendment.* Princeton: Princeton University Press.
6. Schiller and Stewart, *Electing the Senate*, 8.
7. Disputed elections are often referred to as "contested elections." But the term "contested elections" is sometimes interpreted to mean "contested races"—or when two (or more) candidates campaign for a seat in Congress. Thus we use the term "disputed elections" to make clear the phenomenon being studied in this section. This section is based in part on Jeffery A. Jenkins. 2004. "Partisanship and Contested Election Cases in the House of Representatives, 1789–2002." *Studies in American Political Development* 18: 112–35. For a similar examination of the Senate, see Jeffery A. Jenkins. 2005. "Partisanship and Contested Election Cases in the Senate, 1789–2002." *Studies in American Political Development* 19: 53–74.
8. The contested election data in this analysis span the 1st through 112th Congresses (1789–2012). Data were taken from Jenkins, "Contested Election Cases in the House of Representatives," and updated.
9. For an excellent history of how states elect their representatives, see Jay K. Dow. 2017. *Electing the House: The Adoption and Performance of the U.S. Single-Member District Electoral System.* Lawrence: University Press of Kansas.
10. Over time, the ratio of 1 representative for every 30,000 of a state's population has increased significantly. As of the 2010 census, the current ratio is around 1 representative for every 700,000 citizens.
11. This relationship of districts being composed of sets of whole counties is still the standard today. However, as urban areas have grown denser over time, an increasing number of districts have been carved out of parts of *single* counties. For example, Cook County in Illinois—which contains Chicago—is associated with 11 congressional districts. We refer to such densely populated urban counties as *multidistrict counties.*
12. This was based on arguments that the mandate was unconstitutional or that its legal basis was temporary.
13. In the 1840s, the United States was still predominantly an agrarian society. Tuesday was chosen because Sunday was a day of prayer and rest, while Wednesday was market day. Citizens could then use all of Monday to travel to the county seat, where voting would occur.
14. The matching of election dates was supposed to take effect four years after the passage of the act in 1876.
15. For an excellent history of the methods of electing representatives, especially as it relates to voting technology, see Roy G. Saltman. 2006. *The History and Politics of Voting Technology: In Quest of Integrity and Public Confidence.* New York: Palgrave Macmillan.
16. By this time, only two states—Kentucky and Oregon—were still using voice voting at a broad level.

17. This population provision has since been amended by the second section of the Fourteenth Amendment.
18. See Charles W. Eagles. 1990. *Democracy Delayed: Congressional Reapportionment and Urban-Rural Conflict in the 1920s*. Athens: University of Georgia Press.
19. For an excellent history of congressional apportionment methods, and the battles over them, see Michel L. Balinski and H. Peyton Young. 2010. *Fair Representation: Meeting the Ideal of One Man, One Vote*, 2nd ed. Washington: Brookings.
20. See Tables 3-9 and 3-10 in *Vital Statistics on Congress*, Brookings Institution, www .brookings.edu/multi-chapter-report/vital-statistics-on-congress (accessed 5/16/18).
21. Soft-money contributions to the parties were not publicly disclosed until the 1991–92 election cycle.
22. "Criminal Disenfranchisement Laws across the United States." April 18, 2018. Brennan Center for Justice, https://www.brennancenter.org/criminal-disenfranchisement-laws -across-united-states (accessed 6/30/18).
23. "Voter ID History." National Conference of State Legislatures, www.ncsl.org/research /elections-and-campaigns/voter-id-history.aspx (accessed 5/16/18).
24. Nate Cohn. January 26, 2017. "Illegal Voting Claims, and Why They Don't Hold Up." *New York Times*, www.nytimes.com/2017/01/26/upshot/illegal-voting-claims-and-why -they-dont-hold-up.html?_r=0 (accessed 5/16/18); David Cottrell, Michael C. Herron, and Sean J. Westwood. 2018. "An Exploration of Donald Trump's Allegations of Massive Voter Fraud in the 2016 General Election." *Electoral Studies* 51: 123–42.
25. See National Conference of State Legislatures. August 17, 2017. "Absentee and Early Voting." www.ncsl.org/research/elections-and-campaigns/absentee-and-early-voting.aspx (accessed 5/16/18).
26. United States Elections Project. November 6, 2018. "2018 November General Election Early Voting." www.electproject.org/2018_early_vote (accessed 12/17/18).
27. Jerrold Rusk. 1970. "The Effect of the Australian Ballot Reform on Split Ticket Voting: 1876–1908." *American Political Science Review* 64: 1220–38.
28. Erik Engstrom. 2006. "Stacking the States, Stacking the Nation: The Partisan Consequences of Redistricting in the 19th Century." *American Political Science Review* 100: 419–27.
29. In January 2011, DeLay was sentenced to serve three years in prison. He appealed his conviction and was free on bail while the appeal process played out. In September 2013, the Texas Court of Appeals acquitted him and so did the Texas Court of Criminal Appeals (after the state of Texas appealed his first acquittal) in October 2014.
30. Anthony McGann, Charles Anthony Smith, Michael Latner, and Alex Keena. 2016. *Gerrymandering in America: The House of Representatives, the Supreme Court, and the Future of Popular Sovereignty*. New York: Cambridge University Press, 78–80.
31. Aaron Blake. July 27, 2011. "Name That District! (Gerrymandering Edition)." *Washington Post*, www.washingtonpost.com/blogs/the-fix/post/name-that-district-gerrymandering -edition/2011/07/25/gIQA17HucI_blog.html?utm_term=.235a8ec13b96 (accessed 5/16/18).
32. Gary C. Jacobson and Jamie L. Carson. 2016. *The Politics of Congressional Elections*, Ninth Edition. Lanham, MD: Rowman & Littlefield.
33. David Lublin. 2004. *The Republican South: Democratization and Partisan Change*. Princeton: Princeton University Press, 115.
34. The court cases include *Shaw v. Reno* (1993), *Miller v. Johnson* (1995), *Hunt v. Cromartie* (1999), and *Easley v. Cromartie* (2001).
35. *Davis v. Bandemer* (1986).
36. *Vieth v. Jubelirer* (2004).

37. "*Gill v. Whitford.*" January 24, 2018. Brennan Center for Justice, www.brennancenter.org /legal-work/whitford-v-gill (accessed 5/16/18).

38. Vann R. Newkirk II. June 18, 2018. "Partisan Gerrymandering Stands, for Now." *The Atlantic,* http://www.theatlantic.com/politics/archive/2018/06/partisan-gerrymandering -stands-for-now/563063 (accessed 6/30/18).

39. See Alan Ware. 2002. *The American Direct Primary: Party Institutionalization and Transformation in the North.* New York: Cambridge University Press; John F. Reynolds. 2006. *The Demise of the American Convention System, 1880–1911.* New York: Cambridge University Press.

40. Source for the data and party maps is www.fairvote.org (accessed 5/16/18).

41. These percentages have separated a bit in the last three electoral cycles.

42. Jamie L. Carson and Jeffery A. Jenkins. 2011. "Examining the Electoral Connection across Time." *Annual Review of Political Science* 14: 25–46.

43. Samuel Kernell. 1977. "Toward Understanding 19th Century Congressional Careers: Ambition, Competition, and Rotation." *American Journal of Political Science* 21: 669–93.

44. John J. Wallis. 2007. "American Government and the Promotion of Economic Development in the National Era, 1790 to 1860." In *The Role of Government in U.S. Economic History: Essays in Honor of Robert Higgs,* Price Fishback, ed. Chicago: University of Chicago Press.

45. Some of these activities were illegal, and corruption increased with the nation's political-economic development. Major congressional scandals, for example, occurred during the 1870s (during the Grant administration) and the 1920s (during the Harding administration).

46. David Brady, Kara Buckley, and Douglas Rivers. 1999. "The Roots of Careerism in the U.S. House of Representatives." *Legislative Studies Quarterly* 24: 489–510.

47. Carson and Jenkins, "Examining the Electoral Connection across Time."

48. The classic account of political ambition is Joseph Schlesinger. 1966. *Ambition and Politics: Political Careers in the United States.* Chicago: Rand-McNally.

49. David R. Mayhew. 1974. *Congress: The Electoral Connection.* New Haven: Yale University Press.

50. Richard F. Fenno. 1973. *Congressmen in Committees.* Boston: Little, Brown.

51. David T. Canon. 1990. *Actors, Athletes, and Astronauts: Political Amateurs in the United States Congress.* Chicago: University of Chicago Press.

52. See Gary Jacobson and Samuel Kernell. 1981. *Strategy and Choice in Congressional Elections.* New Haven: Yale University Press; Gary Jacobson. 1989. "Strategic Politicians and the Dynamics of U.S. House Elections, 1946–86." *American Political Science Review* 83: 773–93.

53. See Jennifer L. Lawless. 2011. *Becoming a Candidate: Political Ambition and the Decision to Run for Office.* New York: Cambridge University Press; Jennifer L. Lawless. 2015. "Female Candidates and Legislators." *Annual Review of Political Science* 18: 349–66; Jennifer L. Lawless and Richard L. Fox. 2017. *Women, Men & U.S. Politics: 10 Big Questions.* New York: W. W. Norton.

54. This was a time when party ties in elections were weak and split-ticket voting was high.

55. For House and Senate data, see Tables 3-3 and 3-6 in *Vital Statistics on Congress,* Brookings Institution, www.brookings.edu/multi-chapter-report/vital-statistics-on-congress (accessed 5/16/18).

56. Gary W. Cox and Jonathan N. Katz. 2002. *Elbridge Gerry's Salamander: The Electoral Consequences of the Reapportionment Revolution.* New York: Cambridge University Press.

57. Jamie L. Carson, Michael H. Crespin, and Ryan D. Williamson. 2014. "Reevaluating the Effects of Redistricting on Electoral Competition, 1972–2012." *State Politics & Policy Quarterly* 14: 165–77.

58. Robert S. Erikson. 2017. "The Congressional Incumbency Advantage over Sixty Years: Measurement, Trends, and Implications," in *Governing in a Polarized Era: Elections, Par-*

ties, and Political Representation in America, ed. by Alan S. Gerber and Eric Schickler, 65–89. New York: Cambridge University Press.

59. Erikson (2017) offers this argument for why the Retirement Slump measure remains higher during this period: "Retirees had built up electoral immunity, maintaining their incumbency previously earned. The plunge in the vote following their exit revealed the degree to which the party success during their tenure had been incumbency-induced" (81).

60. See Susan Welch and John R. Hibbing. 1997. "The Effect of Charges of Corruption on Voting Behavior in Congressional Elections, 1982–1990." *Journal of Politics* 59: 226–39; Scott J. Basinger. 2013. "Scandals and Congressional Elections in the Post-Watergate Era." *Political Research Quarterly* 66: 335–98.

61. See Rodrigo Praino, Daniel Stockermer, and Vincent Moscardelli. 2013. "The Lingering Effects of Scandals in Congressional Elections: Incumbents, Challengers, and Voters." *Social Science Quarterly* 94: 1045–61. Ethics-tainted House members also retired at a much higher rate.

62. Pennsylvania had lost one seat in the apportionment following the 2010 U.S. Census, and the Republican Senate essentially merged Altmire's 4th district and Critz's 12th district.

63. Jonathan Weisman. April 25, 2012. "2 House Democrats Defeated after Opposing Health Law." *New York Times*, www.nytimes.com/2012/04/26/us/politics/2-house-democrats-defeated-after-opposing-health-law.html (accessed 5/16/18).

64. The effects of the Voting Rights Act took a generation to play out fully. African American registration was initially met with increased white registration. But, in time, the full effects of the African American electorate altered electoral and partisan dynamics in the South.

65. Jennifer Wolak. 2007. "The Influence of Public Preferences on Voluntary Departures from Congress." *Legislative Studies Quarterly* 32: 285–308.

66. Sheryl Gay Stolberg. September 26, 2017. "Tennessee's Bob Corker Announces Retirement from Senate." *New York Times*, www.nytimes.com/2017/09/26/us/politics/tennessees-bob-corker-announces-retirement-from-senate.html (accessed 5/16/18); Ed O'Keefe and David Weigel. October 24, 2017. "Sen. Jeff Flake of Arizona Will Retire, Citing Direction of GOP under Trump." *Washington Post*, www.washingtonpost.com/powerpost/sen-jeff-flake-will-retire-citing-direction-of-gop-under-trump/2017/10/24/f33acdfc-b8ec-11e7-9e58-e6288544af98_story.html?utm_term=.64274c24af5d (accessed 5/16/18).

67. "Departures Resulting in Open Seat Races by Cycle." Center for Responsive Politics, www.opensecrets.org/members-of-congress/departures-by-cycle (accessed 12/17/18).

68. Morris P. Fiorina. 2017. *Unstable Majorities: Polarization, Party Sorting, and Political Stalemate*. Stanford: Hoover Institution Press, 127. In describing this nationalization, Fiorina refers to it as "re-nationalization," believing that "contemporary elections have returned to a pattern that was common in earlier periods of American history."

69. Larry Bartels. 2000. "Partisanship and Voting Behavior, 1952–1996." *American Journal of Political Science* 44: 35–50.

70. See Matthew Levendusky. 2009. *The Partisan Sort: How Liberals Become Democrats and Conservatives Become Republican*. Chicago: University of Chicago Press; Gary Jacobson. 2015. "It's Nothing Personal: The Decline of the Incumbency Advantage in US House Elections." *Journal of Politics* 77: 861–73.

71. Frances Lee. 2016. *Insecure Majorities: Congress and the Perpetual Campaign*. Chicago: University of Chicago Press; James L. Carson and Jason Roberts. 2017. "Congress and the Nationalization of Congressional Elections." Working Paper.

72. On the pluses versus minuses of wave elections, see Fiorina, *Unstable Majorities*, 140.

Chapter 5: Committees

1. Paul Kane. February 16, 2013. "Congress's Committee Chairmen Push to Reassert Their Power." *Washington Post*, www.washingtonpost.com/politics/congresss-committee -chairman-push-to-reassert-their-power/2013/02/16/2acb7770-6a6a-11e2-af53 -7b2b2a7510a8_story.html (accessed 5/13/18).
2. Clay Risen. 2014. *The Bill of the Century: The Epic Battle for the Civil Rights Act.* New York: Bloomsbury Press; Julian Zelizer. 2015. *The Fierce Urgency of Now: Lyndon Johnson, Congress, and the Battle for the Great Society.* New York: Penguin Press.
3. Christopher Deering and Steven Smith. 1997. *Committees in Congress*, 3rd ed. Washington, DC: Congressional Quarterly.
4. Ashley Parker. June 5, 2013. "From a 'Child of the House' to Longest-Serving Member." *New York Times.*
5. John Ferejohn. 1986. "Logrolling in an Institutional Context: A Case Study of Food Stamp Legislation," in *Congress and Policy Change*, ed. by Gerald C. Wright, Leroy N. Rieselbach, and Lawrence C. Dodd, 223–56. New York: Agathon Press.
6. Walter Oleszek. 2014. *Congressional Procedures and the Policy Process*, 9th ed., 114. Washington, DC: CQ Press; Jeffrey Young. September 7, 2005. "Bonilla Bill Targets Eminent Domain." *The Hill*, www.lexisnexis.com.libraries.colorado.edu/lnacui2api/api/version1 /getDocCui?lni=4H2M-GCF0-00BY-M1GS&csi=153182&hl=t&hv=t&hnsd=f&hns =t&hgn=t&oc=00240&perma=true.
7. Barbara Sinclair. 2007. *Unorthodox Lawmaking: New Legislative Processes in the U.S. Congress*, 3rd ed., Table 6.2. Washington, DC: Congressional Quarterly Press.
8. Garry Young and Joseph Cooper. 1993. "Multiple Referral and the Transformation of House Decision Making," in *Congress Reconsidered*, 5th ed., 211–34. Washington, DC: Congressional Quarterly.
9. Garry Young. 1996. "Committee Gatekeeping and Proposal Power under Single and Multiple Referrals." *Journal of Theoretical Politics* 8: 65–78.
10. CQ *Almanac.* 2010. "Landmark Health Care Overhaul: A Long, Acrimonious Journey," in CQ *Almanac 2009*, ed. by Jan Austin, 65th ed. Washington, DC: CQ-Roll Call Group.
11. Oleszek, *Congressional Procedures and the Policy Process*, p. 103.
12. E. Scott Adler. 2002. *Why Congressional Reforms Fail: Reelection and the House Committee System.* Chicago: University of Chicago Press.
13. David King. 1997. *Turf Wars: How Congressional Committees Claim Jurisdictions.* Chicago: University of Chicago Press. Somewhat surprisingly, other research has shown that when legislators take action to avoid the committee of jurisdiction, other legislators—despite not wanting the same thing to happen to their committees—fail to rise to the support of that original committee. See Charles R. Shipan. 1992. "Individual Incentives and Institutional Imperatives: Committee Jurisdiction and Long-Term Health Care." *American Journal of Political Science* 36: 877–95; and Charles R. Shipan. 1996. "Senate Committees and Turf: Do Jurisdictions Matter?" *Political Research Quarterly* 49: 177–89.
14. Rob Margetta. January 6, 2014. "2013 Legislative Summary: Cybersecurity." CQ *Weekly Report*, 59.
15. Jessica Meyers and Kevin Cirilli. January, 1, 2014. "Senate Panels Fight for a Piece of Target." *POLITICO*, www.politico.com/story/2014/01/congress-target-data-breach-security -senate-commerce-judiciary-banking-102179.html (accessed 7/27/18).
16. Julian Hattem. June 8, 2014. "Anti-hacking Legislation Now on the Fritz." TheHill.com, http://thehill.com/policy/technology/208557-anti-hacking-bills-on-the-fritz (accessed 7/27/18).

17. E. Scott Adler and John Wilkerson. 2012. *Congress and the Politics of Problem Solving.* New York: Cambridge University Press.

18. Karen Foerstel and Alan Ota. January 6, 2001. "Early Grief for GOP Leaders in New Committee Rules." CQ *Weekly Report*, 10–14; Alan Ota. February 3, 2001. "Chairman Tauzin Charts a Bold Course for Commerce." CQ *Weekly Report*, 258–66.

19. Gerald Gamm and Kenneth Shepsle. 1989. "Emergence of Legislative Institutions: Standing Committees in the House and Senate, 1810–1825." *Legislative Studies Quarterly* 14: 39–66.

20. Jonathan Katz and Brian Sala. 1996. "Careerism, Committee Assignments and the Electoral Connection." *American Political Science Review* 90: 21–33.

21. David Canon and Charles Stewart. 2009. "Committee Hierarchy and Assignments in the U.S. Congress: Testing Theories of Legislative Organization 1789–1946." Presented at the Conference on Bicameralism, Duke University.

22. Charles Stewart. 1992. "The Growth of the Committee System, from Randall to Gillett," in *The Atomistic Congress: An Interpretation of Congressional Change*. Armonk, NY: M.E. Sharpe, Inc.

23. Stanley Bach and Steven Smith. 1988. *Managing Uncertainty in the House of Representatives: Adaptation and Innovation in Special Rules*. Washington, DC: Brookings Institution; Bruce I. Oppenheimer. 1977. "The Rules Committee: New Arm of Leadership in a Decentralized House," in *Congress Reconsidered*, 96–116. Washington, DC: Congressional Quarterly.

24. David Hawkings. 2014. "The Opaque World of Committee Assignments." *Roll Call Blog: Hawkings Here*, http://blogs.rollcall.com/hawkings/house-committee-assignments/?dcz= (accessed 4/5/15).

25. Tim Groseclose and Charles Stewart. 1998. "The Value of Committee Seats in the House, 1947–1991." *American Journal of Political Science* 42: 453–74.

26. Nelson W. Polsby. 1968. "The Institutionalization of the US House of Representatives." *American Political Science Review* 62: 144–68.

27. John A. Lawrence. 2018. *The Class of '74: Congress after Watergate and the Roots of Partisanship*. Baltimore: Johns Hopkins University Press.

28. James Gimpel. 1996. *Legislating the Revolution: The Contract with America in Its First 100 Days*. Boston: Allyn and Bacon.

29. Kristin Kanthak. 2007. "Crystal Elephants and Committee Chairs Campaign Contributions and Leadership Races in the U.S. House of Representatives." *American Politics Research* 35.3: 389–406, http://dx.doi.org/10.1177/1532673X06298079.

30. Joseph Schatz. January 10, 2005. "Lewis Wins Favor of GOP Leaders—and Coveted Appropriations Chair." CQ *Weekly Report*, 71–73.

31. Norman J. Ornstein and others. 2014. *Vital Statistics on Congress*. Washington, DC: Brookings Institution and the American Enterprise Institute, www.brookings.edu /research/reports/2013/07/vital-statistics-congress-mann-ornstein (accessed 4/5/15).

32. One law—P.L. 114-222, the Justice against Sponsors of Terrorism Act—was enacted over a presidential veto.

33. Adler and Wilkerson, *Congress and the Politics of Problem Solving*.

34. Gregory Korte. March 7, 2014. "Cummings Accepts Issa Apology for Dust-up at Hearing." *USA Today*, www.usatoday.com/story/news/politics/2014/03/07/cummings-accepts -issa-apology-for-microphone-incident/6159273/ (accessed 12/12/14).

35. James M. Curry. 2015. *Legislating in the Dark: Information and Power in the House of Representatives*. Chicago, IL: University of Chicago Press.

36. Ashley Halsey. July 22, 2011. "FAA Faces Partial Shutdown." *Washington Post*, www .washingtonpost.com/local/faa-faces-partial-shutdown/2011/07/22/gIQA64o3TI_story .html (accessed 4/5/15).

37. Eric Bontrager. March 24, 2009. "House Republicans to Push for Guns Amendment to Public Lands Catchall." *New York Times*, section Business/Energy and Environment, www .nytimes.com/gwire/2009/03/24/24greenwire-house-republicans-to-push-for-guns -amendment-t-10263.html (accessed 8/30/18).

38. Associated Press. May 20, 2009. "Congress Votes to Allow Guns in National Parks." *MSNBC.com*, www.nbcnews.com/id/30832809/ns/politics-capitol_hill/t/congress-votes -allow-guns-national-parks (accessed 7/27/18).

39. Kenneth Shepsle and Barry Weingast. 1987. "The Institutional Foundations of Commit- tee Power." *American Political Science Review* 81: 85–104.

40. Elizabeth Williamson. April 25, 2007. "Revival of Oversight Role Sought." *Washington Post*.

41. Richard Oppel. July 27, 2014. "Lawmakers Reach Deal on a Fix for V.A.'s Health Care System." *New York Times*.

42. Shawn Zeller. May 19, 2014. "Probe to Nowhere: Partisanship Hobbles Benghazi Panel." CQ *Weekly Report*, 704–11.

43. Richard Cohen. 1999. "Crackup of the Committees." *Congressional Quarterly Weekly Report* 2210–17.

44. Barbara Sinclair. 2011. *Unorthodox Lawmaking: New Legislative Processes in the U.S. Con- gress*. Washington, DC: CQ Press.

45. Walter Oleszek. December 28, 1999. *The Use of Task Forces in the House*. Washington, DC: Congressional Research Service.

46. Deborah Kalb. March 29, 1995. "The Official Gingrich Task Force List." *The Hill*.

47. Oleszek, *Congressional Procedures and the Policy Process*, 16–17.

48. Sinclair, *Unorthodox Lawmaking*.

49. Nolan McCarty. 2016. "The Decline of Regular Order in Appropriations: Does It Matter?," in *Congress and Policy Making in the 21st Century*, ed. by Jeffery Jenkins and Eric Patashnik, 162–86. New York: Cambridge University Press.

50. Oleszek, *Congressional Procedures and the Policy Process*, 345.

51. CQ Almanac. 2014. "Symbolic Budget Resolutions Set Stage for Spending Deal, Omnibus," in *Congressional Quarterly Almanac, 2013*, 410–14. Washington, DC: CQ Press.

52. Oleszek, *Congressional Procedures and the Policy Process*, Table 8.1.

53. Oleszek, *Congressional Procedures and the Policy Process*, 335.

54. Steven J. Balla and Christopher J. Deering. 2013. "Police Patrols and Fire Alarms: An Empirical Examination of the Legislative Preference for Oversight." *Congress & the Presi- dency* 40.1: 27–40; Keith W. Smith. 2010. "Congressional Use of Authorization and Oversight." *Congress & the Presidency* 37.1: 45–63.

55. Charles Babington. August 22, 2007. "Democrats Pursue Agenda with Inquiries." *Associ- ated Press*.

56. David Mayhew. 2005. *Divided We Govern: Party Control, Lawmaking, and Investigations 1946–2002*, 2nd ed. New Haven, CT: Yale University Press.

57. In Chapter 10, we consider why committees have an incentive to conduct oversight of executive agencies under unified government.

58. Douglas Kriner and Liam Schwartz. 2008. "Divided Government and Congressional Investigations." *Legislative Studies Quarterly* 33.2: 295–321; David Parker and Matthew Dull. 2009. "Divided We Quarrel: The Politics of Congressional Investigations, 1947– 2004." *Legislative Studies Quarterly* 34.3: 319–45.

59. E. Scott Adler and John S. Lapinski. 1997. "Demand-Side Theory and Congressional Committee Composition: A Constituency Characteristics Approach." *American Journal of Political Science* 41: 895–918; Scott A. Frisch and Sean Q. Kelly. 2004. "Self-Selection Recon- sidered: House Committee Assignment Requests and Constituency Characteristics."

Political Research Quarterly 57.2: 325–26; Kenneth Shepsle. 1978, *The Giant Jigsaw Puzzle.* Chicago: University of Chicago Press; Shepsle and Weingast; Barry Weingast and William Marshall. 1988. "The Industrial Organization of Congress; or, Why Legislatures, Like Firms, Are Not Organized as Markets." *Journal of Political Economy.* 96: 132–63.

60. "Senate Tracker: A Close Race in Louisiana." September 18, 2014. *Hereandnow,* http://hereandnow.wbur.org/2014/09/18/senate-tracker-louisiana (accessed 7/27/18).

61. Newsweek Staff. 1995. "Why Newt Is No Joke." *Newsweek,* www.newsweek.com/why-newt-no-joke-181574.

62. John H. Aldrich, Brittany N. Perry, and David W. Rohde. 2012. "House Appropriations after the Republican Revolution." *Congress & the Presidency* 39.3: 229–53.

63. Jonathan Strong. December 3, 2012. "Dissidents Pushed Off Prominent Committees." *Roll Call.*

64. Specifically, we use what is referred to as a "difference-in-medians" test, popularized in Groseclose (1994) and Adler and Lapinski (1997). We compare the actual median NOMINATE score for a specific committee in a given congressional term to that of a pool of 10,000 committees of the same size made up of randomly drawn members of the House. The committee is considered a *conservative* outlier if the actual median score for the panel is higher than 95 percent of the random committees. The committee is considered a *liberal* outlier if the actual median score for the panel is lower than 95 percent of the random committees.

65. See also Forrest Maltzman. 1997 *Competing Principals: Committees, Parties, and the Organization of Congress.* Ann Arbor: University of Michigan Press.

66. Sarah Binder. May 27, 2014. *Polarized We Govern?* Washington, DC: Brookings Institution, www.brookings.edu/research/papers/2014/05/27-polarized-we-govern-congress-legislative-gridlock-polarized-binder (accessed 7/27/18).

67. Jamie Carson, Charles Finocchiaro, and David Rohde. 2010. "Consensus, Conflict, and Partisanship in House Decision Making: A Bill-Level Examination of Committee and Floor Behavior." *Congress & the Presidency* 37.3: 231–53.

Chapter 6: Parties

1. Eleven of the 12 Republicans were from California, New Jersey, and New York—generally considered "high-tax states." These Republican House members were opposed to the provision in the bill that limited the deduction for state and local taxes (to just $10,000).

2. Thomas Kaplan and Alan Rappeport. December 19, 2017. "Republican Tax Bill Passes Senate in 51–48 Vote." *New York Times,* www.nytimes.com/2017/12/19/us/politics/tax-bill-vote-congress.html (accessed 5/21/18); Deirdre Walsh, Phil Mattingly, Ashley Killough, Lauren Fox, and Kevin Liptak. December 20, 2017. "White House, GOP Celebrate Passing Sweeping Tax Bill." CNN, www.cnn.com/2017/12/20/politics/house-senate-trump-tax-bill/index.html (accessed 5/21/18).

3. Josh Kraushaar. 2013. "The Most Divided Congress Ever, at Least Until Next Year." *National Journal,* www.nationaljournal.com/2013-vote-ratings/the-most-divided-congress-ever-at-least-until-next-year-20140206 (accessed 5/21/18).

4. Voteview. December 18, 2016. "The End of the 114th Congress." https://voteviewblog.com/2016/12/18/the-end-of-the-114th-congress/ (accessed 5/21/18).

5. Vital Statistics on Congress. 2017. "Table 8-3 Party Unity Vote in Congress, 1953–2016." Brookings Institution, www.brookings.edu/wp-content/uploads/2017/01/vitalstats_ch8_tbl3.pdf (accessed 5/21/18).

6. John H. Aldrich. 1995. *Why Parties? The Origin and Transformation of Party Politics in America.* Chicago: University of Chicago Press.

7. We use the generic term "caucus" to describe the collection of members of one party in a chamber. Formally, the House and Senate Democrats refer to themselves as a "caucus," while House and Senate Republicans call themselves a "conference."

8. Jeffery A. Jenkins and Charles Stewart. 2013. *Fighting for the Speakership: The House and the Rise of Party Government*. Princeton: Princeton University Press.

9. Prior to 1839, the vote for Speaker was via secret ballot. Partisan defections, which could not be individually traced, eventually led the leadership to make the balloting public. See Jeffery A. Jenkins and Charles Stewart III. 2003. "Out in the Open: The Emergence of Viva Voce Voting in House Speakership Elections." *Legislative Studies Quarterly* 28: 481–508.

10. Jennifer Steinhauer. September 25, 2015. "John Boehner, House Speaker, Will Resign From Congress." *New York Times*, www.nytimes.com/2015/09/26/us/john-boehner-to-resign-from-congress.html (accessed 8/30/18).

11. United States Senate. "Majority and Minority Leaders, United States Senate," www.senate.gov/artandhistory/history/common/briefing/Majority_Minority_Leaders.htm (accessed 5/21/18).

12. Steven V. Roberts. November 29, 1984. "Dole Wins Battle to Be G.O.P. Leader in the New Senate." *New York Times*, www.nytimes.com/1984/11/29/us/dole-wins-battle-to-be-gop-leader-in-the-new-senate.html (accessed 5/21/18).

13. Jonathan Weisman. February 3, 2006. "In an Upset, Boehner Is Elected House GOP Leader." *Washington Post*, www.washingtonpost.com/wp-dyn/content/article/2006/02/02/AR2006020201046.html (accessed 5/21/18).

14. Stephen Jessee and Neil Malhotra. 2010. "Are Congressional Leaders Middlepersons or Extremists? Yes." *Legislative Studies Quarterly* 35(3): 361–92.

15. For research in this area, see Kristin Kanthak. 2007. "Crystal Elephants and Committee Chairs: Campaign Contributions and Leadership Races in the U.S. House of Representatives." *American Politics Research* 35(3): 389–406.

16. Every Republican Is Crucial PAC, 2010 Election cycle, www.opensecrets.org/pacs/expenditures.php?cmte=C00384701&cycle=2010 (accessed 5/21/18).

17. Matt Fuller. 2014. "New House GOP Rules Impact Medals, Gavels—and Paul Ryan?" *Roll Call*, www.rollcall.com/news/policy/new-house-gop-rules-impact-medals-gavels-and-paul-ryan (accessed 5/21/18).

18. Scott Meinke. 2016. *Leadership Organizations in the House of Representatives: Party Participation and Partisan Politics*. Ann Arbor: University of Michigan Press.

19. Michael Koempel, Judy Schneider, and J. Michael Jarrett. 2014. *A Retrospective of House Rules Changes since the 110th Congress*. Washington, DC: Congressional Research Service.

20. Molly E. Reynolds. November 30, 2017. "Retirement from Congress May Be Driven by Term Limits on Committee Chairs." Brookings Institution, www.brookings.edu/blog/fixgov/2017/11/30/committee-chair-term-limits-and-retirements (accessed 5/21/18).

21. Richard Beth. 2013. *Procedures for Considering Changes in Senate Rules*. Washington, DC: Congressional Research Service.

22. Paul Kane. November 21, 2013. "Reid, Democrats Trigger 'Nuclear' Option; Senate Eliminates Most Nominee Filibusters in Party-Line Vote." *Washington Post*, www.washingtonpost.com/politics/senate-poised-to-limit-filibusters-in-party-line-vote-that-would-alter-centuries-of-precedent/2013/11/21/d065cfe8-52b6-11e3-9fe0-fd2ca728e67c_story.html (accessed 6/1/18).

23. Niels Lesniewski. 2014. "How the Nuclear Option Changed the Judiciary." *Roll Call Blog: The World's Greatest Deliberative Body*, http://blogs.rollcall.com/wgdb/nuclear-option-judiciary-nominations/?dcz (accessed 6/1/18).

24. Al Kamen and Paul Kane. December 17, 2014. "Did 'Nuclear Option' Boost Obama's Judicial Appointments?" *Washington Post*, www.washingtonpost.com/blogs/in-the-loop /wp/2014/12/17/did-nuclear-option-boost-obamas-judicial-appointments (accessed 6/1/18).

25. Alexander Bolton. April 6, 2017. "GOP Triggers 'Nuclear Option,' Gutting Filibuster in Gorsuch Fight." TheHill.com, http://thehill.com/homenews/senate/327591-gop-triggers -nuclear-option-gutting-filibuster-in-gorsuch-fight (accessed 5/21/18); Matt Flegen-heimer. April 6, 2017. "Senate Republicans Deploy 'Nuclear Option' to Clear Path for Gorsuch." *New York Times*, www.nytimes.com/2017/04/06/us/politics/neil-gorsuch -supreme-court-senate.html (accessed 5/21/18).

26. Flegenheimer, "Senate Republicans Deploy 'Nuclear Option' to Clear Path for Gorsuch."

27. David Hawkings. 2013. "4 Centrists Get Money Seats in Appropriations Gavel Shuffle." *Roll Call Blog: Hawkings Here*, http://blogs.rollcall.com/hawkings/4-centrists-get-money -seats-in-appropriations-gavel-shuffle (accessed 6/1/18).

28. Emma Dumain. 2015. "Boehner Adds 2 Rules Republicans—Not the Ones He Booted." *Roll Call Blog: 218*, http://blogs.rollcall.com/218/boehner-adds-2-rules-republicans-not -ones-booted (accessed 6/1/18).

29. Marin Cogan. 2015. "The Trade Vote Reignited the War Within the House GOP." *New York Magazine: Daily Intelligencer*, http://nymag.com/daily/intelligencer/2015/06/house -gops-family-feud.html (accessed 8/31/18); Scott Wong. June 16, 2015. "Boehner Takes His Retribution." TheHill.com, http://thehill.com/homenews/house/245136-boehner-takes -his-retribution; Matt Fuller. 2015. "House Conservatives Emboldened, Despite Crack-down Attempt (Video)." *Roll Call Blog: 218*, http://blogs.rollcall.com/218/house -conservatives-emboldened-despite-crackdown/?dcz (accessed 6/1/18).

30. C. Lawrence Evans and Claire Grandy. 2009. "The Whip Systems of Congress," in *Congress Reconsidered*, ed. by Lawrence Dodd and Bruce Oppenheimer, 189–215. Washington, DC: Congressional Quarterly Press.

31. Evans and Grandy, "The Whip Systems of Congress," 203–4; see also Edmund L. Andrews. July 29, 2005. "How Cafta Passed House by 2 Votes." *New York Times*, www .nytimes.com/2005/07/29/politics/how-cafta-passed-house-by-2-votes.html (accessed 5/21/18).

32. Sandra Fish. October 13, 2014. "Republicans Overtake Democrats in Colorado Political Ad Spending," Colorado Public Radio, www.cpr.org/news/story/republicans-overtake -democrats-colorado-political-ad-spending (accessed 8/31/18); Abby Livingston. October 10, 2014. "DCCC Cuts Ad Time in Top Colorado Race." *Roll Call*, www.rollcall.com /news/home/elections-2014-dccc-andrew-romanoff-mike-coffman-ads (accessed 6/1/18).

33. Reid Wilson. September 17, 2010. "Parties Try Divergent Strategies on Ad Spending." *National Journal*, http://0-search.proquest.com.libraries.colorado.edu/docview /751428067/abstract/9F91869A9EFA4028PQ/2 (accessed 6/1/18).

34. Alex Isenstadt. October 10, 2014. "DCCC Pulls $1M in Ads for Romanoff." *POLITICO*, www.politico.com/story/2014/10/andrew-romanoff-dccc-ads-colorado-2014-111799.html (accessed 6/1/18).

35. Naftali Bendavid. November 12, 2006. "The House Rahm Built." *Chicago Tribune*, www .chicagotribune.com/news/local/politics/chi-0611120215nov12-story.html#page=4 (accessed 6/1/18).

36. Kate Nocera. March 10, 2014. "House Democrats Try to Shake Down Members for Dues Payments." *BuzzFeed*, www.buzzfeed.com/katenocera/house-democrats-try -to-shake-down-members-for-dues-payments (accessed 8/31/18); Eric Black. April 18, 2017. "Congressional 'Dues' Help Garner Good Committee Assignments,"

www.minnpost.com/eric-black-ink/2017/04/congressional-dues-help-garner-good
-committee-assignments (accessed 6/1/18).

37. For more on minority party strategy, see Matthew N. Green. 2013. *Underdog Politics: The Minority Party in the U.S. House of Representatives*. New Haven: Yale University Press.

38. Ron Elving. 2010. "GOP's 'Pledge' Echoes 'Contract'; But Much Myth Surrounds '94 Plan," NPR.org, www.npr.org/sections/itsallpolitics/2010/09/23/130068500/watching -washington-gop-pledge (accessed 6/1/18).

39. CQ Almanac. 1996. "104th Congress Ushers in New Era of GOP Rule," in *Congressional Quarterly Almanac 1995*. Washington, DC: CQ Press, http://0-library.cqpress.com .libraries.colorado.edu/cqalmanac/cqal95-1099419 (accessed 6/1/18).

40. Green, *Underdog Politics*.

41. Robert Draper. 2012. *Do Not Ask What Good We Do: Inside the U.S. House of Representatives*, xix. New York: Free Press.

42. Tim Groseclose and Nolan McCarty. 2001. "The Politics of Blame: Bargaining before an Audience." *American Journal of Political Science* 45: 100–19.

43. Steven M. Gillon. 2008. *The Pact: Bill Clinton, Newt Gingrich, and the Rivalry That Defined a Generation*, 1st ed. Oxford; New York: Oxford University Press.

44. Matt Bai. March 28, 2012. "Obama vs. Boehner: Who Killed the Debt Deal?" *New York Times*, www.nytimes.com/2012/04/01/magazine/obama-vs-boehner-who-killed-the-debt -deal.html (accessed 5/21/18).

45. David Corn. 2012. *Showdown: The Inside Story of How Obama Fought Back against Boehner, Cantor, and the Tea Party*. New York: William Morrow.

46. Megan McArdle. March 6, 2012. "The New Louisiana Purchase: Obamacare's $4.3 Bil-lion Boondoggle," *The Atlantic*, www.theatlantic.com/business/archive/2012/03/the-new -louisiana-purchase-obamacares-43-billion-boondoggle/254003/ (accessed 6/1/18); Jor-dan Fabian. February 22, 2010. "Obama Healthcare Plan Nixes Ben Nelson's 'Cornhusker Kickback' deal." TheHill.com, http://thehill.com/blogs/blog-briefing-room/news/82621 -obama-healthcare-plan-nixes-ben-nelsons-cornhusker-kickback-deal (accessed 6/1/18).

47. "President Obama Signs Executive Order on Abortion. March 24, 2010. *PBS News Hour*, www.pbs.org/newshour/health/president-obama-to-sign-executive-order-on-abortion (accessed 5/21/18).

48. Several months later, the final conference report on the legislation played out similarly. The Republicans did not have the necessary votes, and leaders held open the roll call— this time for nearly three hours—until they could obtain a majority.

49. Congressional Quarterly. 2004. "Medicare Revamp Cuts It Close," in CQ *Almanac 2003*. Washington, DC: Congressional Quarterly Press, https://library.cqpress.com/cqalmanac /document.php?id=cqal03-835-24327-1083636&type=toc&num=5 (accessed 6/1/18).

50. Emma Dumain and Matt Fuller. 2015. "GOP Rewrite of 'No Child' Passes on Second Try." *Roll Call Blog: 218*, http://blogs.rollcall.com/218/gop-rewrite-passes-second-try/ ?dcz (accessed 6/1/18).

51. Billy House. 2015. "Three House Republicans Said to Be Punished over Trade Vote." *Bloom-berg Politics*, www.bloomberg.com/politics/articles/2015-06-16/three-house-republicans -said-to-be-punished-over-trade-rule-vote (accessed 8/30/18); Matt Fuller. June 17, 2015. "GOP Leadership Metes Out Retribution for Rules Votes (Updated)." *Roll Call*, www .rollcall.com/news/home/gop-leadership-metes-retribution-rules-votes (accessed 6/1/18).

52. "U.S. Rep. Says Calling Donors for Money Is a Shameful Distraction." April 22, 2016. *CBS News*, www.cbsnews.com/news/preview-dialing-for-dollars (accessed 5/21/18).

53. Heather Caygle. August 17, 2016. "How the GOP Abandoned One of Its Own." *POLIT-ICO*, www.politico.com/story/2016/08/david-jolly-florida-party-fundraising-227020 (accessed 6/1/18).

54. David R. Jones and Monika McDermott. 2004. "The Responsible Party Government Model in House and Senate Elections." *American Journal of Political Science* 48: 1–12; David R. Jones and Monika McDermott. 2009. *Americans, Congress, and Democratic Responsiveness: Public Evaluations of Congress and Electoral Consequences.* Ann Arbor, MI: University of Michigan Press.

55. See David W. Rohde. 1991. *Parties and Leaders in the Postreform House.* Chicago: University of Chicago Press; Aldrich, *Why Parties?*

56. See Gary W. Cox and Mathew D. McCubbins. 1993. *Legislative Leviathan: Party Government in the House.* Berkeley: University of California Press; Gary W. Cox and Mathew D. McCubbins. 2005. *Setting the Agenda: Responsible Party Government in the U.S. House of Representatives.* Cambridge: Cambridge University Press.

57. John Feehery. 2011. "Majority of the Majority." TheHill.com, 2011, http://thehill.com /opinion/columnists/john-feehery/174849-majority-of-the-majority (accessed 6/1/18).

58. Keith Krehbiel. 1998. *Pivotal Politics: A Theory of U.S. Lawmaking.* Chicago: University of Chicago Press.

59. Keith Krehbiel. 1993. "Where's the Party?" *British Journal of Political Science* 23: 235–66.

60. Stephen Ansolabehere, James Snyder, and Charles Stewart. 2001. "The Effects of Party and Preferences on Congressional Roll-Call Voting." *Legislative Studies Quarterly* 26: 533–72; Jeffery A. Jenkins. 1999. "Examining the Bonding Effects of Party: A Comparative Analysis of Roll-Call Voting in the U.S. and Confederate Houses." *American Journal of Political Science* 43: 1144–65; James Snyder and Tim Groseclose. 2000. "Estimating Party Influence in Congressional Roll-Call Voting." *American Journal of Political Science* 44: 193–211; Nolan McCarty, Keith T. Poole, and Howard Rosenthal. 2001. "The Hunt for Party Discipline in Congress." *American Political Science Review* 95: 673–87.

61. Stanley P. Berard. 2012. "Southern Influence in Congress," in *Oxford Handbook of Southern Politics*, ed. by Charles Bullock and Mark Rozell. New York: Oxford University Press, 484–506; David Brady and Charles Bullock. 1980. "Is There a Conservative Coalition in the House?" *Journal of Politics* 42 549–59.

62. John Wilkerson and Barry Pump. 2011. "The Ties That Bind: Coalitions in Congress," in *The Oxford Handbook of the American Congress*, ed. by Eric Schickler and Frances Lee, 618–40. Oxford: Oxford University Press.

63. Brady and Bullock, "Is There a Conservative Coalition in the House?"; Jeffery A. Jenkins and Nathan W. Monroe. 2014. "Negative Agenda Control and the Conservative Coalition in the U.S. House." *Journal of Politics* 76: 1116–27.

64. Cox and McCubbins, *Setting the Agenda*; Ira Katznelson, Kim Geiger, and Daniel Kryder. 1993. "Limiting Liberalism: The Southern Veto in Congress, 1933–1950." *Political Science Quarterly* 108: 283–306.

65. Rebecca Ballhaus. 2014. "A Short History of the Tea Party Movement," *WSJ Blogs— Washington Wire*, http://blogs.wsj.com/washwire/2014/02/27/a-short-history-of-the-tea -party-movement (accessed 6/1/18).

66. Robert Boatright. 2014. "The 2014 Congressional Primaries in Context" (Presented at the What the 2014 Primaries Foretell About the Future of American Politics). Washington, DC: Brookings Institution.

67. Jonathan Martin. June 10, 2014. "Eric Cantor Defeated by David Brat, Tea Party Challenger, in G.O.P. Primary Upset." *New York Times*, www.nytimes.com/2014/06/11/us /politics/eric-cantor-loses-gop-primary.html (accessed 6/1/18).

68. Michael A. Bailey, Jonathan Mummolo, and Hans Noel. 2012. "Tea Party Influence: A Story of Activists and Elites. *American Politics Research* 40: 769–809.

69. Fuller, "House Conservatives Emboldened, Despite Crackdown Attempt (Video)."

70. Frances E. Lee. 2016. "How Party Polarization Affects Governance." *Annual Review of Political Science* 18: 261–82. In effect, these are the two primary conditions of conditional party government.

71. See Keith T. Poole and Howard Rosenthal. 2007. *Ideology and Congress*. New Brunswick, NJ: Transaction Publishers.

72. Katnelson, Geiger, and Kryder, "Limiting Liberalism."

73. Brian Schaffner. 2011. "Party Polarization," in *The Oxford Handbook of the American Congress*, ed. by Eric Schickler and Frances Lee, 527–49. Oxford: Oxford University Press.

74. Laurel Harbridge. 2015. *Is Bipartisanship Dead?: Policy Agreement and Agenda-Setting in the House of Representatives*. New York: Cambridge University Press.

75. Thomas E. Mann and Norman J. Ornstein. 2012. *It's Even Worse Than It Looks: How the American Constitutional System Collided with the New Politics of Extremism*. New York: Basic Books.

76. Elena Schneider. August 2, 2016. "Huelskamp Loses GOP Primary after Ideological Battle." *POLITICO*, www.politico.com/story/2016/08/huelskamp-defeated-in-kansas-primary-226603 (accessed 6/1/18).

Chapter 7: Policy Making

1. Kent Allen. January 3, 2011. "2010 Key House Vote: Immigration Policy." CQ *Weekly*, 72.

2. Alexander Hamilton, James Madison, and John Jay. 2012. *The Federalist Papers*, no. 62, 1st ed., ed. by Richard Beeman. New York: Penguin Books, 2012.

3. Joseph Story. 1891. *Commentaries on the Constitution of the United States*, two volumes, 5th ed., ed. by Melville Bigelow. Boston: Little, Brown.

4. "Biennial Elections." n.d. US House of Representatives: History, Art & Archives, http://history.house.gov/Institution/Origins-Development/Biennial-Elections (accessed 7/14/18).

5. Robert Diamond, ed. 1976. *Origins and Development of Congress*, 40. Washington, DC: Congressional Quarterly.

6. U.S. Senate. n.d. "U.S. Senate: The Senate and the United States Constitution." www.senate.gov/artandhistory/history/common/briefing/Constitution_Senate.htm (accessed 7/5/18).

7. "Constitutional Qualifications." n.d. US House of Representatives: History, Art & Archives, http://history.house.gov/Institution/Origins-Development/Constitutional-Qualifications/http://history.house.gov/Institution/Origins-Development/Constitutional-Qualifications (accessed 7/5/18).

8. Hamilton, Madison, and Jay. *The Federalist Papers*, no. 62.

9. James Madison and Adrienne Koch. 1985. *Notes of Debates in the Federal Convention of 1787*, 2nd ed. Athens, Ohio: Ohio University Press.

10. Alexander Hamilton, James Madison, and John Jay. 2012. *The Federalist Papers*, no. 39, 1st ed., ed. by Richard Beeman. New York: Penguin Books.

11. Alexander Hamilton, James Madison, and John Jay. 2012. *The Federalist Papers*, no. 52, 1st ed., ed. by Richard Beeman. New York: Penguin Books.

12. "Power of the Purse." n.d. US House of Representatives: History, Art & Archives, http://history.house.gov/Institution/Origins-Development/Power-of-the-Purse (accessed 7/5/18).

13. Diamond, *Origins and Development of Congress*, 53–54.

14. Richard F. Fenno. 1982. *The United States Senate: A Bicameral Perspective*, 5. Washington, DC: AEI Press.

15. Hamilton, Madison, and Jay. *The Federalist Papers*. The Federalist Papers, no. 62.

16. Diamond, *Origins and Development of Congress*, 175.

17. Diamond, *Origins and Development of Congress*, 3.

18. Diamond, *Origins and Development of Congress*, 175.
19. George Packer. August 2, 2010. "The Empty Chamber." *New Yorker*, 38–51.
20. Frances E. Lee. 2016. *Insecure Majorities: Congress and the Perpetual Campaign*. Chicago: University of Chicago Press.
21. Chuck Jordan. September 22, 2017. "In the House, If You Don't Like the Rules, Suspend Them." TheHill.com, http://thehill.com/blogs/congress-blog/politics/351963-in-the -house-if-you-dont-like-the-rules-suspend-them (accessed 7/5/18).
22. James Wallner. 2017. "A Beginner's Guide to the Senate's Rules." R Street Policy Study. Washington, DC: R Street Institute. For an explanation of precedents, see Alan Frumin. 1992. *Riddick's Senate Procedure: Precedents and Practices*. Washington, DC: U.S. Government Printing Office.
23. Walter Oleszek. 2014. *Congressional Procedures and the Policy Process*, 9th ed., 171. Washington, DC: CQ Press.
24. Keith Krehbiel. 1991. *Information and Legislative Organization*. Ann Arbor: University of Michigan.
25. Bryan Marshall. 2002. "Explaining the Role of Restrictive Rules in the Postreform House." *Legislative Studies Quarterly* 27: 61–86.
26. Oleszek, *Congressional Procedures and the Policy Process*, 181–82.
27. Molly Reynolds. April 16, 2018. "Procedural Hurdles for the Mueller Protection Bills." *Lawfare* (blog), www.lawfareblog.com/procedural-hurdles-mueller-protection-bills (accessed 7/5/18).
28. Kathryn Pearson and Eric Schickler. 2009. "Discharge Petitions, Agenda Control, and the Congressional Committee System, 1929–76." *Journal of Politics* 71: 1238–56.
29. Catherine Lucey, Kevin Freking, and Matthew Daly. June 27, 2018. "House Rejects Republican Immigration Bill, Ignoring Trump." *Associated Press*, https://wtop.com /government/2018/06/gop-immigration-bill-faces-likely-defeat-in-showdown-vote/ (accessed 7/5/18).
30. Stephen A. Jessee and Sean M. Theriault. 2014. "The Two Faces of Congressional Roll Call Voting." *Party Politics* 20(6): 836–48.
31. CNN, Tal Kopan, Phil Mattingly, and Deirdre Walsh. February 9, 2018. "Trump Signs Massive Budget Deal." CNN politics, www.cnn.com/2018/02/08/politics/budget-vote -congress-shutdown/index.html (accessed 7/5/18).
32. Valerie Heitshusen. 2017. "The Legislative Process on the Senate Floor: An Introduction." CRS Report for Congress. Washington, DC: Congressional Research Service.
33. There are some exceptions where germaneness is required, including on appropriations bills and budget measures, and after cloture has been invoked.
34. "Most Memorable Filibusters in Modern American History." March 6, 2013. Fox News, www.foxnews.com/politics/2013/03/06/most-memorable-filibusters-in-modern -american-history.html; Emily Keeler. September 25, 2013. "Ted Cruz Reads Dr. Seuss and Ayn Rand to Stall Senate." *Los Angeles Times*, http://articles.latimes.com/2013/sep /25/entertainment/la-et-jc-ted-cruz-dr-seuss-ayn-rand-to-stall-senate-20130925 (accessed 9/14/18).
35. Valerie Heitshusen. 2017. "The Legislative Process on the Senate Floor: An Introduction." CRS Report for Congress, 5. Washington, DC: Congressional Research Service.
36. Packer, "The Empty Chamber."
37. Oleszek, *Congressional Procedures and the Policy Process*, 255–57.
38. Evan McMorris-Santoro. February 4, 2010. "Report: Shelby Blocks All Obama Nominations in the Senate over AL Earmarks." *Talking Points Memo* (blog), https://talkingpointsmemo .com/dc/report-shelby-blocks-all-obama-nominations-in-the-senate-over-al-earmarks (accessed 7/5/18).

39. Gregory Koger. 2010. *Filibustering: A Political History of Obstruction in the House and Senate.* Chicago: University of Chicago Press. Note that Koger has a broad list of obstruction tactics that he includes in his count of filibusters. See also the work of Gregory Wawro and Eric Schickler. 2006. *Filibuster: Obstruction and Lawmaking in the U.S. Senate.* Princeton, N.J.: Princeton University Press.

40. David Lightman. February 12, 2010. "Senate Republicans: Filibuster Everything to Win in November?" McClatchy Newspapers, www.mcclatchydc.com/news/politics -government/article24573448.html (accessed 7/5/18).

41. Sarah Binder. November 12, 2013. "What Senate Cloture Votes Tell Us about Obstruction." *Monkey Cage, Washington Post* (blog), www.washingtonpost.com/news/monkey-cage /wp/2013/11/12/what-senate-cloture-votes-tell-us-about-obstruction (accessed 7/5/18).

42. Talking Points Memo. January 27, 2010. "The Rise Of Cloture: How GOP Filibuster Threats Have Changed the Senate." *Talking Points Memo* (blog), https:// talkingpointsmemo.com/dc/the-rise-of-cloture-how-gop-filibuster-threats-have-changed -the-senatehttps://talkingpointsmemo.com/dc/the-rise-of-cloture-how-gop-filibuster -threats-have-changed-the-senate (accessed 7/5/18).

43. Sarah A. Binder and Steven Smith. 1996. *Politics or Principle? Filibustering in the United States Senate.* Washington, DC: Brookings Institution Press.

44. See Lee, *Insecure Majorities: Congress and the Perpetual Campaign*, Chapter 6 for a discussion of majority- and minority-party use of floor votes in the Senate on amendments for purposes of partisan communications.

45. Lisa Mascaro. February 12, 2018. "Senators Begin Freewheeling Immigration Debate, and It's Anyone's Guess Where It Will End Up." *Los Angeles Times* (online), www.latimes.com /politics/la-na-pol-immigration-senate-20180212-story.html (accessed 7/5/18).

46. "Healthy Congress Index." Bipartisan Policy Center, https://bipartisanpolicy.org/congress (accessed 05/28/18).

Chapter 8: The Legislative Effectiveness of Congress and Its Members

1. Lauren French. March 12, 2016. "Congress Setting New Bar for Doing Nothing." *POLITICO*, www.politico.com/story/2016/03/congress-supreme-court-budget-do-nothing- 221057 (accessed 9/14/18); Aaron Blake. December 20, 2016. "The 'Do-Nothing Congress' Graduates to the 'Do-Nothing-Much Congress.'" *The Fix, Washington Post* (blog), www.washingtonpost.com/news/the-fix/wp/2016/12/20/the-do-nothing-congress -graduates-to-the-do-nothing-much-congress/?utm_term=.4f54f8bf48ee (accessed 9/14/18).

2. Cristina Marcos. July 13, 2014. "A 'Do-Nothing Congress'?" TheHill.com, http://thehill .com/blogs/floor-action/212041-a-do-nothing-congress (accessed 9/14/18); Derek Willis. May 28, 2014. "A Do-Nothing Congress? Well, Pretty Close." *New York Times*, www .nytimes.com/2014/05/28/upshot/a-do-nothing-congress-well-pretty-close.html (accessed 9/14/18).

3. Norman Ornstein. July 19, 2011. "Worst. Congress. Ever." *Foreign Policy* (blog).

4. Joseph Cooper and David Brady. 1981. "Toward a Diachronic Analysis of Congress." *American Political Science Review* 75: 988–1012.

5. Thad Hall. 2004. *Authorizing Policy*, 1st ed. Columbus: Ohio State University Press.

6. John Kingdon. 1995. *Agendas, Alternatives, and Public Policies*, 2nd ed. New York: Harper Collins; E. Scott Adler and John Wilkerson. 2012. *Congress and the Politics of Problem Solving.* New York: Cambridge University Press.

7. Rebecca M. Kysar. 2006. "The Sun Also Rises: The Political Economy of Sunset Provisions in the Tax Code." *Georgia Law Review* 40: 335–405.

8. Kysar, "The Sun Also Rises: The Political Economy of Sunset Provisions in the Tax Code."

9. E. Scott Adler, Stefani R. Langehennig, and Ryan W. Bell. 2018. "Congressional Capacity and Reauthorizations." Paper presented at Congressional Capacity Conference, Washington, DC.

10. Danny Vinik. February 3, 2016. "Meet Your Unauthorized Federal Government." *POLITICO*, www.politico.com/agenda/story/2016/02/government-agencies-programs-unauthorized-000036-000037 (accessed 6/19/18).

11. "Causes and Effects of the July–August 2011 Partial Shutdown of the Federal Aviation Administration." March 19, 2012. The Center for the Study of the Presidency & Congress—Presidential Fellows Blog, https://presidentialfellows.wordpress.com/2012/03/19/causes-and-effects-of-the-july-august-2011-partial-shutdown-of-the-federal-aviation-administration/ (accessed 6/19/18).

12. Glen Krutz. 2001. *Hitching a Ride: Omnibus Legislating in the U.S. Congress*. Columbus, OH: Ohio State University Press.

13. Nolan McCarty. 2016. "The Decline of Regular Order in Appropriations: Does It Matter?," in *Congress and Policy Making in the 21st Century*, ed. by Jeffery Jenkins and Eric Patashnik, 162–86. New York: Cambridge University Press.

14. McCarty, "The Decline of Regular Order in Appropriations: Does It Matter?"

15. In his agreement with Congress, President Obama signed legislation (the Budget Control Act of 2011) creating the Joint Select Committee on Deficit Reduction, commonly called the "supercommittee." Its charge was to propose and have Congress enact a reduction in federal spending by $1.2 trillion over 10 years. If it failed in this responsibility, there would be across-the-board cuts in discretionary and defense spending of the same amount. After a flurry of negotiations, a deal was never reached, and the automatic sequestration of funds was implemented.

16. Frances Lee and Timothy Cordova. 2015. "The 'Ins' vs. the 'Outs': The Congressional Politics of the Debt Limit, 1953–2014." Paper given at the History of Congress Conference, Vanderbilt University.

17. Mayhew initially ended the series in 1990, but he has subsequently updated the list at the end of each congressional term.

18. William Howell, Scott Adler, Charles Cameron, and Charles Riemann. "Divided Government and the Legislative Productivity of Congress, 1945–94." *Legislative Studies Quarterly* 25 (2000): 285–312.

19. Joshua Clinton and John S. Lapinski. 2006. "Measuring Legislative Accomplishment, 1877–1994." *American Journal of Political Science* 50: 232–49.

20. Sarah Binder. 2003. *Stalemate: Causes and Consequences of Legislative Gridlock*. Washington, DC: Brookings Institution Press.

21. R. Douglas Arnold. 2016. "Explaining Legislative Achievement," in Congress and Policy Making in the 21st Century, ed. by Jeffery A. Jenkins and Eric M. Patashnik, 301–23. New York: Cambridge University Press.

22. Richard Fenno. 1978. *Home Style: House Members in Their Districts*. Glenview, IL: Scott Foresman & Co.

23. Gary Jacobson. 2012. *The Politics of Congressional Elections*, 8th ed. Boston: Pearson.

24. Craig Volden and Alan E. Wiseman. 2014. *Legislative Effectiveness in the United States Congress: The Lawmakers*, 18. New York, NY: Cambridge University Press.

25. A second and related line of research is to examine the progress of individual bills, which allows us to also examine the characteristics of the bills themselves that contribute to higher probability for passage.

26. Edward B. Hasecke and Jason D. Mycoff. December 1, 2007. "Party Loyalty and Legislative Success: Are Loyal Majority Party Members More Successful in the U.S. House of Repre-

sentatives?" *Political Research Quarterly* 60(4): 607–17; William D. Anderson, Janet M. Box-Steffensmeier, and Valeria Sinclair-Chapman. August 2003. "The Keys to Legislative Success in the U.S. House of Representatives." *Legislative Studies Quarterly* 28(3): 357–86; Gary Cox and William Terry. November 2008. "Legislative Productivity in the 93d–105th Congresses." *Legislative Studies Quarterly* 33: 603–18.

27. Gregory Koger and James Fowler. 2006. "Parties and Agenda-Setting in the Senate, 1973–1998." Manuscript, University of California, San Diego.
28. Cox and Terry, "Legislative Productivity in the 93d–105th Congresses."
29. Adler and Wilkerson, *Congress and the Politics of Problem Solving.*
30. Stephen Frantzich. August 1979. "Who Makes Our Laws? The Legislative Effectiveness of Members of the U. S. Congress." *Legislative Studies Quarterly* 4(3): 409–28; Cox and Terry, "Legislative Productivity in the 93d–105th Congresses." Adler and Wilkerson, *Congress and the Politics of Problem Solving.*
31. Koger and Fowler, "Parties and Agenda-Setting in the Senate, 1973–1998." Anderson, Box-Steffensmeier, and Sinclair-Chapman, "The Keys to Legislative Success in the U.S. House of Representatives." Glen Krutz. 2005. "Issues and Institutions: 'Winnowing' in the U.S. Congress." *American Journal of Political Science* 49: 313–26.
32. Jennifer Lawless and Richard Fox. 2017. *Women, Men & US Politics: Ten Big Questions.* New York: W. W. Norton.
33. Craig Volden, Alan E. Wiseman, and Dana E. Wittmer. 2013. "When Are Women More Effective Lawmakers Than Men?" *American Journal of Political Science* 57: 326–41.
34. Peverill Squire. 1992. "Legislative Professionalization and Membership Diversity in State Legislatures." *Legislative Studies Quarterly* 17: 69–79.
35. Donald Matthews. 1960. *U.S. Senators and Their World.* New York: Vintage Books.
36. Norman Ornstein, Robert Peabody, and David Rohde. 1977. "The Changing Senate: From the 1950s to the 1970s," in *Congress Reconsidered*, 1st ed., ed. by Lawrence Dodd and Bruce Oppenheimer, 3–20. New York: Praeger Publishers; David Rohde, Norman Ornstein, and Robert Peabody. 1985. "Political Change and Legislative Norms in the U.S. Senate, 1957–1974," in *Studies of Congress*, 147–88. Washington, DC: Congressional Quarterly Press.
37. Steven Smith. 1989. *Call to Order: Floor Politics in the House and Senate*, illustrated edition. Washington, DC: Brookings Institution Press.
38. Matthews, *U.S. Senators and Their World.*
39. Richard L. Hall. 1996. *Participation in Congress.* New Haven: Yale University Press.
40. Ralph K. Huitt. 1961. "The Outsider in the Senate: An Alternative Role." *American Political Science Review* 55: 566–75; Eric Schickler. 2012. "The U.S. Senate in the Mid-Twentieth Century," in *The U.S. Senate: From Deliberation to Dysfunction*, ed. by Burdett Loomis, 27–48. Washington, DC: CQ Press.
41. Robert A. Caro. 2002. *Master of the Senate: The Years of Lyndon Johnson III*, 1st ed. New York: Knopf.
42. Barbara Sinclair. 1989. *The Transformation of the U.S. Senate.* Baltimore: Johns Hopkins University Press.
43. Sinclair, *The Transformation of the U.S. Senate.* Smith, *Call to Order: Floor Politics in the House and Senate.*
44. Ornstein, Peabody, and Rohde, "The Changing Senate: From the 1950s to the 1970s."
45. Michele L. Swers. 2013. *Women in the Club: Gender and Policy Making in the Senate.* Chicago, IL: University of Chicago Press.

Chapter 9: Congress and the President

1. This account draws on the time line in CNN Library. December 16, 2016. "2016 Presidential Campaign Hacking Fast Facts." CNN, www.cnn.com/2016/12/26/us/2016-presidential-campaign-hacking-fast-facts/index.html (accessed 7/25/18).

2. David French. March 31, 2017. "A Beginner's Guide to the Trump/Russia Controversy." *National Review*, www.nationalreview.com/article/446339/donald-trump-russia-and-2016-election-controversy-explained (accessed 6/13/18).

3. While these and other prominent Republicans, including Speaker Paul Ryan, supported Obama's actions, they also criticized the actions as being too limited and too long in coming.

4. Evan Perez and Daniella Diaz. January 2, 2017. "White House Announces Retaliation against Russia: Sanctions, Ejecting Diplomats." CNN, www.cnn.com/2016/12/29/politics/russia-sanctions-announced-by-white-house/index.html (accessed 6/13/18).

5. Katie Reilly. May 8, 2017. "Sen. Lindsey Graham: It Was Russia, 'Not Some 400-Pound Guy' That Hacked the 2016 Election." *Time*, http://time.com/4771426/lindsey-graham-election-interference-400-pound-hacker/ (accessed 6/13/18).

6. It was during one of these hearings that the then FBI director James Comey confirmed that the FBI was investigating links between the Trump campaign and Russia. Afterward, Trump fired Comey.

7. Peter Baker and Sophia Kishkovsky. August 2, 2017. "Trump Signs Russian Sanctions into Law, with Caveats." *New York Times*, www.nytimes.com/2017/08/02/world/europe/trump-russia-sanctions.html?_r=0 (accessed 6/13/18).

8. And, in fact, Russian Prime Minister Dmitry Medvedev lashed out on Facebook, sneering that "Trump's administration has demonstrated total impotence by surrendering its executive authority to Congress in the most humiliating way." See *Business Insider*. August 2, 2017. "Russia Reserving Right for More Retaliatory Steps on U.S." https://www.businessinsider.com/ap-russia-reserving-right-for-more-retaliatory-steps-on-us-2017-8 (accessed 7/25/18). In addition, Putin seized American properties and expelled hundreds of U.S. diplomatic workers in Russia.

9. Statement by President Donald J. Trump on the Signing of H.R. 3364. August 2, 2017. White House, www.whitehouse.gov/the-press-office/2017/08/02/statement-president-donald-j-trump-signing-hr-3364 (accessed 6/13/18).

10. Many in Congress viewed this statement warily, seeing it as an indication that Trump planned to ignore the law. For example, Senator Benjamin L. Cardin of Maryland, the senior Democrat on the Foreign Relations Committee and a prime driver behind the legislation, said, "I remain very concerned that this administration will seek to strike a deal with Moscow that is not in the national security interests of the United States." See Baker and Kishkovsky, "Trump Signs Russian Sanctions into Law, with Caveats."

11. Baker and Kishkovsky, "Trump Signs Russian Sanctions into Law, with Caveats."

12. As with nearly every other issue, there was disagreement among the Framers about how much power the president should have. Alexander Hamilton, true to his federalist leanings, preferred a strong executive (see Alexander Hamilton, *The Federalist Papers*, no. 70, 1788), while Thomas Jefferson predictably viewed the position with suspicion. Overall, though, as Dan B. Wood. 2011. "Congress and the Executive Branch: Delegation and Presidential Dominance," in *The Oxford Handbook of the American Congress*, ed. by Eric Schickler and Frances Lee, 789. Oxford: Oxford University Press, has documented, "In many respects, the presidency envisioned by the founders was to be a passive *agent* of Congress."

13. See Richard Neustadt. 1960. *Presidential Power: The Politics of Leadership*. New York: Wiley (as well as the foundations of this view in James Madison's writings in James Madison, *The Federalist Papers*, no. 51, 1787.).

14. As Louis Fisher drily and aptly observes, "the Constitution is remarkable for its laconic treatment of presidential powers" (1981, *The Politics of Shared Power: Congress and the Executive*, 22. Washington, DC: Congressional Quarterly Press).

15. Data drawn from John Woolley and Gerhard Peters. 1999–2018. "Presidential Vetoes." The American Presidency Project. Santa Barbara, CA: University of California. www .presidency.ucsb.edu/data/vetoes.php (accessed 7/25/18). We address changes in the president's nonlegislative powers later in this chapter.

16. See Brian Balogh. 2009. *A Government Out of Sight*. New York: Cambridge University Press; and Paul Frymer. 2017. *Building an American Empire*. Princeton, NJ: Princeton University Press.

17. Fisher, *The Politics of Shared Power: Congress and the Executive*, 16.

18. Of course, Congress has the power of the purse, which means that it controls spending; it can constrain the president's authority to execute the laws by limiting funding to agencies, and it can affect the president's right to effect changes in the military by choosing whether to appropriate funds. In addition, the War Powers Act gives Congress, and not the president, the power to declare war. The point here is that presidents enjoy broad authority to manage the executive branch and this management can entail major decisions, such as when President Truman integrated the military through an executive order.

19. The courts have limited this power, allowing presidents to use the pocket veto only when Congress adjourns *sine die*—that is, for an indefinite period.

20. See the discussion in Louis Fisher. 2007. *Constitutional Conflicts between Congress and the President*, 5th ed., 116–19. Lawrence: University of Kansas Press.

21. In addition, there are other powers that presidents use that do not appear in the Constitution, some of which Congress gave to them (e.g., that the president starts the budget process by formally submitting a budget) and others that they claimed on their own (e.g., signing statements, which we discuss later in this chapter).

22. Ronald Reagan. January 25, 1983. "Address before a Joint Session of the Congress on the State of the Union." The American Presidency Project, www.presidency.ucsb.edu/ws /index.php?pid=41698 (accessed 6/13/18).

23. Paul C. Light. 1982. *The President's Agenda: Domestic Policy Choice from Kennedy to Carter (with Notes on Ronald Reagan)*, 158. Baltimore, MD; London: Johns Hopkins University Press.

24. See, for example, Andrew Rudalevige. 2002. *Managing the President's Program: Presidential Leadership and Legislative Policy Formulation*. Princeton: Princeton University Press; and Jeffrey Cohen. 2012. *The President's Legislative Policy Agenda, 1789–2002*. New York: Cambridge University Press.

25. Neustadt, *Presidential Power: The Politics of Leadership*, 11.

26. Neustadt, *Presidential Power: The Politics of Leadership*, 40.

27. George Edwards. 2009. "Presidential Approval as a Source of Influence in Congress," in *The Oxford Handbook of the American Presidency*, ed. by George C. Edwards and William Howell, 339–61. New York: Oxford University Press.

28. See George C. Edwards. 1980. *Presidential Influence in Congress*, 147–66. San Francisco: W. H. Freeman; and Andrew Rudalevige. May 13, 2005. "The Structure of Leadership: Presidents, Hierarchies, and Information Flow." *Presidential Studies Quarterly* 35(2): 434–6.

29. Patricia H. Conley. 2001. *Presidential Mandates: How Elections Shape the National Agenda*, 86–115. Chicago: University of Chicago Press.

30. Stephen J. Wayne. 2009. "Legislative Skills," in *The Oxford Handbook of the American Presidency*, ed. by George C. Edwards and William Howell, 311–37. New York: Oxford University Press.

31. Michael R. Gordon. October 20, 1990. "The Budget Battle; Cheney May Seek Veto Unless Pentagon Is Heeded on Arms Budget. *New York Times*, www.nytimes.com/1990 /10/20/us/the-budget-battle-cheney-may-seek-veto-unless-pentagon-is-heeded-on-arms -budget.html (accessed 6/13/18)

32. See Laurie L. Rice. 2010. "Statements of Power: Presidential Use of Statements of Administration Policy and Signing Statements in the Legislative Process." *Presidential Studies Quarterly* 40: 686–707, for a more detailed discussion of statements of administrative policy.

33. Leo Shane III. September 8, 2017. "White House Objects to Military Pay, Housing Changes in Senate Budget Bill." *Military Times*, www.militarytimes.com/pay-benefits /2017/09/08/white-house-objects-to-military-pay-housing-changes-in-senate-budget -bill/ (accessed 6/13/18). For the president's statement when signing the bill, see "Statement by President Donald J. Trump on H.R. 2810." Statements and Releases, December 12, 2017, www.whitehouse.gov/briefings-statements/statement-president -donald-j-trump-h-r-2810/ (accessed 7/25/18).

34. Samuel Kernell. 2007. *Going Public: New Strategies of Presidential Leadership*. Washington, DC: CQ Press.

35. The president has such a bully pulpit by virtue of being the single politician in the United States who is elected by the entire country, which, combined with the increasing power of the presidency over time, means that the media pay an enormous amount of attention to whatever presidents say or do.

36. George Skelton. March 14, 1985. "'Make My Day': Reagan Assails Congress, Vows Tax Hike Veto." *LA Times*, www.articles.latimes.com/1985-03-14/news/mn-26514_1 _spending-cuts (accessed 6/13/18).

37. Sean Sullivan, John Wagner, and Kelsey Snell. June 12, 2017. "Trump: 'I Will Be Very Angry' If GOP Senators Don't Pass a Health-Care Bill." *Washington Post*, www .washingtonpost.com/politics/trump-i-will-be-very-angry-if-gop-senators-dont-pass-a -health-care-bill/2017/07/12/cad615ae-673b-11e7-a1d7-9a32c91c6f40_story.html?utm _term=.575788294562&wpisrc=nl_evening&wpmm=1 (accessed 6/13/18).

38. Matthew Eshbaugh-Soha and Thomas Miles. 2011. "Presidential Speeches and the Stages of the Legislative Process." *Congress & the Presidency* 38(3): 301–21.

39. "Minimizing the Economic Burden of the Patient Protection and Affordable Care Act Pending Repeal," Executive Order 13765. January 20, 2017, https://www.federalregister .gov/documents/2017/01/24/2017-01799/minimizing-the-economic-burden-of-the -patient-protection-and-affordable-care-act-pending-repeal (accessed 7/25/18).

40. For example, Barack Obama issued 34.6 executive orders per year, which was the lowest rate among recent presidents, slightly fewer than George W. Bush's 36.4, Bill Clinton's 45.5, George H. W. Bush's 41.5, and Ronald Reagan's 47.6. In the first 13 months of his term, Donald Trump issued 59 executive orders. For perspective, FDR issued an average of 307 executive orders per year! For complete data on executive orders, see Amrita Khalid. June 3, 2016. "The Number of Executive Orders by Every U.S. President." The Daily Dot, www.dailydot.com/layer8/number-of-executive-orders-per -president/ (accessed 7/25/18); and Presidential Actions, www.whitehouse.gov/briefing -room/presidential-actions/executive-orders (accessed 7/25/18). Interestingly, as the overall use of executive orders has decreased since the middle of the twentieth century, the use of presidential memoranda has increased steadily, and the use of presidential proclamations has increased dramatically. See Yu Ouyang and Richard W. Waterman. 2015. "How Legislative (In)Activity, Ideological Divergence, and Divided Government Impact Executive Unilateralism: A Test of Three Theories." *Congress & the Presidency* 42(3): 317–41.

41. For an insightful analysis of the politics of waivers, see Elizabeth K. Mann. 2016. "Presidential Policymaking at the State Level: Revision through Waivers." Dissertation, University of Michigan.

42. See Ian Ostrander and Joel Sievert. 2013. "What's So Sinister about Presidential Signing Statements?" *Presidential Studies Quarterly* 43: 58–80.

43. Regarding the limits to signing statements, see Ostrander and Sievert, "The Logic of Presidential Signing Statements" and Ian Ostrander and Joel Sievert. 2014. "Presidential Signing Statements and the Durability of the Law." *Congress & the Presidency* 41(3): 141–53. For a discussion of the ways in which waivers are not a pure unilateral strategy, see Mann, "Presidential Policymaking at the State Level: Revision through Waivers."

44. Paul E. Rutledge and Heather A. Larsen-Price. 2014. "The President as Agenda Setter-in-Chief: The Dynamics of Congressional and Presidential Agenda Setting." *Policy Studies Journal* 42.3: 443–64.

45. Rudalevige, *Managing the President's Program: Presidential Leadership and Legislative Policy Formulation*.

46. Cohen, *The President's Legislative Policy Agenda, 1789–2002*, 157.

47. See Chamberlain, 1946, 450–53 (discussed in Wayne, "Legislative Skills").

48. James P. Pfiffner. 1996. *The Strategic President: Hitting the Ground Running*, 112. Lawrence: University of Kansas Press.

49. Quoted in Paul C. Light. 1999. *The President's Agenda: Domestic Policy Choice from Kennedy to Clinton*, 3rd edition, 43. Baltimore: Johns Hopkins University Press. Light also notes that *"presidents set their domestic agendas early and repeat them often"* p. 41 (italics in original).

50. George C. Edwards III and Andrew Barrett. 2000. "Presidential Agenda Setting in Congress," in *Polarized Politics: Congress and the President in a Partisan Era*, ed. by Jon Bond and Richard Fleisher, 126. Washington, DC: Congressional Quarterly Press.

51. Edwards and Barrett, "Presidential Agenda Setting in Congress," 126.

52. Barbara Sinclair. 2000. *Unorthodox Lawmaking: New Legislative Processes in the U.S. Congress*, 142. Washington, DC: CQ Press.

53. Mark A. Peterson. 1990. *Legislating Together: The White House and Capitol Hill from Eisenhower to Reagan*, 95–6, 152–7. Cambridge, Massachusetts: Harvard University Press.

54. Heather A. Larsen-Price and Paul Rutledge. 2013. "Follow the Leader: Issue-Dependent Representation in American Political Institutions." *Congress & the Presidency* 40(1): 1.

55. John Lovett, Shaun Bevan, and Frank R. Baumgartner. 2015. "Popular Presidents Can Affect Congressional Attention, for a Little While." *Policy Studies Journal* 43(1): 22–43. Presidents influence congressional attention under unified government when they have approval ratings in the upper 50s or higher. Under divided government, these ratings need to be in the 80s or above to produce a significant change in congressional attention. Roger T. Larocca also finds that the effect fades rather quickly over time (2006, *The Presidential Agenda: Sources of Executive Influence in Congress*. Columbus: Ohio State Press).

56. The quote, as well as the more general claims, come from Rudalevige, *Managing the President's Program: Presidential Leadership and Legislative Policy Formulation*, 63.

57. Other analyses have found similar patterns of success. Peterson, for example, found that presidents won all or part of what they wanted on 54 percent of the items they proposed.

58. See Brandice Canes-Wrone and Scott de Marchi. 2002. "Presidential Approval and Legislative Success." *Journal of Politics* 64(2): 491–509.

59. Tom Raum. July 28, 1981. "Hill Flooded with Phone Calls, Telegrams." Associated Press.

60. See George C. Edwards III. 2003. *On Deaf Ears: The Limits of the Bully Pulpit*. New Haven: Yale University Press; and George C. Edwards III. 2015. *Overreach: Leadership in the Obama Presidency*. Princeton, NJ: Princeton University Press.

61. This section is drawn from Brandice Canes-Wrone. 2001. "The President's Legislative Influence from Public Appeals." *American Journal of Political Science* 45(2): 313–29.

62. Interestingly, the ability to use public appeals to increase success is not limited to popular presidents. Presidents with lower levels of popularity can also increase their chances of legislative success by appealing to the public, although the effect is smaller. See Brandice Canes-Wrone. 2004. "The Public Presidency, Personal Approval Ratings, and Policy Making." *Presidential Studies Quarterly* 34(3): 477–92.

63. See Bryan Marshall. 2012. "Congress and the Executive: Unilateralism and Legislative Bargaining," in *New Directions in Congressional Politics*, ed. by Jamie L. Carson, 183–201. New York: Routledge. See D. Roderick Kiewiet and Matthew D. McCubbins. 1988. "Presidential Influence on Congressional Appropriations Decisions." *American Journal of Political Science* 32(30): 713–36, for an argument that veto threats are more effective at getting Congress to do less (i.e., to cut spending) than to do more (e.g., to increase spending).

64. Howell shows that executive orders increase under divided government, while Kenneth Mayer. 2002. *With the Stroke of a Pen: Executive Orders and Presidential Power.* Princeton, NJ: Princeton University Press, does not. Alexander Bolton and Sharece Thrower. 2016. "Legislative Capacity and Executive Unilateralism." *American Journal of Political Science* 60(3): 649–63 (doi:10.1111/ajps.12190), suggest a middle ground: in the past, divided government led to more executive orders, but this has been less true in recent decades, because Congress now has a greater capacity to constrain the president. Mann, "Presidential Policymaking at the State Level: Revision through Waivers," shows that waivers increase under divided government, contingent on agreement between the president and governors. Christopher S. Kelley and Bryan W. Marshall. 2008. "The Last Word: Presidential Power and the Role of Signing Statements." *Presidential Studies Quarterly* 38: 248–67, find that divided government can lead to an increase in signing statements, while Ian Ostrander and Joel Siewert. 2013. "The Logic of Presidential Signing Statements." *Political Research Quarterly* 66(1) 141–53, contend that this effect is conditional.

65. See Barbara Sinclair. 2006. *Party Wars: Polarization and the Politics of National Policymaking*, 247. Norman: University of Oklahoma Press.

66. Kernell, *Going Public: New Strategies of Presidential Leadership*, 216. Jeff Cummins. 2010. "The Partisan Considerations of the President's Agenda." *Polity* 42(3): 398–422, shows that the State of the Union address increases the president's chance of success regarding the domestic agenda, but only if polarization is average or low and the opposition party does not control Congress.

67. See Daniel Paul Franklin and Michael P. Fix. 2016. "The Best of Times and the Worst of Times: Polarization and Presidential Success in Congress." *Congress & the Presidency* 43(3): 377–94.

68. See William G. Howell and Jon C. Rogowski. 2013. "War, the Presidency, and Legislative Voting Behavior." *American Journal of Political Science* 57: 150–66. Interestingly, they do not find evidence of such an effect during the Korean or Vietnam Wars. William G. Howell, Saul P. Jackman, and Jon C. Rogowski. 2012. "The Wartime President: Insights, Lessons, and Opportunities for Continued Investigation." *Presidential Studies Quarterly* 42.4: 791–810, argue that this effect occurs because national, as opposed to local, considerations are heightened during war, and the president has clear information advantages.

69. For a more nuanced view of these agreements, see Glen S. Krutz and Jeffrey S. Peake. 2009. *Treaty Politics and the Rise of Executive Agreements.* Ann Arbor: University of Michigan Press, who point out that while executive agreements give presidents a bargaining advantage, many of them either are based on statutes or require at least some congressional action.

70. Peterson, *Legislating Together: The White House and Capitol Hill from Eisenhower to Reagan.*

71. Charles Shipan. March 1, 1996. "Senate Committees and Turf: Do Jurisdictions Matter?" *Political Research Quarterly* 49:177–89, demonstrates that the size of the agenda expands

during divided government, indicating that the president's agenda items face competition from those items favored by the opposing party.

72. Jordan Carney. May 23, 2017. "McCain: Trump's Budget 'Dead on Arrival.'" TheHill .com, http://thehill.com/blogs/floor-action/senate/334731-mccain-trumps-budget-dead -on-arrival (accessed 6/13/18).

73. Carney, "McCain: Trump's Budget 'Dead on Arrival.'"

74. This logic, and the following example, is spelled out in Tim Groseclose and Nolan McCarty. 2001. "The Politics of Blame: Bargaining before an Audience." *American Journal of Political Science* 45(1): 100–19.

75. A more recent example occurred in 2015 when Congress was working on an infrastructure bill that included the controversial Keystone Pipeline. After a spokesman for President Obama indicated that the president was unlikely to sign the legislation, Senate Majority Leader Mitch McConnell (R-KY) publicly rebuked the president: "The president threatening to veto the first bipartisan infrastructure bill of the new Congress must come as a shock to the American people who spoke loudly in November in favor of bipartisan accomplishments" (Coral Davenport. January 6, 2015. "With Veto Threat, Obama and Congress Head for Collision over Keystone Pipeline." *New York Times*, www.nytimes.com/2015/01/07/us /politics/with-veto-threat-obama-and-congress-head-for-collision-over-keystone-pipeline .html [accessed 7/25/18]). Congress did pass the bill, which Obama then vetoed.

76. Ostrander and Sievert, "Presidential Signing Statements and the Durability of the Law," show that Congress is much more likely to revise laws for which presidents have issued signing statements.

77. See Hans J. G. Hassell and Samuel Kernell. 2015. "Veto Rhetoric and Legislative Riders." *American Journal of Political Science* 60(4): 845–59 (doi:10.1111/ajps.12217). These threats seem to be effective mainly by holding out the promise that the president's co-partisans in Congress will disrupt the normal legislative process (e.g., engaging in filibusters) unless the rider is softened.

78. For a theoretical foundation for this point, see John Ferejohn and Charles Shipan. 1990. "Congressional Influence on Bureaucracy." *Journal of Law, Economics, and Organization* 6: 1–20.

79. Scott H. Ainsworth, Brian M. Harward, and Kenneth W. Moffett. 2012. "Congressional Response to Presidential Signing Statements." *American Politics Research* 40.6: 1067–91.

80. David Weigel. September 30, 2015. "Boehner's Likely Successor Credits Benghazi Committee for Lowering Hillary Clinton's Poll Numbers." *Washington Post*, www.washington post.com/news/post-politics/wp/2015/09/30/boehners-likely-successor-credits-benghazi -committee-for-lowering-hillary-clintons-poll-numbers/?utm_term=.2c1cb8e2c6de (accessed 6/13/18).

81. Douglas L. Kriner and Eric Schickler. 2016. *Investigating the President: Congressional Checks on Presidential Power*, 6. Princeton, NJ: Princeton University Press.

82. Kriner and Schickler, *Investigating the President: Congressional Checks on Presidential Power*, 113.

83. Andrew McCarty. July 12, 2017. "Trump, Russia, and the Misconduct of Public Men." *National Review*, www.nationalreview.com/article/449401/trump-jr-emails-high-crimes -misdemeanors (accessed 7/25/18). The Framers generally agreed that policy and politics are different, and what Madison referred to as "maladministration," were not legitimate grounds for impeachment. But several Framers pointed to corruption, public misconduct, and illicit entanglements with foreign powers as impeachable offenses under the "High Crimes and Misdemeanors" standard. See Cass R. Sunstein. February 15, 2017. "What Impeachment Meant to the Founders." *Bloomberg*, www.bloomberg.com/view/articles /2017-02-15/what-impeachment-meant-to-the-founders (accessed 7/25/18).

84. Alexander Hamilton, *The Federalist Papers*, no. 65 (1788). Benjamin Franklin supported adding impeachment provisions to the Constitution because he worried that otherwise citizens' only recourse might be assassination. Franklin viewed impeachment of an official who had "rendered himself obnoxious" as far preferable to assassination. See Kat Eschner. December 19, 2016. "Presidents Can Be Impeached Because Benjamin Franklin Thought It Was Better Than Assassination." *Smart News*, www.smithsonianmag.com /smart-news/american-presidents-can-be-impeached-because-benjamin-franklin-thought -it-was-better-assassination-180961500/ (accessed 7/25/18); and Josh Chaffetz. 2010. "Impeachment and Assassination." *Minnesota Law Review* 95: 347–423.

Chapter 10: Congress and the Bureaucracy

1. In the end, no groups that applied were denied 501(c)(4) status. But of the 300 groups that were targeted for extra scrutiny, 75 received this treatment after having been identified by their names. And 25 groups withdrew their applications. See Zachary A. Goldfarb and Karen Tumulty. May 20, 2013. "IRS Admits Targeting Conservatives, for Tax Scrutiny in 2012 Election." *Washington Post*, www.washingtonpost.com/business/economy/irs-admits -targeting-conservatives-for-tax-scrutiny-in-2012-election/2013/05/10/3b6a0ada-b987 -11e2-92f3-f291801936b8_story.html?utm_term=.b54a18635add (accessed 7/19/18).

2. See Kelsey Snell. August 5, 2015. "Two Years after Scandal, the IRS Still Struggling." *Washington Post*, www.washingtonpost.com/news/powerpost/wp/2015/08/05/two-years -after-scandal-the-irs-still-struggling/?utm_term=.4956922e0aa6 (accessed 7/19/18).

3. We obtained information on state budgets from "List of U.S. State Budgets." Wikipedia, https://en.wikipedia.org/wiki/List_of_U.S._state_budgets (accessed 8/6/18).

4. In most cases, these grievances are initially heard by *administrative law judges*, who are bureaucrats empowered to make decisions about specific cases (i.e., they adjudicate these disputes). Eventually these grievances can be appealed to the five-member board at the head of the agency. The findings of the board are then final, subject to judicial review in the appellate courts.

5. The agency's rule, which can be found at "Guidance to Identify Waters Protected by the Clean Water Act," Environmental Protection Agency, https://www.epa.gov/cwa-404 /guidance-identify-waters-protected-clean-water-act (accessed 8/6/18), identifies the parts of the law that refer to "navigable waters."

6. The 115th Congress and President Trump struck down this rule using the Congressional Review Act, which we discuss next.

7. See the agency's discussion and explanation of the rule at "HHS Final Rule and Treasury Notices on Individual Shared Responsibility Provision Exemptions, Minimum Essential Coverage, and Related Topics." June 26, 2013, www.cms.gov/Newsroom /MediaReleaseDatabase/Fact-Sheets/2013-Fact-Sheets-Items/2013-06 26.html?DLPage =1&DLSort=0&DLSortDir=descending%20and%20a%20guidance%20 (accessed 8/6/18). As HHS explains, the "final regulation includes rules that will ease implementation and help to ensure that the shared responsibility payment obligation applies only to the limited group of taxpayers who have ready access to affordable coverage but choose to spend a substantial period of time uninsured." The sections of the law that deputize the secretary to take such actions include Sec. 1411 (b)(5)(a) and Sec. 1501 (d) and (e). See "Compilation of Patient Protection and Affordable Care Act." Office of the Legislative Counsel for the use of the House of Representatives, May 1, 2010, http://housedocs.house.gov /energycommerce/ppacacon.pdf (accessed 8/6/18). For an outstanding discussion of the rules regarding exemptions, see Timothy Jost. June 27, 2013. "Implementing Health Reform: Exemptions From the Individual Mandate." *Health Affairs* (blog), http://

healthaffairs.org/blog/2013/06/27/implementing-health-reform-exemptions-from-the
-individual-mandate/ (accessed 8/6/18).

8. See the press release from the Centers for Medicare & Medicaid Services at "HHS Final
Rule and Treasury Notices on Individual Shared Responsibility Provision Exemptions,
Minimum Essential Coverage, and Related Topics." Centers for Medicare & Medicaid
Services, http://www.cms.gov/CCIIO/Resources/Regulations-and-Guidance/Downloads
/exemptions-guidance-6-26-2013.pdf (accessed 8/6/18).

9. The estimate of the number of pages of laws passed by Congress comes from Christopher
Beam. August 20, 2009. "Paper Weight." *Slate,* www.slate.com/articles/news_and
_politics/explainer/2009/08/paper_weight.html (accessed 8/6/18). For the pages in the
Federal Register, see Pages in the Federal Register (1936–2015), Regulatory Studies,
https://regulatorystudies.columbian.gwu.edu/sites/regulatorystudies.columbian.gwu.edu
/files/downloads/Pages.JPG (accessed 8/6/18). It is worth noting, however, that the number
of what are called "significant rules" (based on their predicted effects or costs) has
dropped in recent years and was much lower under Obama than under his two
predecessors.

10. Pamela J. Clouser McCann. 2016. *The Federal Design Dilemma: Congress and Intergovern-
mental Delegation.* New York: Cambridge University Press.

11. Justin Grimmer, Sean J. Westwood, and Solomon Messing. 2014. *The Impression of Influence.*
Princeton, NJ: Princeton University Press.

12. The House Oversight and Government Reform Committee has broader responsibility for
oversight but is less powerful in any given policy area.

13. Lawrence C. Dodd and Richard L. Schott. 1979. *Congress and the Administrative State.*
New York: Wiley.

14. Stephen Dinan. January 12, 2017. "Paul Ryan Rules Out Donald Trump's 'Deportation
Force.'" *Washington Post,* www.washingtontimes.com/news/2017/jan/12/paul-ryan-rules
-out-donald-trumps-deportation-forc (accessed 7/19/18).

15. See Renae Merle. October 26, 2016. "This Obscure Government Agency Has a Plan to
put Wall Street CEOs in Prison." *Washington Post,* www.washingtonpost.com/news
/business/wp/2016/10/26/this-obscure-government-agency-has-a-plan-to-put-wall-street
-ceos-in-prison/?utm_term=.1832f13d382e (accessed 8/6/18) for a discussion of
SIGTARP.

16. As Anne Joseph O'Connell has pointed out, this dichotomy between executive branch
and independent agencies is an oversimplification (see 2013–14, "Bureaucracy at the
Boundary." *University of Pennsylvania Law Review* 162: 841–927. Many well-known agencies, including the Postal Service, the National Guard, and the U.S. Anti-Doping Agency,
fit into neither category. Still, most of the largest and most prominent agencies fall into
these two classifications.

17. There are other agencies within the executive branch that do not fall within one of the
main cabinet agencies, such as NASA.

18. In some cases, the president can create these agencies by organizing existing departments
and bringing them together into a single agency. Richard Nixon took such an approach
with the creation of the EPA in 1970. Even in that case, however, Congress played a role,
albeit a lesser role than in the case of other executive departments. When Nixon revealed
his plan to bring together units that currently exist in other agencies (e.g., the Department of the Interior, the FDA, the Council on Environmental Quality), the Government
Operations subcommittees in each chamber held hearings about the proposed reorganization and produced reports endorsing the president's idea.

19. David E. Lewis. 2003. *Presidents and the Politics of Agency Design: Political Insulation in the
United States Government Bureaucracy, 1946–1997.* Stanford, CA: Stanford University Press.

20. B. Dan Wood and John Bohte. 2004. "Political Transaction Costs and the Politics of Administrative Design." *Journal of Politics* 66(1): 176–202. See also Lewis, *Presidents and the Politics of Agency Design: Political Insulation in the United States Government Bureaucracy, 1946–1997.*

21. The authors also coded whether Congress gave agencies adjudicatory authority, which they contend also increases autonomy. However, because much of that autonomy relates to the ability of courts to overturn agency actions, here we focus on only the grants of rule-making authority. In their statistical tests, they find similar patterns for adjudication as for rule making.

22. Data on the number of appointees comes from "United States Government Policy and Supporting Positions (Plum Book)." Government Publishing Office, https://m.gpo.gov /plumbook (accessed 8/6/18). The Senate's authority to confirm presidential nominees derives from Article II, Section 2 of the Constitution. Notably, this section also gives Congress the power to create positions that do *not* require Senate approval, stating that "Congress may by Law vest the Appointment of such inferior Officers, as they think proper, in the President alone, in the Courts of Law, or in the Heads of Departments."

23. See Nathanial Rakich. January 10, 2017. "It's Really Hard to Block a Cabinet Nominee." *FiveThirtyEight*, https://fivethirtyeight.com/features/its-really-hard-to-block-a-cabinet -nominee/ (accessed 8/6/18).

24. See Glen S. Krutz, Richard Fleisher, and Jon R. Bond. 1998. "From Abe Fortas to Zoë Baird: Why Some Presidential Nominations Fail in the Senate." *American Political Science Review* 92(4): 871–81.

25. See Krutz, Fleisher, and Bond, "From Abe Fortas to Zoë Baird: Why Some Presidential Nominations Fail in the Senate." New evidence does show, however, that the percentage of cabinet nominations that were rejected or withdrawn has increased recently, from just over 1 percent between 1945 and 2000 to just under 8 percent between 2001 and 2012. See James D. King and James W. Riddlesperger Jr. 2013. "Senate Confirmation of Cabinet Appointments: Congress-Centered, Presidency-Centered, and Nominee-Centered Explanations." *Social Science Journal* 50: 177–88.

26. Osita Nwanevu. January 27, 2017. "What the Hell Is Wrong with Senate Democrats?" *Slate*, www.slate.com/blogs/the_slatest/2017/01/27/what_the_hell_is_wrong_with _senate_democrats.html (accessed 7/19/18).

27. See also Jon R. Bond, Richard Fleisher, and Glen S. Krutz. 2009. "Malign Neglect: Evidence That Delay Has Become the Primary Method of Defeating Presidential Appointments." *Congress & the Presidency* 36: 226–43. In effect, the process of appointments is not fixed, but rather changes, often dramatically, over time.

28. See Ian Ostrander. 2016. "The Logic of Collective Inaction: Senatorial Delay in Executive Nominations." *American Journal of Political Science* 60(4): 1063–76.

29. "How Vacancies are Changing the Federal Reserve." April 26, 2016. *Economist*, www .economist.com/news/business-and-finance/21697594-two-empty-board-seats-are -addling-americas-central-bank-how-vacancies-are-changing (accessed 7/19/18).

30. Russell Berman. January 20, 2017. "How Democrats Paved the Way for the Confirmation of Trump's Cabinet." *The Atlantic*, www.theatlantic.com/politics/archive/2017/01 /democrats-trump-cabinet-senate/513782 (accessed 7/19/18).

31. The number of PAS appointees varies by agency. As of January 2017, some, such as HHS, with 18 PAS appointees, have roughly the same number as the Department of Commerce. Others have far more. The Department of State, for example, has 265, including one position formally known as "the Representative of the United States of America to the United Nations, with the rank and status of Ambassador Extraordinary and Plenipotentiary, and Representative of the United States of America in the Security Council of the United Nations."

32. Matthew Rosenberg. December 12, 2016. "Michael Flynn Is Harsh Judge of C.I.A.'s Role." *New York Times*, www.nytimes.com/2016/12/12/us/politics/donald-trump-cia -michael-flynn.html (accessed 7/19/18).

33. Flynn ended up serving only a little over three weeks in the role, the shortest stint of any-one in this position in history. He resigned over allegations of improper contacts with Russia during the presidential campaign and for having lied to Vice President Mike Pence about these contacts.

34. Presidents also can make interim appointments, which are temporary appointments that do not have to be made during recesses. Although this is an even more effective way for presidents to avoid the Senate (interim appointees can serve for up to 210 days, or even longer if the Senate takes no action), it is a power that Congress gave to presidents with the Vacancies Reform Act.

35. Reuters Staff. February 6, 2013. "Postal Service Will End Saturday Mail Delivery." *Reuters*, www.reuters.com/article/usa-postal-idUSL1N0B63K720130206 (accessed 7/19/18).

36. Elvina Nawaguna. March 21, 2013. "Congress to Force Postal Service to Keep Saturday Delivery." *Reuters*, www.reuters.com/article/us-usa-postal-delivery-idUSBRE92K0OL 20130321 (accessed 7/19/18).

37. Charles Shipan. 2004. "Regulatory Regimes, Agency Actions, and the Conditional Nature of Congressional Influence." *American Political Science Review* 98(3) 467–80.

38. See Hannah Lutz. April 12, 2017. "Criticism Lingers over CFPB's Handling of Auto Lending." Automotive News, www.autonews.com/article/20170412/BLOG13 /304129985/criticism-lingers-over-cfpbs-handling-of-auto-lending (accessed 8/6/18).

39. See Jeremy Gelman. 2017. "Rewarding Dysfunction: Interest Groups and Intended Legis-lative Failure." *Legislative Studies Quarterly* 42(4): 661–92.

40. Interestingly, neither side can point to such things actually occurring (i.e., investigations revealed no instances of terrorist plots being revealed or thwarted, or of any violations of privacy or other misuse of the collected data). See Jeff Stone. June 2, 2015. "What Is 'Metadata'? NSA Loses Surveillance Power on American Phone Calls, But 'Data about Data' Remains Hazy." *International Business Times*, www.ibtimes.com/what-metadata-nsa -loses-surveillance-power-american-phone-calls-data-about-data-1947196 (accessed 8/6/18).

41. Greg Sargent. July 25, 2013. "Reform of NSA Surveillance Is Probably Inevitable." *Wash-ington Post*, www.washingtonpost.com/blogs/plum-line/wp/2013/07/25/reform-of-nsa -surveillance-is-probably-inevitable/?utm_term=.984b627abc62 (accessed 8/6/18); and David Weigel. July 25, 2013. "Killing the NSA Softly." *Slate*, www.slate.com/articles /news_and_politics/politics/2013/07/justin_amash_s_nsa_amendment_almost_passed _congressional_critics_think_they.html (accessed 7/19/18).

42. Jeff Stone. June 2, 2015. "What Is 'Metadata'? NSA Loses Surveillance Power on American Phone Calls, But 'Data about Data' Remains Hazy." *International Business Times*, www.ibtimes.com/what-metadata-nsa-loses-surveillance-power-american-phone -calls-data-about-data-1947196 (accessed 7/19/18).

43. These negative votes differ from regular laws in that Congress does not need to obtain the president's signature.

44. *Immigration and Naturalization Service v. Chadha*, 462 U.S. 919 (1983).

45. Indeed, the 2011 appropriations bill on its own included 36 different legislative veto pro-visions. See Michael J. Berry. 2016. *The Modern Legislative Veto: Macropolitical Conflict and the Legacy of Chadha*. Ann Arbor: University of Michigan Press. Data in Berry's book (see Table 2.5) show that between 1989 and 2012, attempts at resolutions of approval were nearly 20 times more likely to succeed than resolutions of disapproval.

46. See Berry, *The Modern Legislative Veto: Macropolitical Conflict and the Legacy of Chadha*; and also Martin Rosenberg. 2008. "Congressional Review of Agency Rulemaking: An Update and Assessment of the Congressional Review Act after a Decade." Washington, DC: Congressional Review Service.

47. Furthermore, in early 2018, Republicans in Congress began to explore using the CRA to overturn a different type of agency action known as guidance documents. Although guidance documents are statements of agency policy, unlike rules, they do not need to be passed via a formal process. Still, the Government Accountability Office told Congress that it could treat these guidance documents as being equivalent to rules, which meant that they, too, could be overturned through the CRA.

48. See David Epstein and Sharon O'Halloran. 1999. *Delegating Powers*, New York: Cambridge University Press.

49. "Criminal Investigations." Environmental Protection Agency, www.epa.gov/enforcement/criminal-investigations (accessed 8/6/18).

50. Daniel P. Carpenter. 1996. "Adaptive Signal Processing, Hierarchy, and Budgetary Control in Federal Regulation." *American Political Science Review* 90(2): 283–302.

51. Jason A. MacDonald. 2010. "Limitation Riders and Congressional Influence over Bureaucratic Policy Decisions." *American Political Science Review* 104.04: 766–82.

52. Joel D. Aberbach. 1990. *Keeping a Watchful Eye: The Politics of Congressional Oversight.* Washington, DC: Brookings Institution Press.

53. For an insightful analysis of how Congress uses informal means to influence agencies, see Kenneth Lowande. (Forthcoming). "Politicization and Responsiveness in Executive Agencies." *Journal of Politics.*

54. E. Scott Adler and John D. Wilkerson. 2013. *Congress and the Politics of Problem Solving.* New York: Cambridge University Press.

55. Michael Bromwich. January 14, 2017. "The Investigation of James Comey Is Exactly What the Country Needs." *Washington Post*, www.washingtonpost.com/opinions/the-investigation-of-james-comey-is-exactly-what-the-country-needs/2017/01/14/83a558b0-da97-11e6-b8b2-cb5164beba6b_story.html?tid=pm_opinions_pop&utm_term=.99c8da2b6939 (accessed 7/19/18).

56. Thomas E. Mann and Norman J. Ornstein. 2006. *The Broken Branch: How Congress Is Failing America and How to Get It Back on Track*, 155. Washington, DC: Brookings Institution Press.

57. Alan K. Ota. June 7, 2010. "Black Gold for a Veteran Inquisitor." CQ *Weekly*, p. 1392.

58. Morris P. Fiorina. 1981. "Congressional Control of the Bureaucracy: A Mismatch of Incentives and Capabilities," in *Congress Reconsidered*, 2nd ed., eds. Lawrence C. Dodd and Bruce J. Oppenheimer, 332–48. Washington: CQ Press. See also Elaine Kamarck. 2016. "A Congressional Oversight Office: A Proposed Early Warning System for the United States Congress." Center for Effective Public Management, Brookings, www.brookings.edu/wp-content/uploads/2016/07/congressional/oversight.pdf (accessed 10/22/18).

59. Matthew D. McCubbins and Thomas Schwartz. 1984. "Congressional Oversight Overlooked: Police Patrols versus Fire Alarms." *American Journal of Political Science* 28(1): 165–79.

60. The figure originally comes from Jason MacDonald and Robert J. McGrath. 2016. "Retrospective Congressional Oversight and the Dynamics of Legislative Influence over the Bureaucracy." *Legislative Studies Quarterly* 41(4): 899–934. This version of their figure comes from the Kamarck article referenced earlier.

61. See Aberbach, *Keeping a Watchful Eye: The Politics of Congressional Oversight.*

62. In a follow-up study, Aberbach distinguishes between two types of oversight. One type is primary-purpose oversight, which he finds that Congress continued to deploy at high

levels in the 1990s. On the other hand, he also found a decline in the 1990s for hearings dealing with authorizations and reauthorizations. See Joel D. Aberbach. 2002. "What's Happened to the Watchful Eye?" *Congress & the Presidency* 29:1, 3–23.

63. Steven J. Balla and Christopher J. Deering. 2013. "Police Patrols and Fire Alarms: An Empirical Examination of the Legislative Preference for Oversight." *Congress & the Presidency*, 40:1, 27–40.

64. See, for example, John D. Huber and Charles R. Shipan. 2002. *Deliberate Discretion? The Institutional Foundations of Bureaucratic Autonomy.* New York: Cambridge University Press.

65. See Joshua D. Clinton, Anthony Bertelli, Christian R. Grose, David E. Lewis, and David C. Nixon. 2012. "Separated Powers in the United States: The Ideology of Agencies, Presidents, and Congress." *American Journal of Political Science* 56(2): 341–54.

66. See Joshua D. Clinton, David E. Lewis, and Jennifer L. Selin. 2014. "Influencing the Bureaucracy: The Irony of Congressional Oversight." *American Journal of Political Science* 58(2): 387–401.

Chapter 11: Congress and the Courts

1. Burgess Everett and Glenn Thrush. February 13, 2016. "McConnell Throws Down the Gauntlet." *POLITICO*, www.politico.com/story/2016/02/mitch-mcconnell-antonin-scalia -supreme-court-nomination-219248 (accessed 8/9/18).

2. For example, the Courts of Appeals affirmed or reversed more than 25,000 cases in 2014. "Table B-5—U.S. Courts of Appeals Federal Judicial Caseload Statistics," United States Courts, March 31, 2014, www.uscourts.gov/statistics/table/b-5/federal-judicial-caseload -statistics/2014/03/31 (accessed 8/10/18). Meanwhile, the district courts issued decisions in approximately 3,000 cases but addressed another 216,000 that were terminated as a result of some court action before trial (e.g., precedential opinions on summary judgment). www.uscourts.gov/statistics/table/c-4/statistical-tables-federal-judiciary/2015/12/31.

3. See Siobhan Hughes. April 19, 2016. "Why Republican Resistance to Vote on Supreme Court Nominee Remains Strong." *Wall Street Journal*, http://blogs.wsj.com/washwire /2016/04/19/why-republican-resistance-to-vote-on-supreme-court-nominee-remains -strong/ (accessed 8/10/18).

4. See Thomas G. Walker and Lee Epstein. 1993. *The Supreme Court of the United States: An Introduction.* New York: St. Martin's Press.

5. Supporters believed that although they had enough votes to create these courts, trying to force this issue might have imperiled ratification of the Constitution. Thus they were content to empower Congress to create such courts later, knowing that they would likely be successful in the first Congress. See Walker and Epstein, *The Supreme Court of the United States: An Introduction.*

6. District courts are located entirely within state boundaries. The number of district courts within a state ranges from one (e.g., Maine, Colorado) to four (e.g., California, Texas).

7. "Table C-4, Civil Cases Terminated, by Nature of Suit and Action Taken, during the 12-Month Period Ending December 31, 2015." U.S. District Courts, www.uscourts.gov/sites /default/files/data_tables/stfj_c4_1231.2015.pdf; "Table D-4, Criminal Defendants Disposed of, by Type of Disposition and Offense, during the 12-Month Period Ending December 31, 2015." U.S. District Courts, www.uscourts.gov/sites/default/files/data _tables/stfj_d4_1231.2015.pdf (both accessed 9/21/18).

8. *League of Women Voters of N.C. v. North Carolina*, 769 F.3d 224 (4th Cir. 2014).

9. Exceptions include cases where the decisions of government agencies are appealed directly to the DC Court of Appeals.

10. Article III, Section 2 spells out examples of such cases (e.g., disagreements between two states or cases involving ambassadors). Such cases are rare, but they can be important. For

example, in *Kansas v. Nebraska and Colorado*, which was decided in 2015, the Supreme Court adjudicated a dispute over states' rights to the waters of the Republican River Basin.

11. In Hamilton's words in *The Federalist*, no. 78, 1798, "The independence of the judges may be an essential safeguard against the effects of occasional ill humors in the society."

12. Arguing in favor, Hamilton, in *The Federalist*, no. 78 (1798), wrote, "Nothing can contribute so much to its firmness and independence as permanency in office, this quality may therefore be justly regarded as an indispensable ingredient in its constitution, and, in a great measure, as the citadel of the public justice and the public security." Thomas Jefferson, in a letter to William T. Barry (July 2, 1822), took the opposing view: "Let the future appointments of judges be for four or six years, and renewable by the President and Senate. This will bring their conduct, at regular periods, under revision and probation, and may keep them in equipoise between the general and special governments." Thomas Jefferson. "Letter CLXIV.—To William T. Barry, July 2, 1822," in *Memoir, Correspondence, and Miscellanies, from the Papers of Thomas Jefferson*. Project Gutenberg, www.gutenberg.org /files/16784/16784-h/16784-h.htm#link2H_4_0164 (accessed 8/20/18).

13. See, for example, this argument: John Aloysius Farrell. February 23, 2009. "No Supreme Court Term Limits." *US News & World Report*, www.usnews.com/opinion /blogs/john-farrell/2009/02/23/no-supreme-court-term-limits-even-with-partisan -justices-like-scalia-and-thomas (accessed 8/13/18), and this argument against: Adrienne LaFrance. November 12, 2013. "Down with Lifetime Appointments." *Slate*, www.slate .com/articles/technology/future_tense/2013/11/lifetime_appointments_don_t_make _sense_anymore.html (accessed 8/13/18). Stuart N. Taylor. June 2005. "Life Tenure Is Too Long for Supreme Court Justices." *The Atlantic*, www.theatlantic.com/magazine /archive/2005/06/life-tenure-is-too-long-for-supreme-court-justices/304134 (accessed 9/25/18).

14. An additional factor providing for independence was the constitutional provision preventing Congress from cutting judges' salaries. Article III, Section 1 of the Constitution specifies that federal judges shall "receive for their Services a Compensation, which shall not be diminished during their Continuance in Office."

15. See Henry J. Abraham. 1999. *Justices, Presidents, and Senators: A History of U.S. Supreme Court Appointments from Washington to Bush II*. Lanham, MD: Rowman & Littlefield.

16. Abraham, *Justices, Presidents, and Senators: A History of U S. Supreme Court Appointments from Washington to Bush II*, 1059.

17. For details on the role of the Judiciary Committee, see Denis Steven Rutkus. July 6, 2005. "Supreme Court Appointment Process." Congressional Research Service Report for Congress, http://fpc.state.gov/documents/organization/50146.pdf (accessed 8/13/18).

18. For a detailed discussion of the Senate's role in the appointment process, see Denis Steven Rutkus. February 19, 2010. "Supreme Court Appointment Process." Congressional Research Service, www.fas.org/sgp/crs/misc/RL31989.pdf (accessed 8/13/18). Much of this section draws upon this report.

19. The tradition is for the committee to report the nomination to the full Senate regardless of whether it has a favorable view of the nominee, allowing the Senate to always weigh in on the nomination. Indeed, there have been half-a-dozen cases over the past 140 years in which the committee did *not* issue a favorable recommendation but sent the nomination forward anyway, most recently with the nominations of Robert Bork (who received an unfavorable report) and Clarence Thomas (whose nomination was reported without recommendation).

20. Transcript: Sen. Orrin Hatch (R-Utah) Opening Statement. July 13, 2009. *Washington Post: CQ Transcriptions*, www.washingtonpost.com/wp-srv/politics/documents/hatch _openingstatement_sotomayor.html (accessed 8/13/18).

21. See Bryon J. Moraski and Charles R. Shipan. 1999. "The Politics of Supreme Court Nominations: A Theory of Institutional Constraints and Choices." *American Journal of Political Science* 43: 1069–95. Moraski and Shipan argue and show that presidents make appointments with the goal of shifting the median of the Supreme Court, taking the preferences of the Senate into account

22. See Charles M. Cameron, Albert D. Cover, and Jeffrey A. Segal. 1990. "Senate Voting on Supreme Court Nominees: A Neoinstitutional Model." *American Political Science Review* 84: 525–34; Jonathan P. Kastellec, Jeffrey R. Lax, and Justin H. Phillips. 2010. "Public Opinion and Senate Confirmation of Supreme Court Nominees." *Journal of Politics* 72: 767–84.

23. See Charles R. Shipan. 2008. "Partisanship, Ideology, and Senate Voting on Supreme Court Nominees." *Journal of Empirical Legal Studies* 5: 55–76.

24. See Sarah A. Binder and Forrest Maltzman. 2009. *Advice and Dissent: The Struggle to Shape the Federal Judiciary.* Washington, DC: Brookings Institution. Although this system largely remains in place—in particular, if a home-state senator opposes a nominee, that nominee is very unlikely to be confirmed—in recent years, it has become much more common for senators to try to block the appointment of judicial nominees to federal courts in other states.

25. See Barbara Sinclair. 2006. *Party Wars.* Norman: University of Oklahoma Press.

26. Alexander Hamilton, *The Federalist,* no. 78.

27. See, for example, Cliff Sloan and David McKean. 2009. *The Great Decision: Jefferson, Adams, Marshall, and the Battle for the Supreme Court.* New York: PublicAffairs. For a provocative and contrary view that the changes attributed to *Marbury* have been exaggerated and that the decision itself has been greatly misunderstood, see Robert Lowry Clinton. 1989. *Marbury v. Madison and Judicial Review.* Lawrence: University of Kansas Press.

28. These cases include *Martin v. Hunter's Lessee* (14 U.S. 304 [1816]), which asserted Supreme Court jurisdiction and authority over state courts in cases involving federal law; *Ex parte Milligan* (71 U.S. 2 [1866]), which ruled that trying citizens in military courts is unconstitutional in conditions when civilian courts are still operating; and *Texas v. White* (74 U.S. 700 [1869]), which held that a state cannot unilaterally secede from the United States, meaning the Confederacy states never left the Union during the Civil War.

29. Mark A. Graber. 1993. "The Nonmajoritarian Difficulty: Legislative Deference to the Judiciary." *Studies in American Political Development* 7: 35–73. Quote is on p. 37. For example, Graber argues that there is a consensus among scholars that the main object of the Sherman Act was to enable Congress to defer to whatever antitrust policy the courts decided to employ. This allowed politicians to ignore demands for federal economic policy, which helped them avoid disrupting existing political alignments.

30. See Keith E. Whittington. 2007. *Political Foundations of Judicial Supremacy: The Presidency, the Supreme Court, and Constitutional Leadership in U.S. History.* Princeton, NJ: Princeton University Press. Even a case as well known, and infamous, as the Court's *Dred Scott* decision can be seen as an example of the Court carrying out the wishes of members of Congress who preferred not to act themselves.

31. See George Lovell. 2010. *Legislative Deferrals.* New York: Cambridge University Press, for an explication of the conditions under which Congress will prefer to defer to the courts.

32. The Sherman Antitrust Act is perhaps the most prominent law that illustrates many of these goals. In this law, Congress handed the courts the responsibility to determine what constituted an antitrust violation, rather than trying to write legislation that identified such violations. It did so for reasons outlined in the text: to avoid controversy over a difficult issue, to give the courts flexibility, and to allow for passage of the law. See Graber, "The Nonmajoritarian Difficulty: Legislative Deference to the Judiciary."

33. 558 U.S. 310 (2010).

34. "Measures Proposed to Amend the Constitution," United States Senate, www.senate.gov /pagelayout/reference/three_column_table/measures_proposed_to_amend_constitution .htm (accessed 8/13/18).

35. See John Nichols. September 11, 2014. "The Senate Tried to Overturn 'Citizen's United' Today. Guess What Stopped Them?" *The Nation*, www.thenation.com/article/senate -tried-overturn-citizens-united-today-guess-what-stopped-them/ (accessed 8/13/18).

36. For a discussion of this conventional wisdom, see Virginia A. Hettinger and Christopher Zorn. 2005. "Explaining the Incidence and Timing of Congressional Responses to the U.S. Supreme Court." *Legislative Studies Quarterly* 30: 5–28.

37. William N. Eskridge Jr. 1991. "Overriding Supreme Court Statutory Interpretation Decisions." *Yale Law Journal* 101: 331–455.

38. See Richard L. Hasen. 2013. "End of the Dialogue? Political Polarization, the Supreme Court, and Congress." *Southern California Law Review* 86: 205–61.

39. See Matthew R. Christiansen and William N. Eskridge Jr. 2014. "Congressional Over-rides of Supreme Court Statutory Interpretation Decisions, 1967–2011." *Texas Law Review* 92: 1317. For a discussion of these two studies, see Amanda Frost. May 30, 2014. "Academic Highlight: Congressional Overrides of Supreme Court Decisions." *SCOTUSblog*, www.scotusblog.com/2014/05/academic-highlight-congressional-overrides-of-supreme -court-decisions/ (accessed 8/13/18).

40. William Saletan. June 26, 2013. "Anti-Gay Is Yesterday." *Slate*, www.slate.com/articles/news _and_politics/frame_game/2013/06/gay_marriage_polls_and_public_opinion_the_supreme _court_s_rulings_upheld.html (accessed 8/13/18); Josh Gerstein. June 25, 2015. "Conserva-tives Steamed at Chief Justice John Roberts' Betrayal." *POLITICO*, www.politico.com/story /2015/06/gop-conservatives-angry-supreme-court-chief-john-roberts-obamacare-119431.

41. See John Nichols. October 25, 2010. "Congressman Considers Move to Impeach Chief Justice John Roberts." *The Nation*, www.thenation.com/article/congressman-considers -move-impeach-chief-justice-john-roberts (accessed 8/20/18).

42. Congress set the size of the Court at nine in the Judiciary Act of 1869.

43. Howard Gillman. 2002. "How Political Parties Can Use the Courts to Advance Their Agendas: Federal Courts in the United States, 1875–1891." *American Political Science Review* 96.03: 511–24.

44. See *Reorganization of the Federal Judiciary*, 75th Cong., 1st sess., 1937, S. Rep. 711. In part, the plan died because it lacked support from key members of the Senate, such as Senator Henry Ashurst, chair of the Senate Judiciary Committee. It certainly did not help that when the bill was read in the Senate, FDR's vice president, John Garner, "stood in the well of the Senate and, as the plan was read aloud to the senators, Garner held his nose and gestured thumbs down," according to Jeff Shesol. 2010. *Supreme Power: Franklin Roosevelt vs. The Supreme Court.* New York: W. W. Norton. Finally, there is a widespread belief that when Justice Owen Roberts, who had previously voted with the conservative justices to strike down New Deal actions, switched and sided with the liberal faction on a minimum wage case, it relieved pressure on Congress to address the obstruction of the Court. In this view, FDR's pressure had the intended effect of producing a more amenable Court. Recent accounts, such as Shesol's, have cast doubt on this story.

45. Chase, who at the time was a Federalist, drew the ire of the Jeffersonian Democratic-Republicans who controlled the House.

46. Porteous was convicted based on a series of activities that Congress found to be corrupt and impeachable, including lying during his confirmation hearings, financial improprieties, failing to recuse himself from a case involving a former law partner, and accepting cash and other favors from lawyers in cases he presided over. See Jennifer Steinhauer. December 8,

2010. "Senate, for Just the 8th Time, Votes to Oust a Federal Judge." *New York Times*, www.nytimes.com/2010/12/09/us/politics/09judge.html (accessed 8/13/18). More recently, Judge Mark Fuller announced his resignation in 2015 after being informed that the House Judiciary Committee was going to impeach him over charges of domestic abuse.

47. In his outstanding history of the relationship between Congress and the courts, Charles Gardner Geyh observes that "[a]lthough the impeachment process may look like a judicial one, it is commonly characterized as political—and fairly so." Gardner Geyh. 2008. *When Congress and Courts Collide*, 116. Ann Arbor: University of Michigan Press.

48. See Geyh, *When Congress and Courts Collide*, 119.

49. Quoted in Scott Keyes. June 28, 2012. "Republican Congressman Suggests 'Impeachment' for Justice over Obamacare Ruling." *ThinkProgress*, http://thinkprogress.org/justice /2012/06/28/508137/louie-gohmert-impeach-kagan (accessed 8/20/18). See also threats to impeach Justices John Roberts, Sotomayor, and Thomas discussed in Robert Barnes. October 31, 2010. "Impeachment Calls Part of Life for a Supreme Court Justice, but Few Get Very Far." *Washington Post*, www.washingtonpost.com/wp-dyn/content/article/2010 /10/31/AR2010103103379.html (accessed 8/13/18).

50. The most thorough and insightful consideration of court-curbing bills can be found in Tom S. Clark. 2011. *The Limits of Judicial Independence*. New York: Cambridge University Press.

51. Clark, *The Limits of Judicial Independence*, 37–8, for example, notes that "jurisdiction-stripping is generally regarded as the main mechanism by which Congress attacks the Court."

52. Other bills focused on impeachment. Then-congressman Gerald R. Ford, for example, pushed for the impeachment of Justice William O. Douglas because of Douglas's liberal rulings, on the grounds that an "impeachable offense" means "whatever a majority of the House of Representatives considers [it] to be at a given moment in history." Quoted in Geyh, *When Congress and Courts Collide*, 109.

53. Lawrence Baum. 1997. *The Puzzle of Judicial Behavior*. Ann Arbor: University of Michigan Press.

54. James R. Zink, James F. Spriggs II, and John T. Scott. 2009. "Courting the Public: The Influence of Decision Attributes on Individuals' Views of Court Opinions." *Journal of Politics* 71(3): 909–25.

55. See Robert A. Katzmann. 1997. *Courts and Congress*. Washington, DC: Brookings Institution.

56. Jeffrey A. Segal. 1997. "Separation-of-Powers Games in the Positive Theory of Congress and Courts." *American Political Science Review* 91: 28–44.

57. Those finding an effect included Lee Epstein, Jack Knight, and Andrew D. Martin. 2001. "The Supreme Court as a Strategic National Policy Maker." *Emory Law Journal* 50 (2): 583–611 (Symposium) and Pablo T. Spiller and Rafael Gely. 1992. "Congressional Control or Judicial Independence: The Determinants of US Supreme Court Labor-Relations Decisions, 1949–1988." *RAND Journal of Economics* 463–92. Those finding either no effect or very little effect include: James F. Spriggs and Thomas G. Hansford. 2001. "Explaining the Overruling of U.S. Supreme Court Precedent." *Journal of Politics* 63: 1091–1111 and Brian Sala and James F. Spriggs. 2004. "Designing Tests of the Supreme Court and the Separation of Powers." *Political Research Quarterly* 57: 197–208.

58. Lee Epstein and Jack Knight. 1997. *The Choices Justices Make*. Washington, DC: CQ Press. Forrest Maltzman, James F. Spriggs, and Paul J. Wahlbeck. 2000. *Crafting Law on the Supreme Court*. New York: Cambridge University Press.

59. Anna Harvey and Barry Friedman. 2009. "Ducking Trouble: Congressionally Induced Selection Bias in the Supreme Court's Agenda." *Journal of Politics* 71: 574–92. But see also Ryan J. Owens. 2010. "The Separation of Powers, Judicial Independence, and Strategic

Agenda Setting." *American Journal of Political Science* 54(2): 412–27, who finds no evidence that justices' votes are affected by the ideological distance between Congress and the Court.

60. This finding helps to explain why the size of the Court's docket (i.e., the number of cases it agrees to hear each year) has been decreasing over the past few decades. See Kenneth W. Moffett, Forrest Maltzman, Karen Miranda, and Charles R. Shipan. 2016. "Strategic Behavior and Variation in the Supreme Court's Caseload over Time." *Justice System Journal* 37.1: 20–38. See also Anna Harvey. 2014. *A Mere Machine: The Supreme Court, Congress, and American Democracy.* New Haven, CT: Yale University Press.

61. See Clark, *The Limits of Judicial Independence.* Jeffrey L. Segal, Chad Westerland, and Stefanie Lindquist. 2011. "Congress, the Supreme Court, and Judicial Review: Testing a Constitutional Separation of Powers Model." *American Journal of Political Science* 55: 89–104 also find support for an institutional legitimacy argument, showing that the Court is less likely to find laws to be unconstitutional when it is faced with a Congress that is ideologically distant.

62. Michael A. Bailey and Forrest Maltzman. 2010. *The Constrained Court: Law, Politics, and the Decisions Justices Make.* Princeton, NJ: Princeton University Press.

63. Robert A. Katzmann. 2016. *Judging Statutes.* New York: Oxford University Press.

64. See Katzmann, *Courts and Congress.*

65. In an interview, Scalia said, "You will see recited in opinions all the way back that the object of interpretation is to determine the intent of the drafter. I don't believe that. We're not governed by the drafter's intent. We're governed by laws." Pete Williams. August 22, 2012. *NBC News,* http://dailynightly.nbcnews.com/_news/2012/08/22/13416169-scalia-judges-should-interpret-words-not-intent?lite (accessed 8/13/18).

66. 467 U.S. 837 (1984). The Supreme Court ruled that the EPA's definition of the word "source" in the Clean Air Act was a reasonable interpretation of the statute.

67. 401 U.S. 402 (1971). The Department of Transportation approved the use of federal funds to construct Interstate 40 through Overton Park in Memphis, Tennessee. A group called Citizens to Preserve Overton Park filed suit to block this action, which the Supreme Court ultimately upheld, stating that it violated a statute requiring the government to demonstrate that there were no "feasible and prudent" alternatives to building through public lands.

68. For a discussion of these sorts of provisions and how Congress deployed them in the area of communications policy, see Charles R. Shipan. 1997. *Designing Judicial Review: Interest Groups, Congress, and Communications Policy.* Ann Arbor: University of Michigan Press.

69. In addition, between 25 and 30 percent of these laws also specified which courts can conduct reviews, who has standing, whether there are time limits, and the scope of reviews. See Pamela J. Clouser McCann, Charles R. Shipan, and Yuhua Wang. 2018. "Congress and Judicial Review of Agency Actions." Manuscript, University of Michigan.

70. Evidence from a recent study shows that Congress writes more specific laws when members want to constrain the courts (e.g., because of ideological disagreements). See Kirk A. Randazzo, Richard W. Waterman, and Jeffrey A. Fine. 2006. "Checking the Federal Courts: The Impact of Congressional Statutes on Judicial Behavior." *Journal of Politics* 68: 1006–17. Quote on p. 1006.

71. Richard A. Paschal. 1991. "The Continuing Colloquy: Congress and the Finality of the Supreme Court." *Journal of Law & Politics* 8: 143.

Chapter 12: Interest Groups

1. For a list of Republican priorities in the House of Representatives, see Speaker Paul Ryan's "A Better Way" document, https://abetterway.speaker.gov/ (accessed 8/23/18).

2. John Sides. November 18, 2017. "Here's the Incredibly Unpopular GOP Tax Reform Plan—In One Graph." *Washington Post*, www.washingtonpost.com/news/monkey-cage /wp/2017/11/18/heres-the-incredibly-unpopular-gop-tax-reform-plan-in-one-graph /?utm_term=.c2cd5df1d1c9 (accessed 8/7/18).

3. H.R. 1628-American Health Care Act of 2017, Maplight, http://maplight.org/data /passthrough/#legacyurl=http://classic.maplight.org/us-congress/bill/115-hr-1628 /12273735/contributions-by-vote (accessed 8/7/18).

4. Gary Strauss. November 30, 2017. "AARP Opposes Senate Tax Bill." AARP, www.aarp .org/politics-society/advocacy/info-2017/senate-letter-tax-fd.html (accessed 8/7/18).

5. See Suzanne P. Clark. November 20, 2017. "Key Vote Letter: Senate 'Tax Cuts and Jobs Act.'" U.S. Chamber of Commerce, www.uschamber.com/letter/key-vote-letter-senate -tax-cuts-and-jobs-act (accessed 8/7/18); and Joshua Bolten. November 29, 2017. "Business Roundtable Letter to Senate in Support of the Tax Cuts and Jobs Act." Business Round-table, http://businessroundtable.org/resources/business-roundtable-letter-senate-support -the-tax-cuts-and-jobs-act (accessed 8/7/18).

6. A related point is that lobbying has become increasingly partisan in recent years. That is, the proportion of lobbying firms that work for both Democrats and Republicans has decreased over time, while the proportion that specialize in one party has increased. See Kevin Bogardus. February 11, 2014. "K Street's Holdouts Are Partisan, Proud." *The Hill*, http://thehill.com/business-a-lobbying/business-a-lobbying/198012-showing-their-colors -k-streets-holdouts-are-partisan (accessed 8/7/18).

7. Cristina Marcos. November 7, 2017. "GOP Lawmaker: Donors Are Pushing Me to Get Tax Reform Done." TheHill.com, http://thehill.com/homenews/house/359110-gop -lawmaker-donors-are-pushing-me-to-get-tax-reform-done (accessed 8/7/18).

8. Rebecca Savransky. November 9, 2017. "Graham: 'Financial Contributions Will Stop' If GOP Doesn't Pass Tax Reform." TheHill.com, http://thehill.com/policy/finance/359606 -graham-financial-contributions-will-stop-if-gop-doesnt-pass-tax-reform (accessed 8/7/18).

9. James Madison, *Federalist no. 10*, November 23, 1787,

10. *Federalist no. 10*.

11. Throughout the essay, it is clear that one of Madison's main concerns was about class. At several points, he comments on the notion of property as a dividing line, observing that "those who hold and those who are without property have ever formed distinct interests in society," with those owning property also dividing into different groups to pursue their interests: "A landed interest, a manufacturing interest, a mercantile interest, a moneyed interest."

12. James Madison, *Federalist no. 51*, February 8, 1788.

13. Rasmussen Reports. February 16, 2016. "Voters Say Money, Media Have Too Much Political Clout." Rasmussen Reports, www.rasmussenreports.com/public_content/politics /general_politics/february_2016/voters_say_money_media_have_too_much_political _clout (accessed 8/7/18).

14. Andrew Dugan. September 28, 2015. "Majority of Americans See Congresses as Out of Touch, Corrupt." Gallup, http://news.gallup.com/poll/185918/majority-americans -congress-touch-corrupt.aspx (accessed 8/7/18).

15. Jeffrey M. Jones. December 10, 2007. "Lobbyists Debut at Bottom of Honesty and Ethics List." Gallup, http://news.gallup.com/poll/103123/lobbyists-debut-bottom-honesty -ethics-list.aspx (accessed 8/7/18).

16. OpenSecrets.org. 2017. "Top Spenders." Center for Responsive Politics, www.opensecrets .org/lobby/top.php?indexType=s&showYear=2017 (accessed 8/7/18). The next 10 on the list also fall into the same categories: National Association of Broadcasters, Comcast,

Lockheed Martin, National Retail Federation, Business Roundtable, Southern Co., Amazon, Oracle, Verizon, and Northrop Grumman.

17. John F. Kennedy. February 19, 1956. "To Keep the Lobbyist within Bounds." *New York Times Magazine,* reported in *Congressional Record* (March 2, 1956), vol. 102, p. 3802–3.

18. From Ken Kollman. 2017. *The American Political System,* 511. New York: W. W. Norton. Original source: Center for Responsive Politics. "Top Organization Contributors: Hard Money." www.opensecrets.org (accessed 11/13/16).

19. For a list of PACs contributing the most money in 2017–18, see OpenSecrets.org. 2018. "Top PACs." Center for Responsive Politics, www.opensecrets.org/pacs/toppacs.php (accessed 8/7/18).

20. More precisely, multicandidate PACs can give a limit of $5,000 per election to a candidate, while PACs that are non-multicandidate (because they have fewer than 50 contributors or have been registered for less than six months) are limited to $2,700. Overall, members of the House are more reliant on PAC contributions than are senators and Senate candidates. But PAC money has been declining overall as a significant source of funds for all candidates, as we discuss in the following sections.

21. New York Times and CBS News. June 2, 2015. "Americans' View on Money in Politics." *New York Times,* www.nytimes.com/interactive/2015/06/02/us/politics/money-in -politics-poll.html (accessed 8/7/18).

22. As the Sunlight Foundation reported, for example, in the 2016 presidential primaries, a 501(c)(4) called Conservative Solutions spent millions of dollars to promote Senator Marco Rubio's candidacy and was able to do so without revealing the names of individuals who contributed donations. See Libby Watson. January 21, 2016. "6 Years Later, the Impact of *Citizens United* Still Looms Large." Sunlight Foundation, https:// sunlightfoundation.com/2016/01/21/6-years-later-the-impact-of-citizens-united-still -looms-large/ (accessed 8/7/18).

23. See Charles R. Shipan and William R. Lowry. 2001. "Environmental Policy and Party Divergence in Congress." *Political Research Quarterly* 54 (2): 245–63.

24. Gene Karpinski. November 3, 2014. "LCV's Dirty Dozen: The Names Are In." *The Blog,* www.huffingtonpost.com/gene-karpinski/lcvs-dirty-dozen-the-names-are-in_b _6095568.html (accessed 8/7/18).

25. League of Conservative Voters. 2018. "2018 Dirty Dozen." League of Conservation Voters, www.lcv.org/dirty-dozen/ (accessed 8/7/18).

26. Karpinski, "LCV's Dirty Dozen."

27. See Suzanne P. Clark. November 20, 2017. "Key Vote Letter: Senate 'Tax Cuts and Jobs Act.'" U.S. Chamber of Commerce, www.uschamber.com/letter/key-vote-letter-senate -tax-cuts-and-jobs-act (accessed 8/7/18); and Suzanne P. Clark. November 20, 2017. "Key Vote Alert." U.S. Chamber of Commerce, www.uschamber.com/sites/default/files /171120_kv_tax_reform_senate.pdf (accessed 8/7/18).

28. John R. Wright. 1996. *Interest Groups and Congress: Lobbying, Contributions, and Influence.* Boston, MA: Allyn and Bacon.

29. Frank R. Baumgartner and Bryan D. Jones. 1993. *Agenda and Instability in American Politics.* Chicago: University of Chicago Press.

30. Frank R. Baumgartner, Jeffrey M. Berry, Marie Hojnacki, David C. Kimball, and Beth L. Leech. 2009. *Lobbying and Policy Change: Who Wins, Who Loses, and Why.* Chicago: University of Chicago Press.

31. Richard L. Hall. 1996. *Participation in Congress.* New Haven: Yale University Press.

32. Cecilia Kang. November 7, 2017. "Inside the Opposition to a Net Neutrality Repeal." *New York Times,* www.nytimes.com/2017/12/07/technology/net-neutrality-protests-opposition .html?emc=edit_th_20171208&nl=todaysheadlines&nlid=67901470 (accessed 8/7/18).

33. In this section, we focus on the nature and extent of business involvement in politics. Another change worth noting is that in the past, businesses generally got involved in politics through one key trade association (e.g., the American Petroleum Institute) that represented a well-defined industry and market. Nowadays, businesses tend to be involved with multiple associations. These associations have proliferated as the economy has grown more complex, and businesses often have their own presence in Washington, DC, independent of these associations.

34. This section draws heavily on Drutman's rich and insightful book, Lee Drutman. 2015. *The Business of America Is Lobbying: How Corporations Became Politicized and Politics Became More Corporate*. New York: Oxford, particularly Chapter 3.

35. Drutman, *The Business of America Is Lobbying: How Corporations Became Politicized and Politics Became More Corporate*, 48.

36. Drutman, *The Business of America Is Lobbying: How Corporations Became Politicized and Politics Became More Corporate*, 49.

37. See David Vogel. 1989. *Fluctuating Fortunes: The Political Power of Business in America*, 33. New York: Basic Books.

38. Raymond A. Bauer, Ithiel de Sola Pool, and Lewis Anthony Dexter. 1972. *American Business and Public Policy*, 2nd ed. Chicago: Aldine-Atherton.

39. Drutman, *The Business of America Is Lobbying: How Corporations Became Politicized and Politics Became More Corporate*, 56.

40. Timothy LaPira. 2012. "The Allure of Reform: The Increasing Demand for Health Care Lobbying from Clinton's Task Force to Obama's Big [Expletive] Deal," in *Interest Group Politics*, 8th ed., ed. by Allan Cigler and Burdett Loomis, 345–74. Washington, DC: CQ Press.

41. See, for example, Bauer, Pool, and Dexter, *American Business and Public Policy*.

42. Richard L. Hall and Alan V. Deardorff. 2006. "Lobbying as Legislative Subsidy." *American Political Science Review* 100(91): 69–84.

43. Groups also can provide legislators with valuable information about the likelihood that a bill will pass and about how support for or opposition to a bill might affect a legislator's electoral prospects. See Wright, *Interest Groups and Congress: Lobbying, Contributions, and Influence*.

44. Marie Hojnacki and David C. Kimball. 1998. "Organized Interests and the Decision of Whom to Lobby in Congress." *American Political Science Review* 92(4): 775–90.

45. To identify the relevant groups, they drew on a variety of sources, including *Congressional Quarterly*'s Washington Information Directory, issue-related stories in the *National Journal*, and lists of groups that testified at congressional hearings.

46. This finding also is consistent with other studies that argue that the composition of a district can help determine which issues a member is most active on (Hall, *Participation in Congress*; Tracy Sulkin, *Issue Politics in Congress*, New York: Cambridge University Press [2005]).

47. Interestingly, the results also showed no effect for counteractive lobbying. That is, a group's decision about whether to lobby a legislator was unaffected by the number of opposing groups lobbying that legislator. They also showed more lobbying overall on the two issues—grazing and financial reform—that were narrower and less salient to the broader public.

48. See Drutman, *The Business of America Is Lobbying: How Corporations Became Politicized and Politics Became More Corporate* for a more detailed description of these types of lobbyists.

49. See Jeffrey L. Lazarus, Amy McKay, and Lindsey Herbel. 2016. "Who Walks through the Revolving Door? Examining the Lobbying Activity of Former Members of Congress." *Interest Groups and Advocacy* 5(1): 82–100.

50. See Jordi Blanes i Vidal, Mirko Draca, and Christian Fons-Rosen. 2012. "Revolving Door Lobbyists." *American Economic Review* 102(7): 3731–48; and Baumgartner et al., *Lobbying and Policy Change: Who Wins, Who, Loses, and Why*, p. 208.

51. See Timothy M. LaPira and Herschel F. Thomas III. 2017. *Revolving Door Lobbying: Public Service, Private Influence, and the Unequal Representation of Interests*. Lawrence: University Press of Kansas.

52. See Lazarus, McKay, and Herbel, "Who Walks through the Revolving Door? Examining the Lobbying Activity of Former Members of Congress."

53. Catherine Ho. September 20, 2016. "Former Speaker John Boehner Heads to K Street." *Washington Post*, www.washingtonpost.com/news/powerpost/wp/2016/09/20/fomer -speaker-john-boehner-heads-to-k-street/?utm_term=.a848ec569643 (accessed 8/7/18).

54. There are numerous reports of former members being paid thousands or millions of dollars by institutionalized interest groups to lobby. Former members have also registered as foreign agents. For example, at least four former members of Congress were hired by Saudi Arabia to lobby against a bill that would allow families to sue the Saudi government for its involvement in the September 2001 terrorist attacks. See H.R. 1628-American Health Care Act of 2017. Maplight, http://maplight.org/data /passthrough/#legacyurl=http://classic.maplight.org/us-congress/bill/115-hr-1628 /12273735/contributions-by-vote (accessed 8/7/18).

55. See, especially, Timothy M. LaPira and Herschel F. Thomas III, 2014. "Revolving Door Lobbyists and Interest Representation." *Interest Groups and Advocacy* 3(1): 4–29.

56. Cecilia Kang. November 7, 2017. "Inside the Opposition to a Net Neutrality Repeal." *New York Times*, www.nytimes.com/2017/12/07/technology/net-neutrality-protests -opposition.html?emc=edit_th_20171208&nl=todaysheadlines&nlid=67901470 (accessed 8/7/18).

57. For example, Gregory Wawro, 2001, *Legislative Entrepreneurship in the U.S. House of Representatives*, University of Michigan Press, investigated the relationship between campaign contributions and roll call votes on business and labor issues, but he did not find that contributions were a significant predictor of voting.

58. Glenn Thrush. April 24, 2018. "Mulvaney, Watchdog Bureau's Leader, Advises Bankers on Ways to Curtail Agency." *New York Times*, www.nytimes.com/2018/04/24/us /mulvaney-consumer-financial-protection-bureau.html (accessed 8/7/18). Mulvaney also emphasized that his staff always made time to meet with constituents.

59. See LaPira and Thomas, "Revolving Door Lobbyists and Interest Representation."

60. See Richard L. Hall. 1996. *Participation in Congress*. New Haven, CT: Yale University Press.

61. Richard L. Hall and Frank Wayman. September 1990. "Buying Time: Moneyed Interests and the Mobilization of Bias in Congressional Committees." *APSR* 84(3): 797–820.

62. They are careful to adjust for the potential of endogeneity. That is, they make sure that their results show that contributions influence participation, rather than the other way around.

63. See Baumgartner et al., *Lobbying and Policy Change: Who Wins, Who, Loses, and Why*. For an excellent summary and extension of these findings, see Frank R. Baumgartner, Jeffrey M. Berry, Marie Hojnacki, David C. Kimball, and Beth L. Leech. 2014. "Money, Priorities, and Stalemate: How Lobbying Affects Public Policy." *Election Law Journal* 13 (1): 194–209.

64. Furthermore, they showed that this result was robust. They also looked at each side of an issue (with one side wanting change and another opposing it) to see if the side with more combined resources tended to win. Again, they found that more resources didn't matter.

65. In addition, a number of other studies of specific policy areas do show that groups are sometimes able to get the changes they seek, even if those changes are small. See the review article by John M. de Figueiredo and Brian Kelleher Richter. 2014. "Advancing the Empirical Research on Lobbying." *Annual Review of Political Science* 17: 163–85.

66. Norman J. Ornstein and Shirley Elder. 1978. *Interest Groups, Lobbying, and Policymaking,* 77. Washington, DC: CQ Press.

67. Peter Grier. September 28, 2009. "The Lobbyist through History: Villainy and Virtue." *Christian Science Monitor,* www.csmonitor.com/USA/Politics/2009/0928/the-lobbyist -through-history-villainy-and-virtue (accessed 8/7/18).

68. Sarah Smith and Norman Ornstein. February 18, 2007. Sunday Book Review, "The K Street Project." *New York Times,* www.nytimes.com/2007/02/18/books/review/Letters.t-1.html (accessed 8/7/18).

69. Juan Williams. January 11, 2006. "The K Street Project and Jack Abramoff." NPR, www .npr.org/templates/story/story.php?storyId=5148982 (accessed 8/7/18).

70. Jim VandeHei. June 10, 2002. "GOP Monitoring Lobbyists' Politics; White House, Hill Access May Be Affected." *Washington Post,* A01.

71. Richard S. Dunham. June 24, 2002. "The GOP's Wacky War on Dem Lobbyists." Bloomberg, www.bloomberg.com/news/articles/2002-06-23/the-gops-wacky-war-on-dem -lobbyists (accessed 8/7/18).

72. VandeHei, "GOP Monitoring Lobbyists' Politics; White House, Hill Access May Be Affected."

Credits

PHOTOS

Chapter 1

p. 3: CQ Roll Call via AP Images;
p. 9: Bettmann/Getty Images;
p. 13: Tom Williams/CQ Roll Call via AP Images;
p. 16: Richard F. Fenno Jr. Papers, D.359, Rare Books, Special Collections, and Preservation, River Campus Libraries, University of Rochester.

Chapter 2

p. 21: The Miriam and Ira D. Wallach Division of Art, Prints and Photographs: Print Collection, The New York Public Library;
p. 46: Granger-All Rights Reserved;
p. 49: AP Photo;
p. 54: Richard Ellis/AFP/Getty Images;
p. 57: Mike Theiler/UPI/Newscom.

Chapter 3

p. 67: Andrew Lichtenstein/Corbis via Getty Images;
p. 75: Everett Collection/Newscom;
p. 79: Michael Laughlin/South Florida Sun-Sentinel via AP;
p. 89: AP Photo/Andrew Harnik;
p. 90: Tom Williams/CQ Roll Call/Getty Images.

Chapter 4

p. 103: AP Photo/Steve Helber;
p. 120: Bygone Collection/Alamy Stock Photo;
p. 121: Archive PL/Alamy Stock Photo;
p. 123: Bettmann Archive/Getty Images;
p. 124: nationalmap.gov/USGS;
p. 133 top: Keystone Pictures USA/Alamy Stock Photo; **bottom:** Craig Lassig/Reuters/Newscom;

Chapter 5

p. 151: Andrew Harrer/Bloomberg via Getty Images;
p. 154: Mark Wilson/Getty Images;
p. 173: Tom Williams/CQ Roll Call/Getty Images;
p. 184: Mark Wilson/Getty Images.

Chapter 6

p. 197: Kevin Dietsch/UPI/Newscom;
p. 203 left: Tom Williams/CQ Roll Call/Getty Images; **right:** Melina Mara/The Washington Post via Getty Images;
p. 205: Alex Wong/Getty Images;
p. 219: Scott J. Ferrell/Congressional Quarterly/Alamy Stock Photo;
p. 228: ©2016 FreedomWorks. Meadows photo: AP Photo/J.Scott Applewhite.

Chapter 7

p. 237: Bill Clark/CQ Roll Call via AP Images;

p. 246 left: Bill Clark/CQ Roll Call/Getty Images; right: Alex Edelman/picture-alliance/dpa/AP Images;

p. 257: AP Photo/Senate TV;

p. 266: Pete Marovich/ZUMApress.com /Alamy Stock Photo.

Chapter 8

p. 271: Bill Clark/CQ Roll Call via AP Images;

p. 286: Kevin Dietsch/UPI/Newscom;

p. 296: AP Photo/J. Scott Applewhite;

p. 301 top: Gordon Parks/The LIFE Picture Collection/Getty Images; bottom: AP Photo/Joe Marquette.

Chapter 9

p. 305: Twitter;

p. 313: AP Photo/Ron Edmonds;

p. 319: Andrew Harrer/Bloomberg via Getty Images;

p. 329 left: Rick Friedman/Corbis via Getty Images; right: Bill Clark/CQ Roll Call/Getty Images;

p. 337: AP Photo/Pablo Martinez Monsivais.

Chapter 10

p. 343: Douglas Graham/CQ Roll Call via AP Images;

p. 348: Jim Young/Reuters/Newscom;

p. 362: Andrew Harrer/Bloomberg via Getty Images;

p. 374: Douglas Graham/CQ Roll Call via AP Images.

Chapter 11

p. 381: Tom Williams-Pool/Getty Images;

p. 388: Olivier Douliery/Sipa USA via AP Images;

p. 390: Melina Mara/The Washington Post via Getty Images;

p. 397: Clarissa Peterson, The Leadership Conference on Civil and Human Rights;

p. 411: Dana Verkouteren via AP.

Chapter 12

p. 417: Drew Angerer/Getty Images;

p. 420: Alex Wong/Getty Images;

p. 428: Andy Abeyta/Quad-City Times/ZUMA Wire/Alamy Live News;

p. 432: Tom Williams/CQ Roll Call via AP Images;

p. 447: AP Photo/Jim Cole.

TEXT

Figure 2.1: Appendix 1 from Jeffrey A. Jenkins and Timothy Nokken, "Legislative Shirking in the Pre-Twentieth Amendment Era: Presidential Influence, Party Power, and Lame-Duck Sessions of Congress, 1877–1933," *Studies in American Development* 22(1), 111–140 (2008), reproduced with permission of Cambridge University Press.

Figures 3.1 and 3.2: From "The changing face of Congress in 5 charts." Pew Research Center, Washington, D. C. (February 2, 2017) http://www .pewresearch.org/fact-tank/2017/02/02 /the-changing-face-of-congress-in-5 -charts/.

Figure 3.5: Republished with permission of Gallup, Inc, from "Congress and the Public," Gallup Historical Trends, 2018; permission conveyed through Copyright Clearance Center, Inc.

Figure 4.4: Adapted from "Voter ID Enactments 2000–2016," Voter ID History (May 31, 2017), http://www .ncsl.org. Reprinted by permission of the National Conference of State Legislatures.

Figure 4.9: Figure 4.6 from Alan S. Gerber, Eric Schickler (eds.), *Governing in a Polarized Age, Elections, Parties, and Political Representation in America.* © Cambridge University Press 2017. Reprinted by permission of Cambridge University Press.

Figure 5.1: Republished with permission of SAGE College, from "Chapter 6: Why and How the Legislative Process Changed" in *Unorthodox Lawmaking: New Legislative Processes in the U.S. Congress*, Barbara Sinclair, 5th Ed., 2017. Copyright © 2017 by CQ Press, an Imprint of SAGE Publications, Inc; permission conveyed through Copyright Clearance Center, Inc.

Table 6.3: Republished with permission of Gallup, Inc, from "Congressional Job Approval Stays Near Historical Low," Gallup News, Jeffrey M. Jones, August 12, 2014; permission conveyed through Copyright Clearance Center, Inc.

Figure 6.3: Republished with permission of Oxford University Press, from "The Ties That Bind: Coalitions in Congress" in *The Oxford Handbook of the American Congress*, John Wilkerson and Barry Pump, eds. Eric Schickler and Frances Lee, © 2011; permission conveyed through Copyright Clearance Center, Inc.

Figure 6.4: "Party means on the liberal-conservative dimensions over time by chamber" from "Polarization in Congress," VoteView.com, accessed March 11, 2018. Reprinted with permission.

Figure 6.5: "Liberal-conservative partisan polarization by chamber" from "Polarization in Congress," VoteView.com, accessed March 11, 2018. Reprinted with permission.

Figure 7.6: Figure 1 from "The Disappearing Conference Committee: The Use of Procedures by Minority Coalitions to Prevent Conferencing," Josh Ryan, *Congress and the Presidency* 38(1), 2011, American University, Center for Congressional and Presidential Studies. Reprinted by permission of Taylor & Francis Ltd, http://www.tandfonline.com.

Figure 8.1: Republished with permission of Capitol News Company LLC, from "Meet your unauthorized federal government," Danny Vinik, *Politico*, February 3, 2016; permission conveyed through Copyright Clearance Center, Inc.

Figure 8.6: Figure 3 from Binder, Sarah, "Polarized We Govern?", May 2014, Center for Effective Public Management at Brookings. Reprinted by permission of The Brookings Institution.

Figure 8.7: Republished with permission of SAGE College, from "Legislative Effectiveness and Representation" in *Congress Reconsidered*, Craig Volden and Alan Wiseman, 11th Ed., 2017. Copyright © 2017 by CQ Press, an Imprint of SAGE Publications, Inc; permission conveyed through Copyright Clearance Center, Inc.

Figure 9.1: Figure 4.1 from Cohen, J. (2012). The Size of the President's Agenda, 1789–2002. In *The President's Legislative*

Policy Agenda, 1789–2002 (pp. 97-139) © Jeffrey E. Cohen 2012. Reprinted by permission of Cambridge University Press.

Figure 9.3: Figure 1 from "Presidential Speeches Amid a More Centralized and Unified Congress," Ronald J. McGauvran and Matthew Eshbaugh-Soha, *Congress & the Presidency* 44(1), 2017, American University, Center for Congressional and Presidential Studies. Reprinted by permission of Taylor & Francis Ltd, http://www.tandfonline.com.

Figure 9.4: Republished with permission of John Wiley and Sons, Inc., from "Legislative Capacity and Executive Unilateralism," *American Journal of Political Science*, Alexander Bolton and Sharece Thrower, Vol. 60, No. 3, © 2015 Midwest Political Science Association; permission conveyed through Copyright Clearance Center, Inc.

Figure 9.5: Republished with permission of John Wiley and Sons, Inc., from "What's So Sinister about Presidential Signing Statements?", *Presidential Studies Quarterly*, Ian Ostrander and Joel Sievert, Vol. 43, No. 1, © 2013 Center for the Study of the Presidency; permission conveyed through Copyright Clearance Center, Inc.

Figure 9.7: Copyright © 2012. Figure 10.1 from "Chapter 10—Congress and the Executive: Unilateralism and Legislative Bargaining" in *New Directions in Congressional Politics* by Bryan W. Marshall, ed. Jamie L. Carson. Reproduced by permission of Taylor and Francis Group, LLC, a division of Informa plc.

Figure 9.8: Figure 2 from "The Best of Times and the Worst of Times: Polarization and Presidential Success in Congress," Daniel Paul Franklin and Michael P. Fix, *Congress & the Presidency* 43(3), 2016, American University, Center for Congressional and Presidential Studies. Reprinted by permission of Taylor & Francis Ltd, http://www.tandfonline.com.

Figure 9.10: Republished with permission of Princeton University Press, from "Chapter 2: When Congress Investigates" in *Investigating the President: Congressional Checks on Presidential Power*, Eric

Index

A page number in *italics* refers to a figure or table.